2008 SUPPLEMENT

CASES AND MATERIALS

SECURITIES REGULATION

TENTH EDITION

by

JOHN C. COFFEE, JR.
Adolf A. Berle Professor of Law
Columbia University School of Law

JOEL SELIGMAN
President
University of Rochester

HILLARY A. SALE
F. Arnold Daum Professor of Corporate Finance and Law
University of Iowa College of Law

FOUNDATION PRESS
75TH ANNIVERSARY

THOMSON
WEST

This publication was created to provide you with accurate and authoritative information concerning the subject matter covered; however, this publication was not necessarily prepared by persons licensed to practice law in a particular jurisdiction. The publisher is not engaged in rendering legal or other professional advice and this publication is not a substitute for the advice of an attorney. If you require legal or other expert advice, you should seek the services of a competent attorney or other professional.

Nothing contained herein is intended or written to be used for the purposes of 1) avoiding penalties imposed under the federal Internal Revenue Code, or 2) promoting, marketing or recommending to another party any transaction or matter addressed herein.

© 2003, 2004 FOUNDATION PRESS
© 2005, 2007 THOMSON REUTERS/FOUNDATION PRESS
© 2008 By THOMSON REUTERS/FOUNDATION PRESS
395 Hudson Street
New York, NY 10014
Phone Toll Free 1–877–888–1330
Fax (212) 367–6799
foundation-press.com

Printed in the United States of America

ISBN 978–1–59941–466–9

TEXT IS PRINTED ON 10% POST CONSUMER RECYCLED PAPER

PREFACE

The last year has seen important market and legal developments. This Supplement will focus primarily on legal developments, but some important transitions in the markets require at least a brief notice:

A. <u>Globalized Securities Markets</u>. In 2007, although U.S. IPO activity was sluggish, the total global proceeds from IPOs exceeded $287 billion, a record total, as the result of 1,979 IPOs (according to Ernst & Young's Global IPO Trends Report 2008). Brazil, Russia, India and China generated $119 billion in 430 deals (or 41% of worldwide IPO proceeds – a sharp increase from 2004 when these same countries accounted for only 14% of global IPO proceeds). These four countries also accounted for half of the top 20 IPOs in 2007.

90% of IPOs, and 17 of the top 20 IPOs, in 2007 went public on their home country exchange, including such locales as Madrid, Dubai, Sao Paolo, Tokyo, Bogata, Frankfurt, Brussels, Dublin, Shanghai, and Mumbai. A decade earlier, large IPOs were generally conducted in either New York or London, as regional exchanges were then considered incapable of handling large volume offerings. The U.S. dominance in securities offerings appears to have ended.

B. <u>Exchange Consolidation</u>. In January, 2008, the NYSE, which merged with Euronext in 2006, acquired the American Stock Exchange. In March 2008, the Chicago Mercantile Exchange, which had earlier merged with the Chicago Board of Trade, acquired NYMEX, the largest player in a number of commodities markets. In February, 2008, Nasdaq acquired OMX, the principal stock exchange in the Baltic region. In April, 2007, the Deutsche Borse acquired the International Securities Exchange, and also in that year, the Toronto Stock Exchange acquired the Bourse de Montreal. The Tokyo Stock Exchange is currently merging with the Osaka exchange and plans its own IPO in 2009. This wave of consolidation appears unlikely to halt, but the dynamic for the future may lie in the fact that derivative exchanges are growing far faster than stock exchanges (and are trading at higher price/earnings multiples).

C. <u>The Emergence of Sovereign Wealth Funds ("SWFs")</u>. Sovereign wealth funds describe a distinct pool of government-owned or government controlled financial assets. Many are located in the Middle East or Asia (e.g., China and Singapore). With the subprime mortgage crisis peaking in late 2007, several large U.S. financial institutions (including Citibank and Merrill Lynch) turned to SWFs for large infusions of capital (at discounted prices off the public market price). While these capital infusions were much needed, the high visibility of SWFs has raised concern that they may use their large stakes in financial institutions to realize political as well as economic objectives. No evidence of such efforts has yet surfaced, but Congressional hearings continue to focus on the perceived danger.

Major legal developments in 2007-2008 include the following:

(1) <u>New Developments Under Rule 10b-5</u>. Here, the most obvious new developments are the Supreme Court's decisions in <u>Stoneridge</u> and <u>Tellabs</u>. The former decision ends the possibility of "scheme to defraud liability" under the first clause of Rule 10b-5 and makes clear that only those who make a public statement face liability under the Rule. While the <u>Stoneridge</u> decision was written broadly, <u>Tellabs</u> addressed the narrower context of the standards for pleading scienter under the Rule and appears to have struck a careful compromise that only mildly elevates the pleading standard and may be less exacting than the prior law in some Circuits. In 2007, the <u>Credit Suisse</u> decision also established an important principle that transcends Rule 10b-5 but that will have its primary application in Rule 10b-5 litigation: namely that federal securities laws represent a partial implied exemption from the federal antitrust laws. Again, the decision does not deviate significantly from the Court's earlier decisions, but does amplify its earlier holding notably in <u>Gordon</u>. Other significant developments are still in progress. These include (1) the increasing difficulty of obtaining

class certification, and (2) the reduced applicability of the "fraud on the market doctrine."

(2) <u>Judicial Scrutiny of SEC Decision-making</u>. The SEC has had its recent litigation losses, and we include four – <u>Goldstein v. SEC</u>, <u>Chamber of Commerce v. SEC</u>, <u>Financial Planning Association v. SEC</u>, and <u>AFSCME Employees Pension Plan v. AIG, Inc.</u> – both to show the more skeptical, less deferential standard of review and to give an overview of new trends, including the rise of the hedge fund and the regulatory issues it portends;

(3) <u>The Subprime Mortgage Debacle and the Credit Rating Agencies</u>. Extraordinary losses on investment grade debt focused attention in 2008 on the performance of the credit-rating agencies. In 2006, Congress passed the Credit Rating Agency Reform Act to encourage greater competition in a field long dominated by two agencies (Moody's and Standard & Poor's). The Act authorized the SEC to promulgate rules regarding public disclosure, recordkeeping and financial reporting in order to ensure that Nationally Recognized Statistical Rating Organizations ("NRSROs") conducted their activities objective and impartially. After Congressional hearings and broad press coverage suggested that the rating agencies had often been highly optimistic in rating structured finance products (probably in order to win a larger market share in the highly lucrative structured finance market) and that debt issuers frequently shopped for ratings, declining to pay for below investment grade ratings, the SEC issued proposed rules on June 11, 2008. The most controversial provision in these proposed rules would require ratings agencies to differentiate the ratings issued on structured finance products from those issued on corporate bonds, either through use of a different symbols or by a narrative description.

In addition, the Commission's proposed rules would:

- Prohibit a credit rating agency from issuing a rating on a structured product unless information on assets underlying the product was available.
- Prohibit credit rating agencies from structuring the same products that they rate.

- Require credit rating agencies to make all of their ratings and subsequent rating actions publicly available. This data would be required to be provided in a way that will facilitate comparisons of each credit rating agency's performance.

- Restrict the practice of buying favorable ratings by prohibiting anyone who participates in determining a credit rating from negotiating the fee that the issuer pays for it.

- Prohibit gifts from those who receive ratings to those who rate them, in any amount over $25.

- Require credit rating agencies to publish performance statistics for 1, 3, and 10 years within each rating category, in a way that facilitates comparison with their competitors in the industry.

- Require disclosure by the rating agencies of the way they rely on the due diligence of others to verify the assets underlying a structured product.

- Require disclosure of how frequently credit ratings are reviewed; whether different models are used for ratings surveillance than for initial ratings; and whether changes made to models are applied retroactively to existing ratings.

- Require credit rating agencies to make an annual report of the number of ratings actions they took in each ratings class, and require the maintenance of an XBRL database of all rating actions on the rating agency's Web site. That would permit easy analysis of both initial ratings and ratings change data.

- Require the public disclosure of the information a credit rating agency uses to determine a rating on a structured product, including information on the underlying assets. This is intended to permit broad market scrutiny, as well as competitive analysis by other rating agencies that are not paid by the issuer to rate the product.

(4) Developments Under Sarbanes-Oxley and the Continuing Shift Toward Deregulation. Here, the requirements of Section 404 have been relaxed, and new exemptions under the Securities Act appear to be coming. The Commission also appears to be on the verge of new rulemaking with regard to Rule 14a-8 on shareholder proposals in the wake of the AFSCME decision, which found the existing rule not to prohibit a bylaw amendment permitting shareholders to nominate a candidate on the corporation's own proxy statement. Depending on the positions taken, the new rules could significantly affect the ability of activist shareholders to nominate minority directors.

JOHN C. COFFEE, JR.
HILLARY A. SALE

June 12, 2008

TABLE OF CONTENTS

[The page number at which the new material appears in this Supplement is indicated in the right column; the page number of the Casebook at which we suggest the new material should be considered appears in the left column. Many of the footnotes to the cases have been omitted; those retained have not be renumbered. Parallel citations to cases and statutes have also been omitted without so indicating.]

		Page
PREFACE		ii

Casebook Page		Supplement Page No.

Chapter 3

| 212 | An Update on Section 404 and the PCAOB | 1 |

Chapter 9

| 521 | The SEC's Proposed Revisions to Rule 144 and New Exemptions for Small Offerings | 4 |
| | Revised Problems on Rule 144 | 6 |

Chapter 10

| 623 | Implied Antitrust Immunity: Credit Suisse Securities (USA) LLC v. Billing | 16 |

Chapter 11

| 712 | Section 4. The Dividing Line Between Brokers and Investment Advisers: | |
| | Financial Planning Association v. Securities and Exchange Commission | 27 |

Chapter 14

| 1009 | The Fraud on the Market Doctrine Revisited: | |
| | In re Polymedica Corp. Securities Litigation | 36 |

Chapter 15

-vii-

1048	Pleading Scienter: Tellabs Inc. v. Makor Issues & Rights, Ltd.	50
	[This decision should replace Novak v. Kasaks in the Casebook]	
1048	Note on the Impact of Tellabs ------------------------------------	59
1073	Section 1(E). The Changing Law on Class Certification:	
	In re Initial Public Offering Securities Litigation ----------------	61
1095	Section 2(C): The Rise and Fall of Scheme to Defraud Liability:	
	Stoneridge Investment Partners LLC v. Scientific-Atlanta, Inc.	78

Chapter 17

1227	Section 2A. Bylaw Amendments Under Rule 14a-8:	
	AFSCME Employees Pension Plan v. American International Group, Inc. ---	92

Chapter 18

1271	Section 4. Registration:	
	Chamber of Commerce v. Securities and Exchange Commission ---	99
	Goldstein v. Securities and Exchange Commission --------------	109

Chapter 19

1272	The Impact of SLUSA: Merrill Lynch, Pierce Fenner & Smith v. Dabit --------------------	118

APPENDICES

App.

I.	Google Inc. Form S-1 Registration Statement, August 18, 2004 (including Prospectus Subject to Completion) -------------------	126
II.	PIXAR, Underwriting Agreement, November 28, 1995 --------	346
III.	Master Agreement Among Underwriters --------------------------	372
IV.	Master Selected Dealers Agreement --------------------------------	386

CASES AND MATERIALS

SECURITIES REGULATION

An Update on Section 404 and the PCAOB's New Standard

Under Section 404 of the Sarbanes-Oxley Act, a public company must conduct an annual evaluation of the effectiveness of its internal controls and include in its annual report the results of this evaluation. The company auditors must then "attest" to management's findings, a term which the Public Company Accounting Oversight Board ("PCAOB") originally interpreted in Auditing Standard No. 2 to require a full-scale audit.

This procedure has now been in force for large U.S. issuers for some three reporting seasons and has evoked considerable criticism as to its costs and rigidity. Under new rules adopted by the SEC and PCAOB in May, 2007, the process will change in that (1) management will develop its own evaluation process independently of the rules applicable to auditors, and (2) both management and auditors will apply a "top-down, risk-based" approach intended to tailor the evaluation to each company's specific circumstances. As a practical matter, this means that the auditor need only focus on areas that could lead to material misstatement in the company's financial statements.

Both the SEC and PCAOB changed their rules in several important respects:

SEC Rule Changes:

Essentially, the SEC adopted three significant changes. First, it adopted a safe harbor under which management's obligation to evaluate internal control is satisfied if the evaluation is performed in accordance with the SEC's interpretive guidance. This eliminated any possible need to comply with a "rigid" checklist specified in any PCAOB statement. Nonetheless, commentators have disagreed about the utility of this safe harbor, because some feel that principles-based guidelines does not by it nature fix clear compliance standards.

The second change related to the auditors' report on internal control. Under the prior rules, the report had to express two opinions: whether internal control was effective and whether management's assessment of internal control was fairly stated. The amendments eliminate the second opinion, which means that auditor does not need to pass on management's evaluation procedures, but only on the effectiveness of the controls themselves.

Third, the SEC adopted as part of its rules a new definition of the key term "material weakness." The former definition, which was in PCAOB Auditing Standard No. 2, but not the SEC's rules, specified that a control deficiency is a material weakness if the likelihood of a material financial misstatement is "more than remote." Numerous critics of the Section 404 process argued that this definition led to an unnecessary search for low-probability flaws. The new definition adopted by both the SEC and the PCAOB changes the standard from "more than a remote likelihood" to "a reasonable possibility" of a material misstatement. This was a compromise, as business lobbyists had pushed for an even more permissive "reasonably likely" test, but lost.

New PCAOB Standards:

Auditing Standard No. 5 completely replaces Auditing Standard No. 2, which has been in effect since June 2004 and had been criticized as requiring excessive procedures and encouraging an unnecessarily costly approach to reviewing internal controls.

Auditing Standard No. 5 is intended to focus the audit on the most important matters, eliminate "unnecessary" procedures, allow the audit to be "scaled" for smaller companies and simplify the standard's requirements. It is also designed to integrate with the related SEC rules, in part by utilizing a common terminology.

The SEC rule changes and interpretive guidance are now in effect, and PCAOB's

Auditing Standard No. 5 will become effective for fiscal years ending on and after November 15, 2007. The SEC had delayed the application of these requirements for smaller issues, but has now indicated that it will permit no further delay. As a result, smaller issuers (known technically as "non-accelerated filers") will have to prepare a Section 404 report for fiscal years ending on or after December 15, 2007, and the requirement for an auditor's opinion on that report will apply one year later.

Pending PCAOB Constitutional Litigation:

In Free Enterprise Fund v. The Public Company Accounting Oversight Board, 2007 U.S. Dist. LEXIS 24310 (D.C. March 21, 2007), the District Court rejected a constitutional challenged to the creation and existence of the PCAOB based on (1) separation-of-powers principles, (ii) the Appointments Clause of the U.S. Constitution, and (iii) the non-delegation doctrine. That decision was appealed to the D.C. Circuit, where a decision is expected shortly. If the PCAOB were found to violate any of these Constitutional doctrines, an appeal to the Supreme Court seems likely, but the core of the Sarbanes-Oxley Act could find its way back before Congress.

The SEC's Proposed Revisions to Rule 144 and New Exemptions for Small Offerings

A year after the report of the Commission's Advisory Committee on Smaller Public Companies, which was released in April 2006, the Commission voted at an open meeting on May 23, 2007 to propose a series of rule changes indicated to facilitate public and private capital raising for smaller companies:

Revisions to Rule 144. The most noteworthy proposed change would revise Rule 144 to permit sales of restricted securities held by non-affiliates after a holding period of six months in the case of issuers that are reporting companies with current information available. Thereafter, holders who were non-affiliates could make sales without limitation (i.e., the volume limitations of Rule 144(e) would be inapplicable). In the case of other issuers, the holding period would be one year (and in the case of all non-affiliates who had hedged their positions, the holding period would also be one year, even though the issuer was a reporting company with current information available). No release has yet described the specific terms, and it is thus uncertain, for example, (1) what would be the holding period for a non-affiliate holder who acquired from a prior holder who had hedged, and (2) whether non-affiliates who had hedged would be free to sell their entire holdings after a one year holding period if those holdings exceeded 1%.

It was also announced that the manner of sale restrictions under Rule144 would be relaxed in the case of debt securities.

Rule 145. Rule 145's holding periods will also be harmonized with those of Rule 144, by eliminating the presumptive underwriting doctrine in most cases and making the restrictions under Rule 145(d) consistent with those under revised Rule 144.

Revisions to Regulation D. The Commission intends to adopt a new rule – Rule 507 –

that would define a new class of qualified purchasers between "accredited investor" and "qualified institutional buyer" (under Rule 144A). This new category of investor would be required to hold at least $2.5 million of investments or have an annual income of $400,000 (or $600,000 with a spouse); in the case of institutions, the institution would either hold $10 million in investments or currently qualify as an accredited investor without regard to the amount of its assets. Under this new proposed exemption, limited advertising would be permitted, thereby relaxing the restrictions in current Rule 502(c), but only for this new class of larger investor.

Rule 506's definition of "accredited investor" would also be modified to upgrade its assets and earnings requirements to adjust for the impact of inflation (beginning at some point over the next five years); in addition, a new alternative exemption would be added to the definition of "accredited investor" to exempt persons meeting a $750,000 "investments-owned" standard.

Smaller Reporting Companies. A new definition of "smaller reporting companies" would be created to combine the two current categories of "small business issuers" and "non-accelerated filers." This new category would include those issuers with a "public float" of $75 million or less (up from the current category of $25 million for "small business issuers"), and those companies so qualifying would be eligible to provide the more limited disclosures currently permitted for "small business issuers." This proposal would eliminate Regulation S-B and the "SR" forms by merging them into Regulation S-K and the "S" forms. At the same time, these smaller issuers would become eligible to use Forms S-3 and F-3 for primary offerings, including through shelf registration, even though their "public float" fell below $75 million.

Revised Problems to Chapter 9

(Offerings by Underwriters, Affiliates and Dealers)

PROBLEM 9-1
C.B. 495

Your old college roommate and the best man at your wedding has launched a small start-up company in Silicon Valley. He convinces you to invest $200,000, and, because you are "best lawyer he knows" (he was always good at flattery), to write the first draft of the registration statement for a small offering by which his firm is chiefly buying the stock of a rival firm in an exchange offer. But they are also looking for additional financing, and he convinces you to give him the email addresses of 100 or so of your law firm's better heeled clients. He solicits them to invest, and about 20 do. Are you an underwriter?

PROBLEM 9-2
C.B. 496

Your law firm has a unique practice of representing IPO clients on a "stock only" basis. That is, rather than charging the $1 million to $1.5 million fee that comparable firms would, you take stock (valued at the initial offering price) in lieu of cash. Because the offering was initially priced at $25 per share, but the price rose on the first day to $60, your firm has made a bundle and would like to realize its profit as soon as it can. Although your firm's stock was fully registered, you agreed to a lock-up under which you would not to sell any shares until six months after the offering. Are you now an underwriter as one who "participates" in a distribution? What if during the period between one month after the offering and the end of the lock-up agreement, your firm occasionally buys the issuer's stock in the secondary market (because the lead underwriter, who also is buying, advises you that otherwise the stock price will slip)?

PROBLEM 9-3
C.B. 517

Investor A purchases common stock in a private placement by a major airline on March 30, 2001. Following the September, 2001 World Trade Center disaster, which shocked the markets and collapsed the price of airline stocks, sells the shares, claiming that the World Trade Center was totaling unforeseen and represented an historically fundamental change of circumstances. As an attorney in the enforcement division, you are asked to advise the Commission and its staff as to whether this is a legitimate claim that should be accepted.

PROBLEM 9-4
C.B. 517

Ebarka Eban, a 7' 3" center who plays in the European Basketball League, is the first draft choice in the first round of this year's NBA draft. He signs with the New York Knicks on July 30, 2008, which team, as usual, finished last (but this year they did not trade away their draft choice) for $50 million over 5 year plus 1 million shares in the Knicks, which is sold to him on that date in a valid private placement at $1.50 per share (the trading price in the open market was then $8 per share and the 1 million shares represent 5% of the Knicks outstanding shares). A week later, Eban pledges his shares in the Knicks with the Bank of New York as partial collateral for a $60 million loan, which he promptly uses to buy a controlling stake in a franchise in the European Basketball League. Three months later, he decides to play next year for his European team, and thereby (i) breaches his contract with the Knicks, and (ii) defaults on his loan with the Bank of New York. Bank of New York wants to sell the shares it received in the Eban pledge on Nasdaq, which is where it the Knicks are traded. Can it?

PROBLEM 9-5
C.B. 517

In Problem 9-4, assume now that Eban buys 1 million Knick shares from the Knicks after becoming their first draft choice at $1.5 per share (when the market price was $8 per share). Two months later, he is injured in a motorcycle accident, and uncertainty exists about his ability to play next year. Because Eban's employment contract required him not to ride motorcycles (but only Rolls Royces), an employment negotiation follows, at the end of which Eban is traded to the Nets for a second round draft choice in next year's draft, gives back half his cash bonus and sells his million Knick shares back to Mr. J. Dolan, the Knicks's controlling shareholder, for $2.25 a share (when the market price of the Knicks was then $5 per share). The sale of the Knick shares occurs four months after his acquisition of the shares. Any securities law problem here?

PROBLEM 9-6
C.B. 517

The Rutgers family has always controlled Rutgers Industries, a reporting company traded on Nasdaq, since their grandfather, Raritan Rutgers, founded it in 1925. But today they own only 28% of the stock among them. Yet on the nine person Rutgers board, they hold five seats. When the oldest Rutgers director – Brunswick Rutgers – dies suddenly, the family decides to replace him with their family lawyer, Somerset Trenton. Because Trenton owns no Rutgers shares, they cause the company to sell him 2 million shares (or 2% of the outstanding shares) at a price of $3 per share on October 1, 2009 in a private placement. Rutgers is behind in its filing of Exchange Act reports. Nonetheless, on the day of his retirement from his law firm, Trenton sells 1.5 million Rutgers shares on Nasdaq on November 5, 2010 in a brokerage transaction in which his broker solicits orders.

PROBLEM 9-7
C.B. 529

Medium Tech, Inc. is a Nasdaq listed "reporting" company that designs software and web sites for large corporate clients. Becky Gill was hired by Medium Tech two years ago, at which point she purchased 10,000 shares from Medium Tech in a private sale (the purchase price was $120,000 and she paid $20,000 in cash and gave a full recourse promissory note for $100,000, which was secured by a pledge of securities having a market value of $80,000). Becky paid off this note in full three months ago. Becky's title is Director of Web Design for Medium Tech, which is an important creative position, but does not make her an executive officer. Becky now owns 25,000 shares in Medium Tech, having purchased 5,000 shares in the open market on Nasdaq last week and 10,000 shares on the exercise of a stock option three months ago. Becky was awarded the stock option under the company's employee stock option plan, which is a "qualified" plan. She is not quite clear on whether the stock option plan is registered. You are counsel to Merrill, Shearson, the brokerage firm, which she has asked to help her sell all of the stock she can without registration (she wants to buy a ski chalet in Colorado). Medium Tech has 1,400,000 shares outstanding and its trading volume over the last four weeks has been 10,000, 13,000, 16,000, and 14,000 shares, respectively. Advise her as to what she can and cannot now sell.

PROBLEM 9-8
C.B. 530

Same facts as in the preceding problem, except that now (1) Becky Gill has been promoted to Executive Vice President and made a director of Medium Tech, (ii) Becky financed her purchase a year ago of 10,000 Medium Tech shares with a full-recourse bank loan (not a loan from Medium Tech), and the bank received no collateral other than a pledge of the Medium Tech shares, and (iii) Becky gave 2,000 of the 5,000 shares that she recently purchased in the market to her 19 year old son, Ronald, as a birthday present. Ronald sold those shares last week to buy a car. Now, how many shares can Becky sell immediately.

PROBLEM 9-9
C.B. 530

(a) Donald Duck is the Vice Chairman of Disney Enterprises, Inc., the movie studio. On January 10, 2003, he makes a gift of 1 million shares each to his three nephews, Huey, Dewey, and Louie (none of whom live with Donald). The 3 million shares have been held by Donald Duck for over ten years. Disney has 100 million shares of its Common Stock outstanding and its average weekly trading volume is 600,000 shares. On June 30, 2003, both Huey, Dewey, and Louie independently decide to sell 500,000 shares each. Any problem?

(b) Same facts as before, but Huey, Dewey and Louie agree that sales of 500,000 by each of them would depress the market. Thus, they agree that Huey will sell in Week One, Dewey in Week Two, and Louie in Week Three. Any problem now?

(c) Same facts as before, except that Huey, Dewey and Louie – all very eligible bachelors – share a swinging East Side Townhouse.

PROBLEM 9-10
C.B. 530

Widget Corp., a reporting company listed on Nasdaq, has recently done a series of exempt transactions. On September 1, 2008, it sold 50,000 shares (or just under 1% of its Common Stock outstanding) to Bill Jones, a Widget Vice President (who is not a controlling person or affiliate), pursuant to his employment contract, relying on Rule 701 for its exemption. On April 15, 2008, it sold 3 million shares in an intrastate offering under § 3(a)(11), including 30,000 shares to Mike Smith, a retail investor. It is now April 20, 2009, and both shareholders would like to sell and want an opinion from you, their counsel, that they are free to use Rule 144. Can you give it to each of them? What can you advise each?

PROBLEM 9-11
C.B. 531

Assume next that Widget Corporation made a $20 million private placement of its stock in February 2008 under Rule 506, selling to some 60 investors, some accredited and some not. Several of the non-accredited investors would probably not qualify as sophisticated. One of these is Homer Pyle, an ex-Marine Corps veteran and now a member of Congress. Pyle bought 10,000 shares at $15 per share, and would like to sell them at their current price ($14 per share). It is now December, 2008, the Average Weekly Trading Volume in Widget is 50,000 shares, and the resale limitations imposed on Pyle under Rule 502(d) when he purchased have expired. Can he rely on Rule 144?

PROBLEM 9-12
C.B. 531

Bill Smith is a director of Widget and its largest shareholder with 24% of its Common Stock. He wants to cause Mike Jones, Chief Operating Officer of Intel, to join Widget as its new CEO. He is prepared to sell Jones 1% of Widget's stock at a price $2 below the current market price from his own personal holdings. Assume Widget has made all requisite filings with the SEC. Can Smith use Rule 144 to cover this transaction?

PROBLEM 9-13
C.B. 531

Tardy Corp. just listed on Nasdaq 90 days ago, but now it has become six months late in filing its Form 10-Q. Joe Jones, a Tardy salesman (but not an officer or affiliate), owns 10,000 shares of Tardy Common Stock that he purchased six months ago in the open market. Sally Smith, a small but sophisticated investor, bought 10,000 shares of Tardy in a Tardy private placement nine months ago. Prudence Jones, another sophisticated investor, bought 10,000 shares of Tardy one year ago in another private placement. Assume the Average Weekly Trading Volume in Tardy is 50,000 shares. Which of these investors can sell today under Rule 144?

PROBLEM 9-14
C.B. 531

On September 1, 2007, Delta Corp., a privately held non-reporting company, sells 1 million shares of its Common Stock to Tom Prince, its incoming chief executive officer at $10 per share. Prince gives his demand note bearing interest at 10% per annum in return for the shares and also pledges the stock to Delta as collateral for this loan. In early 2008, Delta Corp. does an initial public offering and lists on Nasdaq. Delta Corp. now has 80 million shares outstanding and an Average Weekly Trading Volume of 200,000 shares, and its stock price has risen to $25 per share. On September 15, 2008, Prince secures another loan from City Bank for $10,000,000 and uses that loan to pay off the Delta loan. He pledges half of his Delta stock (or 500,000 shares) to secure the City Bank loan. On September 30, 2008, he sells 150,000 of his shares to Mellon Investors, a hedge fund, at $22 per share in a private sale (i.e., $3 below the then market price). On March 20, 2009, he wishes to sell 200,000 additional Delta shares on Nasdaq. Do you see any problems with either of these sales?

PROBLEM 9-15
C.B. 531

Donald Duck is a senior officer, director and 10% shareholder of Disney, Inc., a publicly held company. He sells one million shares (equal to .9% of Disney's outstanding Common Stock) on January 15, 2008 and then dies of a heart attack on January 20, 2008 (after becoming upset about a commercial that employed the Aflac duck, which he considered "stereotypical"). His only beneficiaries are Huey, Dewey and Louie, who now live separately; each would like to sell the 500,000 shares on February 20, 2008 that each expects to receive from Donald's estate. Can they each make their contemplated sales under Rule 144? What if the executor of Donald's estate were also a director and vice-chairman of Disney, owning 8% himself? Can he sell any of Donald's Disney stock?

PROBLEM 9-16
C.B. 545

United States Industries, a reporting company whose common stock is listed on the New York Stock Exchange, makes a private placement of $100 million in face amount of 10% Convertible Debentures through Goldman Brothers, its placing agent. The bonds were purchased at their face value without any discount. The purchasers are twenty or so large institutional investors, most of whom would satisfy the definition of "qualified institutional buyer" in Rule 144A(a)(i). Both these institutions and United States Industries would like to list these debentures on the Portal system administered by the NASD. Each $1,000 bond is convertible into 20 shares of United States Industries, which on the date that the offering closed was trading at $40 per share. Do these securities qualify for Rule 144A?

PROBLEM 9-17
C.B. 546

(a) Widget Corp., a non-reporting issuer, sells $50 million of its Convertible Debentures through two distributors – Citybank and J.P. Morganbank – who in turn resell to 20 QIBs. Citybank and J.P. Morganbank both indicated on their websites, both preceding and following their purchase from Widget, that they would be offering the Widget Debentures to QIBs. One of these QIBs – Lafayette Securities – resells six months later to five wealthy investors, none of whom are QIBs (although all are accredited investors). What exposure does Lafayette have? And what exposure do Widget, Citybank, and the QIB purchasers (other than Lafayette) face because of Lafayette's sale?

(b) Assume now that one of Lafayette's purchasers was not even an accredited investor and received no information or disclosure document from Lafayette, Widget, Citybank or anyone else. What result now for all the parties?

PROBLEM 9-18
C.B. 546

Quick Chips, a non-reporting company in Silicon Valley that produces microchips, is evaluating two capital raising alternatives. First, it could sell 5 million shares of its Common Stock in a private placement through a local broker dealer, with the purchasers being largely accredited investors (and a few QIBs). Second, it could do a Rule 144A transaction, using a large bank as its "distributor." The small brokerage firm (which lacks the contacts with QIBs to do a Rule 144A offering) argues that it can sell to a wider audience of persons (i.e. non-QIB accredited investors, sophisticated persons, and even unsophisticated persons with a qualified purchaser representative), and it will charge a comparable fee. As securities counsel to Quick Chips, you are asked to explain what the advantages of a Rule 144A offering – both legal and economic – might be?

PROBLEM 9-19
C.B. 568

Belgian Industries is a Belgium incorporated company, listed on the Euronext Stock Exchange, with over 70% of its shareholders being Belgians. It is not a U.S. "reporting" company, but it does occasionally trade on the Nasdaq Bulletin Board, with such trading never accounting for more than 10% of the overall trading in its stock. On December 20, 2007, it makes an offering of 10,000,000 shares of its common stock in Europe pursuant to Rule 903. You may further assume that (i) offering restrictions were implemented, (ii) no "directed selling efforts" were made by anyone in the United States, (iii) all offers and sales were made in "offshore transactions," and (iv) that the securities carry a legend to the effect that transfers are prohibited except in accordance with the provisions of Regulation S or pursuant to an exemption from registration under the Securities Act of 1933. After the offering, 100 million shares of Belgian Industries's common stock are outstanding (and the average weekly trading volume is roughly 50,000 shares a week). Jacques Café, a wealthy Belgian investor, bought 800,000 shares of Belgian's stock in he December offering. He thereafter sells 400,000 shares on January 15, 2008 to a U.S. broker dealer, XYZ Securities, Inc., in a transaction negotiated in Europe. Between January 20th and January 23, 2008, XYZ Securities sells 250,000 Belgian Industries shares over the Nasdaq Bulletin Board to ten different buyers. Are these sales in compliance with the requirements of the Securities Act of 1933? Explain specifically why or why not, discussing the relevant rules and/or exemptions.

PROBLEM 9-20
C.B. 568

Small Co., a Delaware corporation that is not a reporting company, makes an offering of common stock in Europe on January 15, 2008, selling some 5 million shares through a combination of U.S. and European distributors. Offering restrictions are implemented; no directed selling efforts are made in the U.S.; the legend and stop transfer order mandated by Rule 903(b)(3)(iii) are properly complied with; and all offers and sales by the distributors are made in offshore transactions. The Gallic Fund, a French mutual fund, buys 250,000 shares on January 15th, and on February 1, it sells its shares to CalPERS, the California pension fund pursuant to Rule 144A. Is this permissible? Can CalPERS resell and to whom and when?

PROBLEM 9-21
C.B. 568

Assume that Small Co. in Problem 9-20 is a reporting company listed on the New York Stock Exchange. On January 30, 2008, it makes a Regulation S offering of its common stock in Europe through two American investment banks – Merrill, Sachs and Goldman, Lynch – acting as distributors. They sell:

(a) 100,000 shares of Small Co's common stock to the London office of the Hartford Insurance Co., which sells insurance in the U.K. subject to U.K. regulation;

(b) the Quantitative Fund, one of the U.S.'s largest hedge funds, in what purports to be a Rule 144A transaction.

(c) a discretionary account managed by a large U.S. broker-dealer for Count Bernadotte, the billionaire Swedish industrialist.

Which of these sales are permissible under Regulation S?

PROBLEM 9-22
C.B. 568

Small Co. has 100 million shares of its Common Stock outstanding after the above Regulation S offering in January 2008, and its Average Weekly Trading Volume is 500,000 shares. The Little Fund, a small U.S. mutual fund that does not qualify as a QIB, has purchased 2 million shares of Small Co. on February 15, 2008 from the Gallic Fund, a French mutual fund which acquired the shares in the original Regulation S offering by Small Co. but Little Fund quickly sours on its investment. On September 15, it sells 500,000 shares, and on October 1, it sells 300,000 shares, and on October 30, it sells 400,000 shares – all on the New York Stock Exchange. Any problem here? What can it do?

Credit Suisse Securities (USA) LLC v. Billing

Supreme Court of the United States, 2007
127 S. Ct. 2383 (June 18, 2007)

■ JUSTICE BREYER delivered the opinion of the Court.

A group of buyers of newly issued securities have filed an antitrust lawsuit against underwriting firms that market and distribute those issues. The buyers claim that the underwriters unlawfully agreed with one another that they would not sell shares of a popular new issue to a buyer unless that buyer committed (1) to buy additional shares of that security later at escalating prices (a practice called "laddering"), (2) to pay unusually high commissions on subsequent security purchases from the underwriters, or (3) to purchase from the underwriters other less desirable securities (a practice called "tying"). The question before us is whether there is a "'plain repugnancy'" between these antitrust claims and the federal securities law. See *Gordon v. New York Stock Exchange, Inc.*, 422 U.S. 659, 682 (1975) (quoting *United States v. Philadelphia Nat. Bank*, 374 U.S. 321, 350-351 (1963)). We conclude that there is. Consequently we must interpret the securities laws as implicitly precluding the application of the antitrust laws to the conduct alleged in this case. See *422 U.S., at 682, 689, 691*; see also *United States v. National Assn. of Securities Dealers, Inc.*, 422 U.S. 694 (1975) (NASD); *Silver v. New York Stock Exchange*, 373 U.S. 341 (1963).

I

A

The underwriting practices at issue take place during the course of an initial public offering (IPO) of shares in a company. An IPO presents an opportunity to raise capital for a new enterprise by selling shares to the investing public. A group of underwriters will typically form a syndicate to help market the shares. The syndicate will investigate and estimate likely market demand for the shares at various prices. It will then recommend to the firm a price and the number of shares it believes the firm should offer. Ultimately, the syndicate will promise to buy from the firm all the newly issued shares on a specified date at a fixed, agreed-upon price, which price the syndicate will then charge investors when it resells the shares. When the syndicate buys the shares from the issuing firm, however, the firm gives the syndicate a price discount, which amounts to the syndicate's commission. See generally L. Loss & J. Seligman, Fundamentals of Securities Regulation 66-72 (4th ed. 2001).

At the heart of the syndicate's IPO marketing activity lie its efforts to determine suitable initial share prices and quantities. At first, the syndicate makes a preliminary estimate that it submits in a registration statement to the Securities and Exchange Commission (SEC). It then conducts a "road show" during which syndicate underwriters and representatives of the offering firm meet potential investors and engage in a process that the industry calls "book building." During this time, the underwriters and firm representatives present information to investors about the company and the stock. And they attempt to gauge the strength of the investors' interest in purchasing the stock. For this purpose, underwriters might well ask the investors how their interest would vary depending upon price and the number of shares that are offered. They will learn, among other things, which investors might buy shares, in what quantities, at what prices, and for how long each is likely to hold purchased shares before selling them to others.

On the basis of this kind of information, the members of the underwriting syndicate work out final arrangements with the issuing firm, fixing the price per share and specifying the number of shares for which the underwriters will be jointly responsible. As we have said, after buying the shares at a discounted price, the syndicate resells the shares to investors at the fixed price, in effect earning its commission in the process.

B

In January 2002, respondents, a group of 60 investors, filed two antitrust class-action lawsuits against the petitioners, 10 leading investment banks. They sought relief under § 1 of the Sherman Act, ch. 647, 26 Stat. 209, as amended, *15 U.S.C. § 1*; § 2(c) of the Clayton Act, 38 Stat. 730, as amended by the Robinson-Patman Act, 49 Stat. 1527, *15 U.S.C. § 13(c)*; and state antitrust laws. App. 1, 14. The investors stated that between March 1997 and December 2000 the banks had acted as underwriters, forming syndicates that helped execute the IPOs of several hundred technology-related companies. *Id.*, at 22. Respondents' antitrust complaints allege that the underwriters "abused the . . . practice of combining into underwriting syndicates" by agreeing among themselves to impose harmful conditions upon potential investors--conditions that the investors apparently were willing to accept in order to obtain an allocation of new shares that were in high demand. *Id.*, at 12.

These conditions, according to respondents, consist of a requirement that the investors pay "additional anticompetitive charges" over and above the agreed-upon IPO share price plus underwriting commission. In particular, these additional charges took the form of (1) investor promises "to place bids . . . in the aftermarket at prices above the IPO price" (*i.e.*, "laddering" agreements); (2) investor "commitments to purchase other, less attractive securities" (*i.e.*, "tying" arrangements); and (3) investor payment of "non-competitively determined" (*i.e.*, excessive) "commissions," including the "purchas[e] of an issuer's shares in follow-up or 'secondary' public offerings (for which the underwriters would earn underwriting discounts)." *Id.*, at 12-13. The complaint added that the underwriters' agreement to engage in some or all of these practices artificially inflated the share prices of the securities in question. *Id.*, at 32.

The underwriters moved to dismiss the investors' complaints on the ground that federal securities law impliedly precludes application of antitrust laws to the conduct in question. (The antitrust laws at issue include the commercial bribery provisions of the Robinson-Patman Act.) The District Court agreed with petitioners and dismissed the complaints against them. See *In re Initial Public Offering Antitrust Litigation, 287 F. Supp. 2d 497, 524-525 (SDNY 2003) (IPO Antitrust)*. The Court of Appeals for the Second Circuit reversed, however, and reinstated the complaints. *426 F.3d 130, 170, 172 (2005)*. We granted the underwriters' petition for certiorari. And we now reverse the Court of Appeals.

II

A

Sometimes regulatory statutes explicitly state whether they preclude application of the antitrust laws. Compare, *e.g.*, Webb-Pomerene Act, *15 U.S.C. § 62* (expressly providing antitrust immunity) with § 601(b)(1) of the Telecommunications Act of 1996, *47 U.S.C. § 152* (stating that antitrust laws remain applicable). See also *Verizon Communications Inc. v. Law Offices of Curtis V. Trinko, LLP, 540 U.S. 398, 406-407 (2004)* (analyzing the antitrust saving clause of the Telecommunications Act). Where regulatory statutes are silent in respect to antitrust, however, courts must determine whether, and in what respects, they implicitly preclude application of the antitrust laws. Those determinations may vary from statute to statute, depending upon the relation between the antitrust laws and the regulatory program set forth in the particular statute, and the relation of the specific conduct at issue to both sets of laws. Compare *Gordon, 422 U.S., at 689* (finding implied preclusion of antitrust laws); and *NASD, 422 U.S., at 729-730* (same), with *Otter Tail Power Co. v. United States, 410 U.S. 366, 374-375 (1973)* (finding no implied immunity); *Philadelphia Nat. Bank, 374 U.S., at 352* (same); and *Silver, 373 U.S., at 360* (same). See also *Phonotele, Inc. v. American Tel. & Tel. Co., 664 F.2d 716, 727 (CA9 1981)*.

Three decisions from this Court specifically address the relation of securities law to antitrust law. In *Silver* the Court considered a dealer's claim that, by expelling him from the New York Stock Exchange, the Exchange had violated the antitrust prohibition against group "boycott[s]." *373 U.S., at 347*. The Court wrote that, where possible, courts should "reconcil[e] the operation of both [*i.e.*, antitrust and securities] statutory schemes . . . rather than holding one completely ousted." *Id., at 357*. It also set forth a standard, namely that "[r]epeal of the antitrust laws is to be regarded as implied only if necessary to make the Securities Exchange Act work, and even then only to the minimum extent necessary." *Ibid*. And it held that the securities law did *not* preclude application of the antitrust laws to the claimed boycott *insofar as the Exchange denied the expelled dealer a right to fair procedures. Id., at 359-360.*

In reaching this conclusion, the Court noted that the SEC lacked jurisdiction under the securities law "to review particular instances of enforcement of exchange rules"; that "nothing [was] built into the regulatory scheme which performs the antitrust function of insuring" that rules that injure competition are nonetheless "justified as furthering" legitimate regulatory "ends"; that the expulsion "would clearly" violate "the Sherman Act unless justified by reference to the purposes of the Securities Exchange Act"; and that it could find *no such justifying purpose* where the Exchange took "anticompetitive collective action . . . *without according fair procedures.*" *Id., at 357-358, 364* (emphasis added).

In *Gordon* the Court considered an antitrust complaint that essentially alleged "price fixing" among stockbrokers. It charged that members of the New York Stock Exchange had agreed to fix their commissions on sales under $ 500,000. And it sought damages and an injunction forbidding future agreements. *422 U.S., at 661*. The lawsuit was filed at a time when regulatory attitudes toward fixed stockbroker commissions were changing. The fixed commissions challenged in the complaint were applied during a period when the SEC approved of the practice of fixing broker-commission rates. But Congress and the SEC had both subsequently disapproved for the future the fixing of some of those rates. See *id., at 690-691.*

In deciding whether antitrust liability could lie, the Court repeated *Silver*'s general standard in somewhat different terms: It said that an "implied repeal" of the antitrust laws would be found only "where there is a 'plain repugnancy between the antitrust and regulatory provisions.'" *422 U.S., at 682* (quoting *Philadelphia Nat. Bank, supra, at 350-351*. It then held that the securities laws impliedly precluded application of the antitrust laws in the case at hand. The Court rested this conclusion on three sets of considerations. For one thing, the securities law "gave the SEC direct regulatory power over exchange rules and practices with respect to the fixing of reasonable rates of commission." *422 U.S., at 685* (internal quotation marks omitted). For another, the SEC had "taken an active role in review of proposed rate changes during the last 15 years," and had engaged in "continuing activity" in respect to the regulation of commission rates. *Ibid*. Finally, without antitrust immunity, "the exchanges and their members" would be subject to "conflicting standards." *Id., at 689*.

This last consideration--the conflict--was complicated due to Congress', and the agency's, changing views about the validity of fixed commissions. As far as the *past* fixing of rates was concerned, the conflict was clear: The antitrust law had forbidden the very thing that the securities law had then permitted, namely an anticompetitive rate setting process. In respect to the future, however, the conflict was less apparent. That was because the SEC's new (congressionally authorized) prohibition of (certain) fixed rates would take effect in the near-term future. And after that time the SEC and the antitrust law would *both* likely prohibit some of the ratefixing to which the plaintiff's injunction would likely apply. See *id., at 690-691*.

Despite the likely compatibility of the laws in the future, the Court nonetheless expressly found *conflict*. The conflict arose from the fact that the law permitted the SEC to supervise the competitive setting of rates and to "*reintroduc[e] . . . fixed rates,*" *id., at 691* (emphasis added), under certain conditions. The Court consequently wrote that "failure to imply repeal would render nugatory the legislative provision for regulatory agency supervision of exchange commission rates." *Ibid*. The upshot is that, in light of potential future conflict, the Court found that the securities law precluded antitrust liability even in respect to a practice that both antitrust law and securities law might forbid.

In *NASD* the Court considered a Department of Justice antitrust complaint claiming that mutual fund companies had agreed with securities broker-dealers (1) to fix "resale" prices, *i.e.*, the prices at which a broker-dealer would sell a mutual fund's shares to an investor or buy mutual fund shares from a fund investor (who wished to redeem the shares); (2) to fix other terms of sale including those related to when, how, to whom, and from whom the broker-dealers might sell and buy mutual fund shares; and (3) to forbid broker-dealers from freely selling to, and buying shares from, one another. See *422 U.S., at 700-703*.

The Court again found "clear repugnancy," and it held that the securities law, by implication, precluded all parts of the antitrust claim. *Id., at 719*. In reaching this conclusion, the Court found that antitrust law (*e.g.*, forbidding resale price maintenance) and securities law (*e.g.*, permitting resale price maintenance) were in conflict. In deciding that the latter trumped the former, the Court relied upon the same kinds of considerations it found determinative in *Gordon*. In respect to the last set of allegations (restricting a free market in mutual fund shares among brokers), the Court said that (1) the relevant securities law "enables [the SEC] to monitor the activities questioned"; (2) "the history of Commission regulations suggests no laxity in the exercise of this authority"; and hence (3) allowing an antitrust suit to proceed that is "so directly related to the SEC's responsibilities" would present "a substantial danger that [broker-dealers and other defendants] would be subjected to duplicative and inconsistent standards." See *NASD, 422 U.S., at 734-735*.

As to the other practices alleged in the complaint (concerning, *e.g.*, resale price maintenance), the Court emphasized that (1) the securities law "vested in the SEC final authority to determine whether and to what extent" the relevant practices "should be tolerated," *id., at 729*; (2) although the SEC has not actively supervised the relevant practices, that is only because the statute "reflects a clear congressional determination that, subject to Commission oversight, mutual funds should be allowed to retain the initiative in dealing with the potentially adverse effects of disruptive trading practices," *id., at 727*; and (3) the SEC has supervised the funds insofar as its "acceptance of fund-initiated restrictions for more than three decades . . . manifests an informed administrative judgment that the contractual restrictions . . . were appropriate means for combating the problems of the industry," *id., at 728*. The Court added that, in these respects, the SEC had engaged in "precisely the kind of administrative oversight of private practices that Congress contemplated." *Ibid*.

As an initial matter these cases make clear that JUSTICE THOMAS is wrong to regard §§ *77p(a)* and *78bb(a)* as saving clauses so broad as to preserve all antitrust actions. See *post*, (dissenting opinion). The United States advanced the same argument in *Gordon*. See Brief for United States as *Amicus Curiae* in *Gordon* v. *New York Stock Exchange, Inc.*, O. T. 1974, No. 74-304, pp. 8, 42. And the Court, in finding immunity, necessarily rejected it. See also *NASD, supra, at 694* (same holding); *Herman & MacLean v. Huddleston, 459 U.S. 375, 383 (1983)* (finding saving clause applicable to overlap between *securities* laws where that "overlap [was] neither unusual nor unfortunate" (internal quotation marks omitted)). Although one party has made the argument in this Court, it was not presented in the courts below. And we shall not reexamine it.

This Court's prior decisions also make clear that, when a court decides whether securities law precludes antitrust law, it is deciding whether, given context and likely consequences, there is a "clear repugnancy" between the securities law and the antitrust complaint--or as we shall subsequently describe the matter, whether the two are "clearly incompatible." Moreover, *Gordon* and *NASD*, in finding sufficient incompatibility to warrant an implication of preclusion, have treated the following factors as critical: (1) the existence of regulatory authority under the securities law to supervise the activities in question; (2) evidence that the responsible regulatory entities exercise that authority; and (3) a resulting risk that the securities and antitrust laws, if both applicable, would produce conflicting guidance, requirements, duties, privileges, or standards of conduct. We also note (4) that in *Gordon* and *NASD* the possible conflict affected practices that lie squarely within an area of financial market activity that the securities law seeks to regulate.

B

These principles, applied to the complaints before us, considerably narrow our legal task. For the parties cannot reasonably dispute the existence here of several of the conditions that this Court previously regarded as crucial to finding that the securities law impliedly precludes the application of the antitrust laws.

First, the activities in question here--the underwriters' efforts jointly to promote and to sell newly issued securities--is central to the proper functioning of well-regulated capital markets. The IPO process supports new firms that seek to raise capital; it helps to spread ownership of those firms broadly among investors; it directs capital flows in ways that better correspond to the public's demand for goods and services. Moreover, financial experts, including the securities regulators, consider the general kind of joint underwriting activity at issue in this case, including road shows and book-building efforts essential to the successful marketing of an IPO. See Memorandum *Amicus Curiae* of SEC in *IPO Antitrust,* Case No. 01 CIV 2014 (WHP) (SDNY), pp. 15, 39-40, App. D to Pet. for Cert. 124a, 138a, 155a-157a (hereinafter Brief for SEC). Thus, the antitrust complaints before us concern practices that lie at the very heart of the securities marketing enterprise.

Second, the law grants the SEC authority to supervise all of the activities here in question. Indeed, the SEC possesses considerable power to forbid, permit, encourage, discourage, tolerate, limit, and otherwise regulate virtually every aspect of the practices in which underwriters engage. See, *e.g., 15 U.S.C. §§ 77b(a)(3), 77j, 77z-2* (granting SEC power to regulate the process of book-building, solicitations of "indications of interest," and communications between underwriting participants and their customers, including those that occur during road shows); *§ 78o(c)(2)(D)* (granting SEC power to define and prevent through rules and regulations acts and practices that are fraudulent, deceptive, or manipulative); *§ 78i(a)(6)* (similar); *§ 78j(b)* (similar). Private individuals who suffer harm as a result of a violation of pertinent statutes and regulations may also recover damages. See *§§ 78bb, 78u-4, 77k*.

Third, the SEC has continuously exercised its legal authority to regulate conduct of the general kind now at issue. It has defined in detail, for example, what underwriters may and may not do and say during their road shows. Compare, *e.g.,* Guidance Regarding Prohibited Conduct In Connection with *IPO Allocations, 70 Fed. Reg. 19672 (2005),* with Regulation M, *17 CFR §§ 242.100-242.105 (2006)*. It has brought actions against underwriters who have violated these SEC regulations. See Brief for SEC 13-14, App. D to Pet. for Cert. 136a-138a. And private litigants, too, have brought securities actions complaining of conduct virtually identical to the conduct at issue here; and they have obtained damages. See, *e.g., In re Initial Pub. Offering Securities Litigation, 241 F. Supp. 2d 281 (SDNY 2003)*.

The preceding considerations show that the first condition (legal regulatory authority), the second condition (exercise of that authority), and the fourth condition (heartland securities activity) that were present in *Gordon* and *NASD* are satisfied in this case as well. Unlike *Silver,* there is here no question of the existence of appropriate regulatory authority, nor is there doubt as to whether the regulators have exercised that authority. Rather, the question before us concerns the third condition: Is there a conflict that rises to the level of incompatibility? Is an antitrust suit such as this likely to prove practically incompatible with the SEC's administration of the Nation's securities laws?

III

A

Given the SEC's comprehensive authority to regulate IPO underwriting syndicates, its active and ongoing exercise of that authority, and the undisputed need for joint IPO underwriter activity, we do not read the complaints as attacking the bare existence of IPO underwriting syndicates or any of the joint activity that the SEC considers a necessary component of IPO-related syndicate activity. See Brief for SEC 15, 39-40, App. D to Pet. for Cert. 138a, 155a-157a. See also *IPO Antitrust, 287 F. Supp. 2d, at 507* (discussing the history of syndicate marketing of IPOs); App. 12 (complaint attacks underwriters "*abuse*" of "the preexisting practice of combining into underwriting syndicates" (emphasis added)); H. R. Rep. No. 1383, 73d Cong., 2d Sess., 6-7 (1934); S. Rep. No. 792, 73d Cong., 2d Sess., 5 (1934) (law must give to securities agencies freedom to regulate agreements among syndicate members). Nor do we understand the complaints as questioning underwriter agreements to fix the levels of their commissions, whether or not the resulting price is "excessive." See *Gordon, 422 U.S., at 688-689* (securities law conflicts with, and therefore precludes, antitrust attack on the fixing of commissions where SEC has not approved, but later *might* approve, the practice).

We nonetheless can read the complaints as attacking the *manner* in which the underwriters jointly seek to collect "excessive" commissions. The complaints attack underwriter efforts to collect commissions through certain practices (*i.e.*, laddering, tying, collecting excessive commissions in the form of later sales of the issued shares), which according to respondents the SEC itself has already disapproved and, in all likelihood, will not approve in the foreseeable future. In respect to this set of claims, they contend that there is no possible "conflict" since both securities law and antitrust law aim to prohibit the same undesirable activity. Without a conflict, they add, there is no "repugnance" or "incompatibility," and this Court may not imply that securities law precludes an antitrust suit.

B

We accept the premises of respondents' argument--that the SEC has full regulatory authority over these practices, that it has actively exercised that authority, but that the SEC has *disapproved* (and, for argument's sake, we assume that it will continue to disapprove) the conduct that the antitrust complaints attack. Nonetheless, we cannot accept respondents' conclusion. Rather, several considerations taken together lead us to find that, even on these prorespondent assumptions, securities law and antitrust law are clearly incompatible.

First, to permit antitrust actions such as the present one *still* threatens serious securities-related harm. For one thing, an unusually serious legal line-drawing problem remains unabated. In the present context only a fine, complex, detailed line separates activity that the SEC permits or encourages (for which respondents must concede antitrust immunity) from activity that the SEC must (and inevitably will) forbid (and which, on respondents' theory, should be open to antitrust attack).

For example, in respect to "laddering" the SEC forbids an underwriter to "solicit customers prior to the completion of the distribution regarding whether and at what price and in what quantity they intend to place immediate aftermarket orders for IPO stock," *70 Fed. Reg. 19675*-19676 (emphasis deleted); *17 CFR §§ 242.100-242.105*. But at the same time the SEC permits, indeed encourages, underwriters (as part of the "book building" process) to "inquir[e] as to a customer's desired future position in the longer term (for example, three to six months), and the price or prices at which the customer might accumulate that position without reference to immediate aftermarket activity." *70 Fed. Reg. 19676.*

It will often be difficult for someone who is not familiar with accepted syndicate practices to determine with confidence whether an underwriter has insisted that an investor buy more shares in the immediate aftermarket (forbidden), or has simply allocated more shares to an investor willing to purchase additional shares of that issue in the long run (permitted). And who but a securities expert could say whether the present SEC rules set forth a virtually permanent line, unlikely to change in ways that would permit the sorts of "laddering-like" conduct that it now seems to forbid? Cf. *Gordon, supra, at 690-691.*

Similarly, in respect to "tying" and other efforts to obtain an increased commission from future sales, the SEC has sought to prohibit an underwriter "from demanding . . . an offer from their customers of any payment or other consideration [such as the purchase of a different security] in addition to the security's stated consideration." *69 Fed. Reg. 75785 (2004).* But the SEC would permit a firm to "allocat[e] IPO shares to a customer because the customer has separately retained the firm for other services, when the customer has not paid excessive compensation in relation to those services." *Ibid.,* n. 108. The National Association of Securities Dealers (NASD), over which the SEC exercises supervisory authority, has also proposed a rule that would prohibit a member underwriter from "offering or threatening to withhold" IPO shares "as consideration or inducement for the receipt of compensation that is excessive in relation to the services provided." *Id.,* at 77810. The NASD would allow, however, a customer legitimately to compete for IPO shares by increasing the level and quantity of compensation it pays to the underwriter. See *Ibid.* (describing NASD Proposed Rule 2712(a)).

Under these standards, to distinguish what is forbidden from what is allowed requires an understanding of just when, in relation to services provided, a commission is "excessive," indeed, so "excessive" that it will remain *permanently* forbidden, see *Gordon, 422 U.S., at 690-691.* And who but the SEC itself could do so with confidence?

For another thing, evidence tending to show unlawful antitrust activity and evidence tending to show lawful securities marketing activity may overlap, or prove identical. Consider, for instance, a conversation between an underwriter and an investor about how long an investor intends to hold the new shares (and at what price), say a conversation that elicits comments concerning both the investor's short and longer term plans. That exchange might, as a plaintiff sees it, provide evidence of an underwriter's insistence upon "laddering" or, as a defendant sees it, provide evidence of a lawful effort to allocate shares to those who will hold them for a longer time. See Brief for United States as *Amicus Curiae* 27.

....

Now consider these factors together--the fine securities-related lines separating the permissible from the impermissible; the need for securities-related expertise (particularly to determine whether an SEC rule is likely permanent); the overlapping evidence from which reasonable but contradictory inferences may be drawn; and the risk of inconsistent court results. Together these factors mean there is no practical way to confine antitrust suits so that they challenge only activity of the kind the investors seek to target, activity that is presently unlawful and will likely remain unlawful under the securities law. Rather, these factors suggest that antitrust courts are likely to make unusually serious mistakes in this respect. And the threat of antitrust mistakes, *i.e.*, results that stray outside the narrow bounds that plaintiffs seek to set, means that underwriters must act in ways that will avoid not simply conduct that the securities law forbids (and will likely continue to forbid), but also a wide range of joint conduct that the securities law permits or encourages (but which they fear could lead to an antitrust lawsuit and the risk of treble damages). And therein lies the problem.

This kind of problem exists to some degree in respect to other antitrust lawsuits. But here the factors we have mentioned make mistakes unusually likely (a matter relevant to Congress' determination of which institution should regulate a particular set of market activities). And the role that joint conduct plays in respect to the marketing of IPOs, along with the important role IPOs themselves play in relation to the effective functioning of capital markets, means that the securities-related costs of mistakes is unusually high. It is no wonder, then, that the SEC told the District Court (consistent with what the Government tells us here) that a "failure to hold that the alleged conduct was immunized would threaten to disrupt the full range of the Commission's ability to exercise its regulatory authority," adding that it would have a "chilling effect" on "lawful joint activities . . . of tremendous importance to the economy of the country." Brief for SEC 40, App. D to Pet. for Cert. 157a.

We believe it fair to conclude that, where conduct at the core of the marketing of new securities is at issue; where securities regulators proceed with great care to distinguish the encouraged and permissible from the forbidden; where the threat of antitrust lawsuits, through error and disincentive, could seriously alter underwriter conduct in undesirable ways, to allow an antitrust lawsuit would threaten serious harm to the efficient functioning of the securities markets.

Second, any enforcement-related need for an antitrust lawsuit is unusually small. For one thing, the SEC actively enforces the rules and regulations that forbid the conduct in question. For another, as we have said, investors harmed by underwriters' unlawful practices may bring lawsuits and obtain damages under the securities law. See *supra*, at 10-11. Finally, the SEC is itself required to take account of competitive considerations when it creates securities-related policy and embodies it in rules and regulations. And that fact makes it somewhat less necessary to rely upon antitrust actions to address anticompetitive behavior. See *15 U.S.C. § 77b(b)* (instructing the SEC to consider, "in addition to the protection of investors, whether the action will promote efficiency, competition, and capital formation"); *§ 78w(a)(2)* (the SEC "shall consider among other matters the impact any such rule or regulation would have on competition"); *Trinko, 540 U.S., at 412* ("[T]he additional benefit to competition provided by antitrust enforcement will tend to be small" where other laws and regulatory structures are "designed to deter and remedy anticompetitive harm").

We also note that Congress, in an effort to weed out unmeritorious securities lawsuits, has recently tightened the procedural requirements that plaintiffs must satisfy when they file those suits. To permit an antitrust lawsuit risks circumventing these requirements by permitting plaintiffs to dress what is essentially a securities complaint in antitrust clothing. See generally Private Securities Litigation Reform Act of 1995, 109 Stat. 737; Securities Litigation Uniform Standards Act of 1998, 112 Stat. 3227.

In sum, an antitrust action in this context is accompanied by a substantial risk of injury to the securities markets and by a diminished need for antitrust enforcement to address anticompetitive conduct. Together these considerations indicate a serious conflict between, on the one hand, application of the antitrust laws and, on the other, proper enforcement of the securities law.

We are aware that the Solicitor General, while recognizing the conflict, suggests a procedural device that he believes will avoid it (in effect, a compromise between the differing positions that the SEC and Antitrust Division of the Department of Justice took in the courts below). Compare Brief for Dept. of Justice, Antitrust Division, as *Amicus Curiae* in Case No. 01 CIV 2014, p. 23 (seeking no preclusion of the antitrust laws), with Brief for SEC 39-40, App. D to Pet. for Cert. 155a-157a (seeking total preclusion of the antitrust laws). He asks us to remand this case to the District Court so that it can determine "whether respondents' allegations of prohibited conduct can, as a practical matter, be separated from conduct that is permitted by the regulatory scheme," and in doing so, the lower court should decide whether SEC-permitted and SEC-prohibited conduct are "inextricably intertwined." See Brief for United States as *Amicus Curiae* 9. The Solicitor General fears that otherwise, we might read the law as totally precluding application of the antitrust law to underwriting syndicate behavior, even were underwriters, say, overtly to divide markets.

The Solicitor General's proposed disposition, however, does not convincingly address the concerns we have set forth here--the difficulty of drawing a complex, sinuous line separating securities-permitted from securities-forbidden conduct, the need for securities-related expertise to draw that line, the likelihood that litigating parties will depend upon the same evidence yet expect courts to draw different inferences from it, and the serious risk that antitrust courts will produce inconsistent results that, in turn, will overly deter syndicate practices important in the marketing of new issues. (We also note that market divisions appear to fall well outside the heartland of activities related to the underwriting process than the conduct before us here, and we express no view in respect to that kind of activity.)

The upshot is that all four elements present in *Gordon* are present here: (1) an area of conduct squarely within the heartland of securities regulations; (2) clear and adequate SEC authority to regulate; (3) active and ongoing agency regulation; and (4) a serious conflict between the antitrust and regulatory regimes. We therefore conclude that the securities laws are "clearly incompatible" with the application of the antitrust laws in this context.

The Second Circuit's contrary judgment is

Reversed.

....

DISSENT BY: THOMAS

DISSENT:

JUSTICE THOMAS, dissenting.

The Court believes it must decide whether the securities laws implicitly preclude application of the antitrust laws because the securities statutes "are silent in respect to antitrust." See *ante*, at 5. I disagree with that basic premise. The securities statutes are not silent. Both the Securities Act and the Securities Exchange Act contain broad saving clauses that preserve rights and remedies existing outside of the securities laws.

Section 16 of the Securities Act of 1933 states that "the rights and remedies provided by this subchapter shall be in addition to any and all other rights and remedies that may exist in law or in equity." *15 U.S.C. § 77p(a)*. In parallel fashion, *§ 28* of the Securities Exchange Act of 1934 states that "the rights and remedies provided by this chapter shall be in addition to any and all other rights and remedies that may exist at law or in equity." *§ 78bb(a)*. This Court has previously characterized those clauses as "confirm[ing] that the remedies in each Act were to be supplemented by 'any and all' additional remedies." *Herman & MacLean v. Huddleston, 459 U.S. 375, 383, 103 S. Ct. 683, 74 L. Ed. 2d 548 (1983)*.

The Sherman Act was enacted in 1890. See 26 Stat. 209. Accordingly, rights and remedies under the federal antitrust laws certainly would have been thought of as "rights and remedies" that existed "at law or in equity" by the Congresses that enacted that Securities Act and the Securities Exchange Act in the early 1930's. See *§ 77p*; *§ 78bb*. Therefore, both statutes explicitly save the very remedies the Court holds to be impliedly precluded. There is no convincing argument for why these saving provisions should not resolve this case in respondents' favor.

....

[Justice Stevens filed an opinion concurring in the judgment, and Justice Kennedy took no part in the consideration or decision of the case].

Financial Planning Association v. Securities and Exchange Commission

United States Court of Appeals, Fourth District of Columbia Circuit, 2007
482 F.3d 481

Before: ROGERS, GARLAND, and KAVANAUGH, Circuit Judges.

■ ROGERS, CIRCUIT JUDGE: Brokers and dealers are not subject to the requirements of the Investment Advisers Act ("IAA") where their investment advice is (1) "solely incidental to the conduct of [their] business as a broker or dealer," and (2) the broker or dealer "receives no special compensation therefor." *15 U.S.C. § 80b-2(a)(11)(C) (2000)*. The Securities and Exchange Commission, acting pursuant to § 202(a)(11)(F) and § 211(a) of the IAA, *15 U.S.C. §§ 80b-2(a)(11)(F), 80b-11(a)*, promulgated a final rule exempting broker-dealers from the IAA when they receive "special compensation therefor." *See* "Certain Broker-Dealers Deemed Not to be Investment Advisers," *70 Fed. Reg. 20,424 (Apr. 19, 2005)*. The Financial Planning Association ("FPA") petitions for review of the final rule on the ground that the SEC has exceeded its authority. We agree, and we therefore grant the petition and vacate the final rule.

I.

The IAA was enacted by Congress as one title of a bill "to provide for the registration and regulation of investment companies and investment advisers." Pub. L. No. 76-768, tit. II, 54 Stat. 847 (1940). The other title was the Investment Company Act ("ICA"). Pub. L. No. 76-768, tit. I, 54 Stat. 789 (1940). These were the last in a series of congressional enactments designed to eliminate certain abuses in the securities industry that contributed to the stock market crash of 1929 and the depression of the 1930s. Congress had previously enacted the Securities Act of 1933, the Securities Exchange Act of 1934 (hereinafter "the Exchange Act"), the Public Utility Holding Company Act of 1935, and the Trust Indenture Act of 1939.

"A fundamental purpose, common to these statutes, was to substitute a philosophy of full disclosure for the philosophy of *caveat emptor* and thus to achieve a high standard of business ethics in the securities industry." *SEC v. Capital Gains Research Bureau, Inc., 375 U.S. 180, 186 (1963)*. The IAA arose from a consensus between industry and the SEC "that investment advisers could not 'completely perform their basic function - -furnishing to clients on a personal basis competent, unbiased, and continuous advice regarding the sound management of their investments - - unless all conflicts of interest between the investment counsel and the client were removed.'" *Id. at 187* (citation omitted). According to the Committee Reports, "[t]he essential purpose of [the IAA] ... [was] to protect the public from the frauds and misrepresentations of unscrupulous tipsters and touts and to safeguard the honest investment adviser against the stigma of the activities of these individuals by making fraudulent practices by investment advisers unlawful." H.R. Rep. No. 76-2639, at 28 (1940).

> Virtually no limitations or restrictions exist with respect to the honesty and integrity of individuals who may solicit funds to be controlled, managed, and supervised... Individuals assuming to act as investment advisers at present can enter profit-sharing contracts which are nothing more than 'heads I win, tails you lose' arrangements. Contracts with investment advisers which are of a personal nature may be assigned and the control of funds of investors may be transferred to others without the knowledge or consent of the client."

S. Rep. No. 76-1775, at 21-22 (1940).

Under the IAA, investment advisers are required, among other things, to register and to maintain records, *15 U.S.C. § 80b-3(c) & (e)*; to limit the type of contracts they enter, *id. § 80b-5*; and not to engage in certain types of deceptive and fraudulent transactions, *id. § 80b-6*. Congress has amended the IAA on several occasions, *see* VII Louis Loss & Joel Seligman, *Securities Regulation* 3314-15 (3d ed. 2003), but the provisions at issue in this appeal have remained, in relevant part, unchanged.

In *§ 202(a)(11) of the IAA*, Congress broadly defined "investment adviser" as

> any person who, for compensation, engages in the business of advising others, either directly or through publications or writings, as to the value of securities or as to the advisability of investing in, purchasing, or selling securities, or who, for compensation and as part of a regular business, issues or promulgates analyses or reports concerning securities ...."

15 U.S.C. § 80b-2(a)(11). Carving out six exemptions from this broad definition, Congress determined that an "investment adviser" did not include:

> (A) a bank, or any bank holding company as defined in the Bank Holding Company Act of 1956 which is not an investment company, except that the term "investment adviser" includes any bank or bank holding company to the extent that such bank or bank holding company serves or acts as an investment adviser to a registered investment company, but if, in the case of a bank, such services or actions are performed through a separately identifiable department or division, the department or division, and not the bank itself, shall be deemed to be the investment adviser;

> (B) any lawyer, accountant, engineer, or teacher whose performance of such services is solely incidental to the practice of his profession;

> **(C) any broker or dealer [1] whose performance of such services is solely incidental to the conduct of his business as a broker or dealer and [2] who receives no special compensation therefor;**

(D) the publisher of any bona fide newspaper, news magazine or business or financial publication of general and regular circulation;

(E) any person whose advice, analyses, or reports relate to no securities other than securities which are direct obligations of or obligations guaranteed as to principal or interest by the United States, or securities issued or guaranteed by corporations in which the United States has a direct or indirect interest which shall have been designated by the Secretary of the Treasury, pursuant to section 3(a)(12) of the Securities Exchange Act of 1934, as exempted securities for the purposes of that Act; or

(F) such other persons not within the intent of this paragraph, as the Commission may designate by rules and regulations or order.

15 U.S.C. § 80b-2(a)(11) (emphasis added). *Subsections (C) and (F) are at issue in this appeal.*

Before enactment of the IAA, broker-dealers and others who offered investment advice received two general forms of compensation. Some charged only traditional commissions (earning a certain amount for each securities transaction completed). Others charged a separate advice fee (often a certain percentage of the customer's assets under advisement or supervision). *See 11 Fed. Reg. 10,996 (Sept. 27, 1946)*. The Committee Reports recognized that the statutory exemption for broker-dealers reflected this distinction; the Reports explained that the term "investment adviser" was "so defined as specifically to exclude ... brokers (insofar as their advice is merely incidental to brokerage transactions for which they receive only brokerage commissions)." S. Rep. No. 76-1775, at 22 [HA 164]; H. R. Rep. No. 76-2639, at 28 [HA 168].

The final rule took a different approach. After determining in 1999 that certain new forms of fee-contracting adopted by broker-dealers were "not ... fundamentally different from traditional brokerage programs," the SEC proposed a rule very similar to the final rule, *see Notice of Proposed Rulemaking, 64 Fed. Reg. 61,228 (Nov. 10, 1999)* ("1999 NOPR"), stating it would act as if it had already issued the rule, *id.* at 61,227. In adopting the temporary rule, pursuant to *subsection (F)* and its general rulemaking authority under *IAA § 211(a)*, the SEC exempted a new group of broker-dealers from the *IAA. 64 Fed. Reg. 61,226 (Nov. 10, 1999)*. After re-proposing the rule in January 2005, again pursuant to its authority under *subsection (F)* and *§ 211(a)*, the SEC adopted a slightly modified final rule on April 12, 2005, codified at 17 C.F.R. § 275.202(a)(11)-1. *70 Fed. Reg. 20,424, 453-54.*

The final rule provides, generally, in *Paragraph (a)(1)*, on "fee-based programs," that a broker-dealer who (1) receives special compensation will not be deemed an investment adviser if (2) any advice provided is solely incidental to brokerage services provided on a customer's account and (3) specific disclosure is made to the customer. In *Paragraph (a)(2)*, on discount brokerage programs, a broker-dealer will not be deemed to have received special compensation merely because it charges one customer more or less for brokerage services than it charges another customer. *Paragraph (b)* lists three non-exclusive circumstances in which advisory services, for which special compensation is received under *paragraph (a)(1)*, would not be performed "solely incidental to" brokerage: when

(1) a separate fee or contract exists for advice; (2) a customer receives certain financial planning services; and, (3) generally, a broker-dealer has investment discretion over a client's account. *Paragraph (c)* states a "special rule" that broker-dealers registered under the Exchange Act are investment advisers only for those accounts for which they receive compensation that subjects them to the IAA. *Paragraph (d)* defines the term "investment discretion," which appears in *paragraphs (a)(1)* and *(b)(3)*, to have the same meaning as § 3(a)(35) of the Exchange Act, *15 U.S.C. § 78c(a)(35)*, except for "discretion granted by a customer on a temporary or limited basis."

....

The FPA contends that when Congress enacted the IAA, Congress identified in *subsection (C)* the group of broker-dealers it intended to exempt, and that *subsection (F)* was only intended to allow the SEC to exempt new groups from the IAA, not to expand the groups that Congress specifically addressed. The resolution of the FPA's challenge thus turns on whether the SEC is authorized under *§ 202(a)(11)(F)* or *§ 211(a)* to except from IAA coverage an additional group of broker-dealers beyond the broker-dealers exempted by Congress in subsection (C), *15 U.S.C. § 80b-2(a)(11)(C)*. *Subsection (F) of § 202(a)(11)* authorizes the SEC to except from the IAA "such other persons not within the intent of this paragraph, as the Commission may designate by rules and regulations or order." *15 U.S.C. § 80b-2(a)(11)(F)*. As such, we review the SEC's exercise of its authority pursuant to *subsection (F)* under the familiar two-step analysis of *Chevron, USA, Inc. v. Natural Res. Def. Counsel, Inc., 467 U.S. 837, 842-43 (1984)*. Under step one, the court must determine whether Congress has directly spoken to the precise question at issue. "If the intent of Congress is clear, that is the end of the matter; for the court, as well as the agency, must give effect to the unambiguously expressed intent of Congress." *Id.* Under step two, "if the statute is silent or ambiguous with respect to the specific issue, the question for the court is whether the agency's answer is based on a permissible construction of the statute." *Id. at 843*. In reviewing an agency's interpretation of its authority under a statute it administers, the court will uphold that interpretation as long as it is a reasonable interpretation of the statute. *See Village of Bergen v. FERC, 308 U.S. App. D.C. 251, 33 F.3d 1385, 1389 (D.C. Cir. 1994)*.

Applying the "traditional tools of statutory construction," *see Chevron, 467 U.S. at 843 n.9*, the court looks to the text, structure, and the overall statutory scheme, as well as the problem Congress sought to solve. *See PDK Labs. Inc. v. DEA, 360 U.S. App. D.C. 344, 362 F.3d 786, 796 (D.C. Cir. 2004); Sierra Club v. EPA, 352 U.S. App. D.C. 357, 294 F.3d 155, 161 (D.C. Cir. 2002)*. All four elements demonstrate that the SEC has exceeded its authority in promulgating the rule under *§ 202(a)(11)(F)* because Congress has addressed the precise issue at hand.

Section 202(a)(11) lists exemptions (A)-(E) from the broad definition of "investment adviser" for several classes of persons -- including, for example, lawyers, accountants, and others whose advice is "solely incidental" to their regular business; and publishers of newsletters that circulate widely and do not give individually-tailored financial advice. Among the IAA exemptions is *subsection (C)*'s exemption for "*any* broker or dealer whose performance of such [investment advisory] services is solely incidental to the conduct of his business as a broker or dealer and who receives no special compensation therefor." (Emphasis added). Beyond the listed exemptions, *subsection (F)* authorizes the SEC to exempt from the IAA "such *other* persons not within the intent of this paragraph, as the Commission may designate by rules and regulations or order." (Emphasis added).

In the final rule, the SEC purports to use its authority under *subsection (F)* to broaden the exemption for broker-dealers provided under *subsection (C)*. The rule is inconsistent with the IAA, however, because it fails to meet either of the two requirements for an exemption under *subsection (F)*. First, the legislative "intent" does not support an exemption for broker-dealers broader than the exemption set forth in the text of *subsection (C)*; therefore, the final rule does not meet the statutory requirement that exemptions under *subsection (F)* be consistent with the "intent" of *paragraph 11 of section 202(a)*. Second, because broker-dealers are already expressly addressed in *subsection (C)*, they are not "other persons" under *subsection (F)*; therefore the SEC cannot use its authority under *subsection (F)* to establish new, broader exemptions for broker-dealers.

The final rule's exemption for broker-dealers is broader than the statutory exemption for broker-dealers under *subsection (C)*. Although the SEC maintains that the intent of paragraph 11 is to exempt broker-dealers who receive special compensation for investment advice [Red Br. 28; Oral Arg. Tape at 31:50], the plain text of *subsection (C)* exempts only broker-dealers who do not receive special compensation for investment advice. The word "any" is usually understood to be all inclusive. *See New York v. EPA, 370 U.S. App. D.C. 239, 443 F.3d 880, 885 (D.C. Cir. 2006)*. As "[t]he plain meaning of legislation should be conclusive, except in the 'rare cases [in which] the literal application of a statute will produce a result demonstrably at odds with the intentions of its drafters,'" *United States v. Ron Pair Enters., Inc., 489 U.S. 235, 242 (1989)* (quoting *Griffin v. Oceanic Contractors, Inc., 458 U.S. 564, 571 (1982))*, the terms of the IAA establish the precise conditions under which broker-dealers are exempt from the IAA. "To read out of a statutory provision a clause setting forth a specific condition or trigger to the provision's applicability is ... an entirely unacceptable method of construing statutes." *Natural Res. Def. Council v. EPA, 261 U.S. App. D.C. 372, 822 F.2d 104, 113 (D.C. Cir. 1987)*.

No other indicators of congressional intent support the SEC's interpretation of its authority under *subsection (F)*. The relevant language in the committee reports suggests that Congress deliberately drafted the exemption in *subsection (C)* to apply as written. Those reports stated that the "term 'investment adviser' is so defined as specifically to exclude ... brokers (insofar as their advice is merely incidental to brokerage transactions for which they receive *only* brokerage commissions)." S. Rep. No. 76-1775, at 22 (emphasis added) [HA 164]; *see also* H.R. Rep. No. 76-2639, at 28 [HA 168]. By seeking to exempt broker-dealers beyond those who receive only brokerage commissions for investment advice, the SEC has promulgated a final rule that is in direct conflict with both the statutory text and the Committee Reports.

The text of *subsection (F)* confirms this conclusion by the limiting the SEC's exemption authorization to "other persons." We agree with the FPA that when Congress enacted the IAA, Congress identified the specific classes of persons it intended to exempt. As to broker-dealers, *subsection (C)* applied to "*any* broker or dealer." Congress, through the use of contrasting text in *subsection (F)*, signaled that it only authorized the SEC to exempt "*other* persons" when consistent with the intent of the paragraph, and thus only when doing so would not override Congress's determination of the appropriate persons to be exempted from the IAA's requirements.

As the FPA points out, the word "other" connotes "existing besides, or distinct from, that already mentioned or implied." II *The Shorter Oxford English Dictionary* 1391 (2d ed. 1936, republished 1939). *See Key v. Allstate Ins. Co.*, 90 F.3d 1546, 1550 (11th Cir. 1996) (citing *The American Heritage Dictionary* 931 (1981)). There is nothing to suggest that Congress did not intend the words "any" or "other" to have their "ordinary or natural meaning." *Smith v. United States, 508 U.S. 223, 228 (1993)*. So understood, courts have hesitated to allow parties to use language structurally similar to the "other persons" clause in *subsection (F)* to redefine or otherwise avoid specific requirements in existing statutory exceptions. In *Liljeberg v. Health Servs. Acquisition Corp., 486 U.S. 847, 864 n.11 (1988)*, for example, the Supreme Court noted that where *Federal Rule of Civil Procedure 60(b)* contained five explicit grounds for relief, and one non-specific "any *other* reason" clause, (emphasis added) the structure of the clauses suggested that the final clause could not be used to elude or enlarge the first five -- that "clause (6) and clauses (1) through (5) are *mutually exclusive*." (emphasis added). *Accord Pioneer Inv. Servs. Co. v. Brunswick Assocs. Ltd. P'ship, 507 U.S. 380, 393 (1993)*; *Hesling v. CSX Transp. Inc., 396 F.3d 632, 643 (5th Cir. 2005)*; *United States v. Erdoss, 440 F.2d 1221, 1223 (2d Cir. 1971)*. Similarly, in *Am. Bankers Ass'n v. SEC*, this court explained that:

> A universal clause preceding every definition in the statute, which states only "unless the context otherwise requires," cannot provide the authority for one of the agencies whose jurisdictional boundaries are defined in the statute to alter by administrative regulation those very jurisdictional boundaries. To suggest otherwise is to sanction administrative autonomy beyond the control of either Congress or the courts.

256 U.S. App. D.C. 194, 804 F.2d 739, 754 (D.C. Cir. 1986). Our dissenting colleague attempts to distinguish these two cases as limited to situations in which one agency seeks to redraw the jurisdictional boundaries of another agency. *See* Dissenting Op. at [7-9]. That interpretation, however, ignores the underlying principle in each case: where the statutory text is clear, an agency may not use general clauses to redefine the jurisdictional boundaries set by the statute.

Just as the text and structure of paragraph of *202(a)(11)* make it evident that Congress intended to define "investment adviser" broadly and create only a precise exemption for broker-dealers, so does a consideration of the problems Congress sought to address in enacting the IAA. A comprehensive study conducted by the SEC pursuant to the Public Utility Holding Company Act of 1935 indicated that "many investment counsel have 'strayed a great distance from that professed function' of furnishing disinterested, personalized, continuous supervision of investments." Securities and Exchange Commission, *Investment Counsel, Investment Management, Investment Supervisory and Investment Advisory Services*, at 25 (1939) (quoting testimony of brokerage executive James N. White, of Scudder, Stevens & Clark). Floor debate on the IAA called attention to the fact that while this study was being conducted investment trusts and investment companies had perpetrated "some of the most flagrant abuses and grossest violations of fiduciary duty to investors." 86 Cong. Rec. 2844 (daily ed. Mar. 14, 1940) (statement of Sen. Wagner). Congress reiterated throughout its proceedings an intention to protect investors and bona fide investment advisers.

The overall statutory scheme of the IAA addresses the problems identified to Congress in two principal ways: First, by establishing a federal fiduciary standard to govern the conduct of investment advisers, broadly defined, *see Transamerica Mortgage Advisors v. Lewis, 444 U.S. 11, 17 (1979),* and second, by requiring full disclosure of all conflicts of interest. As the Supreme Court noted, Congress's "broad proscription against 'any ... practice ... which operates ... as a fraud or deceit upon any client or prospective client' remained in the bill from beginning to end." *Capital Gains, 375 U.S. at 191.*

> [T]he Committee Reports indicate a desire to ... eliminate conflicts of interest between the investment adviser and the clients as safeguards both to 'unsophisticated investors' and to 'bona fide investment counsel.' The [IAA] thus reflects a ... congressional intent to eliminate, or at least to expose, all conflicts of interest which might incline an investment adviser -- consciously or unconsciously -- to render advice which was not disinterested.

Id. at 191-92. This statutory scheme is inconsistent with a construction of the SEC's authority under *subsection (F)* that would enable persons Congress determined should be subject to the IAA to escape its restrictions.

In an attempt to overcome the plain language of the statute, the SEC asserts that Congress was also concerned about the regulation of broker-dealers under both the IAA and Exchange Act, and that such concern was reflected in the "intent" of the paragraph. *See 70 Fed. Reg. 20,430*; *see also 64 Fed. Reg. 61,228.* The SEC points to no convincing evidence that supports these assertions. At the time Congress enacted the IAA in 1940, broker-dealers were already regulated under the Exchange Act. In the IAA, Congress expressly acknowledged that the broker-dealers it covered could also be subject to other regulation. IAA § 208(b), *15 U.S.C. § 80b-8(b).* The IAA's essential purpose was to "protect the public from the frauds and misrepresentations of unscrupulous tipsters and touts and to safeguard the honest investment adviser against the stigma of the activities of these individuals by making fraudulent practices by investment advisers unlawful." H.R. Rep. No. 76-2639 at 28; *see also id. at 21.* As the FPA emphasizes, there is nothing in the committee reports to suggest that Congress was particularly concerned about the regulatory burdens on broker-dealers.

While the SEC's failure to respect the unambiguous textual limitations marked by the phrase "intent of this paragraph" and "other persons" is fatal to the final rule, an additional weakness exists in the SEC's interpretation: It flouts six decades of consistent SEC understanding of its authority under *subsection (F)*. *Cf. Commodity Futures Trading Comm'n v. Schor, 478 U.S. 833, 844 (1986); Red Lion Broad. Co. v. FCC, 395 U.S. 367, 380-82 (1969). Subsection (F)* is not a catch-all that authorizes the SEC to rewrite the statute. Rather, as *subsection (F)*'s terms provide, the authority conferred must be exercised consistent with the "intent of this paragraph" and apply to "other persons." The SEC cannot point to any instance between the 1940 enactment of the IAA and the commencement of the rulemaking proceedings that resulted in the final rule in 2005, when it attempted to invoke *subsection (F)* to alter or rewrite the exemptions for persons qualifying for exemptions under *subsections (A)-(E)*. Rather, the SEC has historically invoked *subsection (F)* to exempt persons not otherwise addressed in the five exemptions established by Congress: For example, the adviser to a family trust who was otherwise subject to fiduciary duties, Oral Arg. Tape at 39:20-43: 24; or new groups, such as thrift institutions acting in a fiduciary capacity, *69 Fed. Reg. 25,777-90 (May 7, 2004)*, and World Bank instrumentalities that provide advice only to sovereigns, *In re Int'l Bank for Reconstr. & Dev., 2001 SEC LEXIS 1782 (Sept. 4, 2001)*. As the SEC's own actions for the last 65 years suggest, *subsection (F)* serves the clear purpose of authorizing the SEC to address persons or classes involving situations that Congress had not foreseen in the statutory text -- not to broaden the exemptions of the classes of persons (such as broker-dealers) Congress had expressly addressed.

The SEC unconvincingly attempts to defend its expansive interpretation of *subsection (F)* by likening it to section 6(c) of the ICA, *15 U.S.C. § 80a-6(c)*. Section 6(c) of the ICA empowers the SEC to grant exemptions from the ICA, or any rule or regulation adopted under it, "if and to the extent that such exemption is necessary or appropriate in the public interest and consistent with the protection of investors and the purposes fairly intended by the policy and provisions" of the ICA. This court has noted that the SEC "has exercised this authority to exempt persons not within the intent of the [ICA] and generally to adjust its provisions to take account of special situations not foreseen when the [ICA] was drafted." *National Asso. of Sec. Dealers, Inc. v. Securities & Exchange Com.,420 F.2d 83, 92 (D.C. Cir. 1969)*, vacated on other grounds, *Investment Co. Inst. v. Camp, 401 U.S. 617 (1971)*. Reliance on *NASD* does not advance the SEC's position as the plain text of the ICA is far broader than that of IAA *subsection (F)*. The ICA expressly refers to the SEC's view of "the public interest" as a basis for new exemptions. "[W]e assume that in drafting ... legislation, Congress said what it meant." *United States v. LaBonte, 520 U.S. 751, 757 (1997)*. Although Congress amended the IAA in 1970, *see supra*, and repeated the same ICA language highlighted in *NASD* in § 206A of the IAA, *15 U.S.C. § 80b-6a*, the SEC disavows any reliance on *§ 206A* in promulgating the final rule, *see 70 Fed. Reg. 20,453*; Respondent's Br. at 27 n.10, and thus the court has no occasion to express an opinion on the SEC's authority under it, *see SEC v. Chenery Corp., 318 U.S. 80, 95 (1943)*. But the broader language found in *§ 206A* supports the conclusion that *subsection (F)* must be read more narrowly. *Cf. Duncan v. Walker, 533 U.S. 167, 174 (2001)*; *City of Chicago v. EDF, 511 U.S. 328, 338 (1994)*.

In light of the context in which Congress drafted *subsections (C)* and *(F)*, we conclude that, as indicated by the structure of *§ 202(a)(11)* and the problems that Congress addressed in the IAA, as well as the other indicators of Congress's intent, under *Chevron* step one the text of *subsections (C)* and *(F)* is unambiguous, and that, therefore, the SEC has exceeded its authority in promulgating the final rule. Our dissenting colleague's analysis fails to confront two realities of statutory construction. First, "[a]mbiguity is a creature not of definitional possibilities but of statutory context." *Brown v. Gardner, 513 U.S. 115, 118 (1994)*. Congress has used words having ordinary meaning -- "*any* broker or dealer" in *subsection (C)* and " *other* persons" in *subsection (F)* -- and a familiar structure to express its "intent" in addressing problems identified by the industry and the SEC. Second, the absence of a statutory definition of "intent of this paragraph" and "other persons" does not necessarily render their meaning ambiguous. *See Goldstein v. SEC, 371 U.S. App. D.C. 358, 451 F.3d 873, 878 (D.C. Cir. 2006)*. Again, the meaning of the text is defined by its context as set forth in the normal meaning of the words, the structure of paragraph 11, and the problems

Congress sought to address in the IAA. Because the court's duty is to give meaning to each word of a statute, the court cannot properly treat one authorization, under *subsection (F)*, as duplicative of another authorization, under *Section 206A*. *See supra* at [20]; Dissenting Op. at [10]. Consequently, *section 202(a)(11)(F)* does not lend itself to alternative meanings; to conclude otherwise would undermine Congress's purpose in enacting the IAA-to protect consumers and honest investment advisers and to establish fiduciary standards and require full disclosure of all conflicts of interests of "investment advisers," broadly defined. The SEC's suggestion that "new" broker-dealer marketing developments fall within the scope of its authority under *subsection (F)* ignores its own contemporaneous understanding of Congressional intent to capture such developments. *See supra* at [17] and note 7. Although an agency may change its interpretation of an ambiguous statute, all elements of the traditional tools of statutory interpretation confound the SEC's effort to walk away from its long-settled view of the limits of its authority under *subsection (F)* and our dissenting colleague's attempt to find an alternative meaning at this late date.

The SEC's invocation of its general rulemaking authority under *IAA section 211(a)*, is likewise to no avail because it suggests no intention by Congress that the SEC could ignore either of the two requirements in *subsection (C)* for broker-dealers to be exempt from the IAA. *See Am. Bankers, 804 F.2d 739, 755*. Paraphrasing an apt observation, while, in the SEC's view, "[t]he statute may be imperfect, ... the [SEC] has no power to correct flaws that it perceives in the statute it is empowered to administer. Its [*subsection (F)* authority and its] rulemaking power[s] [are] limited to adopting regulations to carry into effect the will of Congress as expressed in the statute." *Bd. of Governors v. Dimension Fin. Corp., 474 U.S. 361, 374 (1986)*.

Accordingly, we grant the petition and vacate the final rule. *See North Carolina v. Fed. Energy Regulatory Comm'n, 730 F.2d 790, 795-96 (D.C. Cir. 1984)*; *cf. K Mart Corp. v. Cartier, Inc., 486 U.S. 281, 294 (1988)*. The final rule does not contain a severability clause; nor does the SEC suggest it is severable. *Paragraph (b)* is expressly tied to *paragraph (a)*. Although, absent *(a)* or *(b)*, *paragraph (c)* merely states the current law, the SEC identifies *paragraph (c)* as one of "three separate, yet related, parts" of the final rule. Respondent's Br. at 11, 13. *Paragraph (d)* defines a term used in *paragraphs (a)* and *(b)*. The SEC release to the final rule states that *paragraph (d)* institutes a policy change based on its interpretation of *subsection (F)*, *see 70 Fed. Reg.20,439*-440, but otherwise identifies *paragraph (d)* in the release as part and parcel of the final rule, *see, e.g., id. at 20,424*.

DISSENT BY: GARLAND

DISSENT: GARLAND, *Circuit Judge*, dissenting:

The Investment Advisers Act contains five specific exceptions, and further authorizes the SEC to exempt "such other persons not within the intent of this paragraph, as the Commission may designate by rules." *15 U.S.C. § 80b-2(a)(11)*. Unlike my colleagues, I cannot derive an unambiguous meaning from the terms "such other persons" and "within the intent of this paragraph." As required by *Chevron*, I would therefore defer to the SEC's reasonable interpretation of the statute it administers and uphold the Commission's fee-based brokerage rule....

In Re Polymedica Corp. Securities Litigation

United States Court of Appeals, First Circuit, 2005
432 F.3d 1

Before: TORRUELLA, CYR, and LIPEZ, Circuit Judges.

■ LIPEZ, CIRCUIT JUDGE: In this appeal pursuant to *Rule 23(f) of the Federal Rules of Civil Procedure* from an order certifying a class in a securities fraud case, we must decide an issue of first impression in this Circuit: the standard for determining whether a market was "efficient" when applying the fraud-on-the-market presumption of investor reliance. We also address the level of inquiry that a district court may pursue at the class-certification stage when making that efficiency determination. Defendants-Appellants PolyMedica Corporation, Liberty Medical Supply, Inc. ("Liberty"), and various officers of both companies (collectively, "PolyMedica") argue that the district court erred in finding that common questions predominated under *Rule 23(b)(3) of the Federal Rules of Civil Procedure*, by determining that the market was efficient for eight months of the class period, from January 2001 through August 2001 (the "Contested Time Period"), and deeming PolyMedica's expert evidence irrelevant to that determination. For the reasons set forth below, we vacate the district court's order certifying the class for the Contested Time Period, and remand for further proceedings.

I.

Thomas Thuma ("Plaintiff") is a purchaser of PolyMedica stock, who seeks to represent a class of all purchasers of PolyMedica stock from October 1998 through August 2001. PolyMedica is the parent company of Liberty, a seller of diabetic testing supplies. According to Plaintiff, PolyMedica reported record revenues and earnings during the class period based primarily on the growth of Liberty's diabetic supplies business, which accounted for up to 80% of PolyMedica's revenues. As a result of these increases in revenue and earnings, the price of PolyMedica's stock, which traded on the NASDAQ and the American Stock Exchange during the class period, increased substantially. In the consolidated complaint, filed on October 9, 2001, Plaintiff alleges that PolyMedica artificially inflated the market price of its stock by misrepresenting sales, revenues, and accounts receivable, and by issuing false press releases, causing Plaintiff and other members of the class to purchase stock at artificially inflated prices. Plaintiff further alleges that when the truth of this fraud became known, PolyMedica's stock lost more than 80% of its value. Plaintiff seeks damages under Section 10(b) of the Securities Exchange Act of 1934, *15 U.S.C. § 78j(b)* (the "Exchange Act") and Rule 10b-5 promulgated thereunder, *17 C.F.R. § 240.10b-5*, and Section 20(a) of the Exchange Act, *15 U.S.C. § 78t(a)*.

On January 28, 2004, following several years of litigation, Plaintiff moved for class certification pursuant to *Fed. R. Civ. P. 23(a)* and *(b)(3)*, asserting that common questions of law and fact predominated, based on the "fraud-on-the-market" theory. As we explain in greater detail below, under the Supreme Court's plurality decision in *Basic, Inc. v. Levinson, 485 U.S. 224 (1988)*, this theory obviates the need for a plaintiff to demonstrate individualized reliance on a defendant's misstatement by permitting a class-wide rebuttable presumption of reliance, thereby enabling a securities fraud class action to meet *Rule 23(b)(3)*'s commonality requirement. PolyMedica opposed the motion, arguing that the fraud- on-the-market presumption of reliance was inapplicable for the Contested Time Period because the market for PolyMedica stock was not "efficient" (a prerequisite for application of the presumption). Both sides submitted expert testimony in support of their respective positions.

Plaintiff's expert, Alan R. Miller, relying upon each of the five widely-accepted market-efficiency factors set forth in *Cammer v. Bloom, 711 F. Supp. 1264 (D.N.J. 1989)*, concluded that the market for PolyMedica stock was efficient. PolyMedica's expert, Dr. Denise Neumann Martin, in turn, concluded that the Polymedica market was not efficient, based on three factors not enumerated in Cammer. A hearing on Plaintiff's motion for class certification was held on July 16, 2004. On September 7, 2004, the district court granted Plaintiff's motion to certify the class for the entire proposed class period, rejecting Dr. Martin's evidence as not relevant to the definition of "market efficiency," which the court derived from Basic. The court also excluded from the class those investors who participated in short-sale transactions (i.e., transactions involving the sale of a borrowed security, as further discussed below), leaving it to "able counsel [to] develop an efficient solution" for identifying short-sellers.

PolyMedica filed an interlocutory appeal from the district court's order certifying the class pursuant to *Rule 23(f)*, which we permitted on February 15, 2005. On appeal, PolyMedica argues that the district court erred in determining that the market for PolyMedica stock was "efficient" during the Contested Time Period, and in concluding that the fraud-on-the-market presumption of reliance was therefore applicable for these months. PolyMedica further argues that the district court erred in certifying the class without a plan for identifying and excluding short-sellers from the class.

II.

A. Standard of Review

We generally review decisions granting or denying class certification under the highly deferential "abuse of discretion" standard. *Smilow v. Southwestern Bell Mobile Sys., Inc., 323 F.3d 32, 37 (1st Cir. 2003)*. Since *Rule 23* contains express legal standards for class certification, "an appeal of a class certification can pose pure issues of law which are reviewed de novo," that is, without deference to the district court. *Tardiff v. Knox County, 365 F.3d 1, 4 (1st Cir. 2004)*. "An error of law is, of course, always an abuse of discretion." *Charlesbank Equity Fund II v. Blinds To Go, Inc., 370 F.3d 151, 158 (1st Cir. 2004)*. Mixed questions of law and fact fall along a degree-of-deference continuum, ranging from non-deferential plenary review for law-dominated questions, to deferential clear-error review for fact-dominated questions. *Johnson v. Watts Regulator Co., 63 F.3d 1129, 1132 (1st Cir. 1995)*.

The formulation of the proper standard for efficiency is a purely legal question reviewed de novo. Reviewing the application of that standard to the facts of a case involves the review of a mixed question of law and fact. See *Cammer, 711 F. Supp. at 1277* (stating that "the question of whether the fraud-on-the-market theory can substitute for direct reliance in any given case is both a legal and a factual one: is the market in which a particular company's stock trades efficient"). Given the various factors relevant to an efficiency determination, and the abundant evidence that can be developed with respect to each factor, the determination of whether a market is efficient is a fact-dominated inquiry. Therefore, deferential clear-error review applies to that determination. The ultimate decision to certify a class is, of course, a discretionary one.

B. Level of Inquiry by the District Court

In determining whether to certify the class, the district court went well beyond the four corners of the pleadings, considering both parties' expert reports and literally hundreds of pages of exhibits focused on market efficiency. Before we can decide whether the district court correctly certified Plaintiff's class based on a finding of market efficiency, we must determine whether this detailed level of inquiry was appropriate at the class-certification stage. Plaintiff, relying on the Second Circuit's decision in *Wal-Mart Stores, Inc. v. Visa USA Inc. (In re Visa Check/MasterMoney Antitrust Litig.), 280 F.3d 124 (2d Cir. 2001)*, argues that a district court should not engage in a weighing of competing evidence at the class-certification stage, and should instead confine its review to the allegations raised in the plaintiff's complaint. At that stage, according to the Second Circuit, "a district court may not weigh conflicting expert evidence or engage in 'statistical dueling' of experts." *Id. at 135* (quoting *Caridad v. Metro-North Commuter R.R., 191 F.3d 283, 292-93 (2d Cir. 1999))*. In support of its position, the Second Circuit looked to *Eisen v. Carlisle & Jacquelin, 417 U.S. 156 (1974)*, in which the Supreme Court held that *Rule 23* did not authorize courts "to conduct a preliminary inquiry into the merits of a suit in order to determine whether it may be maintained as a class action." *Id. at 177*; see also *J.B. ex rel. Hart v. Valdez, 186 F.3d 1280, 1290 n.7 (10th Cir. 1999)* (recognizing that "when deciding a motion for class certification, the district court should accept the allegations contained in the complaint as true").

PolyMedica, on the other hand, argues that we should follow the majority of courts of appeals that have addressed this issue. According to these courts, a district court is not limited to the allegations raised in the complaint, and should instead make whatever legal and factual inquiries are necessary to an informed determination of the certification issues. See *Unger, 401 F.3d at 321* (stating that while "class certification hearings should not be mini-trials on the merits of the class or individual claims. . . . 'going beyond the pleadings is necessary, as a court must understand the claims, defenses, relevant facts, and applicable substantive law in order to make a meaningful determination of the certification issues'") (quoting *Castano v. Am. Tobacco Co., 84 F.3d 734, 744 (5th Cir. 1996))*; accord *Cooper v. Southern Co., 390 F.3d 695, 712 (11th Cir. 2004)*; *Gariety v. Grant Thornton, LLP, 368 F.3d 356, 365 (4th Cir. 2004)*; *West v. Prudential Sec., Inc., 282 F.3d 935, 938 (7th Cir. 2002)* ("Tough questions [at class-certification stage] must be faced and squarely decided, if necessary by holding evidentiary hearings and choosing between competing perspectives."); *Johnston v. HBO Film Mgmt., Inc., 265 F.3d 178, 189 (3rd Cir. 2001)*; see also *Wagner v. Taylor, 266 U.S. App. D.C. 414, 836 F.2d 578, 587 (D.C. Cir. 1987)* (noting that "a decision on class certification cannot be made in a vacuum," and that "some inspection of the circumstances of the case is essential to determine whether the prerequisites of *Federal Civil Rule 23* have been met").

In support of this more demanding inquiry at the class-certification stage, many of these courts rely on *General Telephone Co. of Southwest v. Falcon, 457 U.S. 147 (1982)*, in which the Supreme Court noted that since "the class determination generally involves considerations that are enmeshed in the factual and legal issues comprising the plaintiff's cause of action. . . .

sometimes it may be necessary for the court to probe behind the pleadings before coming to rest on the certification question." *Id. at 160* (internal quotation marks and citations omitted); see also *Amchem, 521 U.S. at 616* (noting that *Rule 23(b)(3)* involves a "close look" at predominance and superiority criteria).

We have already expressed our preference for the majority view. In *Waste Management Holdings, Inc. v. Mowbray, 208 F.3d 288 (1st Cir. 2000)*, we upheld a district court's decision to certify a class, where the court "engaged in a case-specific analysis that went well beyond the pleadings." *Id. at 297*. In that case, we also squared the Supreme Court's holdings in Eisen and Falcon, noting that while Eisen prohibits a district court from inquiring into whether a plaintiff will prevail on the merits at class certification, it "does not foreclose consideration of the probable course of litigation," as contemplated by Falcon. *Id. at 298*. "After all," we explained, "a district court must formulate some prediction as to how specific issues will play out in order to determine whether common or individual issues predominate in a given case." Id.

Three years later, in *Smilow v. Southwestern Bell Mobile Systems, 323 F.3d 32 (1st Cir. 2003)*, we noted that "[a] district court must conduct a rigorous analysis of the prerequisites established by *Rule 23* before certifying a class." *Id. at 38* (citing *Falcon, 457 U.S. at 161*). And last year, in Tardiff, we noted the split between circuits, reasoning that while "it is sometimes taken for granted that the complaint's allegations are necessarily controlling . . . in our view a court has the power to test disputed premises early on if and when the class action would be proper on one premise but not another." *365 F.3d at 4-5*. Therefore, in light of our prior precedent, we conclude that the district court was entitled to look beyond the pleadings in its evaluation of the applicability of the fraud-on-the-market presumption of reliance, and its resolution of the class-certification question.

III.

A. The Fraud-on-the-Market Theory

The Supreme Court has described the "basic elements" of a securities fraud action under *§ 10(b)* of the Exchange Act and *Rule 10b-5* promulgated thereunder as including: (1) "a material misrepresentation (or omission)"; (2) "scienter, i.e., a wrongful state of mind"; (3) "a connection with the purchase or sale of a security"; (4) "reliance"; (5) "economic loss"; and (6) "loss causation." *Brody v. Stone & Webster, Inc. (In re Stone & Webster, Inc., Sec. Litig.), 414 F.3d 187, 193 (1st Cir. 2005)* (quoting *Dura Pharm., Inc. v. Broudo, 544 U.S. 336 (2005))*; see also *Wortley v. Camplin, 333 F.3d 284, 294 (1st Cir. 2003)*. While reliance is typically demonstrated on an individual basis, the Supreme Court has noted that such a rule would effectively foreclose securities fraud class actions because individual questions of reliance would inevitably overwhelm the common ones under *Rule 23(b)(3)*. *Basic, 485 U.S. at 242*.

To avoid this result, the Supreme Court has recognized the fraud-on-the-market theory, which relieves the plaintiff of the burden of proving individualized reliance on a defendant's misstatement, by permitting a rebuttable presumption that the plaintiff relied on the "integrity of the market price" which reflected that misstatement. As the Supreme Court recognized in Basic, "the fraud on the market theory is based on the hypothesis that, in an open and developed securities market, the price of a company's stock is determined by the available material information regarding the company and its business," including any available material misstatements. *Id. at 241* (internal quotation marks and citation omitted). Since investors who purchase or sell stock do so in reliance on "the integrity of the market price," *id. at 247*, they indirectly rely on such misstatements because they purchase or sell stock at a price which necessarily reflects that misrepresentation. Under the fraud-on-the-market theory, "misleading statements will therefore defraud purchasers of stock even if the purchasers do not directly rely on the misstatements." *Id. at 242-43* (quoting *Peil v. Speiser, 806 F.2d 1154, 1160-61 (3d Cir. 1986))*; see also *Shaw v. Digital Equip. Corp., 82 F.3d 1194, 1218 (1st Cir. 1996)* (noting that in cases involving fraud-on-the-market theory, "the statements identified by plaintiffs as actionably misleading are alleged to have caused injury, if at all, not through the plaintiffs' direct reliance upon them, but by dint of the statements' inflating effect on the market price of the security purchased").

Before an investor can be presumed to have relied upon the integrity of the market price, however, the market must be "efficient". See *Basic, 485 U.S. at 248 n.27* (recognizing elements cited by court of appeals for invoking fraud-on-the-market presumption of reliance, including "that the shares were traded on an efficient market"). Efficiency refers to the flow of information in the relevant market and the effect of that information on the price of the stock. See *In re Laser Arms Corp. Sec. Litig., 794 F. Supp. at 490* (stating that "the underlying premise of the fraud on the market theory assumes that the market is a transmission belt which efficiently translates all information concerning a security," including misleading information, "into a price"). In an efficient market, the defendant's misrepresentations are said to have been absorbed into, and are therefore reflected in, the stock price. Conversely, when a market lacks efficiency, there is no assurance that the market price was affected by the defendant's alleged misstatement at all. Instead, the price may reflect information wholly unrelated to the misstatement. See *Freeman v. Laventhol & Horwath, 915 F.2d 193, 198 (6th Cir. 1990)* (stating that "an inefficient market, by definition, does not incorporate into its price all the available information about the value of a security. Investors, therefore, cannot be presumed to rely reasonably on the integrity of the market price of a security that is traded in such a market").

The fraud-on-the-market presumption of reliance and its relationship to market efficiency can thus be reduced to the following syllogism: (a) an investor buys or sells stock in reliance on the integrity of the market price; (b) publicly available information, including material misrepresentations, is reflected in the market price; and therefore, (c) the investor buys or sells stock in reliance on material misrepresentations. This syllogism breaks down, of course, when a market lacks efficiency, and the market does not necessarily reflect the alleged material misrepresentation. With this understanding as background, we must now decide the appropriate standard for determining whether a market is efficient.

B. The Meaning of "Market Efficiency"

The efficient market hypothesis began as an academic attempt to answer the following question: Can an ordinary investor beat the stock market, that is, can such an investor make trading profits on the basis of new information? In an efficient market, the answer is "no," because the information that would have given the investor a competitive edge and allowed the investor to "beat" the market is already reflected in the market price. See Lynn A. Stout, The Mechanisms of Market Inefficiency: An Introduction to the New Finance, *28 Iowa J. Corp. L. 635, 639 (2003)* (stating that "the common definition of market efficiency . . . is really a shorthand for the empirical claim that 'available information' does not support profitable trading strategies or arbitrage opportunities") (internal quotation marks and citation omitted). There is, therefore, no "bargain" from which an investor can benefit. Since the stock price fully reflects the information, an investor cannot take advantage of it by either purchasing the stock (if the information indicates the stock is underpriced) or selling the stock (if the information indicates the stock is overpriced). See Philip H. Dyvig & Stephen A. Ross, Arbitrage, in 1 The New Palgrave Dictionary of Money and Finance 48 (Peter Newman et al. eds., 1992) (stating that "the intuition behind [the efficient market hypothesis] is that if the price does not fully reflect all available information, then there is a profit opportunity available from buying the asset if the asset is underpriced or from selling the asset if the asset is overpriced").

One way information gets absorbed into the market and reflected in stock price is through arbitrageurs, who obtain and analyze information about stocks from a variety of sources, including from the issuer, market analysts, and the financial and trade press. *In re Verifone Sec. Litig., 784 F. Supp. 1471, 1479 (N.D. Cal. 1992)*; see generally Ronald J. Gilson & Reinier H. Kraakman, The Mechanisms of Market Efficiency, *70 Va. L. Rev. 549, 566 (1983)* (discussing variety of mechanisms by which new information is incorporated into stock price). These arbitrageurs immediately attempt to profit from such information (for instance, through short sales,) thereby causing the stock to move to a price which reflects the latest public information concerning the stock, where it is no longer possible to generate profits. See *Eckstein v. Balcor Film Investors, 8 F.3d 1121, 1129 (7th Cir. 1993)*(stating that "competition among savvy investors leads to a price that impounds all available information"); see also *Stout, supra, at 638 n.15* (noting that if arbitrageurs observe a difference between price and value, "they immediately eliminate it by their trading") (internal quotation marks and citation omitted).

The capacity of arbitrageurs to "seek out new information and evaluate its effects on the price of securities" distinguishes them from ordinary investors, who "lack the time, resources, or expertise to evaluate all the information concerning a security," and are thus "unable to act in time to take advantage of opportunities for arbitrage profits." Robert G. Newkirk, Comment, Sufficient Efficiency: Fraud on the Market in the Initial Public Offering Context, *58 U. Chi. L. Rev. 1393, 1409 (1991)*. In an efficient market, then, an ordinary investor "who becomes aware of publicly available information cannot make money by trading on it" because the information will have already been incorporated into the market by arbitrageurs. *Stout, supra, at 640*. "An example would be an investor who decides to sell a stock upon the public announcement of a decline in corporate earnings, who finds that by the time she calls her broker, the price has already dropped." Id.

According to the prevailing definition of market efficiency, an efficient market is one in which market price fully reflects all publicly available information. *Stout, supra, at 639* (citing Eugene F. Fama, Efficient Capital Markets: A Review of Theory and Empirical Work, 25 J. Fin. 383 (1970)). This definition has been adopted by many lower courts as a prerequisite for applying the fraud-on-the-market presumption of reliance. PolyMedica urges us to do likewise, arguing that an "efficient" market is an open and developed one, in which a stock price will move quickly to reflect all publicly available information.

The district court, on the other hand, expressly declined to adopt this prevailing definition of market efficiency. Relying upon language gleaned from the Supreme Court's decision in Basic, the district court held that "the 'efficient' market required for [the] 'fraud on the market' presumption of reliance is simply one in which 'market professionals generally consider most publicly announced material statements about companies, thereby affecting stock market prices'"; it "is not one in which a stock price rapidly reflects all publicly available material information." *In re PolyMedica Corp. Sec. Litig., 224 F.R.D. at 41* (emphasis in original) (quoting *Basic, 485 U.S. at 246 n.24*). Plaintiff agrees with the district court's definition, which, he contends, is drawn directly from language used by the Supreme Court in Basic.

PolyMedica argues that the district court's definition of market efficiency, while rooted in a footnote in Basic, defies the controlling language of Basic, the cases upon which Basic relied, and the subsequent cases interpreting Basic, all of which support the prevailing definition of market efficiency. Specifically, PolyMedica argues that the definition adopted by the district court wrongly focuses on the thought processes of unidentified market professionals and whether stock prices are in some way affected by their consideration of most (but not necessarily all) material public information. The prevailing definition, on the other hand, requires a more searching inquiry into whether stock prices fully reflect all publicly available information. We must assess these conflicting positions of the parties.

C. The Standard for Determining an Efficient Market

1. Basic v. Levinson

While endorsing the fraud-on-the-market presumption of reliance in Basic, the Supreme Court did not explicitly address the meaning of an "efficient" market. See *Gariety, 368 F.3d at 368* (stating that Basic "offers little guidance for determining whether a market is efficient"). PolyMedica points to various passages in Basic purportedly showing a preference for the prevailing definition of an efficient market, noting the Supreme Court's statements that "the market is acting as the unpaid agent of the investor, informing him that given all the information available to it, the value of the stock is worth the market price," and that "the market price of shares traded on well-developed markets reflects all publicly available information, and hence, any material misrepresentations." *Basic, 485 U.S. at 244, 246* (emphasis added) (internal quotation marks and citation omitted).

Elsewhere, however, the Basic decision suggests that something less than "all publicly available information" may be required, noting that an investor's reliance may be presumed "because most publicly available information is reflected in market price," *id. at 247* (emphasis added). In separate footnotes of the decision, the Court further appeared to resist PolyMedica's suggested definition of an efficient market. As pointed out by the district court, the Supreme Court, after listing several academic articles, noted that:

> we need not determine by adjudication what economists and social scientists have debated through the use of sophisticated statistical analysis and the application of economic theory. For purposes of accepting the presumption of reliance in this case, we need only believe that market professionals generally consider most publicly announced material statements about companies, thereby affecting stock market prices.

Id. at 246 n.24. In addition, the Court noted that by accepting a rebuttable presumption of reliance, it "did not intend conclusively to adopt any particular theory of how quickly and completely publicly available information is reflected in market price." *Id. at 249 n.28.*

While the Supreme Court's language in Basic provides support for both the district court's definition of an efficient market as well as the prevailing definition urged by PolyMedica, the cases relied upon by the Supreme Court in Basic favor the latter definition. In Peil, cited extensively in Basic, the Third Circuit noted that "the 'fraud on the market' theory rests on the assumption that there is a nearly perfect market in information, and that the market price of stock reacts to and reflects the available information." *Peil, 806 F.2d at 1161 n.10.* Likewise, in *In re LTV Sec. Litig., 88 F.R.D. 134 (N.D. Tex. 1980),* which the Supreme Court also cited, the district court stated that "the central assumption of the fraud on the market theory [is] that the market price reflects all representations concerning the stock. . . . Efficient capital markets exist when security [sic] prices reflect all available public information about the economy, about financial markets, and about the specific company involved." *Id. at 144.*

Other cases cited in Basic, including the decision of the Sixth Circuit under review in Basic, similarly support the prevailing definition. See *Levinson, 786 F.2d at 750* (stating that "the fraud on the market theory is based on two assumptions: first, that in an efficient market the price of stock will reflect all information available to the public . . . and, second, that an individual relies on the integrity of the market price when dealing in that stock"); *T.J. Raney, Inc. & Sons v. Fort Cobb Irrigation Fuel Auth., 717 F.2d 1330, 1332 (10th Cir. 1983)* (stating that "the [fraud-on-the-market] theory is grounded on the assumption that the market price reflects all known material information").

Given the Supreme Court's disclaimer that it was not adopting any particular economic theory in applying the fraud-on-the-market presumption of reliance, on the one hand, and its embrace of the holdings of cases adopting the prevailing definition of market efficiency on the other hand, the most that can be said of Basic is that it did not directly address the meaning of an efficient market, choosing instead to leave the development of that concept to the lower courts. See *Abell v. Potomac Ins. Co. of Ill., 858 F.2d 1104, 1120 (5th Cir. 1988)* (stating that "Basic essentially allows each of the circuits room to develop its own fraud-on-the-market rules"), vacated on other grounds sub. nom. *Fryar v. Abell, 492 U.S. 914, 109 S. Ct. 3236, 106 L. Ed. 2d 584 (1989).* Basic is therefore not the benchmark for deriving a definition of market efficiency. We must turn to the decisions of the lower courts, post-Basic, for further guidance.

2. Lower Courts' Interpretation of "Market Efficiency"

PolyMedica correctly notes that in the wake of Basic, many lower courts have accepted a definition of market efficiency which requires that stock price fully reflect all publicly available information. The district court conceded as much: "I also note that the definition I have derived from Basic differs from much of the existing case law. Most cases define an 'efficient' market as a market in which prices incorporate rapidly or promptly all publicly available information." *In re PolyMedica Corp. Sec. Litig., 224 F.R.D. at 42.*

The district court's observation was apt. The precedents from other circuits overwhelmingly favor the definition advanced by PolyMedica. See *Gariety, 368 F.3d at 368* (stating that "in an efficient market, 'the market price has integrity[;] . . . it adjusts rapidly to reflect all new information'") (quoting *Macey & Miller, supra, at 1060*); *Greenberg v. Crossroads Sys., Inc., 364 F.3d 657, 662 n.6 (5th Cir. 2004)* (stating that "where securities are traded in an efficient market, it is assumed that all public information concerning a company is known to the market and reflected in the market price of the company's stock"); *No. 84 Employer-Teamster Joint Council Pension Trust Fund v. Am. West Holding Corp., 320 F.3d 920, 947 (9th Cir. 2003)* (stating that "in a modern and efficient securities market, the market price of a stock incorporates all available public information"); *GFL Advantage Fund, Ltd. v. Colkitt, 272 F.3d 189, 208 (3d. Cir. 2001)* (defining "efficient marketplace" as one "in which stock prices reflect all available relevant information about the stock's economic value"); *Joseph v. Wiles, 223 F.3d 1155, 1164 n.2 (10th Cir. 2000)* (stating that in an efficient market "the investor must rely on the market to perform a valuation process which incorporates all publicly available information, including misinformation"); *Kowal v. MCI Communications Corp., 305 U.S. App. D.C. 60, 16 F.3d 1271, 1276 n.1 (D.C. Cir. 1994)* (stating that "in an efficient securities market all publicly available information regarding a company's prospects has been reflected in its shares' price"); *Raab v. Gen. Physics Corp., 4 F.3d 286, 289 (4th Cir. 1993)* (reasoning that fraud-on-the-market presumption of reliance assumes "the market price has internalized all publicly available information"); *Freeman, 915 F.2d at 198* (stating that "the fraud on the market theory rests on the assumption that the price of an actively traded security in an open, well-developed, and efficient market reflects all the available information about the value of a company").

The prevailing definition of an efficient market is also consistent with language in our pre-Basic decision in *Roeder v. Alpha Industries, Inc., 814 F.2d 22 (1st Cir. 1987)*. There, we stated that under the fraud-on-the-market theory, "the market price of stock is taken to be the basis for investment decisions; because the price reflected all available information, investors are presumed to have been misled by the nondisclosure." *Id. at 27.*

3. Other Arguments Supporting the Prevailing Definition of "Market Efficiency"

PolyMedica points to statements made by the United States Securities and Exchange Commission ("SEC") supporting the prevailing definition of market efficiency. See Brief for the Securities and Exchange Commission as Amicus Curiae, *Basic v. Levinson, 485 U.S. 224 (1988)* (No. 86-279), available at 1987 WL 881068, at *22 (stating that fraud-on-the-market theory rests on proposition that "in an active secondary market, the price of company's stock is determined by all material information regarding the company and its business"); see also Arthur Levitt, Chairman, U.S. Securities and Exchange Commission, Testimony before House Subcomm. on Telecomm. & Fin., 104th Cong. 13 (Feb. 10, 1995), available at http://www.sec.gov./news/testimony/testarchive/1995/spch025.txt.

PolyMedica also argues with some force that the district court's definition is logically inconsistent. By requiring that an efficient market need only be affected by most but not all material information in order to be efficient, the district court's definition allows some information to be considered "material" and yet not affect market price. Cf. *In re Burlington Coat Factory Sec. Litig., 114 F.3d 1410, 1425 (3d Cir. 1997)* (stating that "in the context of an 'efficient' market, the concept of materiality translates into information that alters the price of the firm's stock").

4. "Market Efficiency" Defined

On the basis of the authorities and considerations cited, we conclude that the definition of market efficiency adopted by the district court is inconsistent with the presumption of investor reliance at the heart of the fraud-on-the-market theory. By rejecting the prevailing definition of market efficiency advocated by PolyMedica, and focusing instead on the general consideration by market professionals of most publicly announced material statements about companies, the district court applied the wrong standard of efficiency. For application of the fraud-on-the-market theory, we conclude that an efficient market is one in which the market price of the stock fully reflects all publicly available information.

Anticipating the possibility of this definition, Plaintiff complains that it forces him to prove that market price "correctly" reflects a stock's fundamental value before a market will be considered efficient. This argument misconstrues the conclusion that market price must "fully reflect" all publicly available information. The words "fully reflect" have two distinct meanings, each of which points to a different concept of market efficiency.

5. "Informational" v. "Fundamental Value" Efficiency

The first meaning of "fully reflect" focuses on the ability of the market to digest information, thereby preventing trading profits: market price "fully reflects" all publicly available information when "prices respond so quickly to new information that it is impossible for traders to make trading profits on the basis of that information." *Stout, supra, at 651*. This is known as "informational efficiency," and is best understood "as a prediction or implication about the speed with which prices respond to information." *Id. at 640*; see also Daniel R. Fischel, Efficient Capital Markets, the Crash, and the Fraud on the Market Theory, *74 Cornell L. Rev. 907, 913 (1989)* (stating that "under this definition, a market is efficient if it is impossible to devise a trading rule that systematically outperforms the market . . . absent possession of inside information").

"With many professional investors alert to news, markets are efficient in the sense that they rapidly adjust to all public information . . . ." *West, 282 F.3d at 938*. Where the market reacts slowly to new information, it is less likely that misinformation was reflected in market price and therefore relied upon. See *City of Monroe Employees Ret. Sys. v. Bridgestone Corp., 399 F.3d 651, 676 (6th Cir. 2005)* (stating that "in an open and efficient securities market[,] information important to reasonable investors (in effect, the market) is immediately incorporated into stock prices") (internal quotation marks and citation omitted); *Freeman, 915 F.2d at 199* (stating that "an efficient market is one which rapidly reflects new information in price") (quoting *Cammer, 711 F. Supp. at 1276 n.17*); *Fischel, supra, at 912* (stating that "the more rapidly prices reflect publicly-available information, the more sensible it is to apply the [fraud-on-the-market theory]").

Determining whether a market is informationally efficient, therefore, involves analysis of the structure of the market and the speed with which all publicly available information is impounded in price. See *Fischel, supra, at 912* (enumerating factors relevant to determination of "trading-rule" [i.e., "informational"] efficiency, including whether a stock "is actively traded, and whether it is followed by analysts and other market professionals. . . ., [and] the speed of price adjustment to new information [which] can be tested directly by use of widely-accepted statistical techniques").

The second, and much broader meaning of "fully reflect," focuses on the price of the stock as a function of its fundamental value: market price "fully reflects" all publicly available information when it responds to information not only quickly but accurately, such that "market prices mirror the best possible estimates, in light of all available information, of the actual economic values of securities in terms of their expected risks and returns." *Stout, supra, at 640.* This is known as "fundamental value efficiency." See *Fischel, supra, at 913* (stating that fundamental value efficiency "focuses on the extent to which security prices reflect the present value of the net cash flows generated by a firm's assets").

Determining whether a market is fundamental value efficient is a much more technical inquiry than determining informational efficiency. Depending on the method of valuation used, a stock's fundamental value turns on an assessment of various factors, including "present operations, future growth rates, relative risk levels, and the future levels of interest rates." *Newkirk, supra, at 1399*; see, e.g., *Stout, supra, at 641, 643-44* (discussing valuation of stocks based on Capital Asset Pricing Model, which focuses on expected risks and returns); cf. *Fischel, supra, at 914* (stating that the results of certain kinds of tests which measure "how closely prices reflect value," such as those which measure "whether the variability of prices is greater than the variability of dividends over time . . . . have been extremely controversial").

Courts and commentators often use these two concepts of market efficiency interchangeably. See *Newkirk, supra, at 1407* (stating that "the manner in which the courts apply the [efficient market hypothesis] is problematic because courts often fail to distinguish between value efficiency and information efficiency"). In fact, informational and fundamental value efficiency "often are [] made to go hand-in-hand, with fundamental value efficiency flowing naturally from informational efficiency." See *Stout, supra, at 641.* Despite this blurring of concepts, one thing is clear: a market can be information efficient without also being fundamental value efficient. *Stout, supra, at 651* (stating that "informational efficiency and fundamental value efficiency are distinct concepts"); see also *Fischel, supra, at 913-14.* While fundamental value efficiency may be the more comprehensive of the two concepts, encompassing both speed and accuracy, "'efficiency' is not an all-or-nothing phenomenon." *Eckstein, 8 F.3d at 1130.*

Therefore, by requiring that stock price in an efficient market fully reflect all publicly available information in order to establish the fraud-on-the-market presumption, we do not suggest that stock price must accurately reflect the fundamental value of the stock. This distinction is well-supported by the legal and economic commentary. See Jill E. Fisch, Picking a Winner, *20 Iowa J. Corp. L. 451, 464 (1995)* (book review) (stating that "stock prices regularly and persistently depart substantially from present value models as well as from financial variables that would appear to supply most of the information relevant to a calculation of fundamental value"); Baruch Lev & Meiring de Villiers, Stock Prices and 10B-5 Damages: A Legal, Economic, and Policy Analysis, *47 Stan. L. Rev. 7, 20 (1994)* (stating that "overwhelming empirical evidence suggests that capital markets are not fundamentally efficient"); *Newkirk, supra, at 1399* (noting that a "major drawback to fundamental value theory is that it requires a great deal of specific, sometimes unobtainable, information").

Our focus on whether a particular market has absorbed all available information (and misinformation) - such that an ordinary investor cannot beat the market by taking advantage of unexploited profit opportunities - is not a fundamental value inquiry. See *Stout, supra, at 651* (stating that "when finance economists define market efficiency in terms of the difficulty of making arbitrage profits, they have implicitly abandoned the more-powerful claim that efficient markets price securities accurately"). On the contrary, for purposes of establishing the fraud-on-the-market presumption of reliance, investors need only show that the market was informationally efficient. See *In re Verifone Sec. Litig., 784 F. Supp. at 1479 n.7* (stating that the fraud-on-the-market theory does not require "proof that the market correctly reflects some 'fundamental value' of the security. To apply the fraud-on-the-market theory, it is sufficient that the market for a security be 'efficient' only in the sense that market prices reflect the available information about the security."). The fraud-on-the-market theory is concerned with whether a market processes information in such a way as to justify investor reliance, not whether the stock price paid or received by investors was "correct" in the fundamental value sense.

Still, as a matter of logic, we cannot say that fundamental value efficiency has no place in applying the fraud-on-the-market presumption of reliance at the class-certification stage. Evidence bearing on a stock's fundamental value may be relevant to the efficiency determination as, for example, circumstantial evidence that arbitrageurs are not trading in the market, with the result that securities prices do not fully reflect all publicly available information. In other words, evidence of fundamental value may be relevant to the extent that it raises questions about informational efficiency. But there are practical limits on the evidence a court can or should consider during the class-certification proceedings. Courts which choose to consider such fundamental value evidence at the class-certification stage run the risk of turning the class-certification proceeding into a mini-trial on the merits, which must not happen. See *Eisen, 417 U.S. at 178* (stating that "in determining the propriety of a class action, the question is not whether the plaintiff or plaintiffs . . . will prevail on the merits, but rather whether the requirements of *Rule 23* are met") (internal quotation marks and citation omitted).

6. Evidence Necessary to Prove Presumption of Reliance

It is important to remember that the application of the fraud-on-the-market presumption only establishes just that - a presumption of reliance. That reliance can be rebutted at trial. See *Cammer, 711 F. Supp. at 1290* (stating that "if it were concluded after a hearing [that] the market appeared efficient, and [that] plaintiffs could proceed under the rebuttable presumption, [the defendant] would be entitled to prove to a jury that the market was inefficient, thereby rebutting the presumption"); see also *Lehocky v. Tidel Techs., Inc., 220 F.R.D. 491, 505 n.16 (S.D. Tex. 2004)* (stating that "at [the class-certification] stage of the proceedings, the Court need only inquire whether the stock traded in an efficient market and not examine the merits of the case. . . . Thus, the Court will not address whether Defendants' [sic] can rebut the presumption of reliance").

As the notes of the Advisory Committee on *Rule 301 of the Federal Rules of Evidence*, cited in Basic, make clear, a party need only establish "basic facts" in order to invoke the presumption of reliance. See *Basic, 485 U.S. at 245* (citing *Rule 301* and Advisory Committee Notes in support of statement that "presumptions are . . . useful devices for allocating the burden of proof between parties"); see also *Cammer, 711 F. Supp. at 1291 n.48* (stating that under the notes of the Advisory Committee on *Rule 301*, the nonmoving party has the burden of establishing the nonexistence of the presumed fact "once the party invoking the presumption establishes the basic facts giving rise to it") (emphasis in original) (internal quotation marks omitted).

The question of how much evidence of efficiency is necessary for a court to accept the fraud-on-the-market presumption of reliance at the class-certification stage is therefore one of degree. District courts must draw these lines sensibly, mindful that evidence of fundamental value may be relevant to the determination of informational efficiency, but other more accessible and manageable evidence may be sufficient at the certification stage to establish the basic facts that permit a court to apply the fraud-on-the-market presumption.

We have no illusions that this line-drawing is easy. Knowing the high stakes in the class-certification decision, the parties will try to move the court in different directions, with plaintiffs arguing for less evidence of efficiency and defendants for more, some of it highly technical. Exercising its broad discretion, and understanding the correct definition of efficiency and the factors relevant to that determination, the district court must evaluate the plaintiff's evidence of efficiency critically without allowing the defendant to turn the class-certification proceeding into an unwieldy trial on the merits. In this highly variable setting, these generalities are the best we can do.

IV.

Having concluded that the district court adopted the wrong definition of market efficiency, we must now decide whether the court's determination that the market for PolyMedica stock was efficient is nevertheless supportable. As previously discussed, the question of whether a particular market is efficient is a mixed question of law and fact. While the proper definition of market efficiency is a purely legal issue reviewed de novo, application of this definition to the facts of a case requires district courts to make judgments about the structure of the market for a particular stock. These judgments are reviewed for clear error. Many factors bearing on the structure of the market may be relevant to the efficiency analysis, and courts have wide latitude in deciding what factors to apply in a given case, and what weight should be given to those factors.

The district court in this case based its analysis of market efficiency on three factors: "(1) the involvement of market professionals, (2) the degree to and fluidity with which information is disseminated, and (3) whether information affected stock market prices." *In re PolyMedica Corp. Sec. Litig.*, 224 F.R.D. at 42-43. Applying these factors, the district court determined that the market for PolyMedica stock met the court's definition of market efficiency, that is, "one in which market professionals generally considered most publicly announced material statements about PolyMedica, thereby affecting the stock market price." *Id. at 43*. The court explicitly rejected PolyMedica's proffered evidence, which focused on whether market price "fully and rapidly reflected all the publicly available material information," ruling that it was "not relevant to the definition of market 'efficiency'" announced by the court. Id.

PolyMedica argues that by adopting the wrong definition of market efficiency, the district court erroneously refused to consider PolyMedica's evidence and, therefore, erroneously concluded that the market for PolyMedica stock was efficient. Plaintiff argues that regardless of whether the court adopted the wrong definition of efficiency, the factors analyzed by the court were nevertheless sufficient to support a finding of market efficiency under the correct definition of market efficiency that we adopt today. While we agree with Plaintiff that the factors considered by the district court were relevant to the issue of market efficiency, these factors are not exhaustive. See *Unger, 401 F.3d at 323*. If the district court had used the definition of market efficiency that we adopt today, other factors cited by PolyMedica may have also been relevant to the efficiency analysis and may have supported a contrary finding. The district court's error, therefore, was not in analyzing the factors that it did, but in applying an erroneous definition of market efficiency that prevented it from analyzing other arguably relevant evidence. We must therefore vacate its decision and remand for application of the proper standard.

V.

We summarize the essential points of our analysis. The district court was entitled to look beyond the pleadings and consider evidence in its evaluation of the applicability of the fraud-on-the-market presumption of reliance, and in its resolution of the class-certification question. However, the district court adopted a standard of market efficiency at odds with the prevailing standard, holding that market efficiency means that market professionals generally consider most publicly announced material statements about companies, thereby affecting stock market prices. This was error.

For purposes of establishing the fraud-on-the-market presumption of reliance, we adopt the prevailing definition of market efficiency, which provides that an efficient market is one in which the market price of the stock fully reflects all publicly available information. By "fully reflect," we mean that market price responds so quickly to new information that ordinary investors cannot make trading profits on the basis of such information. This is known as "informational efficiency." We reject a second and much broader meaning of "fully reflect," known as "fundamental value efficiency," which requires that a market respond to information not only quickly but accurately, such that the market price of a stock reflects its fundamental value.

While evidence of a stock's fundamental value may be relevant to the extent that it raises questions about informational efficiency, courts which choose to consider such fundamental value evidence at the class-certification stage run the risk of turning the class-certification proceeding into a mini-trial on the merits, which must not happen. The fraud-on-the-market presumption, after all, only establishes a presumption of reliance which can be rebutted at trial. At the class-certification stage, a party need only establish "basic facts" in order to invoke the presumption of reliance. The question of how much evidence of efficiency is necessary to establish the fraud-on-the-market presumption of reliance is one of degree. While district courts have broad discretion to draw these lines, they must do so sensibly, understanding the correct definition of efficiency and the factors relevant to that determination.

Having concluded this analysis, we must **vacate** the district court's order certifying the class for the period beginning January 2001 and ending August 2001, and **remand** for further proceedings consistent with this opinion. Each party shall bear its own costs of appeal.

So ordered.

Tellabs, Inc. v. Makor Issues & Rights, Ltd.

Supreme Court of the United States, 2007
127 S. Ct. __, 2007 WL 1773208 (June 21, 2007)

■ JUSTICE GINSBURG delivered the opinion of the Court.

This Court has long recognized that meritorious private actions to enforce federal antifraud securities laws are an essential supplement to criminal prosecutions and civil enforcement actions brought, respectively, by the Department of Justice and the Securities and Exchange Commission (SEC). See, *e.g.*, *Dura Pharmaceuticals, Inc. v. Broudo, 544 U.S. 336, 345 (2005); J. I. Case Co. v. Borak, 377 U.S. 426, 432 (1964)*. Private securities fraud actions, however, if not adequately contained, can be employed abusively to impose substantial costs on companies and individuals whose conduct conforms to the law. See *Merrill Lynch, Pierce, Fenner & Smith Inc. v. Dabit, 547 U.S. 71, 81 (2006)*. As a check against abusive litigation by private parties, Congress enacted the Private Securities Litigation Reform Act of 1995 (PSLRA), 109 Stat. 737.

Exacting pleading requirements are among the control measures Congress included in the PSLRA. The Act requires plaintiffs to state with particularity both the facts constituting the alleged violation, and the facts evidencing scienter, *i.e.*, the defendant's intention "to deceive, manipulate, or defraud." *Ernst & Ernst v. Hochfelder, 425 U.S. 185, 194, and n. 12 (1976)*; see *15 U.S.C. § 78u-4(b)(1),(2)*. This case concerns the latter requirement. As set out in § 21D(b)(2) of the PSLRA, plaintiffs must "state with particularity facts giving rise to a strong inference that the defendant acted with the required state of mind." *15 U.S.C. § 78u-4(b)(2)*.

Congress left the key term "strong inference" undefined, and Courts of Appeals have divided on its meaning. In the case before us, the Court of Appeals for the Seventh Circuit held that the "strong inference" standard would be met if the complaint "allege[d] facts from which, if true, a reasonable person could infer that the defendant acted with the required intent." *437 F.3d 588, 602 (2006)*. That formulation, we conclude, does not capture the stricter demand Congress sought to convey in § 21D(b)(2). It does not suffice that a reasonable factfinder plausibly could infer from the complaint's allegations the requisite state of mind. Rather, to determine whether a complaint's scienter allegations can survive threshold inspection for sufficiency, a court governed by § 21D(b)(2) must engage in a comparative evaluation; it must consider, not only inferences urged by the plaintiff, as the Seventh Circuit did, but also competing inferences rationally drawn from the facts alleged. An inference of fraudulent intent may be plausible, yet less cogent than other, nonculpable explanations for the defendant's conduct. To qualify as "strong" within the intendment of § 21D(b)(2), we hold, an inference of scienter must be more than merely plausible or reasonable--it must be cogent and at least as compelling as any opposing inference of nonfraudulent intent.

I

Petitioner Tellabs, Inc., manufactures specialized equipment used in fiber optic networks. During the time period relevant to this case, petitioner Richard Notebaert was Tellabs' chief executive officer and president. Respondents (Shareholders) are persons who purchased Tellabs stock between December 11, 2000, and June 19, 2001. They accuse Tellabs and Notebaert (as well as several other Tellabs executives) of engaging in a scheme to deceive the investing public about the true value of Tellabs' stock. *See 437 F.3d at 591;* App. 94-98.

Beginning on December 11, 2000, the Shareholders allege, Notebaert (and by imputation Tellabs) "falsely reassured public investors, in a series of statements . . . that Tellabs was continuing to enjoy strong demand for its products and earning record revenues," when, in fact, Notebaert knew the opposite was true. *Id.,* at 94-95, 98. From December 2000 until the spring of 2001, the Shareholders claim, Notebaert knowingly misled the public in four ways. *437 F.3d at 596.* First, he made statements indicating that demand for Tellabs' flagship networking device, the TITAN 5500, was continuing to grow, when in fact demand for that product was waning. *Id., at 596, 597.* Second, Notebaert made statements indicating that the TITAN 6500, Tellabs' next-generation networking device, was available for delivery, and that demand for that product was strong and growing, when in truth the product was not ready for delivery and demand was weak. *Id., at 596, 597-598.* Third, he falsely represented Tellabs' financial results for the fourth quarter of 2000 (and, in connection with those results, condoned the practice of "channel stuffing," under which Tellabs flooded its customers with unwanted products). *Id., at 596, 598.* Fourth, Notebaert made a series of overstated revenue projections, when demand for the TITAN 5500 was drying up and production of the TITAN 6500 was behind schedule. *Id., at 596, 598-599.* Based on Notebaert's sunny assessments, the Shareholders contend, market analysts recommended that investors buy Tellabs' stock. See *id., at 592.*

The first public glimmer that business was not so healthy came in March 2001 when Tellabs modestly reduced its first quarter sales projections. *Ibid.* In the next months, Tellabs made progressively more cautious statements about its projected sales. On June 19, 2001, the last day of the class period, Tellabs disclosed that demand for the TITAN 5500 had significantly dropped. *Id., at 593.* Simultaneously, the company substantially lowered its revenue projections for the second quarter of 2001. The next day, the price of Tellabs stock, which had reached a high of $ 67 during the period, plunged to a low of $ 15.87. *Ibid.*

On December 3, 2002, the Shareholders filed a class action in the District Court for the Northern District of Illinois. *Ibid.* Their complaint stated, *inter alia,* that Tellabs and Notebaert had engaged in securities fraud in violation of § 10(b) of the Securities Exchange Act of 1934, 48 Stat. 891, *15 U.S.C. § 78j*(b), and SEC Rule 10b-5, 17 CFR § 240.10b-5 (2006), also that Notebaert was a "controlling person" under § 20(a) of the 1934 Act, *15 U.S.C. § 78t*(a), and therefore derivatively liable for the company's fraudulent acts. See App. 98-101, 167-171. Tellabs moved to dismiss the complaint on the ground that the Shareholders had failed to plead their case with the particularity the PSLRA requires. The District Court agreed, and therefore dismissed the complaint without prejudice. App. to Pet. for Cert. 80a-117a; see *Johnson v. Tellabs, Inc., 303 F. Supp. 2d 941, 945 (ND Ill. 2004).*

The Shareholders then amended their complaint, adding references to 27 confidential sources and making further, more specific, allegations concerning Notebaert's mental state. See *437 F.3d at 594;* App. 91-93, 152-160. The District Court again dismissed, this time with prejudice. *303 F. Supp. 2d, at 971.* The Shareholders had sufficiently pleaded that Notebaert's statements were misleading, the court determined, *id., at 955-961,* but they had insufficiently alleged that he acted with scienter, *id., at 954-955, 961-969.*

The Court of Appeals for the Seventh Circuit reversed in relevant part. *437 F.3d at 591.* Like the District Court, the Court of Appeals found that the Shareholders had pleaded the misleading character of Notebaert's statements with sufficient particularity. *Id., at 595-600.* Unlike the District Court, however, the Seventh Circuit concluded that the Shareholders had sufficiently alleged that Notebaert acted with the requisite state of mind. *Id., at 603-605.*

The Court of Appeals recognized that the PSLRA "unequivocally raise[d] the bar for pleading scienter" by requiring plaintiffs to "plea[d] sufficient facts to create a strong inference of scienter." *Id., at 601* (internal quotation marks omitted). In evaluating whether that pleading standard is met, the Seventh Circuit said, "courts [should] examine all of the allegations in the complaint and then . . . . decide whether collectively they establish such an inference." *Ibid.* "[W]e will allow the complaint to survive," the court next and critically stated, "if it alleges facts from which, if true, a reasonable person could infer that the defendant acted with the required intent . . . . If a reasonable person could not draw such an inference from the alleged facts, the defendants are entitled to dismissal." *Id., at 602.*

In adopting its standard for the survival of a complaint, the Seventh Circuit explicitly rejected a stiffer standard adopted by the Sixth Circuit, *i.e.*, that "plaintiffs are entitled only to the most plausible of competing inferences." *Id., at 601, 602* (quoting *Fidel v. Farley, 392 F.3d 220, 227 (CA6 2004)).* The Sixth Circuit's standard, the court observed, because it involved an assessment of competing inferences, "could potentially infringe upon plaintiffs' Seventh Amendment rights." *437 F.3d at 602.* We granted certiorari to resolve the disagreement among the Circuits on whether, and to what extent, a court must consider competing inferences in determining whether a securities fraud complaint gives rise to a "strong inference" of scienter. 549 U.S.   (2007).

II

Section 10(b) of the Securities Exchange Act of 1934 forbids the "use or employ, in connection with the purchase or sale of any security . . ., [of] any manipulative or deceptive device or contrivance in contravention of such rules and regulations as the [SEC] may prescribe as necessary or appropriate in the public interest or for the protection of investors." *15 U.S.C. § 78j(b).*

. . . .

Section 10(b), this Court has implied from the statute's text and purpose, affords a right of action to purchasers or sellers of securities injured by its violation. See, *e.g.*, *Dura Pharmaceuticals, 544 U.S., at 341.* See also *id., at 345* ("The securities statutes seek to maintain public confidence in the marketplace . . . . by deterring fraud, in part, through the availability of private securities fraud actions."); *Borak, 377 U.S., at 432* (private securities fraud actions provide "a most effective weapon in the enforcement" of securities laws and are "a necessary supplement to Commission action"). To establish liability under § 10(b) and Rule 10b-5, a private plaintiff must prove that the defendant acted with scienter, "a mental state embracing intent to deceive, manipulate, or defraud." *Ernst & Ernst, 425 U.S., at 193-194, and n. 12.*

In an ordinary civil action, the Federal Rules of Civil Procedure require only "a short and plain statement of the claim showing that the pleader is entitled to relief." Fed. Rule Civ. Proc. 8(a)(2).

Although the rule encourages brevity, the complaint must say enough to give the defendant "fair notice of what the plaintiff's claim is and the grounds upon which it rests." *Dura Pharmaceuticals, 544 U.S., at 346* (internal quotation marks omitted). Prior to the enactment of the PSLRA, the sufficiency of a complaint for securities fraud was governed not by Rule 8, but by the heightened pleading standard set forth in Rule 9(b). See *Greenstone v. Cambex Corp., 975 F.2d 22, 25 (CA1 1992)* (Breyer, J.) (collecting cases). Rule 9(b) applies to "all averments of fraud or mistake"; it requires that "the circumstances constituting fraud . . . be stated with particularity" but provides that "[m]alice, intent, knowledge, and other condition of mind of a person, may be averred generally."

Courts of Appeals diverged on the character of the Rule 9(b) inquiry in § 10(b) cases: Could securities fraud plaintiffs allege the requisite mental state "simply by stating that scienter existed," *In re GlenFed, Inc. Securities Litigation, 42 F.3d 1541, 1546-1547 (CA9 1994)* (en banc), or were they required to allege with particularity facts giving rise to an inference of scienter? Compare *id., at 1546* ("We are not permitted to add new requirements to Rule 9(b) simply because we like the effects of doing so."), with, *e.g., Greenstone, 975 F.2d at 25* (were the law to permit a securities fraud complaint simply to allege scienter without supporting facts, "a complaint could evade too easily the 'particularity' requirement in Rule 9(b)'s first sentence"). Circuits requiring plaintiffs to allege specific facts indicating scienter expressed that requirement variously....

Setting a uniform pleading standard for § 10(b) actions was among Congress' objectives when it enacted the PSLRA. Designed to curb perceived abuses of the § 10(b) private action--"nuisance filings, targeting of deep-pocket defendants, vexatious discovery requests and manipulation by class action lawyers," *Dabit, 547 U.S., at 81* (quoting H. R. Conf. Rep. No. 104-369, p. 31 (1995) (hereinafter H. R. Conf. Rep.))--the PSLRA installed both substantive and procedural controls. Notably, Congress prescribed new procedures for the appointment of lead plaintiffs and lead counsel. This innovation aimed to increase the likelihood that institutional investors--parties more likely to balance the interests of the class with the long-term interests of the company--would serve as lead plaintiffs. See *id.,* at 33-34; S. Rep. No. 104-98, p. 11 (1995). Congress also "limit[ed] recoverable damages and attorney's fees, provide[d] a 'safe harbor' for forward-looking statements, . . . mandate[d] imposition of sanctions for frivolous litigation, and authorize[d] a stay of discovery pending resolution of any motion to dismiss." *Dabit, 547 U.S., at 81.* And in § 21D(b) of the PSLRA, Congress "impose[d] heightened pleading requirements in actions brought pursuant to § 10(b) and Rule 10b-5." *Ibid.*

Under the PSLRA's heightened pleading instructions, any private securities complaint alleging that the defendant made a false or misleading statement must: (1) "specify each statement alleged to have been misleading [and] the reason or reasons why the statement is misleading," *15 U.S.C. § 78u-4(b)(1)*; and (2) "state with particularity facts giving rise to a strong inference that the defendant acted with the required state of mind," § 78u-4(b)(2). In the instant case, as earlier stated, see *supra*, at 5, the District Court and the Seventh Circuit agreed that the Shareholders met the first of the two requirements: The complaint sufficiently specified Notebaert's alleged misleading statements and the reasons why the statements were misleading. *303 F. Supp. 2d, at 955-961; 437 F.3d at 596-600.* But those courts disagreed on whether the Shareholders, as required by § 21D(b)(2), "state[d] with particularity facts giving rise to a strong inference that [Notebaert] acted with [scienter]," § 78u-4(b)(2). See *supra*, at 5.

The "strong inference" standard "unequivocally raise[d] the bar for pleading scienter," *437 F.3d at 601,* and signaled Congress' purpose to promote greater uniformity among the Circuits, see H. R. Conf. Rep., p. 41. But "Congress did not . . . throw much light on what facts . . . suffice to create [a strong] inference," or on what "degree of imagination courts can use in divining whether" the requisite inference exists. *437 F.3d at 601.* While adopting the Second Circuit's "strong inference" standard, Congress did not codify that Circuit's case law interpreting the standard. See § 78u-4(b)(2). See also Brief for United States as *Amicus Curiae* 18. With no clear guide from Congress other than its "inten[tion] to strengthen existing pleading requirements," H. R. Conf. Rep., p. 41, Courts of Appeals have diverged again, this time in construing the term "strong inference." Among the uncertainties, should courts consider competing inferences in determining whether an inference of scienter is "strong"? See *437 F.3d at 601-602* (collecting cases). Our task is to prescribe a workable construction of the "strong inference" standard, a reading geared to the PSLRA's twin goals: to curb frivolous, lawyer-driven litigation, while preserving investors' ability to recover on meritorious claims.

III

A

We establish the following prescriptions: *First*, faced with a Rule 12(b)(6) motion to dismiss a § 10(b) action, courts must, as with any motion to dismiss for failure to plead a claim on which relief can be granted, accept all factual allegations in the complaint as true. See *Leatherman v. Tarrant County Narcotics Intelligence and Coordination Unit, 507 U.S. 163, 164 (1993).* On this point, the parties agree. See Reply Brief 8; Brief for Respondents 26; Brief for United States as *Amicus Curiae* 8, 20, 21.

Second, courts must consider the complaint in its entirety, as well as other sources courts ordinarily examine when ruling on Rule 12(b)(6) motions to dismiss, in particular, documents incorporated into the complaint by reference, and matters of which a court may take judicial notice. See 5B Wright & Miller § 1357 (3d ed. 2004 and Supp. 2007). The inquiry, as several Courts of Appeals have recognized, is whether *all* of the facts alleged, taken collectively, give rise to a strong inference of scienter, not whether any individual allegation, scrutinized in isolation, meets that standard. See, *e.g., Abrams v. Baker Hughes Inc., 292 F.3d 424, 431 (CA5 2002); Gompper v. VISX, Inc., 298 F.3d 893, 897 (CA9 2002).* See also Brief for United States as *Amicus Curiae* 25.

Third, in determining whether the pleaded facts give rise to a "strong" inference of scienter, the court must take into account plausible opposing inferences. The Seventh Circuit expressly declined to engage in such a comparative inquiry. A complaint could survive, that court said, as long as it "alleges facts from which, if true, a reasonable person could infer that the defendant acted with the required intent"; in other words, only "[i]f a reasonable person could not draw such an inference from the alleged facts" would the defendant prevail on a motion to dismiss. *437 F.3d at 602.* But in § 21D(b)(2), Congress did not merely require plaintiffs to "provide a factual basis for [their] scienter allegations," *ibid.* (quoting *In re Cerner Corp. Securities Litigation, 425 F.3d 1079, 1084, 1085 (CA8 2005)), i.e.,* to allege facts from which an inference of scienter rationally *could* be drawn. Instead, Congress required plaintiffs to plead with particularity facts that give rise to a "strong"--*i.e.*, a powerful or cogent--inference. See American Heritage Dictionary 1717 (4th ed.

2000) (defining "strong" as "[p]ersuasive, effective, and cogent"); 16 Oxford English Dictionary 949 (2d ed. 1989) (defining "strong" as "[p]owerful to demonstrate or convince" (definition 16b)); cf. 7 *id.*, at 924 (defining "inference" as "a conclusion [drawn] from known or assumed facts or statements"; "reasoning from something known or assumed to something else which follows from it").

The strength of an inference cannot be decided in a vacuum. The inquiry is inherently comparative: How likely is it that one conclusion, as compared to others, follows from the underlying facts? To determine whether the plaintiff has alleged facts that give rise to the requisite "strong inference" of scienter, a court must consider plausible nonculpable explanations for the defendant's conduct, as well as inferences favoring the plaintiff. The inference that the defendant acted with scienter need not be irrefutable, *i.e.*, of the "smoking-gun" genre, or even the "most plausible of competing inferences," *Fidel, 392 F.3d at 227* (quoting *Helwig v. Vencor, Inc., 251 F.3d 540, 553 (CA6 2001)* (en banc)). Recall in this regard that § 21D(b)'s pleading requirements are but one constraint among many the PSLRA installed to screen out frivolous suits, while allowing meritorious actions to move forward. See *supra*, at 9, and n. 4. Yet the inference of scienter must be more than merely "reasonable" or "permissible"--it must be cogent and compelling, thus strong in light of other explanations. A complaint will survive, we hold, only if a reasonable person would deem the inference of scienter cogent and at least as compelling as any opposing inference one could draw from the facts alleged.[5]

---

[5] JUSTICE SCALIA objects to this standard on the ground that "[i]f a jade falcon were stolen from a room to which only A and B had access," it could not "*possibly* be said there was a 'strong inference' that B was the thief." *Post*, at 1 (opinion concurring in judgment) (emphasis in original). I suspect, however, that law enforcement officials as well as the owner of the precious falcon would find the inference of guilt as to B quite strong--certainly strong enough to warrant further investigation. Indeed, an inference at least as likely as competing inferences can, in some cases, warrant recovery. See *Summers v. Tice, 33 Cal.2d 80, 84-87, 199 P.2d 1, 3-5 (1948)* (in bank) (plaintiff wounded by gunshot could recover from two defendants, even though the most he could prove was that each defendant was at least as likely to have injured him as the other); Restatement (Third) of Torts § 28(b), Comment *e*, p. 504 (Proposed Final Draft No. 1, Apr. 6, 2005) ("Since the publication of the Second Restatement in 1965, courts have generally accepted the alternative-liability principle of [*Summers* v. *Tice*, adopted in] § 433B(3), while fleshing out its limits."). In any event, we disagree with JUSTICE SCALIA that the hardly stock term "strong inference" has only one invariably right ("natural" or "normal") reading--his. See *post*, at 3.

JUSTICE ALITO agrees with JUSTICE SCALIA, and would transpose to the pleading stage "the test that is used at the summary-judgment and judgment-as-a-matter-of-law stages." *Post*, at 3 (opinion concurring in judgment). But the test at each stage is measured against a different backdrop. It is improbable that Congress, without so stating, intended courts to test pleadings, unaided by discovery, to determine whether there is "no genuine issue as to any material fact." See Fed. Rule Civ. Proc. 56(c). And judgment as a matter of law is a post-trial device, turning on the question whether a party has produced evidence "legally sufficient" to warrant a jury determination in that party's favor. See Rule 50(a)(1).

B

Tellabs contends that when competing inferences are considered, Notebaert's evident lack of pecuniary motive will be dispositive. The Shareholders, Tellabs stresses, did not allege that Notebaert sold any shares during the class period. See Brief for Petitioners 50 ("The absence of any allegations of motive color all the other allegations putatively giving rise to an inference of scienter."). While it is true that motive can be a relevant consideration, and personal financial gain may weigh heavily in favor of a scienter inference, we agree with the Seventh Circuit that the absence of a motive allegation is not fatal. See *437 F.3d at 601*. As earlier stated, *supra*, at 11, allegations must be considered collectively; the significance that can be ascribed to an allegation of motive, or lack thereof, depends on the entirety of the complaint.

Tellabs also maintains that several of the Shareholders' allegations are too vague or ambiguous to contribute to a strong inference of scienter. For example, the Shareholders alleged that Tellabs flooded its customers with unwanted products, a practice known as "channel stuffing." See *supra*, at 3. But they failed, Tellabs argues, to specify whether the channel stuffing allegedly known to Notebaert was the illegitimate kind (*e.g.*, writing orders for products customers had not requested) or the legitimate kind (*e.g.*, offering customers discounts as an incentive to buy). Brief for Petitioners 44-46; Reply Brief 8. See also *id.*, at 8-9 (complaint lacks precise dates of reports critical to distinguish legitimate conduct from culpable conduct). But *see 437 F.3d at 598, 603-604* (pointing to multiple particulars alleged by the Shareholders, including specifications as to timing). We agree that omissions and ambiguities count against inferring scienter, for plaintiffs must "state with particularity facts giving rise to a strong inference that the defendant acted with the required state of mind." § 78u-4(b)(2). We reiterate, however, that the court's job is not to scrutinize each allegation in isolation but to assess all the allegations holistically. See *supra*, at 11; *437 F.3d at 601*. In sum, the reviewing court must ask: When the allegations are accepted as true and taken collectively, would a reasonable person deem the inference of scienter at least as strong as any opposing inference?[6]

IV

---

[6] The Seventh Circuit held that allegations of scienter made against one defendant cannot be imputed to all other individual defendants. *437 F.3d at 602-603*. See also *id.*, at 603 (to proceed beyond the pleading stage, the plaintiff must allege as to each defendant facts sufficient to demonstrate a culpable state of mind regarding his or her violations) (citing *Phillips v. Scientific-Atlanta, Inc., 374 F.3d 1015, 1018 (CA11 2004)*). Though there is disagreement among the Circuits as to whether the group pleading doctrine survived the PSLRA, see, *e.g.*, *Southland Securities Corp. v. Inspire Ins. Solutions Inc., 365 F.3d 353, 364 (CA5 2004)*, the Shareholders do not contest the Seventh Circuit's determination, and we do not disturb it.

Accounting for its construction of § 21D(b)(2), the Seventh Circuit explained that the court "th[ought] it wis[e] to adopt an approach that [could not] be misunderstood as a usurpation of the jury's role." *437 F.3d at 602.* In our view, the Seventh Circuit's concern was undue.[7] A court's comparative assessment of plausible inferences, while constantly assuming the plaintiff's allegations to be true, we think it plain, does not impinge upon the Seventh Amendment right to jury trial.[8]

Congress, as creator of federal statutory claims, has power to prescribe what must be pleaded to state the claim, just as it has power to determine what must be proved to prevail on the merits. It is the federal lawmaker's prerogative, therefore, to allow, disallow, or shape the contours of--including the pleading and proof requirements for--§ 10(b) private actions. No decision of this Court questions that authority in general, or suggests, in particular, that the Seventh Amendment inhibits Congress from establishing whatever pleading requirements it finds appropriate for federal statutory claims. Cf. *Swierkiewicz v. Sorema N. A., 534 U.S. 506, 512-513 (2002); Leatherman, 507 U.S., at 168* (both recognizing that heightened pleading requirements can be established by Federal Rule, citing Fed. Rule Civ. Proc. 9(b), which requires that fraud or mistake be pleaded with particularity).

Our decision in *Fidelity & Deposit Co. of Md. v. United States, 187 U.S. 315 (1902),* is instructive. That case concerned a rule adopted by the Supreme Court of the District of Columbia in 1879 pursuant to rulemaking power delegated by Congress. The rule required defendants, in certain contract actions, to file an affidavit "specifically stating . . ., in precise and distinct terms, the grounds of his defen[s]e." *Id., at 318* (internal quotation marks omitted). The defendant's affidavit was found insufficient, and judgment was entered for the plaintiff, whose declaration and supporting affidavit had been found satisfactory. *Ibid.* This Court upheld the District's rule against the contention that it violated the Seventh Amendment. *Id., at 320.* Just as the purpose of § 21D(b) is to screen out frivolous complaints, the purpose of the prescription at issue in *Fidelity & Deposit Co.* was to "preserve the courts from frivolous defen[s]es," *ibid.* Explaining why the Seventh Amendment was not implicated, this Court said that the heightened pleading rule simply "prescribes the means of making an issue," and that, when "[t]he issue [was] made as prescribed, the right of trial by jury accrues." *Ibid.;* accord *Ex parte Peterson, 253 U.S. 300, 310 (1920)*

---

[7] The Seventh Circuit raised the possibility of a Seventh Amendment problem on its own initiative. The Shareholders did not contend below that dismissal of their complaint under § 21D(b)(2) would violate their right to trial by jury. Cf. *Monroe Employees Retirement System v. Bridgestone Corp., 399 F.3d 651, 683, n. 25 (CA6 2005)* (noting possible Seventh Amendment argument but declining to address it when not raised by plaintiffs).

[8] In numerous contexts, gatekeeping judicial determinations prevent submission of claims to a jury's judgment without violating the Seventh Amendment. See, *e.g., Daubert v. Merrell Dow Pharmaceuticals, Inc., 509 U.S. 579, 589 (1993)* (expert testimony can be excluded based on judicial determination of reliability); *Neely v. Martin K. Eby Constr. Co., 386 U.S. 317, 321 (1967)* (judgment as a matter of law); *Pease v. Rathbun-Jones Engineering Co., 243 U.S. 273, 278 (1917)* (summary judgment).

(Brandeis, J.) (citing *Fidelity & Deposit Co.*, and reiterating: "It does not infringe the constitutional right to a trial by jury [in a civil case], to require, with a view to formulating the issues, an oath by each party to the facts relied upon."). See also *Walker v. New Mexico & Southern Pacific R. Co., 165 U.S. 593, 596 (1897)* (Seventh Amendment "does not attempt to regulate matters of pleading").

In the instant case, provided that the Shareholders have satisfied the congressionally "prescribe[d] . . . means of making an issue," *Fidelity & Deposit Co., 187 U.S., at 320,* the case will fall within the jury's authority to assess the credibility of witnesses, resolve any genuine issues of fact, and make the ultimate determination whether Notebaert and, by imputation, Tellabs acted with scienter. We emphasize, as well, that under our construction of the "strong inference" standard, a plaintiff is not forced to plead more than she would be required to prove at trial. A plaintiff alleging fraud in a § 10(b) action, we hold today, must plead facts rendering an inference of scienter *at least as likely as* any plausible opposing inference. At trial, she must then prove her case by a "preponderance of the evidence." Stated otherwise, she must demonstrate that it is *more likely* than not that the defendant acted with scienter. See *Herman & MacLean v. Huddleston, 459 U.S. 375, 390 (1983).*

* * *

While we reject the Seventh Circuit's approach to § 21D(b)(2), we do not decide whether, under the standard we have described, see *supra*, at 11-14, the Shareholders' allegations warrant "a strong inference that [Notebaert and Tellabs] acted with the required state of mind," *15 U.S.C. § 78u-4(b)(2)*. Neither the District Court nor the Court of Appeals had the opportunity to consider the matter in light of the prescriptions we announce today. We therefore vacate the Seventh Circuit's judgment so that the case may be reexamined in accord with our construction of § 21D(b)(2).

The judgment of the Court of Appeals is vacated, and the case is remanded for further proceedings consistent with this opinion.

It is so ordered.

CONCUR:

JUSTICE SCALIA, concurring in the judgment.

I fail to see how an inference that is merely "at least as compelling as any opposing inference," *ante*, at 2, can conceivably be called what the statute here at issue requires: a "strong inference," *15 U.S.C. § 78u-4(b)(2)*. If a jade falcon were stolen from a room to which only A and B had access, could it *possibly* be said there was a "strong inference" that B was the thief? I think not, and I therefore think that the Court's test must fail. In my view, the test should be whether the inference of scienter (if any) is *more plausible* than the inference of innocence.[*]

---

[*] The Court suggests that "the owner of the precious falcon would find the inference of guilt as to B quite strong." *Ante*, at 13, n. 5. If he should draw such an inference, it would only prove the wisdom of the ancient maxim "*aliquis non debet esse Judex in propria causa*"--no man ought to be a judge of his own cause. *Dr. Bonham's Case, 8 Co. 107a, 114a, 118a, 77 Eng. Rep. 638, 646, 652 (C. P. 1610)*. For it is quite clear (from the dispassionate perspective of one who does not own a jade falcon) that a *possibility*, even a strong possibility, that B is responsible is

....

[Justice Alito also filed a concurring opinion and Justice Stevens dissented].

Note on Tellabs' Impact

The Court's statement in Tellabs that scienter must be plead with sufficient persuasiveness so that a "reasonable person would deem the inference of scienter cogent and at least as compelling as any opposing inference one could draw from the facts alleged" has spawned a host of Circuit Court decisions re-examining their Circuit's pleading standards. Some decisions have recognized that their former standard was too high because it expressly required the inferences favoring the plaintiffs to be stronger than those favoring the defendants. See Mississippi Public Employees' Retirement Sys. v. Boston Scientific Corp., 523 F.3d 75 (1st Cir. 2008) (reversing district court's dismissal and finding scienter to have been adequately pleaded where corporate statements that a product defect with a coronary stent had been "fixed" came just before a recall of the stent). Other cases have, however, found that anonymous source statements must be ignored or heavily discounted and so cannot be balanced against the inferences raised by the defendants. See Higginbotham v. Baxter Int'l Inc., 495 F.3d 753 (7th Cir. 2007); Cent. Laborers' Pension Fund v. Integrated Elec. Sys., 497 F.3d 546 (5th Cir. 2007). Interestingly, on the remand of Tellabs to the Seventh Circuit, the panel reinstated the complaint, finding that the possibility that a manufacturer's false statements resulted from a cascade of innocent mistakes was far less likely than the possibility

---

not a strong *inference* that B is responsible. "Inference" connotes "belief" in what is inferred, and it would be impossible to form a strong belief that it was B and not A, or A and not B.

of scienter at the corporate level at which the statements were made. See Makor Issues & Rights, Ltd. v. Tellabs, Inc., 513 F.3d 702 (7th Cir. 2008).

In general, few cases have involved fact situations in which the inferences favoring each side were nearly in balance. More commonly, the alleged facts have either been highly specific (in which case the complaint is upheld, even in a Circuit with a formerly high pleading standard – see Milton Arbitrage Partners LLC v. Syncor Int'l Corp., Fed. Sec. L. Rep. (CCH) Para. 94,354 (9th Cir. April 18, 2007)) or vague and general (in which case the complaint is dismissed, even in a Circuit with a formerly liberal pleading standard – see ATSI Communs., Inc. v. Shaar Fund, Ltd., 493 F.3d 87 (2d Cir. 2008)).

One pleading issue that has surfaced recurrently in the wake of Tellabs is the current status of the "group pleading" doctrine. That doctrine was a judicial presumption that statements in documents published by a corporation (e.g., annual reports and press releases) were collectively attributable to the officers and directors having day-to-day control over and involvement in the corporation's affairs. The doctrine thus dispensed with the need to show a specific connection of the individual defendant officer or director to the group-published statement. Most Circuits have now held that this doctrine did not survive the specific pleading standards of the PSLRA. See Winer Family Trust v. Queen, 503 F.3d 319 (3d Cir. 2007); Pugh v. Tribune Co., 521 F.3d 686 (7th Cir. 2008). But the doctrine appears to survive to a limited degree in other Circuits. See Mississippi Public Employees Ret. Sys. v. Boston Scientific Corp., 523 F.3d 75, 93 (1st Cir. 2008).

In Re: Initial Public Offering Securities Litigation

United States Court of Appeals, Second Circuit, 2006
471 F.3d 24

Before: NEWMAN, SOTOMAYOR, and HALL, Circuit Judges.

■ NEWMAN, CIRCUIT JUDGE: This appeal primarily concerns the issue, surprisingly unsettled in this Circuit, as to what standards govern a district judge in adjudicating a motion for class certification under *Rule 23 of the Federal Rules of Civil Procedure*. Comprehended within this broad issue are subsidiary issues such as whether a definitive ruling must be made that each *Rule 23* requirement has been met or whether only some showing of a requirement suffices, whether all of the evidence at the class certification stage is to be assessed or whether a class plaintiff's evidence, if not fatally flawed, suffices, and whether the standards for determination of a *Rule 23* requirement are lessened when a *Rule 23* requirement overlaps with an aspect of the merits of the proposed class action. Finally, the appeal presents the question whether granting a motion for class certification in the pending litigation exceeded the District Court's discretion.

These issues arise on an appeal by Defendants-Appellants Merrill Lynch & Co. and others ("the underwriters") from the October 13, 2004, order of the District Court for the Southern District of New York (Shira A. Scheindlin, District Judge) granting in part Plaintiffs-Appellees' motion for class certification in six securities fraud class actions. The six actions were selected by the District Court as "focus cases" out of 310 consolidated class actions, which themselves were consolidations of thousands of separate class actions. All of the lawsuits, including the six at issue on this appeal, involve claims of fraud on the part of several of the nation's largest underwriters in connection with a series of initial public offerings ("IPOs").

We conclude (1) that a district judge may not certify a class without making a ruling that each *Rule 23* requirement is met and that a lesser standard such as "some showing" for satisfying each requirement will not suffice, (2) that all of the evidence must be assessed as with any other threshold issue, (3) that the fact that a *Rule 23* requirement might overlap with an issue on the merits does not avoid the court's obligation to make a ruling as to whether the requirement is met, although such a circumstance might appropriately limit the scope of the court's inquiry at the class certification stage, and (4) that the cases pending on this appeal may not be certified as class actions. We therefore vacate the class certifications and remand for further proceedings.

Background

Throughout 2001, thousands of investors filed class actions against 55 underwriters, 310 issuers, and hundreds of individual officers of the issuing companies, alleging that the Defendants had engaged in a scheme to defraud the investing public in violation of federal securities laws. The Assignment Committee of the Southern District of New York transferred all these suits to Judge Scheindlin for pretrial coordination. Judge Scheindlin consolidated the thousands of cases by issuer, resulting in 310 consolidated actions.

The complaints, as amended, consist of a set of "Master Allegations" applicable to all 310 consolidated actions and a "Class Action Complaint" specific to each of the 310 issuers. The Master

Allegations describe three fraudulent devices used by the underwriters. First, they allege that the underwriters conditioned allocations of shares at the offer price on agreements to purchase shares in the aftermarket (the "Tie-in Agreements"). Second, they allege that the underwriters also required customers who received allocations of shares at the offer price to pay three forms of "Undisclosed Compensation" to the underwriters: (1) paying inflated brokerage commissions, (2) paying commissions on churned transactions in unrelated securities, and (3) purchasing other unwanted securities from the underwriters. Third, the Plaintiffs allege that the underwriters used their analysts in several improper ways: (1) setting unrealistic price targets, (2) promising a "hot" analyst to an issuer in exchange for underwriting the IPO, (3) tying analyst compensation to performance of the investment banking division, (4) allowing analysts to own shares of stocks they were touting, and (5) failing to disclose these conflicts of interest. The Master Allegations also allege that the underwriters facilitated receipt of quick profits by insiders of the issuer and that the issuers (also Defendants) "participated in and benefitted from" the underwriters' misconduct.

The Master Allegations detail the specific activities of each underwriter. These allegations include reports of the tie-in arrangements, undisclosed compensation, and analyst manipulation.

The issuers in the six focus cases involved in the pending appeal are Corvis Corp., Engage Technologies, Inc., FirePond, Inc., iXL Enterprises, Inc., Sycamore Networks, Inc., and VA Software Corp. All six complaints include the following six claims:

* claims under *section 11* of the Securities Act, *15 U.S.C. § 77k*, against the issuer, individual officers, and underwriters for untrue material statements of fact or material omissions from the registration statement, specifically the tie-in agreements and the undisclosed compensation;

* claims under *section 15* of the Securities Act, *15 U.S.C. § 77o*, against individual officers for derivative liability for an issuer's violation of *section 11*;

* claims under *section 10(b)* of the Securities and Exchange Act of 1934 ("the Exchange Act"), *15 U.S.C. § 78j*, and *Rule 10b-5, 17 C.F.R. § 240.10b-5*, against the underwriters for deceptive and manipulative practices in connection with an IPO, specifically the tie-in agreements and the undisclosed compensation;

* claims under *section 10(b)* of the Exchange Act and *Rule 10b-5* against the underwriters for materially false or misleading or material omissions from the registration statement/prospectus, specifically concealment of the tie-in agreements, undisclosed compensation, and analyst conflicts of interest;

* claims under *section 10(b)* of the Exchange Act and *Rule 10b-5* against issuers and individual officers for materially false or misleading statements or material omissions, specifically concealment of the underwriters' wrongdoing; and

* claims under *section 20(a)* of the Exchange Act, *15 U.S.C. § 78t*, against individual officers for derivative liability for an issuer's violation of *Rule 10b-5*.

Two of the complaints, those concerning iXL Enterprises, Inc. and Sycamore Networks, Inc., also included three additional claims related to secondary offerings that occurred with stocks of those issuers:

* claims under *section 11* of the Securities Act against the issuer, individual officers, and underwriters for untrue material statements of fact or material omissions from the registration

statement for the secondary offering, specifically the tie-in agreements and the undisclosed compensation;

* claims under *section 15* of the Securities Act against individual officers for derivative liability for an issuer's violation of *section 11* in connection with the secondary offering; and

* claims under *section 10(b)* of the Exchange Act and *Rule 10b-5* against the underwriters for deceptive and manipulative practices in connection with the secondary offering, specifically the requirement that allocants in the IPO agree to purchase shares in the secondary offering.

Motions to Dismiss. In February 2003, Judge Scheindlin ruled on the Defendants' motions to dismiss. *In re IPO Securities Litigation, 241 F. Supp. 2d 281 (S.D.N.Y. 2003)*. Judge Scheindlin denied the Defendants' motions except with respect to two sets of claims: the *section 11* and *section 15* claims of Plaintiffs who had sold their shares above the offering price, and some of the *Rule 10b-5* claims against issuers and individual officers. *Id. at 296-97*. Judge Scheindlin granted the Plaintiffs leave to re-plead the latter claims. *Id. at 399*.

In December 2003, Judge Scheindlin denied the Underwriter Defendants' renewed motion to dismiss. *In re IPO Securities Litigation, 297 F. Supp. 2d 668 (S.D.N.Y. 2003)*. Judge Scheindlin held that the Plaintiffs' allegations of loss causation were sufficient when they alleged that the Defendants had manipulated the market. She also held that it was fair to infer dissipation of the inflated price over time in a manipulation case, notwithstanding the Second Circuit's intervening decision in *Emergent Capital Investment Management, LLC v. Stonepath Group, Inc., 343 F.3d 189 (2d Cir. 2003)* (holding that, in a material misstatement or omission securities fraud action, plaintiffs must allege a price correction to adequately plead loss causation). *297 F. Supp. 2d at 674-75*.

Class Certification. In October 2004, Judge Scheindlin issued an order granting in part and denying in part the Plaintiffs' motions for class certification in the six focus cases. *In re IPO Securities Litigation ("IPO Dist. Ct."), 227 F.R.D. 65 (S.D.N.Y. 2004)*. For each focus case, Judge Scheindlin defined the class as follows:

> The Class consists of all persons and entities that purchased or otherwise acquired the securities of [Specific Issuer] during the Class Period and were damaged thereby. Excluded from the Class are:
>
> > (1) Defendants herein, each of their respective parents, subsidiaries, and successors, and each of their respective directors, officers and legal counsel during the Class Period, and each such person's legal representatives, heirs, and assigns, members of each such person's immediate family, and any entity in which such person had a controlling interest during the Class Period;
> >
> > (2) all persons and entities that, with respect to [Specific Issuer's] initial public offering: (a) received an allocation, (b) placed orders to purchase shares of that issuer's securities in the aftermarket within four weeks of the

> effective date of the offering, (c) paid any undisclosed compensation to the allocating underwriter(s), and (d) made a net profit (exclusive of commissions and other transaction costs), realized or unrealized, in connection with all of such person's or entity's combined transactions in [Specific Issuer's] securities during the Class Period; and
>
> (3) all persons and entities who satisfy all of the requirements of subparagraph (2) with respect to any of the 309 initial public offerings that are the subject of these coordinated actions, if that offering occurred prior to [Specific Issuer's] offering.

Id. at 102.

Of particular pertinence to this appeal, Judge Scheindlin explicitly considered the issue of the standard of proof that the Plaintiffs must meet to obtain class certification. She noted that the Supreme Court has been silent on the question of what showing plaintiffs must make in support of their motion for class certification. The only parameters established by the Supreme Court in this regard, she further noted, were that a court must conduct a "rigorous analysis" in which it "may be necessary for the court to probe behind the pleadings," *General Telephone Co. of the Southwest v. Falcon, 457 U.S. 147, 160-61, 102 S. Ct. 2364, 72 L. Ed. 2d 740 (1982)*, but the court cannot "conduct a preliminary inquiry into the merits of a suit," *Eisen v. Carlisle & Jacquelin, 417 U.S. 156, 177; IPO (Dist. Ct.), 227 F.R.D. at 90-91*. Judge Scheindlin noted recent decisions by the Fourth and Seventh Circuits that suggested that the plaintiffs must establish the requirements of *Rule 23* by a preponderance of the evidence, even if resolving those issues requires a "preliminary inquiry into the merits," *Szabo v. Bridgeport Machines, Inc., 249 F.3d 672, 676 (7th Cir. 2001)*, or an "overlap with issues on the merits," *Gariety v. Grant Thornton, LLP, 368 F.3d 356, 366 (4th Cir. 2004)*. See *IPO (Dist. Ct.), 227 F.R.D. at 91-92*.

Judge Scheindlin concluded that applying the preponderance standard was inappropriate where those elements were "enmeshed" with the merits, because, as Eisen cautioned, *417 U.S. at 178*, that standard would prejudice a defendant. Instead, she adopted a "some showing" standard, which she derived from this Court's opinions in *Caridad v. Metro-North Commuter Railroad, 191 F.3d 283, 292 (2d Cir. 1999)*, and In re Visa Check/MasterMoney Antitrust Litigation ("Visa Check"), *280 F.3d 124, 134-35 (2d Cir. 2001)*. Judge Scheindlin concluded:

> In order to pass muster, plaintiffs -- who have the burden of proof at class certification -- must make "*some showing*." That showing may take the form of, for example, expert opinions, evidence (by document, affidavit, live testimony, or otherwise), or the uncontested allegations of the complaint.

IPO (Dist. Ct.), 227 F.R.D. at 93.

Judge Scheindlin then analyzed whether, under the "some showing" standard, the Plaintiffs had met the *Rule 23* requirements. As to commonality, she found numerous common factual issues for the class, and noted that, apart from individual calculation of damages, all other individual issues "will arise because of issues *defendants* choose to raise." *Id. at 94*. Even these issues, she concluded, would have common questions, such as whether a certain publication put the Plaintiffs on inquiry notice of the scheme. As to typicality, Judge Scheindlin dispensed with the Defendants' principal argument -- that some class representatives were inappropriate due to their involvement in the scheme -- by altering the class definition to exclude such persons. Judge Scheindlin also found that the class representatives would adequately represent the class. Defendants did not contest that the putative classes were so numerous as to render joinder impracticable.

The implied requirement of ascertainability implicated Judge Scheindlin's revised class definition. The Plaintiffs had conceded that any persons who knowingly participated in the market manipulation would be barred from recovery. Viewing three components of the market manipulation scheme as "necessary," Judge Scheindlin created subparagraph (2) of the class definition, quoted above, which excluded Plaintiffs that had (1) received an allocation, (2) purchased additional shares within four weeks of the IPO, (3) paid undisclosed compensation, and (4) profited with respect to any of the 310 IPOs. The Defendants argued that determining which Plaintiffs had participated "would be a massive undertaking." Judge Scheindlin acknowledged that ascertainment would not be easy, but that the class definition was "objectively determinable," *id. at 104*, which satisfied the ascertainability criterion.

The Defendants raised four arguments relating to *Rule 23(b)(3)*'s requirement that common questions predominate over individual ones. First, they argued that individual questions surrounding transaction causation, or reliance, predominated because the fraud-on-the-market presumption of reliance, recognized in *Basic Inc. v. Levinson, 485 U.S. 224, 245-47 (1988)*, could not apply for lack of an efficient market. Judge Scheindlin rejected this argument, ruling that the Plaintiffs had made "some showing" of market efficiency, *IPO (Dist. Ct.), 227 F.R.D. at 107*, and that knowledge of the Defendants' scheme from publications presented a common question rather than individual ones, *id. at 110*. Second, the Defendants argued that the Plaintiffs' expert report did not establish loss causation. Judge Scheindlin concluded that weighing the competing expert reports was inappropriate and, citing Visa Check, that the Plaintiffs had "satisfied their burden at this stage to articulate a theory of loss causation that is not fatally flawed." *Id. at 115*. Third, Judge Scheindlin accepted the Plaintiffs' contention that they could prove damages class-wide by proposing a formula for the measure of damages over time. *Id. at 116-17*. Fourth, as to the Plaintiffs' *section 11* claims, Judge Scheindlin agreed with the Defendants that once untraceable shares entered the market, the individual questions of whether an investor could trace his shares to the IPO would predominate, and so she ended the class periods with respect to these claims at the time when unregistered shares became tradeable. *Id. at 118-19, 120*.

Finally, Judge Scheindlin concluded that class adjudication was "clearly superior to any other form of adjudication," *id. at 122*, and granted the Plaintiffs' motion for class certification, subject to the modified definition and the limit on class period for *section 11* claims set forth above, id.

Partial Settlement. In February 2005, Judge Scheindlin approved a settlement between the Plaintiff classes and the issuer and the individual officer Defendants in 298 of the 310 consolidated actions. The settlement provided the Plaintiffs with a guaranteed recovery of one billion dollars, offset by whatever amount the Plaintiffs recover from the underwriters.

Appeal. In June 2005, a panel of this Court granted the Defendants' petition for permission to appeal pursuant to *Fed. R. Civ. P. 23(f)*. The order granting permission to appeal directed the parties to address the following issues:

(1) Whether the Second Circuit's "some showing" standard, see *In re Visa Check/MasterMoney Antitrust Litigation, 280 F.3d 124, 134-35 (2d Cir. 2001); Caridad v. Metro-North Commuter Railroad, 191 F.3d 283, 293 (2d Cir. 1999)*, is consistent with the 2003 amendments to *Fed. R. Civ. P. 23*; and

(2) Whether the presumption of reliance established in Basic [Inc.] v. *Levinson, 485 U.S. 224 (1988)*, was properly extended to plaintiffs' claims against non-issuer defendants and to the market manipulation claims.

Discussion

"Provided that the district court has applied the proper legal standards in deciding whether to certify a class, its decision may only be overturned if it constitutes an abuse of discretion." *Caridad, 191 F.3d at 291* (internal quotation marks omitted); accord *Parker v. Time Warner Entertainment Co., 331 F.3d 13, 18 (2d Cir. 2003); Moore v. PaineWebber, Inc., 306 F.3d 1247, 1252 (2d Cir. 2002)*. The statement of this standard of review does not make it clear whether the abuse-of-discretion standard applies only to the trial judge's ultimate conclusion on the class certification motion or also to the subsidiary rulings on each of the six requirements for a *Rule 23(b)(3)* class. Since a district judge "may" certify a class where all the requirements of *Rule 23* are met, see *Fed. R. Civ. P. 23(b)*, it is arguable that review for abuse of discretion refers to the ultimate discretion whether or not to certify a class.

However, the abuse-of-discretion standard has regularly been applied in reviewing a district judge's conclusions with respect to individual requirements of *Rule 23* both by this Court, see, e.g., *Lundquist v. Security Pacific Automotive Financial Services Corp., 993 F.2d 11, 14 (2d Cir. 1993)* (commonality and typicality); *Johnpoll v. Thornburgh, 898 F.2d 849, 852 (2d Cir. 1990)* (adequacy of class definition and adequacy of representation); cf. *In re Drexel Burnham Lambert Group, Inc., 960 F.2d 285, 292 (2d Cir. 1992)* (prohibition against opting out), and by other Circuits, see, e.g., *Pederson v. Louisiana State University, 213 F.3d 858, 867-69 (5th Cir. 2000)* (numerosity); *Castano v. American Tobacco Co., 84 F.3d 734, 752 (5th Cir. 1996)* (superiority); *Hoxworth v. Blinder, Robinson & Co., 980 F.2d 912, 924, 925 (3d Cir. 1992)* (adequacy of representation, predominance, and duration of class period). We will apply the abuse-of-discretion standard both to Judge Scheindlin's ultimate decision on class certification as well as her rulings as to *Rule 23* requirements, bearing in mind that whether an incorrect legal standard has been used is an issue of law to be reviewed de novo, see *Parker, 331 F.3d at 18*.

I. Legal Standards for *Rule 23* Requirements

Our initial inquiry is whether Judge Scheindlin applied proper legal standards in determining the existence of the four prerequisites for every class action: numerosity, commonality, typicality, and adequacy of representation, *Fed. R. Civ. P. 23(a)*, and the two additional requirements for a *(b)(3)* class action: predominance, i.e., law or fact questions common to the class predominate over questions affecting individual members, and superiority, i.e., class action is superior to other methods, id. *23(b)(3)*. Judge Scheindlin ruled that the Plaintiffs were required to make only "some showing" of compliance with these *Rule 23* requirements. We conclude that use of a "some showing" standard was error, but we readily acknowledge that, until now, our Court has been less than clear as to the applicable standards for class certification, and on occasion, as we discuss below, we have used language that understandably led Judge Scheindlin astray. Before considering the relevant opinions of our Court, we start with the guidance provided by the Supreme Court.

Supreme Court decisions. The principal Supreme Court decision on determining *Rule 23* requirements, *General Telephone Co. of the Southwest v. Falcon, 457 U.S. 147 (1982)*, states, "[A] Title VII class action, like any other class action, may only be certified if the trial court is satisfied, after a rigorous analysis, that the prerequisites of *Rule 23(a)* have been satisfied." *Id. at 161.* Although the Court's double use of the word "satisfied" is somewhat perplexing, the important point is that the requirements of *Rule 23* must be met, not just supported by some evidence. As the Court added with respect to the four requirements of *Rule 23(a)*, "[A]ctual, not presumed, conformance with *Rule 23(a)* remains . . . indispensable." *Id. at 160.* Moreover, the certification decision requires "rigorous analysis." *Id. at 161.* Significantly, the Court noted that "the class determination generally involves considerations that are enmeshed in the factual and legal issues comprising the plaintiff's cause of action." *Id. at 160* (internal quotation marks omitted). This last statement is especially important in light of the way circuit and district courts have understood (or, as we point out below, misunderstood) the Supreme Court's earlier decision in Eisen.

In Eisen, the Court stated: "We find nothing in either the language or history of *Rule 23* that gives a court any authority to conduct a preliminary inquiry into the merits of a suit in order to determine whether it may be maintained as a class action." *Eisen, 417 U.S. at 177.* This statement has led some courts to think that in determining whether any *Rule 23* requirement is met, a judge may not consider any aspect of the merits, and has led other courts to think that a judge may not do so at least with respect to a prerequisite of *Rule 23* that overlaps with an aspect of the merits of the case.

However, careful examination of Eisen reveals that there is no basis for thinking that a specific *Rule 23* requirement need not be fully established just because it concerns, or even overlaps with, an aspect of the merits. The oft-quoted statement from Eisen was made in a case in which the district judge's merits inquiry had nothing to do with determining the requirements for class certification. In Eisen, the district court, after determining that the case was appropriate for class certification, was concerned with which side should bear the cost of notice to the class. *Id. at 166-68.* As recounted by the Supreme Court, the district court had ruled that, without a class action, no one plaintiff could bear the cost of the notice, but that it would be unfair to impose the cost on the defendants unless the plaintiffs could show a probability of success on the merits. *Id. at 168.* Concluding that such a probability existed, the district court had ordered the defendants to pay 90 percent of the costs of notice, id., and had devised a scheme of individual notice for some plaintiffs and notice by publication for others, *id. at 167.* The court of appeals had rejected that approach and had required individual notice with the cost borne by the plaintiffs. *Id. at 169*. The court of appeals had also ruled that the action was "unmanageable" and had rejected class certification. Id.

The Supreme Court ruled that *Rule 23* required individual notice. *Id. at 175-77*. Then the Court ruled that the plaintiffs must bear the cost. It was in this context that the Court said that the district court could not "conduct a preliminary inquiry into the merits." *Id. at 177*. Doing so, the Court said, would allow the class representative to obtain a determination on the merits "without any assurance that a class action may be maintained." *Id. at 177-78*. The Court said it was also concerned that the court's tentative findings "may color the subsequent proceedings and place an unfair burden on the defendant." *Id. at 178*. Then, since the class representative had said he would not bear the cost of notice, the Court ordered the class action dismissed. *Id. at 179*.

The point is that the Supreme Court was not faced with determination of any particular *Rule 23* requirement or a requirement that overlapped with the merits. The district court had preliminarily assessed the merits to decide the collateral issue of who should pay for the notice.

The Fifth Circuit case on which the Supreme Court principally relied in Eisen, *Miller v. Mackey International, Inc., 452 F.2d 424 (5th Cir. 1971)*, also did not involve determination of any *Rule 23* requirement or even one that overlapped with a merits inquiry. The Supreme Court said:

> In short, we agree with Judge Wisdom's conclusion in *Miller v. Mackey International, 452 F.2d 424 (5th Cir. 1971),* where the court rejected a preliminary inquiry into the merits of a proposed class action:
>
>> "In determining the propriety of a class action, the question is not whether the plaintiff or plaintiffs have stated a cause of action or will prevail on the merits, but rather whether the requirements of *Rule 23* are met."

Eisen, 417 U.S. at 178.

But the district court in Miller, just like the district court in Eisen, had not looked at the merits in order to determine whether any one of the *Rule 23* requirements was met. Instead, the district court in Miller had simply concluded that because of a deficiency on the merits of the plaintiff's securities claim, i.e., an alleged competitor, omitted from the prospectus, was not in fact in competition with the defendant, a class action was inappropriate. *Miller, 452 F.2d at 426*. Significantly, after ruling that this merits inquiry was not a proper basis for denying class certification, Judge Wisdom's opinion remanded the case to the district court for further proceedings "including a full hearing on the question presented [*Rule 23* certification] and findings by the district judge." *Id. at 431* (emphasis added).

Unfortunately, the statement in Eisen that a court considering certification must not consider the merits has sometimes been taken out of context and applied in cases where a merits inquiry either concerns a *Rule 23* requirement or overlaps with such a requirement. The evolution of case law in our Circuit, to which we now turn, illustrates what has happened.

Case law within the Second Circuit. An early example is *Professional Adjusting Systems of America, Inc. v. General Adjustment Bureau, Inc.*, 64 F.R.D. 35 (S.D.N.Y. 1974), in which then-District Judge Gurfein, explicitly mindful of the admonitions in Eisen and Miller, said that the choice for a district court must be

> somewhere between the pleading and the fruits of discovery . . . . Enough must be laid bare to let the judge survey the factual scene on a kind of sketchy relief map, leaving for later view the myriad of details that cover the terrain. But to find its way, the Court must know something of the commonality of action or frustration that binds the class.

Id. at 38 (emphasis added). Most of Judge Gurfein's statement was expressly quoted by our Court in *Sirota v. Solitron Devices, Inc.*, 673 F.2d 566, 571-72 (2d Cir. 1982), in addition to the no-merits-inquiry language from Eisen itself, *id.* at 570.

Eisen and Sirota were prominently cited in our Circuit's decision in *Caridad*, 191 F.3d at 291, which was principally relied on by Judge Scheindlin in the pending case. As many other decisions have done, Caridad took the "no merits inquiry" language of Eisen out of its context of a merits inquiry unrelated to a specific *Rule 23* class certification requirement and applied it to consideration of the *Rule 23* threshold requirements. In addition, Caridad contained the following sentence, on which Judge Scheindlin based her "some showing" standard for *Rule 23* requirements: "Of course, class certification would not be warranted absent some showing that the challenged practice is causally related to a pattern of disparate treatment or has a disparate impact on African-American employees at Metro-North." *Caridad*, 191 F.3d at 292 (emphasis added). Although it is not entirely clear whether the "some showing" sentence in Caridad is a comment on the standard for satisfying the *Rule 23(a)* requirement of commonality or a requirement concerning the merits issue of causality, it seems clear that the Eisen caution was a major influence on the Caridad decision. Thus, under the influence of Eisen, Caridad condemned "statistical dueling" between experts, id. (internal quotations marks omitted), and ruled that the report of the plaintiffs' expert plus anecdotal evidence "satisfies the Class Plaintiffs' burden of demonstrating commonality for purposes of class certification," *id.* at 293, without requiring the district court to have made a clear determination of commonality in light of all the evidence bearing on that issue that had been presented at the class certification stage. The condemnation of "statistical dueling" by experts was drawn from a careful opinion by District Judge Koeltl, which had noted that the experts' disagreement on the merits -- whether a discriminatory impact could be shown -- was not a valid basis for denying class certification. See *Krueger v. New York Telephone Co.*, 163 F.R.D. 433, 440 (S.D.N.Y. 1995). Caridad, by the imprecision of its language, left unclear whether the merits dispute between the experts was not to be resolved at the class certification stage or whether their dispute about a class certification requirement was not to be resolved at that stage.

Caridad was soon followed by Visa Check, which upheld a district court's conclusion as to commonality on the lenient basis that the plaintiffs' methodology to show common questions of fact "was not fatally flawed," *Visa Check*, 280 F.3d at 135. Visa Check began its consideration of the issue by citing Eisen, *id.* at 133, and quoting Caridad for the proposition, based on Eisen, that "'a motion for class certification is not an occasion for examination of the merits of the case,'" *id. at 135* (quoting *Caridad, 191 F.3d at 291*). Then Visa Check asserted that a district judge "must ensure that the basis of the expert opinion [for the theory supporting common issues subject to classwide determination] is not so flawed that it would be inadmissible as a matter of law." Id. For this proposition, the Court cited *Cruz v. Coach Stores, Inc., No. 96 Civ. 8099, 1998 U.S. Dist. LEXIS 18051, 1998 WL 812045, at *4 n. 3 (S.D.N.Y. Nov. 18, 1998)*, aff'd in part, vacated in part on other grounds, *202 F.3d 560 (2d Cir. 2000)*. In the cited footnote in the district court opinion in Cruz, Judge Rakoff had said that the plaintiff's expert's report, offered to show commonality, was "fatally flawed" and for that reason inadmissible. In affirming in part, our Court said that "[the plaintiff] has not shown that the [district] court abused its discretion in finding the report methodologically flawed." *Cruz, 202 F.3d at 573*. Ultimately, Visa Check approved what it characterized as the district court's conclusion that it was obliged to determine only "whether [the plaintiffs] had shown, based on methodology that was not fatally flawed, that the requirements of *Rule 23* were met." *Visa Check, 280 F.3d at 135*. However, the fact that an expert's report was rejected as admissible evidence in Cruz because it was fatally flawed was not a sufficient basis for saying in Visa Check that a report suffices to establish a *Rule 23* requirement as long as it is not fatally flawed. Visa Check also stated that a district judge, at the class certification stage, "may not weigh conflicting expert evidence or engage in 'statistical dueling' of experts," id. (quoting *Caridad, 191 F.3d at 292-93*), without clarifying whether the district judge should refrain from resolving a merits dispute or a dispute about a class certification requirement.

After Visa Check, our decision in Parker appeared to move away from the lenient approach of Caridad and Visa Check and toward a district court's obligation to determine that *Rule 23* requirements are met. In Parker, we rejected a denial of certification by a district judge who had ruled that a class action was not superior to individual actions where the aggregate liability of the defendant was grossly disproportionate to the harm suffered by each individual. *331 F.3d at 21*. We concluded that the district judge had made assumptions of fact concerning the size of the class, and we remanded for "findings of fact." Id.

More recently, our Court's decision in *Heerwagen v. Clear Channel Communications, 435 F.3d 219 (2d Cir. 2006)*, marked a major shift away from the "some showing" and "not fatally flawed" language of Caridad and Visa Check. Heerwagen began its consideration of the appropriate standard for meeting class certification requirements by repeating the admonitions of Caridad and Visa Check that the court is not "to conduct a preliminary inquiry into the merits of plaintiff's case at the class certification stage." *Id. at 231*. There was even an invocation of Sirota's reliance on Judge Gurfein's statement in Professional Adjusting Systems that a class certification judge need only look "somewhere between the pleading and the fruits of discovery" to make a class certification. See id. (internal quotation marks omitted). However, without mentioning the "some showing" language from Caridad, Heerwagen then asserted that the district court must determine whether *Rule 23* requirements have been met. Heerwagen also referred to "the express language of *Rule 23(b)(3)*, which requires that a court find predominance." *Id. at 233* (emphasis added). Heerwagen somewhat straddled the issue of whether such a determination could include some inquiry into the merits:

> Some overlap with the ultimate review on the merits is an acceptable collateral consequence of the "rigorous analysis" that courts must perform when determining whether *Rule 23*'s requirements have been met, see *Falcon, 457 U.S. at 161, 102 S. Ct.*

2364, so long as it does not stem from a forbidden preliminary inquiry into the merits, *Eisen, 417 U.S. at 177, 94 S. Ct. 2140.*

435 F.3d at 232. Declining to go as far as other circuits in permitting broad inquiry into the merits in order to determine whether *Rule 23* requirements have been met, see id. (citing, e.g., *Gariety, 368 F.3d at 366*; *Szabo, 249 F.3d at 676*), Heerwagen, apparently still laboring under the influence of Eisen, identified one circumstance where the need for findings would not require weighing all the relevant evidence. We relied on Caridad "to prohibit weighing evidence in connection with *Rule 23* determinations to the extent those determinations are effectively identical to merits issues." Id. (emphasis added). Satisfied that the merits issue considered by the district court was not identical with a *Rule 23* requirement, Heerwagen affirmed the denial of class certification. Thus, the Eisen caution was disregarded as to *Rule 23* requirements that somewhat overlap with the merits, but apparently retained as to a requirement that completely overlaps with the merits.

Heerwagen also considered the putative class plaintiff's claim that the district court had improperly required her to meet *Rule 23*'s predominance requirement by a preponderance of the evidence. Initially, we expressed doubt whether the district court had used the preponderance standard. See *id. at 233*. Then, without determining what standard had been used, we said, in what may well have been dictum, that "[e]ven if a preponderance of the evidence standard was invoked, that was not in error." Id. Indeed, we asserted: "Complying with *Rule 23(b)(3)*'s predominance requirement cannot be shown by less than a preponderance of the evidence." Id.

Case law in other circuits. The case law that has developed outside our Circuit since Eisen has generally supported an obligation of the district court to make a determination that the requirements of *Rule 23* are met, and has not accepted a weak "some showing" standard.

Several circuits have strongly supported a requirement of findings that *Rule 23* requirements are met, and some have explicitly rejected the idea that something less than a clear finding is adequate just because a *Rule 23* requirement overlaps with the merits. The Seventh Circuit has stated that "a judge should make whatever factual and legal inquiries are necessary under *Rule 23*" even if "the judge must make a preliminary inquiry into the merits." *Szabo, 249 F.3d at 676.* Judge Easterbrook added, "[T]he judge would receive evidence (if only by affidavit) and resolve the disputes before deciding whether to certify the class." Id. (emphasis added). The Fourth Circuit has followed Szabo and stated that "the factors spelled out in *Rule 23* must be addressed through findings, even if they overlap with issues on the merits." *Gariety, 368 F.3d at 366.* The Third Circuit has also followed Szabo and cited approvingly this statement from 5 *Moore's Federal Practice § 23.46[4]*: "[B]ecause the determination of a certification request invariably involves some examination of factual and legal issues underlying the plaintiffs' cause of action, a court may consider the substantive elements of the plaintiff's case . . . ." *Newton v. Merrill Lynch, Pierce, Fenner & Smith, Inc., 259 F.3d 154, 166 (3d Cir. 2001).* The Eighth Circuit has stated that "in ruling on class certification, a court may be required to resolve disputes concerning the factual setting of the case," including "the resolution of expert disputes concerning the import of evidence." *Blades v. Monsanto Co., 400 F.3d 562, 575 (8th Cir. 2005)* (emphasis added). The Fifth Circuit, following Gariety, has stated that "a careful certification inquiry is required and findings must be made" and has rejected a class certification because the district court "applied too lax a standard of proof," *Unger v. Amedisys, Inc., 401 F.3d 316, 319 (5th Cir. 2005)*. The Eleventh Circuit has stated:

> While it is true that a trial court may not properly reach the merits of a claim when determining whether class certification is warranted, this principle should not be talismanically invoked to artificially limit a trial court's examination of the factors necessary to a reasoned determination of whether a plaintiff has met her burden of establishing each of the *Rule 23* class action requirements.

Love v. Turlington, 733 F.2d 1562, 1564 (11th Cir. 1984) (citation omitted).

The Fourth Circuit in Gariety considered and fully answered the concern expressed in Eisen (with respect to a merits inquiry on an issue unrelated to a *Rule 23* requirement) that a merits inquiry on an issue that is related to the merits would prejudice the defendant. The Fourth Circuit noted that such an inquiry would not bind the ultimate fact-finder. See *Gariety, 368 F.3d at 366*. A trial judge's finding on a merits issue for purposes of a *Rule 23* requirement no more binds the court to rule for the plaintiff on the ultimate merits of that issue than does a finding that the plaintiff has shown a probability of success for purposes of a preliminary injunction.

The First Circuit has expressed a mild disagreement with this strong line of authority. See *In re Polymedica Corp. Securities Litigation, 432 F.3d 1 (1st Cir. 2005)*. Although aligning itself with "the majority view" permitting merits inquiry, see *id. at 6* (citing *Waste Management Holdings, Inc. v. Mowbray, 208 F.3d 288* (lst Cir. 2000)), the First Circuit invoked Eisen for the limited proposition that the Supreme Court "prohibits a district court from inquiring into whether a plaintiff will prevail on the merits at c lass certification," id. (emphasis added). Ultimately, in considering the issue of how much evidence a class plaintiff must present to show the efficient market necessary to invoke the Basic presumption of reliance, the First Circuit stated that the "[t]he question of how much evidence of efficiency is necessary for a court to accept the fraud-on-the-market presumption of reliance at the class-certification stage is . . . one of degree." *Id. at 17*. The court acknowledged that its "generalities" on the issue "are the best we can do." Id.

Significance of the 2003 amendments to *Rule 23*. In 2003, the Civil Rules Advisory Committee made several changes to *Rule 23*, but neither the amended Rule nor the Committee's commentary explicitly resolves the split of authority between our Circuit's ambiguous *Caridad/Visa Check/Heerwagen* approach to determining *Rule 23* requirements and the predominant view of the other circuits that class certification requires findings as to such requirements, even if such findings involve consideration of merits issues. Two changes arguably combine to permit a more extensive inquiry into whether *Rule 23* requirements are met than was previously appropriate. First, the amended rule removes from prior *Rule 23(c)(1)(C)* the provision that class certification "may be conditional." Second, the amended rule replaces the provision of prior *Rule 23(c)(1)(A)* that a class certification decision be made "as soon as practicable" with a provision requiring the decision "at an early practicable time." And the Advisory Committee states that "[a] court that is not satisfied that the requirements of *Rule 23* have been met should refuse certification until they have been met." *Fed. R. Civ. P. 23(c)(1)(C)* Adv. Comm. Notes 2003.

Clarifying the standards for the Second Circuit. The foregoing discussion demonstrates the need for some clarification of a district court's role in assessing a motion for class certification. Obviously, we can no longer continue to advise district courts that "some showing," *Caridad, 191 F.3d at 292*, of meeting *Rule 23* requirements will suffice and that "findings" are required, see *Parker, 331 F.3d at 21*, or that an expert's report will sustain a plaintiff's burden so long as it is not "fatally flawed," see *Visa Check, 280 F.3d at 135*, and that the plaintiff must prove *Rule 23* requirements, see *Heerwagen, 435 F.3d at 233*.

It would seem to be beyond dispute that a district court may not grant class certification without making a determination that all of the *Rule 23* requirements are met. We resist saying that what are required are "findings" because that word usually implies that a district judge is resolving a disputed issue of fact. Although there are often factual disputes in connection with *Rule 23* requirements, and such disputes must be resolved with findings, the ultimate issue as to each requirement is really a mixed question of fact and law. A legal standard, e.g., numerosity, commonality, or predominance, is being applied to a set of facts, some of which might be in dispute. The *Rule 23* requirements are threshold issues, similar in some respects to preliminary issues such as personal or subject matter jurisdiction. We normally do not say that a district court makes a "finding" of subject matter jurisdiction; rather, the district court makes a "ruling" or a "determination" as to whether such jurisdiction exists. The judge rules either that jurisdiction exists or that it does not. Of course, in making such a ruling, the judge often resolves underlying factual disputes, and, as to these disputes, the judge must be persuaded that the fact at issue has been established. The same approach is appropriate for *Rule 23* requirements. For example, in considering whether the numerosity requirement is met, a judge might need to resolve a factual dispute as to how many members are in a proposed class. Any dispute about the size of the proposed class must be resolved, and a finding of the size of the class, e.g., 50, 100, or more than 200, must be made. At that point, the judge would apply the legal standard governing numerosity and make a ruling as to whether that standard, applied to the facts as found, establishes numerosity.

The *Rule 23* requirements differ from other threshold issues in that, once a district court has ruled, the standard for appellate review is whether discretion has been exceeded (or abused). This standard of review implies that a district judge has some leeway as to *Rule 23* requirements, and, unlike rulings as to jurisdiction, may be affirmed in some circumstances for ruling either that a particular *Rule 23* requirement is met or is not met. Of course, this leeway, as with all matters of discretion, is not boundless. To the extent that the ruling on a *Rule 23* requirement is supported by a finding of fact, that finding, like any other finding of fact, is reviewed under the "clearly erroneous" standard. And to the extent that the ruling involves an issue of law, review is de novo. See *Parker, 331 F.3d at 18*. To illustrate, again using the example of numerosity, review of the factual finding as to the size of the proposed class would be for clear error, review of the judge's articulation of the legal standard governing numerosity would be de novo, and review of the ultimate ruling that applied the correct legal standard to the facts as found would be for abuse of discretion. Thus a ruling on numerosity, based on a finding of fact that is not clearly erroneous and with application of a legal standard that is correct, could be affirmed as within allowable discretion, in some circumstances, whether the ruling determined that this *Rule 23* requirement was met or not met.

The more troublesome issue arises when the *Rule 23* requirement overlaps with an issue on the merits. With *Eisen* properly understood to preclude consideration of the merits only when a merits issue is unrelated to a *Rule 23* requirement, there is no reason to lessen a district court's obligation to make a determination that every *Rule 23* requirement is met before certifying a class just because of some or even full overlap of that requirement with a merits issue. We thus align ourselves with *Szabo*, *Gariety*, and all of the other decisions discussed above that have required definitive assessment of *Rule 23* requirements, notwithstanding their overlap with merits issues. As Gariety usefully pointed out, the determination as to a *Rule 23* requirement is made only for purposes of class certification and is not binding on the trier of facts, even if that trier is the class certification judge. *368 F.3d at 366*.

In one respect, however, overlap between a *Rule 23* requirement and a merits issue justifies some adjustment in a district court's procedures at the class certification stage. To avoid the risk that a *Rule 23* hearing will extend into a protracted mini-trial of substantial portions of the underlying litigation, a district judge must be accorded considerable discretion to limit both discovery and the extent of the hearing on *Rule 23* requirements. But even with some limits on discovery and the extent of the hearing, the district judge must receive enough evidence, by affidavits, documents, or testimony, to be satisfied that each *Rule 23* requirement has been met.

In light of the foregoing discussion, we reach the following conclusions: (1) a district judge may certify a class only after making determinations that each of the *Rule 23* requirements has been met; (2) such determinations can be made only if the judge resolves factual disputes relevant to each *Rule 23* requirement and finds that whatever underlying facts are relevant to a particular *Rule 23* requirement have been established and is persuaded to rule, based on the relevant facts and the applicable legal standard, that the requirement is met; (3) the obligation to make such determinations is not lessened by overlap between a *Rule 23* requirement and a merits issue, even a merits issue that is identical with a *Rule 23* requirement; (4) in making such determinations, a district judge should not assess any aspect of the merits unrelated to a *Rule 23* requirement; and (5) a district judge has ample discretion to circumscribe both the extent of discovery concerning *Rule 23* requirements and the extent of a hearing to determine whether such requirements are met in order to assure that a class certification motion does not become a pretext for a partial trial of the merits.

In drawing these conclusions, we add three observations. First, our conclusions necessarily preclude the use of a "some showing" standard, and to whatever extent *Caridad* might have implied such a standard for a *Rule 23* requirement, that implication is disavowed. Second, we also disavow the suggestion in *Visa Check* that an expert's testimony may establish a component of a *Rule 23* requirement simply by being not fatally flawed. A district judge is to assess all of the relevant evidence admitted at the class certification stage and determine whether each *Rule 23* requirement has been met, just as the judge would resolve a dispute about any other threshold prerequisite for continuing a lawsuit. Finally, we decline to follow the dictum in *Heerwagen* suggesting that a district judge may not weigh conflicting evidence and determine the existence of a *Rule 23* requirement just because that requirement is identical to an issue on the merits.

II. Application of the Correct Standards to the Pending Case

In some circumstances, it would be appropriate to remand a case such as this to the District Court for reconsideration of the class certification motion under the proper standards as we have explained them. We conclude, however, that remand is not appropriate because the Plaintiffs' own allegations and evidence demonstrate that the *Rule 23* requirement of predominance of common questions over individual questions cannot be met under the standards as we have explicated them.

Reliance. The predominance requirement fails initially with respect to the issue of reliance. The Plaintiffs recognize that they must establish that they relied on the misrepresentations that they have alleged, and they also recognize that establishing reliance individually by members of the class would defeat the requirement of *Rule 23* that common questions of law or fact predominate over questions affecting only individual members. See *Fed. R. Civ. P. 23(b)(3)*. To satisfy the predominance requirement the Plaintiffs invoke the presumption from the Supreme Court's decision in *Basic, 485 U.S. at 245-47*, that purchasers of securities relied on price in an efficient market. "The fraud-on-the-market doctrine, as described by the Supreme Court in Basic [Inc.] v. Levinson, creates a rebuttable presumption that (1) misrepresentations by an issuer affect the price of securities traded in the open market, and (2) investors rely on the market price of securities as an accurate measure of their intrinsic value." *Hevesi v. Citigroup Inc., 366 F.3d 70, 77 (2d Cir. 2004)*. Applying the lenient "some showing" standard, which we have now discarded, the District Court in the pending case ruled that the Plaintiffs had sufficiently shown the existence of an efficient market to invoke the Basic presumption. *IPO (Dist. Ct.), 227 F.R.D. at 107*. However, the Plaintiffs' own allegations and evidence demonstrate that an efficient market cannot be established in this case under the proper standards set forth in this opinion.

In the first place, the market for IPO shares is not efficient. As the late Judge Timbers of our Court has said, sitting with the Sixth Circuit, "[A] primary market for newly issued [securities] is not efficient or developed under any definition of these terms." *Freeman v. Laventhol & Horwath, 915 F.2d 193, 199 (6th Cir. 1990)* (internal quotation marks omitted); accord *Berwecky v. Bear, Stearns & Co., 197 F.R.D. 65, 68 n. 5 (S.D.N.Y. 2000)* (The fraud-on-the-market "presumption can not logically apply when plaintiffs allege fraud in connection with an IPO, because in an IPO there is no well-developed market in offered securities."). As just one example of why an efficient market, necessary for the Basic presumption to apply, cannot be established with an IPO, we note that during the 25-day "quiet period," analysts cannot report concerning securities in an IPO, see *17 C.F.R. §§ 230.174(d), 242.101(b)(1)*, thereby precluding the contemporaneous "significant number of reports by securities analysts" that are a characteristic of an efficient market. See *Freeman, 915 F.2d at 199*.

Moreover, the Plaintiffs' own allegations as to how slow the market was to correct the alleged price inflation despite what they also allege was widespread knowledge of the scheme indicate the very antithesis of an efficient market. Indeed, the Plaintiffs claim on appeal, in an effort to support their theory of loss causation, that whatever artificially inflated effects on share prices were allegedly caused by the Defendants' conduct continued even past the December 6, 2000, end date of the class period. See Brief for Appellees at 81. It is also doubtful whether the Basic presumption can be extended, beyond its original context, to tie-in trading, underwriter compensation, and analysts' reports. See *West v. Prudential Securities, Inc., 282 F.3d 935, 938 (7th Cir. 2002)*.

Without the Basic presumption, individual questions of reliance would predominate over common questions.

Knowledge. There is no dispute that a *section 10(b)* claimant "must allege and prove" that the claimant traded "in ignorance of the fact that the price was affected by the alleged manipulation." *Gurary v. Winehouse, 190 F.3d 37, 45 (2d Cir. 1999)*. The Plaintiffs must show lack of knowledge to recover on their *section 11* claims as well. *DeMaria v. Andersen, 318 F.3d 170, 175 (2d Cir. 2003)* ("*[Section] 11* provides a cause of action for 'any person acquiring' a security issued pursuant to a materially false registration statement unless the purchaser knew about the false statement at the time of acquisition."). The Plaintiffs' allegations, evidence, and discovery responses demonstrate that the predominance requirement is defeated because common questions of knowledge do not predominate over individual questions. The claim that lack of knowledge is common to the class is thoroughly undermined by the Plaintiffs' own allegations as to how widespread was knowledge of the alleged scheme. Obviously, the initial IPO allocants, who were required to purchase in the aftermarket, were fully aware of the obligation that is alleged to have artificially inflated share prices. Those receiving or seeking allocations number in the thousands. With respect to one IPO alone (Engage Technologies, Inc.), 540 institutions and 1,850 others received allocations. And there were more than 900 IPOs allegedly manipulated by aftermarket purchase requirements. Equally obviously, the requirements would have been known not just to the entities receiving allocations, but also to many thousands of people employed by the institutional investors. In addition, two cable television networks, MSNBC and CNBC, reported on the aftermarket purchase requirements in 1999, and in 2000 the practice was the subject of an SEC Staff Legal Bulletin and a report in Barron's discussing the bulletin. The Plaintiffs themselves refer to the "industry-wide understanding" that those who agreed to purchase in the aftermarket received allocations. See Master Allegations PP 30, 31.

The District Court sought to minimize the extent of individual questions of knowledge by redefining the proposed class to exclude "those investors who exhibit the hallmarks of full participation in the alleged scheme." *227 F.R.D. at 103* (emphasis added). However, that exclusion leaves within the class those who participated in part and those who were required to remain "ready" to purchase in the aftermarket if the underwriters so desired, Master Allegations P 15, all of whom knew of the alleged scheme. Moreover, the exclusion of full participants from the class does nothing to lessen the broad extent of knowledge of the scheme throughout the community of market participants and watchers, and it is this widespread knowledge that would precipitate individual inquiries as to the knowledge of each member of the class, even as redefined.

Payment of undisclosed compensation. Yet a further example of an aspect of this litigation bristling with individual questions is ascertainment of which putative class members have "paid any undisclosed compensation to the allocating underwriter(s)," *IPO (Dist. Ct.), 227 F.R.D. at 102*, a circumstance that, along with others, would exclude them from the class. Passing the somewhat paradoxical point as to how someone is to determine whether compensation that was "undisclosed" was paid, we note that individual issues arise even as to those aspects of compensation that a Plaintiff might be able to determine were within the Plaintiffs' definition of "Undisclosed Compensation." As described in the Master Allegations, such compensation comprises:

> (a) paying inflated brokerage commissions; (b) entering into transactions in otherwise unrelated securities for the primary purpose of generating commissions; and/or (c) purchasing equity offerings underwritten by the Underwriter Defendants, including, but not limited to, secondary (or add-on) offerings that would not be purchased but for the Underwriter Defendants' unlawful scheme.

Id. at 100 (quoting Master Allegations P 17) (emphases added).

Each category of undisclosed compensation would require individualized determinations. Whether a brokerage commission was inflated would depend on a comparison between what brokerage the putative class member was charged and the customary commission for trades of a similar nature. Whether shares unrelated to the IPO were purchased for the purpose of generating commissions and whether shares purchased in the aftermarket would not have been bought but for the allegedly unlawful scheme would require inquiry into the subjective intent of the purchaser. A purchaser would not have paid undisclosed compensation if shares were bought entirely at the behest of the purchaser and because of an independent interest in buying shares of a particular company. Obviously, ascertaining each purchaser's intent would require an individualized determination. See *Simer v. Rios, 661 F.2d 655, 669 (7th Cir. 1981)* (class difficult to ascertain where "membership in the class depends on each individual's state of mind"); *Dunnigan v. Metropolitan Life Insurance Co., 214 F.R.D. 125, 135 (S.D.N.Y. 2003)* ("Where membership in the class requires a subjective determination, the class is not identifiable."). Although it has been stated that class members must be ascertainable "at some point in the case," but not necessarily prior to class certification, see In re Methyl Tertiary Butyl Ether ("MTBE") *Products Liability Litigation, 209 F.R.D. 323, 337 (S.D.N.Y. 2002)* (internal quotation marks omitted), we point out the need for numerous individualized determinations of class membership in order to provide further support for our basic conclusion that individual questions will permeate this litigation. Although ascertainability of the class is an issue distinct from the predominance requirement for a *(b)(3)* class, the problems we have identified on this topic further indicate the obstacles to proceeding with the focus cases as class actions.

Conclusion

Under the standards we have today set forth, it is clear that, with respect to at least the factors of reliance and lack of knowledge of the scheme, the Plaintiffs cannot satisfy the predominance requirement for a *(b)(3)* class action. Accordingly, we vacate the District Court's order granting class certifications in each of the six focus cases and remand for further proceedings.

Stoneridge Investment Partners, LLC v. Scientific-Atlanta, Inc.

Supreme Court of the United States, 2008
128 S. Ct. 761, 169 L. Ed. 627 (January 15, 2008)

■ JUSTICE KENNEDY delivered the opinion of the Court.

We consider the reach of the private right of action the Court has found implied in § 10(b) of the Securities Exchange Act of 1934, and SEC Rule 10b-5. In this suit investors alleged losses after purchasing common stock. They sought to impose liability on entities who, acting both as customers and suppliers, agreed to arrangements that allowed the investors' company to mislead its auditor and issue a misleading financial statement affecting the stock price. We conclude the implied right of action does not reach the customer/supplier companies because the investors did not rely upon their statements or representations. We affirm the judgment of the Court of Appeals.

I

This class-action suit by investors was filed against Charter Communications, Inc., in the United States District Court for the Eastern District of Missouri. Stoneridge Investment Partners, LLC, a limited liability company organized under the laws of Delaware, was the lead plaintiff and is petitioner here.

Charter issued the financial statements and the securities in question. It was a named defendant along with some of its executives and Arthur Andersen LLP, Charter's independent auditor during the period in question. We are concerned, though, with two other defendants, respondents here. Respondents are Scientific-Atlanta, Inc., and Motorola, Inc. They were suppliers, and later customers, of Charter.

For purposes of this proceeding, we take these facts, alleged by petitioner, to be true. Charter, a cable operator, engaged in a variety of fraudulent practices so its quarterly reports would meet Wall Street expectations for cable subscriber growth and operating cash flow. The fraud included misclassification of its customer base; delayed reporting of terminated customers; improper capitalization of costs that should have been shown as expenses; and manipulation of the company's billing cutoff dates to inflate reported revenues. In late 2000, Charter executives realized that, despite these efforts, the company would miss projected operating cash flow numbers by $ 15 to $ 20 million. To help meet the shortfall, Charter decided to alter its existing arrangements with respondents, Scientific-Atlanta and Motorola. Petitioner's theory as to whether Arthur Andersen was altogether misled or, on the other hand, knew the structure of the contract arrangements and was complicit to some degree, is not clear at this stage of the case. The point, however, is neither controlling nor significant for our present disposition, and in our decision we assume it was misled.

Respondents supplied Charter with the digital cable converter (set top) boxes that Charter furnished to its customers. Charter arranged to overpay respondents $ 20 for each set top box it purchased until the end of the year, with the understanding that respondents would return the overpayment by purchasing advertising from Charter. The transactions, it is alleged, had no economic substance; but, because Charter would then record the advertising purchases as revenue and capitalize its purchase of the set top boxes, in violation of generally accepted accounting principles, the transactions would enable Charter to fool its auditor into approving a financial statement showing it met projected revenue and operating cash flow numbers. Respondents agreed to the arrangement.

So that Arthur Andersen would not discover the link between Charter's increased payments for the boxes and the advertising purchases, the companies drafted documents to make it appear the transactions were unrelated and conducted in the ordinary course of business. Following a request from Charter, Scientific-Atlanta sent documents to Charter stating--falsely--that it had increased production costs. It raised the price for set top boxes for the rest of 2000 by $ 20 per box. As for Motorola, in a written contract Charter agreed to purchase from Motorola a specific number of set top boxes and pay liquidated damages of $ 20 for each unit it did not take. The contract was made with the expectation Charter would fail to purchase all the units and pay Motorola the liquidated damages.

To return the additional money from the set top box sales, Scientific-Atlanta and Motorola signed contracts with Charter to purchase advertising time for a price higher than fair value. The new set top box agreements were backdated to make it appear that they were negotiated a month before the advertising agreements. The backdating was important to convey the impression that the negotiations were unconnected, a point Arthur Andersen considered necessary for separate treatment of the transactions. Charter recorded the advertising payments to inflate revenue and operating cash flow by approximately $ 17 million. The inflated number was shown on financial statements filed with the Securities and Exchange Commission (SEC) and reported to the public.

Respondents had no role in preparing or disseminating Charter's financial statements. And their own financial statements booked the transactions as a wash, under generally accepted accounting principles. It is alleged respondents knew or were in reckless disregard of Charter's intention to use the transactions to inflate its revenues and knew the resulting financial statements issued by Charter would be relied upon by research analysts and investors.

Petitioner filed a securities fraud class action on behalf of purchasers of Charter stock alleging that, by participating in the transactions, respondents violated § 10(b) of the Securities Exchange Act of 1934 and SEC Rule 10b-5.

The District Court granted respondents' motion to dismiss for failure to state a claim on which relief can be granted. The United States Court of Appeals for the Eighth Circuit affirmed. *In re Charter Communications, Inc., Securities Litigation, 443 F.3d 987 (2006)*. In its view the allegations did not show that respondents made misstatements relied upon by the public or that they violated a duty to disclose; and on this premise it found no violation of § 10(b) by respondents. *Id., at 992*. At most, the court observed, respondents had aided and abetted Charter's misstatement of its financial results; but, it noted, there is no private right of action for aiding and abetting a § 10(b) violation. See *Central Bank of Denver, N. A. v. First Interstate Bank of Denver, N. A., 511 U.S. 164, 191 (1994)*. The court also affirmed the District Court's denial of petitioner's motion to amend the complaint, as the revised pleading would not change the court's conclusion on the merits. *443 F.3d at 993*.

Decisions of the Courts of Appeals are in conflict respecting when, if ever, an injured investor may rely upon § 10(b) to recover from a party that neither makes a public misstatement nor violates a duty to disclose but does participate in a scheme to violate § 10(b). Compare *Simpson v. AOL Time Warner Inc., 452 F.3d 1040 (CA9 2006)*, with *Regents of Univ. of Cal. v. Credit Suisse First Boston (USA), Inc., 482 F.3d 372 (CA5 2007)*. We granted certiorari. *549 U.S. , 127 S. Ct. 1873 (2007)*.

II

Section 10(b) of the Securities Exchange Act makes it

> "unlawful for any person, directly or indirectly, by the use of any means or instrumentality of interstate commerce or of the mails, or of any facility of any national securities exchange . . . to use or employ, in connection with the purchase or sale of any security . . . any manipulative or deceptive device or contrivance in contravention of such rules and regulations as the Commission may prescribe as necessary or appropriate in the public interest or for the protection of investors." *15 U.S.C. § 78j*.

The SEC, pursuant to this section, promulgated Rule 10b-5, which makes it unlawful

> "(a) To employ any device, scheme, or artifice to defraud,
>
> "(b) To make any untrue statement of a material fact or to omit to state a material fact necessary in order to make the statements made, in the light of the circumstances under which they were made, not misleading, or
>
> "(c) To engage in any act, practice, or course of business which operates or would operate as a fraud or deceit upon any person, "in connection with the purchase or sale of any security." *17 CFR § 240.10b-5*.

Rule 10b-5 encompasses only conduct already prohibited by § 10(b). *United States v. O'Hagan, 521 U.S. 642, 651 (1997)*. Though the text of the Securities Exchange Act does not provide for a private cause of action for § 10(b) violations, the Court has found a right of action implied in the words of the statute and its implementing regulation. *Superintendent of Ins. of N. Y. v. Bankers Life & Casualty Co., 404 U.S. 6, 13, n. 9 (1971)*. In a typical § 10(b) private action a plaintiff must prove (1) a material misrepresentation or omission by the defendant; (2) scienter; (3) a connection between the misrepresentation or omission and the purchase or sale of a security; (4) reliance upon the misrepresentation or omission; (5) economic loss; and (6) loss causation. See *Dura Pharms., Inc. v. Broudo, 544 U.S. 336, 341-342 (2005)*.

In *Central Bank*, the Court determined that § 10(b) liability did not extend to aiders and abettors. The Court found the scope of § 10(b) to be delimited by the text, which makes no mention of aiding and abetting liability. *511 U.S., at 177*. The Court doubted the implied § 10(b) action should extend to aiders and abettors when none of the express causes of action in the securities Acts included that liability. *Id., at 180*. It added the following:

"Were we to allow the aiding and abetting action proposed in this case, the defendant could be liable without any showing that the plaintiff relied upon the aider and abettor's statements or actions. See also *Chiarella* [v. *United States, 445 U.S. 222, 228 (1980)].* Allowing plaintiffs to circumvent the reliance requirement would disregard the careful limits on 10b-5 recovery mandated by our earlier cases." *Ibid.*

The decision in *Central Bank* led to calls for Congress to create an express cause of action for aiding and abetting within the Securities Exchange Act. Then-SEC Chairman Arthur Levitt, testifying before the Senate Securities Subcommittee, cited *Central Bank* and recommended that aiding and abetting liability in private claims be established. S. Hearing No. 103-759, pp. 13-14 (1994). Congress did not follow this course. Instead, in § 104 of the Private Securities Litigation Reform Act of 1995 (PSLRA), it directed prosecution of aiders and abettors by the SEC. *15 U.S.C. § 78t(e)*.

The § 10(b) implied private right of action does not extend to aiders and abettors. The conduct of a secondary actor must satisfy each of the elements or preconditions for liability; and we consider whether the allegations here are sufficient to do so.

III

The Court of Appeals concluded petitioner had not alleged that respondents engaged in a deceptive act within the reach of the § 10(b) private right of action, noting that only misstatements, omissions by one who has a duty to disclose, and manipulative trading practices (where "manipulative" is a term of art, see, *e.g., Santa Fe Industries, Inc. v. Green, 430 U.S. 462, 476-477 (1977))* are deceptive within the meaning of the rule. *443 F.3d at 992.* If this conclusion were read to suggest there must be a specific oral or written statement before there could be liability under § 10(b) or Rule 10b-5, it would be erroneous. Conduct itself can be deceptive, as respondents concede. In this case, moreover, respondents' course of conduct included both oral and written statements, such as the backdated contracts agreed to by Charter and respondents.

A different interpretation of the holding from the Court of Appeals opinion is that the court was stating only that any deceptive statement or act respondents made was not actionable because it did not have the requisite proximate relation to the investors' harm. That conclusion is consistent with our own determination that respondents' acts or statements were not relied upon by the investors and that, as a result, liability cannot be imposed upon respondents.

A

Reliance by the plaintiff upon the defendant's deceptive acts is an essential element of the § 10(b) private cause of action. It ensures that, for liability to arise, the "requisite causal connection between a defendant's misrepresentation and a plaintiff's injury" exists as a predicate for liability. *Basic Inc. v. Levinson, 485 U.S. 224, 243 (1988);* see also *Affiliated Ute Citizens of Utah v. United States, 406 U.S. 128 (1972)* (requiring "causation in fact"). We have found a rebuttable presumption of reliance in two different circumstances. First, if there is an omission of a material fact by one with a duty to disclose, the investor to whom the duty was owed need not provide specific proof of reliance. *Id., at 153-154*. Second, under the fraud-on-the-market doctrine, reliance is presumed when the statements at issue become public. The public information is reflected in the market price of the security. Then it can be assumed that an investor who buys or sells stock at the market price relies upon the statement. *Basic, supra, at 247*.

Neither presumption applies here. Respondents had no duty to disclose; and their deceptive acts were not communicated to the public. No member of the investing public had knowledge, either actual or presumed, of respondents' deceptive acts during the relevant times. Petitioner, as a result, cannot show reliance upon any of respondents' actions except in an indirect chain that we find too remote for liability.

B

Invoking what some courts call "scheme liability," see, *e.g., In re Enron Corp. Secs. v. Enron Corp., 439 F. Supp. 2d 692, 723 (SD Tex. 2006)*, petitioner nonetheless seeks to impose liability on respondents even absent a public statement. In our view this approach does not answer the objection that petitioner did not in fact rely upon respondents' own deceptive conduct.

Liability is appropriate, petitioner contends, because respondents engaged in conduct with the purpose and effect of creating a false appearance of material fact to further a scheme to misrepresent Charter's revenue. The argument is that the financial statement Charter released to the public was a natural and expected consequence of respondents' deceptive acts; had respondents not assisted Charter, Charter's auditor would not have been fooled, and the financial statement would have been a more accurate reflection of Charter's financial condition. That causal link is sufficient, petitioner argues, to apply *Basic*'s presumption of reliance to respondents' acts. See, *e.g., Simpson, 452 F.3d at 1051-1052*; *In re Parmalat Securities Litigation, 376 F. Supp. 2d 472, 509 (SDNY 2005)*.

In effect petitioner contends that in an efficient market investors rely not only upon the public statements relating to a security but also upon the transactions those statements reflect. Were this concept of reliance to be adopted, the implied cause of action would reach the whole marketplace in which the issuing company does business; and there is no authority for this rule.

As stated above, reliance is tied to causation, leading to the inquiry whether respondents' acts were immediate or remote to the injury. In considering petitioner's arguments, we note § 10(b) provides that the deceptive act must be "in connection with the purchase or sale of any security." *15 U.S.C. § 78j(b)*. Though this phrase in part defines the statute's coverage rather than causation (and so we do not evaluate the "in connection with" requirement of § 10(b) in this case), the emphasis on a purchase or sale of securities does provide some insight into the deceptive acts that concerned the enacting Congress. See Black, Securities Commentary: The Second Circuit's Approach to the 'In Connection With' Requirement of Rule 10b-5, *53 Brooklyn L. Rev. 539, 541 (1987)* ("While the 'in connection with' and causation requirements are analytically distinct, they are related to each other, and discussion of the first requirement may merge with discussion of the second"). In all events we conclude respondents' deceptive acts, which were not disclosed to the investing public, are too remote to satisfy the requirement of reliance. It was Charter, not respondents, that misled its auditor and filed fraudulent financial statements; nothing respondents did made it necessary or inevitable for Charter to record the transactions as it did.

The petitioner invokes the private cause of action under § 10(b) and seeks to apply it beyond the securities markets--the realm of financing business--to purchase and supply contracts--the realm of ordinary business operations. The latter realm is governed, for the most part, by state law. It is true that if business operations are used, as alleged here, to affect securities markets, the SEC enforcement power may reach the culpable actors. It is true as well that a dynamic, free economy presupposes a high degree of integrity in all of its parts, an integrity that must be underwritten by rules enforceable in fair, independent, accessible courts. Were the implied cause of action to be extended to the practices described here, however, there would be a risk that the federal power would be used to invite litigation beyond the immediate sphere of securities litigation and in areas already governed by functioning and effective state-law guarantees. Our precedents counsel against this extension. See *Marine Bank v. Weaver, 455 U.S. 551, 556 (1982)* ("Congress, in enacting the securities laws, did not intend to provide a broad federal remedy for all fraud"); *Santa Fe, 430 U.S., at 479-480* ("There may well be a need for uniform federal fiduciary standards . . . . But those standards should not be supplied by judicial extension of § 10(b) and Rule 10b-5 to 'cover the corporate universe'" (quoting Cary, Federalism and Corporate Law: Reflections Upon Delaware, 83 Yale L. J. 663, 700 (1974))). Though § 10(b) is "not 'limited to preserving the integrity of the securities markets,'" *Bankers Life, 404 U.S., at 12*, it does not reach all commercial transactions that are fraudulent and affect the price of a security in some attenuated way.

These considerations answer as well the argument that if this were a common-law action for fraud there could be a finding of reliance. Even if the assumption is correct, it is not controlling. Section 10(b) does not incorporate common-law fraud into federal law. See, *e.g., SEC v. Zandford, 535 U.S. 813, 820 (2002)* ("[Section 10(b)] must not be construed so broadly as to convert every common-law fraud that happens to involve securities into a violation"); *Central Bank, 511 U.S., at 184* ("Even assuming . . . a deeply rooted background of aiding and abetting tort liability, it does not follow that Congress intended to apply that kind of liability to the private causes of action in the securities Acts"); see also *Dura, 544 U.S., at 341*. Just as § 10(b) "is surely badly strained when construed to provide a cause of action . . . to the world at large," *Blue Chip Stamps v. Manor Drug Stores, 421 U.S. 723, 733, n. 5 (1975)*, it should not be interpreted to provide a private cause of action against the entire marketplace in which the issuing company operates.

Petitioner's theory, moreover, would put an unsupportable interpretation on Congress' specific response to *Central Bank* in § 104 of the PSLRA. Congress amended the securities laws to provide for limited coverage of aiders and abettors. Aiding and abetting liability is authorized in actions brought by the SEC but not by private parties. See *15 U.S.C. § 78t(e)*. Petitioner's view of primary liability makes any aider and abettor liable under § 10(b) if he or she committed a deceptive act in the process of providing assistance. Reply Brief for Petitioner 6, n. 2; Tr. of Oral Arg. 24. Were we to adopt this construction of § 10(b), it would revive in substance the implied cause of action against all aiders and abettors except those who committed no deceptive act in the process of facilitating the fraud; and we would undermine Congress' determination that this class of defendants should be pursued by the SEC and not by private litigants. See *Alexander v. Sandoval, 532 U.S. 275, 290 (2001)* ("The express provision of one method of enforcing a substantive rule suggests that Congress intended to preclude others"); *FDA v. Brown & Williamson Tobacco Corp., 529 U.S. 120, 143 (2000)* ("At the time a statute is enacted, it may have a range of plausible meanings. Over time, however, subsequent acts can shape or focus those meanings"); see also *Seatrain Shipbuilding Corp. v. Shell Oil Co., 444 U.S. 572, 596 (1980)* ("While the views of subsequent Congresses cannot override the unmistakable intent of the enacting one, such views are entitled to significant weight, and particularly so when the precise intent of the enacting Congress is obscure" (citations omitted)).

This is not a case in which Congress has enacted a regulatory statute and then has accepted, over a long period of time, broad judicial authority to define substantive standards of conduct and liability. Cf. *Leegin Creative Leather Prods. v. PSKS, Inc., 551 U.S.   , 127 S. Ct. 2705 (2007) (slip op., at 19-20)*. And in accord with the nature of the cause of action at issue here, we give weight to Congress' amendment to the Act restoring aiding and abetting liability in certain cases but not others. The amendment, in our view, supports the conclusion that there is no liability.

The practical consequences of an expansion, which the Court has considered appropriate to examine in circumstances like these, see *Virginia Bankshares, Inc. v. Sandberg, 501 U.S. 1083, 1104-1105 (1991)*; *Blue Chip, 421 U.S., at 737*, provide a further reason to reject petitioner's approach. In *Blue Chip*, the Court noted that extensive discovery and the potential for uncertainty and disruption in a lawsuit allow plaintiffs with weak claims to extort settlements from innocent companies. *Id., at 740-741*. Adoption of petitioner's approach would expose a new class of defendants to these risks. As noted in *Central Bank*, contracting parties might find it necessary to protect against these threats, raising the costs of doing business. See *511 U.S., at 189*. Overseas firms with no other exposure to our securities laws could be deterred from doing business here. See Brief for Organization for International Investment et al. as *Amici Curiae* 17-20. This, in turn, may raise the cost of being a publicly traded company under our law and shift securities offerings away from domestic capital markets. Brief for NASDAQ Stock Market, Inc., et al. as *Amici Curiae* 12-14.

C

The history of the § 10(b) private right and the careful approach the Court has taken before proceeding without congressional direction provide further reasons to find no liability here. The § 10(b) private cause of action is a judicial construct that Congress did not enact in the text of the relevant statutes. See *Lampf, Pleva, Lipkind, Prupis & Petigrow v. Gilbertson, 501 U.S. 350, 358-359 (1991)*; *Blue Chip, supra, at 729*. Though the rule once may have been otherwise, see *J. I. Case Co. v. Borak, 377 U.S. 426, 432-433 (1964)*, it is settled that there is an implied cause of action only if the underlying statute can be interpreted to disclose the intent to create one, see, *e.g., Alexander, supra, at 286-287, 1511*; *Virginia Bankshares, supra, at 1102*; *Touche Ross & Co. v. Redington, 442 U.S. 560, 575 (1979)*. This is for good reason. In the absence of congressional intent the Judiciary's recognition of an implied private right of action

> "necessarily extends its authority to embrace a dispute Congress has not assigned it to resolve. This runs contrary to the established principle that 'the jurisdiction of the federal courts is carefully guarded against expansion by judicial interpretation . . . ,' *American Fire & Casualty Co. v. Finn, 341 U.S. 6, 17 (1951)*, and conflicts with the authority of Congress under Art. III to set the limits of federal jurisdiction." *Cannon v.*

University of Chicago, 441 U.S. 677, 746 (1979) (Powell, J., dissenting) (citations and footnote omitted).

The determination of who can seek a remedy has significant consequences for the reach of federal power. See *Wilder v. Virginia Hosp. Ass'n*, 496 U.S. 498, 509, n. 9 (1990) (requirement of congressional intent "reflects a concern, grounded in separation of powers, that Congress rather than the courts controls the availability of remedies for violations of statutes").

Concerns with the judicial creation of a private cause of action caution against its expansion. The decision to extend the cause of action is for Congress, not for us. Though it remains the law, the § 10(b) private right should not be extended beyond its present boundaries. See *Virginia Bankshares, supra, at 1102* ("The breadth of the [private right of action] once recognized should not, as a general matter, grow beyond the scope congressionally intended"); see also *Central Bank, supra, at 173* (determining that the scope of conduct prohibited is limited by the text of § 10(b)).

This restraint is appropriate in light of the PSLRA, which imposed heightened pleading requirements and a loss causation requirement upon "any private action" arising from the Securities Exchange Act. See *15 U.S.C. § 78u-4(b)*. It is clear these requirements touch upon the implied right of action, which is now a prominent feature of federal securities regulation. See *Merrill Lynch, Pierce, Fenner & Smith Inc. v. Dabit*, 547 U.S. 71, 81-82 (2006); *Dura*, 544 U.S., at 345-346; see also S. Rep. No. 104-98, p. 4-5 (1995) (recognizing the § 10(b) implied cause of action, and indicating the PSLRA was intended to have "Congress . . . reassert its authority in this area"); *id.*, at 26 (indicating the pleading standards covered § 10(b) actions). Congress thus ratified the implied right of action after the Court moved away from a broad willingness to imply private rights of action. See *Merrill Lynch, Pierce, Fenner & Smith, Inc. v. Curran*, 456 U.S. 353, 381-382 and n. 66 (1982); cf. *Borak, supra, at 433*. It is appropriate for us to assume that when *§ 78u-4* was enacted, Congress accepted the § 10(b) private cause of action as then defined but chose to extend it no further.

IV

Secondary actors are subject to criminal penalties, see, *e.g.*, *15 U.S.C. § 78ff*, and civil enforcement by the SEC, see, *e.g.*, *§ 78t(e)*. The enforcement power is not toothless. Since September 30, 2002, SEC enforcement actions have collected over $ 10 billion in disgorgement and penalties, much of it for distribution to injured investors. See SEC, 2007 Performance and Accountability Report, p. 26, http://www.sec.gov/about/secpar2007.shtml (as visited Jan. 2, 2008, and available in Clerk of Court's case file). And in this case both parties agree that criminal penalties are a strong deterrent. See Brief for Respondents 48; Reply Brief for Petitioner 17. In addition some state securities laws permit state authorities to seek fines and restitution from aiders and abettors. See, *e.g.*, Del. Code Ann., Tit. 6, § 7325 (2005). All secondary actors, furthermore, are not necessarily immune from private suit. The securities statutes provide an express private right of action against accountants and underwriters in certain circumstances, see *15 U.S.C. § 77k*, and the implied right of action in § 10(b) continues to cover secondary actors who commit primary violations. *Central Bank, supra, at 191*.

Here respondents were acting in concert with Charter in the ordinary course as suppliers and, as matters then evolved in the not so ordinary course, as customers. Unconventional as the arrangement was, it took place in the marketplace for goods and services, not in the investment sphere. Charter was free to do as it chose in preparing its books, conferring with its auditor, and preparing and then issuing its financial statements. In these circumstances the investors cannot be said to have relied upon any of respondents' deceptive acts in the decision to purchase or sell securities; and as the requisite reliance cannot be shown, respondents have no liability to petitioner under the implied right of action. This conclusion is consistent with the narrow dimensions we must give to a right of action Congress did not authorize when it first enacted the statute and did not expand when it revisited the law.

The judgment of the Court of Appeals is affirmed, and the case is remanded for further proceedings consistent with this opinion.

It is so ordered.

JUSTICE BREYER took no part in the consideration or decision of this case.

DISSENT:

JUSTICE STEVENS, with whom JUSTICE SOUTER and JUSTICE GINSBURG join, dissenting.

Charter Communications, Inc., inflated its revenues by $ 17 million in order to cover up a $ 15 to $ 20 million expected cash flow shortfall. It could not have done so absent the knowingly fraudulent actions of Scientific-Atlanta, Inc., and Motorola, Inc. Investors relied on Charter's revenue statements in deciding whether to invest in Charter and in doing so relied on respondents' fraud, which was itself a "deceptive device" prohibited by § 10(b) of the Securities Exchange Act of 1934. This is enough to satisfy the requirements of § 10(b) and enough to distinguish this case from *Central Bank of Denver, N. A. v. First Interstate Bank of Denver, N. A., 511 U.S. 164 (1994)*.

The Court seems to assume that respondents' alleged conduct could subject them to liability in an enforcement proceeding initiated by the Government, *ante,* at 15, but nevertheless concludes that they are not subject to liability in a private action brought by injured investors because they are, at most, guilty of aiding and abetting a violation of § 10(b), rather than an actual violation of the statute. While that conclusion results in an affirmance of the judgment of the Court of Appeals, it rests on a rejection of that court's reasoning. Furthermore, while the Court frequently refers to petitioner's attempt to "expand" the implied cause of action, --a conclusion that begs the question of the contours of that cause of action--it is today's decision that results in a significant departure from *Central Bank.*

The Court's conclusion that no violation of § 10(b) giving rise to a private right of action has been alleged in this case rests on two faulty premises: (1) the Court's overly broad reading of *Central Bank,* and (2) the view that reliance requires a kind of super-causation--a view contrary to both the

Securities and Exchange Commission's (SEC) position in a recent Ninth Circuit case and our holding in *Basic Inc. v. Levinson, 485 U.S. 224 (1988)*. These two points merit separate discussion.

I

The Court of Appeals incorrectly based its decision on the view that "[a] device or contrivance is not 'deceptive,' within the meaning of § 10(b), absent some misstatement or a failure to disclose by one who has a duty to disclose." *In re Charter Communications, Inc., Securities Litigation, 443 F.3d 987, 992 (CA8 2006)*. The Court correctly explains why the statute covers nonverbal as well as verbal deceptive conduct. *Ante*, at 7. The allegations in this case--that respondents produced documents falsely claiming costs had risen and signed contracts they knew to be backdated in order to disguise the connection between the increase in costs and the purchase of advertising--plainly describe "deceptive devices" under any standard reading of the phrase.

What the Court fails to recognize is that this case is critically different from *Central Bank* because the bank in that case did not engage in any deceptive act and, therefore, did not *itself* violate § 10(b). The Court sweeps aside any distinction, remarking that holding respondents liable would "revive the implied cause of action against all aiders and abettors except those who committed no deceptive act in the process of facilitating the fraud." *Ante*, at 12. But the fact that Central Bank engaged in no deceptive conduct whatsoever--in other words, that it was at most an aider and abettor--sharply distinguishes *Central Bank* from cases that do involve allegations of such conduct. *511 U.S., at 167* (stating that the question presented was "whether private civil liability under § 10(b) extends as well to those who do not engage in the manipulative or deceptive practice, but who aid and abet the violation").

The Central Bank of Denver was the indenture trustee for bonds issued by a public authority and secured by liens on property in Colorado Springs. After default, purchasers of $ 2.1 million of those bonds sued the underwriters, alleging violations of § 10(b); they also named Central Bank as a defendant, contending that the bank's delay in reviewing a suspicious appraisal of the value of the security made it liable as an aider and abettor. *Id., at 167-168*. The facts of this case would parallel those of *Central Bank* if respondents had, for example, merely delayed sending invoices for set-top boxes to Charter. Conversely, the facts in *Central Bank* would mirror those in the case before us today if the bank had knowingly purchased real estate in wash transactions at above-market prices in order to facilitate the appraiser's overvaluation of the security. *Central Bank*, thus, poses no obstacle to petitioner's argument that it has alleged a cause of action under § 10(b).

II

The Court's next faulty premise is that petitioner is required to allege that Scientific-Atlanta and Motorola made it "necessary or inevitable for Charter to record the transactions in the way it did," *ante*, at 10, in order to demonstrate reliance. Because the Court of Appeals did not base its holding on reliance grounds, see *443 F.3d at 992*, the fairest course to petitioner would be for the majority to remand to the Court of Appeals to determine whether petitioner properly alleged reliance, under a correct view of what § 10(b) covers. Because the Court chooses to rest its holding on an absence of reliance, a response is required.

In *Basic Inc., 485 U.S., at 243*, we stated that "reliance provides the requisite causal connection between a defendant's misrepresentation and a plaintiff's injury." The Court's view of the causation required to demonstrate reliance is unwarranted and without precedent.

In *Basic Inc.*, we held that the "fraud-on-the-market" theory provides adequate support for a presumption in private securities actions that shareholders (or former shareholders) in publicly traded companies rely on public material misstatements that affect the price of the company's stock. *Id., at 248*. The holding in *Basic* is surely a sufficient response to the argument that a complaint alleging that deceptive acts which had a material effect on the price of a listed stock should be dismissed because the plaintiffs were not subjectively aware of the deception at the time of the securities' purchase or sale. This Court has not held that investors must be aware of the specific deceptive act which violates § 10b to demonstrate reliance.

The Court is right that a fraud-on-the-market presumption coupled with its view on causation would not support petitioner's view of reliance. The fraud-on-the-market presumption helps investors who cannot demonstrate that they, *themselves*, relied on fraud that reached the market. But that presumption says nothing about causation from the other side: what an individual or corporation must do in order to have "caused" the misleading information that reached the market. The Court thus has it backwards when it first addresses the fraud-on-the-market presumption, rather than the causation required. See, *ante*, at 8. The argument is not that the fraud-on-the-market presumption is enough standing alone, but that a correct view of causation coupled with the presumption would allow petitioner to plead reliance.

Lower courts have correctly stated that the causation necessary to demonstrate reliance is not a difficult hurdle to clear in a private right of action under § 10(b). Reliance is often equated with "'transaction causation.'" *Dura Pharms., Inc. v. Broudo, 544 U.S. 336, 341, 342 (2005)*. Transaction causation, in turn, is often defined as requiring an allegation that but for the deceptive act, the plaintiff would not have entered into the securities transaction. See, *e.g.*, *Lentell v. Merrill Lynch & Co., 396 F.3d 161, 172 (CA2 2005)*; *Binder v. Gillespie, 184 F.3d 1059, 1065-1066 (CA9 1999)*.

Even if but-for causation, standing alone, is too weak to establish reliance, petitioner has also alleged that respondents proximately caused Charter's misstatement of income; petitioner has alleged that respondents knew their deceptive acts would be the basis for statements that would influence the market price of Charter stock on which shareholders would rely. Second Amended Consolidated Class Action Complaint PP 8, 98, 100, 109, App. 19a, 55a-56a, 59a. Thus, respondents' acts had the foreseeable effect of causing petitioner to engage in the relevant securities transactions. The *Restatement (Second) of Torts § 533*, pp. 72-73 (1977), provides that "the maker of a fraudulent misrepresentation is subject to liability . . . if the misrepresentation, although not made directly to the other, is made to a third person and the maker intends or has reason to expect that its terms will be repeated or its substance communicated to the other." The sham transactions described in the complaint in this case had the same effect on Charter's profit and loss statement as a false entry directly on its books that included $ 17 million of gross revenues that had not been received. And respondents are alleged to have known that the outcome of their fraudulent transactions would be communicated to investors.

The Court's view of reliance is unduly stringent and unmoored from authority. The Court first says that if the petitioner's concept of reliance is adopted the implied cause of action "would reach the whole marketplace in which the issuing company does business." *Ante*, at 9. The answer to that objection is, of course, that liability only attaches when the company doing business with the issuing company has *itself* violated § 10(b). The Court next relies on what it views as a strict division between the "realm of financing business" and the "ordinary business operations." *Ante*, at 10. But petitioner's position does not merge the two: A corporation engaging in a business transaction with a partner who transmits false information to the market is only liable where the corporation *itself* violates § 10(b). Such a rule does not invade the province of "ordinary" business transactions.

The majority states that "section 10(b) does not incorporate common-law fraud into federal law," citing *SEC v. Zandford, 535 U.S. 813 (2002)*. *Ante*, at 11. Of course, not every common-law fraud action that happens to touch upon securities is an action under § 10(b), but the Court's opinion in *Zandford* did not purport to jettison all reference to common-law fraud doctrines from § 10(b) cases. In fact, our prior cases explained that to the extent that "the antifraud provisions of the securities laws are not coextensive with common-law doctrines of fraud," it is because common-law fraud doctrines might be too restrictive. *Herman & MacLean v. Huddleston, 459 U.S. 375, 388-389 (1983)*. "Indeed, an important purpose of the federal securities statutes was to rectify perceived deficiencies in the available common-law protections by establishing higher standards of conduct in the securities industry." *Id., at 389, 103 S. Ct. 683, 74 L. Ed. 2d 548*. I, thus, see no reason to abandon common-law approaches to causation in § 10(b) cases.

Finally, the Court relies on the course of action Congress adopted after our decision in *Central Bank* to argue that siding with petitioner on reliance would run contrary to congressional intent. Senate hearings on *Central Bank* were held within one month of our decision. Less than one year later, Senators Dodd and Domenici introduced S. 240, which became the Private Securities Litigation Reform Act of 1995 (PSLRA). Congress stopped short of undoing *Central Bank* entirely, instead adopting a compromise which restored the authority of the SEC to enforce aiding and abetting liability. A private right of action based on aiding and abetting violations of § 10(b) was not, however, included in the PSLRA, despite support from Senator Dodd and members of the Senate Subcommittee on Securities. This compromise surely provides no support for extending *Central Bank* in order to immunize an undefined class of actual violators of § 10(b) from liability in private litigation. Indeed, as Members of Congress--including those who rejected restoring a private cause of action against aiders and abettors--made clear, private litigation under § 10(b) continues to play a vital role in protecting the integrity of our securities markets. That Congress chose not to restore the aiding and abetting liability removed by *Central Bank* does not mean that Congress wanted to exempt from liability the broader range of conduct that today's opinion excludes.

The Court is concerned that such liability would deter overseas firms from doing business in the United States or "shift securities offerings away from domestic capital markets." *Ante*, at 13. But liability for those who violate § 10(b) "will not harm American competitiveness; in fact, investor faith in the safety and integrity of our markets *is* their strength. The fact that our markets are the safest in the world has helped make them the strongest in the world." Brief for Former SEC Commissioners as *Amici Curiae* 9.

Accordingly, while I recognize that the *Central Bank* opinion provides a precedent for judicial policymaking decisions in this area of the law, I respectfully dissent from the Court's continuing campaign to render the private cause of action under § 10(b) toothless. I would reverse the decision of the Court of Appeals.

III

While I would reverse for the reasons stated above, I must also comment on the importance of the private cause of action that Congress implicitly authorized when it enacted the Securities Exchange Act of 1934. A theme that underlies the Court's analysis is its mistaken hostility towards the § 10(b) private cause of action. *Ante,* at 13. The Court's current view of implied causes of action is that they are merely a "relic" of our prior "heady days." *Correctional Services Corp. v. Malesko, 534 U.S. 61, 75, 122 S. Ct. 515, 151 L. Ed. 2d 456 (2001)* (SCALIA, J., concurring). Those "heady days" persisted for two hundred years.

During the first two centuries of this Nation's history much of our law was developed by judges in the common-law tradition. A basic principle animating our jurisprudence was enshrined in state constitution provisions guaranteeing, in substance, that "every wrong shall have a remedy." Fashioning appropriate remedies for the violation of rules of law designed to protect a class of citizens was the routine business of judges. See *Marbury v. Madison, 5 U.S. 137 (1803)*. While it is true that in the early days state law was the source of most of those rules, throughout our history-- until 1975--the same practice prevailed in federal courts with regard to federal statutes that left questions of remedy open for judges to answer. In *Texas & Pacific R. Co. v. Rigsby, 241 U.S. 33, 39 (1916)*, this Court stated the following:

> "A disregard of the command of the statute is a wrongful act, and where it results in damage to one of the class for whose especial benefit the statute was enacted, the right to recover the damages from the party in default is implied, according to a doctrine of the common law expressed in 1 Com. Dig., *tit.* Action upon Statute (F), in these words: 'So, in every case, where a statute enacts, or prohibits a thing for the benefit of a person, he shall have a remedy upon the same statute for the thing enacted for his advantage, or for the recompense of a wrong done to him contrary to the said law.' (*Per* Holt, C. J., *Anon.*, 6 Mod. 26, 27.)"

The concept of a remedy for every wrong most clearly emerged from Sir Edward Coke's scholarship on Magna Carta. See 1 Second Part of the Institutes of the Laws of England (1797). At the time of the ratification of the United States Constitution, Delaware, Massachusetts, Maryland, New Hampshire, and North Carolina had all adopted constitutional provisions reflecting the provision in Coke's scholarship. . . .

In a law-changing opinion written by Justice Brennan in 1975, the Court decided to modify its approach to private causes of action. *Cort v. Ash, 422 U.S. 66* (constraining courts to use a strict four-factor test to determine whether Congress intended a private cause of action). A few years later, in *Cannon v. University of Chicago, 441 U.S. 677 (1979)*, we adhered to the strict approach mandated by *Cort* v. *Ash* in 1975, but made it clear that "our evaluation of congressional action in 1972 must take into account its contemporary legal context." *441 U.S., at 698-699*. That context persuaded the majority that Congress had intended the courts to authorize a private remedy for members of the protected class.

Until *Central Bank,* the federal courts continued to enforce a broad implied cause of action for the violation of statutes enacted in 1933 and 1934 for the protection of investors. . . .

In light of the history of court-created remedies and specifically the history of implied causes of action under § 10(b), the Court is simply wrong when it states that Congress did not impliedly authorize this private cause of action "when it first enacted the statute." *Ante*, at 16. Courts near in time to the enactment of the securities laws recognized that the principle in *Rigsby* applied to the securities laws. Congress enacted § 10(b) with the understanding that federal courts respected the principle that every wrong would have a remedy. Today's decision simply cuts back further on Congress' intended remedy. I respectfully dissent.

American Federation of State, County & Municipal Employees, Employees Pension Plan v. American International Group, Inc.

United States Court of Appeals, Second Circuit, 2006
462 F.3d 121

Before: OAKES, CALABRESI, and WESLEY, Circuit Judges.

■ WESLEY, CIRCUIT JUDGE: This case raises the question of whether a shareholder proposal requiring a company to include certain shareholder-nominated candidates for the board of directors on the corporate ballot can be excluded from the corporate proxy materials on the basis that the proposal "relates to an election" under Securities Exchange Act Rule 14a-8(i)(8), *17 C.F.R. § 240.14a-8* ("election exclusion" or "Rule 14a-8(i)(8)"). Complicating this question is not only the ambiguity of *Rule 14a-8(i)(8)* itself but also the fact that the Securities Exchange Commission (the "SEC" or "Commission") has ascribed two different interpretations to the Rule's language. The SEC's first interpretation was published in 1976, the same year that it last revised the election exclusion. The Division of Corporation Finance (the "Division"), the group within the SEC that handles investor disclosure matters and issues no-action letters, continued to apply this interpretation consistently for fifteen years until 1990, when it began applying a different interpretation, although at first in an ad hoc and inconsistent manner. The result of this gradual interpretive shift is the SEC's second interpretation, as set forth in its amicus brief to this Court. We believe that an agency's interpretation of an ambiguous regulation made at the time the regulation was implemented or revised should control unless that agency has offered sufficient reasons for its changed interpretation. Accordingly, we hold that a shareholder proposal that seeks to amend the corporate bylaws to establish a procedure by which shareholder-nominated candidates may be included on the corporate ballot does not relate to an election within the meaning of the Rule and therefore cannot be excluded from corporate proxy materials under that regulation.

Background

The American Federation of State, County & Municipal Employees ("AFSCME") is one of the country's largest public service employee unions. Through its pension plan, AFSCME holds 26,965 shares of voting common stock of American International Group ("AIG" or "Company"), a multi-national corporation operating in the insurance and financial services sectors. On December 1, 2004, AFSCME submitted to AIG for inclusion in the Company's 2005 proxy statement a shareholder proposal that, if adopted by a majority of AIG shareholders at the Company's 2005 annual meeting, would amend the AIG bylaws to require the Company, under certain circumstances, to publish the names of shareholder-nominated candidates for director positions together with any candidates nominated by AIG's board of directors ("Proposal").[***] AIG sought the input of the Division regarding whether AIG could exclude the Proposal from its proxy statement

---

[***] The AFSCME Proposal states in relevant part:

RESOLVED, pursuant to Section 6.9 of the By-laws (the "Bylaws") of American International Group Inc. ("AIG") and *section 109(a)* of the Delaware General Corporation Law, stockholders hereby amend the Bylaws to add section 6.10:

"The Corporation shall include in its proxy materials for a meeting of stockholders the name, together with the Disclosure and Statement (both defined below), of any person nominated for election to the Board of Directors by a stockholder or group thereof that satisfies the requirements of this section 6.10 (the "Nominator"), and allow stockholders to vote with respect to such nominee on the Corporation's proxy card. Each Nominator may nominate one candidate for election at a meeting.

To be eligible to make a nomination, a Nominator must:

(a) have beneficially owned 3 or more of the Corporation's outstanding common stock (the "Required Shares") for at least one year;

(b) provide written notice received by the Corporation's Secretary within the time period specified in section 1.11 of the Bylaws containing (i) with respect to the nominee, (A) the information required by Items 7(a), (b) and (c) of SEC Schedule 14A (such information is referred to herein as the "Disclosure") and (B) such nominee's consent to being named in the proxy statement and to serving as a director if elected; and (ii) with respect to the Nominator, proof of ownership of the Required Shares; and

(c) execute an undertaking that it agrees (i) to assume all liability of any violation of law or regulation arising out of the Nominator's communications with stockholders, including the Disclosure (ii) to the extent it uses soliciting material other than the Corporation's proxy materials, comply with all laws and regulations relating thereto.

The Nominator shall have the option to furnish a statement, not to exceed 500 words, in support of the nominee's candidacy (the "Statement"), at the time the Disclosure is submitted to the Corporation's Secretary. The Board of Directors shall adopt a procedure for timely resolving disputes over whether notice of a nomination was timely given and whether the Disclosure and Statement comply with this section 6.10 and SEC Rules."

under the election exclusion on the basis that it "relates to an election." The Division issued a no-action letter in which it indicated that it would not recommend an enforcement action against AIG should the Company exclude the Proposal from its proxy statement. *American International Group, Inc., SEC No-Action Letter, 2005 SEC No-Act. LEXIS 235, 2005 WL 372266 (Feb 14, 2005)* ("AIG No-Action Letter"). Armed with the no-action letter, AIG then proceeded to exclude the Proposal from the Company's proxy statement. In response, AFSCME brought suit in the United States District Court for the Southern District of New York (Stanton, J.) seeking a court order compelling AIG to include the Proposal in its next proxy statement. The district court denied AFSCME's motion for a preliminary injunction, concluding that AFSCME's Proposal "on its face 'relates to an election.' Indeed, it relates to nothing else." *AFSCME v. Am. Int'l Group, Inc., 361 F. Supp. 2d 344, 346 (S.D.N.Y. 2005)*. After this Court denied AFSCME's motion for expedited appeal, the parties stipulated that the district court's opinion denying AFSCME's motion for a preliminary injunction "be deemed to contain the Court's complete findings of fact and conclusions of law with respect to all claims asserted by plaintiff in this action" and that it also "be deemed a final judgment on the merits with respect to all claims asserted by plaintiff in this action." Pursuant to this joint stipulation, the district court entered final judgment denying plaintiff's claims for declaratory and injunctive relief and dismissing plaintiff's complaint.

Discussion

Rule 14a-8(i)(8), also known as "the town meeting rule," regulates what are referred to as "shareholders proposals," that is, "recommendation[s] or requirement[s] that the company and/or its board of directors take [some] action, which [the submitting shareholder(s)] intend to present at a meeting of the company's shareholders," *17 C.F.R. § 240.14a-8(a)*. If a shareholder seeking to submit a proposal meets certain eligibility and procedural requirements, the corporation is required to include the proposal in its proxy statement and identify the proposal in its form of proxy, unless the corporation can prove to the SEC that a given proposal may be excluded based on one of thirteen grounds enumerated in the regulations. *Id. § 240.14a-8(i)(1)-(13)*. One of these grounds, Rule 14a-8(i)(8), provides that a corporation may exclude a shareholder proposal "[i]f the proposal relates to an election for membership on the company's board of directors or analogous governing body." *Id. § 240.14a-8(i)(8)*.

We must determine whether, under *Rule 14a-8(i)(8)*, a shareholder proposal "relates to an election" if it seeks to amend the corporate bylaws to establish a procedure by which certain shareholders are entitled to include in the corporate proxy materials their nominees for the board of directors ("proxy access bylaw proposal"). "In interpreting an administrative regulation, as in interpreting a statute, we must begin by examining the language of the provision at issue." *Resnik v. Swartz, 303 F.3d 147, 151-52 (2d Cir. 2002)* (citing *New York Currency Research Corp. v. CFTC, 180 F.3d 83, 92 (2d Cir. 1999))*. The relevant language here -- "relates to an election" -- is not particularly helpful. AFSCME reads the election exclusion as creating an obvious distinction between proposals addressing a particular seat in a particular election (which AFSCME concedes are excludable) and those, like AFSCME's proposal, that simply set the background rules governing elections generally (which AFSCME claims are not excludable). AFSCME's distinction rests on *Rule 14a-8(i)(8)*'s use of the article "an," which AFSCME claims "necessarily implies that the phrase 'relates to an election' is intended to relate to proposals that address *particular elections*, instead of simply 'elections' generally." It is at least plausible that the words "an election" were intended to narrow the scope of the election exclusion, confining its application to proposals relating to "a particular election *and not* elections generally." It is, however, also plausible that the phrase was intended to create a comparatively broader exclusion, one covering "a particular election *or* elections generally" since any proposal that relates to elections in general will necessarily relate to an election in particular. The language of *Rule 14a-8(i)(8)* provides no reason to adopt one interpretation over the other.

When the language of a regulation is ambiguous, we typically look for guidance in any interpretation made by the agency that promulgated the regulation in question. *See Auer v. Robbins, 519 U.S. 452, 461, 117 S. Ct. 905, 137 L. Ed. 2d 79 (1997)* (holding that an agency's interpretation of its own regulation is entitled to deference provided that the regulation is ambiguous); *see also Christensen v. Harris County, 529 U.S. 576, 588 (2000)*. We are aware of two statements published by the SEC that offer informal interpretations of *Rule 14a-8(i)(8)*. The first is a statement appearing in the amicus brief that the SEC filed in this case at our request. The second interpretation is contained in a statement the SEC published in 1976, the last time the SEC revised the election exclusion. Neither of these interpretations has the force of law. But, while agency interpretations that lack the force of law do not warrant deference when they interpret ambiguous *statutes*, they do normally warrant deference when they interpret ambiguous *regulations*. *See Christensen, 529 U.S. at 588* (citing *Auer, 519 U.S. at 461*); *see also Levy v. Southbrook Int'l Invs., Ltd., 263 F.3d 10, 14 (2d Cir. 2001)* (explaining that courts will defer to an agency's interpretation of its own regulation, presented in the agency's amicus brief, unless the interpretation is plainly erroneous or inconsistent with the regulation).

In its amicus brief, the SEC interprets *Rule 14a-8(i)(8)* as permitting the exclusion of shareholder proposals that "would result in contested elections." The SEC explains that "[f]or purposes of *Rule 14a-8*, a proposal would result in a contested election if it is a means either to campaign for or against a director nominee or to require a company to include shareholder-nominated candidates in the company's proxy materials." Under this interpretation, a proxy access bylaw proposal like AFSCME's would be excludable under *Rule 14a-8(i)(8)* because it "is a means to require AIG to include shareholder-nominated candidates in the company's proxy materials." However, that interpretation is plainly at odds with the interpretation the SEC made in 1976.

In that year, the SEC amended *Rule 14a-8(i)(8)* in an effort to clarify the purpose of the existing election exclusion. The SEC explained that "with respect to corporate elections, *Rule 14a-8* is not the proper means for conducting campaigns or effecting reforms in elections of that nature [i.e., "corporate, political or other elections to office"], *since other proxy rules, including Rule 14a-11, are applicable thereto*." Proposed Amendments to Rule 14a-8, Exchange Act Release No. 34-12598, 41 Fed. Reg. 29,982, 29,9845 (proposed July 7, 1976) (emphasis added) ("1976 Statement"). The district court opinion quoted the 1976 Statement but omitted the italicized language and concluded that shareholder proposals were not intended to be used to accomplish any type of election reform. *AFSCME, 361 F. Supp. 2d at 346-47*. Clearly, however, that cannot be what the 1976 Statement means. Indeed, when the SEC finally adopted the revision of *Rule 14a-8(i)(8)* four months after publication of the 1976 Statement, it explained that it was rejecting a previous proposed rule (which would have authorized the exclusion of proposals that "relate[] to a corporate, political or other election to office") in favor of the current version (which authorizes the exclusion of proposals that simply "relate[] to an election") so as to avoid creating "the erroneous belief that the Commission intended to expand the scope of the existing exclusion to cover proposals dealing with matters previously held not excludable by the Commission, such as cumulative voting rights, general qualifications for directors, and political contributions by the issuer." Adoption of Amendments Relating to Proposals by Security Holders, Exchange Act Release No. 34-129999, 41 Fed. Reg. 52,994, 52,998 (Nov. 22, 1976) ("1976 Adoption"). And yet, all three of these shareholder proposal topics -- cumulative voting rights, general qualifications for directors, and political contributions -- fit comfortably within the category "election reform."

In its amicus brief, the SEC places a slightly different gloss on the 1976 Statement than did the district court. The SEC reads the 1976 Statement as implying that the purpose of *Rule 14a-8(i)(8)* is to authorize the exclusion of proposals that seek to effect, not election reform in general, but only certain types of election reform, namely those to which "other proxy rules, including *Rule 14a-11*," are generally applicable. In 1976, *Rule 14a-11* was essentially the equivalent of current *Rule 14a-12*, which requires certain disclosures where a solicitation is made "for the purpose of opposing" a solicitation by any other person "with respect to the election or removal of directors." *17 C.F.R. § 240.14a-12(c)*. The SEC reasons that, based on the 1976 Statement, "a proposal may be excluded pursuant to *Rule 14a-8(i)(8)* if it would result in an immediate election contest (e.g., by making a director nomination for a particular meeting) or would set up a process for shareholders to conduct an election contest in the future by requiring the company to include shareholder director nominees in the company's proxy materials for subsequent meetings."

We agree with the SEC that, based on the 1976 Statement, shareholder proposals can be excluded under the election exclusion if they would result in an immediate election contest. We understand the phrase "since other proxy rules, including *Rule 14a-11*, are applicable thereto" in the 1976 Statement to mean that under *Rule 14a-8(i)(8)*, companies can exclude shareholder proposals dealing with those election-related matters that, if addressed in a proxy solicitation -- the alternative to a shareholder proposal -- would trigger *Rule 14a-12*, or the former *Rule 14a-11*. A proxy solicitation nominating a candidate for a specific election would be made "for the purpose of opposing" the company's proxy solicitation and therefore would clearly trigger *Rule 14a-12*. Accordingly, based on the 1976 Statement, a shareholder proposal seeking to contest management's nominees would be excludable under *Rule 14a-8(i)(8)*.

By contrast, a proxy solicitation seeking to add a proxy access amendment to the corporate bylaws does not involve opposing solicitations dealing with "the election or removal of directors," and therefore *Rule 14a-12*, or, equivalently, the former *Rule 14a-11*, would not apply to a proposal seeking to accomplish the same end. Thus, we cannot agree with the second half of the SEC's interpretation of the 1976 Statement: that a proposal may be excluded under *Rule 14a-8(i)(8)* if it would simply establish a process for shareholders to wage a future election contest.

The 1976 Statement clearly reflects the view that the election exclusion is limited to shareholder proposals used to oppose solicitations dealing with an identified board seat in an upcoming election and rejects the somewhat broader interpretation that the election exclusion applies to shareholder proposals that would institute procedures making such election contests more likely. The SEC suggested as much when, four months after its 1976 Statement, it explained that the scope of the election exclusion does not cover shareholder proposals dealing with matters such as cumulative voting and general director requirements, both of which have the potential to increase the likelihood of election contests. *See* 1976 Adoption, 41 Fed. Reg. at 52,998.

That the 1976 statement adopted this narrower view of the election exclusion finds further support in the fact that it was also the view that the Division adopted for roughly sixteen years following publication of the SEC's 1976 Statement. *See e.g.*, Union Oil Co. of Calif., SEC No-Action Letter, 1983 SEC No-Act. LEXIS 1959, 1983 WL 30873, at *4-5 (Feb. 24, 1983); Mobil Corp., SEC No-Action Letter, 1981 SEC No-Act. LEXIS 3207, 1981 WL 26205, at *22 (Mar. 3, 1981); Union Oil Co. of Calif., SEC No-Action Letter, 1981 SEC No-Act. LEXIS 3001, 1981 WL 24701, at *7 (Jan. 29, 1981); Unicare Servs., SEC No-Action Letter, 1980 SEC No-Act. LEXIS 3289, 1980 WL 15475, at * 7 (May 13, 1980); *see also* Newbury Corp., SEC No-Action Letter, 1986 SEC No-Act. LEXIS 2617, 1986 WL 67178, at *3 (Aug. 11, 1986). It was not until 1990 that the Division first signaled a change of course by deeming excludable proposals that *might* result in contested elections, even if the proposal only purports to alter general procedures for nominating and electing directors. *See, e.g.*, Thermo Electron, SEC No-Action Letter, 1990 SEC No-Act. LEXIS 549, 1990 WL 286329, at *19 (Mar. 22, 1990); Unocal Corp., SEC No-Action Letter, 1990 SEC No-Act. LEXIS 183 , 1990 WL 285946, at *7 (Feb. 6, 1990); Bank of Boston, SEC No-Action Letter, 1990 SEC No-Act. LEXIS 206, 1990 WL 285947, at *14 (Jan. 26, 1990).

Because the interpretation of *Rule 14a-8(i)(8)* that the SEC advances in its amicus brief -- that the election exclusion applies to proxy access bylaw proposals -- conflicts with the 1976 Statement, it does not merit the usual deference we would reserve for an agency's interpretation of its own regulations. *See Thomas Jefferson Univ. v. Shalala, 512 U.S. 504, 515, (1994)* (quoting *INS v. Cardoza-Fonseca, 480 U.S. 421, 446 n. 30 (1987)* (quoting *Watt v. Alaska, 451 U.S. 259, 273 (1981)))* (stating that an agency's interpretation of a regulation that conflicts with a prior interpretation is "'entitled to considerably less deference' than a consistently held agency view"). The SEC has not provided, nor to our knowledge has it or the Division ever provided, reasons for its changed position regarding the excludability of proxy access bylaw proposals. Although the SEC has substantial discretion to adopt new interpretations of its own regulations in light of, for example, changes in the capital markets or even simply because of a shift in the Commission's regulatory approach, it nevertheless has a "duty to explain its departure from prior norms." *Atchison, T. & S. F. Ry. Co v. Wichita Bd. of Trade, 412 U.S. 800, 808 (1973)* (citing *Sec. of Agric. v. United States, 347 U.S. 645, 652-53 (1954))*; *cf. Torrington Extend-A-Care Employee Ass'n v. NLRB, 17 F.3d 580, 589 (2d Cir. 1994)* (stating that "an agency may alter its interpretation of a statute so long as the new rule is consistent with the statute, applies to all litigants, and is supported by a 'reasoned analysis'").

In its amicus submission, the SEC fails to so much as acknowledge a changed position, let alone offer a reasoned analysis of the change. The amicus brief is curiously silent on any Division action prior to 1990 and characterizes the intermittent post-1990 no-action letters which continued to apply the pre-1990 position as mere "mistake[s]." While we by no means wish to imply that the Commission or the Division cannot correct analytical errors following a refinement of their thinking, we have a difficult time accepting the SEC's characterization of a policy that the Division consistently applied for sixteen years as nothing more than a "mistake." Although we are willing to afford the Commission considerable latitude in explaining departures from prior interpretations, its reasoned analysis must consist of something more than *mea culpas*.

Accordingly, we deem it appropriate to defer to the 1976 Statement, which represents the SEC's interpretation of the election exclusion the last time the Rule was substantively revised. *Cf. Watt, 451 U.S. at 272-73* (deferring to an agency's initial interpretation of a statutory provision where the interpretation was made contemporaneously with the provision's original enactment and consequently rejecting the agency's later conflicting interpretation). We therefore interpret the election exclusion as applying to shareholder proposals that relate to a particular election and not to proposals that, like AFSCME's, would establish the procedural rules governing elections generally.

In deeming proxy access bylaw proposals non-excludable under *Rule 14a-8(i)(8)*, we take no side in the policy debate regarding shareholder access to the corporate ballot. There might be perfectly good reasons for permitting companies to exclude proposals like AFSCME's, just as there may well be valid policy reasons for rendering them non-excludable. However, Congress has determined that such issues are appropriately the province of the SEC, not the judiciary.

Conclusion

For the foregoing reasons, we reverse the judgment of the district court and remand the case for entry of judgment in favor of AFSCME.

Chamber of Commerce of the United States of America v. Securities and Exchange Commission

United States Court of Appeals, D.C. Circuit, 2005
412 F.3d 133

Before: GINSBURG, Chief Judge, and ROGERS and TATEL, Circuit Judges.

■ GINSBURG, CHIEF JUDGE: The Chamber of Commerce of the United States petitions for review of a rule promulgated by the Securities and Exchange Commission under the Investment Company Act of 1940 (ICA), *15 U.S.C. § 80a-1 et seq.* The challenged provisions of the rule require that, in order to engage in certain transactions otherwise prohibited by the ICA, an investment company -- commonly referred to as a mutual fund -- must have a board (1) with no less than 75% independent directors and (2) an independent chairman. The Chamber argues the ICA does not give the Commission authority to regulate "corporate governance" and, in any event, the Commission promulgated the rule without adhering to the requirements of the Administrative Procedure Act, *5 U.S.C. § 551 et seq.*

We hold the Commission did not exceed its statutory authority in adopting the two conditions, and the Commission's rationales for the two conditions satisfy the APA. We agree with the Chamber, however, that the Commission did violate the APA by failing adequately to consider the costs mutual funds would incur in order to comply with the conditions and by failing adequately to consider a proposed alternative to the independent chairman condition. We therefore grant in part the Chamber's petition for review.

I. Background

A mutual fund, which is "a pool of assets ... belonging to the individual investors holding shares in the fund," *Burks v. Lasker, 441 U.S. 471, 480 (1979),* is operated by an "investment company" the board of directors of which is elected by the shareholders. Although the board is authorized to operate the fund, it typically delegates that management role to an "adviser," which is a separate company that may have interests other than maximizing the returns to shareholders in the fund. In enacting the ICA, the Congress sought to control "the potential for abuse inherent in the structure of [funds]" arising from the conflict of interests between advisers and shareholders, *id.*; to that end, the ICA prohibits a fund from engaging in certain transactions by which the adviser might gain at the expense of the shareholders. *See generally 15 U.S.C. § 80a-12(a)-(g).* Pursuant to the Commission's long-standing Exemptive Rules, however, a fund that satisfies certain conditions may engage in an otherwise prohibited transaction. *See, e.g.*, Rule 10f-3, *17 C.F.R. § 270.10f-3 (2004)* (when conditions are satisfied, fund may purchase securities in primary offering although adviser-affiliated broker-dealer is member of underwriting syndicate).

Early in 2004 the Commission proposed to amend ten Exemptive Rules by imposing five new or amended conditions upon any fund wishing to engage in an otherwise prohibited transaction. *See Investment Company Governance, Proposed Rule, 69 Fed. Reg. 3472 (Jan. 23, 2004).* Although the

Commission had amended the same ten rules in 2001 to condition exemption upon the fund having a board with a majority of independent directors (that is, directors who are not "interested persons" as defined in *§ 2(a)(19) of the ICA*), *see Role of Independent Directors of Investment Companies, Final Rule, 66 Fed. Reg. 3734 (Jan. 16, 2001)*, by 2004 the Commission had come to believe that more was required. "Enforcement actions involving late trading, inappropriate market timing activities and misuse of nonpublic information about fund portfolios" had brought to light, in the Commission's view, "a serious breakdown in management controls," signaling the need to "revisit the governance of funds." *69 Fed. Reg. at 3472*. Accordingly, the Commission proposed to condition the ten exemptions upon, among other things, the fund having a board of directors (1) with at least 75% independent directors and (2) an independent chairman. *Id. at 3474*.

After a period for comment and a public meeting, the Commission unanimously adopted three of the proposed new conditions and, by a vote of three to two, adopted the two corporate governance conditions challenged here. *See Investment Company Governance, Final Rule, 69 Fed. Reg. 46,378 (Aug. 2, 2004)*. The Commission majority adopted those two conditions in light of recently revealed abuses in the mutual fund industry, reasoning that the Exemptive Rules

> rely on the independent judgment and scrutiny of directors, including independent directors, in overseeing activities that are beneficial to funds and fund shareholders but that involve inherent conflicts of interest between the funds and their managers. ... These further amendments provide for greater fund board independence and are designed to enhance the ability of fund boards to perform their important responsibilities under each of the rules.

Id. at 46,379. Raising the percentage of independent directors from 50% to 75%, the Commission anticipated, would "strengthen the independent directors' control of the fund board and its agenda," *id. at 46,381*, and "help ensure that independent directors carry out their fiduciary responsibilities," *id. at 46,382*. The Commission justified the independent chairman condition on the ground that "a fund board is in a better position to protect the interests of the fund, and to fulfill the board's obligations under the Act and the Exemptive Rules, when its chairman does not have the conflicts of interest inherent in the role of an executive of the fund adviser." *Id.*

The dissenting Commissioners were concerned the two disputed conditions would come at "a substantial cost to fund shareholders," and they believed the existing statutory and regulatory controls ensured adequate oversight by independent directors. *69 Fed. Reg. at 46,390*. Specifically, they faulted the Commission for not giving "any real consideration to the costs" of the 75% condition, *id. at 46,390-46,391*; for failing adequately to justify the independent chairman condition, *id. at 46,391-46,392*; and for not considering alternatives to that condition, *id. at 46,392-46,393*. The Chamber timely petitioned for review, asserting an interest in the new conditions both as an investor and as an association with mutual fund advisers among its members.

II. Analysis

The Chamber makes two arguments on the merits: The Commission had no authority under the ICA to adopt the two conditions; and the Commission violated the APA in the rulemaking by which it promulgated the conditions. Before addressing those arguments, we must assure ourselves of the Chamber's standing, and thus of our jurisdiction.

A. Jurisdiction of the Court

Under Article III of the Constitution the "judicial Power of the United States" is limited to the resolution of "Cases" or "Controversies," a corollary of which is that a party invoking our jurisdiction "must show that the conduct of which he complains has caused him to suffer an 'injury in fact' that a favorable judgment will redress." *Elk Grove Unified School Dist. v. Newdow, 542 U.S. 1 (2004)*. In this case the Chamber claims it is injured by the two challenged conditions because it would like to invest in shares of funds that may engage in transactions regulated by the Exemptive Rules but do not meet those conditions. *See* Dec'l of Stan M. Harrell P 2 (Chamber currently invests in funds, intends to continue doing so, and would like to invest in funds unconstrained by the conditions).

The Chamber cites two cases for the proposition that loss of the opportunity to purchase a desired product is a legally cognizable injury. *Consumer Fed'n of Am. v. FCC, 358 U.S. App. D.C. 271, 348 F.3d 1009, 1011-12 (D.C. Cir. 2003)* (injury-in-fact where merger would deprive plaintiff of opportunity to purchase desired service); *Competitive Enter. Inst. v. Nat'l Highway Traffic Safety Admin., 284 U.S. App. D.C. 1, 901 F.2d 107, 112-13 (D.C. Cir. 1990)* (injury-in-fact where fuel economy regulations foreclosed "opportunity to buy larger passenger vehicles"). The Commission argues in response that there is no evidence a fund of the type in which the Chamber wants to invest would perform better than a fund that conforms to the two corporate governance conditions. In *Consumer Federation*, however, we held "the inability of consumers to buy a desired product ... constituted injury-in-fact even if they could ameliorate the injury by purchasing some alternative product." *348 F.3d at 1012*. Under our precedent, therefore, the Chamber has suffered an injury-in-fact and, because a favorable ruling would redress that injury, it has standing to sue the Commission. And so to the merits.

B. The Commission's Authority under the ICA

The Chamber maintains the Commission did not have authority under the ICA to condition the exemptive transactions as it did. First the Chamber observes rather generally that "matters of corporate governance are traditionally relegated to state law"; and second, it maintains these particular conditions are inconsistent with the statutory requirement that 40% of the directors on the board of an investment company be independent, *see 15 U.S.C. § 80a-10(a)*. The Commission points to § 6(c) of the ICA, *15 U.S.C. § 80a-6(c)*, as the source of its authority.* That provision conspicuously confers upon the Commission broad authority to exempt transactions from rules promulgated under the ICA, subject only to the public interest and the purposes of the ICA.

The thrust of the Chamber's first contention is that *§ 6(c)* should not be read to enable the Commission to leverage the exemptive authority it clearly does have so as to regulate a matter, namely, corporate governance, over which the states, not the Commission, have authority. For support the Chamber relies principally upon two cases from this circuit concerning the Commission's authority under the *Securities and Exchange Act of 1934. Neither of* those cases, however, arose from an exercise of authority analogous to the rulemaking here under review.

In *Business Roundtable v. SEC, 905 F.2d 406, 416-17 (1990)*, we held the Commission did not have authority under the 1934 Act to bar a stock exchange from listing common stock with restricted voting rights. The Commission had invoked the provision of that Act authorizing it to make rules "otherwise in furtherance of the purposes" of the Act. *Id. at 410*. Reasoning that "unless the legislative purpose is defined by reference to the *means* Congress selected, it can be framed at *any* level of generality," and the means the Congress selected in the 1934 Act was disclosure, *id.*, we vacated the rule because it went beyond disclosure to regulate "the substance of what the shareholders may enact," *id. at 411*.

Business Roundtable is of little help to the Chamber because, as the Commission documents, the purposes of the ICA include tempering the conflicts of interest "inherent in the structure of investment companies," *Burks, 441 U.S. at 480*; *see also 15 U.S.C. § 80a-1(b)* ("policy and purposes of [ICA] ... shall be interpreted ... to eliminate" conflicts of interest); and regulation of the governance structure of investment companies is among the means the Congress used to effect that purpose. *See Burks, 441 U.S. at 479* (ICA "functions primarily to impose controls and restrictions on the internal management of investment companies") (emphases removed); *id. at 484* (in enacting ICA Congress "placed the unaffiliated directors in the role of independent watchdogs ... who would furnish an independent check upon the management of investment companies"). Moreover, the Commission's effort to enlarge the role of independent directors on the boards of investment companies accords with "the structure and purpose of the ICA [both of which] indicate that Congress entrusted to the independent directors ... the primary responsibility for looking after the interests of the funds' shareholders." *Id. at 484-85*.

---

* That section provides:

> The Commission, by rules and regulations upon its own motion, or by order upon application, may conditionally or unconditionally exempt any person, security, or transaction, or any class or classes of persons, securities, or transactions, from any provision or provisions of this [Act] or of any rule or regulation thereunder, if and to the extent that such exemption is necessary or appropriate in the public interest and consistent with the protection of investors and the purposes fairly intended by the policy and provisions of this [Act].

In *Teicher v. SEC, 177 F.3d 1016, 1019-20 (1999)*, we held a provision of the 1934 Act authorizing the Commission to "place limitations on the activities or functions" of a person convicted of securities fraud in the broker-dealer industry did not authorize it to place limitations upon the activities or functions of that person in an industry regulated under a different "occupational licensing regime" administered by the Commission. The Commission's authority, we reasoned, must be read with "some concept of the relevant domain" in mind; even the Commission did not "suggest that [provision] allows it to bar one of the offending parties from being a retail shoe salesman, or to exclude him from the Borough of Manhattan." *Id. at 1019*. The present case is different from *Teicher* because here the Commission did not exercise its regulatory authority to effect a purpose beyond that of the statute from which its authority derives.

The Chamber's second contention is that the conditions conflict with the intent of the Congress, expressed in *§ 10(a) of the ICA*, that 40% of the directors of an investment company be independent. *See Chevron, U.S.A., Inc. v. NRDC, 467 U.S. 837, 842-43, 104 S. Ct. 2778, 81 L. Ed. 2d 694 (1984)* ("If the intent of Congress is clear, that is the end of the matter; for the court, as well as the agency, must give effect to the unambiguously expressed intent of Congress"). *Section 10(a)*, however, states only that a fund may have "no more than" 60% inside directors, *15 U.S.C. § 80a-10(a)*, which necessarily means at least 40% must be independent and strongly implies a greater percentage may be; it speaks not at all to authority of the Commission to provide an incentive for investment companies to enhance the role of independent directors and, as the Commission is keen to point out, the challenged conditions apply only to funds that engage in exemptive transactions.

C. The Requirements of the APA

The condemnation of the APA extends to any rule that is "arbitrary, capricious, an abuse of discretion, or otherwise not in accordance with law." *5 U.S.C. § 706(2)(A)*. Although the "scope of review under the 'arbitrary and capricious' standard is narrow and a court is not to substitute its judgment for that of the agency," we must nonetheless be sure the Commission has "examined the relevant data and articulated a satisfactory explanation for its action including a rational connection between the facts found and the choice made." *Motor Vehicle Mfrs. Ass'n v. State Farm Mutual Auto. Ins. Co., 463 U.S. 29, 43 (1983)*; *see also Pub. Citizen v. Fed. Motor Carrier Safety Admin., 374 F.3d 1209, 1216 (D.C. Cir. 2004)*.

The Chamber argues the Commission violated the APA because it (1) failed to show the connection between the abuses that prompted the rulemaking and the conditions newly included in the Exemptive Rules; (2) did not comply with its obligation under the ICA to consider whether those conditions "will promote efficiency, competition, and capital formation," *15 U.S.C. § 80a-2(c)*; *see Pub. Citizen, 374 F.3d at 1216* (rule is "arbitrary and capricious" if agency fails to consider factors "it must consider under its organic statute"); and (3) did not consider reasonable alternatives to the independent chairman condition.

1. Justification for the Rulemaking

The Chamber maintains the "rulemaking is flawed for the elementary reason that the Commission amended ten separate and distinct pre-existing rules [by imposing the two challenged conditions] without any meaningful consideration of them." Similarly, the Chamber argues the Commission did not adequately explain why the conditions it added were necessary in light of the conditions previously contained in the Exemptive Rules. The Commission answers that its stated justification for amending the Exemptive Rules satisfies the standards of the APA. We agree.

In the wake of recent revelations of certain abuses in the mutual fund industry, the Commission was concerned about what it diagnosed as "a serious breakdown in management controls." *See 69 Fed. Reg. at 46,378-46,379; 69 Fed. Reg. at 3472.* Although it is true, as the Chamber repeatedly notes, that none of the documented abuses involved a transaction covered by the Exemptive Rules, the Commission, as we have said, thought it prudent to amend those rules because the particular abuses that had come to light revealed a more general problem with conflicts of interest than it had previously suspected and portended further abuses if that perceived problem was not addressed. The Commission thus viewed strengthening the role of independent directors in relation to exemptive transactions as a prophylactic measure, not a response to a present problem involving abuse of the Exemptive Rules. *See 69 Fed. Reg. at 46,379.*

The Chamber claims the Commission's decision was unreasonable because the conditions for engaging in exemptive transactions had already been tightened in 2001. But that begs the question whether the conditions of 2001 were adequate in view of the new evidence that some boards were failing to prevent egregious conflicts of interest involving late trading and market timing. Might not they also fail to police sufficiently the conflicts of interest inherent in the exemptive transactions? That those transactions were already subject to some regulation does not render unreasonable the Commission's judgment that additional regulation was called for as a prophylactic.

Finally, the Chamber argues the "actual terms" of the conditions were not reasonable in light of "the problems [the Commission] claimed justified the rulemaking." Those problems all trace to the failure of investment company boards, for whatever reason, to guard against advisers' conflicts of interest. *See 69 Fed. Reg. at 3473* ("boards may have simply abdicated their responsibilities, or failed to ask the tough questions of advisers; in other cases, boards may have lacked the information or organizational structure necessary to play their proper role"). So that boards are apprised of the activities of their fund's adviser, the Commission, in a separate proceeding first required funds to designate a chief compliance officer charged with bringing relevant information to the board. *See Compliance Programs of Investment Companies and Investment Advisers, 68 Fed. Reg. 74,714 (Dec. 24, 2003).* The Commission then undertook in the present rulemaking to ensure that independent directors would be in a position to put such information to good use.

To that end, the Commission reasonably concluded that raising the minimum percentage of independent directors from 50% to 75% would "strengthen the hand of the independent directors when dealing with fund management, and may assure that independent directors maintain control of the board and its agenda." *69 Fed. Reg. at 46,382.* Similarly, the Commission concluded that having an independent chairman would be beneficial because the chairman plays "an important role in setting the agenda of the board[,] ... in providing a check on the adviser, in negotiating the best deal for shareholders when considering the advisory contract, and in providing leadership to the board that focuses on the long-term interests of investors." *69 Fed. Reg. at 46,383.* We have no basis upon which to second-guess that judgment.

In sum, the Chamber points to nothing in the ICA to suggest the Congress restricted the authority of the Commission to make "precautionary or prophylactic responses to perceived risks," *Certified Color Mfrs. Ass'n v. Mathews, 543 F.2d 284, 296 (D.C. Cir. 1976)*; and the Commission's effort to prevent future abuses of exemptive transactions was not arbitrary, capricious, or in any way an abuse of its discretion, in violation of the APA.

2. Consideration of Costs

The ICA mandates that when the Commission "engages in rulemaking and is required to consider or determine whether an action is consistent with the public interest [it] shall ... consider ... whether the action will promote efficiency, competition, and capital formation." *15 U.S.C. § 80a-2(c)*. The Chamber argues the Commission violated this mandate, and hence the APA, by failing (1) to develop new, and to consider extant, empirical data comparing the performance of funds respectively led by inside and by independent chairmen; and (2) to consider the costs of the conditions it was imposing, which costs in turn impede efficiency, competition, and capital formation. The Commission denies the charges.

The particulars of the Chamber's first contention are that the Commission should have directed its staff to do a study of the effect of an independent chairman upon fund performance and that when such a study, commissioned by Fidelity Investments, was presented during the comment period, the Commission gave it short shrift. *69 Fed. Reg. at 46,383 n.52*; *see* Geoffrey H. Bobroff and Thomas H. Mack, Assessing the Significance of Mutual Fund Board Independent Chairs (Mar. 10, 2004). As to the former point, although we recognize that an agency acting upon the basis of empirical data may more readily be able to show it has satisfied its obligations under the APA, *see National Asso. of Regulatory Utility Comm'rs v. FCC, 737 F.2d 1096, 1124 (D.C. Cir. 1984)* (in informal rulemaking it is "desirable" that agency "independently amass [and] verify the accuracy of" data), we are acutely aware that an agency need not -- indeed cannot -- base its every action upon empirical data; depending upon the nature of the problem, an agency may be "entitled to conduct ... a general analysis based on informed conjecture." *Melcher v. FCC, 134 F.3d 1143, 1158 (D.C. Cir. 1998)*; *Nat'l Ass'n of Regulatory Util. Comm'rs, 737 F.2d at 1124* (failure to conduct independent study not violative of APA because notice and comment procedures "permit parties to bring relevant information quickly to the agency's attention"); *see also FCC v. Nat'l Citizens Comm. for Broad., 436 U.S. 775, 813-14 (1978)* (FCC, in making "judgmental or predictive" factual determinations, did not need "complete factual support" because "a forecast of the direction in which future public interest lies necessarily involves deductions based on the expert knowledge of the agency").

Here the Commission, based upon "its own and its staff's experience, the many comments received, and other evidence, in addition to the limited and conflicting empirical evidence," concluded an independent chairman "can provide benefits and serve other purposes apart from achieving high performance of the fund." *69 Fed. Reg. at 46,383-46,384*. The Commission's decision not to do an empirical study does not make that an unreasoned decision. *See BellSouth Corp. v. FCC, 333 U.S. App. D.C. 308, 162 F.3d 1215, 1221 (D.C. Cir. 1999)* ("When ... an agency is obliged to make policy judgments where no factual certainties exist or where facts alone do not provide the answer, our role is more limited; we require only that the agency so state and go on to identify the considerations it found persuasive").

Nor did the Commission violate the APA in its consideration of the Fidelity study. Although Chairman Donaldson did, as the Chamber points out, betray a dismissive attitude toward the value of empirical data, SEC Open Meeting, 57-58 (June 23, 2004) ("there are no empirical studies that are worth much. You can do anything you want with numbers and we've seen evidence of that in a number of our submissions"), the Commission did not reject the Fidelity study or decline to do its own study upon that basis. Rather, the Commission concluded the Fidelity study was "unpersuasive" because, as the authors acknowledged, it did not rule out "other important differences [than independence of the chairman] that may have impacted performance results," *69 Fed. Reg. at 46,383 n.52* (quoting study), and because it did not use a reliable method of calculating fund expenses, *id.* The Commission also noted that other commenters reviewing the Fidelity study had concluded funds with an independent chairman did "slightly better in terms of returns, but at lower cost." *Id.* Although a more detailed discussion of the study might have been useful, the Commission made clear enough the limitations of the study, and we have no cause to disturb its ultimate judgment that the study was "unpersuasive evidence." *Cf. Huls Am. Inc. v. Browner, 317 U.S. App. D.C. 333, 83 F.3d 445, 452 (D.C. Cir. 1996)* (court owes "extreme degree of deference to the agency when it is evaluating scientific data within its technical expertise").

We reach a different conclusion with regard to the Commission's consideration of the costs of the conditions. With respect to the 75% independent director condition, the Commission, although describing three methods by which a fund might comply with the condition, claimed it was without a "reliable basis for determining how funds would choose to satisfy the [condition] and therefore it [was] difficult to determine the costs associated with electing independent directors." *69 Fed. Reg. at 46,387.* That particular difficulty may mean the Commission can determine only the range within which a fund's cost of compliance will fall, depending upon how it responds to the condition but, as the Chamber contends, it does not excuse the Commission from its statutory obligation to determine as best it can the economic implications of the rule it has proposed. *See Pub. Citizen, 374 F.3d at 1221* (in face of uncertainty, agency must "exercise its expertise to make tough choices about which of the competing estimates is most plausible, and to hazard a guess as to which is correct, even if ... the estimate will be imprecise").

With respect to the costs of the independent chairman condition, counsel maintains the Commission "was not aware of any costs associated with the hiring of staff because boards typically have this authority under state law, and the rule would not require them to hire employees." The Commission made that observation, however, in regard not to the independent chairman condition but to a condition not challenged here, and we cannot therefore consider counsel's rationalization for the regulation under review. *See Motor Vehicle Mfrs. Ass'n, 463 U.S. at 50* ("courts may not accept appellate counsel's *post hoc* rationalizations for agency action"). In any event, the argument is a *non sequitur*; whether a board is authorized by law to hire additional staff in no way bears upon the contention that, because of his comparative lack of knowledge about the fund, an independent chairman would in fact cause the fund to incur additional staffing costs.

What the Commission itself did was acknowledge in a footnote that an independent chairman "may choose to hire [more] staff" but it stopped there because, it said, it had no "reliable basis for estimating those costs." *69 Fed. Reg. at 46,387 n.81*. Although the Commission may not have been able to estimate the aggregate cost to the mutual fund industry of additional staff because it did not know what percentage of funds with independent chairman would incur that cost, it readily could have estimated the cost to an individual fund, which estimate would be pertinent to its assessment of the effect the condition would have upon efficiency and competition, if not upon capital formation. And, as we have just seen, uncertainty may limit what the Commission can do, but it does not excuse the Commission from its statutory obligation to do what it can to apprise itself -- and hence the public and the Congress -- of the economic consequences of a proposed regulation before it decides whether to adopt the measure.

In sum, the Commission violated its obligation under *15 U.S.C. § 80a-2(c)*, and therefore the APA, in failing adequately to consider the costs imposed upon funds by the two challenged conditions.

3. Consideration of Alternatives

Finally, the Chamber argues the Commission gave "inadequate consideration" to suggested alternatives to the independent chairman condition, citing as an example -- the only significant one, it seems to us -- the proposal, endorsed by the two dissenting Commissioners, that each fund be required prominently to disclose whether it has an inside or an independent chairman and thereby allow investors to make an informed choice. Commission counsel responds by noting generally that the agency is "not required to discuss every alternative raised" and that it did consider the "major alternatives" proposed by commenters, adding more specifically that it had no obligation to consider the dissenters' disclosure alternative because the "Congress rejected a purely disclosure-based approach to regulating conflicts of interest under the [ICA]."

We conclude the Commission's failure to consider the disclosure alternative violated the APA. To be sure, the Commission is not required to consider "every alternative ... conceivable by the mind of man ... regardless of how uncommon or unknown that alternative" may be. *Motor Vehicle Mfrs. Ass'n, 463 U.S. at 51*. Here, however, two dissenting Commissioners raised, as an alternative to prescription, reliance upon disclosure, *see 69 Fed. Reg. at 46,393* -- a familiar tool in the Commission's toolkit -- and several commenters suggested that the Commission should leave the choice of chairman to market forces, making it hard to see how that particular policy alternative was either "uncommon or unknown."

The Commission would nevertheless be excused for failing to consider this alternative if it were, for whatever reason, unworthy of consideration. Commission counsel accordingly suggests one such reason, namely, that in the ICA the Congress rejected a "purely disclosure-based approach." *See also SEC v. Variable Annuity Life Ins. Co., 359 U.S. 65 (1959)* (ICA "passes beyond a simple 'disclosure' philosophy"). Counsel's statement is true but irrelevant; that the Congress required more than disclosure with respect to some matters governed by the ICA does not mean it deemed disclosure insufficient with respect to all such matters. On the contrary, the ICA requires funds to make extensive disclosures. *See, e.g., 15 U.S.C. § 80a-8(b)* (fund must file registration statement with Commission); *id. § 80a-29(e)* (fund must send semiannual report to shareholders); *id. § 80a-44(a)* (fund must make available to public all documents filed with Commission); *see also* Mary M. Frank et al., *Copycat Funds: Information Disclosure Regulation and the Returns to Active*

Fund Management in the Mutual Fund Industry, 47 J.L. & ECON. 515 (2004) ("[ICA] regulates information disclosure by mutual funds"). Indeed, the Commission augmented the disclosure requirements of the ICA even as it was considering the independent chairman condition. *See Final Rule, Shareholder Reports and Quarterly Portfolio Disclosure of Registered Management Investment Companies, 69 Fed. Reg. 11,244, 11,245 (Mar. 9, 2004).*

In sum, the disclosure alternative was neither frivolous nor out of bounds and the Commission therefore had an obligation to consider it. *Cf. Laclede Gas Co. v. FERC, 277 U.S. App. D.C. 237, 873 F.2d 1494, 1498 (D.C. Cir. 1989)* ("where a party raises facially reasonable alternatives ... the agency must either consider those alternatives or give some reason ... for declining to do so") (emphases removed). The Commission may ultimately decide the disclosure alternative will not sufficiently serve the interests of shareholders, but the Commission -- not its counsel and not this court -- is charged by the Congress with bringing its expertise and its best judgment to bear upon that issue. *See SEC v. Chenery Corp., 332 U.S. 194, 196-97 (1947); see also Motor Vehicle Mfrs. Ass'n, 463 U.S. at 54.*

III. Conclusion

For the foregoing reasons, we grant in part the Chamber's petition for review. This matter is remanded to the Commission to address the deficiencies with the 75% independent director condition and the independent chairman condition identified herein. *See Fox Television Stations, Inc. v. FCC, 280 F.3d 1027, 1048-49 (D.C. Cir. 2002); Allied Signal, Inc. v. U.S. Nuclear Regulatory Comm'n, 988 F.2d 146, 150-51 (D.C. Cir. 1993).*

So ordered.

Goldstein v. Securities and Exchange Commission

United States Court of Appeals, D.C. Circuit, 2006
451 F.3d 873

Before: RANDOLPH and GRIFFITH, Circuit Judges, and EDWARDS, Senior Circuit Judge.

■ RANDOLPH, CIRCUIT JUDGE: This is a petition for review of the Securities and Exchange Commission's regulation of "hedge funds" under the Investment Advisers Act of 1940, *15 U.S.C. § 80b-1 et seq. See Registration Under the Advisers Act of Certain Hedge Fund Advisers, 69 Fed. Reg. 72,054 (Dec. 10, 2004)* (codified at 17 C.F.R. pts. 275, 279) ("*Hedge Fund Rule*"). Previously exempt because they had "fewer than fifteen clients," *15 U.S.C. § 80b-3(b)(3)*, most advisers to hedge funds must now register with the Commission if the funds they advise have fifteen or more "shareholders, limited partners, members, or beneficiaries." *17 C.F.R. § 275.203(b)(3)-2(a)*. Petitioners Philip Goldstein, an investment advisory firm Goldstein co-owns (Kimball & Winthrop), and Opportunity Partners L.P., a hedge fund in which Kimball & Winthrop is the general partner and investment adviser (collectively "Goldstein") challenge the regulation's equation of "client" with "investor."

I.

"Hedge funds" are notoriously difficult to define. The term appears nowhere in the federal securities laws, and even industry participants do not agree upon a single definition. *See, e.g.*, SEC Roundtable on Hedge Funds (May 13, 2003) (comments of David A. Vaughan), *available at* http://www.sec.gov/spotlight/hedgefunds/hedge-vaughn.htm (citing fourteen different definitions found in government and industry publications). The term is commonly used as a catch-all for "any pooled investment vehicle that is privately organized, administered by professional investment managers, and not widely available to the public." PRESIDENT'S WORKING GROUP ON FINANCIAL MARKETS, HEDGE FUNDS, LEVERAGE, AND THE LESSONS OF LONG-TERM CAPITAL MANAGEMENT 1 (1999) ("*Working Group Report*"); *see also* IMPLICATIONS OF THE GROWTH OF HEDGE FUNDS: STAFF REPORT TO THE UNITED STATES SECURITIES AND EXCHANGE COMMISSION 3 (2003) ("*Staff Report*") (defining "hedge fund" as "an entity that holds a pool of securities and perhaps other assets, whose interests are not sold in a registered public offering and which is not registered as an investment company under the Investment Company Act").

Hedge funds may be defined more precisely by reference to what they are *not*. The Investment Company Act of 1940, *15 U.S.C. § 80a-1 et seq.*, directs the Commission to regulate any issuer of securities that "is or holds itself out as being engaged primarily . . . in the business of investing, reinvesting, or trading in securities." *Id. § 80a-3(a)(1)(A)*. Although this definition nominally describes hedge funds, most are exempt from the Investment Company Act's coverage because they have one hundred or fewer beneficial owners and do not offer their securities to the public, *id. § 80a-3(c)(1)*, or because their investors are all "qualified" high net-worth individuals or institutions, *id. § 80a-3(c)(7)*. Investment vehicles that remain private and available only to highly sophisticated investors have historically been understood not to present the same dangers to public markets as more widely available investment companies, like mutual funds. *See Staff Report, supra*, at 11-12, 13.

Exemption from regulation under the Investment Company Act allows hedge funds to engage in very different investing behavior than their mutual fund counterparts. While mutual funds, for example, must register with the Commission and disclose their investment positions and financial condition, *id. §§ 80a-8, 80a-29*, hedge funds typically remain secretive about their positions and strategies, even to their own investors. *See Staff Report, supra*, at 46-47. The Investment Company Act places significant restrictions on the types of transactions registered investment companies may undertake. Such companies are, for example, foreclosed from trading on margin or engaging in short sales, *15 U.S.C. § 80a-12(a)(1), (3)*, and must secure shareholder approval to take on significant debt or invest in certain types of assets, such as real estate or commodities, *id. § 80a-13(a)(2)*. These transactions are all core elements of most hedge funds' trading strategies. *See Staff Report, supra*, at 33-43. "Hedging" transactions, from which the term "hedge fund" developed, *see* Willa E. Gibson, *Is Hedge Fund Regulation Necessary?, 73 TEMP. L. REV. 681*, 684-85 & n.18 (2000), involve taking both long and short positions on debt and equity securities to reduce risk. This is still the most frequently used hedge fund strategy, *see Staff Report, supra*, at 35, though there are many others. Hedge funds trade in all sorts of assets, from traditional stocks, bonds, and currencies to more exotic financial derivatives and even non-financial assets. *See, e.g.*, Kate Kelly, *Creative Financing: Defying the Odds, Hedge Funds Bet Billions on Movies*, WALL ST. J., Apr. 29, 2006, at A1. Hedge funds often use leverage to increase their returns.

Another distinctive feature of hedge funds is their management structure. Unlike mutual funds, which must comply with detailed requirements for independent boards of directors, *15 U.S.C. § 80a-10*, and whose shareholders must explicitly approve of certain actions, *id. § 80a-13*, domestic hedge funds are usually structured as limited partnerships to achieve maximum separation of ownership and management. In the typical arrangement, the general partner manages the fund (or several funds) for a fixed fee and a percentage of the gross profits from the fund. The limited partners are passive investors and generally take no part in management activities. *See Staff Report, supra*, at 9-10, 61.

Hedge fund advisers also had been exempt from regulation under the Investment Advisers Act of 1940, *15 U.S.C. § 80b-1 et seq.* ("Advisers Act"), a companion statute to the Investment Company Act, and the statute which primarily concerns us in this case. Enacted by Congress to "substitute a philosophy of full disclosure for the philosophy of *caveat emptor*" in the investment advisory profession, *SEC v. Capital Gains Research Bureau, Inc., 375 U.S. 180, 186, 84 S. Ct. 275, 11 L. Ed. 2d 237 (1963)*, the Advisers Act is mainly a registration and anti-fraud statute. Non-exempt "investment advisers" must register with the Commission, *15 U.S.C. § 80b-3*, and all advisers are prohibited from engaging in fraudulent or deceptive practices, *id. § 80b-6*. By keeping a census of advisers, the Commission can better respond to, initiate, and take remedial action on complaints against fraudulent advisers. *See id. § 80b-4* (authorizing the Commission to examine registered advisers' records).

Hedge fund general partners meet the definition of "investment adviser" in the Advisers Act. *See 15 U.S.C. § 80b-2(11)* (defining "investment adviser" as one who "for compensation, engages in the business of advising others, either directly or through publications or writings, as to the value of securities or as to the advisability of investing in, purchasing, or selling securities"); *Abrahamson v. Fleschner, 568 F.2d 862, 869-71 (2d Cir. 1977)* (holding that hedge fund general partners are "investment advisers"), *overruled in part on other grounds by Transamerica Mortgage Advisors, Inc. v. Lewis, 444 U.S. 11 (1979)*. But they usually satisfy the "private adviser exemption" from registration in § 203(b)(3) of the Act, *15 U.S.C. § 80b-3(b)(3)*. That section exempts "any investment adviser who during the course of the preceding twelve months has had fewer than fifteen clients and who neither holds himself out generally to the public as an investment adviser nor acts as an investment adviser to any investment company registered under [the Investment Company Act]." *Id.* As applied to limited partnerships and other entities, the Commission had interpreted this provision to refer to the partnership or entity itself as the adviser's "client." *See 17 C.F.R. § 275.203(b)(3)-1*. Even the largest hedge fund managers usually ran fewer than fifteen hedge funds and were therefore exempt.

Although the Commission has a history of interest in hedge funds, *see Staff Report, supra*, at app. A, the current push for regulation had its origins in the failure of Long-Term Capital Management, a Greenwich, Connecticut-based fund that had more than $ 125 billion in assets under management at its peak. In late 1998, the fund nearly collapsed. Almost all of the country's major financial institutions were put at risk due to their credit exposure to Long-Term, and the president of the Federal Reserve Bank of New York personally intervened to engineer a bailout of the fund in order to avoid a national financial crisis. *See generally* ROGER LOWENSTEIN, WHEN GENIUS FAILED: THE RISE AND FALL OF LONG-TERM CAPITAL MANAGEMENT (2000).

A joint working group of the major federal financial regulators produced a report recommending regulatory changes to the regime governing hedge funds, and the Commission's staff followed with its own report about the state of hedge fund regulation. Drawing on the conclusions in the *Staff Report*, the Commission -- over the dissent of two of its members -- issued the rule under review in December 2004 after notice and comment. The Commission cited three recent shifts in the hedge fund industry to justify the need for increased regulation. First, despite the failure of Long-Term Capital Management, hedge fund assets grew by 260 percent from 1999 to 2004. *Hedge Fund Rule, 69 Fed. Reg. at 72,055*. Second, the Commission noticed a trend toward "retailization" of hedge funds that increased the exposure of ordinary investors to such funds. This retailization was driven by hedge funds loosening their investment requirements, the birth of "funds of hedge funds" that offered shares to the public, and increased investment in hedge funds by pension funds, universities, endowments, foundations and other charitable organizations. *See id. at 72,057-58*. Third, the Commission was concerned about an increase in the number of fraud actions brought against hedge funds. *See id. at 72,056-57*. Concluding that its "current regulatory program for hedge fund advisers [was] inadequate," *id. at 72,059*, the Commission moved to require hedge fund advisers to register under the Advisers Act so that it could gather "basic information about hedge fund advisers and the hedge fund industry," "oversee hedge fund advisers," and "deter or detect fraud by unregistered hedge fund advisers," *id.*

The *Hedge Fund Rule* first defines a "private fund" as an investment company that (a) is exempt from registration under the Investment Company Act by virtue of having fewer than one hundred investors or only qualified investors, *see 15 U.S.C. § 80a-3(c)(1), (7)*; (b) permits its investors to redeem their interests within two years of investing; and (c) markets itself on the basis of the "skills, ability or expertise of the investment adviser." *17 C.F.R. § 275.203(b)(3)-1(d)(1)*. For these private funds, the rule then specifies that "[f]or purposes of section 203(b)(3) of the [Advisers] Act (*15 U.S.C. § 80b-3(b)(3)*), you must count as clients the shareholders, limited partners, members, or beneficiaries . . . of [the] fund." *Id. § 275.203(b)(3)-2(a)*. The rule had the effect of requiring most hedge fund advisers to register by February 1, 2006.

II.

The dissenting Commissioners disputed the factual predicates for the new rule and its wisdom. Goldstein makes some of the same points but the major thrust of his complaint is that the Commission's action misinterpreted § 203(b)(3) of the Advisers Act, a charge the Commission dissenters also leveled. This provision exempts from registration "any investment adviser who during the course of the preceding twelve months has had fewer than fifteen *clients*." *15 U.S.C. § 80b-3(b)(3)* (emphasis added). The Act does not define "client." Relying on *Chevron U.S.A. Inc. v. NRDC, 467 U.S. 837, 842-43, 104 S. Ct. 2778, 81 L. Ed. 2d 694 (1984)*, the Commission believes this renders the statute "ambiguous as to a method for counting clients." Br. for Resp. 21. There is no such rule of law. The lack of a statutory definition of a word does not necessarily render the meaning of a word ambiguous, just as the presence of a definition does not necessarily make the meaning clear. A definition only pushes the problem back to the meaning of the defining terms. *See Alarm Indus. Commc'ns Comm. v. FCC, 327 U.S. App. D.C. 412, 131 F.3d 1066, 1068-70 (D.C. Cir. 1997)*; *Doris Day Animal League v. Veneman, 354 U.S. App. D.C. 216, 315 F.3d 297, 298-99 (D.C. Cir. 2003)*.

If Congress employs a term susceptible of several meanings, as many terms are, it scarcely follows that Congress has authorized an agency to choose *any* one of those meanings. As always, the "words of the statute should be read in context, the statute's place in the overall statutory scheme should be considered, and the problem Congress sought to solve should be taken into account" to determine whether Congress has foreclosed the agency's interpretation. *PDK Labs. Inc. v. DEA, 360 U.S. App. D.C. 344, 362 F.3d 786, 796 (D.C. Cir. 2004)* ("*PDK I*") (internal quotation marks omitted).

"Client" may mean different things depending on context. The client of a laundry occupies a very different position than the client of a lawyer. Even for professional representation, the specific indicia of a client relationship -- contracts, fees, duties, and the like -- vary with the profession and with the particulars of the situation. An attorney-client relationship, for example, can be formed without any signs of formal "employment." *See* RESTATEMENT (THIRD) OF THE LAW GOVERNING LAWYERS § 14 & cmt. c (2000) ("The client need not necessarily pay or agree to pay the lawyer; and paying a lawyer does not by itself create a client-lawyer relationship . . . ."). Matters may be very different for the client of, say, an architectural firm.

The Commission believes that an amendment to *§ 203(b)(3)* suggests the possibility that an investor in a hedge fund could be counted as a client of the fund's adviser. In 1980, Congress added to *§ 203(b)(3)* the following language: "For purposes of determining the number of clients of an investment adviser under this paragraph, no shareholder, partner, or beneficial owner of a business development company . . . shall be deemed to be a client of such investment adviser unless such person is a client of such investment adviser separate and apart from his status as a shareholder, partner, or beneficial owner." Act of Oct. 21, 1980, Pub. L. No. 96-477, § 202, 94 Stat. 2275, 2290 (1980). This language was inserted against a backdrop of uncertainty created by the Second Circuit's decision in *Abrahamson v. Fleschner*. The *Abrahamson* court held that hedge fund general partners were "investment advisers" under the Advisers Act, *568 F.2d at 869-71*. In its original opinion, the court specified that the general partners were advisers "to the limited partners." *See* Robert C. Hacker & Ronald D. Rotunda, *SEC Registration of Private Investment Partnerships After Abrahamson v. Fleschner*, 78 COLUM. L. REV. 1471, 1484 n.72 (1978). The final published opinion omits those four words, *see Abrahamson, 568 F.2d at 871 n.16*, suggesting that the court expressly declined to resolve any ambiguity in the term "client." If -- as we generally assume -- Congress was aware of this judicial confusion, *see, e.g., Beethoven.com LLC v. Librarian of Congress, 364 U.S. App. D.C. 295, 394 F.3d 939, 945-46 (D.C. Cir. 2005)*, the 1980 amendment could be seen as Congress's acknowledgment that "client" is ambiguous in the context of *§ 203(b)(3)*. There are statements in the legislative history that suggest as much. *See, e.g.,* H.R. REP. NO. 96-1341, at 62 (1980) ("[W]ith respect to persons or firms which *do not* advise business development companies, the . . . amendment . . . is not intended to suggest that each shareholder, partner, or beneficial owner of a company advised by such person or firm *should or should not be* regarded as a client . . . ." (emphasis added)). Although "the views of a subsequent Congress form a hazardous basis for inferring the intent of an earlier one," *PDK I, 362 F.3d at 794-95* (quoting *United States v. Price, 361 U.S. 304, 313 (1960)),* the 1980 amendment might be seen as introducing another definitional possibility into the statute. *See PDK Labs. Inc. v. DEA, 370 U.S. App. D.C. 47, 438 F.3d 1184, 1192-93 (D.C. Cir. 2006).*

On the other hand, a 1970 amendment to *§ 203* appears to reflect Congress's understanding at the time that investment company entities, not their shareholders, were the advisers' clients. In the amendment, Congress eliminated a separate exemption from registration for advisers who advised only investment companies and explicitly made the fewer-than-fifteen-clients exemption unavailable to such advisers. Investment Company Amendments Act of 1970, Pub. L. No. 91-547, § 24, 84 Stat. 1413, 1430 (1970). This latter prohibition would have been unnecessary if the shareholders of investment companies could be counted as "clients."

Another section of the Advisers Act strongly suggests that Congress did not intend "shareholders, limited partners, members, or beneficiaries" of a hedge fund to be counted as "clients." Although the statute does not define "client," it does define "investment adviser" as "any person who, for compensation, engages in the business of advising others, either *directly* or through publications or writings, as to the value of securities or as to the advisability of investing in, purchasing, or selling securities." *15 U.S.C. § 80b-2(11)* (emphasis added). An investor in a private fund may benefit from the adviser's advice (or he may suffer from it) but he does not receive the advice *directly*. He invests a portion of his assets in the fund. The fund manager -- the adviser -- controls the disposition of the pool of capital in the fund. The adviser does not tell the *investor* how to spend his money; the investor made that decision when he invested in the fund. Having bought into the fund, the investor fades into the background; his role is completely passive. If the person or entity controlling the fund is not an "investment adviser" to each individual investor, then *a fortiori* each investor cannot be a "client" of that person or entity. These are just two sides of the same coin.

This had been the Commission's view until it issued the new rule. As recently as 1997, it explained that a "client of an investment adviser typically is provided with individualized advice that is based on the client's financial situation and investment objectives. In contrast, the investment adviser of an investment company need not consider the individual needs of the company's shareholders when making investment decisions, and thus has no obligation to ensure that each security purchased for the company's portfolio is an appropriate investment for each shareholder." Status of Investment Advisory Programs Under the Investment Company Act of 1940, *62 Fed. Reg. 15,098, 15,102 (Mar. 31, 1997)*. The Commission said much the same in 1985 when it promulgated a rule with respect to investment companies set up as limited partnerships rather than as corporations. The "client" for purposes of the fifteen-client rule of § 203(b)(3) is the limited partnership not the individual partners. *See 17 C.F.R. § 275.203(b)(3)-1(a)(2)*. As the Commission wrote in proposing the rule, when "an adviser to an investment pool manages the assets of the pool on the basis of the investment objectives of the participants as a group, it appears appropriate to view the pool -- rather than each participant -- as a client of the adviser." *Safe Harbor Proposed Rule, 50 Fed. Reg. at 8741*.

The Supreme Court embraced a similar conception of the adviser-client relationship when it held in *Lowe v. SEC, 472 U.S. 181, 105 S. Ct. 2557, 86 L. Ed. 2d 130 (1985)*, that publishers of certain financial newsletters were not "investment advisers." *Id. at 211*; *see 15 U.S.C. § 80b-2(11)(D)*. After an extensive discussion of the legislative history of the Advisers Act, the Court held that existence of an advisory relationship depended largely on the character of the advice rendered. Persons engaged in the investment advisory profession "provide personalized advice attuned to a client's concerns." *Lowe, 472 U.S. at 208*. "[F]iduciary, person-to-person relationships" were "characteristic" of the "investment adviser-client relationship[]." *Id. at 210*. The Court thought it "significant" that the Advisers Act "repeatedly" referred to "clients," which signified to the Court "the kind of fiduciary relationship the Act was designed to regulate." *Id. at 208 n.54, 201 n.45*. This type of direct relationship exists between the adviser and the fund, but not between the adviser and the investors in the fund. The adviser is concerned with the fund's performance, not with each investor's financial condition.

The Commission nevertheless is right to point out that the *Lowe* Court was not rendering an interpretation of the word "client." *See Hedge Fund Rule, 69 Fed. Reg. at 72,069 n.174*. Because it was construing an exception to the definition of "investment adviser," we do not read too much into the Court's understanding of the meaning of "client." *See Nat'l Cable & Telecomms. Ass'n v. Brand X Internet Servs., 545 U.S. 967 (2005)*.

As we have noted before, "[i]t may be that . . . the strict dichotomy between clarity and ambiguity is artificial, that what we have is a continuum, a probability of meaning." *PDK I, 362 F.3d at 797*. Here, even if the Advisers Act does not foreclose the Commission's interpretation, the interpretation falls outside the bounds of reasonableness. "An agency construction of a statute cannot survive judicial review if a contested regulation reflects an action that exceeds the agency's authority. It does not matter whether the unlawful action arises because the disputed regulation defies the plain language of a statute or because the agency's construction is utterly unreasonable and thus impermissible." *Aid Ass'n for Lutherans v. United States Postal Serv., 355 U.S. App. D.C.*

221, 321 F.3d 1166, 1174 (D.C. Cir. 2003); see also id. at 1177-78; Am. Library Ass'n v. FCC, 365 U.S. App. D.C. 353, 406 F.3d 689, 699 (D.C. Cir. 2005).

"The 'reasonableness' of an agency's construction depends," in part, "on the construction's 'fit' with the statutory language, as well as its conformity to statutory purposes." *Abbott Labs. v. Young, 287 U.S. App. D.C. 190, 920 F.2d 984, 988 (D.C. Cir. 1990).* As described above, the Commission's interpretation of the word "client" comes close to violating the plain language of the statute. At best it is counterintuitive to characterize the investors in a hedge fund as the "clients" of the adviser. *See Am. Bar Ass'n v. FTC,c 368 U.S. App. D.C. 368, 430 F.3d 457, 471 (D.C. Cir. 2005).* The adviser owes fiduciary duties only to the fund, not to the fund's investors. Section 206 of the Advisers Act, *15 U.S.C. § 80b-6,* makes it unlawful for any investment adviser -- registered or not -- "to engage in any transaction, practice, or course of business which operates as a fraud or deceit upon any client or prospective client." *Id. § 80b-6(2).* In *SEC v. Capital Gains Research Bureau, Inc., 375 U.S. 180 (1963),* the Supreme Court held that this provision created a fiduciary duty of loyalty between an adviser and his client. *See id. at 191-92; id. at 201* ("The statute, in recognition of the adviser's fiduciary relationship to his clients, requires that his advice be disinterested."); *see also Hedge Fund Rule, 69 Fed. Reg. at 72,059 & n.57.* In that case, the duty of loyalty required an adviser to disclose self-interested transactions to his clients. The Commission recognizes more generally that the duty of loyalty "requires advisers to manage their clients' portfolios in the best interest of clients," and imposes obligations to "fully disclose any material conflicts the adviser has with its clients, to seek best execution for client transactions, and to have a reasonable basis for client recommendations." *Id. at 72,054.*

If the investors are owed a fiduciary duty and the entity is also owed a fiduciary duty, then the adviser will inevitably face conflicts of interest. Consider an investment adviser to a hedge fund that is about to go bankrupt. His advice to the fund will likely include any and all measures to remain solvent. His advice to an investor in the fund, however, would likely be to sell. For the same reason, we do not ordinarily deem the shareholders in a corporation the "clients" of the corporation's lawyers or accountants. *See RESTATEMENT, supra, § 96 cmt. b* ("By representing the organization, a lawyer does not thereby also form a client-lawyer relationship with all or any individuals . . . who have an ownership or other beneficial interest in it, such as its shareholders."). While the shareholders may benefit from the professionals' counsel indirectly, their individual interests easily can be drawn into conflict with the interests of the entity. It simply cannot be the case that investment advisers are the servants of two masters in this way.

The Commission's response to this argument is telling. It argues that the *Hedge Fund Rule* amends *only* the method for counting clients under *§ 203(b)(3)*, and that it does not "alter the duties or obligations owed by an investment adviser to its clients." *69 Fed. Reg. at 72,070.* We ordinarily presume that the same words used in different parts of a statute have the same meaning. *See Sullivan v. Stroop, 496 U.S. 478, 484, 110 S. Ct. 2499, 110 L. Ed. 2d 438 (1990).* The Commission cannot explain why "client" should mean one thing when determining to whom fiduciary duties are owed, *15 U.S.C. § 80b-6(1)-(3),* and something else entirely when determining whether an investment adviser must register under the Act, *id. § 80b-3(b)(3). Cf. Mobil Oil Corp. v. EPA, 276 U.S. App. D.C. 352, 871 F.2d 149, 153 (D.C. Cir. 1989).*

The Commission also argues that the organizational form of most hedge funds is merely "legal artifice," Br. for Resp. 41, to shield advisers who want to advise more than fifteen clients and remain exempt from registration. *See Hedge Fund Rule, 69 Fed. Reg. at 72,068*. But as the discussion above shows, form matters in this area of the law because it dictates to whom fiduciary duties are owed.

The *Hedge Fund Rule* might be more understandable if, over the years, the advisory relationship between hedge fund advisers and investors had changed. The Commission cited, as justification for its rule, a rise in the amount of hedge fund assets, indications that more pension funds and other institutions were investing in hedge funds, and an increase in fraud actions involving hedge funds. All of this may be true, although the dissenting Commissioners doubted it. But without any evidence that the role of fund advisers with respect to investors had undergone a transformation, there is a disconnect between the factors the Commission cited and the rule it promulgated. That the Commission wanted a hook on which to hang more comprehensive regulation of hedge funds may be understandable. But the Commission may not accomplish its objective by a manipulation of meaning.

The Commission has, in short, not adequately explained how the relationship between hedge fund investors and advisers justifies treating the former as clients of the latter. *See Shays v. FEC, 367 U.S. App. D.C. 185, 414 F.3d 76, 96-97 (D.C. Cir. 2005)* (explaining that agency interpretation is not "reasonable" if it is "arbitrary and capricious"). The Commission points to its finding that a hedge fund adviser sometimes "may not treat all of its hedge fund investors the same." *Hedge Fund Rule, 69 Fed. Reg. at 72,069-70* (citing different lock-up periods, greater access to information, lower fees, and "side pocket" arrangements). From this the Commission concludes that each account of a hedge fund investor "*may* bear many of the characteristics of separate investment accounts, which, of course, must be counted as separate clients." *Id. at 72,070*. But the Commission's conclusion does not follow from its premise. It may be that different classes of investors have different rights or privileges with respect to their investments. This reveals little, however, about the *relationship* between the investor and the adviser. Even if it did, the Commission has not justified treating *all* investors in hedge funds as clients for the purpose of the rule. If there are certain characteristics present in some investor-adviser relationships that mark a "client" relationship, then the Commission should have identified those characteristics and tailored its rule accordingly.

By painting with such a broad brush, the Commission has failed adequately to justify departing from its own prior interpretation of *§ 203(b)(3)*. *See Mich. Pub. Power Agency v. FERC, 365 U.S. App. D.C. 313, 405 F.3d 8, 12 (D.C. Cir. 2005)* (citing *Greater Boston Television Corp. v. FCC, 143 U.S. App. D.C. 383, 444 F.2d 841, 852 (D.C. Cir. 1970))*. As we have discussed, in 1985 the Commission adopted a "safe harbor" for general partners of limited partnerships, enabling them to count the partnership as a single "client" for the purposes of *§ 203* so long as they provided advice to a "collective investment vehicle" based on the investment objectives of the limited partners as a group. *Safe Harbor Proposed Rule, 50 Fed. Reg. at 8741*. This "safe harbor" remains part of the Commission's rules and has since been expanded to include corporations, limited liability companies, and business trusts (hedge funds sometimes take these less common forms, *see Staff Report, supra,* at 9-10 & n.27). The *Hedge Fund Rule* therefore appears to carve out an exception from this safe harbor solely for investment entities that have fewer than one hundred-one but more than fourteen investors. *Compare 17 C.F.R. § 275.203(b)(3)-1, with id. § 275.203(b)(3)-2.* As discussed above, the Commission does not justify this exception by reference to any change in the nature of investment adviser-client relationships since the safe harbor was adopted. Absent such a justification, its choice appears completely arbitrary. *See Northpoint Technology, Ltd. v. FCC, 366 U.S. App. D.C. 363, 412 F.3d 145, 156 (D.C. Cir. 2005)* ("A statutory interpretation . . . that results from an unexplained departure from prior [agency] policy and practice is not a reasonable one.").

Nor is this choice any more rational when viewed in light of the policy goals underlying the Advisers Act. *See Abbott Labs., 920 F.2d at 988.* The Commission recites Congress's findings in § 201 that investment advisory activities "substantially . . . affect . . . national securities exchanges . . . and the national economy," *15 U.S.C. § 80b-1(3),* and concludes that "[i]n enacting *[section 203(b)(3)]*, Congress exempted from the registration requirements a category of advisers whose activities were not sufficiently large or national in scope." *Hedge Fund Rule, 69 Fed. Reg. at 72,067.* The Commission reasons that because hedge funds are now national in scope, treating the entity as a single client for the purpose of the exemption would frustrate Congress's policy. If Congress did intend the exemption to prevent regulation only of small-scale operations -- a policy goal that is clear from neither the statute's text nor its legislative history -- the Commission's rule bears no rational relationship to achieving that goal. The number of investors in a hedge fund -- the "clients" according to the Commission's rule -- reveals nothing about the scale or scope of the fund's activities. It is the volume of assets under management or the extent of indebtedness of a hedge fund or other such financial metrics that determines a fund's importance to national markets. One might say that if Congress meant to exclude regulation of small operations, it chose a very odd way of accomplishing its objective -- by excluding investment companies with one hundred or fewer investors and investment advisers having fewer than fifteen clients. But the *Hedge Fund Rule* only exacerbates whatever problems one might perceive in Congress's method for determining who to regulate. The Commission's rule creates a situation in which funds with one hundred or fewer investors are exempt from the more demanding Investment Company Act, but those with fifteen or more investors trigger registration under the Advisers Act. This is an arbitrary rule.

* * *

The petition for review is granted, and the *Hedge Fund Rule* is vacated and remanded.

So ordered.

Merrill Lynch, Pierce, Fenner & Smith v. Dabit

Supreme Court of the United States, 2006
547 U.S. 71

■ JUSTICE STEVENS delivered the opinion of the Court.

Title I of the Securities Litigation Uniform Standards Act of 1998 (SLUSA) provides that "[n]o covered class action" based on state law and alleging "a misrepresentation or omission of a material fact in connection with the purchase or sale of a covered security" "may be maintained in any State or Federal court by any private party." § 101(b), 112 Stat. 3227 (codified at *15 U.S.C. § 78bb(f)(1)(A)*). In this case the Second Circuit held that SLUSA only pre-empts state-law class-action claims brought by plaintiffs who have a private remedy under federal law. *395 F.3d 25 (2005)*. A few months later, the Seventh Circuit ruled to the contrary, holding that the statute also pre-empts state-law class-action claims for which federal law provides no private remedy. *Kircher v. Putnam Funds Trust, 403 F.3d 478 (2005)*. The background, the text, and the purpose of SLUSA's pre-emption provision all support the broader interpretation adopted by the Seventh Circuit.

I

Petitioner Merrill Lynch, Pierce, Fenner & Smith, Inc. (Merrill Lynch), is an investment banking firm that offers research and brokerage services to investors. Suspicious that the firm's loyalties to its investment banking clients had produced biased investment advice, the New York attorney general in 2002 instituted a formal investigation into Merrill Lynch's practices. The investigation sparked a number of private securities fraud actions, this one among them.

Respondent, Shadi Dabit, is a former Merrill Lynch broker. He filed this class action in the United States District Court for the Western District of Oklahoma on behalf of himself and all other former or current brokers who, while employed by Merrill Lynch, purchased (for themselves and for their clients) certain stocks between December 1, 1999, and December 31, 2000. See App. 27a-46a. Rather than rely on the federal securities laws, Dabit invoked the District Court's diversity jurisdiction and advanced his claims under Oklahoma state law.

The gist of Dabit's complaint was that Merrill Lynch breached the fiduciary duty and covenant of good faith and fair dealing it owed its brokers by disseminating misleading research and thereby manipulating stock prices. Dabit's theory was that Merrill Lynch used its misinformed brokers to enhance the prices of its investment banking clients' stocks: The research analysts, under management's direction, allegedly issued overly optimistic appraisals of the stocks' value; the brokers allegedly relied on the analysts' reports in advising their investor clients and in deciding whether or not to sell their own holdings; and the clients and brokers both continued to hold their stocks long beyond the point when, had the truth been known, they would have sold. The complaint further alleged that when the truth was actually revealed (around the time the New York attorney general instituted his investigation), the stocks' prices plummeted.

Dabit asserted that Merrill Lynch's actions damaged the class members in two ways: The misrepresentations and manipulative tactics caused them to hold onto overvalued securities, and the brokers lost commission fees when their clients, now aware that they had made poor investments, took their business elsewhere.

In July 2002, Merrill Lynch moved to dismiss Dabit's complaint. It argued, first, that SLUSA pre-empted the action and, second, that the claims alleged were not cognizable under Oklahoma law. The District Court indicated that it was "not impressed by" the state-law argument, but agreed that the federal statute pre-empted at least some of Dabit's claims. *Id.*, at 49a-50a. The court noted that the complaint alleged both "claims and damages based on wrongfully-induced purchases" and "claims and damages based on wrongfully-induced holding." *Ibid.* While the "holding" claims, the court suggested, might not be pre-empted, the "purchasing" claims certainly were. The court dismissed the complaint with leave to amend to give Dabit the opportunity to untangle his "hopeless melange of purchase-related and holding-related assertions." *Ibid.* (punctuation added).

Dabit promptly filed an amended complaint that omitted all direct references to purchases. What began as a class of brokers who "purchased" the subject securities during the class period became a class of brokers who "owned and continued to own" those securities. See *id.*, at 52a.

Meanwhile, dozens of other suits, based on allegations similar to Dabit's, had been filed against Merrill Lynch around the country on both federal- and state-law theories of liability. The Judicial Panel on Multidistrict Litigation transferred all of those cases, along with this one, to the United States District Court for the Southern District of New York for consolidated pretrial proceedings. Merrill Lynch then filed its second motion to dismiss Dabit's complaint. Senior Judge Milton Pollack granted the motion on the ground that the claims alleged fell "squarely within SLUSA's ambit." *Ciccarelli v. Merrill Lynch & Co. (In re Merrill Lynch & Co. Research Reports Sec. Litig.), 2003 U.S. Dist. LEXIS 5999, 2003 WL 1872820, *1 (Apr. 10, 2003).*

The Court of Appeals for the Second Circuit, however, vacated the judgment and remanded for further proceedings. *395 F.3d at 51.* It concluded that the claims asserted by holders did not allege fraud "in connection with the purchase or sale" of securities under SLUSA. Although the court agreed with Merrill Lynch that that phrase, as used in other federal securities laws, has been defined broadly by this Court, it held that Congress nonetheless intended a narrower meaning here--one that incorporates the "standing" limitation on private federal securities actions adopted in *Blue Chip Stamps v. Manor Drug Stores, 421 U.S. 723, 95 S. Ct. 1917, 44 L. Ed. 2d 539 (1975).* Under the Second Circuit's analysis, fraud is only "in connection with the purchase or sale" of securities, as used in SLUSA, if it is alleged by a purchaser or seller of securities. Thus, to the extent that the complaint in this action alleged that brokers were fraudulently induced, not to sell or purchase, but to retain or delay selling their securities, it fell outside SLUSA's pre-emptive scope.

After determining that the class defined in Dabit's amended complaint did not necessarily exclude purchasers, the panel remanded with instructions that the pleading be dismissed without prejudice. The court's order would permit Dabit to file another amended complaint that defines the class to exclude "claimants who purchased in connection with the fraud and who therefore could meet the standing requirement" for a federal damages action, and to include only those "who came to hold [a Merrill Lynch] stock before any relevant misrepresentation." *395 F.3d at 45-46.* Under the Second Circuit's analysis, a class action so limited could be sustained under state law. For the reasons that follow, we disagree.

II

The magnitude of the federal interest in protecting the integrity and efficient operation of the market for nationally traded securities cannot be overstated. In response to the sudden and disastrous collapse in prices of listed stocks in 1929, and the Great Depression that followed, Congress enacted the Securities Act of 1933 (1933 Act), 48 Stat. 74, and the Securities Exchange Act of 1934 (1934 Act), 48 Stat. 881. Since their enactment, these two statutes have anchored federal regulation of vital elements of our economy.

Securities and Exchange Commission (SEC) *Rule 10b-5, 17 CFR § 240.10b-5 (2005)*, promulgated in 1942 pursuant to § 10(b) of the 1934 Act, *15 U.S.C. § 78j(b)*, is an important part of that regulatory scheme. The Rule, like *§ 10(b)* itself, n4 broadly prohibits deception, misrepresentation, and fraud "in connection with the purchase or sale of any security." The SEC has express statutory authority to enforce the Rule. See *15 U.S.C. § 78u (2000 ed. and Supp. III)*. Although no such authority is expressly granted to private individuals injured by securities fraud, in 1946 Judge Kirkpatrick of the United States District Court for the Eastern District of Pennsylvania, relying on "the general purpose" of the Rule, recognized an implied right of action thereunder. *Kardon v. National Gypsum Co., 69 F. Supp. 512, 514*. His holding was adopted by an "overwhelming consensus of the District Courts and Courts of Appeals," *Blue Chip Stamps, 421 U.S., at 730, 95 S. Ct. 1917, 44 L. Ed. 2d 539*, and endorsed by this Court in *Superintendent of Ins. of N. Y. v. Bankers Life & Casualty Co., 404 U.S. 6, 92 S. Ct. 165, 30 L. Ed. 2d 128 (1971)*.

A few years after *Kardon* was decided, the Court of Appeals for the Second Circuit limited the reach of the private right of action under *Rule 10b-5*. In *Birnbaum v. Newport Steel Corp., 193 F.2d 461 (1952)*, a panel composed of Chief Judge Swan and Judges Augustus and Learned Hand upheld the dismissal of a suit brought on behalf of a corporation and a class of its stockholders alleging that fraud "in connection with" a director's sale of his controlling block of stock to third parties violated *Rule 10b-5*. The court held that the Rule could only be invoked by a purchaser or seller of securities to remedy fraud associated with his or her own sale or purchase of securities, and did not protect those who neither purchased nor sold the securities in question but were instead injured by corporate insiders' sales to third parties. *Id., at 464*. While the *Birnbaum* court did not question the plaintiffs' "standing" to enforce *Rule 10b-5*, later cases treated its holding as a standing requirement. See *Eason v. General Motors Acceptance Corp., 490 F.2d 654, 657 (CA7 1973)*.

By the time this Court first confronted the question, literally hundreds of lower court decisions had accepted "*Birnbaum*'s conclusion that the plaintiff class for purposes of *§ 10(b)* and *Rule 10b-5* private damages actions is limited to purchasers and sellers." *Blue Chip Stamps, 421 U.S., at 731-732, 95 S. Ct. 1917, 44 L. Ed. 2d 539*. Meanwhile, however, cases like *Bankers Life & Casualty Co.* had interpreted the coverage of the Rule more broadly to prohibit, for example, "deceptive practices *touching* [a victim's] sale of securities as an investor." *404 U.S., at 12-13* (emphasis added); see *Eason, 490 F.2d at 657* (collecting cases). The "judicial oak which ha[d] grown from little more than a legislative acorn," as then-Justice Rehnquist described the rules governing private *Rule 10b-5* actions, *Blue Chip Stamps, 421 U.S., at 737*, had thus developed differently from the law defining what constituted a substantive violation of *Rule 10b-5*. Ultimately, the Court had to decide whether to permit private parties to sue for any violation of *Rule 10b-5* that caused them harm, or instead to limit the private remedy to plaintiffs who were themselves purchasers or sellers.

Relying principally on "policy considerations" which the Court viewed as appropriate in explicating a judicially crafted remedy, *ibid.*, and following judicial precedent rather than "the many commentators" who had criticized the *Birnbaum* rule as "an arbitrary restriction which unreasonably prevents some deserving plaintiffs from recovering damages," *421 U.S., at 738*, the Court in *Blue Chip Stamps* chose to limit the private remedy. The main policy consideration tipping the scales in favor of precedent was the widespread recognition that "litigation under *Rule 10b-5* presents a danger of vexatiousness different in degree and in kind from that which accompanies litigation in general." *Id., at 739*. Even weak cases brought under the Rule may have substantial settlement value, the Court explained, because "[t]he very pendency of the lawsuit may frustrate or delay normal business activity." *Id., at 740*. Cabining the private cause of action by means of the purchaser-seller limitation would, in the Court's view, minimize these ill effects. The limitation of course had no application in Government enforcement actions brought pursuant to *Rule 10b-5*. See *id., at 751, n. 14*.

III

Policy considerations similar to those that supported the Court's decision in *Blue Chip Stamps* prompted Congress, in 1995, to adopt legislation targeted at perceived abuses of the class-action vehicle in litigation involving nationally traded securities. While acknowledging that private securities litigation was "an indispensable tool with which defrauded investors can recover their losses," the House Conference Report accompanying what would later be enacted as the Private Securities Litigation Reform Act of 1995 (Reform Act), 109 Stat. 737 (codified at *15 U.S.C. §§ 77z-1 and 78u-4*), identified ways in which the class action device was being used to injure "the entire U. S. economy." H. R. Rep. No. 104-369, p 31 (1995). According to the Report, nuisance filings, targeting of deep-pocket defendants, vexatious discovery requests, and "manipulation by class action lawyers of the clients whom they purportedly represent" had become rampant in recent years. *Ibid.* Proponents of the Reform Act argued that these abuses resulted in extortionate settlements, chilled any discussion of issuers' future prospects, and deterred qualified individuals from serving on boards of directors. *Id.*, at 31-32.

Title I of the Reform Act, captioned "Reduction of Abusive Litigation," represents Congress' effort to curb these perceived abuses. Its provisions limit recoverable damages and attorney's fees, provide a "safe harbor" for forward-looking statements, impose new restrictions on the selection of (and compensation awarded to) lead plaintiffs, mandate imposition of sanctions for frivolous litigation, and authorize a stay of discovery pending resolution of any motion to dismiss. See *15 U.S.C. § 78u-4*. Title I also imposes heightened pleading requirements in actions brought pursuant to *§ 10(b)* and *Rule 10b-5*; it "insists that securities fraud complaints 'specify' each misleading statement; that they set forth the facts 'on which [a] belief' that a statement is misleading was 'formed'; and that they 'state with particularity facts giving rise to a strong inference that the defendant acted with the required state of mind.'" *Dura Pharmaceuticals, Inc. v. Broudo, 544 U.S. 336, 345, (2005)* (quoting *15 U.S.C. §§ 78u-4(b)(1), (2)*).

The effort to deter or at least quickly dispose of those suits whose nuisance value outweighs their merits placed special burdens on plaintiffs seeking to bring federal securities fraud class actions. But the effort also had an unintended consequence: It prompted at least some members of the plaintiffs' bar to avoid the federal forum altogether. Rather than face the obstacles set in their path by the Reform Act, plaintiffs and their representatives began bringing class actions under state law, often in state court. The evidence presented to Congress during a 1997 hearing to evaluate the effects of the Reform Act suggested that this phenomenon was a novel one; state-court litigation of class actions involving nationally traded securities had previously been rare. See H. R. Rep. No. 105-640, p 10 (1998); S. Rep. No. 105-182, pp 3-4 (1998). To stem this "shif[t] from Federal to State courts" and "prevent certain State private securities class action lawsuits alleging fraud from being used to frustrate the objectives of" the Reform Act, SLUSA §§ 2(2), (5), 112 Stat. 3227, Congress enacted SLUSA.

IV

The core provision of SLUSA reads as follows:

> "Class Action Limitations.--No covered class action based upon the statutory or common law of any State or subdivision thereof may be maintained in any State or Federal court by any private party alleging--
>
> "(A) a misrepresentation or omission of a material fact in connection with the purchase or sale of a covered security; or
>
> "(B) that the defendant used or employed any manipulative or deceptive device or contrivance in connection with the purchase or sale of a covered security." *Id.*, at 3230 (codified as amended at *15 U.S.C. § 78bb(f)(1)*).

A "covered class action" is a lawsuit in which damages are sought on behalf of more than 50 people. A "covered security" is one traded nationally and listed on a regulated national exchange. Respondent does not dispute that both the class and the securities at issue in this case are "covered" within the meaning of the statute, or that the complaint alleges misrepresentations and omissions of material facts. The only disputed issue is whether the alleged wrongdoing was "in connection with the purchase or sale" of securities.

Respondent urges that the operative language must be read narrowly to encompass (and therefore pre-empt) only those actions in which the purchaser-seller requirement of *Blue Chip Stamps* is met. Such, too, was the Second Circuit's view. But insofar as the argument assumes that the rule adopted in *Blue Chip Stamps* stems from the text of *Rule 10b-5* --specifically, the "in connection with" language, it must be rejected. Unlike the *Birnbaum* court, which relied on *Rule 10b-5*'s text in crafting its purchaser-seller limitation, this Court in *Blue Chip Stamps* relied chiefly, and candidly, on "policy considerations" in adopting that limitation. *421 U.S., at 737*. The *Blue Chip Stamps* Court purported to define the scope of a private right of action under *Rule 10b-5* --not to define the words "in connection with the purchase or sale." *Id., at 749* ("No language in either *[§ 10(b)* or *Rule 10b-5]* speaks at all to the contours of a private cause of action for their violation"). Any ambiguity on that score had long been resolved by the time Congress enacted SLUSA. See *United States v. O'Hagan, 521 U.S. 642, 656, 664 (1997)*; *Holmes v. Securities Investor Protection*

Corporation, 503 U.S. 258, 285 (1992) (O'Connor, J., concurring in part and concurring in judgment); *id., at 289-290, 285* (Scalia, J., concurring in judgment); *United States v. Naftalin, 441 U.S. 768, 774, n. 6 (1979)*; see also *395 F.3d at 39* (acknowledging that "[t]he limitation on standing to bring [a] private suit for damages for fraud in connection with the purchase or sale of securities is unquestionably a distinct concept from the general statutory and regulatory prohibition on fraud in connection with the purchase or sale of securities").

Moreover, when this Court *has* sought to give meaning to the phrase in the context of § *10(b)* and *Rule 10b-5*, it has espoused a broad interpretation. A narrow construction would not, as a matter of first impression, have been unreasonable; one might have concluded that an alleged fraud is "in connection with" a purchase or sale of securities only when the plaintiff himself was defrauded into purchasing or selling particular securities. After all, that was the interpretation adopted by the panel in the *Birnbaum* case. See *193 F.2d at 464*. But this Court, in early cases like *Superintendent of Ins. of N. Y. v. Bankers Life & Casualty Co., 404 U.S. 6 (1971)*, and most recently in *SEC v. Zandford, 535 U.S. 813, 820, 822 (2002)*, has rejected that view. Under our precedents, it is enough that the fraud alleged "coincide" with a securities transaction--whether by the plaintiff or by someone else. See *O'Hagan, 521 U.S., at 651*. The requisite showing, in other words, is "deception 'in connection with the purchase or sale of any security,' not deception of an identifiable purchaser or seller." *Id., at 658, 117 S. Ct. 2199, 138 L. Ed. 2d 724*. Notably, this broader interpretation of the statutory language comports with the longstanding views of the SEC. See *Zandford, 535 U.S., at 819-820*.

Congress can hardly have been unaware of the broad construction adopted by both this Court and the SEC when it imported the key phrase--"in connection with the purchase or sale"--into SLUSA's core provision. And when "judicial interpretations have settled the meaning of an existing statutory provision, repetition of the same language in a new statute indicates, as a general matter, the intent to incorporate its . . . judicial interpretations as well." *Bragdon v. Abbott, 524 U.S. 624, 645 (1998)*; see *Cannon v. University of Chicago, 441 U.S. 677, 696-699 (1979)*. Application of that presumption is particularly apt here; not only did Congress use the same words as are used in § *10(b)* and *Rule 10b-5*, but it used them in a provision that appears in the same statute as § *10(b)*. Generally, "identical words used in different parts of the same statute are . . . presumed to have the same meaning." *IBP, Inc. v. Alvarez, 546 U.S. __, __, 546 U.S. 21, 126 S. Ct. 514, 523, 163 L. Ed. 2d 288 (2005)*.

The presumption that Congress envisioned a broad construction follows not only from ordinary principles of statutory construction but also from the particular concerns that culminated in SLUSA's enactment. A narrow reading of the statute would undercut the effectiveness of the 1995 Reform Act and thus run contrary to SLUSA's stated purpose, viz., "to prevent certain State private securities class action lawsuits alleging fraud from being used to frustrate the objectives" of the 1995 Act. SLUSA § 2(5), 112 Stat. 3227. As the *Blue Chip Stamps* Court observed, class actions brought by holders pose a special risk of vexatious litigation. *421 U.S., at 739*. It would be odd, to say the least, if SLUSA exempted that particularly troublesome subset of class actions from its pre-emptive sweep. See *Kircher, 403 F.3d at 484*.

Respondent's preferred construction also would give rise to wasteful, duplicative litigation. Facts supporting an action by purchasers under *Rule 10b-5* (which must proceed in federal court if at all) typically support an action by holders as well, at least in those States that recognize holder claims. The prospect is raised, then, of parallel class actions proceeding in state and federal court, with different standards governing claims asserted on identical facts. That prospect, which exists to some extent in this very case, squarely conflicts with the congressional preference for "national standards for securities class action lawsuits involving nationally traded securities." SLUSA § 2(5), 112 Stat. 3227.

In concluding that SLUSA pre-empts state-law holder class-action claims of the kind alleged in Dabit's complaint, we do not lose sight of the general "presum[ption] that Congress does not cavalierly pre-empt state-law causes of action." *Medtronic, Inc. v. Lohr, 518 U.S. 470, 485 (1996)*. But that presumption carries less force here than in other contexts because SLUSA does not actually pre-empt any state cause of action. It simply denies plaintiffs the right to use the class action device to vindicate certain claims. The Act does not deny any individual plaintiff, or indeed any group of fewer than 50 plaintiffs, the right to enforce any state-law cause of action that may exist.

Moreover, the tailored exceptions to SLUSA's pre-emptive command demonstrate that Congress did not by any means act "cavalierly" here. The statute carefully exempts from its operation certain class actions based on the law of the State in which the issuer of the covered security is incorporated, actions brought by a state agency or state pension plan, actions under contracts between issuers and indenture trustees, and derivative actions brought by shareholders on behalf of a corporation. *15 U.S.C. §§ 78bb(f)(3)(A)-(C), (f)(5)(C)*. The statute also expressly preserves state jurisdiction over state agency enforcement proceedings. *§ 78bb(f)(4)*. The existence of these carve-outs both evinces congressional sensitivity to state prerogatives in this field and makes it inappropriate for courts to create additional, implied exceptions.

Finally, federal law, not state law, has long been the principal vehicle for asserting class-action securities fraud claims. See, *e.g.*, H. R. Conf. Rep. No. 105-803, p 14 (1998) ("Prior to the passage of the Reform Act, there was essentially no significant securities class action litigation brought in State court"). More importantly, while state-law holder claims were theoretically available both before and after the decision in *Blue Chip Stamps*, the actual assertion of such claims by way of class action was virtually unheard of before SLUSA was enacted; respondent and his *amici* have identified only *one* pre-SLUSA case involving a state-law class action asserting holder claims. n14 This is hardly a situation, then, in which a federal statute has eliminated a historically entrenched state-law remedy. Cf. *Bates v. Dow Agrosciences LLC, 544 U.S. 431, 449 (2005)* (observing that a "long history" of state-law tort remedy "add[ed] force" to the presumption against pre-emption).

V

The holder class action that respondent tried to plead, and that the Second Circuit envisioned, is distinguishable from a typical *Rule 10b-5* class action in only one respect: It is brought by holders instead of purchasers or sellers. For purposes of SLUSA pre-emption, that distinction is irrelevant; the identity of the plaintiffs does not determine whether the complaint alleges fraud "in connection with the purchase or sale" of securities. The misconduct of which respondent complains here--fraudulent manipulation of stock prices--unquestionably qualifies as fraud "in connection with the purchase or sale" of securities as the phrase is defined in *Zandford, 535 U.S., at 820, 822, 122 S. Ct. 1899, 153 L. Ed. 2d 1*, and *O'Hagan, 521 U.S., at 651*.

The judgment of the Court of Appeals for the Second Circuit is vacated, and the case is remanded for further proceedings consistent with this opinion.

It is so ordered.

APPENDIX I

GOOGLE INC. FORM S–1 REGISTRATION STATEMENT, AUGUST 18, 2004

Table of Contents

As filed with the Securities and Exchange Commission on August 18, 2004

Registration No. 333-114984

SECURITIES AND EXCHANGE COMMISSION
Washington, D.C. 20549

AMENDMENT NO. 9
TO
FORM S-1
REGISTRATION STATEMENT
Under
The Securities Act of 1933

GOOGLE INC.
(Exact name of Registrant as specified in its charter)

Delaware	7375	77-0493581
(State or other jurisdiction of incorporation or organization)	(Primary Standard Industrial Classification Code Number)	(I.R.S. Employer Identification Number)

1600 Amphitheatre Parkway
Mountain View, CA 94043
(650) 623-4000

(Address, including zip code, and telephone number, including area code, of Registrant's principal executive offices)

Eric Schmidt
Chief Executive Officer
Google Inc.
1600 Amphitheatre Parkway
Mountain View, CA 94043
(650) 623-4000

(Name, address, including zip code, and telephone number, including area code, of agent for service)

Copies to:

Larry W. Sonsini, Esq.	David C. Drummond, Esq.	William H. Hinman, Jr., Esq.
David J. Segre, Esq.	Jeffery L. Donovan, Esq.	Simpson Thacher & Bartlett LLP
Wilson Sonsini Goodrich & Rosati	Anna Itoi, Esq.	3330 Hillview Avenue
Professional Corporation	Google Inc.	Palo Alto, California 94304
650 Page Mill Road	1600 Amphitheatre Parkway	(650) 251-5000
Palo Alto, California 94304-1050	Mountain View, CA 94043	
(650) 493-9300	(650) 623-4000	

Approximate date of commencement of proposed sale to the public: As soon as practicable after the effective date of this Registration Statement.

If any of the securities being registered on this Form are being offered on a delayed or continuous basis pursuant to Rule 415 under the Securities Act of 1933, as amended (the "Securities Act"), check the following box. ☐

If this Form is filed to register additional securities for an offering pursuant to Rule 462(b) under the Securities Act, please check the following box and list the Securities Act registration number of the earlier effective registration statement for the same offering. ☐

If this Form is a post-effective amendment filed pursuant to Rule 462(c) under the Securities Act, check the following box and list the Securities Act registration number of the earlier effective registration statement for the same offering. ☐

If this Form is a post-effective amendment filed pursuant to Rule 462(d) under the Securities Act, check the following box and list the Securities Act registration statement number of the earlier effective registration statement for the same offering. ☐

If delivery of the prospectus is expected to be made pursuant to Rule 434, check the following box. ☐

The Registrant hereby amends this Registration Statement on such date or dates as may be necessary to delay its effective date until the Registrant shall file a further amendment which specifically states that this Registration Statement shall thereafter become effective in accordance with Section 8(a) of the Securities Act or until the Registration Statement shall become effective on such date as the Securities and Exchange Commission, acting pursuant to said Section 8(a), may determine.

130 APPENDIX I GOOGLE INC. FORM S–1 REGISTRATION STATEMENT

Table of Contents

The information in this prospectus is not complete and may be changed. We may not sell these securities until the registration statement filed with the Securities and Exchange Commission is effective. This prospectus is not an offer to sell these securities and we are not soliciting any offer to buy these securities in any jurisdiction where the offer or sale is not permitted.

Prospectus (Subject to Completion)
Dated August 18, 2004

19,605,052 Shares

Google

Class A Common Stock

Google Inc. is offering 14,142,135 shares of Class A common stock and the selling stockholders are offering 5,462,917 shares of Class A common stock. We will not receive any proceeds from the sale of shares by the selling stockholders. This is our initial public offering and no public market currently exists for our shares. We anticipate that the initial public offering price will be between $85.00 and $95.00 per share.

Following this offering, we will have two classes of authorized common stock, Class A common stock and Class B common stock. The rights of the holders of Class A common stock and Class B common stock are identical, except with respect to voting and conversion. Each share of Class A common stock is entitled to one vote per share. Each share of Class B common stock is entitled to ten votes per share and is convertible at any time into one share of Class A common stock.

Our Class A common stock has been approved for quotation on The Nasdaq National Market under the symbol "GOOG," subject to official notice of issuance.

Investing in our Class A common stock involves risks. See " Risk Factors" beginning on page 4.

Price $ A Share

	Price to Public	Underwriting Discounts and Commissions	Proceeds to Google	Proceeds to Selling Stockholders
Per Share	$	$	$	$
Total	$	$	$	$

The selling stockholders have granted the underwriters the right to purchase up to an additional 2,940,757 shares to cover over-allotments.

The price to the public and allocation of shares will be determined by an auction process. The minimum size for a bid in the auction will be five shares of our Class A common stock. The method for submitting bids and a more detailed description of this auction process are included in "Auction Process" beginning on page 34. As part of this auction process, we are attempting to assess the market demand for our Class A common stock and to set the size and price to the public of this offering to meet that demand. As a result, buyers should not expect to be able to sell their shares for a profit shortly after our Class A common stock begins trading. We will determine the method for allocating shares to bidders who submitted successful bids following the closing of the auction.

The Securities and Exchange Commission and state securities regulators have not approved or disapproved of these securities, or determined if this prospectus is truthful or complete. Any representation to the contrary is a criminal offense.

It is expected that the shares will be delivered to purchasers on or about August   , 2004.

Morgan Stanley   Credit Suisse First Boston

Goldman, Sachs & Co.   **Citigroup**
Lehman Brothers   **Allen & Company LLC**
JPMorgan   **UBS Investment Bank**
WR Hambrecht+Co   **Thomas Weisel Partners LLC**

Table of Contents

TABLE OF CONTENTS

	Page
Prospectus Summary	1
Risk Factors	4
Special Note Regarding Forward-Looking Statements	26
Letter from the Founders	27
Auction Process	34
How to Participate in the Auction for our IPO	42
Use of Proceeds	44
Dividend Policy	44
Cash and Capitalization	44
Dilution	46
Selected Consolidated Financial Data	48
Management's Discussion and Analysis of Financial Condition and Results of Operations	50
Business	73
Management	87
Certain Relationships and Related Party Transactions	100
Principal and Selling Stockholders	102

	Page
Description of Capital Stock	105
Rescission Offer	111
Shares Eligible for Future Sale	113
Underwriters	117
Notice to Canadian Residents	121
Material United States Federal Tax Considerations for Non-U.S. Holders of Common Stock	122
Legal Matters	124
Experts	124
Where You Can Find Additional Information	124
Index to Consolidated Financial Statements	F-1
Index to Financial Statements of Applied Semantics, Inc.	F-39
Index to Condensed Financial Statements of Applied Semantics Inc.	F-55
Appendix A—Meet the Management Presentation	A-1
Appendix B—September 2004 Magazine Article	B-1

You should rely only on the information contained in this prospectus. We have not authorized anyone to provide you with information that is different from that contained in this prospectus. We are offering to sell, and seeking offers to buy, shares of our Class A common stock only in jurisdictions where offers and sales are permitted. The information in this prospectus is complete and accurate only as of the date of the front cover regardless of the time of delivery of this prospectus or of any sale of shares. Except where the context requires otherwise, in this prospectus, the "Company," "Google," "we," "us" and "our" refer to Google Inc., a Delaware corporation, and, where appropriate, its subsidiaries.

We have not undertaken any efforts to qualify this offering for offers to individual investors in any jurisdiction outside the U.S.; therefore, individual investors located outside the U.S. should not expect to be eligible to participate in this offering.

Until   , 2004, 25 days after the date of this offering, all dealers that effect transactions in our shares, whether or not participating in this offering, may be required to deliver a prospectus. This is in addition to the dealers' obligation to deliver a prospectus when acting as underwriters and with respect to their unsold allotments or subscriptions.

Table of Contents

PROSPECTUS SUMMARY

This summary highlights information contained elsewhere in this prospectus and does not contain all of the information you should consider in making your investment decision. You should read this summary together with the more detailed information, including our financial statements and the related notes, elsewhere in this prospectus. You should carefully consider, among other things, the matters discussed in "Risk Factors."

Google Inc.

Google is a global technology leader focused on improving the ways people connect with information. Our innovations in web search and advertising have made our web site a top Internet destination and our brand one of the most recognized in the world. We maintain the world's largest online index of web sites and other content, and we make this information freely available to anyone with an Internet connection. Our automated search technology helps people obtain nearly instant access to relevant information from our vast online index.

We generate revenue by delivering relevant, cost-effective online advertising. Businesses use our AdWords program to promote their products and services with targeted advertising. In addition, the thousands of third-party web sites that comprise our Google Network use our Google AdSense program to deliver relevant ads that generate revenue and enhance the user experience. Advertisers in our AdWords program pay us a fee each time a user clicks on one of their ads displayed either on our web sites or on the web sites of Google Network members that participate in our AdSense program. When a user clicks on an ad displayed on a web site of a Google Network member, we retain only a small portion of the advertiser fee, while most of the fee is paid to the Google Network member.

Our mission is to organize the world's information and make it universally accessible and useful. We believe that the most effective, and ultimately the most profitable, way to accomplish our mission is to put the needs of our users first. We have found that offering a high-quality user experience leads to increased traffic and strong word-of-mouth promotion. Our dedication to putting users first is reflected in three key commitments we have made to our users:

- We will do our best to provide the most relevant and useful search results possible, independent of financial incentives. Our search results will be objective and we will not accept payment for inclusion or ranking in them.

- We will do our best to provide the most relevant and useful advertising. Whenever someone pays for something, we will make it clear to our users. Advertisements should not be an annoying interruption.

- We will never stop working to improve our user experience, our search technology and other important areas of information organization.

We believe that our user focus is the foundation of our success to date. We also believe that this focus is critical for the creation of long-term value. We do not intend to compromise our user focus for short-term economic gain.

Corporate Information

We were incorporated in California in September 1998. In August 2003, we reincorporated in Delaware. Our principal executive offices are located at 1600 Amphitheatre Parkway, Mountain View, California 94043, and our telephone number is (650) 623-4000. We maintain a number of web sites including www.google.com. The information on our web sites is not part of this prospectus.

Google® is a registered trademark in the U.S. and several other countries. Our unregistered trademarks include: AdSense, AdWords, Blogger, Froogle, Gmail, I'm Feeling Lucky and PageRank. All other trademarks, trade names and service marks appearing in this prospectus are the property of their respective holders.

Table of Contents

The Offering

Class A common stock offered:	
By Google	14,142,135 Shares
By the selling stockholders	5,462,917 Shares
Total	19,605,052 Shares
Class A common stock to be outstanding after this offering	33,603,386 Shares
Class B common stock to be outstanding after this offering	237,616,257 Shares
Total common stock to be outstanding after this offering	271,219,643 Shares
Use of proceeds	We intend to use the net proceeds from this offering for general corporate purposes, including working capital, and possible acquisitions of complementary businesses, technologies or other assets. We will not receive any of the proceeds from the sale of shares by the selling stockholders. See "Use of Proceeds" for additional information.
Proposed Nasdaq symbol	GOOG

The number of shares of Class A and Class B common stock that will be outstanding after this offering is based on the number of shares outstanding at June 30, 2004 and includes (i) 2,700,000 shares of Class A common stock issued to Yahoo! Inc. in connection with a settlement arrangement, (ii) 62,187 shares of Class A common stock that will be sold in the offering by one of our selling stockholders following exercise of a warrant to purchase Class B common stock and (iii) the conversion of the shares of Class B common stock into Class A common stock in connection with this sale, and excludes:

- 1,933,953 shares of Class B common stock issuable upon the exercise of warrants outstanding at June 30, 2004, at a weighted average exercise price of $0.62 per share.

- 6,276,573 shares of Class A common stock issuable upon the exercise of options outstanding at June 30, 2004, at a weighted average exercise price of $9.42 per share.

- 10,456,084 shares of Class B common stock issuable upon the exercise of options outstanding at June 30, 2004, at a weighted average exercise price of $2.68 per share.

- 3,891,192 shares of common stock available for future issuance under our stock option plans at June 30, 2004.

Unless otherwise indicated, all information in this prospectus assumes that the underwriters do not exercise the over-allotment option to purchase 2,940,757 additional shares of Class A common stock in this offering and that all shares of our preferred stock are converted into Class B common stock prior to this offering.

The Auction Process

The auction process being used for our initial public offering differs from methods that have been traditionally used in most other underwritten initial public offerings in the U.S. In particular, the initial public offering price and the allocation of shares will be determined by an auction process conducted by us and our underwriters. You should be aware that we have selected an underwriting group that serves a broad range of the investing public, and each member of the underwriting group makes different suitability determinations with respect to investors participating in the auction process. We encourage you to discuss any questions you have regarding underwriter requirements with the underwriter through which you intend to bid because these requirements could affect your ability to submit a bid. For more information about the auction process, see "Auction Process."

APPENDIX I GOOGLE INC. FORM S–1 REGISTRATION STATEMENT

Summary Consolidated Financial Data

The following table summarizes financial data regarding our business and should be read together with "Management's Discussion and Analysis of Financial Condition and Results of Operations" and our consolidated financial statements and the related notes included elsewhere in this prospectus.

	Year Ended December 31,					Six Months Ended June 30,	
	1999	2000	2001	2002	2003	2003	2004
	(in thousands, except per share data)					(unaudited)	
Consolidated Statements of Operations Data:							
Revenues	$ 220	$ 19,108	$ 86,426	$439,508	$1,465,934	$559,817	$1,351,835
Costs and expenses:							
Cost of revenues	908	6,081	14,228	131,510	625,854	204,596	641,775
Research and development	2,930	10,516	16,500	31,748	91,228	29,997	80,781
Sales and marketing	1,677	10,385	20,076	43,849	120,328	42,589	104,681
General and administrative	1,221	4,357	12,275	24,300	56,699	22,562	47,083
Stock-based compensation	--	2,506	12,383	21,635	229,361	70,583	151,234
Total costs and expenses	6,736	33,845	75,462	253,042	1,123,470	370,327	1,025,554
Income (loss) from operations	(6,516)	(14,737)	10,964	186,466	342,464	189,490	326,281
Interest income (expense) and other, net	440	47	(896)	(1,551)	4,190	719	(1,198)
Income (loss) before income taxes	(6,076)	(14,690)	10,068	184,915	346,654	190,209	325,083
Provision for income taxes	—	—	3,083	85,259	241,006	132,241	182,047
Net income (loss)	$(6,076)	$(14,690)	$ 6,985	$ 99,656	$ 105,648	$ 57,968	$ 143,036
Net income (loss) per share:							
Basic	$ (0.14)	$ (0.22)	$ 0.07	$ 0.86	$ 0.77	$ 0.44	$ 0.93
Diluted	$ (0.14)	$ (0.22)	$ 0.04	$ 0.45	$ 0.41	$ 0.23	$ 0.54
Number of shares used in per share calculations:							
Basic	42,445	67,032	94,523	115,242	137,697	131,525	153,263
Diluted	42,445	67,032	186,776	220,633	256,638	253,024	265,223

The following table presents a summary of our balance sheet data at June 30, 2004:

- On an actual basis.

- On a pro forma as adjusted basis to give effect to the conversion of all outstanding shares of our preferred stock into shares of Class B common stock prior to the closing of this offering and to further give effect to the sale by us of shares of our Class A common stock at an assumed initial public offering price of $ 90.00 per share, and the receipt of the net proceeds from this offering, after deducting estimated underwriting discounts and commissions and estimated offering expenses payable by us, as set forth under "Use of Proceeds" and "Cash and Capitalization."

	At June 30, 2004	
	Actual	Pro Forma as Adjusted
	(in thousands) (unaudited)	
Consolidated Balance Sheet Data:		
Cash, cash equivalents and short-term investments	$ 548,687	$1,775,876
Total assets	1,328,022	2,555,211
Total long-term liabilities	58,766	58,766
Deferred stock-based compensation	(352,815)	(352,815)
Total stockholders' equity	1,016,999	2,244,188

3

RISK FACTORS

An investment in Google involves significant risks. You should read these risk factors carefully before deciding whether to invest in our company. The following is a description of what we consider our key challenges and risks.

Risks Related to Our Business and Industry

We face significant competition from Microsoft and Yahoo.

We face formidable competition in every aspect of our business, and particularly from other companies that seek to connect people with information on the web and provide them with relevant advertising. Currently, we consider our primary competitors to be Microsoft and Yahoo. Microsoft has announced plans to develop a new web search technology that may make web search a more integrated part of the Windows operating system. We expect that Microsoft will increasingly use its financial and engineering resources to compete with us. Yahoo has become an increasingly significant competitor, having acquired Overture Services, which offers Internet advertising solutions that compete with our AdWords and AdSense programs, as well as the Inktomi, AltaVista and AllTheWeb search engines. Since June 2000, Yahoo has used, to varying degrees, our web search technology on its web site to provide web search services to its users. We have notified Yahoo of our election to terminate our agreement effective July 2004. This agreement with Yahoo accounted for less than 3% of our revenues for the year ended December 31, 2003 and less than 2% of our revenues for the six months ended June 30, 2004.

Both Microsoft and Yahoo have more employees than we do (in Microsoft's case, currently more than 20 times as many). Microsoft also has significantly more cash resources than we do. Both of these companies also have longer operating histories and more established relationships with customers. They can use their experience and resources against us in a variety of competitive ways, including by making acquisitions, investing more aggressively in research and development and competing more aggressively for advertisers and web sites. Microsoft and Yahoo also may have a greater ability to attract and retain users than we do because they operate Internet portals with a broad range of products and services. If Microsoft or Yahoo are successful in providing similar or better web search results compared to ours or leverage their platforms to make their web search services easier to access than ours, we could experience a significant decline in user traffic. Any such decline in traffic could negatively affect our revenues.

We face competition from other Internet companies, including web search providers, Internet advertising companies and destination web sites that may also bundle their services with Internet access.

In addition to Microsoft and Yahoo, we face competition from other web search providers, including companies that are not yet known to us. We compete with Internet advertising companies, particularly in the areas of pay-for-performance and keyword-targeted Internet advertising. Also, we may compete with companies that sell products and services online because these companies, like us, are trying to attract users to their web sites to search for information about products and services.

We also compete with destination web sites that seek to increase their search-related traffic. These destination web sites may include those operated by Internet access providers, such as cable and DSL service providers. Because our users need to access our services through Internet access providers, they have direct relationships with these providers. If an access provider or a computer or computing device manufacturer offers online services that compete with ours, the user may find it more convenient to use the services of the access provider or manufacturer. In addition, the access provider or manufacturer may make it hard to access our services by not listing them in the access provider's or manufacturer's own menu of offerings. Also, because the access provider gathers information from the user in connection with the establishment of a billing relationship, the access provider may be more effective than we are in tailoring services and advertisements to the specific tastes of the user.

Table of Contents

There has been a trend toward industry consolidation among our competitors, and so smaller competitors today may become larger competitors in the future. If our competitors are more successful than we are at generating traffic, our revenues may decline.

We face competition from traditional media companies, and we may not be included in the advertising budgets of large advertisers, which could harm our operating results.

In addition to Internet companies, we face competition from companies that offer traditional media advertising opportunities. Most large advertisers have set advertising budgets, a very small portion of which is allocated to Internet advertising. We expect that large advertisers will continue to focus most of their advertising efforts on traditional media. If we fail to convince these companies to spend a portion of their advertising budgets with us, or if our existing advertisers reduce the amount they spend on our programs, our operating results would be harmed.

We expect our growth rates to decline and anticipate downward pressure on our operating margin in the future.

We expect that in the future our revenue growth rate will decline and anticipate that there will be downward pressure on our operating margin. We believe our revenue growth rate will decline as a result of increasing competition and the inevitable decline in growth rates as our revenues increase to higher levels. We believe our operating margin will decline as a result of increasing competition and increased expenditures for all aspects of our business as a percentage of our revenues, including product development and sales and marketing expenses. Our operating margin may decline to the extent the proportion of our revenues generated from our Google Network members increases. The margin on revenue we generate from our Google Network members is generally significantly less than the margin on revenue we generate from advertising on our web sites. Additionally, the margin we earn on revenue generated from our Google Network could decrease in the future if our Google Network members require a greater portion of the advertising fees.

Our operating results may fluctuate, which makes our results difficult to predict and could cause our results to fall short of expectations.

Our operating results may fluctuate as a result of a number of factors, many of which are outside of our control. For these reasons, comparing our operating results on a period-to-period basis may not be meaningful, and you should not rely on our past results as an indication of our future performance. Our quarterly and annual expenses as a percentage of our revenues may be significantly different from our historical or projected rates. Our operating results in future quarters may fall below expectations. Any of these events could cause our stock price to fall. Each of the risk factors listed in this "Risk Factors" section, and the following factors, may affect our operating results:

- Our ability to continue to attract users to our web sites.
- Our ability to attract advertisers to our AdWords program.
- Our ability to attract web sites to our AdSense program.
- The mix in our revenues between those generated on our web sites and those generated through our Google Network.
- The amount and timing of operating costs and capital expenditures related to the maintenance and expansion of our businesses, operations and infrastructure.
- Our focus on long term goals over short term results.
- The results of our investments in risky projects.
- General economic conditions and those economic conditions specific to the Internet and Internet advertising.

Table of Contents

- Our ability to keep our web sites operational at a reasonable cost and without service interruptions.
- Our ability to forecast revenue from agreements under which we guarantee minimum payments.
- Geopolitical events such as war, threat of war or terrorist actions.

Because our business is changing and evolving, our historical operating results may not be useful to you in predicting our future operating results. In addition, advertising spending has historically been cyclical in nature, reflecting overall economic conditions as well as budgeting and buying patterns. For example, in 1999, advertisers spent heavily on Internet advertising. This was followed by a lengthy downturn in ad spending on the web. Also, user traffic tends to be seasonal. Our rapid growth has masked the cyclicality and seasonality of our business. As our growth slows, we expect that the cyclicality and seasonality in our business may become more pronounced and may in the future cause our operating results to fluctuate.

If we do not continue to innovate and provide products and services that are useful to users, we may not remain competitive, and our revenues and operating results could suffer.

Our success depends on providing products and services that people use for a high quality Internet experience. Our competitors are constantly developing innovations in web search, online advertising and providing information to people. As a result, we must continue to invest significant resources in research and development in order to enhance our web search technology and our existing products and services and introduce new high-quality products and services that people will use. If we are unable to predict user preferences or industry changes, or if we are unable to modify our products and services on a timely basis, we may lose users, advertisers and Google Network members. Our operating results would also suffer if our innovations are not responsive to the needs of our users, advertisers and Google Network members, are not appropriately timed with market opportunity or are not effectively brought to market. As search technology continues to develop, our competitors may be able to offer search results that are, or that are perceived to be, substantially similar or better than those generated by our search services. This may force us to compete on bases in addition to quality of search results and to expend significant resources in order to remain competitive.

We generate our revenue almost entirely from advertising, and the reduction in spending by or loss of advertisers could seriously harm our business.

We generated approximately 97% of our revenues in 2003 and 98% of our revenues in the six months ended June 30, 2004 from our advertisers. Our advertisers can generally terminate their contracts with us at any time. Advertisers will not continue to do business with us if their investment in advertising with us does not generate sales leads, and ultimately customers, or if we do not deliver their advertisements in an appropriate and effective manner. If we are unable to remain competitive and provide value to our advertisers, they may stop placing ads with us, which would negatively affect our revenues and business.

We rely on our Google Network members for a significant portion of our revenues, and otherwise benefit from our association with them. The loss of these members could prevent us from receiving the benefits we receive from our association with these Google Network members, which could adversely affect our business.

We provide advertising, web search and other services to members of our Google Network. The revenues generated from the fees advertisers pay us when users click on ads that we have delivered to our Google Network members' web sites represented approximately 43% of our revenues in 2003, and approximately 50% of our revenues for the six months ended June 30, 2004. We consider this network to be critical to the future growth of our revenues. However, some of the participants in this network may compete with us in one or more areas. Therefore, they may decide in the future to terminate their agreements with us. If our Google Network members decide to use a competitor's or their own web search or advertising services, our revenues would decline.

Our agreements with a few of the largest Google Network members account for a significant portion of revenues derived from our AdSense program. In addition, advertising and other fees generated from one Google

Table of Contents

Network member, America Online, Inc., primarily through our AdSense program accounted for approximately 15%, 16% and 13% of our revenues in 2002, 2003 and in the six months ended June 30, 2004. Also, certain of our key network members operate high-profile web sites, and we derive tangible and intangible benefits from this affiliation. If one or more of these key relationships is terminated or not renewed, and is not replaced with a comparable relationship, our business would be adversely affected.

Our business and operations are experiencing rapid growth. If we fail to effectively manage our growth, our business and operating results could be harmed and we may have to incur significant expenditures to address the additional operational and control requirements of this growth.

We have experienced, and continue to experience, rapid growth in our headcount and operations, which has placed, and will continue to place, significant demands on our management, operational and financial infrastructure. If we do not effectively manage our growth, the quality of our products and services could suffer, which could negatively affect our brand and operating results. To effectively manage this growth, we will need to continue to improve our operational, financial and management controls and our reporting systems and procedures. These systems enhancements and improvements will require significant capital expenditures and allocation of valuable management resources. If the improvements are not implemented successfully, our ability to manage our growth will be impaired and we may have to make significant additional expenditures to address these issues, which could harm our financial position. The required improvements include:

- Enhancing our information and communication systems to ensure that our offices around the world are well coordinated and that we can effectively communicate with our growing base of users, advertisers and Google Network members.
- Enhancing systems of internal controls to ensure timely and accurate reporting of all of our operations.
- Documenting all of our information technology systems and our business processes for our ad systems and our billing systems.
- Improving our information technology infrastructure to maintain the effectiveness of our search systems.

If we fail to maintain an effective system of internal controls, we may not be able to accurately report our financial results or prevent fraud. As a result, current and potential stockholders could lose confidence in our financial reporting, which would harm our business and the trading price of our stock.

Effective internal controls are necessary for us to provide reliable financial reports and effectively prevent fraud. If we cannot provide reliable financial reports or prevent fraud, our brand and operating results could be harmed. We have in the past discovered, and may in the future discover, areas of our internal controls that need improvement. For example, during our 2002 audit, our external auditors brought to our attention a need to increase restrictions on employee access to our advertising system and automate more of our financial processes. The auditors identified these issues together as a "reportable condition," which means that these were matters that in the auditors' judgment could adversely affect our ability to record, process, summarize and report financial data consistent with the assertions of management in the financial statements. In 2003, we devoted significant resources to remediate and improve our internal controls. Although we believe that these efforts have strengthened our internal controls and addressed the concerns that gave rise to the "reportable condition" in 2002, we are continuing to work to improve our internal controls, including in the areas of access and security. We cannot be certain that these measures will ensure that we implement and maintain adequate controls over our financial processes and reporting in the future. Any failure to implement required new or improved controls, or difficulties encountered in their implementation, could harm our operating results or cause us to fail to meet our reporting obligations. Inferior internal controls could also cause investors to lose confidence in our reported financial information, which could have a negative effect on the trading price of our stock.

Table of Contents

We intend to migrate critical financial functions to a third-party provider. If this potential transition is not successful, our business and operations could be disrupted and our operating results would be harmed.

We have entered into an arrangement to transfer our worldwide billing, collection and credit evaluation functions to a third-party service provider, Bertelsmann AG; however, we cannot be sure that the arrangement will be completed and implemented. The third-party provider will also track, on an automated basis, a majority of our growing number of AdSense revenue share agreements. These functions are critical to our operations and involve sensitive interactions between us and our advertisers and members of our Google Network. If we do not successfully implement this project, our business, reputation and operating results could be harmed. We have no experience managing and implementing this type of large-scale, cross-functional, international infrastructure project. We also may not be able to integrate our systems and processes with those of the third-party service provider on a timely basis, or at all. Even if this integration is completed on time, the service provider may not perform to agreed upon service levels. Failure of the service provider to perform satisfactorily could result in customer dissatisfaction, disrupt our operations and adversely affect operating results. We will have significantly less control over the systems and processes than if we maintained and operated them ourselves, which increases our risk. If we need to find an alternative source for performing these functions, we may have to expend significant resources in doing so, and we cannot guarantee this would be accomplished in a timely manner or without significant additional disruption to our business.

Our business depends on a strong brand, and if we are not able to maintain and enhance our brand, our ability to expand our base of users, advertisers and Google Network members will be impaired and our business and operating results will be harmed.

We believe that the brand identity that we have developed has significantly contributed to the success of our business. We also believe that maintaining and enhancing the "Google" brand is critical to expanding our base of users, advertisers and Google Network members. Maintaining and enhancing our brand may require us to make substantial investments and these investments may not be successful. If we fail to promote and maintain the "Google" brand, or if we incur excessive expenses in this effort, our business, operating results and financial condition will be materially and adversely affected. We anticipate that, as our market becomes increasingly competitive, maintaining and enhancing our brand may become increasingly difficult and expensive. Maintaining and enhancing our brand will depend largely on our ability to be a technology leader and to continue to provide high quality products and services, which we may not do successfully. To date, we have engaged in relatively little direct brand promotion activities. This enhances the risk that we may not successfully implement brand enhancement efforts in the future.

People have in the past expressed, and may in the future express, objections to aspects of our products. For example, people have raised privacy concerns relating to the ability of our recently announced Gmail email service to match relevant ads to the content of email messages. Some people have also reacted negatively to the fact that our search technology can be used to help people find hateful or derogatory information on the web. Aspects of our future products may raise similar public concerns. Publicity regarding such concerns could harm our brand. In addition, members of the Google Network and other third parties may take actions that could impair the value of our brand. We are aware that third parties, from time to time, use "Google" and similar variations in their domain names without our approval, and our brand may be harmed if users and advertisers associate these domains with us.

Proprietary document formats may limit the effectiveness of our search technology by preventing our technology from accessing the content of documents in such formats which could limit the effectiveness of our products and services.

An increasing amount of information on the Internet is provided in proprietary document formats such as Microsoft Word. The providers of the software application used to create these documents could engineer the document format to prevent or interfere with our ability to access the document contents with our search technology. This would mean that the document contents would not be included in our search results even if the contents were directly relevant to a search. These types of activities could assist our competitors or diminish the

Table of Contents

value of our search results. The software providers may also seek to require us to pay them royalties in exchange for giving us the ability to search documents in their format. If the software provider also competes with us in the search business, they may give their search technology a preferential ability to search documents in their proprietary format. Any of these results could harm our brand and our operating results.

New technologies could block our ads, which would harm our business.

Technologies may be developed that can block the display of our ads. Most of our revenues are derived from fees paid to us by advertisers in connection with the display of ads on web pages. As a result, ad-blocking technology could, in the future, adversely affect our operating results.

Our corporate culture has contributed to our success, and if we cannot maintain this culture as we grow, we could lose the innovation, creativity and teamwork fostered by our culture, and our business may be harmed.

We believe that a critical contributor to our success has been our corporate culture, which we believe fosters innovation, creativity and teamwork. As our organization grows, and we are required to implement more complex organizational management structures, we may find it increasingly difficult to maintain the beneficial aspects of our corporate culture. This could negatively impact our future success. In addition, this offering may create disparities in wealth among Google employees, which may adversely impact relations among employees and our corporate culture in general.

Our intellectual property rights are valuable, and any inability to protect them could reduce the value of our products, services and brand.

Our patents, trademarks, trade secrets, copyrights and all of our other intellectual property rights are important assets for us. There are events that are outside of our control that pose a threat to our intellectual property rights. For example, effective intellectual property protection may not be available in every country in which our products and services are distributed or made available through the Internet. Also, the efforts we have taken to protect our proprietary rights may not be sufficient or effective. Any significant impairment of our intellectual property rights could harm our business or our ability to compete. Also, protecting our intellectual property rights is costly and time consuming. Any increase in the unauthorized use of our intellectual property could make it more expensive to do business and harm our operating results.

We seek to obtain patent protection for our innovations. It is possible, however, that some of these innovations may not be protectable. In addition, given the costs of obtaining patent protection, we may choose not to protect certain innovations that later turn out to be important. Furthermore, there is always the possibility, despite our efforts, that the scope of the protection gained will be insufficient or that an issued patent may be deemed invalid or unenforceable.

We also face risks associated with our trademarks. For example, there is a risk that the word "Google" could become so commonly used that it becomes synonymous with the word "search." If this happens, we could lose protection for this trademark, which could result in other people using the word "Google" to refer to their own products, thus diminishing our brand.

We also seek to maintain certain intellectual property as trade secrets. The secrecy could be compromised by third parties, or intentionally or accidentally by our employees, which would cause us to lose the competitive advantage resulting from these trade secrets.

We are, and may in the future be, subject to intellectual property rights claims, which are costly to defend, could require us to pay damages and could limit our ability to use certain technologies in the future.

Companies in the Internet, technology and media industries own large numbers of patents, copyrights, trademarks and trade secrets and frequently enter into litigation based on allegations of infringement or other

9

violations of intellectual property rights. As we face increasing competition, the possibility of intellectual property rights claims against us grows. Our technologies may not be able to withstand any third-party claims or rights against their use. Any intellectual property claims, with or without merit, could be time-consuming, expensive to litigate or settle and could divert management resources and attention. In addition, many of our agreements with members of our Google Network require us to indemnify these members for third-party intellectual property infringement claims, which would increase our costs as a result of defending such claims and may require that we pay damages if there were an adverse ruling in any such claims. An adverse determination also could prevent us from offering our products and services to others and may require that we procure substitute products or services for these members.

With respect to any intellectual property rights claim, we may have to pay damages or stop using technology found to be in violation of a third party's rights. We may have to seek a license for the technology, which may not be available on reasonable terms and may significantly increase our operating expenses. The technology also may not be available for license to us at all. As a result, we may also be required to develop alternative non-infringing technology, which could require significant effort and expense. If we cannot license or develop technology for the infringing aspects of our business, we may be forced to limit our product and service offerings and may be unable to compete effectively. Any of these results could harm our brand and operating results.

From time to time, we receive notice letters from patent holders alleging that certain of our products and services infringe their patent rights. Some of these have resulted in litigation against us. For example, Overture Services (now owned by Yahoo) sued us, claiming that the Google AdWords program infringes certain claims of an Overture Services patent. It also claimed that the patent relates to Overture Services' own bid-for-ad placement business model and its pay-for-performance technologies. We recently settled this dispute.

Companies have also filed trademark infringement and related claims against us over the display of ads in response to user queries that include trademark terms. The outcomes of these lawsuits have differed from jurisdiction to jurisdiction. A court in France has held us liable for allowing advertisers to select certain trademarked terms as keywords. We have appealed this decision. We were also subject to two lawsuits in Germany on similar matters where one court preliminarily reached a similar conclusion as the court in France, while another court held that we are not liable for the actions of our advertisers prior to notification of trademark rights. We are litigating similar issues in other cases in the U.S., France, Germany and Italy.

In order to provide users with more useful ads, we have recently revised our trademark policy in the U.S. and Canada. Under our new policy, we no longer disable ads due to selection by our advertisers of trademarks as keyword triggers for the ads. As a result of this change in policy, we may be subject to more trademark infringement lawsuits. Defending these lawsuits could take time and resources. Adverse results in these lawsuits may result in, or even compel, a change in this practice which could result in a loss of revenue for us, which could harm our business.

We have also been notified by third parties that they believe features of certain of our products, including Google WebSearch, Google News and Google Image Search, violate their copyrights. Generally speaking, any time that we have a product or service that links to or hosts material in which others allege to own copyrights, we face the risk of being sued for copyright infringement or related claims. Because these products and services comprise the majority of our products and services, the risk of potential harm from such lawsuits is substantial.

Expansion into international markets is important to our long-term success, and our inexperience in the operation of our business outside the U.S. increases the risk that our international expansion efforts will not be successful.

We opened our first office outside the U.S. in 2001 and have only limited experience with operations outside the U.S. Expansion into international markets requires management attention and resources. In addition, we face the following additional risks associated with our expansion outside the U.S.:

- Challenges caused by distance, language and cultural differences.

Table of Contents

- Longer payment cycles in some countries.
- Credit risk and higher levels of payment fraud.
- Legal and regulatory restrictions.
- Currency exchange rate fluctuations.
- Foreign exchange controls that might prevent us from repatriating cash earned in countries outside the U.S.
- Political and economic instability and export restrictions.
- Potentially adverse tax consequences.
- Higher costs associated with doing business internationally.

These risks could harm our international expansion efforts, which would in turn harm our business and operating results.

We compete internationally with local information providers and with U.S. competitors who are currently more successful than we are in various markets, and if we fail to compete effectively in international markets, our business will be harmed.

We face different market characteristics and competition outside the U.S. In certain markets, other web search, advertising services and Internet companies have greater brand recognition, more users and more search traffic than we have. Even in countries where we have a significant user following, we may not be as successful in generating advertising revenue due to slower market development, our inability to provide attractive local advertising services or other factors. In order to compete, we need to improve our brand recognition and our selling efforts internationally and build stronger relationships with advertisers. We also need to better understand our international users and their preferences. If we fail to do so, our global expansion efforts may be more costly and less profitable than we expect.

Our business may be adversely affected by malicious third-party applications that interfere with our receipt of information from, and provision of information to, our users, which may impair our users' experience with our products and services.

Our business may be adversely affected by malicious applications that make changes to our users' computers and interfere with the Google experience. These applications have in the past attempted, and may in the future attempt, to change our users' Internet experience, including hijacking queries to Google.com, altering or replacing Google search results, or otherwise interfering with our ability to connect with our users. The interference often occurs without disclosure to or consent from users, resulting in a negative experience that users may associate with Google. These applications may be difficult or impossible to uninstall or disable, may reinstall themselves and may circumvent other applications' efforts to block or remove them. The ability to reach users and provide them with a superior experience is critical to our success. If our efforts to combat these malicious applications are unsuccessful, our reputation may be harmed, and our communications with certain users could be impaired. This could result in a decline in user traffic and associated ad revenues, which would damage our business.

If we fail to detect click-through fraud, we could lose the confidence of our advertisers, thereby causing our business to suffer.

We are exposed to the risk of fraudulent clicks on our ads by persons seeking to increase the advertising fees paid to our Google Network members. We have regularly refunded revenue that our advertisers have paid to us and that was later attributed to click-through fraud, and we expect to do so in the future. Click-through fraud occurs when a person clicks on a Google AdWords ad displayed on a web site in order to generate the revenue share payment to the Google Network member rather than to view the underlying content. If we are unable to stop this fraudulent activity, these refunds may increase. If we find new evidence of past fraudulent clicks we may have to issue refunds retroactively of amounts previously paid to our Google Network members. This would negatively affect our profitability, and these types of fraudulent activities could hurt our brand. If fraudulent clicks are not detected, the affected advertisers may experience a reduced return on their investment in our advertising programs because the fraudulent clicks will not lead to potential revenue for the advertisers. This could lead the advertisers to become dissatisfied with our advertising programs, which could lead to loss of advertisers and revenue.

Index spammers could harm the integrity of our web search results, which could damage our reputation and cause our users to be dissatisfied with our products and services.

There is an ongoing and increasing effort by "index spammers" to develop ways to manipulate our web search results. For example, because our web search technology ranks a web page's relevance based in part on the importance of the web sites that link to it, people have attempted to link a group of web sites together to manipulate web search results. We take this problem very seriously because providing relevant information to users is critical to our success. If our efforts to combat these and other types of index spamming are unsuccessful, our reputation for delivering relevant information could be diminished. This could result in a decline in user traffic, which would damage our business.

Privacy concerns relating to elements of our technology could damage our reputation and deter current and potential users from using our products and services.

From time to time, concerns may be expressed about whether our products and services compromise the privacy of users and others. Concerns about our collection, use or sharing of personal information or other privacy-related matters, even if unfounded, could damage our reputation and operating results. Recently, several groups have raised privacy concerns in connection with our Gmail free email service which we announced in April 2004 and these concerns have attracted a significant amount of public commentary and attention. The concerns relate principally to the fact that Gmail uses computers to match advertisements to the content of a user's email message when email messages are viewed using the Gmail service. Privacy concerns have also arisen with our products that provide improved access to personal information that is already publicly available, but that we have made more readily accessible by the public.

Our business is subject to a variety of U.S. and foreign laws, which could subject us to claims or other remedies based on the nature and content of the information searched or displayed by our products and services, and could limit our ability to provide information regarding regulated industries and products.

The laws relating to the liability of providers of online services for activities of their users are currently unsettled both within the U.S. and abroad. Claims have been threatened and filed under both U.S. and foreign law for defamation, libel, invasion of privacy and other data protection claims, tort, unlawful activity, copyright or trademark infringement, or other theories based on the nature and content of the materials searched and the ads posted or the content generated by our users. From time to time we have received notices from individuals who do not want their names or web sites to appear in our web search results when certain keywords are searched. It is also possible that we could be held liable for misinformation provided over the web when that information appears in our web search results. If one of these complaints results in liability to us, it could be potentially costly, encourage similar lawsuits, distract management and harm our reputation and possibly our business. In addition, increased attention focused on these issues and legislative proposals could harm our reputation or otherwise affect the growth of our business.

The application to us of existing laws regulating or requiring licenses for certain businesses of our advertisers, including, for example, distribution of pharmaceuticals, adult content, financial services, alcohol or firearms, can be unclear. Existing or new legislation could expose us to substantial liability, restrict our ability to

Table of Contents

deliver services to our users, limit our ability to grow and cause us to incur significant expenses in order to comply with such laws and regulations.

Several other federal laws could have an impact on our business. Compliance with these laws and regulations is complex and may impose significant additional costs on us. For example, the Digital Millennium Copyright Act has provisions that limit, but do not eliminate, our liability for listing or linking to third-party web sites that include materials that infringe copyrights or other rights, so long as we comply with the statutory requirements of this act. The Children's Online Protection Act and the Children's Online Privacy Protection Act restrict the distribution of materials considered harmful to children and impose additional restrictions on the ability of online services to collect information from minors. In addition, the Protection of Children from Sexual Predators Act of 1998 requires online service providers to report evidence of violations of federal child pornography laws under certain circumstances. Any failure on our part to comply with these regulations may subject us to additional liabilities.

We also face risks associated with international data protection. The interpretation and application of data protection laws in Europe and elsewhere are still uncertain and in flux. It is possible that these laws may be interpreted and applied in a manner that is inconsistent with our data practices. If so, in addition to the possibility of fines, this could result in an order requiring that we change our data practices, which in turn could have a material effect on our business.

We also face risks from legislation that could be passed in the future. For example, at least two states have introduced legislation that could interfere with or prohibit our Gmail free advertising-supported email service that was recently announced as a test service. The legislation, as originally proposed in California and Massachusetts, would make it more difficult for us to operate or would prohibit the aspects of the service that uses computers to match advertisements to the content of a user's email message when email messages are viewed using the Gmail service. While the California legislation has been modified since being introduced so that it does not inhibit the operation of the Gmail service, the legislation has not been finally adopted. If this legislation is adopted as originally introduced, or other similar legislation is adopted, it could prevent us from implementing the Gmail service in the affected states. This could impair our ability to compete in the email services market.

If we were to lose the services of Eric, Larry, Sergey or our senior management team, we may not be able to execute our business strategy.

Our future success depends in a large part upon the continued service of key members of our senior management team. In particular, our CEO Eric Schmidt and our founders Larry Page and Sergey Brin are critical to the overall management of Google as well as the development of our technology, our culture and our strategic direction. All of our executive officers and key employees are at-will employees, and we do not maintain any key-person life insurance policies. The loss of any of our management or key personnel could seriously harm our business.

The initial option grants to many of our senior management and key employees are fully vested. Therefore, these employees may not have sufficient financial incentive to stay with us, we may have to incur costs to replace key employees that leave, and our ability to execute our business model could be impaired if we cannot replace departing employees in a timely manner.

Many of our senior management personnel and other key employees have become, or will soon become, substantially vested in their initial stock option grants. While we often grant additional stock options to management personnel and other key employees after their hire dates to provide additional incentives to remain employed by us, their initial grants are usually much larger than follow-on grants. Employees may be more likely to leave us after their initial option grant fully vests, especially if the shares underlying the options have significantly appreciated in value relative to the option exercise price. We have not given any additional grants to Eric, Larry or Sergey. Larry and Sergey are fully vested, and only a small portion of Eric's stock is subject to

Table of Contents

future vesting. If any members of our senior management team leave the company, our ability to successfully operate our business could be impaired. We also may have to incur significant costs in identifying, hiring, training and retaining replacements for departing employees.

We rely on highly skilled personnel and, if we are unable to retain or motivate key personnel or hire qualified personnel, we may not be able to grow effectively.

Our performance is largely dependent on the talents and efforts of highly skilled individuals. Our future success depends on our continuing ability to identify, hire, develop, motivate and retain highly skilled personnel for all areas of our organization. Competition in our industry for qualified employees is intense, and we are aware that certain of our competitors have directly targeted our employees. Our continued ability to compete effectively depends on our ability to attract new employees and to retain and motivate our existing employees.

We have in the past maintained a rigorous, highly selective and time-consuming hiring process. We believe that our approach to hiring has significantly contributed to our success to date. As we grow, our hiring process may prevent us from hiring the personnel we need in a timely manner. In addition, as we become a more mature company, we may find our recruiting efforts more challenging. The incentives to attract, retain and motivate employees provided by our option grants or by future arrangements, such as through cash bonuses, may not be as effective as in the past. If we do not succeed in attracting excellent personnel or retaining or motivating existing personnel, we may be unable to grow effectively.

Our CEO and our two founders run the business and affairs of the company collectively, which may harm their ability to manage effectively.

Eric, our CEO, and Larry and Sergey, our founders and presidents, currently provide leadership to the company as a team. Our bylaws provide that our CEO and our presidents will together have general supervision, direction and control of the company, subject to the control of our board of directors. As a result, Eric, Larry and Sergey tend to operate the company collectively and to consult extensively with each other before significant decisions are made. This may slow the decision-making process, and a disagreement among these individuals could prevent key strategic decisions from being made in a timely manner. In the event our CEO and our two founders are unable to continue to work well together in providing cohesive leadership, our business could be harmed.

We have a short operating history and a relatively new business model in an emerging and rapidly evolving market. This makes it difficult to evaluate our future prospects, may increase the risk that we will not continue to be successful and increases the risk of your investment.

We first derived revenue from our online search business in 1999 and from our advertising services in 2000, and we have only a short operating history with our cost-per-click advertising model, which we launched in 2002. As a result, we have very little operating history for you to evaluate in assessing our future prospects. Also, we derive nearly all of our revenues from online advertising, which is an immature industry that has undergone rapid and dramatic changes in its short history. You must consider our business and prospects in light of the risks and difficulties we will encounter as an early-stage company in a new and rapidly evolving market. We may not be able to successfully address these risks and difficulties, which could materially harm our business and operating results.

We may have difficulty scaling and adapting our existing architecture to accommodate increased traffic and technology advances or changing business requirements, which could lead to the loss of users, advertisers and Google Network members, and cause us to incur expenses to make architectural changes.

To be successful, our network infrastructure has to perform well and be reliable. The greater the user traffic and the greater the complexity of our products and services, the more computing power we will need. In 2004, we expect to spend substantial amounts to purchase or lease data centers and equipment and to upgrade our technology and network infrastructure to handle increased traffic on our web sites and to roll out new products and services. This expansion is going to be expensive and complex and could result in inefficiencies or operational failures. If we do not implement this expansion successfully, or if we experience inefficiencies and operational failures during the implementation, the quality of our products and services and our users' experience could decline. This could damage our reputation and lead us to lose current and potential users, advertisers and Google Network members. The costs associated with these adjustments to our architecture could harm our operating results. Cost increases, loss of traffic or failure to accommodate new technologies or changing business requirements could harm our operating results and financial condition.

We rely on bandwidth providers, data centers or other third parties for key aspects of the process of providing products and services to our users, and any failure or interruption in the services and products provided by these third parties could harm our ability to operate our business and damage our reputation.

We rely on third-party vendors, including data center and bandwidth providers. Any disruption in the network access or co-location services provided by these third-party providers or any failure of these third-party providers to handle current or higher volumes of use could significantly harm our business. Any financial or other difficulties our providers face may have negative effects on our business, the nature and extent of which we cannot predict. We exercise little control over these third party vendors, which increases our vulnerability to problems with the services they provide. We license technology and related databases from third parties to facilitate aspects of our data center and connectivity operations including, among others, Internet traffic management services. We have experienced and expect to continue to experience interruptions and delays in service and availability for such elements. Any errors, failures, interruptions or delays experienced in connection with these third-party technologies and information services could negatively impact our relationship with users and adversely affect our brand and our business and could expose us to liabilities to third parties.

Our systems are also heavily reliant on the availability of electricity, which also comes from third-party providers. If we were to experience a major power outage, we would have to rely on back-up generators. These back-up generators may not operate properly through a major power outage and their fuel supply could also be inadequate during a major power outage. This could result in a disruption of our business.

Interruption or failure of our information technology and communications systems could impair our ability to effectively provide our products and services, which could damage our reputation and harm our operating results.

Our provision of our products and services depends on the continuing operation of our information technology and communications systems. Any damage to or failure of our systems could result in interruptions in our service. Interruptions in our service could reduce our revenues and profits, and our brand could be damaged if people believe our system is unreliable. Our systems are vulnerable to damage or interruption from earthquakes, terrorist attacks, floods, fires, power loss, telecommunications failures, computer viruses, computer denial of service attacks or other attempts to harm our systems, and similar events. Some of our data centers are located in areas with a high risk of major earthquakes. Our data centers are also subject to break-ins, sabotage and intentional acts of vandalism, and to potential disruptions if the operators of these facilities have financial difficulties. Some of our systems are not fully redundant, and our disaster recovery planning cannot account for all eventualities. The occurrence of a natural disaster, a decision to close a facility we are using without adequate notice for financial reasons or other unanticipated problems at our data centers could result in lengthy interruptions in our service.

We have experienced system failures in the past and may in the future. For example, in November 2003 we failed to provide web search results for approximately 20% of our traffic for a period of about 30 minutes. Any unscheduled interruption in our service puts a burden on our entire organization and would result in an immediate loss of revenue. If we experience frequent or persistent system failures on our web sites, our reputation and brand could be permanently harmed. The steps we have taken to increase the reliability and redundancy of our systems are expensive, reduce our operating margin and may not be successful in reducing the frequency or duration of unscheduled downtime.

More individuals are using non-PC devices to access the Internet, and versions of our web search technology developed for these devices may not be widely adopted by users of these devices.

The number of people who access the Internet through devices other than personal computers, including mobile telephones, hand-held calendaring and email assistants, and television set-top devices, has increased dramatically in the past few years. The lower resolution, functionality and memory associated with alternative devices make the use of our products and services through such devices difficult. If we are unable to attract and retain a substantial number of alternative device users to our web search services or if we are slow to develop products and technologies that are more compatible with non-PC communications devices, we will fail to capture a significant share of an increasingly important portion of the market for online services.

If we account for employee stock options using the fair value method, it could significantly reduce our net income.

There has been ongoing public debate whether stock options granted to employees should be treated as a compensation expense and, if so, how to properly value such charges. On March 31, 2004, the Financial Accounting Standard Board (FASB) issued an Exposure Draft, *Share-Based Payment: an amendment of FASB Statements No. 123 and 95*, which would require a company to recognize, as an expense, the fair value of stock options and other stock-based compensation to employees beginning in 2005 and subsequent reporting periods. Currently, we record deferred stock-based compensation to the extent that the reassessed value for accounting purposes of the stock on the date of grant exceeds the exercise price of the option. We recognize compensation expense as we amortize the deferred stock-based compensation amounts on an accelerated basis over the related vesting periods. If we had used the fair value method of accounting for stock options granted to employees prior to July 1, 2004 using a Black Scholes option valuation formula, our net income would have been $2.4 million less than reported in the year ended December 31, 2003 and $2.8 million less than reported in the six months ended June 30, 2004. If we elect or are required to record an expense for our stock-based compensation plans using the fair value method as described in the Exposure Draft, we could have on-going accounting charges significantly greater than those we would have recorded under our current method of accounting for stock options. See Note 1 of Notes to Consolidated Financial Statements included in this prospectus for a more detailed presentation of accounting for stock-based compensation plans.

Payments to certain of our Google Network members has exceeded the related fees we receive from our advertisers.

We have entered into, and may continue to enter into, minimum fee guarantee agreements with a small number of Google Network members. In these agreements, we promise to make minimum payments to the Google Networks member for a pre-negotiated period of time, typically from three months to a year or more. It is difficult to forecast with certainty the fees that we will earn under our agreements, and sometimes the fees we earn fall short of the minimum guarantee payment amounts. Also, increasing competition for arrangements with web sites that are potential Google Network members could result in our entering into more of these minimum fee guarantee agreements under which guaranteed payments exceed the fees we receive from advertisers whose ads we place on those Google Network member sites. In each period to date, the aggregate fees we have earned under these agreements have exceeded the aggregate amounts we have been obligated to pay to the Google Network members. However, individual agreements have resulted in guaranteed minimum and other payments to a Google Network member in excess of the related fees we receive from advertisers. In 2003, we recognized $22.5 million in cost of revenues related to such payments in excess of revenues for such agreements. In the six months ended June 30, 2004, we recognized $18.2 million in cost of revenues related to such payments in excess of revenues for such agreements. At December 31, 2003 and June 30, 2004, our

Table of Contents

aggregate outstanding minimum guarantee commitments totaled approximately $477.0 million and $369.4 million. These commitments expire between 2004 and 2007. We may recognize cost of revenues related to payments to certain Google Network members in excess of the related fees we receive from advertisers in the future in connection with certain AdSense agreements, which could adversely affect our profitability.

To the extent our revenues are paid in foreign currencies, and currency exchange rates become unfavorable, we may lose some of the economic value of the revenues in U.S. dollar terms.

As we expand our international operations, more of our customers may pay us in foreign currencies. Conducting business in currencies other than U.S. dollars subjects us to fluctuations in currency exchange rates. If the currency exchange rates were to change unfavorably, the value of net receivables we receive in foreign currencies and later convert to U.S. dollars after the unfavorable change would be diminished. This could have a negative impact on our reported operating results. Hedging strategies, such as forward contracts, options and foreign exchange swaps related to transaction exposures, that we may implement to mitigate this risk may not eliminate our exposure to foreign exchange fluctuations. Additionally, hedging programs expose us to risks that could adversely affect our operating results, including the following:

- We have limited experience in implementing or operating hedging programs. Hedging programs are inherently risky and we could lose money as a result of poor trades.

- We may be unable to hedge currency risk for some transactions because of a high level of uncertainty or the inability to reasonably estimate our foreign exchange exposures.

- We may be unable to acquire foreign exchange hedging instruments in some of the geographic areas where we do business, or, where these derivatives are available, we may not be able to acquire enough of them to fully offset our exposure.

We rely on insurance to mitigate some risks and, to the extent the cost of insurance increases or we are unable to maintain sufficient insurance to mitigate the risks, our operating results may be diminished.

We contract for insurance to cover potential risks and liabilities. In the current environment, insurance companies are increasingly specific about what they will and will not insure. It is possible that we may not be able to get enough insurance to meet our needs, may have to pay very high prices for the coverage we do get or may not be able to acquire any insurance for certain types of business risk. This could leave us exposed to potential claims. If we were found liable for a significant claim in the future, our operating results could be negatively impacted. Also, to the extent the cost of maintaining insurance increases, our operating results will be negatively affected.

Acquisitions could result in operating difficulties, dilution and other harmful consequences.

We do not have a great deal of experience acquiring companies and the companies we have acquired have been small. We have evaluated, and expect to continue to evaluate, a wide array of potential strategic transactions. From time to time, we may engage in discussions regarding potential acquisitions. Any of these transactions could be material to our financial condition and results of operations. In addition, the process of integrating an acquired company, business or technology may create unforeseen operating difficulties and expenditures and is risky. The areas where we may face risks include:

- The need to implement or remediate controls, procedures and policies appropriate for a larger public company at companies that prior to the acquisition lacked these controls, procedures and policies.

- Diversion of management time and focus from operating our business to acquisition integration challenges.

- Cultural challenges associated with integrating employees from the acquired company into our organization.

Table of Contents

- Retaining employees from the businesses we acquire.

- The need to integrate each company's accounting, management information, human resource and other administrative systems to permit effective management.

Foreign acquisitions involve unique risks in addition to those mentioned above, including those related to integration of operations across different cultures and languages, currency risks and the particular economic, political and regulatory risks associated with specific countries. Also, the anticipated benefit of many of our acquisitions may not materialize. Future acquisitions or dispositions could result in potentially dilutive issuances of our equity securities, the incurrence of debt, contingent liabilities or amortization expenses, or write-offs of goodwill, any of which could harm our financial condition. Future acquisitions may require us to obtain additional equity or debt financing, which may not be available on favorable terms or at all.

We occasionally become subject to commercial disputes that could harm our business by distracting our management from the operation of our business, by increasing our expenses and, if we do not prevail, by subjecting us to potential monetary damages and other remedies.

From time to time we are engaged in disputes regarding our commercial transactions. These disputes could result in monetary damages or other remedies that could adversely impact our financial position or operations. Even if we prevail in these disputes, they may distract our management from operating our business and the cost of defending these disputes would reduce our operating results.

We have to keep up with rapid technological change to remain competitive in our rapidly evolving industry.

Our future success will depend on our ability to adapt to rapidly changing technologies, to adapt our services to evolving industry standards and to improve the performance and reliability of our services. Our failure to adapt to such changes would harm our business. New technologies and advertising media could adversely affect us. In addition, the widespread adoption of new Internet, networking or telecommunications technologies or other technological changes could require substantial expenditures to modify or adapt our services or infrastructure.

Our business depends on increasing use of the Internet by users searching for information, advertisers marketing products and services and web sites seeking to earn revenue to support their web content. If the Internet infrastructure does not grow and is not maintained to support these activities, our business will be harmed.

Our success will depend on the continued growth and maintenance of the Internet infrastructure. This includes maintenance of a reliable network backbone with the necessary speed, data capacity and security for providing reliable Internet services. Internet infrastructure may be unable to support the demands placed on it if the number of Internet users continues to increase, or if existing or future Internet users access the Internet more often or increase their bandwidth requirements. In addition, viruses, worms and similar programs may harm the performance of the Internet. The Internet has experienced a variety of outages and other delays as a result of damage to portions of its infrastructure, and it could face outages and delays in the future. These outages and delays could reduce the level of Internet usage as well as our ability to provide our solutions.

Shares issued and options granted under our stock plans exceeded limitations in federal and state securities laws, the result of which is that the holders of these shares and/or options may have rescission rights that could require us to reacquire the shares and/or options for an aggregate repurchase price of up to $25.9 million.

Shares issued and options granted under our 1998 Stock Plan, our 2003 Stock Plan, our 2003 Stock Plan (No. 2) and our 2003 Stock Plan (No. 3) from September 2001 through July 2004 may not have been exempt from registration or qualification under federal securities laws and the securities laws of certain states. Certain

Table of Contents

of the shares issued during this period may not have been exempt from registration and qualification requirements under Rule 701 under the Securities Act of 1933 and under those state securities laws that provide an exemption to the extent the requirements under Rule 701 are met. We became aware that we were approaching the numeric limitations prescribed by Rule 701 in September 2002 and thereafter determined that we could not continue to count on being able to rely on Rule 701 to provide an exemption from the registration requirements of the Securities Act of 1933. In addition, continued compliance under Rule 701 would have required broad dissemination of detailed financial information regarding our business, which would have been strategically disadvantageous to our company. In evaluating how to issue stock upon exercise of outstanding options in light of these limitations we determined we would utilize "private placement" exemptions provided by Section 4(2) of the Securities Act of 1933 in order to exempt these issuances from federal registration requirements notwithstanding the factual and legal uncertainties inherent in Section 4(2). These uncertainties arise because analyzing whether or not issuances of securities qualify for the exemptions afforded by Section 4(2) involves a number of subjective determinations including whether the number of offerees constitutes a general solicitation, the financial sophistication of offerees and their access to information regarding the issuer, as well as whether the offering was designed to result in a distribution of shares to the general public. We considered various alternatives in determining to rely on the exemption provided by Section 4(2) despite its inherent uncertainties. We considered ceasing granting options and shares to service providers. However, we determined that this would be detrimental to our development, as equity compensation was an essential ingredient to building our company. We also considered becoming a reporting company for the purposes of federal securities laws. We determined that this too would be contrary to the best interests of our stockholders. We therefore concluded that relying on Section 4(2) despite its uncertainties was in the best interest of our security holders. Because of this uncertainty, the options we granted and the shares issued upon exercise of these options during this period may have been issued in violation of either federal or state securities laws, or both, and may be subject to rescission. In order to address this issue, we intend to make a rescission offer to the holders of these shares and options as soon as practicable after the completion of the offering of our Class A common stock and, in any event within 30 days of the effective date of this registration statement, assuming the offering has been completed at such time. We will be making this rescission offer to 1,406 persons who are or were residents of Arkansas, California, Colorado, Connecticut, the District of Columbia, Georgia, Illinois, Maryland, Massachusetts, Michigan, Nevada, New Hampshire, New Jersey, New York, North Carolina, Pennsylvania, Texas, Virginia and Washington.

If this rescission offer is accepted, we could be required to make aggregate payments to the holders of these shares and options of up to $25.9 million, which includes statutory interest. For options, this exposure reflects the costs of offering to rescind the issuance of the outstanding options by paying an amount equal to 20% of the aggregate exercise price for the entire option, plus statutory interest. However, it is possible that an optionholder could argue that this does not represent an adequate remedy for the issuance of the option in violation of applicable securities laws, and if a court were to impose a greater remedy, our exposure as a result of the rescission offer could be higher. For issuances of common stock, this exposure is calculated by reference to the acquisition price of the common stock, plus statutory interest. Federal securities laws do not provide that a rescission offer will terminate a purchaser's right to rescind a sale of stock that was not registered as required or was not otherwise exempt from such registration requirements. If any or all of the offerees reject the rescission offer, we may continue to be liable under federal and state securities laws for up to an amount equal to the value of all options and common stock granted or issued since September 2001 plus any statutory interest we may be required to pay. We also understand that the Securities and Exchange Commission has initiated an informal inquiry into this matter and certain state regulators, including California, have requested additional information. If it is determined that we offered securities without properly registering them under federal or state law, or securing an exemption from registration, regulators could impose monetary fines or other sanctions as provided under these laws. See "Rescission Offer."

Risks Related to the Auction Process for Our Offering

Our stock price could decline rapidly and significantly.

Our initial public offering price will be determined by an auction process conducted by us and our underwriters. We believe this auction process will provide information with respect to the market demand for our

Table of Contents

Class A common stock at the time of our initial public offering. However, this information may have no relation to market demand for our Class A common stock once trading begins. We expect that the bidding process will reveal a clearing price for shares of our Class A common stock offered in the auction. The auction clearing price is the highest price at which all of the shares offered (including shares subject to the underwriters' over-allotment option) may be sold to potential investors. Although we and our underwriters may elect to set the initial public offering price below the auction clearing price, we intend to set an initial public offering price that is equal to the clearing price. If there is little or no demand for our shares at or above the initial public offering price once trading begins, the price of our shares would decline following our initial public offering.

The auction process for our public offering may result in a phenomenon known as the "winner's curse," and, as a result, investors may experience significant losses.

The auction process for our initial public offering may result in a phenomenon known as the "winner's curse." At the conclusion of the auction, bidders that receive allocations of shares in this offering (successful bidders) may infer that there is little incremental demand for our shares above or equal to the initial public offering price. As a result, successful bidders may conclude that they paid too much for our shares and could seek to immediately sell their shares to limit their losses should our stock price decline. In this situation, other investors that did not submit successful bids may wait for this selling to be completed, resulting in reduced demand for our Class A common stock in the public market and a significant decline in our stock price. Therefore, we caution investors that submitting successful bids and receiving allocations may be followed by a significant decline in the value of their investment in our Class A common stock shortly after our offering.

The auction process for our initial public offering may result in a situation in which less price sensitive investors play a larger role in the determination of our offering price and constitute a larger portion of the investors in our offering, and, therefore, the offering price may not be sustainable once trading of our Class A common stock begins.

In a typical initial public offering, a majority of the shares sold to the public are purchased by professional investors that have significant experience in determining valuations for companies in connection with initial public offerings. These professional investors typically have access to, or conduct their own independent, research and analysis regarding investments in initial public offerings. Other investors typically have less access to this level of research and analysis, and as a result, may be less sensitive to price in participating in our auction process. Because of our auction process and the broad consumer awareness of Google, these less price sensitive investors may have a greater influence in setting our initial public offering price and may have a higher level of participation in our offering than is normal for initial public offerings. This, in turn, could cause our auction process to result in an initial public offering price that is higher than the prices professional investors are willing to pay. As a result, our stock price may decrease once trading of our Class A common stock begins. Also, because professional investors may have a substantial degree of influence on the trading price of our shares over time, the price of our Class A common stock may decline after our offering. Further, if our initial public offering price is above the level that investors determine is reasonable for our shares, some investors may attempt to short the stock after trading begins, which would create additional downward pressure on the trading price of our Class A common stock.

Successful bidders should not expect to sell our shares for a profit shortly after our Class A common stock begins trading.

During the bidding process, we and our managing underwriters will monitor the master order book to evaluate the demand that exists for our initial public offering. Based on this information, we and our underwriters may revise the price range for our initial public offering set forth on the cover of this prospectus. In addition, we and the selling stockholders may decide to change the number of shares of Class A common stock offered through this prospectus. These increases in the initial public offering price and the number of shares offered may result in there being little or no demand for our shares at or above the initial public offering price. If this were to occur, the price of our shares would decline following this offering. If your objective is to make a short term profit by selling the shares you purchase in the offering shortly after trading begins, you should not submit a bid in the auction.

Table of Contents

Successful bidders may receive the full number of shares subject to their bids, so potential investors should not make bids for more shares than they are prepared to purchase.

We and our underwriters will conduct an auction to assess the demand for our shares of Class A common stock. We intend to set the initial public offering price equal to the auction clearing price. If we do this, the number of shares represented by successful bids will likely equal the number of shares offered by this prospectus, and successful bidders may be allocated all of the shares that they bid for in the auction. Therefore, we caution investors against submitting a bid that does not accurately represent the number of shares of our Class A common stock that they are willing and prepared to purchase.

Our initial public offering price may have little or no relationship to the price that would be established using traditional valuation methods, and therefore, the initial public offering price may not be sustainable once trading begins.

We intend to set an initial public offering price that is equal to the auction clearing price. The offering price of our shares may have little or no relationship to the price that would be established using traditional indicators of value, such as our future prospects and those of our industry in general; our sales, earnings and other financial and operating information; multiples of earnings, cash flows and other operating metrics; market prices of securities and other financial and operating information of companies engaged in activities similar to ours; and the views of research analysts. As a result, our initial public offering price may not be sustainable once trading begins, and the price of our Class A common stock may decline.

If research analysts publish or establish target prices for our Class A common stock that are below the initial public offering price or then current trading market price of our shares, the price of our shares of Class A common stock may fall.

Although the initial public offering price of our shares may have little or no relationship to the price determined using traditional valuation methods, we believe that research analysts will rely upon these methods to establish target prices for our Class A common stock. If research analysts, including research analysts affiliated with our underwriters, publish target prices for our Class A common stock that are below our initial public offering price or the then current trading market price of our shares, it could cause our stock price to decline significantly.

Submitting a bid does not guarantee an allocation of shares of our Class A common stock, even if a bidder submits a bid at or above the initial public offering price.

Our underwriters may require that bidders confirm their bids before the auction for our initial public offering closes. If a bidder is requested to confirm a bid and fails to do so, that bid will be rejected and will not receive an allocation of shares even if the bid is at or above the initial public offering price. In addition, we, in consultation with our underwriters, may determine, in our sole discretion, that some bids that are at or above the initial public offering price are manipulative and disruptive to the bidding process, in which case such bids will be rejected.

The systems and procedures used to implement our auction and the results of our auction could harm our business and our brand.

Only a small number of initial public offerings have been accomplished using auction processes in the U.S. and other countries, and none on the scale of our offering. We expect our auction structure to face scalability and operational challenges. Our underwriters' systems that manage the auction process could fail to operate as anticipated. This could require us to delay our initial public offering, potentially even after our underwriters have started taking bids, and harm our brand. Our underwriters must modify their internal systems and procedures to accommodate our auction process. This could increase the risk that our underwriters' systems or procedures fail to operate as anticipated.

Table of Contents

Many of our users may submit bids in our auction with the hope of becoming stockholders. If these users either do not receive share allocations in our offering or if our share price immediately declines after the offering, our brand could be tarnished and users and investors could become frustrated with us, potentially decreasing their use of our products and services. If this occurs, our business could suffer.

Risks Related to Our Offering

If our involvement in a September 2004 magazine article about Google were held to be in violation of the Securities Act of 1933, we could be required to repurchase securities sold in this offering. You should rely only on statements made in this prospectus in determining whether to purchase our shares.

Information about Google has been published in an article appearing in the September 2004 issue of *Playboy Magazine* and entitled "Playboy Interview: Google Guys." The text of the article, which is included in this prospectus as Appendix B, contains information derived from an interview of Larry and Sergey conducted in April 2004, prior to the filing of our registration statement of which this prospectus is a part. The article includes quotations from Larry and Sergey, and has been reprinted by a number of news media outlets. The article presented certain statements about our company in isolation and did not disclose many of the related risks and uncertainties described in this prospectus. As a result, the article should not be considered in isolation and you should make your investment decision only after reading this entire prospectus carefully.

You should carefully evaluate all the information in this prospectus, including the risks described in this section and throughout the prospectus. We have in the past received, and may continue to receive, a high degree of media coverage, including coverage that is not directly attributable to statements made by our officers and employees. You should rely only on the information contained in this prospectus in making your investment decision.

We do not believe that our involvement in the *Playboy Magazine* article constitutes a violation of Section 5 of the Securities Act of 1933. However, if our involvement were held by a court to be in violation of the Securities Act of 1933, we could be required to repurchase the shares sold to purchasers in this offering at the original purchase price, plus statutory interest from the date of purchase, for a period of one year following the date of the violation. We would contest vigorously any claim that a violation of the Securities Act occurred. The SEC has also requested additional information concerning the publication of the article.

Investors should be aware of the following modifications and updates to the article's content:

- The article states that our Gmail service, with one gigabyte of storage, has 200 times more storage than our primary competitors. While at the time of its introduction, Gmail had such a substantial storage capacity advantage over competitive offerings, competitors have substantially narrowed the gap.

- The article indicates that we had about 1,000 employees. Currently, we have approximately 2,292 employees.

- The article states that more than 65 million people use our search engine each day. We believe that, based on data compiled by an unrelated third party research organization, this number represents monthly, not daily, domestic visitors data.

Our stock price may be volatile, and you may not be able to resell shares of our Class A common stock at or above the price you paid.

Prior to this offering, our common stock has not been traded in a public market. We cannot predict the extent to which a trading market will develop or how liquid that market might become. The initial public offering price may not be indicative of prices that will prevail in the trading market. The trading price of our Class A common stock following this offering is therefore likely to be highly volatile and could be subject to wide fluctuations in price in response to various factors, some of which are beyond our control. These factors include:

- Quarterly variations in our results of operations or those of our competitors.

- Announcements by us or our competitors of acquisitions, new products, significant contracts, commercial relationships or capital commitments.

Table of Contents

- Disruption to our operations or those of our Google Network members or our data centers.
- The emergence of new sales channels in which we are unable to compete effectively.
- Our ability to develop and market new and enhanced products on a timely basis.
- Commencement of, or our involvement in, litigation.
- Any major change in our board or management.
- Changes in governmental regulations or in the status of our regulatory approvals.
- Changes in earnings estimates or recommendations by securities analysts.
- General economic conditions and slow or negative growth of related markets.

In addition, the stock market in general, and the market for technology companies in particular, have experienced extreme price and volume fluctuations that have often been unrelated or disproportionate to the operating performance of those companies. Such fluctuations may be even more pronounced in the trading market shortly following this offering. These broad market and industry factors may seriously harm the market price of our Class A common stock, regardless of our actual operating performance. In addition, in the past, following periods of volatility in the overall market and the market price of a company's securities, securities class action litigation has often been instituted against these companies. This litigation, if instituted against us, could result in substantial costs and a diversion of our management's attention and resources.

Future sales of shares by our stockholders could cause our stock price to decline.

We cannot predict the effect, if any, that market sales of shares or the availability of shares for sale will have on the market price prevailing from time to time. Sales of our Class A common stock in the public market after the restrictions described in this prospectus lapse, or the perception that those sales may occur, could cause the trading price of our stock to decrease or to be lower than it might be in the absence of those sales or perceptions. Based on shares outstanding as of June 30, 2004, upon completion of this offering, we will have outstanding 271,219,643 shares of common stock, assuming no exercise of the underwriters' over-allotment option. We have entered into contractual lock-up agreements with our officers, directors and certain employees and other securityholders, representing the holders of substantially all of our outstanding capital stock. We may, in our sole discretion, permit our officers, directors, employees and current stockholders who are subject to contractual lock-up agreements with us to sell shares prior to the expiration of their lock-up agreements. None of our officers, directors, employees or stockholders have entered into contractual lock-up agreements with the underwriters in connection with this offering. In addition, our employees can only sell vested shares.

We have filed or plan to file shortly after the offering registration statements on Form S-8 and Form S-8/S-3, and a registration statement on Form S-1 relating to our rescission offer. As a result of these registration statements, the selling restriction agreements between us and our stockholders that are described in "Shares Eligible For Future Sale" and the provisions of Rules 144, 144(k) and 701, the restricted securities will first become available for sale in the public market as follows:

Days After the Date of this Prospectus	Additional Shares Eligible for Public Sale
At 15 days after the date of this prospectus and various times thereafter	4,575,048
At 90 days after the date of this prospectus and various times thereafter	39,081,106
At 120 days after the date of this prospectus and various times thereafter	24,874,091
At 150 days after the date of this prospectus and various times thereafter	24,874,091
At 180 days after the date of this prospectus and various times thereafter	176,876,866

147,349,935 of these shares are held by directors, executive officers and other affiliates and will be subject to volume limitations under Rule 144 under the Securities Act of 1933 and various vesting agreements. If these additional shares are sold, or if it is perceived that they will be sold, in the public market, the trading price of our common stock could decline. The selling restriction agreements between us and our stockholders will allow significantly more shares to become freely tradeable soon after completion of the offering than is typical of initial public offerings.

In addition, we have agreed with our underwriters not to sell any shares of our common stock for a period of 180 days after the date of this prospectus. However, this agreement is subject to a number of exceptions, including an exception that allows us to issue an unlimited number of shares in connection with mergers and acquisition transactions, joint ventures or other strategic transactions. Morgan Stanley & Co. Incorporated and Credit Suisse First Boston LLC, on behalf of the underwriters, may release us from this lock-up arrangement without notice at any time. After the expiration of the 180-day period, there is no contractual restriction on our ability to issue additional shares. Any sales of common stock by us, or the perception that such sales could occur, could cause our stock price to decline.

We may apply the proceeds of this offering to uses that do not improve our operating results or increase the value of your investment.

We intend to use the net proceeds from this offering for general corporate purposes, including working capital and capital expenditures. We may also use a portion of the net proceeds to acquire or invest in companies and technologies that we believe will complement our business. However, we do not have more specific plans for the net proceeds from this offering and will have broad discretion in how we use the net proceeds of this offering. These proceeds could be applied in ways that do not improve our operating results or increase the value of your investment.

Purchasers in this offering will experience immediate and substantial dilution in the book value of their investment.

The initial public offering price of our Class A common stock is substantially higher than the net tangible book value per share of our Class A common stock immediately after this offering. Therefore, if you purchase our Class A common stock in this offering, you will incur an immediate dilution of $82.11 in net tangible book value per share from the price you paid, based on the initial offering price of $90.00 per share. The exercise of outstanding options and warrants will result in further dilution. For a further description of the dilution that you will experience immediately after this offering, please see "Dilution."

We do not intend to pay dividends on our common stock.

We have never declared or paid any cash dividend on our capital stock. We currently intend to retain any future earnings and do not expect to pay any dividends in the foreseeable future.

We will incur increased costs as a result of being a public company.

As a public company, we will incur significant legal, accounting and other expenses that we did not incur as a private company. We will incur costs associated with our public company reporting requirements. We also anticipate that we will incur costs associated with recently adopted corporate governance requirements, including requirements under the Sarbanes-Oxley Act of 2002, as well as new rules implemented by the Securities and Exchange Commission and the NASD. We expect these rules and regulations to increase our legal and financial compliance costs and to make some activities more time-consuming and costly. We also expect these new rules and regulations may make it more difficult and more expensive for us to obtain director and officer liability insurance and we may be required to accept reduced policy limits and coverage or incur substantially higher costs to obtain the same or similar coverage. As a result, it may be more difficult for us to attract and retain qualified individuals to serve on our board of directors or as executive officers. We are currently evaluating and monitoring developments with respect to these new rules, and we cannot predict or estimate the amount of additional costs we may incur or the timing of such costs.

The concentration of our capital stock ownership with our founders, executive officers, employees, and our directors and their affiliates will limit your ability to influence corporate matters.

After our offering, our Class B common stock will have ten votes per share and our Class A common stock, which is the stock we are selling in this offering, will have one vote per share. We anticipate that our founders,

Table of Contents

executive officers, directors (and their affiliates) and employees will together own approximately 84.8% of our Class B common stock, representing approximately 83.6% of the voting power of our outstanding capital stock. In particular, following this offering, our two founders and our CEO, Larry, Sergey and Eric, will control approximately 38.1% of our outstanding Class B common stock, representing approximately 37.6% of the voting power of our outstanding capital stock. Larry, Sergey and Eric will therefore have significant influence over management and affairs and over all matters requiring stockholder approval, including the election of directors and significant corporate transactions, such as a merger or other sale of our company or its assets, for the foreseeable future. In addition, because of this dual class structure, our founders, directors, executives and employees will continue to be able to control all matters submitted to our stockholders for approval even if they come to own less than 50% of the outstanding shares of our common stock. This concentrated control will limit your ability to influence corporate matters and, as a result, we may take actions that our stockholders do not view as beneficial. As a result, the market price of our Class A common stock could be adversely affected.

Provisions in our charter documents and under Delaware law could discourage a takeover that stockholders may consider favorable.

Provisions in our certificate of incorporation and bylaws, as amended and restated upon the closing of this offering, may have the effect of delaying or preventing a change of control or changes in our management. These provisions include the following:

- Our certificate of incorporation provides for a dual class common stock structure. As a result of this structure our founders, executives and employees will have significant influence over all matters requiring stockholder approval, including the election of directors and significant corporate transactions, such as a merger or other sale of our company or its assets. This concentrated control could discourage others from initiating any potential merger, takeover or other change of control transaction that other stockholders may view as beneficial.

- Our board of directors has the right to elect directors to fill a vacancy created by the expansion of the board of directors or the resignation, death or removal of a director, which prevents stockholders from being able to fill vacancies on our board of directors.

- Our stockholders may not act by written consent. As a result, a holder, or holders, controlling a majority of our capital stock would not be able to take certain actions without holding a stockholders' meeting.

- Our certificate of incorporation prohibits cumulative voting in the election of directors. This limits the ability of minority stockholders to elect director candidates.

- Stockholders must provide advance notice to nominate individuals for election to the board of directors or to propose matters that can be acted upon at a stockholders' meeting. These provisions may discourage or deter a potential acquiror from conducting a solicitation of proxies to elect the acquiror's own slate of directors or otherwise attempting to obtain control of our company.

- Our board of directors may issue, without stockholder approval, shares of undesignated preferred stock. The ability to authorize undesignated preferred stock makes it possible for our board of directors to issue preferred stock with voting or other rights or preferences that could impede the success of any attempt to acquire us.

As a Delaware corporation, we are also subject to certain Delaware anti-takeover provisions. Under Delaware law, a corporation may not engage in a business combination with any holder of 15% or more of its capital stock unless the holder has held the stock for three years or, among other things, the board of directors has approved the transaction. Our board of directors could rely on Delaware law to prevent or delay an acquisition of us. For a description of our capital stock, see "Description of Capital Stock."

25

Table of Contents

SPECIAL NOTE REGARDING FORWARD-LOOKING STATEMENTS

This prospectus includes forward-looking statements. All statements other than statements of historical facts contained in this prospectus, including statements regarding our future financial position, business strategy and plans and objectives of management for future operations, are forward-looking statements. The words "believe," "may," "will," "estimate," "continue," "anticipate," "intend," "expect" and similar expressions are intended to identify forward-looking statements. We have based these forward-looking statements largely on our current expectations and projections about future events and financial trends that we believe may affect our financial condition, results of operations, business strategy, short term and long term business operations and objectives, and financial needs. In addition, a number of our "objectives," "intentions," "expectations" or "goals" described in "Auction Process" for qualification of bidders, the bidding process, the auction closing process, the pricing process and the allocation process are also forward-looking statements. These statements are based on current expectations or objectives of the auction process being used for our initial public offering that are inherently uncertain. These forward-looking statements are subject to a number of risks, uncertainties and assumptions, including those described in "Risk Factors."

In light of these risks, uncertainties and assumptions, the forward-looking events and circumstances discussed in this prospectus may not occur and actual results could differ materially and adversely from those anticipated or implied in the forward-looking statements.

Table of Contents

LETTER FROM THE FOUNDERS
"AN OWNER'S MANUAL" FOR GOOGLE'S SHAREHOLDERS[1]

INTRODUCTION

Google is not a conventional company. We do not intend to become one. Throughout Google's evolution as a privately held company, we have managed Google differently. We have also emphasized an atmosphere of creativity and challenge, which has helped us provide unbiased, accurate and free access to information for those who rely on us around the world.

Now the time has come for the company to move to public ownership. This change will bring important benefits for our employees, for our present and future shareholders, for our customers, and most of all for Google users. But the standard structure of public ownership may jeopardize the independence and focused objectivity that have been most important in Google's past success and that we consider most fundamental for its future. Therefore, we have implemented a corporate structure that is designed to protect Google's ability to innovate and retain its most distinctive characteristics. We are confident that, in the long run, this will benefit Google and its shareholders, old and new. We want to clearly explain our plans and the reasoning and values behind them. We are delighted you are considering an investment in Google and are reading this letter.

Sergey and I intend to write you a letter like this one every year in our annual report. We'll take turns writing the letter so you'll hear directly from each of us. We ask that you read this letter in conjunction with the rest of this prospectus.

SERVING END USERS

Sergey and I founded Google because we believed we could provide an important service to the world—instantly delivering relevant information on virtually any topic. Serving our end users is at the heart of what we do and remains our number one priority.

Our goal is to develop services that significantly improve the lives of as many people as possible. In pursuing this goal, we may do things that we believe have a positive impact on the world, even if the near term financial returns are not obvious. For example, we make our services as widely available as we can by supporting over 90 languages and by providing most services for free. Advertising is our principal source of revenue, and the ads we provide are relevant and useful rather than intrusive and annoying. We strive to provide users with great commercial information.

We are proud of the products we have built, and we hope that those we create in the future will have an even greater positive impact on the world.

LONG TERM FOCUS

As a private company, we have concentrated on the long term, and this has served us well. As a public company, we will do the same. In our opinion, outside pressures too often tempt companies to sacrifice long term opportunities to meet quarterly market expectations. Sometimes this pressure has caused companies to manipulate financial results in order to "make their quarter." In Warren Buffett's words, "We won't 'smooth' quarterly or annual results: If earnings figures are lumpy when they reach headquarters, they will be lumpy when they reach you."

If opportunities arise that might cause us to sacrifice short term results but are in the best long term interest of our shareholders, we will take those opportunities. We will have the fortitude to do this. We would request that our shareholders take the long term view.

---

[1] Much of this was inspired by Warren Buffett's essays in his annual reports and his "An Owner's Manual" to Berkshire Hathaway shareholders.

Table of Contents

You might ask how long is long term? Usually we expect projects to have some realized benefit or progress within a year or two. But, we are trying to look forward as far as we can. Despite the quickly changing business and technology landscape, we try to look at three to five year scenarios in order to decide what to do now. We try to optimize total benefit over these multi-year scenarios. While we are strong advocates of this strategy, it is difficult to make good multi-year predictions in technology.

Many companies are under pressure to keep their earnings in line with analysts' forecasts. Therefore, they often accept smaller, predictable earnings rather than larger and less predictable returns. Sergey and I feel this is harmful, and we intend to steer in the opposite direction.

Google has had adequate cash to fund our business and has generated additional cash through operations. This gives us the flexibility to weather costs, benefit from opportunities and optimize our long term earnings. For example, in our ads system we make many improvements that affect revenue in both directions. These are in areas like end user relevance and satisfaction, advertiser satisfaction, partner needs and targeting technology. We release improvements immediately rather than delaying them, even though delay might give "smoother" financial results. You have our commitment to execute quickly to achieve long term value rather than making the quarters more predictable.

Our long term focus does have risks. Markets may have trouble evaluating long term value, thus potentially reducing the value of our company. Our long term focus may simply be the wrong business strategy. Competitors may be rewarded for short term tactics and grow stronger as a result. As potential investors, you should consider the risks around our long term focus.

We will make business decisions with the long term welfare of our company and shareholders in mind and not based on accounting considerations.

Although we may discuss long term trends in our business, we do not plan to give earnings guidance in the traditional sense. We are not able to predict our business within a narrow range for each quarter. We recognize that our duty is to advance our shareholders' interests, and we believe that artificially creating short term target numbers serves our shareholders poorly. We would prefer not to be asked to make such predictions, and if asked we will respectfully decline. A management team distracted by a series of short term targets is as pointless as a dieter stepping on a scale every half hour.

RISK VS REWARD IN THE LONG RUN

Our business environment changes rapidly and needs long term investment. We will not hesitate to place major bets on promising new opportunities.

We will not shy away from high-risk, high-reward projects because of short term earnings pressure. Some of our past bets have gone extraordinarily well, and others have not. Because we recognize the pursuit of such projects as the key to our long term success, we will continue to seek them out. For example, we would fund projects that have a 10% chance of earning a billion dollars over the long term. Do not be surprised if we place smaller bets in areas that seem very speculative or even strange when compared to our current businesses. Although we cannot quantify the specific level of risk we will undertake, as the ratio of reward to risk increases, we will accept projects further outside our current businesses, especially when the initial investment is small relative to the level of investment in our current businesses.

We encourage our employees, in addition to their regular projects, to spend 20% of their time working on what they think will most benefit Google. This empowers them to be more creative and innovative. Many of our significant advances have happened in this manner. For example, AdSense for content and Google News were both prototyped in "20% time." Most risky projects fizzle, often teaching us something. Others succeed and become attractive businesses.

Table of Contents

As we seek to maximize value in the long term, we may have quarter-to-quarter volatility as we realize losses on some new projects and gains on others. We would love to better quantify our level of risk and reward for you going forward, but that is very difficult. Even though we are excited about risky projects, we expect to devote the vast majority of our resources to improvements to our main businesses (currently search and advertising). Most employees naturally gravitate toward incremental improvements in core areas so this tends to happen naturally.

EXECUTIVE ROLES

We run Google as a triumvirate. Sergey and I have worked closely together for the last eight years, five at Google. Eric, our CEO, joined Google three years ago. The three of us run the company collaboratively with Sergey and me as Presidents. The structure is unconventional, but we have worked successfully in this way.

To facilitate timely decisions, Eric, Sergey and I meet daily to update each other on the business and to focus our collaborative thinking on the most important and immediate issues. Decisions are often made by one of us, with the others being briefed later. This works because we have tremendous trust and respect for each other and we generally think alike. Because of our intense long term working relationship, we can often predict differences of opinion among the three of us. We know that when we disagree, the correct decision is far from obvious. For important decisions, we discuss the issue with a larger team appropriate to the task. Differences are resolved through discussion and analysis and by reaching consensus. Eric, Sergey and I run the company without any significant internal conflict, but with healthy debate. As different topics come up, we often delegate decision-making responsibility to one of us.

We hired Eric as a more experienced complement to Sergey and me to help us run the business. Eric was CTO of Sun Microsystems. He was also CEO of Novell and has a Ph.D. in computer science, a very unusual and important combination for Google given our scientific and technical culture. This partnership among the three of us has worked very well and we expect it to continue. The shared judgments and extra energy available from all three of us has significantly benefited Google.

Eric has the legal responsibilities of the CEO and focuses on management of our vice presidents and the sales organization. Sergey focuses on engineering and business deals. I focus on engineering and product management. All three of us devote considerable time to overall management of the company and other fluctuating needs. We also have a distinguished board of directors to oversee the management of Google. We have a talented executive staff that manages day-to-day operations in areas such as finance, sales, engineering, human resources, public relations, legal and product management. We are extremely fortunate to have talented management that has grown the company to where it is today—they operate the company and deserve the credit.

CORPORATE STRUCTURE

We are creating a corporate structure that is designed for stability over long time horizons. By investing in Google, you are placing an unusual long term bet on the team, especially Sergey and me, and on our innovative approach.

We want Google to become an important and significant institution. That takes time, stability and independence. We bridge the media and technology industries, both of which have experienced considerable consolidation and attempted hostile takeovers.

In the transition to public ownership, we have set up a corporate structure that will make it harder for outside parties to take over or influence Google. This structure will also make it easier for our management team to follow the long term, innovative approach emphasized earlier. This structure, called a dual class voting structure, is described elsewhere in this prospectus. The Class A common stock we are offering has one vote per share, while the Class B common stock held by many current shareholders has 10 votes per share.

Table of Contents

The main effect of this structure is likely to leave our team, especially Sergey and me, with increasingly significant control over the company's decisions and fate, as Google shares change hands. After the IPO, Sergey, Eric and I will control 37.6% of the voting power of Google, and the executive management team and directors as a group will control 61.4% of the voting power. New investors will fully share in Google's long term economic future but will have little ability to influence its strategic decisions through their voting rights.

While this structure is unusual for technology companies, similar structures are common in the media business and has had a profound importance there. The New York Times Company, The Washington Post Company and Dow Jones, the publisher of *The Wall Street Journal*, all have similar dual class ownership structures. Media observers have pointed out that dual class ownership has allowed these companies to concentrate on their core, long term interest in serious news coverage, despite fluctuations in quarterly results. Berkshire Hathaway has implemented a dual class structure for similar reasons. From the point of view of long term success in advancing a company's core values, we believe this structure has clearly been an advantage.

Some academic studies have shown that from a purely economic point of view, dual class structures have not harmed the share price of companies. Other studies have concluded that dual class structures have negatively affected share prices, and we cannot assure you that this will not be the case with Google. The shares of each of our classes have identical economic rights and differ only as to voting rights.

Google has prospered as a private company. We believe a dual class voting structure will enable Google, as a public company, to retain many of the positive aspects of being private. We understand some investors do not favor dual class structures. Some may believe that our dual class structure will give us the ability to take actions that benefit us, but not Google's shareholders as a whole. We have considered this point of view carefully, and we and the board have not made our decision lightly. We are convinced that everyone associated with Google—including new investors—will benefit from this structure. However, you should be aware that Google and its shareholders may not realize these intended benefits.

In addition, we have recently expanded our board of directors to include three additional members. John Hennessy is the President of Stanford and has a Doctoral degree in computer science. Art Levinson is CEO of Genentech and has a Ph.D. in biochemistry. Paul Otellini is President and COO of Intel. We could not be more excited about the caliber and experience of these directors.

We believe we have a world class management team impassioned by Google's mission and responsible for Google's success. We believe the stability afforded by the dual class structure will enable us to retain our unique culture and continue to attract and retain talented people who are Google's life blood. Our colleagues will be able to trust that they themselves and their labors of hard work, love and creativity will be well cared for by a company focused on stability and the long term.

As an investor, you are placing a potentially risky long term bet on the team, especially Sergey and me. The two of us, Eric and the rest of the management team recognize that our individual and collective interests are deeply aligned with those of the new investors who choose to support Google. Sergey and I are committed to Google for the long term. The broader Google team has also demonstrated an extraordinary commitment to our long term success. With continued hard work and good fortune, this commitment will last and flourish.

When Sergey and I founded Google, we hoped, but did not expect, it would reach its current size and influence. Our intense and enduring interest was to objectively help people find information efficiently. We also believed that searching and organizing all the world's information was an unusually important task that should be carried out by a company that is trustworthy and interested in the public good. We believe a well functioning society should have abundant, free and unbiased access to high quality information. Google therefore has a responsibility to the world. The dual class structure helps ensure that this responsibility is met. We believe that fulfilling this responsibility will deliver increased value to our shareholders.

Table of Contents

IPO PRICING AND ALLOCATION

It is important to us to have a fair process for our IPO that is inclusive of both small and large investors. It is also crucial that we achieve a good outcome for Google and its current shareholders. This has led us to pursue an auction-based IPO for our entire offering. Our goal is to have a share price that reflects an efficient market valuation of Google that moves rationally based on changes in our business and the stock market. (The auction process is discussed in more detail elsewhere in this prospectus.)

Many companies going public have suffered from unreasonable speculation, small initial share float, and stock price volatility that hurt them and their investors in the long run. We believe that our auction-based IPO will minimize these problems, though there is no guarantee that it will.

An auction is an unusual process for an IPO in the United States. Our experience with auction-based advertising systems has been helpful in the auction design process for the IPO. As in the stock market, if people bid for more shares than are available and bid at high prices, the IPO price will be higher. Of course, the IPO price will be lower if there are not enough bidders or if people bid lower prices. This is a simplification, but it captures the basic issues. Our goal is to have the price of our shares at the IPO and in the aftermarket reflect an efficient market price—in other words, a price set by rational and informed buyers and sellers. We seek to achieve a relatively stable price in the days following the IPO and that buyers and sellers receive an efficient market price at the IPO. We will try to achieve this outcome, but of course may not be successful. Our goal of achieving a relatively stable market price may result in Google determining with our underwriters to set the initial public offering price below the auction clearing price.

We are working to create a sufficient supply of shares to meet investor demand at IPO time and after. We are encouraging current shareholders to consider selling some of their shares as part of the offering. These shares will supplement the shares the company sells to provide more supply for investors and hopefully provide a more stable price. Sergey and I, among others, are currently planning to sell a fraction of our shares in the IPO. The more shares current shareholders sell, the more likely it is that they believe the price is not unfairly low. The supply of shares available will likely have an effect on the clearing price of the auction. Since the number of shares being sold is likely to be larger at a high price and smaller at a lower price, investors will likely want to consider the scope of current shareholder participation in the IPO. We may communicate from time to time that we are sellers rather than buyers at certain prices.

While we have designed our IPO to be inclusive for both small and large investors, for a variety of reasons described in "Auction Process" not all interested investors will be able to receive an allocation of shares in our IPO.

We would like you to invest for the long term, and you should not expect to sell Google shares for a profit shortly after Google's IPO. We encourage investors not to invest in Google at IPO or for some time after, if they believe the price is not sustainable over the long term. Even in the long term, the trading price of Google's stock may decline.

We intend to take steps to help ensure shareholders are well informed. We encourage you to read this prospectus, especially the Risk Factors section. We think that short term speculation without paying attention to price is likely to lose you money, especially with our auction structure. In particular, we caution you that investing in Google through our auction could be followed by a significant decline in the value of your investment after the IPO.

GOOGLERS

Our employees, who have named themselves Googlers, are everything. Google is organized around the ability to attract and leverage the talent of exceptional technologists and business people. We have been lucky to recruit many creative, principled and hard working stars. We hope to recruit many more in the future. We will reward and treat them well.

We provide many unusual benefits for our employees, including meals free of charge, doctors and washing machines. We are careful to consider the long term advantages to the company of these benefits. Expect us to add

Table of Contents

benefits rather than pare them down over time. We believe it is easy to be penny wise and pound foolish with respect to benefits that can save employees considerable time and improve their health and productivity.

The significant employee ownership of Google has made us what we are today. Because of our employee talent, Google is doing exciting work in nearly every area of computer science. We are in a very competitive industry where the quality of our product is paramount. Talented people are attracted to Google because we empower them to change the world; Google has large computational resources and distribution that enables individuals to make a difference. Our main benefit is a workplace with important projects, where employees can contribute and grow. We are focused on providing an environment where talented, hard working people are rewarded for their contributions to Google and for making the world a better place.

DON'T BE EVIL

Don't be evil. We believe strongly that in the long term, we will be better served—as shareholders and in all other ways—by a company that does good things for the world even if we forgo some short term gains. This is an important aspect of our culture and is broadly shared within the company.

Google users trust our systems to help them with important decisions: medical, financial and many others. Our search results are the best we know how to produce. They are unbiased and objective, and we do not accept payment for them or for inclusion or more frequent updating. We also display advertising, which we work hard to make relevant, and we label it clearly. This is similar to a well-run newspaper, where the advertisements are clear and the articles are not influenced by the advertisers' payments. We believe it is important for everyone to have access to the best information and research, not only to the information people pay for you to see.

MAKING THE WORLD A BETTER PLACE

We aspire to make Google an institution that makes the world a better place. In pursuing this goal, we will always be mindful of our responsibilities to our shareholders, employees, customers and business partners. With our products, Google connects people and information all around the world for free. We are adding other powerful services such as Gmail, which provides an efficient one gigabyte Gmail account for free. We know that some people have raised privacy concerns, primarily over Gmail's targeted ads, which could lead to negative perceptions about Google. However, we believe Gmail protects a user's privacy. By releasing services, such as Gmail, for free, we hope to help bridge the digital divide. AdWords connects users and advertisers efficiently, helping both. AdSense helps fund a huge variety of online web sites and enables authors who could not otherwise publish. Last year we created Google Grants—a growing program in which hundreds of non-profits addressing issues, including the environment, poverty and human rights, receive free advertising. And now, we are in the process of establishing the Google Foundation. We intend to contribute significant resources to the foundation, including employee time and approximately 1% of Google's equity and profits in some form. We hope someday this institution may eclipse Google itself in terms of overall world impact by ambitiously applying innovation and significant resources to the largest of the world's problems.

SUMMARY AND CONCLUSION

Google is not a conventional company. Eric, Sergey and I intend to operate Google differently, applying the values it has developed as a private company to its future as a public company. Our mission and business description are available in the rest of this prospectus; we encourage you to carefully read this information. We will optimize for the long term rather than trying to produce smooth earnings for each quarter. We will support selected high-risk, high-reward projects and manage our portfolio of projects. We will run the company collaboratively with Eric, our CEO, as a team of three. We are conscious of our duty as fiduciaries for our shareholders, and we will fulfill those responsibilities. We will continue to strive to attract creative, committed new employees, and we will welcome support from new shareholders. We will live up to our "don't be evil" principle by keeping user trust and not accepting payment for search results. We have a dual class structure that is biased toward stability and independence and that requires investors to bet on the team, especially Sergey and me.

32

Table of Contents

In this letter we have talked about our IPO auction method and our desire for stability and access for all investors. We have discussed our goal to have investors who invest for the long term. Finally, we have discussed our desire to create an ideal working environment that will ultimately drive the success of Google by retaining and attracting talented Googlers.

We have tried hard to anticipate your questions. It will be difficult for us to respond to them given legal constraints during our offering process. We look forward to a long and hopefully prosperous relationship with you, our new investors. We wrote this letter to help you understand our company.

We have a strong commitment to our users worldwide, their communities, the web sites in our network, our advertisers, our investors, and of course our employees. Sergey and I, and the team will do our best to make Google a long term success and the world a better place.

Larry Page *Sergey Brin*

33

AUCTION PROCESS

The auction process being used for our initial public offering differs from methods that have been traditionally used in most other underwritten initial public offerings in the United States. In particular, we and our underwriters will conduct an auction to determine the initial public offering price and the allocation of shares in the offering. We plan to conduct this auction in five stages - Qualification; Bidding; Auction Closing; Pricing; and Allocation. Investors that do not submit bids through the auction process will not be eligible for an allocation of shares in our offering. Please see the risks related to the auction process for our offering beginning on page 19.

The Qualification Process

Our objective is to conduct an auction in which you submit informed bids. Before you can submit a bid, you will be required to obtain a bidder ID. Your bidder ID will be issued electronically only after you have visited a web site where you can obtain a bidder ID and followed the steps described at www.ipo.google.com and "How to Participate in the Auction for Our IPO" on page 42. Before you register for a bidder ID, you should:

- Read this prospectus, including all the risk factors.

- Understand that our initial public offering price is expected to be set at the auction clearing price, and, if there is little or no demand for our shares at or above the initial public offering price once trading begins, the price of our shares would decline.

- Understand that we may modify the price range and the size of our offering multiple times in response to investor demand.

- Understand that our current stockholders, including our founders and members of our management team, are selling, not buying, shares of Class A common stock as part of our initial public offering.

- Understand that we, in consultation with our underwriters, will have the ability to reject bids that we believe have the potential to manipulate or disrupt the bidding process, and that if you submit such a bid, all of the bids you have submitted will be rejected in which case you will not receive an allocation of shares in our initial public offering.

- Understand that 4,575,048 of our shares become available for sale starting as early as 15 days after our initial public offering and that additional shares become available at various times thereafter such that 270,281,202 shares are available for sale within 180 days after our initial public offering. Please carefully review the disclosure set forth under "Shares Eligible for Future Sale" on page 113.

You may obtain a bidder ID from www.ipo.google.com. We expect the qualification process to end soon. After the qualification process ends, you will not be able to obtain a bidder ID. If you do not obtain a bidder ID, you will not be able to bid in our auction.

We seek to enable all interested investors to have the opportunity to qualify to bid and, following qualification, place bids in the auction for our initial public offering. To help meet this objective, we have selected an underwriter group that serves a broad range of the investing public.

We caution you that our Class A common stock may not be a suitable investment for you even if you obtain a bidder ID. Moreover, even if you obtain a bidder ID, you may not be able to bid in the auction if you do not meet the suitability requirements of the underwriter through which you are seeking to place a bid or as a result of other regulatory requirements as described below. Because each of the brokerage firms makes its own suitability determinations, we encourage you to discuss with your brokerage firm any questions you have regarding their requirements. Finally, even if you obtain a bidder ID and place a bid in the auction, you may not receive an allocation of shares in our offering for a number of reasons described below.

We have not undertaken any efforts to register this offering in any jurisdiction outside the U.S. Except to the limited extent that this offering will be open to certain non-U.S. investors under private placement exemptions in certain countries other than the U.S., individual investors located outside the U.S. should not expect to be eligible

APPENDIX I GOOGLE INC. FORM S–1 REGISTRATION STATEMENT

Table of Contents

to participate in this offering. We would have liked to have made the offering more broadly available internationally, but myriad international securities regulations and compliance requirements made this impracticable.

The Bidding Process

Once the auction begins, all investors that have qualified to bid may submit bids in our offering through one of our underwriters. In connection with submitting a bid, you must provide the following information:

- The number of shares you are interested in purchasing.

- The price per share you are willing to pay.

- Additional information to enable the underwriter to identify you, confirm your eligibility and suitability for participating in our initial public offering, and, if you submit a successful bid, consummate a sale of shares to you.

To submit a bid, you should contact one of the following underwriters:

Morgan Stanley & Co. Incorporated
Credit Suisse First Boston LLC
Allen & Company LLC
Citigroup Global Markets Inc.
Goldman, Sachs & Co.
J.P. Morgan Securities Inc.
Lehman Brothers Inc.
UBS Securities LLC
Thomas Weisel Partners LLC
WR Hambrecht + Co., LLC
Deutsche Bank Securities Inc.
Lazard Freres & Co. LLC
Ameritrade, Inc.
M.R. Beal & Company
William Blair & Company L.L.C.
Blaylock & Partners, L.P.
Cazenove Inc.
E*TRADE Securities LLC
Epoch Securities, Inc. (distributed by Charles Schwab & Co., Inc.*)
Fidelity Capital Markets, a division of National Financial Services, LLC
HARRISdirect, LLC
Needham & Company, Inc.
Piper Jaffray & Co.
Samuel A. Ramirez & Co., Inc.
Muriel Siebert & Co. Inc.
Utendahl Capital Group, L.L.C.
Wachovia Capital Markets, LLC
Wells Fargo Securities, LLC

---

* Charles Schwab & Co., Inc., pursuant to a distribution agreement with Epoch Securities, Inc., is acting solely as a distribution agent with respect to this offering. Charles Schwab & Co., Inc. will receive no compensation for the distribution of Google's Class A common stock.

Bids may be within, above or below the estimated price range for our initial public offering on the cover of this prospectus. Bid prices may be in any increment, including pennies. The minimum size of any bid is generally

Table of Contents

five shares. However, the minimum size of any bid submitted through HARRISdirect, one of our underwriters, is 100 shares.

The bidding policies of our underwriters vary. Accordingly, the number of bids you may submit through any one underwriter will depend on the bidding policies of that underwriter. Most of our underwriters will permit you to submit an unlimited number of bids. However, UBS Securities, Charles Schwab & Co. and Fidelity Capital Markets will permit bidders to submit only one bid per account. HARRISdirect will permit bidders to submit up to three bids per account. E*TRADE Securities will permit bidders to submit up to five bids per account; however, bidders submitting bids through E*TRADE Securities may not submit bids for more than an aggregate of 10,000 shares per account. Ameritrade will permit bidders to submit up to 30 bids per account. If you decide to submit a bid in our offering, we encourage you to contact the underwriter through which you will submit your bid.

Each underwriter has the ability to receive bids from its customers through one or more of the following means: over the Internet, by telephone, by facsimile or in person. To participate in the auction for our initial public offering, you will be required to agree to accept electronic delivery of this prospectus, the final prospectus, any amendments to this prospectus or the final prospectus, and other communications related to this offering. If you do not consent to electronic delivery, or subsequently revoke that consent prior to the time at which our underwriters accept your bids, you will not be able to submit a bid or participate in our offering. If you revoke your consent after the underwriters accept your bid, a copy of the final prospectus will be delivered to you via U.S. mail. Your consent to electronic delivery of these documents does not constitute consent by you to electronic delivery of other information about us not related to this offering, such as proxy statements and quarterly and annual reports, during and after completion of this offering.

If you are interested in submitting a bid but do not currently have a brokerage account with any of the underwriters named above, you may contact one of these underwriters to inquire about opening an account and submitting a bid. You should be aware that, due to each underwriter's requirements for new customer accounts, you may not be able to open an account with a particular underwriter. Even if you are a customer of one of our underwriters, and even if you have obtained a bidder ID, you may not be permitted to submit a bid if the underwriter through which you wish to submit your bid determines that you do not meet such underwriter's suitability standards or that you are otherwise prohibited from participating in the offering due to regulatory requirements, such as the rules and regulations of the National Association of Securities Dealers.

We encourage you to discuss any questions regarding your bid and the suitability determinations that will be applied to your bid with the underwriter through which you expect to submit a bid. Each of our underwriters makes its own suitability determinations. This could affect your ability to submit a bid. For example, one of our underwriters may view a bid for 100 shares at $90.00 per share as suitable for an investor, while another of our underwriters could determine that such a bid is unsuitable for that same investor. If an underwriter determines that a bid is not suitable for an investor, the underwriter will not submit that bid in the auction, and you may not be informed that your bid was not submitted in the auction.

Our managing underwriters will manage the master order book, to which we will have concurrent access, that will aggregate all bids collected by our underwriters and will include the identity of the bidders. Our master order book will not be available for viewing by bidders. Neither we nor our underwriters will inform you that we have rejected your bids.

You should consider all the information in this prospectus in determining whether to submit a bid, the number of shares you seek to purchase and the price per share you are willing to pay. We, in consultation with our underwriters, will have the ability to reject bids that have the potential to manipulate or disrupt the bidding process. These bids include bids that we, in consultation with our underwriters, believe in our sole discretion do not reflect the number of shares that you actually intend to purchase, or a series of bids that we, in consultation with our underwriters, consider disruptive to the auction process.

Table of Contents

The shares offered by this prospectus may not be sold, nor may offers to buy be accepted, prior to the time that the registration statement filed with the SEC becomes effective. A bid received by any underwriter involves no obligation or commitment of any kind by the bidder until our underwriters have notified you that your bid is successful by sending you a notice of acceptance. Therefore, you will be able to withdraw a bid at any time until it has been accepted. You may withdraw your bid by contacting the underwriter through which you submitted your bid.

During the bidding process, we and our managing underwriters will monitor the master order book to evaluate the demand that exists for our initial public offering. Based on this information and other factors, we and our underwriters may revise the public offering price range for our initial public offering set forth on the cover of this prospectus. In addition, we and the selling stockholders may decide to change the number of shares of Class A common stock offered through this prospectus. It is very likely that the number of shares offered will increase if the price range increases. You should be aware that we have the ability to make multiple such revisions. These increases in the public offering price range or the number of shares offered through this prospectus may result in there being little or no demand for our shares of Class A common stock at or above the initial public offering price following this offering. Therefore, the price of our shares of Class A common stock could decline following this offering, and investors should not expect to be able to sell their shares for a profit shortly after trading begins. You should consider whether to modify or withdraw your bid as a result of developments during the auction process, including changes in the price range or number of shares offered.

Reconfirmations of Bids

We will require that bidders reconfirm the bids that they have submitted in the offering if either of the following events shall occur:

- More than 15 business days have elapsed since the bidder submitted his bid in the offering.

- There is a material change in the prospectus that requires recirculation of the prospectus by us and the underwriters.

If a reconfirmation of bids is required, we will send an electronic notice to everyone who received a bidder ID notifying them that they must reconfirm their bids by contacting the underwriters with which they have their brokerage accounts. If bidders do not reconfirm their bids when requested, we and the underwriters will disregard their bids in the auction, and they will be deemed to have been withdrawn.

Changes in the Price Range Prior to Effectiveness of the Registration Statement

If, prior to the date on which the SEC declares our registration statement effective, there is a change in the price range or the number of shares to be sold in our offering, in each case in a manner that is not otherwise material to our offering, we and the underwriters will:

- Provide notice on our offering web site of the revised price range or number of shares to be sold in our offering, as the case may be.

- Issue a press release announcing the revised price range or number of shares to be sold in our offering, as the case may be.

- Send an electronic notice to everyone who received a bidder ID notifying them of the revised price range or number of shares to be sold in our offering, as the case may be.

In these situations, the underwriters could accept your bid after the SEC declares the registration statement effective without requiring you to reconfirm. However, the underwriters may decide at any time to require you to reconfirm your bid, and if you fail to do so, your bid will be invalid.

Table of Contents

The Auction Closing Process

We can close the auction at any time. You will have the ability to modify any bid until the auction is closed. You will have the ability to withdraw your bid until your bid is accepted. This will occur when and if you are sent a notice of acceptance. If you are requested to reconfirm a bid and fail to do so, your bid will be rejected.

When we submit our request that the SEC declare the registration statement effective, we and the underwriters will also send an electronic notice to everyone who received a bidder ID informing them of our request. Once the registration statement is effective, you will be sent an electronic notice informing you that the registration statement is effective. Bidders may still withdraw their bids after the underwriters send this notice of effectiveness. You should be aware that the following underwriters may require that you deposit funds or securities in your brokerage account with value sufficient to cover the aggregate dollar amount of your bid:

- WR Hambrecht + Co.
- Ameritrade
- M.R. Beal & Company
- E*TRADE Securities
- Charles Schwab & Co.
- Samuel A. Ramirez & Co.
- Muriel Siebert & Co.
- Utendahl Capital Group
- Wells Fargo Securities

In the event these underwriters require you to make deposits, you will need to do so within 24 hours after the registration statement is declared effective. However, if the registration statement is declared effective on Friday, such funds will be due 72 hours after the registration statement is declared effective. If you submit a bid after effectiveness, you will be required to fund your account by the later of the deadline described above or the time you submit a bid.

If you do not provide the required funds or securities in your account within the required time, these underwriters may cancel your bid. However, we and our underwriters may decide to accept successful bids in as little as one hour after the SEC declares the registration statement effective regardless of whether bidders have deposited funds or securities in their brokerage accounts. In this case, as well as all other cases in which notices of acceptance have been sent, successful bidders would be obligated to purchase the shares allocated to them in the allocation process. For the remaining underwriters not listed above, you will be required to deposit funds in your brokerage account prior to settlement, which we expect to occur three or four business days after the underwriters send the notices of acceptance to successful bidders.

The Pricing Process

We expect that the bidding process will reveal a clearing price for the shares of Class A common stock offered in our auction. The clearing price is the highest price at which all of the shares offered (including shares subject to the underwriters' over-allotment option) may be sold to potential investors, based on bids in the master order book that have not been withdrawn or rejected at the time we and our underwriters close the auction.

The initial public offering price will be determined by us and our underwriters after the auction closes. We intend to use the auction clearing price to determine the initial public offering price and, therefore, to set an initial public offering price that is equal to the clearing price. However, we and our underwriters have discretion to set the initial public offering price below the auction clearing price. We may do this in an effort to achieve a broader distribution of our Class A common stock or to potentially reduce the downward price volatility in the trading price of our shares in the period shortly following our offering relative to what would be experienced if

38

Table of Contents

the initial public offering price were set at the auction clearing price. We cannot assure you that setting the initial public offering price below the auction clearing price would achieve this result. In addition, although setting the initial public offering price below the clearing price may achieve a broader distribution of our shares, it may not result in allocations of shares in our offering to specific types of investors, such as professional investors. Even if the initial public offering price is set below the auction clearing price, the trading price of our Class A common stock could still drop significantly after the offering.

We caution you that our initial public offering price may have little or no relationship to the price that would be established using traditional indicators of value, such as:

- Our future prospects and those of our industry in general.
- Our sales, earnings and other financial and operating information.
- Multiples of our earnings, cash flows and other operating metrics.
- Market prices of securities and other financial and operating information of companies engaged in activities similar to ours.
- Research analyst views.

You should understand that the trading price of our Class A common stock could vary significantly from the initial public offering price. Therefore, we caution you not to submit a bid in the auction process for our offering unless you are willing to take the risk that our stock price could decline significantly.

The pricing of our initial public offering will occur after we have closed the auction and after the registration statement has been declared effective. We will issue a press release to announce the initial public offering price. The price will also be included in the notice of acceptance and the final prospectus will be sent to the purchasers of Class A common stock in our offering.

Acceptance of Bids

If the initial public offering price is at or above the bottom of the price range on the cover of the prospectus and no more than 20% above the top of the range, the underwriters can accept all bids at or above the initial public offering price by sending electronic notices of acceptance to successful bidders. As a result of the varying delivery times involved in sending emails over the Internet, some bidders may receive these notices of acceptance before others. In this case, the underwriters can accept your bid without reconfirmation.

If the initial public offering price is less than the bottom of the price range on the cover of the prospectus or more than 20% above the top of the range, we and the underwriters will:

- Provide notice on our offering web site of the final offering price.
- Issue a press release announcing the final offering price.
- Send an electronic notice to everyone who received a bidder ID notifying them of the final offering price.

Under these circumstances, the underwriters would not require the bidders to reconfirm their bids unless there is a material change in the prospectus that requires a recirculation of the prospectus. If reconfirmation is not required, the underwriters may accept successful bids by sending an electronic notice of acceptance in as little as one hour after we and the underwriters send the electronic notice of the final offering price and you will have the ability to withdraw your bid until it is accepted.

You should be aware that the underwriters will accept successful bids by sending an electronic notice of acceptance, and bidders who submitted successful bids will be obligated to purchase the shares allocated to them regardless of (1) whether such bidders are aware that the registration statement has been declared effective or (2) whether they are aware that the electronic notice of acceptance of that bid has been sent. Once the underwriters have accepted a bid by sending out an electronic notice of acceptance, they will not cancel or reject this bid.

The Allocation Process

Once the initial public offering price has been determined, we and our underwriters will begin the allocation process. All investors who submitted successful bids will receive an allocation of shares in our offering. All shares will be sold at the initial public offering price. The allocation process will not give any preference to successful bids based on bid price.

If the initial public offering price is equal to the auction clearing price, all successful bidders will be offered share allocations that are equal or nearly equal to the number of shares represented by their successful bids. Therefore, we caution you against submitting a bid that does not accurately represent the number of shares of our Class A common stock that you are willing and prepared to purchase. If we, in consultation with our underwriters, believe in our sole discretion that your bid does not reflect the number of shares you actually intend to purchase, we may determine that your bid is manipulative or disruptive. If any of your bids are deemed manipulative or disruptive, all of the bids that you have submitted will be rejected, in which case you will not receive an allocation of shares in our initial public offering. Furthermore, neither we nor our underwriters will inform you that we have rejected your bids.

In the event that the number of shares represented by successful bids exceeds the number of shares we and the selling stockholders are offering, the offered shares will need to be allocated across the successful bidder group. We, in consultation with our underwriters, expect to use one of two methods to do so—pro rata allocation or maximum share allocation. With either method, our objective is to set an initial public offering price where successful bidders receive at least 80% of the shares they successfully bid for in the auction. We do not intend to publicly disclose the allocation method that we ultimately employ. Once we choose an allocation method, we will not change it.

Pro Rata Allocation. With pro rata allocation, successful bidders will receive share allocations on a pro rata basis based on the following rules:

- The pro rata allocation percentage will be determined by dividing the number of shares we and the selling stockholders are offering (including shares subject to the underwriters' over-allotment option) by the number of shares represented by successful bids.

- Each bidder who has a successful bid will be allocated a number of shares equal to the pro rata allocation percentage multiplied by the number of shares represented by the successful bid, rounded to the nearest whole number of shares.

The following simplified, hypothetical example illustrates how pro rata allocation might work in practice:

Assumptions

Shares Offered	20,000
Total Shares Subject to Successful Bids	21,200
Pro Rata Allocation Percentage	94.34%

Successful Bidder	Shares Represented by Successful Bid	Pro Rata Allocation
A	100	94
B	2,100	1,981
C	4,000	3,774
D	4,500	4,245
E	5,000	4,717
F	5,500	5,189
Totals	21,200	20,000

Table of Contents

Maximum Share Allocation. With maximum share allocation, successful bidders will receive share allocations based on an algorithm. Under this method, successful bidders with smaller bid sizes would receive share allocations for their entire bid amounts, while successful bidders with larger bid sizes would receive no more than a maximum share allocation to be determined using the following algorithm:

- The total of all share allocations must equal the total number of shares we and the selling stockholders are offering (including any shares subject to the over-allotment option).

- Each successful bidder will receive a share allocation equal to the lesser of the number of shares represented by their successful bid and the maximum share allocation.

- The maximum share allocation would be a number of shares that results in the full allocation of shares being offered.

The following simplified, hypothetical example illustrates how maximum share allocation might work in practice:

Assumptions

Shares Offered	20,000
Total Shares Subject to Successful Bids	21,200
Maximum Share Allocation	4,650

Successful Bidder	Shares Represented by Successful Bids	Share Allocation
A	100	100
B	2,100	2,100
C	4,000	4,000
D	4,500	4,500
E	5,000	4,650
F	5,500	4,650
Totals	21,200	20,000

We may designate "tiers" of bidders for purposes of allocation. Although we will not be able to determine whether or how we would implement a tiered allocation structure until the closing of the auction, the tiers would not be a factor in establishing the initial public offering price or in determining the size of the offering. If we were to implement a tiered allocation structure, we would divide the successful bidders into segments, or "tiers," and assign bidders to tiers based on the size of their bids. This would require us to determine how many shares to allocate to each tier. The portion of the total shares offered in our initial public offering that are allocated to a tier may be different from the portion of the total shares successfully bid for in our auction that were bid for by bidders in that tier. Following the assignment of shares to each tier, we would apply either the maximum share or pro rata allocation within each tier. Our objective is that, regardless of any tiering allocations that we may implement, no successful bidder will be allocated less than 80% of the shares he or she successfully bid for in the auction.

Following the allocation process, our underwriters will provide successful bidders with a final prospectus and confirmations that detail their purchases of shares of our Class A common stock and the purchase price. The final prospectus will be delivered electronically and confirmation will be delivered by regular mail, facsimile or email. Successful bidders can expect to receive their allocated shares in their brokerage accounts three or four business days after the final offering price is established by us and the underwriters.

Table of Contents

HOW TO PARTICIPATE IN THE AUCTION FOR OUR IPO

If you want to participate in the auction for our IPO, you will need to do the following:

1. Have or open a brokerage account at a brokerage firm affiliated with one of our underwriters listed on page 35 of this prospectus.

2. Understand that you should carefully review our entire prospectus. We also recommend that you view the "Meet the Management" presentation available at www.ipo.google.com.

3. Obtain a bidder ID. You will need to go to www.ipo.google.com and follow the directions for registering for a bidder ID. To obtain a bidder ID, you will have to:

    - Provide personal information, including your tax identification number (usually your social security number) and a valid email address. If the email address you provide differs from the one you have on file with your brokerage firm, we suggest that you provide your brokerage firm with the email address you will use for this offering.

    - Acknowledge that you have received an electronic copy of the preliminary prospectus.

    - Consent to electronic delivery of communications related to the offering, including amendments to the prospectus.

    - Accept the Privacy Policy and Terms of Use that are described on the web site.

    - Receive a confirmation email from www.ipo.google.com and click on the link in the email to receive your bidder ID. You are not registered until you click on this link and obtain your bidder ID.

    > You will not be able to receive a bidder ID once the auction begins.

4. Contact your brokerage firm to find out when the auction will open and to place a bid.

    > Because each of the brokerage firms makes its own suitability determinations, we encourage you to discuss with your brokerage firm any questions that you have regarding their requirements because this could impact your ability to submit a bid. For example, while one of our underwriters may view a bid for 100 shares at $90.00 per share as suitable for an investor, another of our underwriters could determine that such a bid is unsuitable for that same investor and, therefore, not submit the bid in the auction.

5. If you choose to submit a bid, contact your brokerage firm while the auction is open.

    - You may bid within, above or below the price range found on the cover of our preliminary prospectus.

    - Each bid must contain both the price per share you are willing to pay and the number of shares for which you are bidding.

    - The minimum size of any bid is generally five shares. However, the minimum size of any bid submitted through HARRISdirect, one of our underwriters, is 100 shares.

    - If you bid, only submit a bid for the number of shares you intend to purchase and the price per share you are willing to pay. If we, in consultation with our underwriters, determine that your bid is manipulative or disruptive, all of the bids that you have submitted will be rejected. You will not be informed if your bids are rejected.

    - Most of our underwriters will permit you to submit an unlimited number of bids. However, UBS Securities, Charles Schwab & Co. and Fidelity Capital Markets will permit bidders to submit only one bid per account. HARRISdirect will permit bidders to submit up to three bids per account. E*TRADE Securities will permit bidders to submit up to five bids per account; however, bidders submitting bids through E*TRADE Securities may not submit bids for more than an aggregate of 10,000 shares per account. Ameritrade will permit bidders to submit up to 30 bids per account.

- You should understand that, if you submit more than one bid, all of your bids could be accepted. This means that you may be allocated shares for any or all of your bids that you have not withdrawn prior to their acceptance by the underwriters. You will be financially obligated for the total value of the shares allocated to you.

> Do not submit bids that add up to more than the amount of money you want to invest in the IPO. This is a very important point. For example, suppose you want to invest, at most, $1,000 in our IPO. Let's assume that you place two bids: one bid for 11 shares at $90.00 (for a total value of $990) and another bid for 7 shares at $93.25 (for a total value of $652.75). If the IPO price were set at $89.25, the underwriters would accept all of your bids and you would be legally obligated to purchase 18 shares for $1,606.50.

6. Keep in contact with your brokerage firm, frequently monitor your email account and check www.ipo.google.com for notifications related to the offering, including:

- *Notice of Recirculation/Request for Reconfirmation.* Notification that we have made material changes to the prospectus for this offering that require you to reconfirm your bid by contacting your brokerage firm.

- *Notice of Change in Price Range or Number of Shares Offered.* Notification that we have changed the price range or size of the offering.

- *Notice of Intent to go Effective.* Notification that we have asked the SEC to declare our registration statement effective.

- *Notice of Effectiveness.* Notification that the SEC has declared our registration statement effective.

- *Notice of Auction Closing.* Notification that the auction has closed.

- *Notice of Final Price.* Notification of the initial public offering price, if the offering price is less than the bottom of the price range on the cover of the prospectus or more than 20% above the top of the range.

- *Notice of Acceptance.* Notification as to whether any of your bids are successful and have been accepted by the underwriters. This notification will include the initial public offering price.

Please be careful only to trust emails relating to the auction that come from your brokerage firm or from www.ipo.google.com. Emails from us will not ask for any personal information (such as social security number or credit card numbers). If you are not sure whether to trust an email, please contact your brokerage firm directly.

7. You may submit, change or withdraw a bid at any time before the auction is closed. You may also withdraw a bid at any time (even after the auction is closed) until a notice of acceptance of that bid is sent to your email account. In all cases, contact your brokerage firm to change or withdraw a bid.

8. Once our registration statement is effective, your brokerage firm may require that, within 24 hours following the effectiveness of the registration statement, you deposit funds or securities in your brokerage account with value sufficient to cover the aggregate dollar amount of your bid. If you do not provide the required funds or securities in your account within the required time, your bid may be rejected. However, we and our underwriters may determine to accept successful bids in as little as one hour after the SEC declares the registration statement effective regardless of whether bidders have deposited funds or securities in their brokerage accounts. In this case, as well as all other cases in which notices of acceptance have been sent, successful bidders would be obligated to purchase the shares allocated to them in the allocation process.

Table of Contents

9. In certain circumstances, you may be required to reconfirm your bid. If this occurs, you should contact your brokerage firm. If you fail to reconfirm your bid when requested, your bid will no longer be valid.

10. If your bids have been accepted by the underwriters, you are bound to purchase all of the shares for which you have bid at or above the initial public offering price. Your brokerage firm will contact you with respect to your exact allocation.

For more information on the auction process, see "Auction Process" beginning on page 34 of this prospectus.

USE OF PROCEEDS

We estimate that we will receive net proceeds of $1,227.2 million from our sale of the 14,142,135 shares of Class A common stock offered by us in this offering, based upon an assumed initial public offering price of $90.00 per share, after deducting estimated underwriting discounts and commissions and estimated offering expenses payable by us. We will not receive any of the net proceeds from the sale of the shares by the selling stockholders.

The principal purposes of this offering are to obtain additional capital, to create a public market for our common stock and to facilitate our future access to the public equity markets.

We currently have no specific plans for the use of the net proceeds of this offering. We anticipate that we will use the net proceeds received by us from this offering for general corporate purposes, including working capital. In addition, we may use a portion of the proceeds of this offering for acquisitions of complementary businesses, technologies or other assets. We have no current agreements or commitments with respect to any material acquisitions.

Pending such uses, we plan to invest the net proceeds in highly liquid, investment grade securities.

DIVIDEND POLICY

We have never declared or paid any cash dividend on our capital stock. We currently intend to retain any future earnings and do not expect to pay any dividends in the foreseeable future.

CASH AND CAPITALIZATION

The following table sets forth our cash, cash equivalents, short-term investments and capitalization at June 30, 2004, as follows:

- On an actual basis, 162,856,233 shares of Class B common stock and 12,359,204 shares of Class A common stock are outstanding.

- On a pro forma basis to reflect the conversion of all of our outstanding preferred stock into an aggregate of 79,099,884 shares of Class B common stock, which will occur prior to the completion of the offering.

- On a pro forma as adjusted basis to give effect to receipt of the net proceeds from the sale by us in this offering of shares of Class A common stock at an assumed initial public offering price of $90.00 per share, after deducting estimated underwriting discounts and commissions and estimated offering expenses.

Table of Contents

You should read this table in conjunction with "Selected Consolidated Financial Data," "Management's Discussion and Analysis of Financial Condition and Results of Operations" and our financial statements and related notes included elsewhere in this prospectus.

	At June 30, 2004		
	Actual	Pro Forma	Pro Forma As Adjusted
	(in thousands, except par value) (unaudited)		
Cash, cash equivalents and short-term investments	$ 548,687	$ 548,687	$1,775,876
Long-term liabilities	58,766	58,766	58,766
Stockholders' equity:			
Convertible preferred stock, $0.001 par value, issuable in series: 164,782 shares authorized, 79,099 shares issued and outstanding, actual; 100,000 shares authorized, none issued and outstanding, pro forma and pro forma as adjusted	79,860	—	—
Class A and B common stock, $0.001 par value: 700,000 shares authorized, 165,012 shares issued and outstanding, actual; 9,000,000 shares authorized, 244,111 shares issued and outstanding, pro forma and 258,254 shares pro forma as adjusted	165	244	258
Additional paid in capital	956,882	1,036,663	2,263,838
Deferred stock-based compensation	(352,815)	(352,815)	(352,815)
Accumulated other comprehensive income	(1,481)	(1,481)	(1,481)
Retained earnings	334,388	334,388	334,388
Total stockholders' equity	1,016,999	1,016,999	2,244,188
Total capitalization	$1,075,765	$1,075,765	$2,302,954

The table above excludes the following shares:

- 10,203,007 shares of Class A and Class B common stock subject to repurchase that were granted and exercised subsequent to March 21, 2002 (see Note 1 of Notes to Consolidated Financial Statements included as part of this prospectus).

- 1,996,140 shares of Class B common stock issuable upon the exercise of warrants outstanding at June 30, 2004, with a weighted average exercise price of $0.62 per share.

- 6,276,573 shares of Class A common stock issuable upon the exercise of options outstanding at June 30, 2004, at a weighted average exercise price of $9.42 per share.

- 10,456,084 shares of Class B common stock issuable upon the exercise of options outstanding at June 30, 2004, at a weighted average exercise price of $2.68 per share.

- 3,891,192 shares of common stock available for future issuance under our stock option plans at June 30, 2004.

- 2,700,000 shares of Class A common stock issued to Yahoo in connection with a settlement arrangement.

DILUTION

If you invest in our Class A common stock, your interest will be diluted to the extent of the difference between the initial public offering price per share of our Class A common stock and the pro forma as adjusted net tangible book value per share of our Class A and Class B common stock immediately after this offering. Pro forma net tangible book value per share represents the amount of our total tangible assets less total liabilities, divided by the number of shares of Class A and Class B common stock outstanding at June 30, 2004 after giving effect to the conversion of all of our preferred stock into Class B common stock, which will occur immediately prior to the completion of the offering.

Investors participating in this offering will incur immediate, substantial dilution. Our pro forma net tangible book value was $913.2 million, computed as total stockholders' equity less goodwill and other intangible assets, or $3.55 per share of Class A and Class B common stock and preferred stock outstanding at June 30, 2004. Assuming the sale by us of shares of Class A common stock offered in this offering at an initial public offering price of $90.00 per share, and after deducting estimated underwriting discounts and commissions and estimated offering expenses, our pro forma as adjusted net tangible book value at June 30, 2004, would have been $2,140.4 million, or $7.89 per share of common stock. This represents an immediate increase in pro forma net tangible book value of $4.34 per share of common stock to our existing stockholders and an immediate dilution of $82.11 per share to the new investors purchasing shares in this offering. The following table illustrates this per share dilution:

Assumed initial public offering price per share of Class A common stock		$90.00
Pro forma net tangible book value per share at June 30, 2004	$3.55	
Increase in pro forma net tangible book value per share attributable to this offering	4.34	
Pro forma as adjusted net tangible book value per share after the offering		7.89
Dilution per share to new investors		$82.11

The following table sets forth on a pro forma as adjusted basis, at June 30, 2004, the number of shares of Class A common stock purchased or to be purchased from us, the total consideration paid or to be paid and the average price per share paid or to be paid by existing holders of common stock, by holders of options and warrants outstanding at June 30, 2004, and by the new investors, before deducting estimated underwriting discounts and estimated offering expenses payable by us.

	Shares Purchased		Total Consideration		Average Price Per Share
	Number	Percent	Amount	Percent	
	(dollars in thousands, except per share amounts)				
Existing stockholders	257,077,508	94.8%	$ 89,523	6.6%	$ 0.35
New investors	14,142,135	5.2%	1,272,792	93.4%	$ 90.00
Total	271,219,643	100.0%	$1,362,315	100.0%	

The discussion and tables above are based on the number of shares of common stock and preferred stock outstanding at June 30, 2004.

The discussion and tables above includes 62,187 shares of Class B common stock issuable upon exercise of a warrant that will be exercised in connection with the offering and 2,700,000 shares of Class A common stock issued to Yahoo in connection with a settlement arrangement. The adjusted tangible book value does not assume any change that will result from this settlement arrangement. Note 14 of Notes to Consolidated Financial Statements included as part of this prospectus provides a preliminary pro forma stockholders' equity as if the settlement had occurred on December 31, 2003. The discussion and table below excludes the following shares:

- 1,933,953 shares of Class B common stock issuable upon the exercise of warrants outstanding, at June 30, 2004, at a weighted average exercise price of $0.62 per share.

46

- 6,276,573 shares of Class A common stock issuable upon the exercise of options outstanding at June 30, 2004, at a weighted average exercise price of $9.42 per share.
- 10,456,084 shares of Class B common stock issuable upon the exercise of options outstanding at June 30, 2004, at a weighted average exercise price of $2.68 per share.
- 3,891,192 shares of common stock available for future issuance under our stock option plans at June 30, 2004.

To the extent outstanding options and warrants are exercised, new investors will experience further dilution.

SELECTED CONSOLIDATED FINANCIAL DATA

You should read the following selected consolidated financial data in conjunction with "Management's Discussion and Analysis of Financial Condition and Results of Operations" and our consolidated financial statements and the related notes appearing elsewhere in this prospectus.

The consolidated statements of operations data for the years ended December 31, 2001, 2002 and 2003, and the consolidated balance sheet data at December 31, 2002 and 2003, are derived from our audited consolidated financial statements appearing elsewhere in this prospectus. The consolidated statements of operations data for the years ended December 31, 1999 and December 31, 2000, and the consolidated balance sheet data at December 31, 1999, 2000 and 2001, are derived from our audited consolidated financial statements that are not included in this prospectus. The consolidated statements of operations data for the six months ended June 30, 2003 and 2004 and the consolidated balance sheet data at June 30, 2004 are derived from our unaudited consolidated financial statements included in this prospectus. The unaudited consolidated financial statements include, in the opinion of management, all adjustments that management considers necessary for the fair presentation of the financial information set forth in those statements. The historical results are not necessarily indicative of the results to be expected in any future period.

	\multicolumn{5}{c}{Year Ended December 31,}	\multicolumn{2}{c}{Six Months Ended June 30,}
	1999	2000	2001	2002	2003	2003	2004
	\multicolumn{5}{c}{(in thousands, except per share data)}	\multicolumn{2}{c}{(unaudited)}
Consolidated Statements of Operations Data:							
Revenues	$ 220	$ 19,108	$ 86,426	$439,508	$1,465,934	$559,817	$1,351,835
Costs and expenses:							
Cost of revenues	908	6,081	14,228	131,510	625,854	204,596	641,775
Research and development	2,930	10,516	16,500	31,748	91,228	29,997	80,781
Sales and marketing	1,677	10,385	20,076	43,849	120,328	42,589	104,681
General and administrative	1,221	4,357	12,275	24,300	56,699	22,562	47,083
Stock-based compensation(1)	—	2,506	12,383	21,635	229,361	70,583	151,234
Total costs and expenses	6,736	33,845	75,462	253,042	1,123,470	370,327	1,025,554
Income (loss) from operations	(6,516)	(14,737)	10,964	186,466	342,464	189,490	326,281
Interest income (expense) and other, net	440	47	(896)	(1,551)	4,190	719	(1,198)
Income (loss) before income taxes	(6,076)	(14,690)	10,068	184,915	346,654	190,209	325,083
Provision for income taxes	—	—	3,083	85,259	241,006	132,341	182,047
Net income (loss)	$(6,076)	$(14,690)	$ 6,985	$ 99,656	$ 105,648	$ 57,968	$ 143,036
Net income (loss) per share(2):							
Basic	$ (0.14)	$ (0.22)	$ 0.07	$ 0.86	$ 0.77	$ 0.44	$ 0.93
Diluted	$ (0.14)	$ (0.22)	$ 0.04	$ 0.45	$ 0.41	$ 0.23	$ 0.54
Number of shares used in per share calculations(2):							
Basic	42,445	67,032	94,523	115,242	137,697	131,525	153,263
Diluted	42,445	67,032	186,776	220,633	256,638	253,024	265,223

(1) Stock-based compensation, consisting of amortization of deferred stock-based compensation and the fair value of options issued to non-employees for services rendered, is allocated as follows:

	\multicolumn{5}{c}{Year Ended December 31,}	\multicolumn{2}{c}{Six Months Ended June 30,}
	1999	2000	2001	2002	2003	2003	2004
	\multicolumn{5}{c}{(in thousands)}	\multicolumn{2}{c}{(unaudited)}
Cost of revenues	$ —	$ 167	$ 876	$ 1,065	$ 8,557	$ 2,813	$ 7,622
Research and development	—	1,573	4,440	8,746	138,377	38,237	92,102
Sales and marketing	—	514	1,667	4,934	44,607	14,711	27,576
General and administrative	—	252	5,400	6,890	37,820	14,822	23,934
	$ —	$ 2,506	$ 12,383	$ 21,635	$ 229,361	$ 70,583	$ 151,234

(2) See Note 1 of Notes to Consolidated Financial Statements included in this prospectus for information regarding the computation of per share amounts.

48

Table of Contents

	\multicolumn{5}{c}{At December 31,}	At June 30, 2004
	1999	2000	2001	2002	2003	
	\multicolumn{5}{c}{(in thousands)}	(unaudited)
Consolidated Balance Sheet Data:						
Cash, cash equivalents and short-term investments	$20,038	$19,101	$ 33,589	$146,231	$ 334,718	$ 548,687
Total assets	25,808	46,872	84,457	286,892	871,458	1,328,022
Total long-term liabilities	3,096	7,397	8,044	9,560	33,365	58,766
Redeemable convertible preferred stock warrant	—	—	—	13,871	13,871	—
Deferred stock-based compensation	—	(8,457)	(15,833)	(35,401)	(369,668)	(352,815)
Total stockholders' equity	20,009	27,234	50,152	173,953	588,770	1,016,999

49

Table of Contents

MANAGEMENT'S DISCUSSION AND ANALYSIS OF
FINANCIAL CONDITION AND RESULTS OF OPERATIONS

The following discussion and analysis of the financial condition and results of our operations should be read in conjunction with the consolidated financial statements and the notes to those statements included elsewhere in this prospectus. This discussion contains forward-looking statements reflecting our current expectations that involve risks and uncertainties. Actual results and the timing of events may differ materially from those contained in these forward-looking statements due to a number of factors, including those discussed in the section entitled "Risk Factors" and elsewhere in this prospectus.

Overview

Google is a global technology leader focused on improving the ways people connect with information. Our innovations in web search and advertising have made our web site a top Internet destination and our brand one of the most recognized in the world. Our mission is to organize the world's information and make it universally accessible and useful. We serve three primary constituencies:

- *Users.* We provide users with products and services that enable people to more quickly and easily find, create and organize information that is useful to them.

- *Advertisers.* We provide advertisers our Google AdWords program, an auction-based advertising program that enables them to deliver relevant ads targeted to search results or web content. Our AdWords program provides advertisers with a cost-effective way to deliver ads to customers across Google sites and through the Google Network under our AdSense program.

- *Web sites.* We provide members of our Google Network our Google AdSense program, which allows these members to deliver AdWords ads that are relevant to the search results or content on their web sites. We share most of the fees these ads generate with our Google Network members—creating an important revenue stream for them.

We were incorporated in California in September 1998 and reincorporated in Delaware in August 2003. We began licensing our WebSearch product in the first quarter of 1999. We became profitable in 2001 following the launch of our Google AdWords program.

How We Generate Revenue

We derive most of our revenues from fees we receive from our advertisers.

Our original business model consisted of licensing our search engine services to other web sites. In the first quarter of 2000, we introduced our first advertising program. Through our direct sales force we offered advertisers the ability to place text-based ads on our web sites targeted to our users' search queries under a program called Premium Sponsorships. Advertisers paid us based on the number of times their ads were displayed on users' search results pages, and we recognized revenue at the time these ads appeared. In the fourth quarter of 2000, we launched Google AdWords, an online self-service program that enables advertisers to place targeted text-based ads on our web sites. AdWords customers originally paid us based on the number of times their ads appeared on users' search results pages. In the first quarter of 2002, we began offering AdWords exclusively on a cost-per-click basis, so that an advertiser pays us only when a user clicks on one of its ads. AdWords is also available through our direct sales force. Our AdWords agreements are generally terminable at any time by our advertisers. We recognize as revenue the fees charged advertisers each time a user clicks on one of the text-based ads that appear next to the search results on our web sites.

Effective January 1, 2004, we terminated the Premium Sponsorships program and now offer a single pricing structure to all of our advertisers based on the AdWords cost-per-click model. We do not expect that this change to one pricing structure will have a negative effect on our revenues because most of our advertisers switched to

Table of Contents

the AdWords cost-per-click model. Our AdWords cost-per-click program is the advertising program through which we generate revenues by serving ads on our web sites and on Google Network member web sites through our AdSense program.

Google AdSense is the program through which we distribute our advertisers' AdWords ads for display on the web sites of our Google Network members. Our AdSense program includes AdSense for search and AdSense for content. AdSense for search, launched in the first quarter of 2002, is our service for distributing relevant ads from our advertisers for display with search results on our Google Network members' sites. AdSense for content, launched in the first quarter of 2003, is our service for distributing ads from our advertisers that are relevant to content on our Google Network members' sites. Our advertisers pay us a fee each time a user clicks on one of our advertisers' ads displayed on Google Network members' web sites. In the past, we have paid most of these advertiser fees to the members of the Google Network, and we expect to continue doing so for the foreseeable future. We recognize these advertiser fees as revenue and the portion of the advertiser fee we pay to our Google Network members as cost of revenue. In some cases, we guarantee our Google Network members minimum revenue share payments. Members of the Google Network do not pay any fees associated with the use of our AdSense program on their web sites. Some of our Google Network members separately license our web search technology and pay related licensing fees to us. Our agreements with Google Network members consist largely of uniform online "click-wrap" agreements that members enter into by interacting with our registration web sites. Agreements with our larger members are individually negotiated. The standard agreements have no stated term and are terminable at will. The negotiated agreements vary in duration. Both the standard agreements and the negotiated agreements contain provisions requiring us to share with the Google Network member a portion of the advertiser fees generated by users clicking on ads on the Google Network member's web site. The standard agreements have uniform revenue share terms. The negotiated agreements vary as to revenue share terms and are heavily negotiated.

We believe the factors that influence the success of our advertising programs include the following:

- The relevance, objectivity and quality of our search results.

- The number of searches initiated at our web sites or our Google Network members' web sites.

- The relevance and quality of advertisements displayed with search results on our web sites and of Google Network members' web sites, or with the content on our Google Network members' web sites.

- The total number of advertisements displayed on our web sites and on web sites of Google Network members.

- The rate at which people click on advertisements.

- The number of advertisers.

- The total and per click advertising spending budgets of an advertiser.

- *Our minimum fee per click, which is currently $0.05.*

- The advertisers' return on investment from advertising campaigns on our web sites or on the web sites of our Google Network members compared to other forms of advertising.

Advertising revenues made up 77%, 94%, 97% and 98% of our revenues in 2001, 2002, 2003 and in the six months ended June 30, 2004. We derive the balance of our revenues from the license of our web search technology, the license of our search solutions to enterprises and the sale and license of other products and services.

Trends in Our Business

Our business has grown rapidly since inception, and we anticipate that our business will continue to grow. This growth has been characterized by substantially increased revenues. However, our revenue growth rate has declined, and we expect that it will continue to decline as a result of increasing competition and the inevitable decline in growth rates as our revenues increase to higher levels. In addition, steps we take to improve the relevance of the ads displayed, such as removing ads that generate low click-through rates, could negatively affect our near-term advertising revenues.

The operating margin we realize on revenues generated from the web sites of our Google Network members through our AdSense program is significantly lower than that generated from paid clicks on our web sites. This lower operating margin arises because most of the advertiser fees from our AdSense agreements are shared with our Google Network members, leaving only a portion of these fees for us. The growth in advertising revenues from our Google Network members' web sites has historically exceeded that from our web sites. This has resulted in an increased portion of our revenue being derived from our Google Network members' web sites and has had a negative impact on operating margins. The relative rate of growth in revenues from our web sites compared to the rate of growth in revenues from our Google Network members' web sites is likely to vary over time. For example, in the second quarter of 2004, growth in advertising revenues from our web sites exceeded that from our Google Network members' web sites.

Our operating margin was greater in the six months ended June 30, 2004 compared to the year ended December 31, 2003. However we believe that our operating margin may decline in 2004 compared to 2003 as a result of an anticipated increase in costs and expenses, other than stock-based compensation, as a percentage of revenues. This decrease may be wholly or partially offset to the extent revenue growth from our Google web sites exceeds that of our Google Network members, as well as from an anticipated decrease in stock-based compensation as a percentage of net revenues in 2004 compared to 2003. The expected increase in cost and expenses, other than stock-based compensation, as a percentage of revenues is primarily a result of building the necessary employee and systems infrastructures required to manage our anticipated growth.

We have a large and diverse base of advertisers and Google Network members. No advertiser generated more than 3% of our revenues in 2001, and no more than 2% in 2002, 2003 or in the six months ended June 30, 2004. In addition, advertising and other revenues generated from one Google Network member, America Online, Inc., primarily through our AdSense programs, accounted for approximately 15%, 16% and 13% of our revenues in 2002, 2003 and in the six months ended June 30, 2004; no other Google Network members' web sites generated advertising fees of more than 10% of our revenues. We expect our base of advertisers and Google Network members to remain large and diverse for the foreseeable future.

We have experienced and expect to continue to experience substantial growth in our operations as we seek to expand our user, advertiser and Google Network members bases and continue to expand our presence in international markets. This growth has required the continued expansion of our human resources and substantial investments in property and equipment. Our full-time employee headcount has grown from 284 at December 31, 2001, to 682 at December 31, 2002, to 1,628 at December 31, 2003 and to 2,292 at June 30, 2004. In addition, we have employed a significant number of temporary employees in the past and expect to continue to do so in the foreseeable future. Our capital expenditures have grown from $13.1 million in 2001, to $37.2 million in 2002, to $176.8 million in 2003 and to $182.3 million in the six months ended June 30, 2004. We currently expect to spend at least $300 million on capital equipment, including information technology infrastructure, to manage our operations during 2004. In addition, we anticipate that the growth rate of our costs and expenses, other than stock-based compensation, may exceed the growth rate of our revenues during 2004. Management of this growth will continue to require the devotion of significant employee and other resources. We may not be able to manage this growth effectively.

In early 2003, we decided to invest significant resources to begin the process of comprehensively documenting and analyzing our system of internal controls. We have identified areas of our internal controls requiring improvement, and we are in the process of designing enhanced processes and controls to address any issues identified through this review. Areas for improvement include streamlining our domestic and international billing processes, further limiting internal access to certain data systems and continuing to improve coordination across business functions. During our 2002 audit, our external auditors brought to our attention a need to increase restrictions on employee access to our advertising system and automate more of our financial processes. The auditors identified these issues together as a "reportable condition," which means that these were matters that in the auditors' judgment could adversely affect our ability to record, process, summarize and report financial data consistent with the assertions of management in our financial statements. In 2003, we devoted significant resources to remediate and improve our internal controls. Although we believe that these efforts have strengthened our internal controls and addressed the concerns that gave rise to the "reportable condition" in 2002, we are continuing to work to improve our internal controls, including in the areas of access and security. We plan to continue to invest the resources necessary to ensure the effectiveness of our internal controls and procedures, including in the areas of access and security.

The portion of our revenues derived from international markets has increased. Our international revenues have grown as a percentage of our total revenues from 22% in 2002 to 29% in 2003, and have grown from 28% in the six months ended June 30, 2003 to 31% in the six months ended June 30, 2004. This increase in the portion of our revenues derived from international markets results largely from increased acceptance of our advertising programs in international markets, an increase in our direct sales resources in international markets and services as well as customer support operations and our continued progress in developing versions of our products tailored for these markets.

Results of Operations

The following is a more detailed discussion of our financial condition and results of operations for the periods presented.

The following table presents our historical operating results as a percentage of revenues for the periods indicated:

	Year Ended December 31, 2001	Year Ended December 31, 2002	Year Ended December 31, 2003	Three Months Ended March 31, 2004	Three Months Ended June 30, 2004	Six Months Ended June 30, 2003	Six Months Ended June 30, 2004
				(unaudited)			
Consolidated Statements of Income Data:							
Revenues	100.0%	100.0%	100.0%	100.0%	100.0%	100.0%	100.0%
Costs and expenses:							
Cost of revenues	16.5	29.9	42.7	48.4	46.6	36.5	47.5
Research and development	19.1	7.2	6.2	5.4	6.5	5.4	6.0
Sales and marketing	23.2	10.0	8.2	7.4	8.1	7.6	7.7
General and administrative	14.2	5.5	3.9	3.3	3.7	4.0	3.5
Stock-based compensation	14.3	4.9	15.6	11.7	10.7	12.6	11.2
Total costs and expenses	87.3	57.5	76.6	76.2	75.6	66.1	75.9
Income from operations	12.7	42.5	23.4	23.8	24.4	33.9	24.1
Interest income (expense) and other, net	(1.0)	(0.4)	0.2	0.1	(0.2)	0.1	(0.1)
Income before income taxes	11.7	42.1	23.6	23.9	24.2	34.0	24.0
Provision for income taxes	3.6	19.4	16.4	14.1	12.9	23.6	13.4
Net income	8.1%	22.7%	7.2%	9.8%	11.3%	10.4%	10.6%

Revenues

The following table presents our revenues, by revenue source, for the periods presented:

	Year Ended December 31, 2001	2002	2003	Three Months Ended March 31, 2004	June 30, 2004	Six Months Ended June 30, 2003	June 30, 2004
				(dollars in thousands)		(unaudited)	
Advertising revenues:							
Google web sites	$66,932	$306,978	$ 792,063	$303,532	$343,442	$341,002	$ 646,974
Google Network web sites	—	103,937	628,600	333,752	346,226	198,801	679,978
Total advertising revenues	66,932	410,915	1,420,663	637,284	689,668	539,803	1,326,952
Licensing and other revenues	19,494	28,593	45,271	14,339	10,544	20,014	24,883
Revenues	$86,426	$439,508	$1,465,934	$651,623	$700,212	$559,817	$1,351,835

The following table presents our revenues, by revenue source, as a percentage of total revenues for the periods presented:

	Year Ended December 31, 2001	2002	2003	Three Months Ended March 31, 2004	June 30, 2004	Six Months Ended June 30, 2003	June 30, 2004
					(unaudited)		
Advertising revenues:							
Google web sites	77%	70%	54%	47%	49%	61%	48%
Google Network web sites	—	24	43	51	49	35	50
Total advertising revenues	77	94	97	98	98	96	98
Google web sites as % of advertising revenues	100	75	56	48	50	63	49
Google Network web sites as % of advertising revenues	—	25	44	52	50	37	51
Licensing and other revenues	23%	6%	3%	2%	2%	4%	2%

Growth in our revenues from 2002 to 2003, and from the three months ended March 31, 2004 to the three months ended June 30, 2004, resulted primarily from growth in advertising revenues from ads on our Google Network members web sites and growth in revenues from ads on our web sites. The advertising revenue growth resulted primarily from increases in the total number of paid clicks and advertisements displayed through our programs, rather than from changes in the fees charged. Revenue growth was driven to a lesser extent by our introduction late in the first quarter of 2003 of AdSense for content. Growth in our revenues from the six months ended June 30, 2003 compared to the six months ended June 30, 2004 resulted primarily from growth in advertising revenues from ads on our Google Network members' web sites and growth in revenues from ads on our web sites. This increase was the result of increases in the number of paid clicks rather than from changes in the fees charged. The increase in the number of paid clicks was due to an increase in the number of Google Network members and aggregate traffic at their web sites and on our web sites. Our revenues grew by 27.2% from the three month period ended December 31, 2003 to the three month period ended March 31, 2004, but grew by only 7.5% for the three month period ended March 31, 2004 to the three month period ended June 30, 2004. The reasons for the decline in growth in revenues are described in the following paragraphs.

Growth in advertising revenues from our Google Network members web sites from the three months ended March 31, 2004 to the three months ended June 30, 2004 was $12.5 million or 3.7%, compared to $78.4 million or 30.7% from the three months ended December 31, 2003 to the three months ended March 31, 2004. This decrease in the growth rate was the result of slower growth in the number of page views and search queries, and ultimately paid clicks, on our Google Network member web sites due to seasonality. In addition, we entered into no new significant AdSense for search arrangements in the three months ended June 30, 2004.

Table of Contents

Growth in advertising revenues from our web sites from the three months ended March 31, 2004 to the three months ended June 30, 2004 was $39.9 million or 13.2% compared to $59.7 million or 24.5% from the three months ended December 31, 2003 to the three months ended March 31, 2004 due to seasonality.

Licensing and other revenues decreased by $3.8 million from the three months ended March 31, 2004 to the three months ended June 30, 2004 primarily as a result of fewer search queries served by us on Yahoo's web sites and fewer search queries on certain licensee web sites due to seasonality.

Growth in our revenues from 2001 to 2002 resulted primarily from growth in advertising revenues from ads on our web sites. The growth in advertising revenues resulted primarily from increases in the total number of paid clicks under our cost-per-click programs and the total number of advertisements displayed through our cost-per-displayed ad programs, rather than from changes in the fees charged. The revenue growth was driven in part by our introduction of our cost-per-click revenue model in the early part of 2002, which contributed to a significant increase in the number of our advertisers and by our introduction of AdSense for search in the first quarter of 2002.

We believe the increases in revenues described above were the result of the relevance and quality of both the search results and advertisements displayed, which resulted in more searches, advertisers and Google Network members, and ultimately more paid clicks.

Revenues by Geography

Domestic and international revenues as a percentage of consolidated revenues, determined based on the billing addresses of our advertisers, are set forth below.

	Year Ended December 31,			Three Months Ended		Six Months Ended	
	2001	2002	2003	March 31, 2004	June 30, 2004	June 30, 2003	June 30, 2004
				(unaudited)			
United States	82%	78%	71%	69%	69%	72%	69%
International	18%	22%	29%	31%	31%	28%	31%

The growth in international revenues is the result of our efforts to provide search results to international users and deliver more ads from non-U.S. advertisers. We expect that international revenues will continue to grow as a percentage of our total revenues during 2004 and in future periods. While international revenues accounted for approximately 29% of our total revenues in 2003 and 31% in the six months ended June 30, 2004, more than half of our user traffic came from outside the U.S. See Note 12 of Notes to Consolidated Financial Statements included as part of this prospectus for additional information about geographic areas.

Costs and Expenses

Cost of Revenues. Cost of revenues consists primarily of traffic acquisition costs. Traffic acquisition costs consist of payments made to our Google Network members. These payments are primarily based on revenue share arrangements under which we pay our Google Network members most of the fees we receive from our advertisers whose ads we place on those Google Network member sites. In addition, certain AdSense agreements obligate us to make guaranteed minimum revenue share payments to Google Network members based on their achieving defined performance terms, such as number of search queries or advertisements displayed. We amortize guaranteed minimum revenue share prepayments (or accrete an amount payable to our Google Network member if the payment is due in arrears) based on the number of search queries or advertisements displayed on the Google Network member's web site. In addition, concurrent with the commencement of certain AdSense agreements we have purchased certain items from, or provided other consideration to, our Google Network members. These amounts are amortized on a pro-rata basis over the related term of the agreement.

The following table presents our traffic acquisition costs (in millions), traffic acquisition costs as a percentage of advertising revenues from Google Network web sites and traffic acquisition costs as a percentage of advertising revenues, for the periods presented.

	Year Ended December 31,			Three Months Ended		Six Months Ended	
	2001	2002	2003	March 31, 2004	June 30, 2004	June 30, 2003	June 30, 2004
		(unaudited)		(unaudited)		(unaudited)	
Traffic acquisition costs	—	$94.5	$526.5	$271.0	$277.0	$166.7	$548.0
Traffic acquisition costs as a percentage of advertising revenues from Google Network web sites	—	91%	84%	81%	80%	84%	81%
Traffic acquisition costs as a percentage of advertising revenues	—	23%	37%	43%	40%	31%	41%

In addition, cost of revenues consists of the expenses associated with the operation of our data centers, including depreciation, labor, energy and bandwidth costs. Cost of revenues also includes credit card and other transaction fees related to processing customer transactions, as well as amortization of expenses related to purchased and licensed technologies.

Cost of revenues increased by $11.0 million to $326.4 million (or 46.6% of revenues) in the three months ended June 30, 2004, from $315.4 million (or 48.4% of revenues) in the three months ended March 31, 2004. This increase in dollars was primarily the result of additional traffic acquisition costs and the depreciation of additional information technology assets purchased in the current and prior periods and additional data center costs required to manage more Internet traffic, advertising transactions and new products and services. There was an increase in traffic acquisition costs of $6.0 million and an increase in data center costs of $4.9 million primarily resulting from the depreciation of additional information technology assets purchased in the current and prior periods.

Cost of revenues increased by $437.2 million to $641.8 million (or 47.5% of revenues) in the six months ended June 30, 2004, from $204.6 million (or 36.5% of revenues) in the six months ended June 30, 2003. This increase was primarily the result of additional traffic acquisition costs and the depreciation of additional information technology assets purchased in the current and prior periods and additional data center costs required to manage more Internet traffic, advertising transactions and new products and services. There was an increase in traffic acquisition costs of $381.3 million and in data center costs of $39.6 million primarily resulting from the depreciation of additional information technology assets purchased in the current and prior periods. In addition, there was an increase in credit card and other transaction processing fees of $13.1 million resulting from more advertiser fees generated through AdWords.

Cost of revenues increased by $494.4 million to $625.9 million (or 42.7% of revenues) in 2003, from $131.5 million (or 29.9% of revenues) in 2002. This increase was primarily the result of increased traffic acquisition costs and additional data center costs required to manage more Internet traffic, advertising transactions and new products and services. Traffic acquisition costs increased $432.0 million due to an increase in the number of paid clicks on our Google Network members web sites. There was an increase in data center costs of $39.9 million primarily resulting from depreciation of additional information technology assets purchased in current and prior periods. In addition, there was an increase of $15.7 million in credit card and other transaction processing fees and an increase of $4.9 million related to amortization of developed technology resulting from acquisitions in 2003.

Cost of revenues increased by $117.3 million to $131.5 million (or 29.9% of revenues) in 2002, from $14.2 million (or 16.5% of revenues) in 2001. This increase was primarily the result of traffic acquisition costs and additional data center costs required to manage more Internet traffic, advertising transactions and new products and services. Traffic acquisition costs related to AdSense first introduced in 2002 totaled $94.5 million.

Table of Contents

There was an increase in data center costs of $15.3 million primarily resulting from depreciation of additional information technology assets purchased in current and prior periods. In addition, there was an increase in credit card and other transactional processing fees of $6.7 million.

In each period to date, the aggregate fees we have earned under our AdSense agreements have exceeded the aggregate amounts we have been obligated to pay our Google Network members. However, individual agreements have resulted in guaranteed minimum and other payments to Google Network members in excess of the related fees we receive from advertisers. In 2003 and in the six months ended June 30, 2004, we made guaranteed minimum and other payments of $22.5 million and $18.2 million in excess of the related fees we received from our advertisers.

We expect cost of revenues to increase in dollars and as a percentage of revenues in 2004 compared to 2003 primarily as a result of forecasted increases in traffic acquisition costs, and in our data center costs required to manage increased traffic, advertising transactions and new products and services. Also, increasing competition for arrangements with web sites that are potential Google Network members could result in our entering into more AdSense agreements under which guaranteed payments to Google Network members exceed the fees we receive from advertisers.

Research and Development. Research and development expenses consist primarily of compensation and related costs for personnel responsible for the research and development of new products and services, as well as significant improvements to existing products and services. We expense research and development costs as they are incurred.

Research and development expenses increased by $10.8 million to $45.8 million (or 6.5% of revenues) in the three months ended June 30, 2004, from $35.0 million (or 5.4% of revenues) in the three months ended March 31, 2004. This increase was primarily due to an increase in labor and facilities related costs of $7.2 million as a result of an 18% increase in research and development headcount. In addition, depreciation and related expenses increased by $2.3 million primarily as a result of additional information technology assets purchased over the six months ended June 30, 2004.

Research and development expenses increased by $50.8 million to $80.8 million (or 6.0% of revenues) in the six months ended June 30, 2004, from $30.0 million (or 5.4% of revenues) in the six months ended June 30, 2003. This increase was primarily due to an increase in labor and facilities related costs of $35.3 million as a result of a 100% increase in research and development headcount. The increase in headcount was a result of the rapid growth of our business between these periods. In addition, depreciation and related expenses increased by $13.7 million primarily as a result of additional information technology assets purchased over the eighteen-month period ended June 30, 2004.

Research and development expenses increased by $59.5 million to $91.2 million (or 6.2% of revenues) in 2003, from $31.7 million (or 7.2% of revenues) in 2002. This increase in dollars was primarily due to an increase in labor and facilities related costs of $34.3 million as a result of a 101% increase in research and development headcount. In addition, we recognized $11.6 million of in-process research and development expenses during 2003 as a result of an acquisition. Note 4 of Notes to Consolidated Financial Statements included as part of this prospectus describes further purchased in-process research and development expenses and other acquisitions.

Research and development expenses increased by $15.2 million to $31.7 million (or 7.2% of revenues) in 2002, from $16.5 million (or 19.1% of revenues) in 2001. This increase was primarily due to an increase in labor and facilities related costs of $13.2 million, principally as a result of an 83% increase in research and development headcount.

We anticipate that research and development expenses will increase in dollar amount and may increase as a percentage of revenues in 2004 and future periods because we expect to hire more research and development personnel and build the infrastructure required to support the development of new, and improve existing, products and services.

Table of Contents

Sales and Marketing. Sales and marketing expenses consist primarily of compensation and related costs for personnel engaged in customer service and sales and sales support functions, as well as advertising and promotional expenditures.

Sales and marketing expenses increased $8.9 million to $56.8 million (or 8.1% of revenues) in the three months ended June 30, 2004, from $47.9 million (or 7.4% of revenues) in the three months ended March 31, 2004. This increase was primarily due to an increase in labor and facilities related costs of $5.5 million mostly as a result of a 19% increase in sales and marketing headcount. In addition, advertising and promotional expenses increased $3.8 million. The increase in sales and marketing personnel and advertising and promotional expenses was a result of our on-going efforts to secure new—and to provide support to our existing—users, advertisers and Google Network members, on a worldwide basis.

Sales and marketing expenses increased $62.1 million to $104.7 million (or 7.7% of revenues) in the six months ended June 30, 2004, from $42.6 million (or 7.6% of revenues) in the six months ended June 30, 2003. This increase was primarily due to an increase in labor and facilities related costs of $42.9 million mostly as a result of a 100% increase in sales and marketing headcount. In addition, advertising and promotional expenses increased $10.9 million and travel-related expenses increased $1.9 million. The increase in sales and marketing personnel and advertising, promotional and travel-related expenses was a result of our on-going efforts to secure new, and to provide support to our existing, users, advertisers and Google Network members, on a worldwide basis.

Sales and marketing expenses increased $76.5 million to $120.3 million (or 8.2% of revenues) in 2003, from $43.8 million (or 10.0% of revenues) in 2002. This increase in dollars was primarily due to an increase in labor and facilities related costs of $54.4 million mostly as a result of a 149% increase in sales and marketing headcount. In addition, advertising and promotional expenses increased $12.9 million and travel related expenses increased $3.2 million, primarily in the second half of 2003. The increase in sales and marketing personnel and advertising, promotional and travel-related expenses was a result of our on-going efforts to secure new, and to provide support to our existing, advertisers and Google Network members, on a worldwide basis. For instance, we have hired personnel to help our advertisers maximize their return on investment through the selection of appropriate keywords and have promoted the distribution of the Google Toolbar to Internet users in order to make our search services easier to access.

Sales and marketing expenses increased $23.7 million to $43.8 million (or 10.0% of revenues) in 2002, from $20.1 million (or 23.2% of revenues) in 2001. This increase in dollars was primarily due to increases in labor and facilities related costs of $19.5 million, primarily as a result of a 202% increase in headcount. Also, advertising and promotional expenses increased $1.7 million and travel related expenses increased $1.3 million.

We anticipate sales and marketing expenses will increase in dollar amount and may increase as a percentage of revenues in 2004 and future periods as we continue to expand our business on a worldwide basis. A significant portion of these increases relate to our plan to add support personnel to increase the level of service we provide to our advertisers and Google Network members.

General and Administrative. General and administrative expenses consist primarily of compensation and related costs for personnel and facilities related to our finance, human resources, facilities, information technology and legal organizations, and fees for professional services. Professional services are principally comprised of outside legal, audit and information technology consulting. To date, we have not experienced any significant amount of bad debts.

General and administrative expenses increased $4.1 million to $25.6 million (or 3.7% of revenues) in the three months ended June 30, 2004, from $21.5 million (or 3.3% of revenues) in the three months ended March 31, 2004. This increase was primarily due to an increase in labor and facilities related costs of $1.2 million, primarily as a result of a 27% increase in headcount, and an increase in professional services fees of $2.0 million. The additional personnel and professional services fees are the result of the growth of our business.

Table of Contents

General and administrative expenses increased $24.5 million to $47.1 million (or 3.5% of revenues) in the six months ended June 30, 2004, from $22.6 million (or 4.0% of revenues) in the six months ended June 30, 2003. This increase in dollars was primarily due to an increase in labor and facilities related costs of $12.8 million, primarily as a result of a 93% increase in headcount, and an increase in professional services fees of $7.0 million. The additional personnel and professional services fees are the result of the growth of our business.

General and administrative expenses increased $32.4 million to $56.7 million (or 3.9% of revenues) in 2003, from $24.3 million (or 5.5% of revenues) in 2002. This increase in dollars was primarily due to an increase in labor and facilities related costs of $16.7 million, primarily as a result of a 194% increase in headcount, and an increase in professional services fees of $10.0 million, primarily in the second half of 2003. The additional personnel and professional services fees are the result of the growth of our business.

General and administrative expenses increased $12.0 million to $24.3 million (or 5.5% of revenues) in 2002, from $12.3 million (or 14.2% of revenues) in 2001. This increase in dollars was primarily due to an increase in labor and facilities related costs of $7.8 million, mostly as a result of a 96% increase in headcount and an increase in professional services fees of $3.9 million. The additional personnel and professional services fees are the result of the growth of our business.

As we expand our business and incur additional expenses associated with being a public company, we believe general and administrative expenses will increase in dollar amount and may increase as a percentage of revenues in 2004 and in future periods.

Stock-Based Compensation. We have granted stock options at exercise prices equal to the value of the underlying stock as determined by our board of directors on the date of option grant. For purposes of financial accounting, we have applied hindsight within each year to arrive at reassessed values for the shares underlying our options. We recorded the difference between the exercise price of an option awarded to an employee and the reassessed value of the underlying shares on the date of grant as deferred stock-based compensation. The determination of the reassessed value of stock underlying options is discussed in detail below in "Critical Accounting Policies and Estimates—Stock-Based Compensation." We recognize compensation expense as we amortize the deferred stock-based compensation amounts on an accelerated basis over the related vesting periods, generally four or five years. In addition, we have awarded options to non-employees to purchase our common stock. Stock-based compensation related to non-employees is measured on a fair-value basis using the Black-Scholes valuation model as the options are earned.

Stock-based compensation in the three months ended June 30, 2004 decreased $1.7 million to $74.8 million (or 10.7% of revenues) from $76.5 million (or 11.7% of revenues) in the three months ended March 31, 2004. The decrease was primarily due to a decrease of $3.9 million of stock-based compensation related to the modification of terms of former employees' stock option agreements and a decrease in the level of stock option grants in the three months ended June 30, 2004, and smaller differences between the exercise prices and the reassessed values of the underlying common stock on the dates of grant, partially offset by the amortization of deferred stock-based compensation amounts from prior periods recognized in the current period.

Stock-based compensation in the six months ended June 30, 2004 increased $80.6 million to $151.2 million (or 11.2% of revenues) from $70.6 million (or 12.6% of revenues) in the six months ended June 30, 2003. The increase in dollars was primarily driven by the larger differences between the exercise prices and the reassessed values of the underlying common stock on the dates of grant, partially offset by a decrease in the level of stock option grants, in recent periods. The increase was also driven by the recognition of $3.9 million of stock-based compensation related to the modification of terms of former employees' stock option agreements in the three months ended March 31, 2004. No such modifications were made in the three months ended March 31, 2003.

Stock-based compensation increased $207.8 million to $229.4 million (or 15.6% of revenues) in 2003 from $21.6 million (or 4.9% of revenues) in 2002. The increase was primarily driven by the the larger differences between the exercise prices and the reassessed values of the underlying common stock on the dates of grant and, to a lesser extent, an increase in the level of stock option grants in 2003. Stock-based compensation increased $9.2 million to $21.6 million (or 4.9% of revenues) in 2002 from $12.4 million (or 14.3% of revenues) in 2001. The increase in dollars was primarily driven by the larger differences between the exercise prices and the reassessed values of the underlying common stock on the dates of grant, partially offset by a decrease in the level of stock option grants in 2002.

We expect stock-based compensation to be $117.2 million for the remaining six months of 2004, $137.7 million in 2005, $66.9 million in 2006, $24.1 million in 2007, $5.2 million in 2008 and $1.7 million thereafter, related to the deferred stock-based compensation on the balance sheet at June 30, 2004. These amounts do not include stock-based compensation related to options granted to non-employees and any options granted to employees and directors subsequent to June 30, 2004 at exercise prices less than the reassessed value on the date of grant and any additional compensation expense that may be required as a result of any changes in the stock option accounting rules. These amounts also assume the continued employment throughout the referenced periods of the recipient of the options that gave rise to the deferred stock-based compensation.

At December 31, 2003, there were 500,150 unvested options held by non-employees with a weighted average exercise price of $0.69, a weighted average 48-month remaining vesting period and a weighted average 4-year remaining expected life. The options generally vest on a monthly and ratable basis subsequent to December 31, 2003. Depending on the fair market value of these options on their vesting dates, which will depend in significant part on the then current trading price of our Class A common stock, the related charge could be significant during 2004 and subsequent periods. We recognized $5.4 million of stock-based compensation related to these options that vest over time in the six months ended June 30, 2004. No options that vest over time were granted to non-employees in the six months ended June 30, 2004.

Interest Income (Expense) and Other, Net

Interest income (expense) and other of $1.2 million of expense in the six months ended June 30, 2004 was primarily the result of $3.4 million of foreign exchange losses from net receivables denominated in currencies other than U.S. dollars as a result of generally weakening foreign currencies against the U.S. dollar during the six months ended June 30, 2004, and approximately $500,000 of interest expense incurred on equipment leases, including the amortization of the fair value of warrants issued to lenders in prior years. This was partially offset by $2.7 million of interest income and realized gains earned on cash, cash equivalents and short-term investments balances.

Interest income (expense) and other of $700,000 in the six months ended June 30, 2003 was primarily the result of approximately $1.2 million of interest income earned on cash, cash equivalents and short-term investments balances and approximately $700,000 of net foreign exchange gains from net receivables denominated in currencies other than U.S. dollars as a result of generally strengthening foreign currencies against the U.S. dollar during the six months ended June 30, 2003. These income sources were partially offset by approximately $1.0 million of interest expense incurred on equipment loans and leases, including the amortization of the fair value of warrants issued to lenders in prior years, and approximately $200,000 of losses incurred on the disposal of certain assets.

Interest income (expense) and other of $4.2 million in 2003 was primarily the result of $2.7 million of interest income earned on cash, cash equivalents and short-term investments balances, and $2.1 million of net foreign exchange gains from net receivables denominated in currencies other than U.S. dollars as a result of generally strengthening foreign currencies against the U.S. dollar throughout 2003. In addition, we recognized $1.4 million of other income in 2003, primarily related to a gain recorded for certain upfront fees paid by advertisers whose ads were not delivered during the related contract periods. These income sources were partially offset by $1.9 million of interest expense incurred on equipment loans and leases, including the amortization of the fair value of warrants issued to lenders in prior years.

Table of Contents

Interest income (expense) and other of $900,000 of expense and $1.6 million of expense in 2001 and 2002 was primarily the result of interest expense incurred on equipment loans and leases, including the amortization of the fair value of warrants issued to lenders, partially offset by interest income on cash, cash equivalents and short-term investments balances.

Provision for Income Taxes

Our provision for income taxes decreased to $90.4 million or an effective tax rate of 53% in the three months ended June 30, 2004, from $91.7 million, or an effective tax rate of 59% in the three months ended March 31, 2004. In addition, our provision for income taxes increased to $182.0 million, or an effective tax rate of 56% in the six months ended June 30, 2004 from $132.2 million, or an effective tax rate of 70%, in the six months ended June 30, 2003. The decrease in our effective tax rate in the three months ended June 30, 2004 compared to the three months ended March 31, 2004 was primarily due to a decrease in forecasted stock-based compensation expense as a percentage of income before income taxes in 2004. Our provision for income taxes increased to $241.0 million or an effective tax rate of 70% during 2003, from $85.3 million or an effective tax rate of 46% during 2002, and from $3.1 million or an effective tax rate of 31% during 2001. The increases in provision for income taxes primarily resulted from increases in Federal and state income taxes, driven by higher taxable income year over year. Our effective tax rate is our provision for income taxes expressed as a percentage of our income before income taxes. Our effective tax rate is higher than the statutory rate because, in arriving at income before income taxes, we include in our costs and expenses significant non-cash expenses related to stock-based compensation, which are recognized for financial reporting purposes, but are not deductible for income tax purposes. The increases in our effective tax rates over each of 2001, 2002 and 2003 were primarily the result of an increase in stock-based compensation amounts.

We expect our effective tax rate to decrease in 2004, primarily as a result of an expected decrease in stock-based compensation charges as a percentage of pre-tax income in 2004 compared to 2003. Furthermore, once there is a public market for our stock, we may reduce our tax provision based on benefits we may realize upon exercise of certain options outstanding. Any such reduction would lower our effective tax rate.

A reconciliation of the federal statutory income tax rate to our effective tax rate is set forth in Note 11 of Notes to Consolidated Financial Statements included in this prospectus.

Settlement of Disputes with Yahoo

On August 9, 2004, we and Yahoo entered into a settlement agreement resolving two disputes that had been pending between us. The first dispute concerned a lawsuit filed by Yahoo's wholly-owned subsidiary, Overture Services, Inc., against us in April 2002 asserting that certain services infringed Overture's U.S. Patent No. 6,269,361. In our court filings, we denied that we infringed the patent and alleged that the patent was invalid and unenforceable.

The second dispute concerned a warrant held by Yahoo to purchase 3,719,056 shares of our stock in connection with a June 2000 services agreement. Pursuant to a conversion provision in the warrant, in June 2003 we issued 1,229,944 shares to Yahoo. Yahoo contended it was entitled to a greater number of shares, while we contended that we had fully complied with the terms of the warrant.

As part of the settlement, Overture will dismiss its patent lawsuit against us and has granted us a fully-paid, perpetual license to the patent that was the subject of the lawsuit and several related patent applications held by Overture. The parties also mutually released any claims against each other concerning the warrant dispute. In connection with the settlement of these two disputes, we issued to Yahoo 2,700,000 shares of Class A common stock.

We will incur a non-cash charge in the third quarter of 2004 related to this settlement. Based on an assumed per share value of the settlement consideration equal to the midpoint of the proposed initial public offering price range included in this prospectus, we preliminarily estimate that this non-cash charge will be between

Table of Contents

$195 million and $215 million in the three months ending September 30, 2004. The non-cash charge will include, among other items, the value of shares associated with the settlement of the warrant dispute. The non-cash charge associated with these shares is required because they are being issued after the warrant was converted. We will also realize an income tax benefit in the third quarter, based on preliminary estimates, of between $75 million and $85 million related to this non-cash charge. The charge will result in a net loss for us in the three months ending September 30, 2004. We anticipate that we will capitalize various intangible assets obtained in this settlement and that these amounts will be amortized ratably over their useful lives, preliminarily expected to be between one and five years. The issuance of 2,700,000 shares represents approximately one percent of the number of shares currently expected to be used in the diluted per share calculation for the three and nine months ending September 30, 2004 and for the year ending December 31, 2004. The foregoing estimates of the amounts to be expensed, the associated tax benefit and the periods over which the capitalized assets will be amortized, are preliminary. As a result, they are subject to further review and may change materially. In finalizing these amounts, we expect to use the actual initial public offering price to determine the reported value of the settlement consideration. We will also engage a third party valuation consultant to assist management in the allocation of the settlement amount and the determination of the useful lives of the capitalized assets and expect to complete these analyses during the third quarter of 2004.

Quarterly Results of Operations

You should read the following tables presenting our quarterly results of operations in conjunction with the consolidated financial statements and related notes contained elsewhere in this prospectus. We have prepared the unaudited information on the same basis as our audited consolidated financial statements. You should also keep in mind, as you read the following tables, that our operating results for any quarter are not necessarily indicative of results for any future quarters or for a full year.

The following table presents our unaudited quarterly results of operations for the ten quarters ended June 2004. This table includes all adjustments, consisting only of normal recurring adjustments, that we consider necessary for fair presentation of our financial position and operating results for the quarters presented. We believe that we experience increased levels of Internet traffic focused on commercial transactions in the fourth quarter and decreased levels of Internet traffic in the summer months. Prior to the second quarter of 2004, these seasonal trends may have been masked by the substantial quarter over quarter growth in our revenues.

	Mar 31, 2002	Jun 30, 2002	Sep 30, 2002	Dec 31, 2002	Mar 31, 2003	Jun 30, 2003	Sep 30, 2003	Dec 31, 2003	Mar 31, 2004	Jun 30, 2004
	(In thousands, except per share amounts) (unaudited)
Consolidated Statements of Income Data:
Revenues	$42,285	$78,525	$130,787	$187,911	$248,618	$311,199	$393,942	$512,175	$651,623	$700,212
Costs and expenses:
Cost of revenues	5,692	20,407	39,622	65,789	87,195	117,401	170,390	250,868	315,398	326,377
Research and development(1)	6,183	6,457	9,053	10,055	12,505	17,492	32,774	28,457	35,019	45,762
Sales and marketing	7,294	11,176	11,704	13,675	17,767	24,822	36,575	41,164	47,904	56,777
General and administrative	4,135	5,653	7,313	7,199	10,027	12,535	13,853	20,284	21,506	25,577
Stock-based compensation(2)	3,774	3,735	6,182	7,944	36,418	34,165	73,794	84,984	76,473	74,761
Total costs and expenses	27,078	47,428	73,874	104,662	163,912	206,415	327,386	425,757	496,300	529,254
Income from operations	15,207	31,097	56,913	83,249	84,706	104,784	66,556	86,418	155,323	170,958
Interest income, expense and other, net	(501)	(310)	(677)	(63)	(47)	766	464	3,007	300	(1,498)
Income before income taxes	14,706	30,787	56,236	83,186	84,659	105,550	67,020	89,425	155,623	169,460
Provision for income taxes	6,780	14,194	25,929	38,356	58,859	73,382	46,594	62,171	91,650	90,397
Net income	$7,926	$16,593	$30,307	$44,830	$25,800	$32,168	$20,426	$27,254	$63,973	$79,063
Net income per share:
Basic	$0.07	$0.15	$0.26	$0.37	$0.20	$0.24	$0.14	$0.19	$0.42	$0.51
Diluted	$0.04	$0.08	$0.13	$0.19	$0.10	$0.12	$0.08	$0.10	$0.24	$0.30

(1) The results for the quarter ended September 30, 2003 includes $11.6 million of in-process research and development expense related to an acquisition.

APPENDIX I GOOGLE INC. FORM S–1 REGISTRATION STATEMENT

Table of Contents

(2) Stock-based compensation, consisting of amortization of deferred stock-based compensation and the reassessed value of options issued to non-employees for services rendered, is allocated in the table that follows. Stock-based compensation in any quarter is affected by the number of grants in the current and prior quarters, and the difference between the values determined by the board of directors on the date of grant and the reassessed values used for financial accounting purposes. The use of the accelerated basis of amortization results in significantly greater stock-based compensation in the first year of vesting compared to subsequent years.

	Mar 31, 2002	Jun 30, 2002	Sep 30, 2002	Dec 31, 2002	Mar 31, 2003	Jun 30, 2003	Sep 30, 2003	Dec 31, 2003	Mar 31, 2004	Jun 30, 2004
					(in thousands) (unaudited)					
Cost of revenues	$ 146	$ 158	$ 343	$ 418	$ 1,452	$ 1,361	$ 3,008	$ 2,736	$ 5,076	$ 2,546
Research and development	1,242	1,415	2,802	3,287	19,423	18,814	43,878	56,262	46,265	45,836
Sales and marketing	473	827	1,528	2,106	7,618	7,093	15,819	14,077	14,146	13,431
General and administrative	1,913	1,335	1,509	2,133	7,925	6,897	11,089	11,909	10,986	12,948
	$ 3,774	$ 3,735	$ 6,182	$ 7,944	$ 36,418	$ 34,165	$ 73,794	$ 84,984	$ 76,473	$ 74,761

The following table presents our unaudited quarterly results of operations as a percentage of revenues for the ten quarters ended June 30, 2004.

	Mar 31, 2002	Jun 30, 2002	Sep 30, 2002	Dec 31, 2002	Mar 31, 2003	Jun 30, 2003	Sep 30, 2003	Dec 31, 2003	Mar 31, 2004	Jun 30, 2004
As Percentage of Revenues:										
Revenues	100.0%	100.0%	100.0%	100.0%	100.0%	100.0%	100.0%	100.0%	100.0%	100.0%
Costs and expenses:										
Cost of revenues	13.5	26.0	30.3	35.0	35.1	37.7	43.3	49.0	48.4	46.6
Research and development(1)	14.6	8.2	6.9	5.4	5.0	5.6	8.3	5.5	5.4	6.5
Sales and marketing	17.2	14.2	9.0	7.3	7.2	8.0	9.3	8.0	7.4	8.1
General and administrative	9.8	7.2	5.6	3.8	4.0	4.0	3.5	4.0	3.3	3.7
Stock-based compensation(2)	8.9	4.8	4.7	4.2	14.6	11.0	18.7	16.6	11.7	10.7
Total costs and expenses	64.0	60.4	56.5	55.7	65.9	66.3	83.1	83.1	76.2	75.6
Income from operations	36.0	39.6	43.5	44.3	34.1	33.7	16.9	16.9	23.8	24.4
Interest income, expense and other, net	(1.2)	(0.4)	(0.5)	(0.0)	(0.0)	0.2	0.1	0.6	0.1	(0.2)
Income before income taxes	34.8	39.2	43.0	44.3	34.1	33.9	17.0	17.5	23.9	24.2
Net income	18.7%	21.1%	23.2%	23.9%	10.4%	10.3%	5.2%	5.3%	9.8%	11.3%

(1) The results for the quarter ended September 30, 2003 includes $11.6 million of in-process research and development expense related to an acquisition.

(2) Stock-based compensation, consisting of amortization of deferred stock-based compensation and the reassessed value of options issued to non-employees for services rendered, is allocated in the table that follows. Stock-based compensation in any quarter is affected by the number of grants in the current and prior quarters, and the difference between the values determined by the board of directors on the date of grant and the reassessed values used for financial accounting purposes. The use of the accelerated basis of amortization results in significantly greater stock-based compensation in the first year of vesting compared to subsequent years.

	Mar 31, 2002	Jun 30, 2002	Sep 30, 2002	Dec 31, 2002	Mar 31, 2003	Jun 30, 2003	Sep 30, 2003	Dec 31, 2003	Mar 31, 2004	Jun 30, 2004
Cost of revenues	0.4%	0.2%	0.3%	0.2%	0.6%	0.4%	0.8%	0.5%	0.8%	0.4%
Research and development	2.9	1.8	2.1	1.8	7.8	6.1	11.1	11.0	7.1	6.5
Sales and marketing	1.1	1.1	1.2	1.1	3.0	2.3	4.0	2.8	2.1	1.9
General and administrative	4.5	1.7	1.1	1.1	3.2	2.2	2.8	2.3	1.7	1.9
	8.9%	4.8%	4.7%	4.2%	14.6%	11.0%	18.7%	16.6%	11.7%	10.7%

Liquidity and Capital Resources

In summary, our cash flows were:

	Year Ended December 31, 2001	Year Ended December 31, 2002	Year Ended December 31, 2003	Six Months Ended June 30, 2003	Six Months Ended June 30, 2004
		(in thousands)		(unaudited)	
Net cash provided by operating activities	$ 31,089	$ 155,265	$ 395,445	$177,174	$ 370,604
Net cash used in investing activities	(29,091)	(109,717)	(313,954)	(92,059)	(294,994)
Net cash provided by (used in) financing activities	(2,439)	(5,473)	8,090	3,899	32,327

Since inception, we have financed our operations primarily through internally generated funds, private sales of preferred stock totaling $37.6 million and the use of our lines of credit with several financial institutions. At June 30, 2004, we had $548.7 million of cash, cash equivalents and short-term investments, compared to $334.7 million, $146.3 million and $33.6 million at December 31, 2003, 2002 and 2001, respectively. Cash equivalents and short-term investments are comprised of highly liquid debt instruments of the U.S. government and its agencies and municipalities. Note 2 of Notes to Consolidated Financial Statements included as part of this prospectus describes further the composition of our short-term investments.

Our principal sources of liquidity are our cash, cash equivalents and short-term investments, as well as the cash flow that we generate from our operations. At June 30, 2004 and December 31, 2003, we had unused letters of credit for approximately $14.9 million and $12.2 million. We believe that our existing cash, cash equivalents, short-term investments and cash generated from operations will be sufficient to satisfy our currently anticipated cash requirements through at least the next 12 months. Our liquidity could be negatively affected by a decrease in demand for our products and services. In addition, we may make acquisitions or license products and technologies complementary to our business and may need to raise additional capital through future debt or equity financing to the extent necessary to fund any such acquisitions and licensing activities. Additional financing may not be available at all or on terms favorable to us.

Cash provided by operating activities primarily consists of net income adjusted for certain non-cash items including depreciation, amortization, stock-based compensation, and the effect of changes in working capital and other activities. Cash provided by operating activities in the six months ended June 30, 2004 was $370.6 million and consisted of net income of $143.0 million, adjustments for non-cash items of $206.9 million and $20.7 million provided by working capital and other activities. Working capital and other activities primarily consisted of an increase in income tax liabilities, net, of $43.0 million (before a reduction in income taxes payable of $93.2 million due to warrant exercises), partially offset by an increase of $36.5 million in accounts receivable due to the growth in fees billed to our advertisers.

Cash provided by operating activities in the six months ended June 30, 2003 was $177.2 million and consisted of net income of $58.0 million, adjustments for non-cash items of $93.3 million and $25.9 million provided by working capital and other activities. Working capital and other activities primarily consisted of an increase in income tax liabilities, net, of $16.6 million and an increase of $35.9 million in accrued revenue share due to the growth in our AdSense programs and the timing of payments made to our Google Network members, partially offset by an increase of $34.2 million in accounts receivable due to the growth in fees billed our advertisers.

Cash provided by operating activities in 2003 was $395.4 million and consisted of net income of $105.6 million, adjustments for non-cash items of $296.0 million and $6.2 million used by working capital and other activities. Working capital and other activities primarily consisted of an increase of $90.4 million in accounts receivable due to the growth in fees billed our advertisers and an increase of $58.9 million in prepaid revenue share, expenses and other assets, due primarily to an increase of $35.5 million related to prepaid revenue share, as a result of several significant prepayments made in the fourth quarter of 2003, as well as an increase of

Table of Contents

$11.0 million of restricted cash relating to our operating leases. This was partially offset by an increase of $74.6 million in accrued revenue share due to the growth in our AdSense programs and the timing of payments made to our Google Network members and an increase of $31.1 million in accrued expenses and other liabilities primarily due to an increase in annual bonuses as a result of the growth in the number of employees. These bonuses were paid in the first quarter of 2004.

Cash provided by operating activities in 2002 was $155.3 million and consisted of net income of $99.7 million, adjustments for non-cash items of $50.6 million and $5.0 million provided by working capital and other activities. Cash provided by operating activities in 2001 was $31.1 million and consisted of net income of $7.0 million, adjustments for non-cash items of $26.6 million and $2.5 million used by working capital and other activities.

As warrants to purchase an additional 1,996,140 shares of our stock, and as certain options to purchase additional shares of Class A and Class B common stock, are exercised as anticipated over the current and future years, we expect to realize significant reductions in our tax liabilities. In addition, we expect to realize a significant reduction in our tax liabilities in the three months ended September 30, 2004 as a result of the issuance of 2,700,000 shares of our Class A common stock pursuant to the settlement of certain disputes with Yahoo in August 2004. Note 14 of Notes to Consolidated Financial Statements included as part of this prospectus provides further disclosure of this settlement and a preliminary estimate of the tax benefit. The reduction in our tax liability is computed based on the applicable statutory rates and the difference between the value of our stock on the date of exercise or issuance, as determined by our board of directors or the market, and the price paid for those shares.

Also, as we expand our business internationally, we may offer payment terms to certain advertisers that are standard in their locales, but longer than terms we would generally offer to our domestic advertisers. This may increase our working capital requirements and may have a negative effect on cash flow provided by our operating activities. In addition, we expect that, once we are a public company, our cash-based compensation per employee will likely increase (in the form of variable bonus awards and other incentive arrangements) in order to retain and attract employees.

Cash used in investing activities in the six months ended June 30, 2004 of $295.0 million was attributable to capital expenditures of $182.3 million, net purchases of short-term investments of $109.2 million and cash consideration used in acquisitions of $3.5 million. Cash used in investing activities in the six months ended June 30, 2003 of $92.1 million was attributable to capital expenditures of $60.6 million and net purchases of short-term investments of $7.9 million. Capital expenditures are mainly for the purchase of information technology assets. Cash used in investing activities in 2003 of $314.0 million was attributable to capital expenditures of $176.8 million, net purchases of short-term investments of $97.2 million and net cash consideration used in acquisitions of $40.0 million. Cash used in investing activities in 2002 of $109.7 million was primarily attributable to net purchases of short-term investments of $72.6 million and capital expenditures of $37.2 million. Cash used in investing activities in 2001 of $29.1 million was primarily attributable to net purchases of short-term investments of $14.9 million and capital expenditures of $13.1 million. In order to manage expected increases in Internet traffic, advertising transactions and new products and services, and to support our overall global business expansion, we will continue to invest heavily in data center operations, technology, corporate facilities and information technology infrastructure. We currently expect to spend at least $300 million on capital equipment, including information technology infrastructure comprised primarily of production servers and network equipment, to manage our operations during 2004.

Cash provided by financing activities in the six months ended June 30, 2004 of $32.3 million was due primarily to proceeds from the issuance of common and convertible preferred stock pursuant to warrant exercises of $21.9 million, as well as to proceeds from the issuance of common stock pursuant to stock option exercises of $8.6 million, net of repurchases, and a $4.3 million payment received from a stockholder on a note receivable, offset by repayment of capital lease obligations of $2.4 million. Cash provided by financing activities in the six months ended June 30, 2003 of $3.9 million was due to proceeds from the issuance of common stock pursuant to stock option exercises of $7.8 million, net of repurchases, offset by repayment of equipment loans and capital lease obligations of $3.9 million. Cash provided by financing activities in 2003 of $8.1 million was due to proceeds from the issuance of common stock pursuant to stock option exercises of $15.5 million, net of repurchases, offset by repayment of equipment loan and lease obligations of $7.4 million. Cash used in financing activities in 2002 of $5.5 million was due to repayment of equipment loan and capital lease obligations of $7.7 million, partially offset by proceeds from the issuance of common stock pursuant to stock option exercises of $2.3 million, net of repurchases. Cash used in financing activities in 2001 of $2.4 million was primarily due to repayment of equipment loan and capital lease obligations of $4.5 million partially offset by proceeds from the issuance of convertible preferred stock of $1.0 million and the issuance of common stock pursuant to stock option exercises of $1.0 million, net of repurchases. We estimate that we will receive significant net proceeds from our sale of shares of Class A common stock offered by us in this offering. We currently have no specific plans for the use of these net proceeds. See "Use of Proceeds" above. Pending such uses, we plan to invest the net proceeds in highly liquid, investment grade securities.

Contractual Obligations

Contractual obligations at December 31, 2003 are as follows:

	Total	Less than 12 months	13-48 months	49-60 months	More than 60 months
			(in millions) (unaudited)		
Guaranteed minimum revenue share payments	$477.0	$ 205.1	$271.9	$ —	$ —
Capital lease obligations	7.4	5.3	2.1	—	—
Operating lease obligations	146.7	7.4	50.9	18.8	69.6
Purchase obligations	11.9	8.8	3.1	—	—
Other long-term liabilities reflected on our balance sheet under GAAP	1.5	—	0.2	0.2	1.1
Total contractual obligations	$644.5	$ 226.6	$328.2	$19.0	$ 70.7

Guaranteed Minimum Revenue Share Payments

In connection with our AdSense revenue share agreements, we are periodically required to make non-cancelable guaranteed minimum revenue share payments to a small number of our Google Network members over the term of the respective contracts. Under our contracts, these guaranteed payments can vary based on our Google Network members achieving defined performance terms, such as number of advertisements displayed or search queries. In some cases, certain guaranteed amounts will be adjusted downward if our Google Network members do not meet their performance terms and, in some cases, these amounts will be adjusted upward if they exceed their performance terms. Upward adjustments are capped at total advertiser fees generated under an AdSense agreement during the guarantee period. The amounts included in the table above assume that the historical upward performance adjustments with respect to each contract will continue, but do not make a similar assumption with respect to downward adjustments. We believe these amounts best represent a reasonable estimate of the future minimum guaranteed payments. Actual guaranteed payments may differ from the estimates presented above. To date, total advertiser fees generated under these AdSense agreements have exceeded the total guaranteed minimum revenue share payments. Five of our Google Network members account for approximately 70% of the total future guaranteed minimum revenue share payments and 10 of our Google Network members account for 91% of these payments. In 2003, we made $108.8 million of non-cancellable minimum guaranteed revenue payments. At June 30, 2004, our aggregate outstanding non-cancellable minimum guarantee commitments totaled $369.4 million through 2007.

In addition, in connection with some other AdSense agreements, we have agreed to make an aggregate of $51.9 million of minimum revenue share payments through 2006. This amount is not included in the above table

Table of Contents

since we generally have the right to cancel these agreements at any time. Because we sometimes cancel agreements that perform poorly, we do not expect to make all of these minimum revenue share payments. At June 30, 2004, this amount had decreased to $27.5 million.

Capital Lease Obligations

At December 31, 2003, we had capital lease obligations of $7.4 million (comprised of $6.6 million of principal and $800,000 of interest) related to several of our equipment leases. These amounts will come due under the terms of the arrangements at various dates through October 2005.

Operating Leases

During 2003, we entered into a nine-year sublease for our headquarters in Mountain View, California. According to the terms of the sublease, we will begin making payments in July 2005 and payments will increase at 3% per annum thereafter. We recognize rent expense on our operating leases on a straight-line basis as of the commencement of the lease. The lease terminates on December 31, 2012; however, we may exercise two five-year renewal options at our discretion. We have an option to purchase the property for approximately $172.4 million, which is exercisable in 2006.

In addition, we have entered into various other non-cancelable operating lease agreements for our offices and certain of our data centers throughout the U.S. and internationally with original lease periods expiring between 2004 and 2015. We recognize rent expense on our operating leases on a straight-line basis at the commencement of the lease. Certain of these leases have free or escalating rent payment provisions. We recognize rent expense under such leases on a straight-line basis. Total payments relating to leases having an initial or remaining non-cancelable term of less than one year are $2.3 million and are not included in the table above.

Subsequent to December 31, 2003, we entered into additional non-cancelable operating lease agreements with future minimum commitment payments as follows: $900,000 due in less than 12 months, $11.7 million due in 13-48 months, $6.6 million due in 49-60 months and $10.6 million due in more than 60 months which are not included in the above table.

Purchase Obligations

Purchase obligations in the above table represent non-cancelable contractual obligations at December 31, 2003. In addition, we had $24.9 million of open purchase orders for which we have not received the related services or goods at December 31, 2003. This amount is not included in the above table since we have the right to cancel the purchase orders upon 10 days notice prior to the date of delivery. The majority of our purchase obligations are related to data center operations.

Acquisition of Applied Semantics

In April 2003, we acquired all of the outstanding capital stock of Applied Semantics, Inc., a privately held provider of content-targeted advertising programs. The total purchase price consisted of a cash payment of $41.5 million and 2,382,800 shares of, and options to purchase, Class A common stock. The transaction was accounted for as a business combination. For additional information, see Note 4 of Notes to Consolidated Financial Statements included as part of this prospectus.

Off-Balance Sheet Entities

At December 31, 2003 and 2002, we did not have any relationships with unconsolidated entities or financial partnerships, such as entities often referred to as structured finance or special purpose entities, which would have been established for the purpose of facilitating off balance sheet arrangements or other contractually narrow or limited purposes.

Critical Accounting Policies and Estimates

We prepare our consolidated financial statements in accordance with accounting principles generally accepted in the U.S. In doing so, we have to make estimates and assumptions that affect our reported amounts of assets, liabilities, revenues and expenses, as well as related disclosure of contingent assets and liabilities. In many cases, we could reasonably have used different accounting policies and estimates. In some cases changes in the accounting estimates are reasonably likely to occur from period to period. Accordingly, actual results could differ materially from our estimates. To the extent that there are material differences between these estimates and actual results, our financial condition or results of operations will be affected. We base our estimates on past experience and other assumptions that we believe are reasonable under the circumstances, and we evaluate these estimates on an ongoing basis. We refer to accounting estimates of this type as critical accounting policies and estimates, which we discuss further below. Our management has reviewed our critical accounting policies and estimates with our board of directors.

Stock-based Compensation

Accounting for Stock-Based Awards to Employees

We have granted stock options at exercise prices equal to the value of the underlying stock as determined by our board of directors on the date of option grant. For purposes of financial accounting, we have applied hindsight to arrive at reassessed values for the shares underlying our options and issued under other transactions. There are two measures of value of our common stock that are relevant to our accounting for equity compensation relating to our compensatory equity grants:

- The "board-determined value" is the per share value of our common stock determined by our board of directors at the time the board makes an equity grant, taking into account a variety of factors, including our historical and projected financial results, comparisons of comparable companies, risks facing us, as well as the liquidity of the common stock.

- The "reassessed value" is the per share value of our common stock determined by us in hindsight solely for the purpose of financial accounting for employee stock-based compensation.

We record deferred stock-based compensation to the extent that the reassessed value of the stock at the date of grant exceeds the exercise price of the option. The reassessed values for accounting purposes were determined based on a number of factors and methodologies. One of the significant methods we used to determine the reassessed values for the shares underlying options is through a comparison of price multiples of our historical and forecasted earnings to certain public companies involved in the same or similar lines of business. The market capitalizations of these companies has increased significantly since January 2003 which contributed significantly to the increase in the reassessed values of our shares. We also considered our financial performance and growth, primarily since January 2003. Our revenue and earnings growth rates contributed significantly to the increase in the reassessed values of our shares. The reassessed values of our shares increased more significantly in dollar and percentage terms in earlier periods compared to later ones which is reflective of the related revenue and earnings growth rates. We also retained third party advisors to provide two contemporaneous valuation analyses since January 2003 and used this information to support our own valuation analyses. Please note that these reassessed values are inherently uncertain and highly subjective. If we had made different assumptions, our deferred stock-based compensation amount, stock-based compensation expense, in-process research and development expense, net income, net income per share and recorded goodwill amounts could have been significantly different.

Table of Contents

The table below shows the computation of deferred stock-based compensation amounts arising from restricted shares and unvested stock options granted to employees for each of the three month periods set forth below:

	Three Months Ended					Three Months Ended	
	March 31, 2003	June 30, 2003	September 30, 2003	December 31, 2003	2003 Total	March 31, 2004	June 30, 2004
	(unaudited)	(unaudited)	(unaudited)	(unaudited)		(unaudited)	(unaudited)
Options granted to employees	10,262,100	1,431,552	5,785,185	1,281,895	18,760,732	1,004,780	965,520
Weighted average exercise price	$ 0.49	$ 3.30	5.17	$ 9.62		$ 16.27	$ 38.43
Weighted average reassessed value of underlying stock	$ 13.09	$ 33.99	52.33	$ 75.05		$ 88.13	97.03
Weighted average reassessed deferred stock-based compensation per option	$ 12.60	$ 30.69	47.16	$ 65.43		$ 71.86	58.60
Deferred stock-based compensation related to options (in millions)	$ 129.3	43.9	272.8	$ 83.9	529.9	72.2	56.6
Restricted shares granted to employees		120,000	114,999		234,999		16,175
Weighted average reassessed value of restricted shares		$ 25.96	66.41				$ 95.09
Deferred stock-based compensation related to restricted shares (in millions)		$ 3.1	7.6		$ 10.7		$ 1.5
Deferred stock-based compensation related to option modifications (in millions)				$ 10.8	$ 10.8	3.9	
Total deferred stock-based compensation (in millions)	$ 129.3	$ 47.0	280.4	$ 94.7	551.4	$ 76.1	58.1

We recognize compensation expense as we amortize the deferred stock-based compensation amounts on an accelerated basis over the related vesting periods. The table below shows employee and non-employee stock-based compensation expense recognized during 2001, 2002, 2003 and through the six months ended June 30, 2004. In addition, the table presents the expected stock-based compensation expense for options granted to employees prior to July 1, 2004, for the second half of 2004 and for each of the next four years and thereafter, assuming no change in the stock option accounting rules and assuming all employees remain employed by us for their remaining vesting periods. These amounts are compared to the expense and expected expense we would have recognized had we amortized deferred stock-based compensation on a straight-line basis.

	Stock-based compensation expense Year Ended December 31,								
	2001	2002	2003	2004	2005	2006	2007	2008	thereafter
					(in millions)				
Accelerated basis	$12.4	$21.6	$229.4	$268.4	$137.7	$ 66.9	$ 24.1	$ 5.2	$ 1.7
Straight-line basis	$ 5.9	$13.3	$120.5	$170.5	$164.2	$153.8	$101.7	$30.4	$ 8.3

We have elected to not record stock-based compensation expense for employee stock option awards using the Black-Scholes option-pricing model. This model was developed for use in estimating the fair value of freely traded options that have no vesting restrictions and are fully transferable. In addition, this model requires the input of highly subjective assumptions including the expected life of options and our expected stock price volatility. Because our employee stock options have characteristics significantly different from those of freely traded options, and because changes in the subjective input assumptions can materially affect the fair value estimate, in our opinion, this model does not provide a reliable measure of the fair value of our employee stock options. Note 1 of Notes to Consolidated Financial Statements included as part of this prospectus describes what the impact would have been had we expensed employee stock awards under the fair value method using the Black-Scholes option-pricing model.

Accounting for Stock-Based Awards to Non-employees

We measure the fair value of options to purchase our common stock granted to non-employees throughout the vesting period as they are earned, at which time we recognize a charge to stock-based compensation. The fair value is determined using the Black-Scholes option-pricing model, which considers the exercise price relative to the reassessed value of the underlying stock, the expected stock price volatility, the risk-free interest rate and the dividend yield. As discussed above, the reassessed value of the underlying stock were based on assumptions of matters that are inherently highly uncertain and subjective. As there has been no public market for our stock, our assumptions about stock-price volatility are based on the volatility rates of comparable publicly held companies. These rates may or may not reflect our stock-price volatility should we become a publicly held company. If we had made different assumptions about the reassessed value of our stock or stock-price volatility rates, the related stock-based compensation expense and our net income and net income per share amounts could have been significantly different.

Effect of Recent Accounting Pronouncements

In November 2002, the EITF reached a consensus on Issue 00-21, *Accounting for Multiple Element Revenue Arrangements*, addressing how to account for arrangements that involve the delivery or performance of multiple products, services, and/or rights to use assets. Revenue arrangements with multiple deliverables are divided into separate units of accounting if the deliverables in the arrangement meet the following criteria: (1) the delivered item has value to the customer on a standalone basis; (2) there is objective and reliable evidence of the fair value of undelivered items; and (3) delivery of any undelivered item is probable. Arrangement consideration should be allocated among the separate units of accounting based on their relative fair values, with the amount allocated to the delivered item limited to the amount that is not contingent on the delivery of additional items or meeting other specified performance conditions. The guidance in Issue 00-21 is effective for revenue arrangements entered into in fiscal periods after June 15, 2003. The adoption of Issue 00-21 did not have an impact on our financial statements. See the further discussion in Note 1 of Notes to the Consolidated Financial Statements included as part of this prospectus.

During November 2002, the FASB issued Interpretation No. 45, *Guarantor's Accounting and Disclosure Requirements for Guarantees, Including Indirect Guarantees of Indebtedness to Others, an interpretation of FASB Statements No. 5, 57 and 107 and a rescission of FASB Interpretation No. 34* (FIN 45). FIN 45 elaborates on the existing disclosure requirements for a guarantor in its interim and annual financial statements regarding its obligations under guarantees issued. It also clarifies that at the time a guarantee is issued, the guarantor must recognize an initial liability for the fair value of the obligations it assumes under the guarantee and must disclose that information in its financial statements. The initial recognition and measurement provisions apply on a prospective basis to guarantees of third party obligations issued or modified after December 31, 2002, and the disclosure requirements apply to such guarantees outstanding at December 31, 2002. The Company adopted the provisions of FIN 45 at January 1, 2003. The adoption of this Interpretation did not have an impact on our operating results. See further discussion regarding indemnifications in Note 7 to the Notes to the Consolidated Financial Statements included with this prospectus.

In January 2003, the FASB issued Interpretation No. 46, *Consolidation of Variable Interest Entities*. Interpretation No. 46 clarifies the application of Accounting Research Bulletin No. 51. This Interpretation requires variable interest entities to be consolidated if the equity investment at risk is not sufficient to permit an entity to finance its activities without support from other parties or the equity investors lack specified characteristics. We do not have any variable interest entities.

Table of Contents

In May 2003, the FASB issued SFAS No. 150, *Accounting for Certain Financial Instruments with Characteristics of both Liabilities and Equity*. SFAS No. 150 establishes standards for how a company classifies and measures certain financial instruments with characteristics of both liabilities and equity. It requires that an issuer classify certain financial instruments as a liability (or as an asset in some circumstances). SFAS No. 150 is effective for financial instruments entered into or modified after May 31, 2003, and otherwise is effective at the beginning of the first interim period beginning after June 15, 2003. The adoption of SFAS No. 150 did not have an impact on our financial statements.

Qualitative and Quantitative Disclosures about Market Risk

We are exposed to financial market risks, including changes in currency exchange rates, interest rates and marketable equity security prices.

Foreign Exchange Risk

Our exposure to foreign currency transaction gains and losses is the result of certain net receivables of the U.S. parent due from its subsidiaries and customers being denominated in currencies other than the U.S. dollar, primarily the British Pound, the Euro and the Japanese Yen. Our foreign subsidiaries conduct their businesses in local currency. Effective January 2004, we began to bill our international online sales through a foreign subsidiary, which will lower our exposure to foreign currency transaction gains and losses. In addition, effective January 2004 our board of directors approved a foreign exchange hedging program designed to minimize the future potential impact due to changes in foreign currency exchange rates. The program allows for the hedging of transaction exposures. The types of derivatives that can be used under the policy are forward contracts, options and foreign exchange swaps. The primary vehicle we expect to use will be forward contracts. We also generate revenue in certain countries in Asia where there are limited forward currency exchange markets, thus making these exposures difficult to hedge. In the three months ended June 30, 2004, we entered into forward foreign exchange contracts to offset the foreign exchange risk on certain existing intercompany assets. The notional principal of forward exchange contracts to purchase U.S. dollars with Euros was $116.9 million at June 30, 2004. There were no other forward foreign exchange contracts outstanding at June 30, 2004.

Our exposure to foreign currency translation gains and losses arises from the translation of certain net assets of our subsidiaries to U.S. dollars during consolidation. During 2003, we recognized a foreign currency translation gain of $1.7 million as a result of greater aggregate net assets of our subsidiaries and stronger foreign currencies compared to the U.S. dollar at December 31, 2003 than at December 31, 2002.

We considered the historical trends in currency exchange rates and determined that it was reasonably possible that adverse changes in exchange rates of 10% for all currencies could be experienced in the near term. These changes would have resulted in an adverse impact on income before taxes of approximately $18.7 million and $4.5 million at June 30, 2004 and December 31, 2003. These reasonably possible adverse changes in exchange rates of 10% were applied to total monetary assets denominated in currencies other than the local currencies at the balance sheet dates to compute the adverse impact these changes would have had on our income before taxes in the near term. The increase in the reasonably possible adverse impact of $18.7 million and $4.5 million at June 30, 2004 and December 31, 2003 were primarily the result of an increase in intercompany receivables and cash held by our Irish subsidiary denominated in foreign currencies. The transaction gains and losses that netted to a $2.8 million loss and a $2.1 million gain in the three months and year ended June 30, 2004 and December 31, 2003 are a function of the exchange rates on the dates these transactions were entered into and the dates they were settled or the balance sheet dates.

Table of Contents

Interest Rate Risk

We invest in a variety of securities, consisting primarily of investments in interest-bearing demand deposit accounts with financial institutions, tax-exempt money market funds and highly liquid debt securities of corporations and municipalities. By policy, we limit the amount of credit exposure to any one issuer.

Investments in both fixed rate and floating rate interest earning products carry a degree of interest rate risk. Fixed rate securities may have their fair market value adversely impacted due to a rise in interest rates, while floating rate securities may produce less income than predicted if interest rates fall. Due in part to these factors, our income from investments may decrease in the future.

We considered the historical volatility of short term interest rates and determined that it was reasonably possible that an adverse change of 100 basis points could be experienced in the near term. A hypothetical 1.00% (100 basis-point) increase in interest rates would have resulted in a decrease in the fair values of our investment securities of approximately $3.2 million and $1.9 million at June 30, 2004 and December 31, 2003.

Table of Contents

BUSINESS

Overview

Google is a global technology leader focused on improving the ways people connect with information. Our innovations in web search and advertising have made our web site a top Internet destination and our brand one of the most recognized in the world. We maintain the world's largest online index of web sites and other content, and we make this information freely available to anyone with an Internet connection. Our automated search technology helps people obtain nearly instant access to relevant information from our vast online index.

We generate revenue by delivering relevant, cost-effective online advertising. Businesses use our AdWords program to promote their products and services with targeted advertising. In addition, the thousands of third-party web sites that comprise our Google Network use our Google AdSense program to deliver relevant ads that generate revenue and enhance the user experience.

Our Mission

Our mission is to organize the world's information and make it universally accessible and useful. We believe that the most effective, and ultimately the most profitable, way to accomplish our mission is to put the needs of our users first. We have found that offering a high-quality user experience leads to increased traffic and strong word-of-mouth promotion. Our dedication to putting users first is reflected in three key commitments we have made to our users:

- We will do our best to provide the most relevant and useful search results possible, independent of financial incentives. Our search results will be objective and we will not accept payment for inclusion or ranking in them.

- We will do our best to provide the most relevant and useful advertising. If any element on a result page is influenced by payment to us, we will make it clear to our users. Advertisements should not be an annoying interruption.

- We will never stop working to improve our user experience, our search technology and other important areas of information organization.

We believe that our user focus is the foundation of our success to date. We also believe that this focus is critical for the creation of long-term value. We do not intend to compromise our user focus for short-term economic gain.

How We Provide Value to Users, Advertisers and Web Sites

Our Users

We serve our users by developing products that enable people to more quickly and easily find, create and organize information. We place a premium on products that matter to many people and have the potential to improve their lives, especially in areas in which our expertise enables us to excel.

Search is one such area. People use search frequently and the results are often of great importance to them. For example, people search for information on medical conditions, purchase decisions, technical questions, long-lost friends and other topics about which they care a great deal. Delivering quality search results requires significant computing power, advanced software and complex processes—areas in which we have expertise and a high level of focus.

Communication is another such area. People increasingly rely on the Internet to communicate with each other. Gmail, our new email service (still in test mode), offers a gigabyte of free storage for each user, along with email search capabilities and relevant advertising. Delivering an improved user experience in Gmail has similar computing and software requirements as our search service.

Table of Contents

Some of the key benefits we offer to users include:

Relevant and Useful Information. Our technologies sort through a vast and growing amount of information to deliver relevant and useful search results in response to user queries. This is an area of continual development for us. When we started the company five years ago, our web index contained approximately 30 million documents. We now index more than 4 billion web pages, or more than 100 times as much information. We are also constantly developing new functionality. Recent enhancements include personalization, which lets users specify interests to help our technology generate customized search results; and local search, which lets users look for web pages and businesses based on a certain geographic location. We also provide convenient links to specialized information, such as definitions, maps and travel information.

Objectivity. We believe it is very important that the results users get from Google are produced with only their interests in mind. We do not accept money for search result ranking or inclusion. We do accept fees for advertising, but it does not influence how we generate our search results. The advertising is clearly marked and separated. This is similar to a newspaper, where the articles are independent of the advertising. Some of our competitors charge web sites for inclusion in their indices or for more frequent updating of pages. Inclusion and frequent updating in our index are open to all sites free of charge. We apply these principles to each of our products and services. We believe it is important for users to have access to the best available information and research, not just the information that someone pays for them to see.

Global Access. We strive to provide Google to everyone in the world. Users from around the world visit our destination sites at Google.com and our 95 other international domains, such as Google.de, Google.fr, Google.co.uk, Google.co.jp and Google.ca. The Google interface is available in more than 90 languages. Through Google News, we offer an automated collection of frequently updated news stories tailored to 10 international audiences. We also offer automatic translation of content between various languages. We provide localized versions of Google in many developing countries. Although we do not currently recover our costs in these countries, we believe providing our products and services is an important social good and a valuable long-term business investment.

Ease of Use. We have always believed that the most useful and powerful search technology hides its complexity from users and provides them with a simple, intuitive way to get the information they want. We have devoted significant efforts to create a streamlined and easy-to-use interface based on a clean search box set prominently on a page free of commercial clutter. We have also created many features that enhance the user experience. Our products present these features when we believe they will be most useful, rather than promoting them unnecessarily. For example, Google WebSearch offers maps when a search appears to be for a geographic location.

Pertinent, Useful Commercial Information. The search for information online often involves an interest in commercial information—researching a purchase, comparing products and services or actively shopping. We help people find commercial information through our search services and by presenting ads that are relevant to the information people seek. To ensure we display only the most relevant commercial information, our technology automatically rewards ads that users prefer and removes ads that users do not find helpful. For example, among our search services, we offer Froogle, a search engine for finding products for sale online.

Our Advertisers

As more people spend additional time and money online, advertisers are increasingly turning to the Internet to market their products and services to consumers. For these advertisers, we offer Google AdWords, an auction-based advertising program that enables them to deliver relevant ads targeted to search results or web content. Our AdWords program provides advertisers with a cost-effective way to deliver ads to customers across Google sites and through the Google Network. The advertisers using AdWords range from small businesses targeting local customers to many of the world's largest global enterprises.

Table of Contents

The AdWords program offers advertisers the following benefits:

Effective Return on Investment. Many advertising dollars are wasted because they are spent delivering messages that are ignored or that reach too broad an audience. With Google AdWords, businesses can achieve greater cost-effectiveness with their marketing budgets for two reasons— AdWords shows ads only to people seeking information related to what the advertisers are selling, and advertisers pay us only when a user clicks on one of their ads. Because we offer a simple ad format, advertisers can avoid incurring significant design, copywriting or other production costs associated with creating ads. As a result, even small advertisers find AdWords cost-effective for connecting with potential customers. In addition, advertisers can easily create many different ads, increasing the likelihood that an ad is exactly suited to a user's search. Users can find advertisements for exactly what they are seeking, and advertisers can find users who want exactly what they are offering. When the interests of users and advertisers align, both are well served.

Access to the Google Network. We serve AdWords ads to the thousands of third-party web sites that make up the Google Network. As a result, advertisers that use our AdWords program can target users on our sites and on search and content sites across the web. This gives advertisers increased exposure to people who are likely to be interested in their offerings. The Google Network significantly enhances our ability to attract interested users.

Precise Campaign Control. Google AdWords gives advertisers hands-on control over most elements of their ad campaigns. Advertisers can specify the relevant search or content topics for each of their ads. Advertisers can also manage expenditures by setting a maximum daily budget and determining how much they are willing to pay whenever a user clicks on an ad. Our online tracking tools and reports give advertisers timely updates on how well their campaigns are performing and enable them to make changes or refinements quickly. Advertisers can also target their campaigns by neighborhood, city, country, region or language.

Global Support. We provide customer service to our advertiser base through our global support organization as well as through field sales offices in 11 countries. AdWords is available on a self-service basis with email support. Advertisers with more extensive needs and budgets can request strategic support services, which include an account team of experienced professionals to help them set up, manage and optimize their campaigns.

Web Sites

Nearly every web site in the world is indexed and made searchable by Google. Our users do searches and are directed to relevant web sites. Google provides a significant amount of traffic to web sites with which we have no business relationship. Many web sites are able to generate revenue from that traffic, but others have difficulty doing so. We are enthusiastic about helping sites make money and thereby facilitating the creation of better content to search. If there is better content on the web, people are likely to do more searches, and we expect that will be good for our business and for users. To address this opportunity, we created Google AdSense. Our Google AdSense program enables the web sites—large and small—that make up the Google Network to deliver AdWords ads that are relevant to the search results or content on their pages. We share most of the revenue generated from ads shown by a member of the Google Network with that member—creating an additional revenue stream for them. Web sites can also license our Google WebSearch product to offer the Google search experience to their users. The key benefits we offer to web sites in the Google Network include:

Access to Advertisers. Many small web site companies do not have the time or resources to develop effective programs for generating revenue from online advertising. Even larger sites, with dedicated sales teams, may find it difficult to generate revenue from pages with specialized content. We believe that Google AdSense enables Google Network members to generate revenue from their sites more effectively and efficiently. Google AdSense promotes effective revenue generation by providing Google Network members immediate access to Google's base of advertisers and their broad collection of ads. As soon as a web site joins the Google Network, our technology automatically begins delivering ads for posting on the member's web site. The automated nature of our advertising programs promotes efficient revenue generation. Our online registration systems enable web

Table of Contents

sites to easily join the Google Network and our ad serving technology allows automated delivery of ads for posting on the member's site. The Google Network member determines the placement of the ads on its web site and controls and directs the nature of ad content.

Improved User Satisfaction. In their quest for revenue, many Internet companies have cluttered their web sites with intrusive or untargeted advertising that may distract or confuse users and may undermine users' ability to find the information they want. Some web sites have adopted practices we consider to be abusive, including pop-up ads or ads that take over web pages. We believe these tactics can cause dissatisfaction with Internet advertising and reduce use of the Internet overall. Our AdSense program extends our commitment to improving the overall web experience for users by enabling web sites to display AdWords ads in a fashion that we believe people find useful rather than disruptive.

Products and Services

Our product development philosophy is centered on rapid and continuous innovation, with frequent releases of test products that we seek to improve with every iteration. We often make products available early in their development stages by posting them on Google Labs, at test locations online or directly on Google.com. If our users find a product useful, we promote it to "beta" status for additional testing. Our beta testing periods often last a year or more. Once we are satisfied that a product is of high quality and utility, we remove the beta label and make it a core Google product. Our current principal products and services are described below.

Google.com

We are focused on building products and services that benefit our users and enable them to find relevant information quickly and easily. We offer, free of charge, all of the following services at Google.com and many of them at our international sites.

Google WebSearch. In addition to providing easy access to more than 4 billion web pages, we have integrated special features into Google WebSearch to help people find exactly what they are looking for on the web. The Google.com search experience also includes:

- Advanced Search Functionality—enables users to construct more complex queries, for example by using Boolean logic or restricting results to languages, countries or web sites.

- Spell Checker—suggests alternate search terms when a search appears to contain misspellings or typing errors.

- Web Page Translation—automatically translates web pages published in French, German, Italian, Portuguese and Spanish into English, or vice versa.

- Stock Quotes—provides links to stock and mutual fund information.

- Street Maps—provides links to street maps and directions.

- Calculator—solves math problems involving basic arithmetic, complicated math or physical constants and converts between units of measure.

- Definitions—provides definitions for words or phrases based on content we have indexed.

- PhoneBook—provides U.S. street addresses and phone numbers for U.S. businesses and residences.

- Search by Number—enables people to conduct quick searches by entering FedEx, UPS and USPS package tracking numbers, vehicle ID numbers, product codes, telephone area codes, patent numbers, FAA airplane registration numbers and FCC equipment ID numbers.

- Travel Information—enables people to check the status of U.S. airline flights and see delays and weather conditions at U.S. airports.

Table of Contents

- Cached Links—provides snapshots of web pages taken when the pages were indexed, enabling web users to view web pages that are no longer available.

Google Image Search. Google Image Search is our searchable index of 880 million images found across the web. To extend the usefulness of Google Image Search, we offer advanced features, such as searching by image size, format and coloration and restricting searches to specific web sites or domains.

Google News. Google News gathers information from nearly 10,000 news sources worldwide and presents news stories in a searchable format within minutes of their publication on the web. The leading stories are presented as headlines on the Google News home page. These headlines are selected for display entirely by a computer algorithm, without regard to political viewpoint or ideology. Google News uses an automated process to pull together related headlines, which enables people to see many different viewpoints on the same story. Because topics are updated continuously throughout the day, people generally see new stories each time they check Google News. We currently provide our Google News service tailored to 10 international audiences.

Google Toolbar. The Google Toolbar makes our search technology constantly and easily available as people browse the web. The Google Toolbar is available as a free, fast download and can improve people's web experience through several innovative features, including:

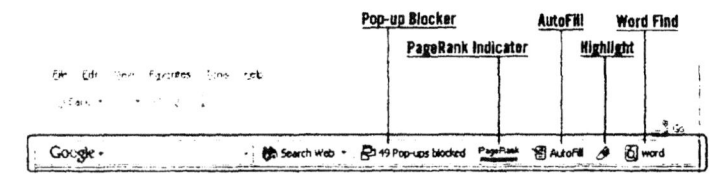

- Pop-up Blocker—blocks pop-up advertising while people use the web.
- PageRank Indicator—displays Google's ranking of any page on the web.
- AutoFill—completes web forms with information saved securely on a user's own computer.
- Highlight—highlights search terms where they appear on a web page, with each term marked in a different color.
- Word Find—finds search terms wherever they appear on a web page.

Froogle. Froogle enables people to easily find products for sale online. By focusing entirely on product search, Froogle applies the power of our search technology to a very specific task—locating stores that sell the items users seek and pointing them directly to the web sites where they can shop. Froogle users can sort results by price, specify a desired price range and view product photos. Froogle accepts data feeds directly from merchants to ensure that product information is up-to-date and accurate. Most online merchants are also automatically included in Froogle's index of shopping sites. Because we do not charge merchants for inclusion in Froogle, our users can browse product categories or conduct product searches with confidence that the results we provide are relevant and unbiased. As with many of our products, Froogle displays relevant advertising separately from search results.

Google Groups. Google Groups enables easy participation in Internet discussion groups by providing users with tools to search, read and browse these groups and to post messages of their own. Google Groups contains the entire archive of Usenet Internet discussion groups dating back to 1981 – more than 845 million posted messages. The discussions in these groups cover a broad range of discourse and provide a comprehensive look at evolving viewpoints, debate and advice on many subjects.

Table of Contents

Google Wireless. Google Wireless offers people the ability to search and view both the "mobile web," consisting of 5 million pages created specifically for wireless devices, and the entire Google index of more than 4 billion web pages. Google Wireless works on devices that support WAP, WAP 2.0, i-mode or j-sky mobile Internet protocols. Google Wireless is available through many wireless and mobile phone services worldwide.

Google Web Directory. Google Web Directory enables people to browse and search through web sites that have been organized into categories. Our directory combines Google's search technology with the categorization developed by the Open Directory Project and is available in 73 languages.

Google Local. Google Local enables users to find relevant local information based on zip codes, cities or specific addresses. Google Local results include neighborhood business listings, addresses, phone numbers, maps and directions.

Google Answers. Google Answers provides people with help finding information and answering questions. Users set a fee they are willing to pay and submit questions to the Google Answers service. One of more than 500 carefully screened freelance researchers responds, usually within 24 hours. Google Answers researchers are experienced web searchers with strong communication skills who often have expertise in various fields. An extensive collection of past responses is available to our users free of charge.

Google Catalogs. With Google Catalogs, we provide access to the full content of more than 6,600 mail-order catalogs, many of which were previously unavailable online.

Google Print. Google Print brings information online that had previously not been available to web searchers. Under this program, we have been experimenting with a number of publishers to host their content and rank their publications in our search results using the same technology we use to evaluate web sites. On Google Print pages, we provide links to book sellers that may offer the full versions of these publications for sale, and we show content-targeted ads that are served through the Google AdSense program.

Google Labs. Google Labs is our playground for our engineers and for adventurous Google users. On Google Labs, we post product prototypes and solicit feedback on how the technology could be used or improved. Current Google Labs examples include:

- Google Personalized Search—provides customized search results based on an individual user's interests.
- Google Deskbar—enables people to search with Google from the taskbar of their computer without launching a web browser.
- Voice Search—enables people to dial a phone number, tell our system what they are looking for and hear Google search results read to them by a computer.
- Froogle Wireless—gives people the ability to search for product information from their mobile phones and other wireless devices.

Blogger. Blogger is a leading web-based publishing tool that gives people the ability to publish to the web instantly using weblogs, or "blogs." Blogs are web pages usually made up of short, informal, frequently updated posts that are arranged chronologically. Blogs can facilitate communications among small groups or to a worldwide audience in a way that is simpler and easier to follow than traditional email or discussion forums.

Picasa. We recently acquired Picasa, Inc., a digital photo management company. Picasa enables users to manage and share digital photographs and helps support our mission of making information universally accessible and useful.

Limited Availability Services. Some of our product offerings are in their initial test phases and are currently available to limited audiences. Examples include Gmail, our free email service, and Orkut, an invitation-based online meeting place where people can socialize, make new acquaintances and find others who share their interests.

Table of Contents

Google AdWords

Google AdWords is our global advertising program, which enables advertisers to present ads to people at the precise moment those people are looking for information related to what the advertiser has to offer. Advertisers use our automated tools, often with little or no assistance from us, to create text-based ads, bid on the keywords that will trigger the display of their ads and set daily spending budgets. AdWords features an automated, low-cost online signup process that enables advertisers to implement ad campaigns that can become live in 15 minutes or less. The total sign-up cost for becoming an AdWords advertiser is only $5.00.

Ads are ranked for display in AdWords based on a combination of the maximum cost per click (CPC) set by the advertiser and click-through rates and other factors used to determine the relevance of the ads. This favors the ads that are most relevant to users, improving the experience for both the person looking for information and the advertiser looking for interested customers. AdWords has many features that make it easy to set up and manage ad campaigns for maximum efficiency and effectiveness:

- *Campaign management.* Advertisers can target multiple ads to a given keyword and easily track individual ad performance to see which ads are the most effective. The campaign management tools built into AdWords enable advertisers to quickly shift their budgets to ads that deliver the best results.

- *Keyword targeting.* Businesses can deliver targeted ads based on specific search terms (keywords) entered by users or found in the content on a web page. We also offer tools that suggest synonyms and useful phrases to use as keywords or ad text. These suggestions can improve ad click-through rates and the likelihood of a user becoming a customer of the advertiser.

- *Traffic estimator.* This tool estimates the number of searches and potential costs related to advertising on a particular keyword or set of keywords. These estimates can help advertisers optimize their campaigns.

- *Budgeted delivery.* Advertisers can set daily budgets for their campaigns and control the timing for delivery of their ads.

- *Performance reports.* We provide continuous, timely reporting of the effectiveness of each ad campaign.

- *Multiple payment options.* We accept credit and debit cards and, for selected advertisers, we offer several options for credit terms and monthly invoicing. We accept payments in 48 currencies.

- *AdWords discounter.* This feature gives advertisers the freedom to increase their maximum CPCs because it automatically adjusts pricing so that they never pay more than one cent over the next highest bid. The AdWords discounter is described in detail below under the heading "Technology—Advertising Technology—Google AdWords Action System."

For larger advertisers, we offer additional services that help to maximize returns on their Internet marketing investments and improve their ability to run large, dynamic campaigns. These include:

- *Creative maximization.* Our AdWords specialists help advertisers select relevant keywords and create more effective ads. This can improve advertisers' ability to target customers and to increase the click-through rates and conversion rates for their ads.

- *Vertical market experts.* Specialists with experience in particular industries offer guidance on how to most effectively target potential customers.

- *Bulk posting.* We assist businesses in launching and managing large ad campaigns with hundreds or even thousands of targeted keywords.

- *Dedicated client service representatives.* These staff members continuously look for ways to better structure their clients' campaigns and to address the challenges large advertisers face.

Table of Contents

Google AdSense

Our Google AdSense program enables the web sites in our Google Network to serve targeted ads from our AdWords advertisers. Targeting can be based on search results or on web content. We share most of the revenue generated from ads shown by a member of the Google Network with that member. Most of the web sites that make up the Google Network sign up with us online, under agreements with no required term. We also engage in direct selling efforts to convince web sites with significant traffic to join the Google Network, under agreements that vary in duration. For our network members, we offer:

Google AdSense for search. For Internet companies with potentially large search audiences, we offer Google AdSense for search. Web sites use AdSense for search to generate additional revenue by serving relevant AdWords ads targeted to search results. Because we also offer to license our web search technology along with Google AdSense for search, companies without their own search service can offer Google WebSearch to improve the usefulness of their web sites for their users while increasing their revenue.

Google AdSense for content. Google AdSense for content enables web sites to generate revenue from advertising by serving relevant AdWords ads targeted to web content. Our automated technology analyzes the meaning of web content and serves relevant advertising, usually in a fraction of a second. We believe that some of the best content on the web comes from web sites aiming to reach small but highly targeted audiences. AdSense for content can help these web sites offset some of their publishing costs. We believe this may help them continue to publish by tapping into the value of their content. There is no charge for web sites to participate in our AdSense for content program. Using our automated sign-up process, web sites can quickly display AdWords ads on their sites. We share the majority of the revenues generated from click-throughs on these ads with the Google Network members that display the ads. For web sites with more than 20 million page views per month, we provide customization services.

Google Search Appliance

We provide our search technology for use within enterprises through the Google Search Appliance (GSA). The GSA is a complete software and hardware solution that companies can easily implement to extend Google's search performance to their internal or external information. The GSA can often be installed and launched in as little as one day. It leverages our search technology to identify the most relevant pages on intranet and public web sites, making it easy for people to find the information they need. The GSA offers several useful features, including automated spell-checking, cached pages, dynamic snippets, indented results and automatic conversion of Microsoft Office and PDF files to HTML. The GSA is available in three models: the GB-1001, for departments and mid-sized companies; the GB-5005, for dedicated, high-priority search services such as customer-facing web sites and company-wide intranet applications; and the GB-8008, for centralized deployments supporting global business units. List prices for our GSA models start at $32,000 for the GB-1001, $230,000 for the GB-5005 and $525,000 for the GB-8008.

Technology

We began as a technology company and have evolved into a software, technology, Internet, advertising and media company all rolled into one. We take technology innovation very seriously. We compete aggressively for talent, and our people drive our innovation, technology development and operations. We strive to hire the best computer scientists and engineers to help us solve very significant challenges across systems design, artificial intelligence, machine learning, data mining, networking, software engineering, testing, distributed systems, cluster design and other areas. We work hard to provide an environment where these talented people can have fulfilling jobs and produce technological innovations that have a positive effect on the world through daily use by millions of people. We employ technology whenever possible to increase the efficiency of our business and to improve the experience we offer our users.

We provide our web search and targeted advertising technology using a large network of commodity computers running custom software developed in-house. Some elements of our technology include:

Table of Contents

Web Search Technology

Our web search technology uses a combination of techniques to determine the importance of a web page independent of a particular search query and to determine the relevance of that page to a particular search query. We do not explain how we do ranking in great detail because some people try to manipulate our search results for their own gain, rather than in an attempt to provide high-quality information to users.

PageRank and Ranking Technology. One element of our technology for ranking web pages is called PageRank. While we developed much of our ranking technology after the company was formed, PageRank was developed at Stanford University with the involvement of our founders, and was therefore published as research. Most of our current ranking technology is protected as trade-secret. PageRank is a query-independent technique for determining the importance of web pages by looking at the link structure of the web. PageRank treats a link from web page A to web page B as a "vote" by page A in favor of page B. The PageRank of a page is the sum of the PageRank of the pages that link to it. The PageRank of a web page also depends on the importance (or PageRank) of the other web pages casting the votes. Votes cast by important web pages with high PageRank weigh more heavily and are more influential in deciding the PageRank of pages on the web.

Text-Matching Techniques. Our technology employs text-matching techniques that compare search queries with the content of web pages to help determine relevance. Our text-based scoring techniques do far more than count the number of times a search term appears on a web page. For example, our technology determines the proximity of individual search terms to each other on a given web page, and prioritizes results that have the search terms near each other. Many other aspects of a page's content are factored into the equation, as is the content of pages that link to the page in question. By combining query independent measures such as PageRank with our text-matching techniques, we are able to deliver search results that are relevant to what people are trying to find.

Advertising Technology

Our advertising program serves millions of relevant, targeted ads each day based on search terms people enter or content they view on the web. The key elements of our advertising technology include:

Google AdWords Auction System. We use the Google AdWords auction system to enable advertisers to automatically deliver relevant, targeted advertising. Every search query we process involves the automated execution of an auction, resulting in our advertising system often processing hundreds of millions of auctions per day. To determine whether an ad is relevant to a particular query, this system weighs an advertiser's willingness to pay for prominence in the ad listings (the CPC) and interest from users in the ad as measured by the click-through rate and other factors. If an ad does not attract user clicks, it moves to a less prominent position on the page, even if the advertiser offers to pay a high amount. This prevents advertisers with irrelevant ads from "squatting" in top positions to gain exposure. Conversely, more relevant, well-targeted ads that are clicked on frequently move up in ranking, with no need for advertisers to increase their bids. Because we are paid only when users click on ads, the AdWords ranking system aligns our interests equally with those of our advertisers and our users. The more relevant and useful the ad, the better for our users, for our advertisers and for us.

The AdWords auction system also incorporates our AdWords discounter, which automatically lowers the amount advertisers actually pay to the minimum needed to maintain their ad position. Consider a situation where there are three advertisers—Pat, Betty and Joe—each bidding on the same keyword for ads that will be displayed on Google.com. These advertisers have ads with equal click-through rates and bid $1.00 per click, $0.60 per click and $0.50 per click, respectively. With our AdWords discounter, Pat would occupy the first ad position and pay only $0.61 per click, Betty would occupy the second ad position and pay only $0.51 per click, and Joe would occupy the third ad position and pay the minimum bid of $0.05 per click. The AdWords discounter saves money for advertisers by minimizing the price they pay per click, while relieving them of the need to constantly monitor and adjust their CPCs. Advertisers can experience greater discounts through the application of our smart pricing technology introduced in April 2004. This technology can reduce the price of clicks for ads served across the Google Network based on the expected value of the click to the advertiser.

Table of Contents

AdSense Contextual Advertising Technology. Our AdSense technology employs techniques that consider factors such as keyword analysis, word frequency, font size and the overall link structure of the web to analyze the content of individual web pages and to match ads to them almost instantaneously. With this ad targeting technology, we can automatically serve contextually relevant ads. To do this, Google Network members embed a small amount of custom HTML code on web pages that generates a request to Google's AdSense service whenever a user views the web page. Upon receiving a request, our software examines the content of web pages and performs a matching process that identifies advertisements that we believe are relevant to the content of the specific web page. The relevant ads are then returned to the web pages in response to the request. We employ similar techniques for matching advertisements to other forms of textual content, such as email messages and Google Groups postings. For example, our technology can serve ads offering tickets to fans of a specific sports team on a news story about that team.

Large-Scale Systems Technology

Our business relies on our software and hardware infrastructure, which provides substantial computing resources at low cost. We currently use a combination of off-the-shelf and custom software running on clusters of commodity computers. Our considerable investment in developing this infrastructure has produced several key benefits. It simplifies the storage and processing of large amounts of data, eases the deployment and operation of large-scale global products and services and automates much of the administration of large-scale clusters of computers.

Although most of this infrastructure is not directly visible to our users, we believe it is important for providing a high-quality user experience. It enables significant improvements in the relevance of our search and advertising results by allowing us to apply superior search and retrieval algorithms that are computationally intensive. We believe the infrastructure also shortens our product development cycle and allows us to pursue innovation more cost effectively.

We constantly evaluate new hardware alternatives and software techniques to help further reduce our computational costs. This allows us to improve our existing products and services and to more easily develop, deploy and operate new global products and services.

Sales and Support

We have put significant effort into developing our sales and support infrastructure. We maintain 21 sales offices in 11 countries, and we deploy specialized sales teams across 18 vertical markets. We bring businesses into our advertising network through both online and direct sales channels. In all cases, we use technology and automation wherever possible to improve the experience for our advertisers and to grow our business cost-effectively. The vast majority of our advertisers use our automated online AdWords program to establish accounts, create ads, target users and launch and manage their advertising campaigns. Our direct advertising sales team focuses on attracting and supporting companies around the world with sizeable advertising budgets. Our AdSense program follows a similar model. Most of the web sites in the Google Network sign up for AdSense using an automated online process. Our direct sales force focuses on building AdSense relationships with leading Internet companies. Our global support organization concentrates on helping our advertisers and Google Network members get the most out of their relationships with us.

Marketing

We have always believed that building a trusted, highly-recognized brand begins with providing high-quality products and services that make a notable difference in people's lives. Our user base has grown primarily by word-of-mouth, which can work very well for products that inspire a high level of user loyalty because users are likely to share their positive experiences with their friends and families. Our early marketing efforts focused on feeding this word-of-mouth momentum and used public relations efforts to accelerate it. Through these efforts and people's increased usage of Google worldwide, we have been able to build our brand with relatively low

Table of Contents

marketing costs as a percentage of our revenues. Today, we use the quality of our own products and services as our most effective marketing tool, and word-of-mouth momentum continues to drive consumer awareness and user loyalty worldwide. We do not promote products before they are successful for our users, preferring to test them until they achieve broad acceptance. We also engage in targeted marketing efforts, such as those we deliver to our advertising clients, designed to inform potential advertisers, Google Network members and enterprises of the benefits they can achieve through Google. In addition, we sponsor industry conferences and have promoted the distribution of the Google Toolbar to Internet users in order to make our search services easier to access.

Competition

We face formidable competition in every aspect of our business, and particularly from other companies that seek to connect people with information on the web and provide them with relevant advertising. Currently, we consider our primary competitors to be Microsoft and Yahoo.

We also face competition from other web search providers, including companies that are not yet known to us. We compete with Internet advertising companies, particularly in the areas of pay-for-performance and keyword-targeted Internet advertising. We may compete with companies that sell products and services online because these companies, like us, are trying to attract users to their web sites to search for information about products and services. In addition to Internet companies, we face competition from companies that offer traditional media advertising opportunities.

We compete to attract and retain relationships with users, advertisers and web sites. The bases on which we compete differ among the groups.

- *Users.* We compete to attract and retain users of our search and communication products and services. Most of the products and services we offer to users are free, so we do not compete on price. Instead, we compete in this area on the basis of the relevance and usefulness of our search results and the features, availability and ease of use of our products and services.

- *Advertisers.* We compete to attract and retain advertisers. We compete in this area principally on the basis of the return on investment realized by advertisers using our AdWords program. We also compete based on the quality of customer service, features and ease of use of AdWords.

- *Web sites.* We compete to attract and retain web sites as members of our Google Network based on the size and quality of our advertiser base, our ability to help our Google Network members generate revenues from advertising on their web sites and the terms of agreements with our Google Network members.

We believe that we compete favorably on the factors described above. However, our industry is evolving rapidly and is becoming increasingly competitive. Larger, more established companies than us are increasingly focusing on search businesses that directly compete with us.

Intellectual Property

We rely on a combination of patent, trademark, copyright and trade secret laws in the U.S. and other jurisdictions as well as confidentiality procedures and contractual provisions to protect our proprietary technology and our brand. We also enter into confidentiality and invention assignment agreements with our employees and consultants and confidentiality agreements with other third parties, and we rigorously control access to proprietary technology.

Google is a registered trademark in the U.S. and several other countries. Our unregistered trademarks include: AdSense, AdWords, Blogger, Froogle, Gmail, I'm Feeling Lucky and PageRank.

The first version of the PageRank technology was created while Larry and Sergey attended Stanford University, which owns a patent to PageRank. The PageRank patent expires in 2017. We hold a perpetual license to this patent. In October 2003, we extended our exclusivity period to this patent through 2011, at which point our license is non-exclusive.

Table of Contents

Circumstances outside our control could pose a threat to our intellectual property rights. For example, effective intellectual property protection may not be available in every country in which our products and services are distributed. Also, the efforts we have taken to protect our proprietary rights may not be sufficient or effective. Any significant impairment of our intellectual property rights could harm our business or our ability to compete. Also, protecting our intellectual property rights is costly and time consuming. Any increase in the unauthorized use of our intellectual property could make it more expensive to do business and harm our operating results.

Companies in the Internet, technology and media industries own large numbers of patents, copyrights and trademarks and frequently enter into litigation based on allegations of infringement or other violations of intellectual property rights. As we face increasing competition, the possibility of intellectual property claims against us grows. Our technologies may not be able to withstand any third-party claims or rights against their use.

Government Regulation

We are subject to a number of foreign and domestic laws that affect companies conducting business on the Internet. In addition, because of the increasing popularity of the Internet and the growth of online services, laws relating to user privacy, freedom of expression, content, advertising, information security and intellectual property rights are being debated and considered for adoption by many countries throughout the world.

In the U.S., laws relating to the liability of providers of online services for activities of their users are currently being tested by a number of claims, which include actions for defamation, libel, invasion of privacy and other data protection claims, tort, unlawful activity, copyright or trademark infringement, or other theories based on the nature and content of the materials searched and the ads posted or the content generated by users. In addition, several other federal laws could have an impact on our business. For example, the Digital Millennium Copyright Act has provisions that limit, but do not eliminate, our liability for listing or linking to third-party web sites that include materials that infringe copyrights or other rights, so long as we comply with the statutory requirements of this act. The Children's Online Protection Act and the Children's Online Privacy Protection Act restrict the distribution of materials considered harmful to children and impose additional restrictions on the ability of online services to collect information from minors. In addition, the Protection of Children from Sexual Predators Act of 1998 requires online service providers to report evidence of violations of federal child pornography laws under certain circumstances.

In addition, the application of existing laws regulating or requiring licenses for certain businesses of our advertisers, including, for example, distribution of pharmaceuticals, adult content, financial services, alcohol or firearms, can be unclear. Existing or new legislation could expose us to substantial liability and restrict our ability to deliver services to our users.

At least two states have recently introduced proposed legislation that could interfere with or prohibit our Gmail free advertising-supported web mail service, which was recently announced as a test service. The legislation, as originally proposed in California and Massachusetts, would make it more difficult for us to operate or would prohibit the aspects of the service that process the contents of users' e-mail messages for the purpose of identifying and displaying ads relevant to that content. While the California legislation has been modified since being introduced so that it does not inhibit the operation of the Gmail service, the legislation has not been finally adopted. If this legislation is adopted as originally proposed, or other similar legislation is adopted, it could prevent us from implementing the Gmail service in the affected states. The company worked with legislators in the state in which the proposed legislation was amended to craft legislation that is narrowly tailored to privacy concerns. Google intends to address privacy related concerns and future proposed legislation by educating the public and legislators about the Google products and services, and by working closely with legislators to craft laws that are not overly broad.

We are also subject to international laws associated with data protection in Europe and elsewhere and the interpretation and application of data protection laws is still uncertain and in flux. In addition, because our services are accessible worldwide, foreign jurisdictions may claim that we are required to comply with their laws.

Table of Contents

Culture and Employees

We take great pride in our company culture and embrace it as one of our fundamental strengths. We remain steadfast in our commitment to constantly improve the technology we offer to our users and advertisers and to web sites in the Google Network. We have assembled what we believe is a highly talented group of employees. Our culture encourages the iteration of ideas to address complex technical challenges. In addition, we embrace individual thinking and creativity. As an example, we encourage our engineers to devote 20% of their time to work on independent projects. Many of our significant new products have come from these independent projects, including Google News, AdSense for content and Orkut.

Despite our rapid growth, we constantly seek to maintain a small-company feel that promotes interaction and the exchange of ideas among employees. We try to minimize corporate hierarchy to facilitate meaningful communication among employees at all levels and across departments, and we have developed software to help us in this effort. We believe that considering multiple viewpoints is critical to developing effective solutions, and we attempt to build consensus in making decisions. While teamwork is one of our core values, we also significantly reward individual accomplishments that contribute to our overall success. As we grow, we expect to continue to provide compensation structures that are more similar to those offered by start-ups than established companies. We will focus on very significant rewards for individuals and teams that build amazing things that provide significant value to us and our users.

At June 30, 2004, we had 2,292 employees, consisting of 705 in research and development, 1,141 in sales and marketing and 446 in general and administrative. All of Google's employees, except temporary employees and contractors, are also equityholders, with significant collective employee ownership. As a result, many employees are highly motivated to make the company more successful.

Legal Proceedings

On August 9, 2004, we and Yahoo entered into a settlement agreement resolving two disputes that had been pending between us. The first dispute concerned a lawsuit filed by Yahoo's wholly-owned subsidiary, Overture Services, Inc., against us in April 2002 asserting that certain services infringed Overture's U.S. Patent No. 6,269,361. In our court filings, we denied that we infringed the patent and alleged that the patent was invalid and unenforceable.

The second dispute concerned a warrant held by Yahoo to purchase 3,719,056 shares of our stock in connection with a June 2000 services agreement. Pursuant to a conversion provision in the warrant, in June 2003 we issued 1,229,944 shares to Yahoo. Yahoo contended it was entitled to a greater number of shares, while we contended that we had fully complied with the terms of the warrant.

As part of the settlement, Overture will dismiss its patent lawsuit against us and has granted us a fully-paid, perpetual license to the patent that was the subject of the lawsuit and several related patent applications held by Overture. The parties also mutually released any claims against each other concerning the warrant dispute. In connection with the settlement of these two disputes, we issued to Yahoo 2,700,000 shares of Class A common stock.

Companies have also filed trademark infringement and related claims against us over the display of ads in response to user queries that include trademark terms. The outcomes of these lawsuits have differed from jurisdiction to jurisdiction. A court in France has held us liable for allowing advertisers to select certain trademarked terms as keywords. We have appealed this decision. We were also subject to two lawsuits in Germany on similar matters where one court preliminarily reached a similar conclusion as the court in France while another court held that we are not liable for the actions of our advertisers prior to notification of trademark rights. We are litigating similar issues in other cases in the U.S., France, Germany and Italy. Adverse results in these lawsuits may result in, or even compel, a change in this practice which could result in a loss of revenue for us, which could harm our business.

From time to time, we may also become a party to other litigation and subject to claims incident to the ordinary course of business. For example, because our products and services link to or host material in which

Table of Contents

others allege to own copyrights, from time to time third parties have asserted copyright infringement or related claims against us. Although the results of litigation and claims cannot be predicted with certainty, we believe that the final outcome of the matters discussed above will not have a material adverse effect on our business. Regardless of the outcome, litigation can have an adverse impact on us because of defense costs, diversion of management resources and other factors.

Facilities

We lease approximately 506,000 square feet of space in our headquarters in Mountain View, California under a lease that expires in 2012. We also lease additional research and development, sales and support offices in Amsterdam, Atlanta, Bangalore, Boston, Chicago, Dallas, Denver, Detroit, Dublin, Hamburg, Hyderabad, London, Los Angeles, Madrid, Milan, Mountain View, New York, Paris, Santa Monica, Seattle, Sydney, Tokyo, Toronto and Zurich. We operate data centers in the United States and the European Union pursuant to various lease agreements and co-location arrangements.

Table of Contents

MANAGEMENT

Executive Officers and Directors

Our executive officers and directors, and their ages and positions as of June 30, 2004 are as follows:

Name	Age	Position
Eric Schmidt	49	Chairman of the Executive Committee, Chief Executive Officer and Director
Sergey Brin	30	President of Technology, Assistant Secretary and Director
Larry Page	31	President of Products, Assistant Secretary and Director
Omid Kordestani	40	Senior Vice President of Worldwide Sales and Field Operations
Wayne Rosing	57	Vice President of Engineering
David C. Drummond	41	Vice President of Corporate Development, Secretary and General Counsel
George Reyes	50	Vice President and Chief Financial Officer
Jonathan J. Rosenberg	42	Vice President of Product Management
Shona L. Brown	38	Vice President of Business Operations
L. John Doerr	53	Director
John L. Hennessy	51	Director
Arthur D. Levinson	54	Director
Michael Moritz	49	Director
Paul S. Otellini	53	Director
K. Ram Shriram	47	Director

Eric Schmidt has served as our Chief Executive Officer since July 2001 and served as Chairman of our board of directors from March 2001 to April 2004. In April 2004, Eric was named Chairman of the Executive Committee of our board of directors. Prior to joining us, from April 1997 to November 2001, Eric served as Chairman of the board of Novell, a computer networking company, and, from April 1997 to July 2001, as the Chief Executive Officer of Novell. From 1983 until March 1997, Eric held various positions at Sun Microsystems, a supplier of network computing solutions, including Chief Technology Officer from February 1994 to March 1997 and President of Sun Technology Enterprises from February 1991 until February 1994. Eric is also a director of Siebel Systems. Eric has a Bachelor of Science degree in electrical engineering from Princeton University, and a Masters degree and Ph.D. in computer science from the University of California at Berkeley.

Sergey Brin, one of our founders, has served as a member of our board of directors since our inception in September 1998 and as our President of Technology since July 2001. From September 1998 to July 2001, Sergey served as our President. Sergey holds a Masters degree in computer science from Stanford University, a Bachelor of Science degree with high honors in mathematics and computer science from the University of Maryland at College Park and is currently on leave from the Ph.D. program in computer science at Stanford University.

Larry Page, one of our founders, has served as a member of our board of directors since our inception in September 1998 and as our President of Products since July 2001. From September 1998 to July 2001, Larry served as our Chief Executive Officer and from September 1998 to July 2002 as our Chief Financial Officer. Larry holds a Masters degree in computer science from Stanford University, a Bachelor of Science degree with high honors in engineering, with a concentration in computer engineering, from the University of Michigan and is currently on leave from the Ph.D. program in computer science at Stanford University.

Table of Contents

Omid Kordestani has served as our Senior Vice President of Worldwide Sales and Field Operations since May 1999. Prior to joining us, from 1995 to 1999, Omid served as Vice President of Business Development at Netscape, an Internet software and services company. Omid holds a Masters of Business Administration degree from Stanford University and a Bachelor of Science degree in electrical engineering from San Jose State University.

Wayne Rosing has served as our Vice President of Engineering since November 2000. From November 1996 to April 2000, Wayne served as Chief Technology Officer and Vice President of Engineering at Caere Corporation, an optical character recognition software company. From 1985 to 1994, Wayne served in various executive engineering positions at Sun Microsystems. From 1992 to 1994, Wayne headed the team that developed the technology base for Java as the president of FirstPerson, and, from 1990 through 1991, was President of Sun Microsystems Laboratories, both subsidiaries of Sun Microsystems. From 1985 to 1990, Wayne was a Vice President of Engineering at Sun Microsystems and, from 1980 to 1985, he was director of engineering for the Apple Computer Lisa and Apple II divisions. Prior to 1980, he held management positions at Digital Equipment Corporation and Data General.

David C. Drummond has served as our Vice President of Corporate Development, Secretary and General Counsel since February 2002. Prior to joining us, from July 1999 to February 2002, David served as Chief Financial Officer of SmartForce, an educational software applications company. Prior to that, David was a partner at the law firm of Wilson Sonsini Goodrich & Rosati, our outside counsel. David holds a J.D. from Stanford University and a Bachelor of Arts degree in history from Santa Clara University. On July 20, 2004, David was advised by the staff of the SEC that it intends to recommend that the SEC bring a civil injunction action against David, alleging violation of federal securities laws, including the anti-fraud provisions. The SEC's recommendation arises out of David's prior employment as Chief Financial Officer of SmartForce, and involves certain disclosure and accounting issues relating to SmartForce's financial statements. None of the allegations involve Google. The staff of the SEC has, in accordance with its customary practices, offered David the opportunity to make a Wells Submission setting forth why David believes that such action should not be brought. David intends to make this submission.

George Reyes has served as our Chief Financial Officer since July 2002. Prior to joining us, George served as Interim Chief Financial Officer for ONI Systems, a provider of optical networking equipment, from February 2002 until June 2002. From April 1999 to September 2001, George served as Vice President and Treasurer of Sun Microsystems, a supplier of networking computing solutions, and as Vice President, Corporate Controller of Sun Microsystems from April 1994 to April 1999. George is also a director of BEA Systems, an application infrastructure software company, and Symantec, an information security company. George holds a Masters of Business Administration degree from Santa Clara University and a Bachelor of Arts degree in accounting from the University of South Florida.

Jonathan J. Rosenberg has served as our Vice President of Product Management since February 2002. Prior to joining us, from October 2001 to February 2002, Jonathan served as Vice President of Software of palmOne, a provider of handheld computer and communications solutions. From November 2000 until October 2001, Jonathan was not formally employed. From March 1996 to November 2000, Jonathan held various executive positions at Excite@Home, an Internet media company, most recently as its Senior Vice President of Online Products and Services. Jonathan holds a Masters of Business Administration degree from the University of Chicago and a Bachelor of Arts degree with honors in economics from Claremont McKenna College.

Shona L. Brown has served as our Vice President of Business Operations since September 2003. Prior to joining us, from October 1995 to August 2003, Shona was at McKinsey & Company, a management consulting firm where she had been a partner since December 2000. Shona holds a Ph.D. and Post-Doctorate in industrial engineering and engineering management from Stanford University, a Masters of Arts degree from Oxford University (as a Rhodes Scholar), and a Bachelor of Science degree in computer systems engineering from Carleton University.

L. John Doerr has served as a member of our board of directors since May 1999. John has been a General Partner of Kleiner Perkins Caufield & Byers, a venture capital firm, since August 1980. John is also a director of

Table of Contents

Amazon.com, an Internet retail company, drugstore.com, an Internet retail company, Homestore.com, a provider of real estate media and technology solutions, Intuit, a provider of business and financial management software, palmOne, a provider of handheld computer and communications solutions, and Sun Microsystems, a supplier of networking computing solutions. John holds a Masters of Business Administration degree from Harvard Business School and a Masters of Science degree in electrical engineering and computer science and a Bachelor of Science degree in electrical engineering from Rice University.

John L. Hennessy has served as a member of our board of directors since April 2004. Since September 2000, John has served as the President of Stanford University. From 1994 to August 2000, John held various positions at Stanford, including Dean of the Stanford University School of Engineering and Chair of the Stanford University Department of Computer Science. John has been a member of the board of directors of Cisco Systems, a networking equipment company, since January 2002 and chairman of the board of directors of Atheros Communications, a wireless semiconductor company since May 1998. John holds a Master's degree and Doctoral degree in computer science from the State University of New York, Stony Brook and a Bachelor of Science degree in electrical engineering from Villanova University.

Arthur D. Levinson has served as a member of our board of directors since April 2004. Since 1995, Art has served as a member of the board of directors of Genentech, a biotechnology company, and has served as its Chairman and Chief Executive Officer since September 1999. Prior to 1999 Art held various executive positions at Genentech, including Senior Vice President of R&D. Art has been a member of the board of directors of Apple Computer, a computer hardware and software company, since 2000. Art was a Postdoctoral Fellow in the Department of Microbiology at the University of California, San Francisco. Art holds a Ph.D. in biochemistry from Princeton University and a Bachelor of Science degree in molecular biology from the University of Washington.

Michael Moritz has served as a member of our board of directors since May 1999. Michael has been a General Partner of Sequoia Capital, a venture capital firm, since 1986. Michael has served as a member of the board of directors of Saba Software, a provider of human capital development and management solutions, since August 1998 and as a member of the board of directors of Flextronics International, a contract electronics manufacturer, since July 1993. Michael has also served as a member of the board of directors of RedEnvelope, an online retailer of upscale gifts, since July 1999 and as its Chairman of the Board since April 2003. Michael holds a Masters of Arts degree from Christ Church, University of Oxford.

Paul S. Otellini has served as a member of our board of directors since April 2004. Paul has been a member of the board of directors of Intel, a semiconductor manufacturing company, and has served as its President and Chief Operating Officer since 2002. From 1974 to 2002, Paul held various positions at Intel, including Executive Vice President and General Manager of Intel Architecture Group and Executive Vice President and General Manager of Sales and Marketing Group. Paul holds a Master's degree from the University of California at Berkeley and a Bachelors degree in economics from the University of San Francisco.

K. Ram Shriram has served as a member of our board of directors since September 1998. Since January 2000, Ram has served as managing partner of Sherpalo, an angel venture investment company. Prior to that, from August 1998 to September 1999, Ram served as Vice President of Business Development at Amazon.com, an Internet retail company. Prior to that, Ram served as President at Junglee, a provider of database technology, acquired by Amazon.com in 1998. Ram was an early member of the Netscape executive team. Ram holds a Bachelor of Science degree from the University of Madras, India.

Board of Directors

Our bylaws provide that the authorized size of our board of directors, which is currently nine (9) members, is to be determined from time to time by resolution of the board of directors. Our current directors were elected in the manner described in our certificate of incorporation. The holders of a majority of our preferred stock, voting as a single class, elected L. John Doerr and Michael Moritz to the board of directors, and the holders of a

Table of Contents

majority of our common stock, voting as a single class, elected Sergey Brin, Larry Page and K. Ram Shriram to the board of directors. John Hennessy, Arthur Levinson and Paul Otellini were appointed by the board of directors to fill vacancies created by the increase in the size of the board of directors. The remaining director, Eric Schmidt, was elected pursuant to a voting agreement that we entered into with certain holders of our common stock and holders of our preferred stock, which provides for the election of a joint director nominated by a majority of the preferred stock and by a majority of the common stock held by Sergey and Larry. Upon the closing of this offering, these board representation rights will terminate and none of our stockholders will have any special rights regarding the election or designation of board members.

Committees of the Board of Directors

Our board of directors has established four committees: an audit committee, a leadership development and compensation committee, a corporate governance and nominating committee and an executive committee.

Audit Committee

Our audit committee's main function will be to oversee our accounting and financial reporting processes, internal systems of control, independent auditor relationships and the audits of our financial statements. This committee's responsibilities will include the following:

- Selecting and hiring our independent auditors.

- Evaluating the qualifications, independence and performance of our independent auditors.

- Approving the audit and non-audit services to be performed by our independent auditors.

- Reviewing the design, implementation, adequacy and effectiveness of our internal controls and our critical accounting policies.

- Overseeing and monitoring the integrity of our financial statements and our compliance with legal and regulatory requirements as they relate to financial statements or accounting matters.

- Reviewing with management and our auditors any earnings announcements and other public announcements regarding our results of operations.

- Preparing the report that the SEC requires in our annual proxy statement.

Our audit committee is comprised of Ram, Paul and Michael, each of whom is a non-employee member of our board of directors. Paul will be our audit committee financial expert as currently defined under SEC rules. Ram will be the chairman of our audit committee. Our board of directors has determined that each of the directors serving on our audit committee is independent within the meaning of the rules of the SEC and the listing standards of The Nasdaq Stock Market. We intend to comply with future audit committee requirements as they become applicable to us.

Leadership Development and Compensation Committee

Our leadership development and compensation committee's purpose will be to assist our board of directors in determining the development plans and compensation of our senior management, directors and employees and recommend these plans to our board. This committee's responsibilities will include:

- Reviewing the employee wide compensation philosophy.

- Reviewing the budget and structure of our employee wide variable cash compensation plans.

- Reviewing the budget and structure of our employee wide equity based compensation plans.

- Periodically reviewing the leadership development plans for the Company.

- Reviewing and recommending compensation and benefit plans for our executive officers and board members.

Table of Contents

- Reviewing the terms of offer letters and employment agreements and arrangements with our officers.
- Setting performance goals for our officers and reviewing their performance against these goals.
- Periodically reviewing executive succession plans and executive education and development plans.
- Evaluating the competitiveness of our executive compensation plans.
- Independently accessing externally provided market information on industry compensation practices.
- Preparing the report that the SEC requires in our annual proxy statement.

Our Leadership Development and Compensation Committee consists of John Doerr and Art, each of whom is a non-employee member of our board of directors. Our Leadership Development and Compensation Committee does not have a chairman. Each member of our Leadership Development and Compensation Committee will be an "outside" director as that term is defined in 162(m) of the Internal Revenue Code of 1986, as amended, and a "non-employee" director within the meaning of Rule 16b-3 of the rules under the Securities Exchange Act of 1934. Our board of directors has determined that each of the directors serving on our Leadership Development and Compensation Committee is independent within the listing standards of The Nasdaq Stock Market.

Corporate Governance and Nominating Committee

Our corporate governance and nominating committee's purpose will be to assist our board by identifying individuals qualified to become members of our board of directors consistent with criteria set by our board and to develop our corporate governance principles. This committee's responsibilities will include:

- Evaluating the composition, size and governance of our board of directors and its committees and make recommendations regarding future planning and the appointment of directors to our committees.
- Establishing a policy for considering stockholder nominees for election to our board of directors.
- Recommending ways to enhance communications and relations with our stockholders.
- Evaluating and recommending candidates for election to our board of directors.
- Overseeing our board of directors performance and self-evaluation process and developing continuing education programs for our directors.
- Reviewing our corporate governance principles and providing recommendations to the board regarding possible changes.
- Reviewing and monitoring compliance with our code of ethics and our insider trading policy.

Our Corporate Governance and Nominating Committee consists of John Doerr and John Hennessy, each of whom is a non-employee member of our board of directors. Our board of directors has determined that each of the directors serving on our Corporate Governance and Nominating Committee is independent within the existing standards of The Nasdaq Stock Market.

Executive Committee

The Executive Committee will serve as an administrative committee of the board that is available to facilitate the approval of certain corporate actions that do not require consideration by the full board.

Chairman of the Board

Our current charter documents provide that the chairman of our board of directors may not be an employee or officer of our company, and may not have been an employee or officer for the last three years, unless the appointment is approved by two-thirds of the members of our board of directors. We currently do not have a chairman of our board of directors.

Compensation Committee Interlocks and Insider Participation

None of the members of our compensation committee is an officer or employee of our company. None of our executive officers currently serves, or in the past year has served, as a member of the board of directors or compensation committee of any entity that has one or more executive officers serving on our board of directors or compensation committee.

Director Compensation

We do not currently compensate our directors in cash for their service as members of our board of directors. We do reimburse our directors for reasonable expenses in connection with attendance at board and committee meetings. Additionally, our directors are eligible to receive and have received stock options under our stock plans.

In April 2004, our newly elected directors, John, Art and Paul each received an option to purchase 65,000 shares of common stock subject to vesting over a term of five years and otherwise pursuant to the terms of our 2000 Stock Plan and 2003 Stock Plan (No. 2).

Executive Compensation

The following table sets forth information regarding the compensation that we paid to our Chief Executive Officer and each of our four other most highly compensated executive officers during the year ended December 31, 2003. We refer to these officers in this prospectus as the named executive officers.

Summary Compensation Table

Name and Principal Position	Salary	Bonus(1) (2)	Securities Underlying Options	All Other Compensation
Eric Schmidt, Chief Executive Officer and Director	$250,000	$301,556	—	$ 2,894(3)
Sergey Brin, President of Technology and Director	150,000	206,556	—	14,440(4)
Larry Page, President of Products and Director	150,000	206,556	—	11,327(5)
Omid Kordestani, Senior Vice President of Worldwide Sales and Field Operations	175,000	394,456(6)	—	2,704(7)
Wayne Rosing, Vice President of Engineering	175,000	151,314	—	2,704(8)

(1) We generally pay bonuses in the year following the year in which they were earned. Unless otherwise noted, bonus amounts presented represent employee performance bonuses and are reported for the year in which they were earned, though they may have been paid in the following year.

(2) Each of the bonuses presented include a holiday bonus in the amount of $1,556.

(3) Includes $2,200 contributed to Eric's account under our 401(k) plan and $694 of insurance premiums paid for his benefit.

(4) Includes $14,008 of engineering patent awards and $432 of insurance premiums paid for Sergey's benefit.

(5) Includes $10,895 of engineering patent awards and $432 of insurance premiums paid for Larry's benefit.

(6) Includes $347,900 of sales commissions.

(7) Includes $2,200 contributed to Omid's account under our 401(k) plan and $504 of insurance premiums paid for his benefit.

(8) Includes $2,200 contributed to Wayne's account under our 401(k) plan and $504 of insurance premiums paid for his benefit.

Table of Contents

Stock Option Grants in Last Fiscal Year

The following table sets forth information regarding the granting of stock options to the named executive officers during 2003. The percentage of total options set forth below is based on an aggregate of 18,681,260 options granted to employees for the year ended December 31, 2003.

Option/SAR Grants in Last Fiscal Year

	Individual Grants					Potential Realizable Value at Assumed Annual Rate of Stock Price Appreciation for Option Term	
Name and Principal Position	Number of Shares Common Stock	Percentage of Total Options Granted to Employees in 2003	Exercise or Base Price Per Share	Expiration Date	5%	10%
Eric Schmidt Chief Executive Officer and Director	—	—	—		—	—
Sergey Brin President of Technology and Director	—	—	—	—	—	—
Larry Page President of Products and Director	—	—	—	—	—	—
Omid Kordestani Senior Vice President of Worldwide Sales and Field Operations	—	—	—	—	—	—
Wayne Rosing(1) Vice President of Engineering	128,000	0.7%	$ 5.00	7/18/13	$18,124,866	$29,239,913

(1) Shares subject to this option will begin vesting on November 23, 2004 and will vest as follows: (i) 15 percent on the one year anniversary of the vesting commencement date, (ii) 17.5 percent in the second year of vesting, (iii) 20 percent in the third year of vesting, (iv) 22.5 percent in the fourth year of vesting, and (v) 25 percent in the fifth year of vesting; provided that shares vesting in each of the years following the one year anniversary of Wayne's vesting commencement date will vest in the respective amounts described above ratably at the end of each month of Wayne's continued employment with us. Wayne's option was granted at the fair market value of our Class B common stock as determined by our board of directors on the date of grant. Wayne's option has a term of 10 years, subject to earlier termination in certain events related to the cessation of Wayne's employment with us.

The amounts shown in the table above for Wayne as potential realizable value represent hypothetical gains that could be achieved for the respective options if exercised at the end of the option term. These amounts represent assumed rates of appreciation in the value of our common stock from the fair market value on the date of grant. Potential realizable values in the table above are calculated by:

- Multiplying the number of shares of our common stock subject to the option by the assumed initial public offering price per share of $90.00.

- Assuming that the aggregate stock value derived from that calculation compounds at the annual 5% or 10% rates shown in the table for the entire 10-year term of the option.

- Subtracting from that result the total option exercise price.

The 5% and 10% assumed rates of appreciation are suggested by the rules of the SEC and do not represent our estimate or projection of the future common stock price. Actual gains, if any, on stock option exercises will be dependent on the future performance of our common stock.

Table of Contents

Option Exercises in Last Fiscal Year and Fiscal Year-End Option Values

The following table provides option exercise information for the executive offices named in the summary compensation table. The table shows the number of shares acquired and the value realized upon exercise of stock options during 2003 and the exercisable and unexercisable options held at December 31, 2003. The "Value Realized" and the "Value of Unexercised In-the-Money Options" shown in the table represents an amount equal to the difference between an assumed initial public offering price of $90.00 per share and the option exercise price, multiplied by the number of shares acquired on exercise and the number of unexercised in-the-money options. These calculations do not take into account the effect of any taxes that may be applicable to the option exercises.

Name and Principal Position	Shares Acquired on Exercise	Value Realized	Number of Unexercised Options at Fiscal Year-End Exercisable (1)	Unexercisable	Value of Unexercised In-the-Money Options at Fiscal Year-End Exercisable	Unexercisable
Eric Schmidt Chairman and Chief Executive Officer	—	—	—	—	—	—
Sergey Brin President of Technology and Director	—	—	—	—	—	—
Larry Page President of Products and Director	—	—	—	—	—	—
Omid Kordestani(2) Senior Vice President of Worldwide Sales and Field Operations	80,000	$7,196,000	1,420,000	—	$127,400,000	—
Wayne Rosing(3) Vice President of Engineering	—	—	148,000	—	12,674,000	—

(1) All of our stock options granted to U.S. residents may be exercised prior to their vesting. Upon the exercise of an option prior to vesting, the optionee is required to enter into a restricted stock purchase agreement with us that provides that we have a right to repurchase the shares purchased upon exercise of the option at the original exercise price; provided, however, that our right to repurchase these shares will lapse in accordance with the original vesting schedule included in the optionee's option agreement.

(2) Omid's option was vested as to 669,666 shares Class B common stock and unvested as to 750,334 shares at December 31, 2003.

(3) Wayne's option was vested as to 8,333 shares Class B common stock and unvested as to 139,667 shares at December 31, 2003.

Employee Benefit Plans

1998 Stock Plan, 2003 Stock Plan, 2003 Stock Plan (No. 2) and 2003 Stock Plan (No. 3)

Our 1998 Stock Plan was adopted by our board of directors in September 1998 and subsequently approved by our stockholders. At June 30, 2004, options to purchase a total of 6,295,431 shares of Class B common stock were outstanding under the 1998 Stock Plan at a weighted average exercise price of $0.29 per share.

Our 2003 Stock Plan was adopted by our board of directors in February 2003 and subsequently approved by our stockholders. At June 30, 2004, options to purchase a total of 2,756,359 shares of Class A common stock were outstanding under the 2003 Stock Plan at a weighted average exercise price of $1.23 per share.

Our 2003 Stock Plan (No. 2) was adopted by our board of directors in July 2003 and subsequently approved by our stockholders. At June 30, 2004, options to purchase a total of 3,875,653 shares of Class B common stock were outstanding under the 2003 Stock Plan (No. 2) at a weighted average exercise price of $6.39 per share.

Table of Contents

Our 2003 Stock Plan (No. 3) was adopted by our board of directors in July 2003, and it was subsequently approved by our stockholders. At June 30, 2004, options to purchase a total of 3,494,095 shares of Class A common stock were outstanding under the 2003 Stock Plan (No. 3) at a weighted average exercise price of $15.95 per share.

Our plans generally provide for the grant of options and stock purchase rights. Incentive stock options within the meaning of Section 422 of the Internal Revenue Code may be granted only to our employees or employees of our subsidiaries. Stock purchase rights may only be granted under the 1998 Stock Plan to our employees, officers, directors, consultants, independent contractors and advisors and those of any of our subsidiaries. Nonstatutory stock options may be granted to our employees, officers, directors, consultants, independent contractors and advisors and those of any of our subsidiaries. Consultants, independent contractors and advisors are only eligible to receive awards if they render bona fide services not in connection with the offer and sale of securities in a capital-raising transaction.

Our board of directors administers the plans. The administrator has the authority to determine the terms and conditions of the options and stock purchase rights granted under these plans, and may reduce the exercise price of an option to the then current fair market value of our common stock or institute a program whereby outstanding options are exchanged for options with a lower exercise price.

The maximum term of the options under these plans is ten years. The awards granted under these plans may not be transferred in any manner other than by will or by the laws of descent and distribution and may be exercised during the lifetime of the optionee only by the optionee.

These plans provide that in the event of our merger with or into another corporation, or a sale of substantially all of our assets, the successor corporation or its parent or subsidiary will assume or substitute each stock purchase right and option. If the outstanding stock purchase rights or options are not assumed or substituted, they will become fully vested and exercisable for a 15-day period from the date the administrator provides notice of such transaction and shall terminate at the end of such 15-day period.

Generally, in the event of our change in control, the successor corporation will assume each option or replace it with a cash incentive program that preserves the spread associated with the option. If the outstanding options are not assumed or substituted after a change in control, the options vesting will accelerate in full.

2000 Stock Plan

Our 2000 Stock Plan was adopted by our board of directors in November 2000, and it was subsequently approved by our stockholders. At June 30, 2004, options to purchase a total of 285,000 shares of Class B common stock were outstanding under the 2000 Stock Plan at a weighted average exercise price of $4.79 per share. The terms of our 2000 Stock Plan are substantially the same as the terms described above, except that the 2000 Stock Plan does not share in the collective authorized share pool applicable to the plans described above.

1999 Stock Option/Stock Issuance Plan

Our 1999 Stock Option/Stock Issuance Plan was assumed by us in connection with our acquisition of Applied Semantics, Inc. in April 2003. At June 30, 2004, options to purchase a total of 24,827 shares of Class A common stock were outstanding under the 1999 Stock Option/Stock Issuance Plan at a weighted average exercise price of $0.38 per share. At June 30, 2004, no shares of Class A common stock remained available for future issuance under our 1999 Stock Option/Stock Issuance Plan.

2003 Equity Incentive Plan

Our 2003 Equity Incentive Plan was assumed by us in connection with our acquisition of Ignite Logic, Inc. in April 2004. At June 30, 2004, options to purchase a total of 1,292 shares of Class A common stock were outstanding under the 2003 Equity Incentive Plan at a weighted average exercise price of $28.78 per share. At June 30, 2004, no shares of Class A common stock remained available for future issuance under our 2003 Equity Incentive Plan.

2004 Stock Plan

Our board of directors adopted the 2004 Stock Plan in April 2004, and it was subsequently approved by our stockholders. The 2004 Stock Plan provides for the grant of incentive stock options, within the meaning of Section 422 of the Code, to our employees and nonstatutory stock options, restricted stock, stock appreciation rights, performance units, performance shares, restricted stock units and other stock based awards to our employees, directors, and consultants. No awards have yet been issued pursuant to the 2004 Stock Plan.

Number of Shares of Common Stock Available Under the 2004 Stock Plan. A total of 9,499,500 shares of our Class A common stock were reserved for issuance pursuant to our 2004 Stock Plan. The number of shares reserved for issuance under the 2004 Stock Plan will be reduced by the number of shares subject to options that are granted after December 31, 2003 under the Company's 1998 Stock Plan, 1999 Stock Option/Stock Issuance Plan, 2000 Stock Plan, 2003 Stock Plan, 2003 Stock Plan (No. 2) and 2003 Stock Plan (No. 3).

If an option, grant of restricted stock, stock appreciation right, performance unit, performance share, restricted stock unit or other stock based award (each, an "award") expires or is terminated or canceled without having been exercised or settled in full, is forfeited back to or repurchased by the Company, the terminated portion of the award (or forfeited or repurchased shares subject to the award) will become available for future grant or sale under our plan (unless our plan has terminated). Shares are not deemed to be issued under the 2004 Stock Plan with respect to any portion of an award that is settled in cash. If the exercise or purchase price of an award is paid for through the tender of shares, or withholding obligations are met through the tender or withholding of shares, those shares tendered or withheld will again be available for issuance under the 2004 Stock Plan. However, shares that have actually been transferred to a financial institution or other person or entity selected by the plan administrator, will not be returned to the 2004 Stock Plan, will not be returned to our plan and will not be available for future distribution under our plan.

Administration of the 2004 Stock Plan. Our board of directors, or one or more committees appointed by our board, will administer our 2004 Stock Plan. In the case of awards intended to qualify as "performance based compensation" within the meaning of Section 162(m) of the Internal Revenue Code of 1986, as amended, the committee will consist of two or more "outside directors" within the meaning of Section 162(m). The administrator has the power to determine the terms of the awards, including the exercise price (which may be changed by the administrator after the date of grant), the number of shares subject to each award, the exercisability of the awards and the form of consideration payable upon exercise. The administrator also has the power to implement an award exchange program, an award transfer program, whereby awards may be transferred to a financial institution or other person or entity selected by the plan administrator, and a program through which participants may reduce cash compensation payable in exchange for awards, and to create other stock based awards that are valued in whole or in part by reference to (or are otherwise based on) shares of our Class A Common Stock (or the cash equivalent of such shares).

Options. A stock option is the right to purchase shares of our common stock at a fixed exercise price for a fixed period of time. The administrator will determine the exercise price of options granted under our 2004 Stock Plan, but with respect to nonstatutory stock options intended to qualify as "performance-based compensation" within the meaning of Section 162(m) of the Code and all incentive stock options, the exercise price generally must be at least equal to the fair market value of our common stock on the date of grant. After termination of one of our employees, directors or consultants, he or she may exercise his or her option for the period of time stated in the option agreement. If termination is due to death or disability, the option generally will remain exercisable for 12 months following such termination. In all other cases, the option generally will remain exercisable for three months. However, an option may never be exercised later than the expiration of its term. The term of an

Table of Contents

incentive stock option may not exceed ten years, except that with respect to any participant who owns 10% of the voting power of all classes of our outstanding capital stock, the term must not exceed five years and the exercise price must equal at least 110% of the fair market value on the date of grant. The administrator determines the term of all other options.

Restricted Stock. Restricted stock awards are awards of shares of our common stock that vest in accordance with terms and conditions established by the administrator. The administrator may impose whatever conditions to vesting it determines to be appropriate. The administrator will determine the number of shares of restricted stock granted to any employee. The administrator determines the purchase price of any grants of restricted stock and, unless the administrator determines otherwise, shares that do not vest typically will be subject to forfeiture or to our right of repurchase, which we may exercise upon the voluntary or involuntary termination of the purchaser's service with us for any reason including death or disability.

Stock Appreciation Rights. A stock appreciation right is the right to receive the appreciation in the fair market value of our common stock between the exercise date and the date of grant, for that number of shares of our common stock with respect to which the stock appreciation right is exercised. We may pay the appreciation in either cash, in shares of our common stock with equivalent value, or in some combination, as determined by the administrator. The administrator determines the exercise price of stock appreciation rights, the vesting schedule and other terms and conditions of stock appreciation rights; however, stock appreciation rights expire under the same rules that apply to stock options.

Performance Shares and Performance Units. Performance units and performance shares are awards that will result in a payment to a participant only if performance goals established by the administrator are achieved or the awards otherwise vest. The administrator will establish performance goals in its discretion, which, depending on the extent to which they are met, will determine the number and/or the value of performance units and performance shares to be paid out to participants. The performance goals may be based upon the achievement of company-wide, divisional or individual goals (including solely continued service), applicable securities laws or other basis determined by the administrator. Payment for performance units and performance shares may be made in cash or in shares of our common stock with equivalent value, or in some combination, as determined by the administrator. Performance units will have an initial dollar value established by the administrator prior to the grant date. Performance shares will have an initial value equal to the fair market value of our common stock on the grant date.

Restricted Stock Units. Restricted stock units are awards of restricted stock, performance shares or performance units that are paid out in installments or on a deferred basis. The administrator determines the terms and conditions of restricted stock units.

Other Stock Based Awards. The administrator has the authority to create awards under the 2004 Stock Plan in addition to those specifically described in the 2004 Stock Plan. These awards must be valued in whole or in part by reference to, or must otherwise be based on, the shares of our Class A common stock (or the cash equivalent of such shares).

Transferability of Awards. Unless the administrator determines otherwise, our 2004 Stock Plan does not allow for the transfer of awards other than by will or by the laws of descent and distribution, and only the participant may exercise an award during his or her lifetime.

Adjustments upon Merger or Change in Control. Our 2004 Stock Plan provides that in the event of a merger with or into another corporation or our "change in control," including the sale of all or substantially all of our assets, the successor corporation will assume or substitute an equivalent award for each outstanding award. Unless determined otherwise by the administrator, any outstanding options or stock appreciation rights not assumed or substituted for will be fully vested and exercisable, including as to shares that would not otherwise have been vested and exercisable, for a period of up to 15 days from the date of notice to the optionee. The option or stock appreciation right will terminate at the end of such period. Unless determined otherwise by the

Table of Contents

administrator, any restricted stock, performance shares, performance units, restricted stock units or other stock based awards not assumed or substituted for will be fully vested as to all of the shares subject to the award, including shares which would not otherwise be vested. In the event an outside director is terminated immediately prior to or following a change in control, other than pursuant to a voluntary resignation, the awards he or she received under the 2004 Stock Plan will fully vest and become immediately exercisable.

Amendment and Termination of Our 2004 Stock Plan. Our 2004 Stock Plan will automatically terminate in 2014, unless we terminate it sooner. In addition, our board of directors has the authority to amend, suspend or terminate our 2004 Stock Plan provided it does not adversely affect any award previously granted under our plan.

Employment Agreements and Change in Control Arrangements

Eric Schmidt Employment Agreement

On March 15, 2001, we entered into an employment agreement with Eric Schmidt, our chief executive officer. The agreement does not provide a specific term for Eric's employment, rather, Eric's employment with us is "at-will" and may be terminated at any time with or without notice, for any or no reason, at either Eric's or our option. The agreement provides that Eric will receive a base salary of $250,000. Eric was also granted an option to purchase 14,331,708 shares of Class B common stock at an exercise price of $0.30 per share pursuant to this agreement and was permitted to purchase 426,892 shares of Series C preferred stock at a purchase price of $2.3425 per share. Eric may also earn a yearly performance bonus of up to 60% of his base salary if he meets the performance criteria set by our board of directors. If Eric is terminated without cause, he will receive 12 months' base salary, six months' accelerated vesting of any options and the greater of his performance bonus for the year of termination or for the prior year. If Eric resigns for good reason or if he is terminated without cause within 12 months after our change in control, then instead of the 6 months accelerated vesting of options, he will receive 12 months accelerated vesting of options. For purposes of this employment agreement, our change in control includes our merger or combination with or into a third party, the sale of all or substantially all our assets or a change in our board composition over a two-year period resulting in fewer than a majority of directors remaining as incumbent directors. For purposes of this employment agreement, a termination "without cause" means a termination for reasons other than an act of material dishonesty in performing his duties, a felony conviction or plea of no contest to a felony or gross misconduct. For purposes of this employment agreement, "good reason" means a material reduction in Eric's base salary, performance bonus or in responsibilities or a relocation to more than 50 miles from our current facility.

In connection with his stock option exercise on September 28, 2001, we entered into a promissory note and security agreement with Eric. On April 28, 2004, Eric repaid the note in its entirety and the stock previously pledged as collateral was released from the security agreement. This arrangement is further described in "Certain Relationships and Related Party Transactions—Indebtedness of Management."

Limitation on Liability and Indemnification Matters

Our certificate of incorporation contains provisions that limit the liability of our directors for monetary damages to the fullest extent permitted by Delaware law. Consequently, our directors will not be personally liable to us or our stockholders for monetary damages for any breach of fiduciary duties as directors, except liability for the following:

- Any breach of their duty of loyalty to our company or our stockholders.

- Acts or omissions not in good faith or which involve intentional misconduct or a knowing violation of law.

- Unlawful payments of dividends or unlawful stock repurchases or redemptions as provided in Section 174 of the Delaware General Corporation Law.

- Any transaction from which the director derived an improper personal benefit.

Table of Contents

Our bylaws provide that we are required to indemnify our directors and officers and may indemnify our employees and other agents to the fullest extent permitted by Delaware law. Our bylaws also provide that we shall advance expenses incurred by a director or officer in advance of the final disposition of any action or proceeding, and permit us to secure insurance on behalf of any officer, director, employee or other agent for any liability arising out of his or her actions in that capacity, regardless of whether our bylaws would otherwise permit indemnification. We have entered and expect to continue to enter into agreements to indemnify our directors, executive officers and other employees as determined by the board of directors. These agreements provide for indemnification for related expenses including attorneys' fees, judgments, fines and settlement amounts incurred by any of these individuals in any action or proceeding. We believe that these bylaw provisions and indemnification agreements are necessary to attract and retain qualified persons as directors and officers. We also maintain directors' and officers' liability insurance.

The limitation of liability and indemnification provisions in our certificate of incorporation and bylaws may discourage stockholders from bringing a lawsuit against our directors for breach of their fiduciary duty. They may also reduce the likelihood of derivative litigation against our directors and officers, even though an action, if successful, might benefit us and other stockholders. Furthermore, a stockholder's investment may be adversely affected to the extent that we pay the costs of settlement and damage awards against directors and officers as required by these indemnification provisions. At present, there is no pending litigation or proceeding involving any of our directors, officers or employees regarding which indemnification is sought, and we are not aware of any threatened litigation that may result in claims for indemnification.

Insofar as the provisions of our certificate of incorporation or bylaws provide for indemnification of directors or officers for liabilities arising under the Securities Act of 1933, we have been informed that in the opinion of the Securities and Exchange Commission this indemnification is against public policy as expressed in the Securities Act of 1933 and is therefore unenforceable.

Table of Contents

CERTAIN RELATIONSHIPS AND RELATED PARTY TRANSACTIONS

Since January 1, 2001, we have not been a party to, and we have no plans to be a party to, any transaction or series of similar transactions in which the amount involved exceeded or will exceed $60,000 and in which any current director, executive officer, holder of more than 5% of our capital stock, or entities affiliated with them, had or will have a material interest, other than as described above in the section captioned "Management" and in the transactions described below.

Investor Rights Agreement

We have entered into an Investor Rights Agreement with the purchasers of our outstanding preferred stock, and certain holders of warrants to purchase our common stock and preferred stock, including entities with which certain of our directors are affiliated. The holders of 80,821,014 shares of our common stock, including the shares of common stock issuable upon the automatic conversion of our preferred stock, and the holders of 621,876 shares of our common stock issuable upon exercise of warrants are entitled to rights with respect to the registration of their shares under the Securities Act of 1933. Certain stockholders who are a party to this agreement are entitled to certain financial information regarding us and to visit and inspect our properties and books of account. These information and inspection rights will terminate upon the closing of this offering. In addition, stockholders who are a party to this agreement are provided certain rights to demand registration of shares of common stock issuable upon conversion of their preferred stock or upon exercise of their warrants and to participate in a registration of our common stock that we may decide to do, from time to time. These registration rights will survive this offering and will terminate as to any holder at such time as all of such holders' securities can be sold within a three month period without compliance with the registration requirements of the Securities Act of 1933 pursuant to Rule 144, but in any event no later than the five-year anniversary of this offering. These demand registration rights, however, may not be exercised until six months after this offering. Certain of our directors and executive officers and holders of 5% of our capital stock are parties to this agreement and, as a group, these directors (and their affiliates), executive officers and shareholders represent 64.6% of the shares subject to this agreement. Eric Schmidt, Sergey Brin, Larry Page, Omid Kordestani and David C. Drummond each hold shares representing less than one percent of the shares subject to the agreement. Ram Shriram and entities affiliated with L. John Doerr and Michael Moritz hold shares representing 4.2%, 29.3% and 29.3% of the shares subject to the agreement, respectively. Parties to the Investor Rights Agreement are subject to selling restrictions as more fully described in "Shares Eligible for Future Sale".

Indemnification Agreements

We have entered into an indemnification agreement with each of our directors and officers. The indemnification agreements and our certificate of incorporation and bylaws require us to indemnify our directors and officers to the fullest extent permitted by Delaware law.

Shares Issued to Insiders

The following table summarizes purchases of our stock since January 1, 2001 by our executive officers, directors and holders of more than 5% of our common stock other than compensatory arrangements.

Name	Date of Issuance	Type of Security	Number of Shares	Purchase Price
Eric Schmidt	7/13/01	Series C preferred stock	426,892	$999,994.51

Each share of our preferred stock will be converted automatically into one share of our Class B common stock upon the closing of this offering.

Indebtedness of Management

In September 2001, in connection with the exercise of an option to purchase 14,331,708 shares of our Class B common stock, Eric Schmidt, our chief executive officer, delivered to us a full recourse promissory note

100

Table of Contents

dated September 28, 2001 in the aggregate principal amount of approximately $4.3 million secured by shares of Class B common stock. Interest on the loan accrued at a rate of 7.38% per annum, compounded semi-annually. The loan was secured by a security interest in 14,331,708 shares of our Class B common stock. The largest aggregate amount of indebtedness outstanding pursuant to the note was approximately $5.2 million, which represented the full amount of principal and interest outstanding at April 28, 2004, the date the loan was repaid in full.

Corporate Use of Personal Aircraft

Eric Schmidt owns an interest in a jet that is managed and operated by Apex Aviation and which is made commercially available for lease to consumers. Until recently, Eric owned a second jet, also managed and operated by Apex Aviation. Eric allows certain of our executive officers to use his aircraft for time-critical business trips that cannot be accommodated by commercial airline services. In 2003, we used these planes for business-related travel services for certain of our executive officers and for which services we paid Apex market rates. Eric is entitled to receive a portion of the profits earned by Apex resulting from its management and operation of these planes. Eric has agreed to pay us any and all annual net profits distributed to him as a result of his ownership of an interest in the jets. In 2003, we paid Apex $278,119 and reimbursed Eric $20,214 for the use of these planes. The reimbursements to Eric related to business flights where Eric was billed directly by Apex for use of the planes. These payments were approved by our board of directors and, based upon a competitive analysis of comparable leased aircraft, our board of directors determined that the amounts billed for our use of the aircraft and pilots were at or below market rates for the charter of similar aircraft.

PRINCIPAL AND SELLING STOCKHOLDERS

The following table sets forth certain information with respect to the beneficial ownership of our common stock at June 30, 2004, and as adjusted to reflect the sale of Class A common stock offered by us in this offering, for

- Each person who we know beneficially owns more than five percent of our common stock.
- Each of our directors.
- Each of our named executive officers.
- All of our directors and executive officers as a group.
- All selling stockholders.

Unless otherwise noted below, the address of each beneficial owner listed in the table is c/o Google Inc., 1600 Amphitheatre Parkway, Mountain View, California 94043.

We have determined beneficial ownership in accordance with the rules of the SEC. Except as indicated by the footnotes below, we believe, based on the information furnished to us, that the persons and entities named in the table below have sole voting and investment power with respect to all shares of Class B common stock that they beneficially own, subject to applicable community property laws.

Applicable percentage ownership is based on 12,359,204 shares of Class A common stock and 241,956,117 shares of Class B common stock outstanding at June 30, 2004, assuming the conversion of all outstanding shares of preferred stock into Class B common stock. For purposes of the table below, we have assumed that 33,603,386 shares of Class A common stock and 237,616,257 shares of Class B common stock will be outstanding upon completion of this offering. In computing the number of shares of common stock beneficially owned by a person and the percentage ownership of that person, we deemed outstanding shares of common stock subject to options or warrants held by that person that are currently exercisable or exercisable within 60 days of June 30, 2004. We did not deem these shares outstanding, however, for the purpose of computing the percentage ownership of any other person. Beneficial ownership representing less than one percent is denoted with an "*."

	Shares Beneficially Owned Prior to Offering						Shares Beneficially Owned After Offering				
	Class A Common Stock		Class B Common Stock		% Total Voting Power (1)	Shares Being Offered	Class A Common Stock		Class B Common Stock		% Total Voting Power (1)
Name of Beneficial Owner	Shares	%	Shares	%			Shares	%	Shares	%	
Officers and Directors											
Eric Schmidt	0	*	14,758,600	6.1	6.1	368,965	0	*	14,389,635	6.1	6.0
Sergey Brin	0	*	38,489,048	15.9	15.8	481,113	0	*	38,007,935	16.0	15.8
Larry Page	0	*	38,593,200	16.0	15.9	482,415	0	*	38,110,785	16.0	15.8
Omid Kordestani(2)	0	*	4,810,520	2.0	2.0	240,526	0	*	4,569,994	1.9	1.9
Wayne Rosing(3)	0	*	1,468,000	*	*	70,149	0	*	1,397,851	*	*
L. John Doerr(4)	0	*	21,043,711	8.7	8.7	0	0	*	21,043,711	8.9	8.7
John Hennessy(5)	0	*	65,000	*	*	0	0	*	65,000	*	*
Arthur Levinson(5)	0	*	65,000	*	*	0	0	*	65,000	*	*
Michael Moritz(6)	0	*	23,893,800	9.9	9.8	0	0	*	23,893,800	10.1	9.9
Paul Otellini(5)	0	*	65,000	*	*	0	0	*	65,000	*	*
K. Ram Shriram	0	*	5,324,660	2.2	2.2	266,233	0	*	5,058,427	2.1	2.1
All executive officers and directors as a group(7) (15 persons)	157,000	1.0	151,281,553	62.0	61.7	2,044,651	157,000	*	149,236,902	62.3	61.4
5% Security Holders											
Entities affiliated with Kleiner Perkins Caufield & Byers(4)	0	*	21,043,711	8.7	8.7	0	0	*	21,043,711	8.9	8.7
Entities affiliated with Sequoia Capital (6)	0	*	23,893,800	9.9	9.8	0	0	*	23,893,800	10.1	9.9
Gilad Elbaz	1,046,834	7.0	0	*	*	0	1,046,834	3.1	0	*	*
Yahoo! Inc.(8)	2,700,000	17.9	5,498,884	2.3	2.4	1,610,758	1,639,130	4.9	4,948,996	2.1	2.1

102

Table of Contents

Name of Beneficial Owner	Shares Beneficially Owned Prior to Offering - Class A Common Stock Shares	%	Class B Common Stock Shares	%	% Total Voting Power (1)	Shares Being Offered (18)	Shares Beneficially Owned After Offering - Class A Common Stock Shares	%	Class B Common Stock Shares	%	% Total Voting Power (1)
Selling Stockholders											
America Online, Inc.(9)	0	*	7,437,452	3.1	3.1	743,745	0	*	6,693,707	2.8	2.8
Entities affiliated with Angel Investors (10)	0	*	830,736	*	*	83,073	0	*	747,663	*	*
Andreas Bechtolsheim	0	*	3,614,080	1.5	1.5	361,408	0	*	3,252,672	1.4	1.3
David Cheriton	0	*	3,404,360	1.4	1.4	340,436	0	*	3,063,924	1.3	1.3
David C. Drummond	0	*	1,002,764	*	*	50,138	0	*	952,626	*	*
Roger J. Ebert and Chaz Ebert	0	*	20,192	*	*	2,019	0	*	18,173	*	*
fundfundfund.com, LLC(11)	0	*	100,000	*	*	10,000	0	*	90,000	*	*
Michael James Homer Trust, DTD 6/3/98(12)	0	*	100,960	*	*	10,096	0	*	90,864	*	*
Rackable Systems, Inc.(13)	0	*	42,688	*	*	4,268	0	*	38,420	*	*
George Reyes	0	*	851,750	*	*	42,587	0	*	809,163	*	*
Jonathan J. Rosenberg	0	*	850,500	*	*	42,525	0	*	807,975	*	*
Spalding & Associates(14)	0	*	18,000	*	*	1,800	0	*	16,200	*	*
The Board of Trustees of the Leland Stanford Junior University(15)	7,574	*	1,834,496	*	*	184,207	7,574	*	1,650,289	*	*
VLLI Holdings II, LLC(16)	0	*	621,876	*	*	62,187	0	*	559,689	*	*
The Babak & Lisa Marie Yazdani Trust UTA dtd 4/27/00(17)	0	*	42,692	*	*	4,269	0	*	38,423	*	*

(1) Percentage total voting power represents voting power with respect to all shares of our Class A and Class B common stock, as a single class. Each holder of Class B common stock shall be entitled to ten votes per share of Class B common stock and each holder of Class A common stock shall be entitled to one vote per share of Class A common stock on all matters submitted to our stockholders for a vote. The Class A common stock and Class B common stock vote together as a single class on all matters submitted to a vote of our stockholders, except as may otherwise be required by law. The Class B common stock is convertible at any time by the holder into shares of Class A common stock on a share-for-share basis.

(2) Includes 1,420,000 shares issuable upon exercise of options that are exercisable within 60 days of June 30, 2004. The options provide for exercise prior to vesting, and any unvested shares that are exercised are subject to a lapsing repurchase right in our favor. 859,000 of the shares are vested and 561,000 of the shares are unvested.

(3) Includes 148,000 shares issuable upon exercise of options that are exercisable within 60 days of June 30, 2004. The options provide for exercise prior to vesting, and any unvested shares that are exercised are subject to a lapsing repurchase right in our favor. 11,000 of the shares are vested and 137,000 of the shares are unvested.

(4) Includes 18,111,504 shares held by Kleiner Perkins Caufield & Byers IX-A, L.P., 559,112 shares held by Kleiner Perkins Caufield & Byers IX-B, L.P., 597,344 shares held by KPCB Information Sciences Zaibatsu Fund II, L.P. and 1,775,751 shares held by Vallejo Ventures Trust. L. John Doerr is a manager of the general partners of the Kleiner Perkins Caufield & Byers funds and has shared voting and investment power over these shares. Mr. Doerr is also trustee of the Vallejo Ventures Trust and has voting and investment authority over the shares held by the Trust. However, Mr. Doerr disclaims beneficial ownership of these shares except to the extent of his pecuniary interest arising therein. Shares are held for convenience in the name of "KPCB Holdings, Inc. as nominee" for the account of entities affiliated with Kleiner Perkins Caufield & Byers and others. KPCB Holdings, Inc. has no voting, dispositive or pecuniary interest in any such shares. The address for all entities and individuals affiliated with Kleiner Perkins Caufield & Byers is 2750 Sand Hill Rd., Menlo Park, CA 94025.

(5) In April 2004, each of John, Art and Paul were granted options to purchase 65,000 shares that are exercisable within 60 days of the date of grant, none of which will then be vested. The options provide for exercise prior to vesting, and any unvested shares that are exercised are subject to a lapsing repurchase right in our favor.

(6) Includes 21,654,952 shares held by Sequoia Capital VIII; 1,433,624 shares held by Sequoia International Technology Partners VIII(Q); 477,872 shares held by CMS Partners LLC; 274,784 shares held by Sequoia International Technology Partners VIII; and 52,568 shares held by Sequoia 1997. SC VIII LLC is the general partner of Sequoia Capital VIII, Sequoia International Technology Partners VIII(Q) and Sequoia International Technology Partners VIII. Michael is one of the managing members, including Douglas Leone, Mark Stevens and Michael Goguen, of SC VIII

LLC and exercises shared voting and investment power over the shares held by the Sequoia entities. Michael disclaims beneficial ownership of the shares held by the Sequoia entities except to the extent of his pecuniary interest in these entities. The address of the entities affiliated with Sequoia Capital and Michael is 3000 Sand Hill Road, Bldg. 4, Suite 180, Menlo Park, California 94025.

(7) Includes 2,043,967 shares issuable upon exercise of options that are exercisable within 60 days of June 30, 2004, of which 870,000 shares are vested and 1,173,967 shares are unvested.

(8) Yahoo! Inc. is a publicly held corporation. The address of this entity is 701 1st Avenue, Sunnyvale, California 94089.

(9) America Online, Inc. is a wholly-owned subsidiary of a publicly held corporation.

(10) Includes 223,120 shares held by Angel Investors L.P.; 49,180 shares held by Angel Investors II L.P.; 180,720 shares held by Angel (Q) Investors L.P.; and 377,716 shares held by Angel (Q) Investors II L.P. Shared voting and investment power over the shares held by Angel Investors is exercised by Ron Conway, Casey McGlynn and Bob Bozeman, its managing directors.

(11) Voting and investment power over the shares held by fundfundfund.com LLC is exercised by Alexandria Real Estate Equities, L.P., its sole member and a wholly owned subsidiary of Alexandria Real Estate Equities, Inc., a publicly held corporation.

(12) Voting and investment power over the shares held by Michael James Homer Trust is exercised by Mr. Homer, its trustee.

(13) Voting and investment power over the shares held by Rackable Systems, Inc. is exercised by its board of directors, which includes Marc Rubin, Brian Golson, Thomas Barton and Giovanni Coglitori.

(14) Voting and investment power over the shares held by Spalding & Associates is exercised by Elyse Spalding, its sole proprietor.

(15) Voting and investment power over the shares held by The Board of Trustees of the Leland Stanford Junior University is exercised by the Stanford Management Company, a division of the university. The executive officers of Stanford Management Company include Michael G. McCaffery, Michael L. Ross and Mark Taborsky.

(16) Voting and investment power over the shares held by VLLI Holding II, LCC is exercised by Westech Investment Advisors, Inc. The principals of Westech Investment Advisors are Ronald W. Swenson and Salvador O. Gutierrez.

(17) Voting and investment power over the shares held by The Babak & Lisa Marie Yazdani UTA dtd 4/27/00 is exercised by Mr. and Mrs. Yazdani, its co-trustees.

(18) If the underwriters' overallotment option is exercised in full, the additional shares sold would be allocated among the selling stockholders as follows:

Selling Stockholders	Shares Subject to the Overallotment Option
K. Ram Shriram	125,000
The Board of Trustees of the Leland Stanford Junior University	283,393
America Online, Inc.	1,144,214
Entities affiliated with Angel Investors	127,804
Andreas Bechtolsheim	90,352
David Cheriton	340,436
Michael James Homer Trust, DTD 6/3/98	15,532
Rackable Systems, Inc.	6,567
Spalding & Associates	2,769
Yahoo! Inc.	709,018
VLLI Holdings II, LLC	95,672

If the underwriters' overallotment option is exercised in part, the additional shares sold would be allocated pro rata based upon the share amounts set forth in the preceding table.

Table of Contents

DESCRIPTION OF CAPITAL STOCK

General

The following is a summary of the rights of our common stock and preferred stock and related provisions of our certificate of incorporation and bylaws, as they will be in effect upon the closing of this offering. For more detailed information, please see our certificate of incorporation, bylaws and Investor Rights Agreement, which are filed as exhibits to the registration statement of which this prospectus is a part.

Our certificate of incorporation provides that, upon the closing of the offering, we will have two classes of common stock: Class A common stock, which will have one vote per share, and Class B common stock, which will have ten votes per share. Any holder of Class B common stock may convert his or her shares at any time into shares of Class A common stock on a share-for-share basis. Otherwise the rights of the two classes of common stock will be identical. The rights of these classes of common stock are discussed in greater detail below.

Immediately following the closing of this offering, our authorized capital stock will consist of 9,100,000,000 shares, each with a par value of $0.001 per share, of which:

- 6,000,000,000 shares are designated as Class A common stock.
- 3,000,000,000 shares are designated as Class B common stock.
- 100,000,000 shares are designated as preferred stock.

At June 30, 2004, we had outstanding 12,359,204 shares of Class A common stock, held of record by 865 stockholders and 241,956,117 shares of Class B common stock, held of record by 1,242 stockholders. These amounts assume the conversion of all outstanding shares of our preferred stock, totaling 79,099,884 shares, into Class B common stock. Each share of our outstanding preferred stock will convert into one share of Class B common stock.

In addition, as of June 30, 2004, 16,732,657 shares of our common stock were subject to outstanding options, and 1,996,140 shares of our capital stock were subject to outstanding warrants. At June 30, 2004, 17,774,176 unvested shares of our outstanding common stock were held by our employees and consultants. These shares are subject to a lapsing right of repurchase in our favor, under which we may repurchase these shares upon the termination of the holder's employment or consulting relationship.

Common Stock

Voting Rights

Holders of our Class A and Class B common stock have identical rights, except that holders of our Class A common stock are entitled to one vote per share and holders of our Class B common stock are entitled to ten votes per share. Holders of shares of Class A common stock and Class B common stock will vote together as a single class on all matters (including the election of directors) submitted to a vote of stockholders, unless otherwise required by law. Delaware law could require either our Class A common stock or Class B common stock to vote separately as a single class in the following circumstances:

- If we amended our certificate of incorporation to increase the authorized shares of a class of stock, or to increase or decrease the par value of a class of stock, then that class would be required to vote separately to approve the proposed amendment.

- If we amended our certificate of incorporation in a manner that altered or changed the powers, preferences or special rights of a class of stock in a manner that affects them adversely then that class would be required to vote separately to approve the proposed amendment.

We have not provided for cumulative voting for the election of directors in our certificate of incorporation.

Table of Contents

Dividends

Subject to preferences that may apply to any shares of preferred stock outstanding at the time, the holders of Class A common stock and Class B common stock shall be entitled to share equally in any dividends that our board of directors may determine to issue from time to time. In the event a dividend is paid in the form of shares of common stock or rights to acquire shares of common stock, the holders of Class A common stock shall receive Class A common stock, or rights to acquire Class A common stock, as the case may be, and the holders of Class B common stock shall receive Class B common stock, or rights to acquire Class B common stock, as the case may be.

Liquidation Rights

Upon our liquidation, dissolution or winding-up, the holders of Class A common stock and Class B common stock shall be entitled to share equally all assets remaining after the payment of any liabilities and the liquidation preferences on any outstanding preferred stock.

Conversion

Our Class A common stock is not convertible into any other shares of our capital stock.

Each share of Class B common stock is convertible at any time at the option of the holder into one share of Class A common stock. In addition, each share of Class B common stock shall convert automatically into one share of Class A common stock upon any transfer, whether or not for value, except for certain transfers described in our certificate of incorporation, including the following:

- Transfers between Larry and Sergey, our founders.
- Transfers for tax and estate planning purposes, including to trusts, corporations and partnerships controlled by a holder of Class B common stock.

In addition, partnerships or limited liability companies that hold more than 5% of the total outstanding shares of Class B common stock as of the closing of the offering may distribute their Class B common stock to their respective partners or members (who may further distribute the Class B common stock to their respective partners or members) without triggering a conversion to Class A common stock. Such distributions must be conducted in accordance with the ownership interests of such partners or members and the terms of any agreements binding the partnership or limited liability company.

The death of any holder of Class B common stock who is a natural person will result in the conversion of his or her shares of Class B common stock to Class A common stock. However, either of our founders may transfer voting control of shares of Class B common stock to the other founder contingent or effective upon their death without triggering a conversion to Class A common stock, provided that the shares of Class B common stock so transferred shall convert to Class A common stock nine months after the death of the transferring founder.

Once transferred and converted into Class A common stock, the Class B common stock shall not be reissued. No class of common stock may be subdivided or combined unless the other class of common stock concurrently is subdivided or combined in the same proportion and in the same manner.

Preferred Stock

Upon the closing of this offering, each outstanding share of our preferred stock will be converted into one share of Class B common stock.

Following the closing of this offering, our board of directors will have the authority, without approval by the stockholders, to issue up to a total of 100,000,000 shares of preferred stock in one or more series. Our board of

Table of Contents

directors may establish the number of shares to be included in each such series and may fix the designations, preferences, powers and other rights of the shares of a series of preferred stock. Our board could authorize the issuance of preferred stock with voting or conversion rights that could dilute the voting power or rights of the holders of common stock. The issuance of preferred stock, while providing flexibility in connection with possible acquisitions and other corporate purposes, could, among other things, have the effect of delaying, deferring or preventing a change in control of Google and might harm the market price of our common stock. We have no current plans to issue any shares of preferred stock.

Warrants

At June 30, 2004, we had outstanding warrants to purchase 1,996,140 shares of our common stock assuming automatic conversion of our preferred stock into common stock upon the closing of this offering at exercise prices ranging from $0.30 to $2.34.

Registration Rights

The holders of 80,821,014 shares of our common stock, including the shares of common stock issuable upon the automatic conversion of our preferred stock, and the holders of 621,876 shares of our common stock issuable upon exercise of warrants are entitled to rights with respect to the registration of their shares under the Securities Act. These registration rights are contained in our third amended and restated investors' rights agreement and are described below. The registration rights under the investors' rights agreement will expire five years following the completion of this offering, or, with respect to an individual holder, when such holder is able to sell all of its shares pursuant to Rule 144 under the Securities Act in any three month period.

Demand Registration Rights

At any time following six months after the closing of this offering, the holders of shares of common stock having demand registration rights under the investors' rights agreement have the right to require that we register their common stock, provided such registration relates to not less than 40% in aggregate of our then outstanding shares of common stock having demand registration rights. We are only obligated to effect two registrations in response to these demand registration rights. We may postpone the filing of a registration statement for up to 90 days once in any 12-month period if our board of directors determines in good faith that the filing would be seriously detrimental to our stockholders or us. The underwriters of any underwritten offering have the right to limit the number of shares to be included in a registration statement filed in response to the exercise of these demand registration rights. We must pay all expenses, except for underwriters' discounts and commissions, incurred in connection with these demand registration rights.

Piggyback Registration Rights

If we register any securities for public sale, the stockholders with piggyback registration rights under the investors' rights agreement have the right to include their shares in the registration, subject to specified exceptions. The underwriters of any underwritten offering have the right to limit the number of shares registered by these stockholders due to marketing reasons, provided that the number of shares held by stockholders with piggyback registration rights may not be limited to less than 30% of the total number of shares to be included in the registration. We must pay all expenses, except for underwriters' discounts and commissions, incurred in connection with these piggyback registration rights.

S-3 Registration Rights

If we are eligible to file a registration statement on Form S-3, the stockholders with S-3 registration rights under the investors' rights agreement can request that we register their shares, provided that the total price of the shares of common stock offered to the public is at least $250,000. A holder of S-3 registration rights may not require us to file a registration statement on Form S-3 if we have already effected two registrations on Form S-3 at the request of such holder. We may postpone the filing of a Form S-3 registration statement for up to 90 days once in any 12-month period if our board of directors determines in good faith that the filing would be seriously detrimental to our stockholders or us. The holders of S-3 registration rights must pay all expenses associated with any registrations on Form S-3.

Compliance with Exchange Governance Rules

Both the Nasdaq and the NYSE have adopted rules that provide that listed companies which are controlled by a single person or a group of persons are not required to comply with certain corporate governance rules and requirements of these exchanges. In particular, a "controlled company" may elect to be exempt from certain rules that require a majority of the board of directors of companies listed on the Nasdaq or NYSE to be independent, as defined by these rules, and which mandate independent director representation on certain committees of the board. In particular, the NYSE requires that a company listed on that exchange must have a nominating/corporate governance committee, a compensation committee and an audit committee comprised exclusively of directors who are independent under the rules of the NYSE. In addition, the NYSE requires that the audit committee must have at least three members and must otherwise be in compliance with rules established for audit committees of public companies under the Exchange Act. The Nasdaq requires that a company listed on that market must have an audit committee comprised of at least three members all of whom are independent under the rules of the Nasdaq and that is otherwise in compliance with the rules established for audit committees of public companies under the Exchange Act. In addition, the Nasdaq requires that director nominees must be selected, or recommended to the board of directors for selection, by a majority of directors who are independent under the rules of the Nasdaq, or a nominations committee comprised solely of independent directors, and that compensation for executive officers must be determined, or recommended to the board of directors for determination, by a majority of independent directors or a nominations committee comprised solely of independent directors.

In the event we are listed on either the Nasdaq or the NYSE, our charter provides that our stockholders will not be permitted to elect to rely upon these "controlled company" exemptions without first obtaining the prior approval of stockholders representing at least 66 $2/3$% of the total voting power of our outstanding capital stock.

In the event we obtain this approval and elect to rely on the "controlled company" exemptions provided by the Nasdaq and the NYSE, our charter documents provide that for so long we continue to be listed on either of these exchanges, then the Board shall be constituted such that a majority of the directors on our board, and the members of our compensation committee and our corporate governance and nominating committee, must not be current employees of Google, and may not have been employees of Google for at least three years.

The provision in our certificate of incorporation that establish these requirements may be amended or repealed only with the unanimous consent of our board of directors and the consent of stockholders representing at least 66 $2/3$% of the total voting power of our outstanding capital stock.

Separation of Office of Chairman and CEO

Our certificate of incorporation provides that the Chairman of our board of directors may not be an employee or officer of our company, and may not have been an employee or officer for the last three years, unless the appointment is approved by two-thirds of the members of our board of directors.

Anti-Takeover Effects of Delaware Law and Our Certificate of Incorporation and Bylaws

Certain provisions of Delaware law, our certificate of incorporation and our bylaws contain provisions that could have the effect of delaying, deferring or discouraging another party from acquiring control of us. In particular, our dual class common stock structure will concentrate ownership of our voting stock in the hands of

Table of Contents

our founders, board members, and employees. These provisions, which are summarized below, are expected to discourage coercive takeover practices and inadequate takeover bids. These provisions are also designed to encourage persons seeking to acquire control of us to first negotiate with our board of directors. We believe that the benefits of increased protection of our potential ability to negotiate with an unfriendly or unsolicited acquiror outweigh the disadvantages of discouraging a proposal to acquire us because negotiation of these proposals could result in an improvement of their terms.

Dual Class Structure

As discussed above, our Class B common stock has ten votes per share, while our Class A common stock, which is the class of stock we are selling in this offering and which will be the only class of stock which is publicly traded, has one vote per share. After the offering, 62.9% of our Class B common stock will be controlled by our founders, executive officers and employees, representing 62.0% of the voting power of our outstanding capital stock. Because of our dual class structure, our founders, executives and employees will continue to be able to control all matters submitted to our stockholders for approval even if they come to own significantly less than 50% of the shares of our outstanding common stock. This concentrated control could discourage others from initiating any potential merger, takeover or other change of control transaction that other stockholders may view as beneficial.

Special Approval for Change in Control Transactions

In the event a person seeks to acquire us by means of a merger or consolidation transaction, a purchase of all or substantially all of our assets, or an issuance of stock which constitutes 2% or more of our outstanding shares at the time of issuance and which results in any person or group owning more than 50% of our outstanding voting power, then these types of acquisition transactions must be approved by our stockholders at an annual or special meeting. At this meeting, we must obtain the approval of stockholders representing the greater of:

- A majority of the voting power of our outstanding capital stock; and

- 60% of the voting power of the shares of capital stock present in person or represented by proxy at the stockholder meeting and entitled to vote.

Limits on Ability of Stockholders to Act by Written Consent

We have provided in our certificate of incorporation and bylaws that our stockholders may not act by written consent. This limit on the ability of our stockholders to act by written consent may lengthen the amount of time required to take stockholder actions. As a result, a holder controlling a majority of our capital stock would not be able to amend our bylaws or remove directors without holding a stockholders meeting.

Undesignated Preferred Stock

The ability to authorize undesignated preferred stock makes it possible for our board of directors to issue preferred stock with voting or other rights or preferences that could impede the success of any attempt to acquire us. These and other provisions may have the effect of deferring hostile takeovers or delaying changes in control or management of our company.

Requirements for Advance Notification of Stockholder Nominations and Proposals

Our bylaws establish advance notice procedures with respect to stockholder proposals and the nomination of candidates for election as directors, other than nominations made by or at the direction of the board of directors or a committee of the board of directors. The bylaws do not give the board of directors the power to approve or disapprove stockholder nominations of candidates or proposals regarding business to be conducted at a special or annual meeting of the stockholders. However, our bylaws may have the effect of precluding the conduct of

Table of Contents

certain business at a meeting if the proper procedures are not followed. These provisions may also discourage or deter a potential acquiror from conducting a solicitation of proxies to elect the acquirer's own slate of directors or otherwise attempting to obtain control of our company.

Delaware Anti-Takeover Statute

We will be subject to the provisions of Section 203 of the Delaware General Corporation Law regulating corporate takeovers. In general, Section 203 prohibits a publicly-held Delaware corporation from engaging under certain circumstances, in a business combination with an interested stockholder for a period of three years following the date the person became an interested stockholder unless:

- Prior to the date of the transaction, the board of directors of the corporation approved either the business combination or the transaction which resulted in the stockholder becoming an interested stockholder.

- Upon completion of the transaction that resulted in the stockholder becoming an interested stockholder, the stockholder owned at least 85% of the voting stock of the corporation outstanding at the time the transaction commenced, excluding for purposes of determining the number of shares outstanding (1) shares owned by persons who are directors and also officers and (2) shares owned by employee stock plans in which employee participants do not have the right to determine confidentially whether shares held subject to the plan will be tendered in a tender or exchange offer.

- On or subsequent to the date of the transaction, the business combination is approved by the board and authorized at an annual or special meeting of stockholders, and not by written consent, by the affirmative vote of at least 66 2/3% of the outstanding voting stock which is not owned by the interested stockholder.

Generally, a business combination includes a merger, asset or stock sale, or other transaction resulting in a financial benefit to the interested stockholder. An interested stockholder is a person who, together with affiliates and associates, owns or, within three years prior to the determination of interested stockholder status, did own 15% or more of a corporation's outstanding voting securities. We expect the existence of this provision to have an anti-takeover effect with respect to transactions our board of directors does not approve in advance. We also anticipate that Section 203 may also discourage attempts that might result in a premium over the market price for the shares of common stock held by stockholders.

The provisions of Delaware law, our certificate of incorporation and our bylaws could have the effect of discouraging others from attempting hostile takeovers and, as a consequence, they may also inhibit temporary fluctuations in the market price of our common stock that often result from actual or rumored hostile takeover attempts. These provisions may also have the effect of preventing changes in our management. It is possible that these provisions could make it more difficult to accomplish transactions that stockholders may otherwise deem to be in their best interests.

Transfer Agent and Registrar

The transfer agent and registrar for our common stock is EquiServe Trust Company, N.A., located at 150 Royall Street, Canton, Massachusetts 02021.

Listing

Our Class A common stock has been approved for quotation on The Nasdaq National Market under the symbol "GOOG," subject to official notice of issuance. Our Class B common stock will not be listed on any stock market or exchange.

Table of Contents

RESCISSION OFFER

From September 2001 through June 2004, we granted under our 1998 Stock Plan, 2003 Stock Plan, 2003 Stock Plan (No. 2) and 2003 Stock Plan (No. 3) to residents of the United States options to purchase 37,079,623 shares of our common stock with a weighted average per share exercise price of $2.86, of which, 12,743,816 shares remain subject to outstanding options. As of June 2004, we issued 23,702,819 shares of our common stock upon the exercise of certain of these options, of which 23,240,668 shares remain outstanding, subject to our right to repurchase certain of these shares in limited circumstances. Options we granted during this period may not have been exempt from the registration or qualification requirements under the securities laws of some states. In addition, certain shares issued upon exercise of options granted during this period may not have been exempt from the registration or qualification requirements under Rule 701 under the Securities Act of 1933 and under those state securities laws that provide an exemption to the extent the requirements under Rule 701 are met. We became aware that we were approaching the numeric limitations prescribed by Rule 701 in September 2002 and thereafter determined that we could not continue to count on being able to rely on Rule 701 to provide an exemption from the registration requirements of the Securities Act of 1933. In addition, continued compliance under Rule 701 would have required broad dissemination of detailed financial information regarding our business, which would have been strategically disadvantageous to our company. In evaluating how to issue stock upon exercise of outstanding options in light of these limitations we determined we would utilize "private placement" exemptions provided by Section 4(2) of the Securities Act of 1933 in order to exempt these issuances from federal registration requirements notwithstanding the factual and legal uncertainties inherent in Section 4(2). These uncertainties arise because analyzing whether or not issuances of securities qualify for the exemptions afforded by Section 4(2) involves a number of subjective determinations including whether the number of offerees constitutes a general solicitation, the financial sophistication of offerees and their access to information regarding the issuer, as well as whether the offering was designed to result in a distribution of shares to the general public. We considered various alternatives in determining to rely on the exemption provided by Section 4(2) despite its inherent uncertainties. We considered ceasing granting options and shares to service providers. However, we determined that this would be detrimental to our development, as equity compensation was an essential ingredient to building our company. We also considered becoming a reporting company for the purposes of federal securities laws. We determined that this too would be contrary to the best interests of our stockholders. We therefore concluded that relying on Section 4(2) despite its uncertainties was in the best interest of our security holders. Because of the uncertainty in relying on Section 4(2), the options we granted and the shares issued upon exercise of these options during this period may have been issued in violation of either federal or state securities laws, or both, and may be subject to rescission. In order to address this issue, we intend to make a rescission offer soon after the effective date of this offering to all holders of any outstanding options and shares who we believe may be entitled to argue for rescission and, pursuant to this rescission offer, we will offer to repurchase these options and shares then outstanding from the holder. We will be making this rescission offer to 1,406 persons who are or were residents of Arkansas, California, Colorado, Connecticut, the District of Columbia, Georgia, Illinois, Maryland, Massachusetts, Michigan, Nevada, New Hampshire, New Jersey, New York, North Carolina, Pennsylvania, Texas, Virginia and Washington. If our rescission offer is accepted by all offerees, we could be required to make an aggregate payment to the holders of these options and shares of up to approximately $25.9 million, which includes statutory interest.

Our anticipated rescission offer will cover an aggregate of approximately 23,240,668 shares of common stock issued and outstanding under our 1998 Stock Plan, 2003 Stock Plan, 2003 Stock Plan (No. 2) and 2003 Stock Plan (No. 3), and options outstanding under these plans to purchase 5,592,248 shares of common stock. These securities represent all of the options we granted to residents of the United States pursuant to these plans during the period from September 2001 through June 2004 that we believe may not been qualified under state securities laws and the shares issued upon exercise of options granted during this period (other than options and shares returned to these plans, whether by cancellation, repurchase or otherwise). These options and shares are held by our current and former employees, including one of our executive officers, and our current and former consultants. We intend to make the rescission offer to the holders of these shares and options as soon as practicable after the completion of the offering of our Class A common stock and, in any event, within 30 days of the effective date of this registration statement, assuming the offering has been completed at such time. The

111

Table of Contents

rescission offer will be kept open for at least 20 business days and will be registered under the Securities Act and qualified in each state where such qualification is required under applicable state securities laws.

We will offer to rescind prior purchases of our common stock acquired through the exercise of options that are subject to the rescission offer for an amount equal to the price paid for the shares plus interest, calculated from the date of the exercise through the date on which the rescission offer expires, at the applicable statutory interest rate per year. With respect to outstanding options to purchase our common stock that are subject to the rescission offer, we will offer to rescind the entire option grant, regardless of whether the option is vested, in exchange for an amount equal to 20% of the aggregate exercise price for the entire option, plus interest, calculated from the date of grant of the option through the date on which the rescission offer expires, at the applicable statutory interest rate per year.

If all holders of shares of our common stock and options subject to the rescission offer elected to accept our rescission offer, we would be required to make an aggregate payment of approximately $25.9 million to these holders. We believe this amount represents our aggregate exposure under federal and state securities laws for not seeking to register or qualify these shares or options under these laws. Our aggregate exposure under just state securities laws (and not federal securities laws) for failing to register or qualify these shares and options is approximately $11.7 million. Our exposure for state securities laws violations is less than our exposure for federal securities laws violations because many of the shares and options that were issued without registration or qualification under federal securities laws were issued under available exemptions from state registration and qualification requirements provided by state securities laws. Our anticipated rescission offers to be made in the various states in which we may not have complied with applicable securities laws will cover an aggregate of approximately 21,706,238 shares of common stock, and outstanding options to purchase 5,592,248 shares of common stock, which were issued under our 1998 Stock Plan and 2003 Stock Plan. Our state rescission liability could require us to make an aggregate payment of approximately $11.7 million to holders of shares of our common stock and options subject to rescission under state securities laws. Because these holders will be offered either the option of having their shares or options, as the case may be, repurchased under provisions of either federal or applicable state laws (but not both), the $11.7 million aggregate liability under state securities laws is included in the aggregate $25.9 million amount discussed above, which is our aggregate exposure under both federal and state securities laws at June 30, 2004.

Our making this rescission offer may not terminate a purchaser's right to rescind a sale of securities that was not registered or qualified under the Securities Act or applicable state securities laws and was not otherwise exempt from registration or qualification. Accordingly, should the rescission offer be rejected by any or all offerees, we may continue to be contingently liable under the Securities Act of 1933 and applicable state securities laws for the purchase price of these shares and the value of the options up to an aggregate amount of approximately $25.9 million, which includes statutory interest. In addition, it is possible that an optionholder could argue that offering to rescind the issuance of outstanding options for an amount equal to 20% of the aggregate exercise price, plus interest, does not represent an adequate remedy for the issuance of the option in violation of applicable securities laws. If a court were to impose a greater remedy, our exposure as a result of the rescission offer could be higher. In addition, if it is determined that we offered securities without properly registering them under federal or state law, or securing an exemption from registration, regulators could impose monetary fines or other sanctions as provided under these laws. We understand that the Securities and Exchange Commission has initiated an informal inquiry into this matter and certain state regulators, including California, have requested additional information.

We expect that we will be able to fund any costs related to our rescission offer from our current cash balances. Furthermore, we do not believe our rescission offer would affect our ability to obtain financing in the future, due to our belief that it is unlikely that the rescission offer will be accepted by our stockholders or option holders in an amount that would represent a material expenditure by us. This belief is based on the fact that our rescission offer will offer to repurchase shares and options at a weighted average price of $2.86, while our current estimated initial public offering price is between $85.00 and $95.00.

Table of Contents

SHARES ELIGIBLE FOR FUTURE SALE

Prior to this offering, there has been no public market for our stock. We cannot predict the effect, if any, that market sales of shares or the availability of shares for sale will have on the market price prevailing from time to time. Sales of our Class A common stock in the public market after the restrictions lapse as described below, or the perception that those sales may occur, could cause the prevailing market price to decrease or to be lower than it might be in the absence of those sales or perceptions.

Sale of Restricted Shares

Upon completion of this offering, we will have outstanding 271,219,643 shares of common stock. The shares of Class A common stock being sold in this offering will be freely tradable, other than by any of our "affiliates" as defined in Rule 144 (a) under the Securities Act, without restriction or registration under the Securities Act. All remaining shares, and all shares subject to outstanding options and warrants, were issued and sold by us in private transactions and are eligible for public sale if registered under the Securities Act or sold in accordance with Rule 144 or Rule 701 under the Securities Act. These remaining shares are "restricted securities" within the meaning of Rule 144 under the Securities Act.

As a result of the selling restriction agreements, the provisions of Rules 144, 144(k) and 701 and the registration statements described below (assuming the registration statement relating to our rescission offer is declared effective by the Securities and Exchange Commission), the restricted securities will first become available for sale in the public market as follows (in all cases subject to the requirement that no unvested shares may be sold before they vest):

Days After the Date of this Prospectus	Additional Shares Eligible for Public Sale	Comments
On the date of this prospectus	0	
At 15 days after the date of this prospectus and various times thereafter	4,575,048	Does not include any shares held by our executive officers or other parties to our Investor Rights Agreement. Includes shares eligible for sale under Rule 144(k), pursuant to our registration statements on Form S-8 and Form S-8/S-3 and under our rescission offer registration statement on Form S-1 described below.
At 90 days after the date of this prospectus and various times thereafter	39,081,106	Shares eligible for sale under Rules 144, 144(k) and 701 and our registration statement on Form S-8 and under our rescission offer registration statement on Form S-1 described below.
At 120 days after the date of this prospectus and various times thereafter	24,874,091	Represents shares held only by parties to our Investor Rights Agreement, eligible for sale under Rules 144 and 144(k).
At 150 days after the date of this prospectus and various times thereafter	24,874,091	Represents shares held only by parties to our Investor Rights Agreement, eligible for sale under Rules 144 and 144(k).
At 180 days after the date of this prospectus and various times thereafter	176,876,866	Includes shares eligible for sale under Rules 144, 144(k) and 701 and our registration statement on Form S-8 and under our rescission offer registration statement on Form S-1 described below.

Table of Contents

Selling Restriction Agreements

We have entered into agreements with the parties to our Investor Rights Agreement, except for our executive officers, that provides that they will limit sales of any common stock owned by them following the date of this prospectus, as follows: one third of their shares held after any sales they make in this offering become eligible for sale 90 days after the date of this prospectus; one third of their shares become eligible for sale 120 days after the date of this prospectus; and one third of their shares become eligible for sale 150 days after the date of this prospectus. Certain parties to our Investors Rights Agreement agreed to limit sales of 10% of their shares (an aggregate of 4,493,751 shares) for a period of 180 days after the date of this prospectus—and, for these holders, the portions restricted for 90, 120 and 150 days are calculated after subtracting the 180 day restricted shares.

We have entered into agreements with our executive officers which provide that they will limit sales of any common stock beneficially owned by them for 180 days following the date of this prospectus, except that 5% of their current equity holdings including options (10% in the case of any executive officer who does not hold vested shares or options as of the date of this prospectus) will become eligible for sale 90 days after the date of this prospectus. This is in addition to any shares our executive officers sell in the offering.

We have entered into agreements with the remaining holders of substantially all of our common stock which provide that they will limit sales of any common stock beneficially owned by them for 180 days following the date of this prospectus, except that they may sell a portion of their shares earlier, as follows:

- 5% of their current equity holdings including options become eligible for sale beginning 15 days after the date of this prospectus.

- 10% of their current equity holdings including options become eligible for sale beginning 90 days after the date of this prospectus.

- Employees can only sell vested shares. Employees who do not hold vested shares, including shares subject to options, upon expiration of these selling restrictions will not be able to sell shares until they vest.

As these shares become available for sale and are sold into the market, the market price of our Class A common stock could decline. After a restricted person's holding of common stock have been released from the restrictions on sale described above they will be available for sale to the public subject satisfaction of the requirements of Rule 144 or Rule 701, which are described below.

Lock-Up Arrangements

We have agreed with the underwriters that for a period of 180 days after the date of this prospectus, we will not sell any shares of our common stock, or securities convertible into shares of our common stock, without the prior written consent of Morgan Stanley & Co. Incorporated and Credit Suisse First Boston LLC. This agreement is subject to certain exceptions, including an exception allowing us to issue an unlimited number of shares in connection with mergers or acquisition transactions, joint ventures or other strategic corporate transactions. Morgan Stanley & Co. Incorporated and Credit Suisse First Boston LLC may release us from these lock-up arrangements at any time without notice. This agreement is subject to extension as set forth in "Underwriters."

None of our officers, directors, employees or stockholders have entered into contractual lock-up agreements with the underwriters in connection with this offering. We have entered into contractual lock-up agreements with our officers and directors and certain of our employees and other securityholders, representing the holders of substantially all of our outstanding capital stock.

Rule 144

In general, under Rule 144, as currently in effect, a person who owns shares that were acquired from us or an affiliate of us at least one year prior to the proposed sale is entitled to sell upon expiration of the selling restrictions described above, within any three-month period beginning September 27, 2004, a number of shares that does not exceed the greater of:

- 1% of the number of shares of common stock then outstanding, which will equal approximately 369,959 shares immediately after this offering; or

Table of Contents

- The average weekly trading volume of the common stock during the four calendar weeks preceding the filing of a notice on Form 144 with respect to such sale.

Sales under Rule 144 are also subject to certain manner of sale provisions and notice requirements and to the availability of current public information about us. Rule 144 also provides that our affiliates who sell shares of our common stock that are not restricted shares must nonetheless comply with the same restrictions applicable to restricted shares with the exception of the holding period requirement.

Rule 144(k)

Under Rule 144(k), a person who is not deemed to have been one of our affiliates for purposes of the Securities Act at any time during the 90 days preceding a sale and who has beneficially owned the shares proposed to be sold for at least two years, including the holding period of any prior owner other than our affiliates, is entitled to sell such shares without complying with the manner of sale, public information, volume limitation or notice provisions of Rule 144. Therefore, unless otherwise restricted, "144(k) shares" may be sold immediately upon the completion of this offering.

Rule 701

In general, under Rule 701 as currently in effect, any of our employees, consultants or advisors who purchases shares from us in connection with a compensatory stock or option plan or other written agreement in a transaction that was completed in reliance on Rule 701 and complied with the requirements of Rule 701 is eligible to resell such shares beginning September 27, 2004 in reliance on Rule 144, but without compliance with certain restrictions, including the holding period, contained in Rule 144.

Stock Options

We intend to file a registration statement on Form S-8 under the Securities Act for shares of our common stock subject to options outstanding or reserved for issuance under our stock plans and shares of our common stock issued upon the exercise of options by employees. We expect to file this registration statement as soon as practicable after this offering. In addition, we intend to file a registration statement on Form S-8 or such other form as may be required under the Securities Act for the resale of shares of our common stock issued upon the exercise of options that were not granted under Rule 701. We expect to file this registration statement as soon as permitted under the Securities Act. However, none of the shares registered on Form S-8 will be eligible for resale until expiration of the selling restriction agreements to which they are subject.

Registration Rights

The holders of 81,442,890 shares of our common stock, assuming the exercise of outstanding warrants to purchase registrable securities, may demand that we register their shares under the Securities Act or, if we file another registration statement under the Securities Act, may elect to include their shares in such registration. If these shares are registered, they will be freely tradable without restriction under the Securities Act. For additional information, see "Description of Capital Stock—Registration Rights."

Registration Statements

We have filed a registration statement on Form S-8 registering the issuance of shares of our Class A common stock and Class B common stock issuable upon the exercise of outstanding options and options that may be issued in the future under our stock plans. Shares covered by the Form S-8 will be available for sale immediately upon issuance, subject to the selling restrictions described above.

We plan to file immediately following the completion of the offering a registration statement on Form S-8/S-3 registering the resale of shares of our Class A common stock (including shares issuable upon

Table of Contents

conversion of Class B common stock) that were issued to service providers. Shares registered under the Form S-8/S-3 will be immediately transferable upon the effectiveness of the Form S-8/S-3, subject to the selling restrictions described above.

We intend to make a registered rescission offer shortly after the offering with respect to shares we have issued in the past in violation of state and federal securities laws as a result of the limited ability to use Rule 701 of the Securities Act of 1933 to exempt service provider grants. Shares covered by the rescission offer will be freely transferable upon effectiveness of the registration statement relating to the rescission offer. See the section above under the caption "Rescission Offer" for a more detailed discussion of the rescission offer.

Table of Contents

UNDERWRITERS

Under the terms and subject to the conditions contained in an underwriting agreement dated the date of this prospectus, the underwriters named below, for whom Morgan Stanley & Co. Incorporated and Credit Suisse First Boston LLC are acting as representatives, have severally agreed to purchase, and we and the selling stockholders have agreed to sell to them, the number of shares of Class A common stock indicated below. The obligation of each underwriter to purchase shares from us and the selling stockholders set forth below is not dependent on the number of shares allocated to that underwriter's customers in respect of successful bids.

Name	Number of Shares
Morgan Stanley & Co. Incorporated	
Credit Suisse First Boston LLC	
Allen & Company LLC	
Citigroup Global Markets Inc.	
Goldman, Sachs & Co.	
J.P. Morgan Securities Inc.	
Lehman Brothers Inc.	
UBS Securities LLC	
Thomas Weisel Partners LLC	
WR Hambrecht + Co., LLC	
Deutsche Bank Securities Inc.	
Lazard Freres & Co. LLC	
Ameritrade, Inc.	
M.R. Beal & Company	
William Blair & Company L.L.C.	
Blaylock & Partners, L.P.	
Cazenove Inc.	
E*TRADE Securities LLC	
Epoch Securities, Inc.	
Fidelity Capital Markets, a division of National Financial Services, LLC	
HARRISdirect, LLC	
Needham & Company, Inc.	
Piper Jaffray & Co.	
Samuel A. Ramirez & Co., Inc.	
Muriel Siebert & Co. Inc.	
Utendahl Capital Group, L.L.C.	
Wachovia Capital Markets, LLC	
Wells Fargo Securities, LLC	
Total	19,605,052

The underwriters are offering the shares of Class A common stock subject to their acceptance of the shares from us and the selling stockholders and subject to prior sale. The underwriting agreement provides that the obligations of the several underwriters to pay for and accept delivery of the shares of Class A common stock offered by this prospectus are subject to the approval of certain legal matters by their counsel and to certain other conditions. The underwriters are obligated to take and pay for all of the shares of Class A common stock offered by this prospectus if any such shares are taken. However, the underwriters are not required to take or pay for the shares covered by the underwriters' over-allotment option described below.

The underwriters initially propose to offer part of the shares of our Class A common stock directly to the public at the public offering price listed on the cover page of this prospectus. After the initial offering of the shares of our Class A common stock, the offering price and other selling terms may from time to time be varied by the representatives of the underwriters.

Table of Contents

The selling stockholders have granted to the underwriters an option, exercisable for 30 days from the date of this prospectus, to purchase up to an aggregate of 2,940,757 additional shares of our Class A common stock at the public offering price listed on the cover page of this prospectus, less underwriters discounts and commissions. The underwriters may exercise this option solely for the purpose of covering over-allotments, if any, made in connection with the offering of the shares of Class A common stock offered by this prospectus. To the extent the option is exercised, each underwriter will become obligated, subject to certain conditions, to purchase about the same percentage of the additional shares of Class A common stock as the number listed next to the underwriter's name in the preceding table bears to the total number of shares of Class A common stock listed next to the names of all underwriters in the preceding table.

If the underwriters' option is exercised in full, the total price to the public of all the shares of Class A common stock sold would be $2,029.1 million, the total underwriting discounts and commissions would be $65.0 million, and the total proceeds to us would be $1,227.2 million. We will not receive any of the proceeds from the sale of the Class A common stock by the selling stockholders.

The following table shows the per share and total underwriting discounts and commissions to be paid by us and the selling stockholders in connection with this offering. These amounts are shown assuming both no exercise and full exercise of the underwriters' over-allotment option.

	Per Share		Total	
Underwriting discounts and commissions to be paid by	No Exercise	Full Exercise	No Exercise	Full Exercise
Google	$	$	$	$
Selling stockholders	$	$	$	$

The expenses of this offering payable by us, not including underwriting discounts and commissions, are estimated to be approximately $4.8 million, which includes legal, accounting and printing costs and various other fees associated with registration and listing of our Class A common stock.

The underwriters have informed us and the selling stockholders that they will not confirm sales of Class A common stock to any accounts over which they exercise discretionary authority without first receiving a written consent from those accounts.

Our Class A common stock has been approved for quotation on The Nasdaq National Market under the symbol "GOOG," subject to official notice of issuance.

We have agreed that, without the prior written consent of Morgan Stanley & Co. Incorporated and Credit Suisse First Boston LLC on behalf of the underwriters, we will not, during the period ending 180 days after the date of this prospectus:

- Offer, pledge, sell, contract to sell, sell any option or contract to purchase, purchase any option or contract to sell, grant any option, right or warrant to purchase, lend or otherwise transfer or dispose of directly or indirectly, any shares of Class A common stock or any securities convertible into or exercisable or exchangeable for such Class A common stock.

- Enter into any swap or other arrangement that transfers to another, in whole or in part, any of the economic consequences of ownership of the Class A common stock.

whether any transaction described above is to be settled by delivery of such common stock or such other securities, in cash or otherwise. The restrictions described in this paragraph do not apply to:

- The sale of shares of Class A common stock to the underwriters.

- The issuance of shares of common stock or the grant of options to purchase shares of Class B common stock under our employee stock purchase plan and/or our equity incentive plan.

118

Table of Contents

- The issuance by us of shares of common stock upon the exercise of an option or a warrant or the conversion of a security outstanding on the date of this prospectus of which the underwriters have been advised in writing or which is otherwise described in this prospectus.

- The issuance by us of shares of our common stock, or securities convertible into our common stock, in connection with mergers or acquisition transactions, joint ventures or other strategic corporate transactions.

The 180-day restricted period described in the preceding paragraphs will be extended if:

- During the last 17 days of the 180-day restricted period we issue an earnings release or material news or a material event relating to our company occurs; or

- Prior to the expiration of the 180-day restricted period, we announce that we will release earnings results during the 16-day period beginning on the last day of the 180-day period;

in which case the restrictions described in the preceding paragraph will continue to apply until the expiration of the 18-day period beginning on the issuance of the earnings release or the occurrence of the material news or material event.

None of our officers, directors, employees or stockholders have entered into contractual lock-up agreements with the underwriters in connection with this offering.

In order to facilitate the offering of our Class A common stock, the underwriters may engage in transactions that stabilize, maintain or otherwise affect the price of the Class A common stock. Specifically, the underwriters may sell more shares than they are obligated to purchase under the underwriting agreement, creating a short position in our Class A common stock for their own account. A short sale is "covered" if the short position is no greater than the number of shares available for purchase by the underwriters under the over-allotment option. The underwriters can close out a covered short sale by exercising the over-allotment option or purchasing shares of Class A common stock in the open market. In determining the source of shares to close out a covered short sale, the underwriters will consider, among other things, the open market price of shares of Class A common stock compared to the price available under the over-allotment option. The underwriters may also sell shares of Class A common stock in excess of the over-allotment option, creating a naked short position. The underwriters must close out any naked short position by purchasing shares in the open market. A naked short position is more likely to be created if the underwriters are concerned that there may be downward pressure on the price of our Class A common stock in the open market after pricing that could adversely affect investors who purchase in the offering. As an additional means of facilitating the offering, the underwriters may bid for, and purchase, shares of our Class A common stock in the open market to stabilize the price of our Class A common stock. These activities may raise or maintain the market price of the Class A common stock above independent market levels. The underwriters are not required to engage in these activities, and may end any of these activities at any time. Each underwriter will be responsible for shares of Class A common stock for which payment from its customers has not been received prior to the closing of this offering.

From time to time, certain of the underwriters have provided, and continue to provide, investment banking and other services to us, our affiliates and employees, for which they receive customary fees and commissions.

A prospectus in electronic format, from which you can view a presentation by our management and obtain your bidder ID through embedded hyperlinks will be made available on a web site. You must obtain a bidder ID in order to participate in this offering. See "Auction Process" for an explanation of how to obtain a bidder ID. A prospectus in electronic format may also be made available on the web sites maintained by one or more of the other underwriters.

We, the selling stockholders and the underwriters have agreed to indemnify each other against certain liabilities, including liabilities under the Securities Act arising out of any untrue statement or alleged untrue statement or caused by any omission or alleged omission of a material fact required to be stated in this

119

Table of Contents

prospectus. Pursuant to an agreement with the underwriters, we will be reimbursed for some of our expenses incurred in the offering.

Each of the underwriters severally represents and agrees that:

- it has not offered or sold and prior to the expiry of a period of six months from the closing date, will not offer or sell any Class A common stock to persons in the United Kingdom except to persons whose ordinary activities involve them in acquiring, holding, managing or disposing of investments (as principal or agent) for the purposes of their businesses or otherwise in circumstances which have not resulted and will not result in an offer to the public in the United Kingdom within the meaning of the Public Offers of Securities Regulations 1995;

- it has only communicated or caused to be communicated and will only communicate or cause to be communicated any invitation or inducement to engage in investment activity (within the meaning of section 21 of the Financial Services and Markets Act 2000, or the FSMA) received by it in connection with the issue or sale of any any Class A common stock in circumstances in which section 21(1) of the FSMA does not apply to us; and

- it has complied and will comply with all applicable provisions of the FSMA with respect to anything done by it in relation to any Class A common stock in, from or otherwise involving the United Kingdom.

120

Table of Contents

NOTICE TO CANADIAN RESIDENTS

Resale Restrictions

The distribution of the Class A common stock in Canada is being made only on a private placement basis exempt from the requirement that we and the selling stockholders prepare and file a prospectus with the securities regulatory authorities in each province where trades of Class A common stock are made. Any resale of the Class A common stock in Canada must be made under applicable securities laws which will vary depending on the relevant jurisdiction, and which may require resales to be made under available statutory exemptions or under a discretionary exemption granted by the applicable Canadian securities regulatory authority. Purchasers are advised to seek legal advice prior to any resale of the Class A common stock.

Representations of Purchasers

By purchasing Class A common stock in Canada and accepting a purchase confirmation a purchaser is representing to us, the selling stockholders and the dealer from whom the purchase confirmation is received that:

- The purchaser is entitled under applicable provincial securities laws to purchase the Class A common stock without the benefit of a prospectus qualified under those securities laws.
- Where required by law, that the purchaser is purchasing as principal and not as agent.
- The purchaser has reviewed the text above under Resale Restrictions.

Rights of Action—Ontario Purchasers Only

Under Ontario securities legislation, a purchaser who purchases a security offered by this prospectus during the period of distribution will have a statutory right of action for damages, or while still the owner of the Class A common stock, for rescission against us and the selling stockholders in the event that this circular contains a misrepresentation. A purchaser will be deemed to have relied on the misrepresentation. The right of action for damages is exercisable not later than the earlier of 180 days from the date the purchaser first had knowledge of the facts giving rise to the cause of action and three years from the date on which payment is made for the Class A common stock. The right of action for rescission is exercisable not later than 180 days from the date on which payment is made for the Class A common stock. If a purchaser elects to exercise the right of action for rescission, the purchaser will have no right of action for damages against us or the selling stockholders. In no case will the amount recoverable in any action exceed the price at which the Class A common stock was offered to the purchaser and if the purchaser is shown to have purchased the securities with knowledge of the misrepresentation, we and the selling stockholders will have no liability. In the case of an action for damages, we and the selling stockholders will not be liable for all or any portion of the damages that are proven to not represent the depreciation in value of the Class A common stock as a result of the misrepresentation relied upon. These rights are in addition to, and without derogation from, any other rights or remedies available at law to an Ontario purchaser. The foregoing is a summary of the rights available to an Ontario purchaser. Ontario purchasers should refer to the complete text of the relevant statutory provisions.

Enforcement of Legal Rights

All of our directors and officers as well as the experts named herein and the selling stockholders may be located outside of Canada and, as a result, it may not be possible for Canadian purchasers to effect service of process within Canada upon us or those persons. All or a substantial portion of our assets and the assets of those persons may be located outside of Canada and, as a result, it may not be possible to satisfy a judgment against us or those persons in Canada or to enforce a judgment obtained in Canadian courts against us or those persons outside of Canada.

Taxation and Eligibility for Investment

Canadian purchasers of Class A common stock should consult their own legal and tax advisors with respect to the tax consequences of an investment in the Class A common stock in their particular circumstances and about the eligibility of the for investment by the purchaser under relevant Canadian legislation.

Table of Contents

MATERIAL UNITED STATES FEDERAL TAX CONSIDERATIONS FOR NON-U.S. HOLDERS OF COMMON STOCK

This section summarizes certain material U.S. federal income and estate tax considerations relating to the ownership and disposition of common stock. This summary does not provide a complete analysis of all potential tax considerations. The information provided below is based on existing authorities. These authorities may change, or the IRS might interpret the existing authorities differently. In either case, the tax considerations of owning or disposing of common stock could differ from those described below. For purposes of this summary, a "non-U.S. holder" is any holder other than a citizen or resident of the United States, a corporation organized under the laws of the United States or any state, a trust that is (i) subject to the primary supervision of a U.S. court and the control of one or more U.S. persons or (ii) has a valid election in effect under applicable U.S. Treasury regulations to be treated as a U.S. person or an estate whose income is subject to U.S. income tax regardless of source. If a partnership or other flow-through entity is a beneficial owner of common stock, the tax treatment of a partner in the partnership or an owner of the entity will depend upon the status of the partner or other owner and the activities of the partnership or other entity. The summary generally does not address tax considerations that may be relevant to particular investors because of their specific circumstances, or because they are subject to special rules. Finally, the summary does not describe the effects of any applicable foreign, state, or local laws.

INVESTORS CONSIDERING THE PURCHASE OF COMMON STOCK SHOULD CONSULT THEIR OWN TAX ADVISORS REGARDING THE APPLICATION OF THE U.S. FEDERAL INCOME AND ESTATE TAX LAWS TO THEIR PARTICULAR SITUATIONS AND THE CONSEQUENCES OF FOREIGN, STATE, OR LOCAL LAWS, AND TAX TREATIES.

Dividends

Any dividend paid to a non-U.S. holder on our common stock will generally be subject to U.S. withholding tax at a 30 percent rate. The withholding tax might not apply, however, or might apply at a reduced rate, under the terms of an applicable income tax treaty between the United States and the non-U.S. holder's country of residence. A non-U.S. holder must demonstrate its entitlement to treaty benefits by certifying its nonresident status. A non-U.S. holder can meet this certification requirement by providing a Form W-8BEN or appropriate substitute form to us or our paying agent. If the holder holds the stock through a financial institution or other agent acting on the holder's behalf, the holder will be required to provide appropriate documentation to the agent. The holder's agent will then be required to provide certification to us or our paying agent, either directly or through other intermediaries. For payments made to a foreign partnership or other flow-through entity, the certification requirements generally apply to the partners or other owners rather than to the partnership or other entity, and the partnership or other entity must provide the partners' or other owners' documentation to us or our paying agent. Special rules, described below, apply if a dividend is effectively connected with a U.S. trade or business conducted by the non-U.S. holder.

Sale of Common Stock

Non-U.S. holders will generally not be subject to U.S. federal income tax on any gains realized on the sale, exchange, or other disposition of common stock. This general rule, however, is subject to several exceptions. For example, the gain would be subject to U.S. federal income tax if:

- the gain is effectively connected with the conduct by the non-U.S. holder of a U.S. trade or business (in which case the special rules described below apply);
- the non-U.S. holder was a citizen or resident of the United States and thus is subject to special rules that apply to expatriates; or
- the rules of the Foreign Investment in Real Property Tax Act (or FIRPTA) (described below) treat the gain as effectively connected with a U.S. trade or business.

Table of Contents

The FIRPTA rules may apply to a sale, exchange or other disposition of common stock if we are, or were within five years before the transaction, a "U.S. real property holding corporation" (or USRPHC). In general, we would be a USRPHC if interests in U.S. real estate comprised most of our assets. We do not believe that we are a USRPHC or that we will become one in the future.

Dividends or Gain Effectively Connected With a U.S. Trade or Business

If any dividend on common stock, or gain from the sale, exchange or other disposition of common stock, is effectively connected with a U.S. trade or business conducted by the non-U.S. holder, then the dividend or gain will be subject to U.S. federal income tax at the regular graduated rates. If the non-U.S. holder is eligible for the benefits of a tax treaty between the United States and the holder's country of residence, any "effectively connected" dividend or gain would generally be subject to U.S. federal income tax only if it is also attributable to a permanent establishment or fixed base maintained by the holder in the United States. Payments of dividends that are effectively connected with a U.S. trade or business, and therefore included in the gross income of a non-U.S. holder, will not be subject to the 30 percent withholding tax. To claim exemption from withholding, the holder must certify its qualification, which can be done by filing a Form W-8ECI. If the non-U.S. holder is a corporation, that portion of its earnings and profits that is effectively connected with its U.S. trade or business would generally be subject to a "branch profits tax." The branch profits tax rate is generally 30 percent, although an applicable income tax treaty might provide for a lower rate.

U.S. Federal Estate Tax

The estates of nonresident alien individuals are generally subject to U.S. federal estate tax on property with a U.S. situs. Because we are a U.S. corporation, our common stock will be U.S. situs property and therefore will be included in the taxable estate of a nonresident alien decedent. The U.S. federal estate tax liability of the estate of a nonresident alien may be affected by a tax treaty between the United States and the decedent's country of residence.

Backup Withholding and Information Reporting

The Code and the Treasury regulations require those who make specified payments to report the payments to the IRS. Among the specified payments are dividends and proceeds paid by brokers to their customers. The required information returns enable the IRS to determine whether the recipient properly included the payments in income. This reporting regime is reinforced by "backup withholding" rules. These rules require the payors to withhold tax from payments subject to information reporting if the recipient fails to cooperate with the reporting regime by failing to provide his taxpayer identification number to the payor, furnishing an incorrect identification number, or repeatedly failing to report interest or dividends on his returns. The withholding tax rate is currently 28 percent. The backup withholding rules do not apply to payments to corporations, whether domestic or foreign.

Payments to non-U.S. holders of dividends on common stock will generally not be subject to backup withholding, and payments of proceeds made to non-U.S. holders by a broker upon a sale of common stock will not be subject to information reporting or backup withholding, in each case so long as the non-U.S. holder certifies its nonresident status. Some of the common means of certifying nonresident status are described under "—Dividends." We must report annually to the IRS any dividends paid to each non-U.S. holder and the tax withheld, if any, with respect to such dividends. Copies of these reports may be made available to tax authorities in the country where the non-U.S. holder resides.

Any amounts withheld from a payment to a holder of common stock under the backup withholding rules can be credited against any U.S. federal income tax liability of the holder.

THE PRECEDING DISCUSSION OF U.S. FEDERAL INCOME TAX CONSIDERATIONS IS FOR GENERAL INFORMATION ONLY. IT IS NOT TAX ADVICE. EACH PROSPECTIVE INVESTOR SHOULD CONSULT ITS OWN TAX ADVISOR REGARDING THE PARTICULAR U.S. FEDERAL, STATE, LOCAL, AND FOREIGN TAX CONSEQUENCES OF PURCHASING, HOLDING, AND DISPOSING OF OUR COMMON STOCK, INCLUDING THE CONSEQUENCES OF ANY PROPOSED CHANGE IN APPLICABLE LAWS.

Table of Contents

LEGAL MATTERS

The validity of the shares of Class A common stock offered hereby will be passed upon for us by Wilson Sonsini Goodrich & Rosati, Professional Corporation, Palo Alto, California. Certain legal matters in connection with this offering will be passed upon for the underwriters by Simpson Thacher & Bartlett LLP, Palo Alto, California. Certain members of, and investment partnerships comprised of members of, and persons associated with, Wilson Sonsini Goodrich & Rosati beneficially hold an aggregate of 197,132 shares of our Class B common stock, which represents less than 0.1% of our outstanding shares of Class B common stock.

EXPERTS

Ernst & Young LLP, independent registered public accounting firm, have audited our consolidated financial statements (and schedule) at December 31, 2002 and 2003, and for each of the three years in the period ended December 31, 2003, as set forth in their report. We've included our consolidated financial statements (and schedule) in the prospectus and elsewhere in the registration statement in reliance on Ernst & Young LLP's report, given on their authority as experts in accounting and auditing.

WHERE YOU CAN FIND ADDITIONAL INFORMATION

We have filed with the SEC a registration statement on Form S-1 under the Securities Act with respect to the shares of common stock offered hereby. This prospectus, which constitutes a part of the registration statement, does not contain all of the information set forth in the registration statement or the exhibits and schedules filed therewith. For further information about us and the Class A common stock offered hereby, reference is made to the registration statement and the exhibits and schedules filed therewith. Statements contained in this prospectus regarding the contents of any contract or any other document that is filed as an exhibit to the registration statement are not necessarily complete, and each such statement is qualified in all respects by reference to the full text of such contract or other document filed as an exhibit to the registration statement. A copy of the registration statement and the exhibits and schedules filed therewith may be inspected without charge at the public reference room maintained by the SEC, located at 450 Fifth Street, N.W., Room 1200, Washington, D.C. 20549, and copies of all or any part of the registration statement may be obtained from such offices upon the payment of the fees prescribed by the SEC. Please call the SEC at 1-800-SEC-0330 for further information about the public reference room. The SEC also maintains an Internet web site that contains reports, proxy and information statements and other information regarding registrants that file electronically with the SEC. The address of the site is www.sec.gov.

Additionally, on April 29, 2004 we filed with the SEC a registration statement on Form 10 pursuant to Section 12(g) of the Exchange Act. On June 28, 2004, this registration statement became effective and consequently we are subject to the information and periodic reporting requirements of the Securities Exchange Act of 1934, and, in accordance therewith, will file periodic reports, proxy statements and other information with the SEC. Such periodic reports, proxy statements and other information will be available for inspection and copying at the public reference room and web site of the SEC referred to above.

Table of Contents

Google Inc.

INDEX TO CONSOLIDATED FINANCIAL STATEMENTS

Contents

Report of Ernst & Young LLP, Independent Registered Public Accounting Firm	F-2
Financial Statements	
Consolidated Balance Sheets	F-3
Consolidated Statements of Income	F-4
Consolidated Statements of Redeemable Convertible Preferred Stock Warrant and Stockholders' Equity	F-5
Consolidated Statements of Cash Flows	F-7
Notes to Consolidated Financial Statements	F-8

Table of Contents

REPORT OF ERNST & YOUNG LLP, INDEPENDENT REGISTERED PUBLIC ACCOUNTING FIRM

The Board of Directors and Stockholders
Google Inc.

We have audited the accompanying consolidated balance sheets of Google Inc. as of December 31, 2002 and 2003, and the related consolidated statements of income, redeemable convertible preferred stock warrant and stockholders' equity and cash flows for each of the three years in the period ended December 31, 2003. Our audits also included the financial statement schedule listed at Item 16(b). These financial statements and schedule are the responsibility of the Company's management. Our responsibility is to express an opinion on these financial statements and schedule based on our audits.

We conducted our audits in accordance with the standards of the Public Company Accounting Oversight Board (United States). Those standards require that we plan and perform the audit to obtain reasonable assurance about whether the financial statements are free of material misstatement. An audit includes examining, on a test basis, evidence supporting the amounts and disclosures in the financial statements. An audit also includes assessing the accounting principles used and significant estimates made by management, as well as evaluating the overall financial statement presentation. We believe that our audits provide a reasonable basis for our opinion.

In our opinion, the financial statements referred to above present fairly, in all material respects, the consolidated financial position of Google Inc. at December 31, 2002 and 2003, and the consolidated results of its operations and its cash flows for each of the three years in the period ended December 31, 2003, in conformity with U.S. generally accepted accounting principles. Also, in our opinion, the related consolidated financial statement schedule, when considered in relation to the basic financial statements taken as a whole, presents fairly in all material respects the information set forth therein.

/s/ ERNST & YOUNG LLP

San Francisco, California

April 20, 2004, except as to
  Note 13 as to which the date
  is June 25, 2004

Google Inc.

CONSOLIDATED BALANCE SHEETS
(In thousands, except par value)

	December 31, 2002	December 31, 2003	As of June 30, 2004 Actual	As of June 30, 2004 Pro Forma
			(unaudited)	
Assets				
Current assets:				
Cash and cash equivalents	$ 57,752	$ 148,995	$ 254,698	
Short-term investments	88,579	185,723	293,989	
Accounts receivable, net of allowance of $2,297, $4,670 and $5,611	61,994	154,690	191,187	
Income taxes receivable	—	—	45,047	
Deferred income taxes	12,646	22,105	30,334	
Prepaid revenue share, expenses and other assets	10,825	48,721	66,634	
Total current assets	231,796	560,234	881,889	
Property and equipment, net	53,873	188,255	320,718	
Goodwill	—	87,442	87,442	
Intangible assets, net	96	18,114	16,313	
Prepaid revenue share, expenses and other assets, non-current	1,127	17,413	21,660	
Total assets	$286,892	$ 871,458	$1,328,022	
Liabilities, Redeemable Convertible Preferred Stock Warrant and Stockholders' Equity				
Current liabilities:				
Accounts payable	$ 9,394	$ 46,175	$ 61,830	
Accrued compensation and benefits	14,528	33,522	33,931	
Accrued expenses and other current liabilities	10,810	26,411	41,054	
Accrued revenue share	13,100	88,672	93,435	
Deferred revenue	11,345	15,346	18,256	
Income taxes payable	25,981	20,705	—	
Current portion of equipment leases	4,350	4,621	3,751	
Total current liabilities	89,508	235,452	252,257	
Long-term portion of equipment leases	6,512	1,988	456	
Deferred revenue, long-term	1,901	5,014	6,023	
Liability for stock options exercised early, long-term	567	6,341	8,576	
Deferred income taxes	580	18,510	42,199	
Other long-term liabilities	—	1,512	1,512	
Commitments and contingencies				
Redeemable convertible preferred stock warrant	13,871	13,871	—	
Stockholders' equity:				
Convertible preferred stock, $0.001 par value, issuable in series: 166,896, 164,782 and 164,782 shares authorized at December 31, 2002 and 2003 and June 30, 2004, 70,432, 71,662 and 79,099 shares issued and outstanding at December 31, 2002 and 2003 and June 30, 2004, no shares issued and outstanding pro forma; aggregate liquidation preference of $40,815 and $62,458 at December 31, 2003 and June 30, 2004	44,346	44,346	79,860	—
Class A and Class B common stock, $0.001 par value: 700,000 shares authorized, 145,346, 160,866, and 165,012 shares issued and outstanding, excluding 3,281, 11,987, and 10,203 shares subject to repurchase (see Note 9) at December 31, 2002 and 2003 and June 30, 2004 and 244,111 shares outstanding pro forma	145	161	165	244
Additional paid-in capital	83,410	725,219	956,882	1,036,663
Note receivable from officer/stockholder	(4,300)	(4,300)	—	—
Deferred stock-based compensation	(35,401)	(369,668)	(352,815)	(352,815)
Accumulated other comprehensive income	49	1,660	(1,481)	(1,481)
Retained earnings	85,704	191,352	334,388	334,388
Total stockholders' equity	173,953	588,770	1,016,999	$1,016,999
Total liabilities, redeemable convertible preferred stock warrant and stockholders' equity	$286,892	$ 871,458	$1,328,022	

See accompanying notes.

Google Inc.

CONSOLIDATED STATEMENTS OF INCOME
(In thousands, except per share amounts)

	Year Ended December 31, 2001	Year Ended December 31, 2002	Year Ended December 31, 2003	Six Months Ended June 30, 2003	Six Months Ended June 30, 2004
				(unaudited)	(unaudited)
Revenues	$ 86,426	$439,508	$1,465,934	$559,817	$1,351,835
Costs and expenses:					
Cost of revenues	14,228	131,510	625,854	204,596	641,775
Research and development	16,500	31,748	91,228	29,997	80,781
Sales and marketing	20,076	43,849	120,328	42,589	104,681
General and administrative	12,275	24,300	56,699	22,562	47,083
Stock-based compensation(1)	12,383	21,635	229,361	70,583	151,234
Total costs and expenses	75,462	253,042	1,123,470	370,327	1,025,554
Income from operations	10,964	186,466	342,464	189,490	326,281
Interest income (expense) and other, net	(896)	(1,551)	4,190	719	(1,198)
Income before income taxes	10,068	184,915	346,654	190,209	325,083
Provision for income taxes	3,083	85,259	241,006	132,241	182,047
Net income	$ 6,985	$ 99,656	$ 105,648	$ 57,968	$ 143,036
Net income per share:					
Basic	$ 0.07	$ 0.86	$ 0.77	$ 0.44	$ 0.93
Diluted	$ 0.04	$ 0.45	$ 0.41	$ 0.23	$ 0.54
Pro forma basic (unaudited)			$ 0.51		$ 0.63
Number of shares used in per share calculations:					
Basic	94,523	115,242	137,697	131,525	153,263
Diluted	186,776	220,633	256,638	253,024	265,223
Pro forma basic (unaudited)			208,825		227,366

(1) Stock-based compensation is allocated as follows (see Note 1):

	Year Ended December 31, 2001	Year Ended December 31, 2002	Year Ended December 31, 2003	Six Months Ended June 30, 2003	Six Months Ended June 30, 2004
				(unaudited)	(unaudited)
Cost of revenues	$ 876	$ 1,065	$ 8,557	$ 2,813	$ 7,622
Research and development	4,440	8,746	138,377	38,237	92,102
Sales and marketing	1,667	4,934	44,607	14,711	27,576
General and administrative	5,400	6,890	37,820	14,822	23,934
	$ 12,383	$ 21,635	$ 229,361	$ 70,583	$ 151,234

See accompanying notes.

Google Inc.

CONSOLIDATED STATEMENTS OF REDEEMABLE CONVERTIBLE PREFERRED STOCK WARRANT AND STOCKHOLDERS' EQUITY
(in thousands)

	Redeemable Convertible Preferred Stock Warrant Shares	Redeemable Convertible Preferred Stock Warrant Amount	Convertible Preferred Stock Shares	Convertible Preferred Stock Amount	Class A and Class B Common Stock Shares	Class A and Class B Common Stock Amount	Additional Paid-In Capital Amount	Notes Receivable from Officer/Stockholders	Deferred Stock-Based Compensation	Accumulated Other Comprehensive Income	Retained Earnings (Accumulated Deficit)	Total Stockholders' Equity
Balance at December 31, 2000	—	$ —	69,988	$ 42,873	119,940	$ 120	$ 13,669	$ (34)	$ (8,457)	$ —	$ (20,937)	$ 27,234
Issuance of Series C convertible preferred stock	—	—	444	1,042	—	—	—	—	—	—	—	1,042
Issuance of Class B common stock upon exercise of stock options for cash and notes receivable, net of repurchases	—	—	—	—	17,312	17	5,271	(4,300)	—	—	—	988
Payments of notes receivable from stockholders	—	—	—	—	—	—	—	34	—	—	—	34
Issuance of Class B common stock	—	—	—	—	132	—	114	—	—	—	—	114
Issuance of Series C convertible preferred stock warrants	—	—	—	232	—	—	—	—	—	—	—	232
Issuance of Class B common stock warrants	—	—	—	—	—	—	1,140	—	—	—	—	1,140
Value of options granted to non-employees	—	—	—	—	—	—	186	—	—	—	—	186
Deferred stock-based compensation related to options granted to employees	—	—	—	—	—	—	19,954	—	(19,954)	—	—	—
Amortization of deferred stock-based compensation, net of reversals for terminated employees	—	—	—	—	—	—	(381)	—	12,578	—	—	12,197
Net income and comprehensive income	—	—	—	—	—	—	—	—	—	—	6,985	6,985
Balance at December 31, 2001	—	—	70,432	44,147	137,384	137	39,953	(4,300)	(15,833)	—	(13,952)	50,152
Issuance of Class B common stock upon exercise of stock options for cash, net of unvested stock options exercised early and repurchases	—	—	—	—	7,962	8	2,254	—	—	—	—	2,262
Issuance of Series C convertible preferred stock warrants	—	—	—	199	—	—	—	—	—	—	—	199
Issuance of Series D redeemable convertible preferred stock warrant	—	13,871	—	—	—	—	—	—	—	—	—	—
Value of options granted to non-employees	—	—	—	—	—	—	1,460	—	—	—	—	1,460
Deferred stock-based compensation related to options granted to employees	—	—	—	—	—	—	40,141	—	(40,141)	—	—	—
Amortization of deferred stock-based compensation, net of reversals for terminated employees	—	—	—	—	—	—	(398)	—	20,573	—	—	20,175
Comprehensive income:												
Change in unrealized gain on available-for-sale investments	—	—	—	—	—	—	—	—	—	49	—	49
Net income	—	—	—	—	—	—	—	—	—	—	99,656	99,656
Total comprehensive income												99,705
Balance at December 31, 2002	—	$ 13,871	70,432	$ 44,346	145,346	$ 145	$ 83,410	$ (4,300)	$ (35,401)	$ 49	$ 85,704	$173,953

See accompanying notes.

Google Inc.

CONSOLIDATED STATEMENTS OF REDEEMABLE CONVERTIBLE PREFERRED STOCK WARRANT AND STOCKHOLDERS' EQUITY—(Continued)
(in thousands)

	Redeemable Convertible Preferred Stock Warrant		Convertible Preferred Stock		Class A and Class B Common Stock		Additional Paid-In Capital	Notes Receivable from Officer/ Stockholders	Deferred Stock-Based Compensation	Accumulated Other Comprehensive Income	Retained Earnings (Accumulated Deficit)	Total Stockholders' Equity
	Shares	Amount	Shares	Amount	Shares	Amount	Amount					
Balance at December 31, 2002	—	$13,871	70,432	$—	44,346	$145	$83,410	$(4,300)	$(35,401)	$49	$85,704	$173,953
Issuance of Class A and Class B common stock upon exercise of stock options for cash, net of unvested stock options exercised early and repurchases	—	—	—	—	9,896	10	3,710	—	—	—	—	3,720
Issuance of Series C convertible preferred stock	—	—	1,230	—	—	—	—	—	—	—	—	—
Vesting of shares exercised early (see Note 9)	—	—	—	—	3,078	3	934	—	—	—	—	937
Issuance of fully vested common stock and stock options in connection with acquisitions	—	—	—	—	2,265	3	72,674	—	—	—	—	72,677
Issuance of fully vested common stock and stock options in connection with licensed technology	—	—	—	—	46	—	863	—	—	—	—	863
Issuance of restricted shares to employees in connection with acquisitions	—	—	—	—	235	—	10,752	—	(10,752)	—	—	—
Value of options granted to non-employees	—	—	—	—	—	—	15,816	—	—	—	—	15,816
Deferred stock-based compensation related to options granted to employees	—	—	—	—	—	—	540,673	—	(540,673)	—	—	—
Amortization of deferred stock-based compensation, net of reversals for terminated employees	—	—	—	—	—	—	(3,613)	—	217,158	—	—	213,545
Comprehensive income:												
Change in unrealized gain on available-for-sale investments	—	—	—	—	—	—	—	—	—	(51)	—	(51)
Foreign currency translation adjustment	—	—	—	—	—	—	—	—	—	1,662	—	1,662
Net income	—	—	—	—	—	—	—	—	—	—	105,648	105,648
Total comprehensive income	—	—	—	—	—	—	—	—	—	—	—	107,259
Balance at December 31, 2003	—	13,871	71,662	—	44,346	160,866	161	725,219	(4,300)	(369,668)	1,660	191,352	588,770
Issuance of Class A and Class B common stock upon exercise of stock options and warrants for cash, net of unvested stock options exercised early and repurchases (unaudited)	—	—	—	—	1,197	1	662	—	—	—	—	663
Vesting of shares exercised early (see Note 9) (unaudited)	—	—	—	—	2,930	3	2,948	—	—	—	—	2,951
Issuance of Series D preferred stock upon exercise of warrant (unaudited)	(13,871)	7,437	35,514	—	—	—	—	—	—	—	—	35,514
Issuance of fully vested common stock and stock options in connection with an acquisition (unaudited)	—	—	—	—	3	—	428	—	—	—	—	428
Issuance of restricted shares to an employee in connection with an acquisition (unaudited)	—	—	—	—	16	—	1,538	—	(1,538)	—	—	—
Tax benefits from exercise of warrants (unaudited)	—	—	—	—	—	—	93,244	—	—	—	—	93,244
Value of options granted to non-employees (unaudited)	—	—	—	—	—	—	5,431	—	—	—	—	5,431
Deferred stock-based compensation related to options granted to employees (unaudited)	—	—	—	—	—	—	132,668	—	(132,668)	—	—	—
Amortization of deferred stock-based compensation, net of reversals for terminated employees (unaudited)	—	—	—	—	—	—	(5,256)	—	151,059	—	—	145,803

Payment of stockholder's note receivable (unaudited)	—	—	—	—	—	4,300	—	—	—	4,300
Comprehensive income:	—	—	—	—	—	—	—	—	—	—
Change in unrealized gain on available-for-sale investments (unaudited)	—	—	—	—	—	—	—	(907)	—	(907)
Foreign currency translation adjustment (unaudited)	—	—	—	—	—	—	—	(2,234)	—	(2,234)
Net income (unaudited)	—	—	—	—	—	—	—	—	143,036	143,036
Total comprehensive income (unaudited)	—	—	—	—	—	—	—	—	—	139,895
Balance at June 30, 2004 (unaudited)	— $	—	79,099 $	79,860 165,012	$ 165	$956,882 $	—	$(352,815) $	(1,481) $	334,388 $1,016,999

See accompanying notes.

F-6

Table of Contents

Google Inc.
CONSOLIDATED STATEMENTS OF CASH FLOWS
(In thousands)

	Year Ended December 31, 2001	Year Ended December 31, 2002	Year Ended December 31, 2003	Six Months Ended June 30, 2003	Six Months Ended June 30, 2004
				(unaudited)	(unaudited)
Operating activities					
Net income	$ 6,985	$ 99,656	$ 105,648	$ 57,968	$ 143,036
Adjustments to reconcile net income to net cash provided by operating activities:					
Depreciation and amortization of property and equipment	9,831	17,815	43,851	15,885	49,824
Amortization of warrants	4,157	10,953	4,864	4,732	62
Amortization of intangibles	194	215	6,334	2,114	4,801
In-process research and development	—	—	11,618	—	950
Stock-based compensation	12,383	21,635	229,361	70,583	151,234
Changes in assets and liabilities, net of effects of acquisitions:					
Accounts receivable	(11,736)	(43,877)	(90,385)	(34,174)	(36,497)
Income taxes, net	2,398	11,517	(6,319)	16,619	42,950
Prepaid revenue share, expenses and other assets	(22)	(5,875)	(58,913)	(13,750)	(21,946)
Accounts payable	1,643	5,645	36,699	10,727	15,642
Accrued expenses and other liabilities	4,207	15,393	31,104	6,232	11,866
Accrued revenue share	—	13,100	74,603	35,923	4,763
Deferred revenue	1,049	9,088	6,980	4,315	3,919
Net cash provided by operating activities	31,089	155,265	395,445	177,174	370,604
Investing activities					
Purchases of property and equipment	(13,060)	(37,198)	(176,801)	(60,553)	(182,283)
Purchase of short-term investments	(26,389)	(93,061)	(316,599)	(89,528)	(471,081)
Maturities and sales of short-term investments	11,460	20,443	219,404	97,474	361,908
Acquisitions, net of cash acquired	—	—	(39,958)	(39,452)	(3,538)
Change in other assets	(1,102)	99	—	—	—
Net cash used in investing activities	(29,091)	(109,717)	(313,954)	(92,059)	(294,994)
Financing activities					
Proceeds from issuance of convertible preferred stock, net	1,042	—	—	—	—
Proceeds from exercise of stock options, net	988	2,262	15,476	7,845	8,553
Proceeds from exercise of warrants	—	—	—	—	21,877
Payments of notes receivable from stockholders	34	—	—	—	4,300
Payments of principal on capital leases and equipment loans	(4,503)	(7,735)	(7,386)	(3,946)	(2,403)
Net cash provided by (used in) financing activities	(2,439)	(5,473)	8,090	3,899	32,327
Effect of exchange rate changes on cash and cash equivalents	—	—	1,662	(689)	(2,234)
Net increase (decrease) in cash and cash equivalents	(441)	40,075	91,243	88,325	105,703
Cash and cash equivalents at beginning of year	18,118	17,677	57,752	57,752	148,995
Cash and cash equivalents at end of period	$ 17,677	$ 57,752	$ 148,995	$146,077	$ 254,698
Supplemental disclosures of cash flow information					
Property and equipment acquired under equipment leases	$ 7,679	$ 7,303	$ —		
Cash paid for interest	$ 1,677	$ 2,285	$ 1,739		
Cash paid for taxes	$ 685	$ 73,763	$ 247,422		
Note receivable from officer/stockholder in exchange for common stock	$ 4,300	$ —	$ —		
Issuance of redeemable convertible preferred stock warrant in conjunction with an AdSense agreement	$ —	$ 13,871	$ —		
Issuance of convertible preferred stock warrants in conjunction with capital lease arrangements	$ 232	$ 199	$ —		
Issuance of common stock warrants in connection with recruitment fees	$ 1,140	$ —	$ —		
Acquisition related activities:					
Issuance of common stock in connection with acquisitions, net of deferred stock-based compensation	$ 114	$ —	$ 73,540		
Reduction in income taxes payable due to warrant exercises	$ —	$ —	$ —	$ —	$ 93,241

See accompanying notes.

Google Inc.

NOTES TO CONSOLIDATED FINANCIAL STATEMENTS
(Information as of June 30, 2004 and for the six months ended June 30, 2003 and 2004 is unaudited)

Note 1. The Company and Summary of Significant Accounting Policies

Nature of Operations

Google Inc. ("Google" or the "Company") was incorporated in California on September 1998. The Company re-incorporated in the State of Delaware in August 2003. The Company offers highly targeted advertising solutions, global Internet search solutions through its own destination Internet site and intranet solutions via an enterprise search appliance.

Basis of Consolidation

The consolidated financial statements include the accounts of Google and its wholly-owned subsidiaries. All intercompany balances and transactions have been eliminated. The Company has included the results of operations of acquired entities from the date of acquisition (see Note 4).

Unaudited Interim Financial Information

The accompanying unaudited interim consolidated balance sheet as of June 30, 2004, the consolidated statements of income for the six months ended June 30, 2003 and 2004, the consolidated statements of cash flows for the six months ended June 30, 2003 and 2004 and the consolidated statement of redeemable convertible preferred stock warrant and stockholders' equity for the six months ended June 30, 2004 are unaudited. These unaudited interim consolidated financial statements have been prepared in accordance with U.S. generally accepted accounting principles. In the opinion of the Company's management, the unaudited interim consolidated financial statements have been prepared on the same basis as the audited consolidated financial statements and include all adjustments necessary for the fair presentation of the Company's statement of financial position at June 30, 2004, its results of operations and its cash flows for the six months ended June 30, 2003 and 2004. The results for the six months ended June 30, 2004 are not necessarily indicative of the results to be expected for the year ending December 31, 2004.

Use of Estimates

The preparation of consolidated financial statements in conformity with accounting principles generally accepted in the United States requires management to make estimates and assumptions that affect the amounts reported and disclosed in the financial statements and the accompanying notes. Actual results could differ materially from these estimates.

On an ongoing basis, the Company evaluates its estimates, including those related to accounts receivable allowance, fair value of investments, fair value of acquired intangible assets and goodwill, useful lives of intangible assets and property and equipment, the value of common stock for the purpose of determining stock-based compensation (see below), and income taxes, among others. The Company bases its estimates on historical experience and on various other assumptions that are believed to be reasonable, the results of which form the basis for making judgments about the carrying values of assets and liabilities.

The Company has granted stock options at exercise prices equal to the value of the underlying stock as determined by its board of directors on the date of option grant. For purposes of financial accounting for stock-based compensation, management has applied hindsight within each year to arrive at reassessed values for the shares underlying the options and issued under other transactions that are higher than the values determined by the board. These reassessed values were determined based on a number of factors, including input from advisors, the Company's historical and forecasted operating results and cash flows, and comparisons to publicly-held

F-8

Table of Contents

Google Inc.

NOTES TO CONSOLIDATED FINANCIAL STATEMENTS—(Continued)
(Information as of June 30, 2004 and for the six months ended June 30, 2003 and 2004 is unaudited)

companies. The reassessed values were used to determine the amount of stock-based compensation recognized related to stock and stock option grants to employees and non-employees, the amount of expense related to stock warrants issued to third-parties (see Note 9) and the purchase prices of the Company's acquisitions (see Note 4).

Revenue Recognition

The following table presents the Company's revenues (in thousands):

	Year Ended December 31,			Six Months Ended June 30,	
	2001	2002	2003	2003	2004
				(unaudited)	
Advertising revenues:					
Google web sites	$66,932	$306,978	$ 792,063	$341,002	$ 646,974
Google Network web sites	—	103,937	628,600	198,801	679,978
Total advertising revenues	66,932	410,915	1,420,663	539,803	1,326,952
Licensing and other revenues	19,494	28,593	45,271	20,014	24,883
Revenues	$86,426	$439,508	$1,465,934	$559,817	$1,351,835

In the first quarter of 2000, the Company introduced its first advertising program through which it offered advertisers the ability to place text-based ads on Google web sites targeted to users' search queries. Advertisers paid the Company based on the number of times their ads were displayed on users' search results pages and the Company recognized revenue at the time these ads appeared. In the fourth quarter of 2000, the Company launched Google AdWords, an online self-service program that enables advertisers to place text-based ads on Google web sites. AdWords advertisers originally paid the Company based on the number of times their ads appeared on users' search results pages. In the first quarter of 2002, the Company began offering AdWords exclusively on a cost-per-click basis, so that an advertiser pays the Company only when a user clicks on one of its ads. The Company recognizes as revenue the fees charged advertisers each time a user clicks on one of the text-based ads that are displayed next to the search results on Google web sites. Effective January 1, 2004, the Company now offers a single pricing structure to all of its advertisers based on the AdWords cost-per-click model.

Google AdSense is the program through which the Company distributes its advertisers' text-based ads for display on the web sites of the Google Network members. In accordance with Emerging Issues Task Force ("EITF") Issue No. 99-19, *Reporting Revenue Gross as a Principal Versus Net as an Agent*, the Company recognizes as revenues the fees it receives from its advertisers. This revenue is reported gross primarily because the Company is the primary obligor to its advertisers.

The Company generates fees from search services through a variety of contractual arrangements, which include per-query search fees and search service hosting fees. Revenues from set-up and support fees and search service hosting fees are recognized on a straight-line basis over the term of the contract, which is the expected period during which these services will be provided. The Company's policy is to recognize revenues from per-query search fees in the period queries are made and results are delivered.

The Company provides search services pursuant to certain AdSense agreements. Management believes that search services and revenue share arrangements represent separate units of accounting pursuant to EITF 00-21 *Revenue Arrangements with Multiple Deliverables*. These separate services are provided simultaneously to the Google Network member and are recognized as revenues in the periods provided.

F-9

Google Inc.

NOTES TO CONSOLIDATED FINANCIAL STATEMENTS—(Continued)
(Information as of June 30, 2004 and for the six months ended June 30, 2003 and 2004 is unaudited)

The Company also generates fees from the sale and license of its Search Appliance, which includes hardware, software and 12 to 24 months of post-contract support. As the elements are not sold separately, sufficient vendor-specific objective evidence does not exist for the allocation of revenue. As a result, the entire fee is recognized ratably over the term of the post-contract support arrangement in accordance with Statement of Position 97-2, *Software Revenue Recognition*, as amended.

Deferred revenue is recorded when payments are received in advance of the Company's performance in the underlying agreement on the accompanying consolidated balance sheets.

Cost of Revenues

Cost of revenues consists primarily of traffic acquisition costs. Traffic acquisition costs consist of payments made to Google Network members. These payments are primarily based on revenue share arrangements under which the Company pays its Google Network members most of the fees it receives from its advertisers. In addition, certain AdSense agreements obligate the Company to make guaranteed minimum revenue share payments to Google Network members based on their achieving defined performance terms, such as number of search queries or advertisements displayed. The Company amortizes guaranteed minimum revenue share prepayments (or accretes an amount payable to its Google Network member if the payment is due in arrears) based on the number of search queries or advertisements displayed on the Google Network member's web site. In addition, concurrent with the commencement of certain AdSense agreements the Company purchased certain items from, or provided other consideration to, its Google Network members. These amounts are amortized on a pro-rata basis over the related term of the agreement.

Traffic acquisition costs were $94.5 million and $526.5 million in 2002 and 2003, and $166.7 million and $548.0 million in the six months ended June 30, 2003 and 2004. There were no traffic acquisition costs in 2001.

In addition, cost of revenues consists of the expenses associated with the operation of the Company's data centers, including depreciation, labor, energy and bandwidth costs. Cost of revenues also includes credit card and other transaction fees relating to processing customer transactions.

Reclassification

Revenues and cost of revenues amounts have been reclassified in all periods presented to reflect the reporting of revenues equal to the advertiser fees received by the Company. The Company had previously reported revenues net of payments and amounts owed to its Google Network members under its AdSense program.

Google Inc.

NOTES TO CONSOLIDATED FINANCIAL STATEMENTS—(Continued)
(Information as of June 30, 2004 and for the six months ended June 30, 2003 and 2004 is unaudited)

Stock-based Compensation

Stock-based compensation as shown on the accompanying consolidated income statements consists of amortization of deferred stock-based compensation related to restricted shares and options to purchase Class A and Class B common stock to employees and the values of options to purchase such stock issued to non-employees.

As permitted by Statement of Financial Accounting Standards ("SFAS") No. 123, *Accounting for Stock-based Compensation* ("SFAS 123"), the Company accounts for employee stock-based compensation in accordance with Accounting Principles Board Opinion ("APB") No. 25, *Accounting for Stock Issued to Employees* ("APB 25"), and related interpretations. Under APB 25, deferred compensation for options granted to employees is equal to its intrinsic value, determined as the difference between the exercise price and the reassessed value for accounting purposes of the underlying stock on the date of grant.

For purposes of financial accounting for employee stock-based compensation, management has applied hindsight within each year to arrive at reassessed values for the shares underlying the options. The Company has recorded deferred stock-based compensation equal to the difference between these reassessed values and the exercise prices.

In connection with restricted shares and unvested stock options granted to employees, the Company recorded deferred stock-based compensation costs of $20.0 million, $40.1 million, $551.4 million and $134.2 million in 2001, 2002, 2003 and the six months ended June 30, 2004. The deferred stock-based compensation amounts arising from these equity activities for each of the six three month periods ended June 30, 2004 were computed as follows:

	Three Months Ended				2003 Total	Three Months Ended	
	March 31, 2003	June 30, 2003	September 30, 2003	December 31, 2003		March 31, 2004	June 30, 2004
	(unaudited)	(unaudited)	(unaudited)	(unaudited)		(unaudited)	(unaudited)
Options granted to employees	10,262,100	1,431,552	5,785,185	1,281,895	18,760,732	1,004,780	965,520
Weighted average exercise price	$ 0.49	$ 3.30	$ 5.17	$ 9.62		$ 16.27	$ 38.43
Weighted average reassessed value of underlying stock	$ 13.09	$ 33.99	$ 52.33	$ 75.05		$ 88.13	$ 97.03
Weighted average reassessed deferred stock-based compensation per option	$ 12.60	$ 30.69	$ 47.16	$ 65.43		$ 71.86	$ 58.60
Deferred stock-based compensation related to options (in millions)	$ 129.3	$ 43.9	$ 272.8	$ 83.9	$ 529.9	72.2	$ 56.6
Restricted shares granted to employees		120,000	114,999		234,999		16,175
Weighted average reassessed value of restricted shares		$ 25.96	$ 66.41				$ 95.09
Deferred stock-based compensation related to restricted shares (in millions)		$ 3.1	$ 7.6		$ 10.7		$ 1.5
Deferred stock-based compensation related to option modifications (in millions)				$ 10.8	$ 10.8	3.9	
Total deferred stock-based compensation (in millions)	$ 129.3	$ 47.0	$ 280.4	$ 94.7	$ 551.4	76.1	$ 58.1

Net amortization of deferred stock-based compensation totaled $12.2 million, $20.2 million, $213.5 million and $145.8 million in 2001, 2002, 2003 and the six months ended June 30, 2004. The deferred stock-based compensation is being amortized using the accelerated vesting method, in accordance with SFAS 123.

Google Inc.

NOTES TO CONSOLIDATED FINANCIAL STATEMENTS—(Continued)
(Information as of June 30, 2004 and for the six months ended June 30, 2003 and 2004 is unaudited)

EITF 96-18, *Accounting for Equity Instruments That Are Issued to Other Than Employees for Acquiring, or in connection with Selling, Goods or Services* ("EITF 96-18"), and Financial Accounting Standards Board ("FASB") Interpretation ("FIN") No. 28, over the vesting period of each respective restricted share and stock option, generally over four or five years. The remaining unamortized, deferred stock-based compensation for all restricted shares and stock option grants through June 30, 2004 assuming no change in the stock option accounting rules and assuming all employees remain employed at Google for their remaining vesting periods will be expensed as follows over the remaining six months of 2004 and each of the next four years and thereafter (in millions):

	(unaudited)
2004	$ 117.2
2005	137.7
2006	66.9
2007	24.1
2008	5.2
Thereafter	1.7
	$ 352.8

The Company accounts for stock awards issued to non-employees in accordance with the provisions of SFAS 123 and EITF 96-18. Under SFAS 123 and EITF 96-18, the Company uses the Black-Scholes method to measure the value of options granted to non-employees at each vesting date to determine the appropriate charge to stock-based compensation.

The Company recorded stock-based compensation expense of $186,000, $1.5 million, $15.8 million and $5.4 million for the value of stock options earned by non-employees in 2001, 2002, 2003 and the six months ended June 30, 2004.

At December 31, 2003, there were 500,150 unvested options to purchase shares of Class B common stock held by non-employees with a weighted-average exercise price of $0.69 and a weighted-average 48 month remaining vesting period. These options will generally vest on a monthly and ratable basis subsequent to December 31, 2003. No options that vest over time were granted to non-employees in the six months ended June 30, 2004.

Pro forma information regarding net income has been determined as if the Company had accounted for its employee stock options under the method prescribed by SFAS 123. The resulting effect on pro forma net income disclosed may not be representative of the effects on net income on a pro forma basis in future years.

F-12

Google Inc.

NOTES TO CONSOLIDATED FINANCIAL STATEMENTS—(Continued)
(Information as of June 30, 2004 and for the six months ended June 30, 2003 and 2004 is unaudited)

Had compensation cost for options granted under the option plans (see Note 9) been determined based on the fair value method prescribed by SFAS 123, the Company's net income and net income per share would have been adjusted to the pro forma amounts below (in thousands, except per share data):

	Year Ended December 31,			Six Months Ended June 30,	
	2001	2002	2003	2003	2004
				(unaudited)	
Net income, as reported	$ 6,985	$ 99,656	$ 105,648	$ 57,968	$ 143,036
Add: Stock-based employee compensation expense included in reported net income	12,197	20,175	213,545	64,989	145,803
Deduct: Total stock-based employee compensation expense under the fair value based method for all awards	(14,648)	(22,390)	(215,946)	(65,709)	(148,599)
Net income, pro forma	$ 4,534	$ 97,441	$ 103,247	$ 57,248	$ 140,240
Net income per share:					
As reported—basic	$ 0.07	$ 0.86	$ 0.77	$ 0.44	$ 0.93
Pro forma—basic	$ 0.05	$ 0.85	$ 0.75	$ 0.44	$ 0.92
As reported—diluted	$ 0.04	$ 0.45	$ 0.41	$ 0.23	$ 0.54
Pro forma—diluted	$ 0.02	$ 0.44	$ 0.40	$ 0.23	$ 0.53

For purposes of the above pro forma calculation, the value of each option granted through June 30, 2004 was estimated on the date of grant using the Black-Scholes pricing model with the following weighted-average assumptions:

	Year Ended December 31,			Six Months Ended June 30,	
	2001	2002	2003	2003	2004
				(unaudited)	
Risk-free interest rate	4.38%	3.34%	2.11%	1.87%	2.51%
Expected volatility	100%	75%	75%	75%	75%
Expected life (in years)	4	3	3	3	3
Dividend yield	—	—	—	—	—

The weighted-average fair value of an option granted in 2001, 2002 and 2003, and in the six months ended June 30, 2003 and 2004, was $0.91, $2.79 and $29.12, $16.18 and $73.17, using the Black-Scholes pricing model.

Stock Options Exercised Early

The Company typically allows employees to exercise options prior to vesting. Upon the exercise of an option prior to vesting, the exercising optionee is required to enter into a restricted stock purchase agreement with the Company, which provides that the Company has a right to repurchase the shares purchased upon exercise of the option at the original exercise price; provided, however, that its right to repurchase these shares will lapse in accordance with the vesting schedule included in the optionee's option agreement. In accordance with EITF 00-23, *Issues Related to Accounting for Stock Compensation under APB Opinion No. 25 and FASB Interpretation No. 44*, stock options granted or modified after March 21, 2002, which are subsequently exercised for cash prior to vesting are treated differently from prior grants and related exercises. The consideration received for an exercise of an

F-13

Google Inc.

NOTES TO CONSOLIDATED FINANCIAL STATEMENTS—(Continued)
(Information as of June 30, 2004 and for the six months ended June 30, 2003 and 2004 is unaudited)

option granted after the effective date of this guidance is considered to be a deposit of the exercise price and the related dollar amount is recorded as a liability. The shares and liability are only reclassified into equity on a ratable basis as the award vests. The Company has applied this guidance and recorded a liability on the consolidated balance sheets relating to 3,281,004, 11,987,482 and 10,203,007 of options granted subsequent to March 21, 2002 that were exercised and are unvested at December 31, 2002 and 2003 and at June 30, 2004. Furthermore, these shares are not presented as outstanding on the accompanying consolidated statements of redeemable convertible preferred stock warrant and stockholders' equity and consolidated balance sheets. Instead, these shares are disclosed as outstanding options in the footnotes to these financial statements.

Stock Split

In February and June 2003, the Company affected separate two-for-one stock splits. In addition, the Company affected other splits in prior years. All references to Class A and Class B common stock and preferred stock shares and per share amounts including options and warrants to purchase Class A and Class B common stock have been retroactively restated to reflect the stock split as if such split had taken place at the inception of the Company.

Net Income Per Share

The Company computes net income per share in accordance with SFAS 128, *Earnings per Share*. Under the provisions of SFAS 128, basic net income per share is computed using the weighted average number of Class A and Class B common shares outstanding during the period except that it does not include unvested Class A and Class B common shares subject to repurchase or cancellation. Diluted net income per share is computed using the weighted average number of Class A and Class B common shares and, if dilutive, potential Class A and Class B common shares outstanding during the period. Potential Class A and Class B common shares consist of the incremental Class A and Class B common shares issuable upon the exercise of stock options, warrants, unvested common shares subject to repurchase or cancellation and convertible preferred stock. The dilutive effect of outstanding stock options and warrants is reflected in diluted earnings per share by application of the treasury stock method. Convertible preferred stock is reflected on an if-converted basis.

Table of Contents

Google Inc.

NOTES TO CONSOLIDATED FINANCIAL STATEMENTS—(Continued)
(Information as of June 30, 2004 and for the six months ended June 30, 2003 and 2004 is unaudited)

The following table sets forth the computation of basic and diluted net income per share (in thousands, except per share amounts):

	Year Ended December 31, 2001	2002	2003	Six Months Ended June 30, 2003	2004
				(unaudited)	
Basic and diluted net income per share:					
Numerator:					
Net income	$ 6,985	$ 99,656	$105,648	$ 57,968	$143,036
Denominator:					
Weighted average Class A and Class B common shares outstanding	125,135	143,317	168,093	164,346	174,317
Less: Weighted average unvested Class A and Class B common shares subject to repurchase or cancellation	(30,612)	(28,075)	(30,396)	(32,821)	(21,054)
Denominator for basic calculation	94,523	115,242	137,697	131,525	153,263
Effect of dilutive securities Add:					
Weighted average convertible preferred shares	70,432	70,432	71,128	70,593	74,103
Weighted average stock options and warrants and unvested Class A and Class B common shares subject to repurchase or cancellation	21,821	34,959	47,813	50,906	37,857
Denominator for diluted calculation	186,776	220,633	256,638	253,024	265,223
Net income per share, basic	$ 0.07	$ 0.86	$ 0.77	$ 0.44	$ 0.93
Net income per share, diluted	$ 0.04	$ 0.45	$ 0.41	$ 0.23	$ 0.54

Pro Forma Net Income Per Share (unaudited)

Pro forma basic net income per share have been computed to give effect to the conversion of convertible preferred stock into Class B common stock upon the closing of the Company's initial public offering on an if-converted basis for the year ended December 31, 2003 and for the six months ended June 30, 2004.

Google Inc.

NOTES TO CONSOLIDATED FINANCIAL STATEMENTS—(Continued)
(Information as of June 30, 2004 and for the six months ended June 30, 2003 and 2004 is unaudited)

The following table sets forth the computation of pro forma basic net income per share (in thousands, except per share amounts):

	Year Ended December 31, 2003	Six Months Ended June 30, 2004
	(unaudited)	(unaudited)
Numerator:		
Net income	$ 105,648	$ 143,036
Denominator:		
Weighted average Class A and Class B common shares outstanding	168,093	174,317
Less: Weighted average unvested Class A and Class B common shares subject to repurchase or cancellation	(30,396)	(21,054)
Add: Adjustments to reflect the weighted average effect of the assumed conversion of preferred stock from the date of issuance	71,128	74,103
Denominator for basic pro forma calculation	208,825	227,366
Pro forma net income per common share, basic	$ 0.51	$ 0.63

We have not included pro forma diluted net income per share in the table above or on the accompanying statements of income because it is the same as diluted net income per share.

Certain Risks and Concentrations

The Company's revenues are principally derived from online advertising, the market for which is highly competitive and rapidly changing. Significant changes in this industry or changes in customer buying behavior could adversely affect the Company's operating results.

Financial instruments that potentially subject the Company to concentrations of credit risk consist principally of cash equivalents, investments and accounts receivable. Cash equivalents consist of money market funds. Short term investments consist primarily of agency notes, market auction preferred securities, municipal auction rate receipts and municipal bonds held with five financial institutions. Accounts receivable are typically unsecured and are derived from revenues earned from customers primarily located in the U.S. In 2003 and in the six months ended June 30, 2004, the Company generated approximately 71% and 69% of its revenues from customers based in the U.S. with the majority of customers outside of the U.S. located in Japan and Europe. Many of the Company's Network members are in the Internet industry. To appropriately manage this risk, the Company performs ongoing evaluations of customer credit and limits the amount of credit extended, but generally no collateral is required. The Company maintains reserves for estimated credit losses and these losses have generally been within management's expectations.

Advertising and other revenues generated from America Online, Inc., which is also a stockholder, accounted for 15%, 16% and 13% of revenues, primarily through the Company's AdSense program, in 2002, 2003 and the six months ended June 30, 2004. No other Google Network member web sites generated advertising revenues for greater than 10% of revenues in these periods.

Fair Value of Financial Instruments

The carrying amounts of the Company's financial instruments, including cash and cash equivalents, short-term investments, accounts receivable, accounts payable and accrued liabilities, approximate fair value because

Google Inc.

NOTES TO CONSOLIDATED FINANCIAL STATEMENTS—(Continued)
(Information as of June 30, 2004 and for the six months ended June 30, 2003 and 2004 is unaudited)

of their short maturities. The carrying amounts of the Company's equipment loans and capital leases approximate fair value of these obligations based upon management's best estimates of interest rates that would be available for similar debt obligations at December 31, 2002 and 2003.

Cash and Cash Equivalents and Short-Term Investments

The Company invests its excess cash in money market funds and in highly liquid debt instruments of the U.S. government, its agencies and municipalities. All highly liquid investments with stated maturities of three months or less from date of purchase are classified as cash equivalents; all highly liquid investments with stated maturities of greater than three months are classified as short-term investments.

Management determines the appropriate classification of its investments in debt and marketable equity securities at the time of purchase and reevaluates such designation at each balance sheet date. The Company's debt and marketable equity securities have been classified and accounted for as available-for-sale. The Company does not intend to hold securities with stated maturities greater than twelve months until maturity. In response to changes in the availability of and the yield on alternative investments as well as liquidity requirements, the Company occasionally sells these securities prior to their stated maturities. These securities are carried at fair value, with the unrealized gains and losses, net of taxes, reported as a component of stockholders' equity. Any realized gains or losses on the sale of short-term investments are determined on a specific identification method, and such gains and losses are reflected as a component of interest income or expense.

Accounts Receivable

Accounts receivable are recorded at the invoiced amount and are non-interest bearing. The Company maintains an allowance for doubtful accounts to reserve for potentially uncollectible receivables. Management reviews the accounts receivable by aging category to identify specific customers with known disputes or collectibility issues. In determining the amount of the reserve, management makes judgments about the creditworthiness of significant customers based on ongoing credit evaluations. The Company also maintains a sales allowance to reserve for potential credits issued to customers. The amount of the reserve is determined based on historical credits issued.

Property and Equipment

Property and equipment are stated at cost less accumulated depreciation and amortization. Depreciation is computed using the straight-line method over the estimated useful lives of the assets, generally two to five years. Equipment under capital leases and leasehold improvements are amortized over the shorter of the lease term or the estimated useful lives of the assets. Construction in process is primarily related to the building of production equipment servers and lease-hold improvements. Depreciation for these assets commences once they are placed in service.

Long-Lived Assets Including Goodwill and Other Acquired Intangible Assets

The Company reviews property and equipment and certain identifiable intangibles, excluding goodwill, for impairment whenever events or changes in circumstances indicate the carrying amount of an asset may not be recoverable. Recoverability of these assets is measured by comparison of its carrying amounts to future undiscounted cash flows the assets are expected to generate. If property and equipment and certain identifiable intangibles are considered to be impaired, the impairment to be recognized equals the amount by which the carrying value of the asset exceeds its fair market value. The Company has made no adjustments to its long-lived assets in any of the years presented.

F-17

Google Inc.

NOTES TO CONSOLIDATED FINANCIAL STATEMENTS—(Continued)
(Information as of June 30, 2004 and for the six months ended June 30, 2003 and 2004 is unaudited)

The Company has adopted SFAS No. 142, *Goodwill and Other Intangible Assets*. SFAS No. 142 requires that goodwill and intangible assets with indefinite useful lives no longer be amortized, but instead be tested for impairment at least annually or sooner whenever events or changes in circumstances indicate that they may be impaired. The Company completed its first goodwill impairment test at November 30, 2003, and found no impairment. The test was based on the Company's single operating segment and reporting unit structure.

SFAS No. 142 also requires that intangible assets with definite lives be amortized over their estimated useful lives and reviewed for impairment whenever events or changes in circumstances indicate an asset's carrying value may not be recoverable in accordance with SFAS No. 144, *Accounting for the Impairment of Long-Lived Assets and for Long-Lived Assets to Be Disposed Of*. The Company is currently amortizing its acquired intangible assets with definite lives over periods ranging from 2 to 3 years. The Company believes no events or changes in circumstances have occurred that would require an impairment test for these assets.

Income Taxes

The Company recognizes income taxes under the liability method. Deferred income taxes are recognized for differences between the financial reporting and tax bases of assets and liabilities at enacted statutory tax rates in effect for the years in which the differences are expected to reverse. The effect on deferred taxes of a change in tax rates is recognized in income in the period that includes the enactment date.

Foreign Currency

Generally, the functional currency of the Company's international subsidiaries is the local currency. The financial statements of these subsidiaries are translated to U.S. dollars using month-end rates of exchange for assets and liabilities, and average rates of exchange for revenues, costs and expenses. Translation gains (losses) are deferred and recorded in accumulated other comprehensive income as a component of stockholders' equity. The Company recorded $1.7 million of net translation gains in 2003. There was no translation gain or loss in 2001 and 2002. Net gains and losses resulting from foreign exchange transactions are included in the consolidated income statements. The Company recognized $2.1 million of net gains resulting from foreign exchange transactions in 2003. Net transaction gains and losses recognized during 2001 and 2002 were not material.

Derivative Financial Instruments

The Company hedges certain net asset and liability exposures with forward foreign exchange contracts to reduce the risk that our cash flows and earnings will be adversely affected by foreign currency exchange rate fluctuations. This program is not designed for trading or speculative purposes. No foreign currency hedge transactions were entered into prior to the six months ended June 30, 2004.

In accordance with SFAS No. 133, *Accounting for Derivative Instruments and Hedging Activities*, the Company recognizes derivative instruments and hedging activities as either assets or liabilities on the balance sheet at fair value. Neither the cost nor the fair value of these forward foreign exchange contracts was material at June 30, 2004. Changes in the fair value of these instruments are recorded as interest income (expense) and other, net and were not material in the six months ended June 30, 2004. The notional principal of forward foreign exchange contracts to purchase U.S. dollars with Euros was $116.9 million at June 30, 2004. There were no other forward foreign exchange contracts outstanding at June 30, 2004.

Table of Contents

Google Inc.

NOTES TO CONSOLIDATED FINANCIAL STATEMENTS—(Continued)
(Information as of June 30, 2004 and for the six months ended June 30, 2003 and 2004 is unaudited)

Advertising Expenses

The Company expenses advertising costs in the period in which they are incurred. For the years ended December 31, 2001, 2002 and 2003 advertising expenses totaled approximately $5.3 million, $7.0 million and $20.9 million, including $2.8 million and $1.4 million of warrant amortization expense in 2001 and 2002 and none in 2003.

Comprehensive Income

Comprehensive income is comprised of net income and other comprehensive income. Other comprehensive income includes unrealized gains and losses on foreign exchange and unrealized gains and losses on available-for-sale investments. The differences between total comprehensive income and net income as disclosed on the consolidated statement of redeemable convertible preferred stock warrant and stockholders' equity for 2001, 2002 and 2003 were insignificant.

Recent Accounting Pronouncements

In November 2002, the EITF reached a consensus on Issue 00-21, *Accounting for Multiple Element Revenue Arrangements*, addressing how to account for arrangements that involve the delivery or performance of multiple products, services, and/or rights to use assets. Revenue arrangements with multiple deliverables are divided into separate units of accounting if the deliverables in the arrangement meet the following criteria: (1) the delivered item has value to the customer on a standalone basis; (2) there is objective and reliable evidence of the fair value of undelivered items; and (3) delivery of any undelivered item is probable. Arrangement consideration should be allocated among the separate units of accounting based on their relative fair values, with the amount allocated to the delivered item being limited to the amount that is not contingent on the delivery of additional items or meeting other specified performance conditions. The guidance in Issue 00-21 is effective for revenue arrangements entered into in fiscal periods after June 15, 2003. The adoption of Issue 00-21 did not have an impact on the Company's financial statements.

During November 2002, the FASB issued FIN 45, *Guarantor's Accounting and Disclosure Requirements for Guarantees, Including Indirect Guarantees of Indebtedness to Others*, an interpretation of FASB Statements No. 5, 57 and 107 and a rescission of FASB Interpretation No. 34. FIN 45 elaborates on the existing disclosure requirements for a guarantor in its interim and annual financial statements regarding its obligations under guarantees issued. It also clarifies that at the time a guarantee is issued, the guarantor must recognize an initial liability for the fair value of the obligations it assumes under the guarantee and must disclose that information in its financial statements. The initial recognition and measurement provisions apply on a prospective basis to guarantees issued or modified after December 31, 2002, and the disclosure requirements apply to guarantees outstanding at December 31, 2002. The Company adopted the provisions of FIN 45 at January 1, 2003. The adoption of this Interpretation did not have an impact on the Company's operating results. See further discussion regarding indemnifications in Note 7.

In January 2003, the FASB issued FIN 46, *Consolidation of Variable Interest Entities*. FIN 46 clarifies the application of Accounting Research Bulletin No. 51. This Interpretation requires variable interest entities to be consolidated if the equity investment at risk is not sufficient to permit an entity to finance its activities without support from other parties or the equity investors lack specified characteristics. The Company does not have any variable interest entities.

In May 2003, the FASB issued SFAS 150, *Accounting for Certain Financial Instruments with Characteristics of both Liabilities and Equity*. SFAS 150 establishes standards for how a company classifies and

F-19

Google Inc.

NOTES TO CONSOLIDATED FINANCIAL STATEMENTS—(Continued)
(Information as of June 30, 2004 and for the six months ended June 30, 2003 and 2004 is unaudited)

measures certain financial instruments with characteristics of both liabilities and equity. It requires that an issuer classify certain financial instruments as a liability (or as an asset in some circumstances). SFAS No. 150 is effective for financial instruments entered into or modified after May 31, 2003, and otherwise is effective at the beginning of the first interim period beginning after June 15, 2003. The adoption of SFAS No. 150 did not have an impact on the Company's financial statements.

Note 2. Cash, Cash Equivalents and Short-term Investments

Cash, cash equivalents and short-term investments consist of the following (in thousands):

	As of December 31, 2002	As of December 31, 2003	As of June 30, 2004
			(unaudited)
Cash and cash equivalents	$ 57,752	$148,995	$254,698
Short-term investments:			
Municipal securities	86,979	166,538	277,629
Market auction preferred securities(1)	1,600	8,000	3,000
U.S. government notes	—	11,185	13,360
Total short-term investments	88,579	185,723	293,989
Total cash, cash equivalents and short-term investments	$146,331	$334,718	$548,687

(1) Market auction preferred securities are securities with perpetual maturities that are structured with short-term reset dates of generally less than 90 days. At the end of the reset period, investors can sell or continue to hold the securities at par. These securities are classified in the table below based on their stated maturity dates.

The Company has not experienced any significant realized gains or losses on its investments in the periods presented. Gross unrealized gains and losses at December 31, 2002 and 2003 and at June 30, 2004 were not material.

The following table summarizes the estimated fair value of our securities held in short-term investments classified by the stated maturity date of the security (in thousands):

	As of December 31, 2002	As of December 31, 2003	As of June 30, 2004
			(unaudited)
Due within 1 year	$ 17,744	$ 29,381	$ 28,641
Due within 1 year through 5 years	—	81,830	163,683
Due within 5 years through 10 years	—	11,382	14,831
Due after 10 years	70,835	63,130	86,834
Total	$ 88,579	$185,723	$293,989

In addition, at December 31, 2002 and at both December 31, 2003 and June 30, 2004, the Company had $376,000 and $11.0 million of restricted cash and investment securities classified as other current assets which are included in "prepaid revenue share, expenses and other assets" in the accompanying consolidated balance sheets.

F-20

Google Inc.

NOTES TO CONSOLIDATED FINANCIAL STATEMENTS—(Continued)
(Information as of June 30, 2004 and for the six months ended June 30, 2003 and 2004 is unaudited)

Note 3. Interest Income (Expense) and Other

	Year Ended December 31,			Six Months Ended June 30,	
	2001	2002	2003	2003	2004
	(in thousands)			(unaudited)	
Interest income	$ 861	$ 1,215	$ 2,663	$ 1,176	$ 2,747
Interest expense	(1,758)	(2,570)	(1,931)	(1,028)	(540)
Other	1	(196)	3,458	571	(3,405)
Interest income (expense) and other, net	$ (896)	$(1,551)	$ 4,190	$ 719	$(1,198)

Note 4. Acquisitions

Applied Semantics, Inc.

In April 2003, the Company acquired all of the voting interests of Applied Semantics, Inc. ("ASI") to strengthen its search and advertising programs, including content-targeted advertising programs. The transaction was accounted for as a business combination.

The total purchase price was $102.4 million and consisted of a cash payment of $41.5 million, including direct transaction costs of $400,000, and the issuance of 1,825,226 fully vested shares of the Company's Class A common stock and 557,574 fully vested and unvested options to purchase the Company's Class A common stock valued at $60.9 million. This value was based on a reassessed value per share determined by management as of April 2003 through the application of hindsight. The intrinsic value of the unvested options to purchase 81,352 shares of Class A common stock on the date of acquisition was recorded as deferred stock-based compensation and is being amortized as compensation expense on an accelerated basis over the related vesting periods of three to 47 months contingent upon each individual's continued employment with the Company.

The fair values of the assets and liabilities acquired, including intangible assets, were determined by management with input from an advisor. The total purchase price was allocated as follows (in thousands):

Goodwill	$ 84,192
Developed technology	16,600
Customer contracts and other	4,100
Net tangible assets acquired	3,612
Deferred tax asset	1,074
Deferred stock-based compensation	1,933
Deferred tax liabilities	(9,074)
Total	$102,437

Goodwill includes but is not limited to the synergistic value and potential competitive benefits that could be realized by the Company from the acquisition, any future products that may arise from ASI's technology when combined with the Company's technology, as well as ASI's skilled and specialized workforce. The goodwill amount is not deductible for tax purposes.

The developed technology and customer contracts and other have a weighted-average useful life of three and two years, and a combined weighted average life of 2.81 years.

Google Inc.

NOTES TO CONSOLIDATED FINANCIAL STATEMENTS—(Continued)
(Information as of June 30, 2004 and for the six months ended June 30, 2003 and 2004 is unaudited)

Cash consideration of $900,000 may be paid over the next four years to certain former employees of ASI contingent upon their continued employment with the Company and will be recognized as expense as it is earned by the employees. As of December 31, 2003, the Company had paid approximately $300,000 of this amount.

The results of operations of ASI have been included in the Company's consolidated income statements since the completion of the acquisition on April 23, 2003. The following unaudited pro forma information presents a summary of the results of operations of the Company assuming the acquisition of ASI occurred on January 1, 2002 (in thousands, except per share amounts):

	Year Ended December 31, 2002	Year Ended December 31, 2003
	(unaudited)	(unaudited)
Revenues	$445,695	$1,468,753
Net income	$ 94,749	$ 105,072
Net income per share—basic	$ 0.81	$ 0.76
Net income per share—diluted	$ 0.43	$ 0.41

Other Acquisitions

During the year ended December 31, 2003 the Company acquired all of the voting interests of three other companies. Two of the companies were accounted for as business combinations. Because the third company was considered a development stage enterprise, the transaction was accounted for as an asset purchase in accordance with EITF Issue No. 98-3, *Determining Whether a Nonmonetary Transaction Involves Receipt of Productive Assets or of a Business*.

The total purchase price for the three acquisitions was $15.3 million and consisted of a cash payment of $1.5 million and the issuance of 440,000 fully vested shares of the Company's Class A common stock valued at $13.8 million. The total purchase price was allocated as follows (in thousands):

Goodwill	$ 3,250
Developed technology	3,651
Net liabilities assumed	(1,759)
Deferred tax liabilities	(1,487)
Purchased in-process research and development	11,618
Total	$15,273

Purchased in-process research and development of $11.6 million was expensed upon acquisition because technological feasibility had not been established and no future alternative uses existed. That amount is included in research and development expenses on the accompanying consolidated income statement and is not deductible for tax purposes.

Goodwill includes but is not limited to the synergistic value and potential competitive benefits that could be realized by the Company from the acquisitions, any future products that may arise from the related technology, as well as the skilled and specialized workforce acquired. The goodwill amount is not deductible for tax purposes.

The developed technology has a weighted-average useful life of three years.

In addition in conjunction with the acquisitions, the Company issued 234,999 restricted shares of the Company's Class A common stock valued at approximately $10.7 million. The fair value of the restricted shares

F-22

Table of Contents

Google Inc.

NOTES TO CONSOLIDATED FINANCIAL STATEMENTS—(Continued)
(Information as of June 30, 2004 and for the six months ended June 30, 2003 and 2004 is unaudited)

was recorded as deferred stock-based compensation and will be amortized to compensation expense on an accelerated basis over the related vesting periods of two to five years, contingent upon each individual's continued employment with the Company.

Note 5. Goodwill and Other Intangible Assets

The changes in the carrying amount of goodwill for the year ended December 31, 2003, are as follows (in thousands):

Balance as of January 1, 2003	$ --
Goodwill acquired during year	87,442
Balance as of December 31, 2003	$87,442

Information regarding the Company's acquisition-related intangible assets that are being amortized is as follows (in thousands):

	As of December 31, 2003		
	Gross Carrying Amount	Accumulated Amortization	Net Carrying Value
Developed technology	$ 20,917	$ 5,514	$ 15,403
Customer contracts and other	4,100	1,389	2,711
Total	$ 25,017	$ 6,903	$ 18,114

Amortization expense of acquisition-related intangible assets for the year ended December 31, 2003 was $6.3 million.

Estimated amortization expense for acquisition-related intangible assets on the Company's December 31, 2003 consolidated balance sheet for the fiscal years ending December 31, is as follows (in thousands):

2004	$ 8,767
2005	7,423
2006	1,924
	$18,114

Note 6. Property and Equipment

Property and equipment consist of the following (in thousands):

	As of December 31,		As of June 30, 2004
	2002	2003	(unaudited)
Information technology assets	$78,764	$204,417	$363,018
Furniture and fixtures	1,835	6,803	10,232
Leasehold improvements	908	7,677	9,530
Construction in process	5,379	42,940	61,271
Total	86,886	261,837	444,051
Less accumulated depreciation and amortization	33,013	73,582	123,333
Property and equipment, net	$53,873	$188,255	$320,718

Google Inc.

NOTES TO CONSOLIDATED FINANCIAL STATEMENTS—(Continued)
(Information as of June 30, 2004 and for the six months ended June 30, 2003 and 2004 is unaudited)

Note 7. Commitments and Contingencies

Capital Leases

In June 2001, the Company entered into a master equipment lease agreement with a financial institution. The agreement provided for an initial equipment lease line of credit not to exceed $5.0 million. In October 2001, the same financial institution provided for the syndication of another equipment lease line of credit not to exceed $10.0 million. Through December 31, 2003 and June 30, 2004, $15.0 million had been borrowed cumulatively under these equipment lease lines of credit.

The equipment financed under the capital lease arrangement is included in property and equipment and the related amortization is included in depreciation and amortization expense. The cost of assets financed under the capital lease was $15.0 million at December 31, 2002 and 2003. The related amortization expense was $728,000, $4.1 million and $5.0 million during 2001, 2002 and 2003 and accumulated amortization was $4.8 million and $9.8 million at December 31, 2002 and 2003. The equipment leases have payment terms of 36 months.

The Company has issued warrants to purchase 179,956 shares of Series C convertible preferred stock in connection with its draw on the equipment lease lines (see Note 9).

Operating Leases

During 2003, the Company entered into a nine year sublease agreement for its headquarters in Mountain View, California. According to the terms of the sublease, the Company will begin making payments in July 2005 and payments will increase at 3% per annum thereafter. The Company recognizes rent expense under this arrangement on a straight line basis. The lease terminates on December 31, 2012, however, the Company may exercise two five year renewal options at its discretion. The Company has an option to purchase the property for approximately $172.4 million, which is exercisable in 2006. In connection with the lease, the Company has a letter of credit which requires it to maintain $9.0 million of cash and investment securities as collateral. This required collateral effectively expires in April 2004. As a result, it is classified as other current assets, which is included in "prepaid revenue share, expenses and other assets" on the accompanying consolidated balance sheets. At December 31, 2003, the Company was in compliance with its financial covenants under the lease.

In addition, the Company has entered into various non-cancelable operating lease agreements for certain of its offices and data centers throughout the U.S. and for international subsidiaries with original lease periods expiring between 2004 and 2015. The Company is committed to pay a portion of the buildings' operating expenses as determined under the agreements. Certain of these arrangements have free or escalating rent payment provisions. The Company recognizes rent expense under such arrangements on a straight line basis. Total payments relating to leases having an initial or remaining non-cancelable term less than one year are $2.3 million and are not included in the table below. Rent expense was $2.0 million, $3.7 million, and $9.8 million in 2001, 2002, and 2003.

Table of Contents

Google Inc.

NOTES TO CONSOLIDATED FINANCIAL STATEMENTS—(Continued)
(Information as of June 30, 2004 and for the six months ended June 30, 2003 and 2004 is unaudited)

At December 31, 2003, future payments under capital leases and minimum payments under non-cancelable operating leases with a remaining term greater than one-year are as follows over each of the next five years and thereafter (in thousands):

	Capital Leases	Operating Leases
2004	$5,304	$ 7,378
2005	2,080	13,596
2006	—	18,620
2007	—	18,774
2008	—	18,769
Thereafter	—	69,592
Total minimum payments required	7,384	$146,729
Less amounts representing interest	775	
Minimum future payments of principal	6,609	
Current portion	4,621	
Long-term portion	$1,988	

AdSense Agreements

In connection with our AdSense revenue share agreements, the Company is periodically required to make non-cancelable guaranteed minimum revenue share payments to a small number of its Google Network members over the term of the respective contracts. Under some of our contracts, these guaranteed payments can vary based on the Google Network members achieving defined performance terms, such as number of advertisements displayed or search queries. In some cases, certain guaranteed amounts will be adjusted downward if the Google Network members do not meet their performance terms and, in some cases, these amounts will be adjusted upward if they exceed their performance terms. In all but one of these AdSense agreements, if a Google Network member were unable to perform under the contract, such as being unable to provide search queries, as defined under the terms of that agreement, then the Company would not be obligated to make any non-cancelable guaranteed minimum revenue share payments to that member.

Under one AdSense agreement, the Company is obligated to make $5.6 million of non-cancelable guaranteed minimum revenue share payments through 2005 irrespective of whether or not the Google Network member achieves defined performance goals. The only circumstance in which the non-cancelable guaranteed minimum revenue share payments would not be due to this Google Network member would be material breach, as defined in the agreement.

Management believes future non-cancelable guaranteed minimum revenue share payments will be significantly greater than the contractual minimum of $5.6 million. To date, total advertiser fees generated under these AdSense agreements have exceeded the total guaranteed minimum revenue share payments. In 2003, the Company made $108.8 million of non-cancelable minimum guaranteed revenue payments.

Purchase Obligations

Additionally, the Company had $11.9 million of other non-cancelable contractual obligations and $24.9 million of open purchase orders for which we have not received the related services or goods at

F-25

Google Inc.

NOTES TO CONSOLIDATED FINANCIAL STATEMENTS—(Continued)
(Information as of June 30, 2004 and for the six months ended June 30, 2003 and 2004 is unaudited)

December 31, 2003. The Company has the right to cancel these open purchase orders upon 10 days notice prior to the date of delivery. The majority of these purchase obligations are related to data center operations.

Letters of Credit

At December 31, 2003 and associated with several leased facilities, the Company has unused letters of credit for $12.2 million and related compensating cash balances of $11.0 million as included in "prepaid revenue share, expenses and other assets" in the accompanying consolidated balance sheets. At December 31, 2003, the Company was in compliance with its financial covenants under the letters of credit.

Indemnifications

While the Company has various guarantees included in contracts in the normal course of business, primarily in the form of indemnities, these guarantees do not represent significant commitments or contingent liabilities of the indebtedness of others. Accordingly, the Company has not recorded a liability related to indemnification provisions.

Legal Matters

See Note 14 for a discussion of a settlement agreement entered into between the Company and Yahoo.

Certain companies have filed trademark infringement and related claims against the Company over the display of ads in response to user queries that include trademark terms. The outcomes of these lawsuits have differed from jurisdiction to jurisdiction. A court in France has held the Company liable for allowing advertisers to select certain trademarked terms as keywords. The Company has appealed this decision. The Company is also subject to two lawsuits in Germany on similar matters where one court preliminarily reached a similar conclusion as the court in France while another court held that the Company is not liable for the actions of our advertisers prior to notification of trademark rights. The Company is litigating similar issues in other cases in the U.S., France, Germany and Italy. Management believes that any adverse results in these lawsuits may result in, or even compel, a change in this practice which could result in a loss of revenues on a prospective basis. As the proceedings related to these lawsuits are currently at a relatively early stage, the magnitude of any unfavorable outcome cannot be reasonably estimated at this time.

Currently, there is no other significant litigation pending against the Company other than as disclosed in the paragraph above. From time to time, the Company may become a party to litigation and subject to claims incident to the ordinary course of the Company's business. Although the results of such litigation and claims in the ordinary course of business cannot be predicted with certainty, the Company believes that the final outcome of such matters will not have a material adverse effect on the Company's business, results of operations or financial condition. Regardless of outcome, litigation can have an adverse impact on the Company because of defense costs, diversion of management resources and other factors.

Note 8. Redeemable Convertible Preferred Stock Warrant

As a part of an AdSense agreement entered into during 2002, the Company issued to the Google Network member fully vested warrants to purchase 7,437,452 shares of Series D convertible preferred stock. The warrants have an exercise price of $2.91 and a life of five years. These warrants expire in 2012. See Note 14.

The Company determined the fair value of the warrants to be $13.9 million. At December 31, 2003, the warrants have been fully amortized.

Google Inc.

NOTES TO CONSOLIDATED FINANCIAL STATEMENTS—(Continued)
(Information as of June 30, 2004 and for the six months ended June 30, 2003 and 2004 is unaudited)

Under certain circumstances, the Company could be required to pay the holder of the warrant the lesser of (i) the fair value of the warrants (as calculated and defined in the warrant agreement using a Black-Scholes pricing model) and (ii) $5.82 per share for maximum payment of approximately $43.3 million.

As a result of the redemption feature of the warrant, the fair value of the warrants has been classified outside of stockholders' equity. Currently, the circumstances necessary for this warrant to be redeemable are not probable and, therefore, the warrant has not been classified as a liability and the value has not been adjusted from the calculated amount. In the future, should a redemption event become probable, the warrant value would be reclassified as a liability and its value adjusted. Any adjustments in value would be recorded as a deemed dividend.

Note 9. Stockholders' Equity

Convertible Preferred Stock

Convertible preferred stock consists of the following (in thousands):

	As of December 31, 2002 Shares Authorized	2002 Shares Issued and Outstanding	2003 Shares Authorized	2003 Shares Issued and Outstanding	2003 Aggregate Liquidation Preference	As of June 30, 2004 Shares Authorized	(unaudited) Shares Issued and Outstanding	Aggregate Liquidation Preference
Series A	15,360	15,360	15,360	15,360	$ 960	15,360	15,360	$ 960
Series A-1	15,360	—	15,360	—	—	15,360	—	—
Series B	50,651	49,823	50,445	49,823	24,677	50,445	49,823	24,677
Series B-1	50,651	—	50,445	—	—	50,445	—	—
Series C	10,000	5,249	9,149	6,479	15,178	9,149	6,479	15,178
Series C-1	10,000	—	9,149	—	—	9,149	—	—
Series D	7,437	—	7,437	—	—	7,437	7,437	21,643
Series D-1	7,437	—	7,437	—	—	7,437	—	—
	166,896	70,432	164,782	71,662	$ 40,815	164,782	79,099	$ 62,458

Significant terms of the Series A, A-1, B, B-1, C, C-1, D and D-1 convertible preferred stock are as follows:

- Holders of Series A, Series B, Series C and Series D convertible preferred stock are entitled to noncumulative dividends of $0.00625, $0.0496, $0.2343 and $0.2910 per share, respectively, if and when declared by the board of directors in preference to holders of common stock. No dividends have been declared through December 31, 2003.

- In the event of liquidation, dissolution, or winding up of the Company, either voluntarily or involuntarily, stockholders will receive distributions of $0.0625 for each share of Series A or A-1 convertible preferred stock, $0.4953 for each share of Series B or B-1 convertible preferred stock, and $2.3425 for each share of Series C or C-1 convertible preferred stock, and $2.91 for each share of Series D or D-1 convertible preferred stock. All remaining assets will be shared on a prorata basis between the Class A and Class B common stockholders.

- Each share of the convertible preferred stock is convertible into one share of Class B common stock of the Company at the option of the holder and carries voting rights equivalent to the Class B common stock on a share-for-share basis. The conversion rate of the convertible preferred stock is

Google Inc.

NOTES TO CONSOLIDATED FINANCIAL STATEMENTS—(Continued)
(Information as of June 30, 2004 and for the six months ended June 30, 2003 and 2004 is unaudited)

subject to adjustment in the event of, among other things, stock splits and stock dividends. Each share of convertible preferred stock automatically converts into Class B common stock in the event of a public offering o the Company's common stock in which the gross proceeds and the offering price per share exceed certain minimum amounts.

- The holders of Series A, B, C, and D convertible preferred stock are entitled to the right of first offer with respect to equity financings of the Company (which does not include an initial public offering of the Company's stock). If the stockholders do not exercise this right in the event of an equity financing at a price per share less than the original respective issue price of Series A, B, C and D convertible preferred stock, then shares of Series A, B, C and D convertible preferred stock will be automatically converted into an equivalent number of shares of Series A-1, B-1, C-1, or D-1 convertible preferred stock, respectively.

Class A and Class B Common Stock

The Company's Board of Directors has authorized two classes of common stock, Class A and Class B. The Company had authorized 400,000,000 and 300,000,000 shares and at December 31, 2003 there were 11,220,718 and 161,632,445 shares legally outstanding of Class A and Class B common stock. The rights of the holders of Class A and Class B common stock are identical, except with respect to voting. Each share of Class A common stock is entitled to one vote per share. Each share of Class B common stock is entitled to ten votes per share. Shares of Class B common stock may be converted at any time at the option of the stockholder and automatically convert upon sale or transfer to Class A common stock. See Note 13.

At December 31, 2003 and June 30, 2004 there were 115,986,783 and 111,922,880 shares of Class A and Class B common stock reserved for future issuance, as presented in the following table:

	December 31, 2003	June 30, 2004
		(unaudited)
Outstanding convertible preferred stock	71,662,432	79,099,884
Outstanding options to purchase Class A and Class B common stock	17,363,122	16,732,657
Options to purchase Class A and Class B common stock available for grant	5,440,155	3,891,192
Warrants to purchase Class B common stock	1,294,308	1,194,308
Warrants to purchase convertible preferred stock	8,239,284	801,832
Unvested shares related to options granted and exercised subsequent to March 21, 2002 to purchase Class A and Class B common stock	11,987,482	10,203,007
Total Class A and Class B common stock reserved for future issuance	115,986,783	111,922,880

Stock Plans

The Company maintains the 1998 Stock Plan, the 2000 Stock Plan, the 2003 Stock Plan, the 2003 Stock Plan (No. 2) and the 2003 Stock Plan (No. 3) and plans assumed through acquisitions which are collectively referred to as the "Stock Plans." Under the Company's Stock Plans, incentive and nonqualified stock options or rights to purchase Class A and Class B common stock may be granted to eligible participants. Options must generally be priced to be at least 85% of the Class A or Class B common stock's fair market value at the date of grant as determined by the board of directors (100% in the case of incentive stock options). Options are generally granted for a term of ten years. Initial options granted under the Stock Plans generally vest 25% after the first year of service and ratably each month over the remaining 36-month period. Additional options granted under the Stock Plans generally vest 20% after the first year of service and ratably each month over the remaining 48-

Google Inc.

NOTES TO CONSOLIDATED FINANCIAL STATEMENTS—(Continued)
(Information as of June 30, 2004 and for the six months ended June 30, 2003 and 2004 is unaudited)

month period. Typically, options may be exercised prior to vesting. Sales of stock under stock purchase rights are made pursuant to restricted stock purchase agreements. There are 24,205,579 shares of Class A and Class B common stock outstanding and subject to repurchase related to the Stock Plans at December 31, 2003. Of this total, 12,218,097 and 11,987,482 shares are related to options granted through and after March 21, 2002, in accordance with EITF 00-23, respectively.

The following table summarizes the activity under the Company's Stock Plans:

	Shares Available for Grant	Options Outstanding Number of Shares	Weighted-Average Exercise Price
Balance at December 31, 2000	18,884,848	8,477,488	$ 0.25
Additional options authorized	15,241,708	—	—
Options granted	(26,990,768)	26,990,768	$ 0.30
Options exercised	—	(17,754,728)	$ 0.30
Options canceled	898,000	(898,000)	$ 0.24
Options repurchased	443,740	—	$ 0.06
Balance at December 31, 2001	8,477,528	16,815,528	$ 0.28
Additional options authorized	14,400,000	—	—
Options granted	(14,980,716)	14,980,716	$ 0.30
Options exercised	—	(8,520,668)	$ 0.28
Options canceled	351,100	(351,100)	$ 0.30
Options repurchased	557,772	—	$ 0.25
Balance at December 31, 2002	8,805,684	22,924,476	$ 0.29
Additional options authorized	16,034,880	—	—
Options granted	(19,846,158)	19,846,158	$ 2.65
Options exercised	—	(13,145,075)	$ 0.54
Options canceled	274,955	(274,955)	$ 1.50
Options repurchased	170,794	—	$ 0.29
Balance at December 31, 2003	5,440,155	29,350,604	$ 2.47
Additional options authorized	64,338	—	—
Options granted (unaudited)	(1,973,111)	1,973,111	$ 27.14
Options exercised (unaudited)	—	(4,138,473)	$ 3.67
Options canceled (unaudited)	249,578	(249,578)	$ 2.69
Options repurchased (unaudited)	110,232	—	$ 0.45
Balance at June 30, 2004 (unaudited)	3,891,192	26,935,664	$ 5.21

The number of options outstanding at December 31, 2002 and 2003 and June 30, 2004 includes 3,281,004, 11,987,482 and 10,203,007 of options granted and exercised subsequent to March 21, 2002 that are unvested at December 31, 2002 and 2003 and June 30, 2004, in accordance with EITF 00 23, *Issues related to the accounting for stock compensation under APB Opinion No. 25 and FASB Interpretation No. 44*.

F-29

Google Inc.

NOTES TO CONSOLIDATED FINANCIAL STATEMENTS—(Continued)
(Information as of June 30, 2004 and for the six months ended June 30, 2003 and 2004 is unaudited)

The following table summarizes additional information regarding outstanding and exercisable options at December 31, 2003:

Range of Exercise Prices	Total Number of Shares	Unvested options granted and exercised subsequent to March 21, 2002	Number of Shares	Weighted-Average Remaining Life (Years)	Weighted-Average Exercise Price	Number of Shares	Weighted-Average Exercise Price
$ 0.01–$ 2.00	21,080,838	10,548,989	10,531,849	8.1	$ 0.40	10,304,146	$ 0.40
$ 3.50–$ 3.50	1,211,262	540,214	671,048	9.4	$ 3.50	597,648	$ 3.50
$ 5.00–$ 7.00	5,771,739	628,559	5,143,180	9.5	$ 5.15	5,037,530	$ 5.15
$ 9.00–$ 9.00	476,050	155,508	320,542	9.8	$ 9.00	291,742	$ 9.00
$10.00–$10.00	810,715	114,212	696,503	9.9	$ 10.00	664,203	$ 10.00
$ 0.01–$10.00	29,350,604	11,987,482	17,363,122	8.7	$ 2.47	16,895,269	$ 2.45

The number of options exercisable at December 31, 2001 and 2002 were 16,815,528 and 22,924,476.

The following table summarizes additional information regarding outstanding and exercisable options at June 30, 2004 (unaudited):

Range of Exercise Prices	Total Number of Shares	Unvested options granted and exercised subsequent to March 21, 2002	Number of Shares	Weighted-Average Remaining Life (Years)	Weighted-Average Exercise Price	Number of Shares	Weighted-Average Exercise Price
$ 0.01–$ 9.00	24,180,607	9,687,734	14,492,873	8.2	$ 2.28	14,163,166	$ 2.27
$10.00–$19.78	1,260,587	408,275	852,312	9.5	$ 10.76	809,562	$ 10.77
$20.00–$28.80	794,657	74,405	720,252	9.7	$ 21.52	659,902	$ 21.30
$30.73–$39.57	386,975	28,493	358,482	9.8	$ 34.20	345,557	$ 34.20
$42.39–$44.71	173	—	173	9.7	$ 43.41	173	$ 43.41
$50.00–$50.00	139,200	1,600	137,600	9.9	$ 50.00	130,100	$ 50.00
$60.00–$60.00	173,465	2,500	170,965	9.9	$ 60.00	156,340	$ 60.00
$ 0.01–$60.00	26,935,664	10,203,007	16,732,657	8.4	$ 5.21	16,264,800	$ 5.08

Note Receivable from Stockholder / Officer

In connection with the exercise of employee stock options, the Company has a $4.3 million loan receivable at December 31, 2003. This outstanding balance is for a loan that was made in 2001, to the Company's Chief Executive Officer pursuant to a full recourse promissory note and stock pledge agreement. The note accrues interest at 7.38% compounded semi-annually and is repayable in full on September 28, 2005. See Note 14.

Google Inc.

NOTES TO CONSOLIDATED FINANCIAL STATEMENTS—(Continued)
(Information as of June 30, 2004 and for the six months ended June 30, 2003 and 2004 is unaudited)

Warrants to Purchase Class B Common and Preferred Stock

Warrant Types	Shares Subject to Purchase at December 31, 2003	Weighted-Average Exercise Price Per Share	Shares Subject to Purchase at June 30, 2004	Weighted-Average Exercise Price Per Share
			(unaudited)	
Class B Common	1,294,308	$ 0.46	1,194,308	$ 0.30
Series B Convertible Preferred	621,876	$ 0.72	621,876	$ 0.72
Series C Convertible Preferred	179,956	$ 2.34	179,956	$ 2.34
Series D Convertible Preferred	7,437,452	$ 2.91	—	
Total	9,533,592	$ 2.42	1,996,140	$ 0.62

The Company determined the value of these warrants at the date of grant using the Black-Scholes option pricing model based on the estimated fair value of the underlying stock, a volatility rate of 100% or 75%, no dividends, a risk-free interest rate ranging from 4.93% to 6.84%, and an expected life of three to ten years which coincides with the maximum exercise periods of the warrants.

Class B Common

In 2001, the Company issued fully vested, nonforfeitable warrants to purchase 1,194,308 shares of Class B common stock at a price of $0.30 per share in connection with recruitment fees. The Company determined the value of the warrants to be $1.1 million. The entire fair value of the warrants was expensed during 2001 as general and administrative expense on the accompanying consolidated income statements. Also, in October 2000, the Company issued fully vested, nonforfeitable warrants to purchase 100,000 shares of Class B common stock at a price of $2.34 per share. See Note 14. The above warrants expire in 2006 and 2005.

Series B Preferred

In 1999, the Company issued fully vested, nonforfeitable warrants to purchase 403,840 shares of Series B convertible preferred stock in connection with an equipment line of credit. The warrants have an exercise price of $0.495. The Company determined the fair value of the warrants to be $157,000. In connection with additional drawdowns on the equipment line of credit during 2000, the Company issued 74,216 and 143,820 warrants to purchase Series B convertible preferred stock with an exercise price of $0.62 and $1.42, respectively. The Company determined the fair value of these warrants to be $28,000 and $269,000. The cost of the warrants was expensed as additional interest expense over the life of the loan arrangement. These warrants remain outstanding and expire in 2005.

Series C Preferred

In June 2000, the Company issued warrants to purchase shares of Series C convertible preferred stock to a customer in connection with a Branding and Promotion Agreement whereby the customer provided advertising to the Company over a two-year period. The warrants had an exercise price of $2.34 per share. The Company determined the fair value of the warrants to be $5.7 million. The entire fair value of the warrants was expensed ratably over the two years of the agreement as sales and marketing expense on the accompanying consolidated income statements. In June 2003, the warrant converted in accordance with its terms into 1,229,944 shares of Series C convertible preferred stock. The conversion of this warrant was the subject of a dispute that was settled as described in Note 14.

F-31

Google Inc.

NOTES TO CONSOLIDATED FINANCIAL STATEMENTS—(Continued)
(Information as of June 30, 2004 and for the six months ended June 30, 2003 and 2004 is unaudited)

In 2001, the Company issued fully vested, nonforfeitable warrants to purchase 108,260 shares of Series C convertible preferred stock in connection with draw downs on the Company's equipment lease lines of credit. The warrants have an exercise price of $2.345. The Company determined the fair value of the warrants to be $232,000. The cost of the warrants is being expensed as additional interest expense over the life of the lease arrangement. These warrants expire in 2011.

In 2002, the Company issued fully vested, nonforfeitable warrants to purchase 71,696 shares of Series C convertible preferred stock in connection with draw downs on the Company's equipment lease lines of credit discussed in Note 7. The warrants have an exercise price of $2.345. The Company determined the fair value of the warrants to be $199,000. The cost of the warrants is being expensed as additional interest expense over the life of the lease arrangement. These warrants expire in 2012.

Series D Preferred

In 2002, the Company issued 7,437,452 redeemable warrants to purchase Series D convertible preferred stock to a customer in connection with a revenue-share agreement (see Note 8 and Note 14).

Note 10. 401(k) Plan

The Company has a 401(k) Savings Plan (the "401(k) Plan") that qualifies as a deferred salary arrangement under Section 401(k) of the Internal Revenue Code. Under the 401(k) Plan, participating employees may elect to contribute up to 15% of their eligible compensation, subject to certain limitations. The Company matches employee contributions up to the lesser of 3.5% of the employee's salary or $2,200. Employee and Company contributions are fully vested when contributed. The Company contributed approximately $329,000, $663,000 and $1.7 million during 2001, 2002 and 2003, respectively.

Note 11. Income Taxes

Income from continuing operations before income taxes included income/(loss) from foreign operations of approximately $500,000 and $(6.5) million for 2002 and 2003. Pretax income from foreign operations was immaterial for 2001.

The provision for (benefit from) income taxes consisted of the following (in thousands):

	Year Ended December 31,		
	2001	2002	2003
Current:			
Federal	$ 4,260	$74,081	$187,686
State	1,017	19,683	52,336
Foreign	--	1,367	965
Total	5,277	95,131	240,987
Deferred:			
Federal	(1,782)	(8,504)	712
State	(412)	(1,368)	(693)
Foreign	--	--	--
Total	(2,194)	(9,872)	19
Provision for income taxes	$ 3,083	$85,259	$241,006

F-32

Table of Contents

Google Inc.

NOTES TO CONSOLIDATED FINANCIAL STATEMENTS—(Continued)
(Information as of June 30, 2004 and for the six months ended June 30, 2003 and 2004 is unaudited)

The reconciliation of federal statutory income tax rate to the Company's effective income tax rate is as follows (in thousands):

	Year Ended December 31,		
	2001	2002	2003
Expected provision at federal statutory rate, 35%	$ 3,524	$64,720	$121,329
State taxes, net of federal benefit	393	11,905	33,568
Stock based compensation expense	4,334	7,572	79,764
Foreign rate differential	—	--	3,249
In-process research and development	—	—	4,066
Valuation allowance (utilized)/provided	(5,558)	(461)	—
Other individually immaterial items	390	1,523	(970)
Provision for income taxes	$ 3,083	$85,259	$241,006

Deferred Tax Assets

Deferred income taxes reflect the net effects of temporary differences between the carrying amounts of assets and liabilities for financing reporting purposes and the amounts used for income tax purposes. Significant components of the Company's deferred tax assets and liabilities are as follows (in thousands):

	As of December 31,	
	2002	2003
Deferred tax assets:		
Net operating loss carryforwards	$ 210	$ 482
Deferred compensation	4,054	5,661
State taxes	6,216	15,947
Deferred revenue	834	775
Accruals and reserves not currently deductible	4,725	4,684
Tax credits	--	291
Other	42	28
Total deferred tax assets	16,081	27,868
Deferred tax liabilities:		
Depreciation	(3,959)	(15,778)
Identified intangibles	—	(8,223)
Other	(56)	(272)
Total deferred tax liabilities	(4,015)	(24,273)
Net deferred tax assets	$12,066	$ 3,595

The net valuation allowance decreased by approximately $5.6 million and $500,000 during the years ended December 31, 2001 and 2002 respectively.

At December 31, 2003, the Company had federal and state net operating loss carryforwards of approximately $604,000 and $5.3 million, respectively. As of December 31, 2003, the Company had federal credit carryforwards of approximately $291,000. The net operating loss and credit carryforwards will begin to expire in 2006, if not utilized.

Google Inc.

NOTES TO CONSOLIDATED FINANCIAL STATEMENTS—(Continued)
(Information as of June 30, 2004 and for the six months ended June 30, 2003 and 2004 is unaudited)

Utilization of the net operating loss and credit carryforwards may be subject to substantial annual limitation due to the ownership change limitations provided by the Internal Revenue Code of 1986, as amended, and similar state provisions. The annual limitation may result in the expiration of net operating losses before utilization.

Note 12. Information about Geographic Areas

The Company's chief operating decision-makers (i.e., chief executive officer and his direct reports) review financial information presented on a consolidated basis, accompanied by disaggregated information about revenues by geographic region for purposes of allocating resources and evaluating financial performance. There are no segment managers who are held accountable for operations, operating results and plans for levels or components below the consolidated unit level. Accordingly, the Company considers itself to be in a single reporting segment and operating unit structure.

Revenues by geography are based on the billing address of the advertiser. The following table sets forth revenues and long-lived assets by geographic area (in thousands):

	Year Ended December 31,			Six Months Ended June 30,	
	2001	2002	2003	2003	2004
				(unaudited)	
Revenues:					
United States	$71,029	$341,570	$1,038,409	$404,478	$928,921
International	15,397	97,938	427,525	155,339	422,914
Total revenues	$86,426	$439,508	$1,465,934	$559,817	$1,351,835

	As of December 31,		
	2001	2002	2003
Long-lived assets:			
United States	$28,217	$55,009	$267,348
International	—	87	43,876
Total long-lived assets	$28,217	$55,096	$311,224

Note 13. Subsequent Event

Class A and Class B Common Stock

The Company's certificate of incorporation previously provided that upon an initial public offering meeting certain criteria, the Company's Class A Senior common stock, which has ten votes per share, would automatically convert into common stock, which has one vote per share. In April 2004, the Company's Board of Directors authorized, and on June 25, 2004 its stockholders approved, certain amendments to the Company's certificate of incorporation. Pursuant to these amendments, each share of Class A Senior common stock was reclassified as one share of Class B common stock and each share of common stock was reclassified as one share of Class A common stock. In addition, these amendments changed the conversion rights of the Class A Senior common stock (now Class B common stock) to provide that these shares would no longer automatically convert into shares of common stock (now Class A common stock) upon an initial public offering. Also, shares of Class B common stock may be converted at any time at the option of the stockholder into Class A common stock and

F-34

Table of Contents

Google Inc.

NOTES TO CONSOLIDATED FINANCIAL STATEMENTS—(Continued)
(Information as of June 30, 2004 and for the six months ended June 30, 2003 and 2004 is unaudited)

automatically convert upon any sale or transfer (subject to certain exceptions set forth in the certificate of incorporation). These amendments have been reflected in the accompanying consolidated financial statements as if they had been made at the inception of the Company. See Note 9.

Note 14. Events Subsequent to Date of Independent Registered Public Accounting Firm's Report (unaudited)

Initial Public Offering and 2004 Stock Plan

In April 2004, the Company's board of directors approved the filing of a registration statement with the Securities and Exchange Commission for an initial public offering of the Company's Class A common stock. In April 2004, the Company's board of directors adopted, and on June 25, 2004, its stockholders approved, the 2004 Stock Plan. The 2004 Stock Plan provides for the grant of incentive stock options to the Company's employees and nonstatutory stock options, restricted stock, stock appreciation rights, performance units, performance shares, restricted stock units and other stock based awards to the Company's employees, directors, and consultants. No awards have yet been issued pursuant to the 2004 Stock Plan.

Rescission Offer

Shares issued and options granted under the Company's 1998 Stock Plan, 2003 Stock Plan, 2003 Stock Plan (No. 2) and 2003 Stock Plan (No. 3) may not have been exempt from registration or qualification under federal securities laws and the securities laws of certain states. As a result, the Company intends to make a rescission offer to the holders of these shares and options beginning approximately 30 days after the effective date of this registration statement. If this rescission is accepted, the Company could be required to make aggregate payments to the holders of these shares and options of up to $25.9 million, which includes statutory interest, based on shares and options outstanding as of June 30, 2004. In addition, if it is determined that the Company offered securities without properly registering them under federal law or state law, or securing an exemption from registration, federal or state regulators could impose fines or other sanctions as provided under these laws. Federal securities laws do not provide that a rescission offer will terminate a purchaser's right to rescind a sale of stock that was not registered as required. If any or all of the offerees reject the rescission offer, the Company may continue to be liable for this amount under federal and state securities laws. As management believes there is only a remote possibility the rescission offer will be accepted by any of the Company's option holders and stockholders in an amount that would result in a material expenditure by the Company, no liability has been recorded. Management does not believe that this rescission offer will have a material effect on the Company's results of operations, cash flows or financial position.

Note Receivable from Stockholder/Officer

In April 2004, the Company's Chief Executive Officer fully repaid the principal and accrued interest due under a full recourse promissory note. See Note 9.

Redeemable Convertible Preferred Stock Warrant

In May 2004, the redeemable warrant to purchase 7,437,452 shares of Series D convertible preferred stock was fully exercised by the holder through a cash payment of $21.6 million. See Note 8.

Google Inc.

NOTES TO CONSOLIDATED FINANCIAL STATEMENTS—(Continued)
(Information as of June 30, 2004 and for the six months ended June 30, 2003 and 2004 is unaudited)

Class B Common Stock Warrant

In May 2004, a warrant to purchase 100,000 shares of Class B common stock was fully exercised by the holder through a cash payment of $234,000.

Settlement of Disputes with Yahoo

On August 9, 2004, the Company and Yahoo entered into a settlement agreement resolving two disputes that had been pending between them. The first dispute concerned a lawsuit filed by Yahoo's wholly-owned subsidiary, Overture Services, Inc., against the Company in April 2002 asserting that certain services infringed Overture's U.S. Patent No. 6,269,361. In its court filings, the Company denied that it infringed the patent and alleged that the patent was invalid and unenforceable.

The second dispute concerned a warrant held by Yahoo to purchase 3,719,056 shares of the Company's stock in connection with a June 2000 services agreement. Pursuant to a conversion provision in the warrant, the Company in June 2003 issued 1,229,944 shares to Yahoo. Yahoo contended it was entitled to a greater number of shares, while the Company contended that it had fully complied with the terms of the warrant.

As part of the settlement, Overture will dismiss its patent lawsuit against the Company and has granted the Company a fully-paid, perpetual license to the patent that was the subject of the lawsuit and several related patent applications held by Overture. The parties also mutually released any claims against each other concerning the warrant dispute. In connection with the settlement of these two disputes, the Company issued to Yahoo 2,700,000 shares of Class A common stock.

The Company will incur a non-cash charge in the third quarter of 2004 related to this settlement. Based on an assumed per share value of the settlement consideration equal to the midpoint of the proposed initial public offering price range included in this prospectus, the Company preliminarily estimates that this non-cash charge will be between $195 million and $215 million in the three months ending September 30, 2004. The non-cash charge will include, among other items, the value of shares associated with the settlement of the warrant dispute. The non-cash charge associated with these shares is required because the shares are being issued after the warrant was converted. The Company will also realize an income tax benefit in the third quarter, based on preliminary estimates, of between $75 million and $85 million related to this non-cash charge. The charge will result in a net loss for the Company in the three months ending September 30, 2004. The Company anticipates that it will capitalize various intangible assets obtained in this settlement and that these amounts will be amortized ratably over their useful lives, preliminarily expected to be between one and five years. The issuance of 2,700,000 shares represents approximately one percent of the number of shares currently expected to be used in the diluted per share calculation for the three and nine months ending September 30, 2004 and for the year ending December 31, 2004. The foregoing estimates of the amounts to be expensed, the associated tax benefit and the periods over which the capitalized assets will be amortized, are preliminary. As a result, these estimates are subject to further review and may change materially. In finalizing these amounts, the Company expects to use the actual initial public offering price to determine the reported value of the settlement consideration. The Company will also engage a third party valuation consultant to assist management in the allocation of the settlement amount and the determination of the useful lives of the capitalized assets and expects to complete these analyses during the third quarter of 2004.

F-36

Table of Contents

Google Inc.

NOTES TO CONSOLIDATED FINANCIAL STATEMENTS—(Continued)
(Information as of June 30, 2004 and for the six months ended June 30, 2003 and 2004 is unaudited)

The unaudited pro forma information below presents net income (loss) and per share amounts assuming the settlement had occurred on January 1, 2003 and balance sheet data assuming it had occurred on December 31, 2003. For the purposes of the settlement we have assumed a per share value of the settlement consideration equal to the midpoint of the proposed initial public offering price range included in this prospectus.

The unaudited pro forma adjustments were derived from the preliminary estimates discussed above and in the related footnotes below. These estimates are subject to further review and may change materially. The following data is in thousands, except per share and footnote amounts:

	Year Ended December 31, 2003			Six Months Ended June 30, 2004		
	Actual	Pro Forma Adjustments	Pro Forma	Actual	Pro Forma Adjustments	Pro Forma
	(unaudited)	(unaudited)	(unaudited)	(unaudited)	(unaudited)	(unaudited)
		$ (205,000)(a)			$ —	
		80,000 (b)			—	
		(13,000)(c)			(6,500)(c)	
		4,000 (d)			2,000 (d)	
Net income (loss)	$105,648	$ (134,000)	$ (28,352)	$143,036	$ (4,500)	$138,536
Net income (loss) per share— basic	$ 0.77		$ (0.20)	$ 0.93		$ 0.89
Shares used in per share calculation—basic	137,697	2,700 (e)	140,397	153,263	2,700 (e)	155,963
Net income per share—diluted	$ 0.41		— (h)	$ 0.54		$ 0.52
Shares used in per share calculation—diluted	256,638		— (h)	265,223	2,700 (e)	267,923

	December 31, 2003		
	Actual	Pro Forma Adjustments	Pro Forma
		(unaudited)	(unaudited)
Total assets	$871,458	$ 38,000 (f)	$ 909,458
Total liabilities	268,817	(80,000)(b)	188,817
		(205,000)(a)	
		80,000 (b)	
		243,000 (g)	
Total stockholders' equity	588,770	118,000	706,770

(a) To reflect the one-time non-cash charge related to the settlement of the warrant dispute and other items assumed to be equal to the midpoint of the preliminarily estimated range of between $195 million and $215 million.

(b) To reflect the income tax benefit related to the non-cash charge (noted in (a) above) assumed to be equal to the midpoint of the preliminarily estimated range of between $75 million and $85 million.

(c) To reflect the amortization expense related to the various intangible assets obtained in this settlement based on a preliminarily estimated average amortization period of approximately 3 years.

(d) To reflect the income tax benefit resulting from the amortization expense related to the various intangible assets obtained in this settlement.

(e) To reflect the 2,700,000 shares of Class A common stock issued to Yahoo in connection with this settlement.

(f) To reflect the capitalization of various intangible assets obtained in this settlement.

(g) To reflect the value of the 2,700,000 shares of Class A common stock issued to Yahoo in connection with this settlement based on an assumed per share value of $90.00 which is equal to the midpoint of the proposed initial public offering price range included in this prospectus.

(h) The "income per share—diluted" amount for the year ended December 31, 2003 pro forma is not provided because the effect of the additional shares is anti-dilutive.

Table of Contents

Google Inc.

NOTES TO CONSOLIDATED FINANCIAL STATEMENTS—(Continued)
(Information as of June 30, 2004 and for the six months ended June 30, 2003 and 2004 is unaudited)

The following table provides a preliminary allocation of the preliminarily estimated $243 million ascribed to the value of the shares issued in connection with this settlement. These estimates are subject to further review and may change materially.

	(In thousands) (unaudited)	
Settlement of warrant dispute and other items	$ 205,000	(see footnote (a) above)
Intangible assets	38,000	(see footnote (f) above)
Total consideration	$ 243,000	

Magazine Article

Information about the Company has been published in an article appearing in the September 2004 issue of Playboy Magazine and entitled "Playboy Interview: Google Guys." This article includes quotations from Larry and Sergey, and has been reprinted by a number of news media outlets. The Company does not believe that its involvement in the Playboy Magazine article constitutes a violation of Section 5 of the Securities Act of 1933. However, if the Company's involvement were held by a court to be in violation of the Securities Act of 1933, the Company could be required to repurchase the shares sold to purchasers in this offering included in this Registration Statement at the original purchase price, plus statutory interest from the date of purchase, for a period of one year following the date of the violation. The Company would contest vigorously any claim that a violation of the Securities Act occurred. Management currently believes there is only a remote possibility that the ultimate outcome with respect to any such claim that might be made would materially adversely affect the operating results, financial position or liquidity of the Company.

Table of Contents

Applied Semantics, Inc.

INDEX TO FINANCIAL STATEMENTS
Year ended December 31, 2002

Contents

Report of Ernst & Young LLP, Independent Registered Public Accounting Firm	F-40
Audited Financial Statements	
Balance Sheet	F-41
Statement of Operations	F-42
Statement of Redeemable Convertible Preferred Stock and Net Capital Deficiency	F-43
Statement of Cash Flows	F-44
Notes to Financial Statements	F-45

Table of Contents

REPORT OF ERNST & YOUNG LLP, INDEPENDENT REGISTERED PUBLIC ACCOUNTING FIRM

The Board of Directors and Stockholders
Applied Semantics, Inc.

We have audited the accompanying balance sheet of Applied Semantics, Inc. as of December 31, 2002 and the related statements of operations, redeemable convertible preferred stock and net capital deficiency, and cash flows for the year then ended. These financial statements are the responsibility of the Company's management. Our responsibility is to express an opinion on these financial statements based on our audits.

We conducted our audit in accordance with the standards of the Public Company Accounting Oversight Board (United States). Those standards require that we plan and perform the audit to obtain reasonable assurance about whether the financial statements are free of material misstatement. An audit includes examining, on a test basis, evidence supporting the amounts and disclosures in the financial statements. An audit also includes assessing the accounting principles used and significant estimates made by management, as well as evaluating the overall financial statement presentation. We believe that our audit provides a reasonable basis for our opinion.

In our opinion, the financial statements referred to above present fairly, in all material respects, the financial position of Applied Semantics, Inc. at December 31, 2002, and the results of its operations and its cash flows for the year then ended, in conformity with U.S. generally accepted accounting principles.

/s/ ERNST & YOUNG LLP

San Francisco, California
June 20, 2003

Applied Semantics, Inc.

BALANCE SHEET
(In thousands, except per share data)

	December 31, 2002
Assets	
Current assets:	
Cash and cash equivalents	$ 1,953
Accounts receivable, net of allowance of $11	3,659
Prepaid expenses and other current assets	74
Total current assets	5,686
Property and equipment, net	526
Other assets	6
Total assets	$ 6,218
Liabilities, redeemable convertible preferred stock, and net capital deficiency	
Current liabilities:	
Accounts payable	$ 36
Accrued revenue share	2,278
Accrued commissions	196
Other accrued expenses	145
Deferred revenue	246
Income taxes payable	25
Current portion of equipment leases	28
Total current liabilities	2,954
Noncurrent portion of equipment leases	60
Commitments	
Series B redeemable convertible preferred stock, par value $0.001 (liquidation preference of $5,453); 2,536 shares authorized; 1,976 issued and outstanding	5,394
Net capital deficiency:	
Undesignated preferred stock, par value $0.001; 6,504 authorized; none outstanding	
Series A-1 convertible preferred stock, par value $0.001; 500 shares authorized, issued, and outstanding (liquidation preference of $500)	500
Series A-2 convertible preferred stock, par value $0.001; 100 shares authorized, issued, and outstanding (liquidation preference of $125)	125
Series A-3 convertible preferred stock, par value $0.001; 360 shares authorized; 205 issued, and outstanding (liquidation preference of $410)	410
Common stock, par value $0.001; 40,000 shares authorized; 10,202 shares issued and outstanding	2,936
Deferred stock-based compensation	(413)
Accumulated deficit	(5,748)
Total net capital deficiency	(2,190)
Total liabilities, redeemable convertible preferred stock, and net capital deficiency	$ 6,218

See accompanying notes.

Applied Semantics, Inc.
STATEMENT OF OPERATIONS
(In thousands)

	Year ended December 31, 2002
Net revenues	$ 6,187
Costs and expenses:	
Cost of revenues	566
Research and development expenses	1,711
Selling and marketing expense	1,483
General and administrative expenses(1)	2,361
Total costs and expenses	6,121
Income from operations	66
Interest income	8
Interest expense and other	(5)
Income before income taxes	69
Provision for income taxes	25
Net income	$ 44

(1) Includes stock-based compensation expense of $1,029 consisting of amortization of deferred stock-based compensation and the fair value of options and warrants issued to nonemployees for services rendered.

See accompanying notes.

F-42

Applied Semantics, Inc.
STATEMENT OF REDEEMABLE CONVERTIBLE PREFERRED STOCK AND NET CAPITAL DEFICIENCY
(In thousands)

	Redeemable Convertible Preferred Stock Series B Shares	Amount	Series A-1 Shares	Amount	Series A-2 Shares	Amount	Series A-3 Shares	Amount	Common Stock Shares	Amount	Deferred Stock-Based Compensation	Accumulated Deficit	Net Capital Deficiency
Balance at December 31, 2001	1,976	$5,394	500	$500	100	$125	205	$410	10,202	$2,450	$(956)	$(5,792)	$(3,263)
Fair value of options granted to nonemployees	—	—	—	—	—	—	—	—	—	26	—	—	26
Deferred stock-based compensation	—	—	—	—	—	—	—	—	—	460	(460)	—	—
Amortization of deferred stock-based compensation	—	—	—	—	—	—	—	—	—	—	1,003	—	1,003
Net income and comprehensive income	—	—	—	—	—	—	—	—	—	—	—	44	44
Balance at December 31, 2002	1,976	$5,394	500	$500	100	$125	205	$410	10,202	$2,936	$(413)	$(5,748)	$(2,190)

See accompanying notes.

F-43

Applied Semantics, Inc.
STATEMENT OF CASH FLOWS
(In thousands)

	Year ended December 31, 2002
Operating activities	
Net income	$ 44
Adjustments to reconcile net income to net cash provided by operating activities:	
Depreciation and amortization	496
Loss on disposal of property and equipment	5
Stock-based compensation	1,029
Changes in assets and liabilities:	
Accounts receivable	(2,694)
Prepaid expenses and other current assets	(21)
Accounts payable	12
Accrued revenue share	1,929
Other accrued expenses	224
Deferred revenue	209
Income taxes payable	25
Net cash provided by operating activities	1,258
Investing activities	
Purchases of property and equipment	(151)
Decrease in other assets	37
Net cash used in investing activities	(114)
Financing activities	
Payments of principal on equipment leases	(22)
Net cash used in financing activities	(22)
Net increase in cash and cash equivalents	1,122
Cash and cash equivalents at beginning of year	831
Cash and cash equivalents at end of year	$ 1,953
Supplemental disclosures of cash flow information	
Property and equipment acquired under capital leases	$ 108
Cash paid for interest	$ 2

See accompanying notes.

F-44

Table of Contents

Applied Semantics, Inc.

NOTES TO FINANCIAL STATEMENTS
December 31, 2002

1. Summary of the Company and Significant Accounting Policies

Nature of Operations

Applied Semantics, Inc. (the "Company"), a California corporation, formerly known as Oingo, Inc., is a developer and provider of software technology solutions that enable businesses, their customers, and their employees to create value by better organizing, managing, and retrieving unstructured information in enterprise, Web-enabled, and e-commerce environments. The Company's solutions are based on its CIRCA Technology, which understands, organizes, and extracts knowledge from unstructured content in a way that mimics human thought and language, allowing for more effective information retrieval. Focusing on specific markets, the Company has introduced products through each of its business units: Naming Solutions (DomainAppraise, DomainPark, DomainSense, Error Page Assistant) and Enterprise Solutions (Auto-Categorizer, Metadata Creator, and Page Summarizer).

Use of Estimates

The preparation of financial statements in conformity with accounting principles generally accepted in the United States requires management to make estimates and assumptions that affect the amounts reported and disclosed in the financial statements and the accompanying notes. Actual results could differ materially from these estimates.

Revenue Recognition

The Company primarily derives its revenue from revenue share agreements for application services. These are three-way revenue share arrangements wherein the Company receives advertising content from one of its content providers, and then subsequently distributes that content to a third party's ("Partner") Web sites. Revenue is generated when end users click-through to the content providers' advertisements listed on the Partner's Web sites. The revenues earned by the Company from its customers under these types of arrangements are reported net of the payment due to partners. The Company's gross revenues and cost of revenues would have been $6.4 million higher for the year ended December 31, 2002, if these transactions had been accounted for on a gross basis. Amounts due to partners under these revenue share arrangements are reported as accrued revenue share in the accompanying balance sheet. The Company also has revenue from licensing agreements. Revenues from the licensing agreements are recognized on a straight-line basis over the term of the related contracts. These amounts, however, have not been a significant revenue stream to date. Any set-up and support fees are also recognized on a straight-line basis over the service period.

Deferred revenue is recorded when payments are received in advance of the Company's performance in the underlying agreement.

Cost of Revenues

Cost of revenues consists primarily of the expenses associated with the operation of the Company's server networks, including depreciation of hardware, amortization of capitalized computer software for internal use, datacenter expenses, and royalties related to a patent license agreement.

Cash and Cash Equivalents

Cash and cash equivalents include all highly liquid investments having an original maturity of three months or less.

Applied Semantics, Inc.

NOTES TO FINANCIAL STATEMENTS—(Continued)
December 31, 2002

Certain Risks and Concentrations

Certain financial instruments potentially subject the Company to concentrations of credit risk. These financial instruments consist primarily of cash and cash equivalents and accounts receivable. The Company places its cash and cash equivalents with high-credit quality financial institutions and has not experienced losses with respect to these items. Cash equivalents consist of cash on deposit with a bank and money market deposits. As of December 31, 2002, two customers represented approximately 64% and 19% of accounts receivable. For the year ended December 31, 2002, two customers represented approximately 53% and 16% of total revenues. The Company regularly evaluates its customers' ability to satisfy credit obligations and maintains an allowance for potential credit losses, when deemed necessary. Credit and losses incurred to date have not been significant.

Property and Equipment

Property and equipment are stated at cost. Depreciation is computed using the straight-line method over the estimated useful lives of the related assets, which range from three to seven years. Leasehold improvements are amortized on a straight-line basis over the shorter of the lease term or estimated useful life of the asset. Equipment under capital leases is amortized over the shorter of the estimated useful life or the related lease term.

Long-Lived Assets

The Company assesses the impairment of long-lived assets whenever events or changes in circumstances indicate that the carrying amount of an asset may not be recoverable. An impairment loss would be recognized when estimated future cash flows expected to result from the use of the asset and its eventual disposition are less than its carrying amount.

Fair Value of Financial Instruments

The carrying amounts of the Company's financial instruments, including cash and cash equivalents, accounts receivable, accounts payable, and accrued liabilities approximate fair value because of their short maturities. The carrying amounts of the Company's equipment leases approximate fair value of these obligations based upon management's best estimates of interest rates that would be available for similar debt obligations at December 31, 2002.

Income Taxes

The Company recognizes income taxes under the liability method. Deferred income taxes are recognized for differences between the financial statements and tax bases of assets and liabilities at enacted statutory tax rates in effect for the years in which the differences are expected to reverse. In addition, valuation allowances are established when necessary to reduce deferred taxes to the amounts expected to be realized.

Stock-Based Compensation

As permitted by the Financial Accounting Standards Board ("FASB") Statement of Financial Accounting Standards No. 123, *Accounting for Stock-Based Compensation* ("FAS 123"), as amended, the Company accounts for employee stock-based compensation using the intrinsic-value method in accordance with Accounting Principles Board Opinion No. 25, *Accounting for Stock Issued to Employees* ("APB 25"), and related interpretations. Under APB 25, when the exercise price of the Company's employee stock options equals the market price of the underlying stock on the date of the grant, no compensation expense is recognized. Deferred

Applied Semantics, Inc.

NOTES TO FINANCIAL STATEMENTS—(Continued)
December 31, 2002

compensation for options granted to employees is determined as the difference between the deemed fair value of the Company's stock on the date options were granted and the exercise price.

Pro forma information regarding net income (loss) has been determined as if the Company had accounted for its employee stock options under the fair-value method prescribed by FAS 123. The resulting effect on pro forma net income (loss) disclosed is not likely to be representative of the effects of income (loss) on a pro forma basis in future years due to additional grants and vesting in subsequent years.

Had compensation cost for options granted under the Company's option plan been determined based on the fair value at the grant dates for the awards under a method prescribed by FAS 123, the Company's net income (loss) would have been adjusted to the pro forma amounts below (in thousands):

	Year ended December 31, 2002
Net income, as reported	$ 44
Add: Stock-based employee compensation expense included in reported net income, net of related tax effects	1,003
Deduct: Total stock-based employee compensation expense under the fair-value-based method for all rewards, net of related tax effects	(1,120)
Net income (loss), pro forma	$ (73)

1. The fair value of each option granted was estimated on the date of grant using the minimum-value method with the following weighted-average assumptions:

	Year ended December 31, 2002
Risk-free interest rate	4.65%
Expected life (in years)	5
Dividend yield	—

The weighted-average deemed fair market value of an option granted during 2002 was $0.36.

The Company accounts for stock awards issued to nonemployees in accordance with the provisions of FAS 123 and Emerging Issues Task Force ("EITF") Issue No. 96-18, *Accounting for Equity Instruments That Are Issued to Other Than Employees for Acquiring, or in Conjunction with Selling, Goods or Services* ("EITF 96-18"). Under FAS 123 and EITF 96-18, stock awards to nonemployees are accounted for at their fair value using the Black-Scholes method. The fair value of options granted to nonemployees is periodically remeasured as the underlying options vest.

Advertising Expenses

The Company expenses advertising costs in the period in which they are incurred. For the year ended December 31, 2002, advertising expenses totaled approximately $5,000.

Comprehensive Income

Comprehensive income generally represents all changes in net capital deficiency except those resulting from investments or contributions by shareholders. To date, the Company's comprehensive income has equaled its net income.

Applied Semantics, Inc.

NOTES TO FINANCIAL STATEMENTS—(Continued)
December 31, 2002

Reclassifications

Certain prior-period amounts have been reclassified to conform to the current-period presentation.

Recent Accounting Pronouncements

In November 2002, the EITF reached a consensus on Issue 00-21, *Accounting for Multiple Element Revenue Arrangements*, addressing how to account for arrangements that involve the delivery or performance of multiple products, services, and/or rights to use assets. Revenue arrangements with multiple deliverables are divided into separate units of accounting if the deliverables in the arrangement meet the following criteria: (1) the delivered item has value to the customer on a stand-alone basis; (2) there is objective and reliable evidence of the fair value of undelivered items; and (3) delivery of any undelivered item is probable. Arrangement consideration should be allocated among the separate units of accounting based on their relative fair values, with the amount allocated to the delivered item being limited to the amount that is not contingent on the delivery of additional items or meeting other specified performance conditions. The final consensus will be applicable to agreements entered into in fiscal periods beginning after June 15, 2003, with early adoption permitted. The Company is evaluating the impact of this consensus on its financial position and operating results.

In November 2002, the FASB issued Interpretation No. 45 (or "FIN 45"), *Guarantor's Accounting and Disclosure Requirements for Guarantees, Including Indirect Guarantees of Indebtedness of Others* - an interpretation of FASB Statements No. 5, 57, and 107 and rescission of FASB Interpretation No. 34. FIN 45 elaborates on the existing disclosure requirements for most guarantees, including residual value guarantees issued in conjunction with operating lease agreements. It also clarifies that at the time a company issues a guarantee, the company must recognize an initial liability for the fair value of the obligation it assumes under that guarantee and must disclose that information in its interim and annual financial statements. The disclosure requirements are effective for interim periods or fiscal years ending after December 15, 2002, and have been adopted. The initial recognition and measurement provisions apply on a prospective basis to guarantees issued or modified after December 31, 2002. The Company is evaluating the impact of this interpretation on the Company's financial position and operating results.

In December 2002, the FASB issued FAS No. 148, *Accounting for Stock-Based Compensation — Transition and Disclosure* ("FAS 148"). This statement amends FAS 123 to provide alternative methods of transition for a voluntary change to the fair-value-based method of accounting for stock-based employee compensation. While FAS 148 does not amend FAS 123 to require companies to account for employee stock options using the fair-value method, the disclosure provisions of FAS 148 are applicable to all companies with stock-based employee compensation, regardless of whether they account for that compensation using the fair-value method of FAS 123 or the intrinsic-value method of APB 25. Since the Company accounts for stock-based compensation under APB 25 and has no current plans to switch to FAS 123, the impact of FAS 148 will be limited to the reporting of the effects on net income (loss) if the Company accounted for stock-based compensation under FAS 123. FAS 148 is effective for fiscal years ending after December 15, 2002, and the disclosure provisions have been reflected in these financial statements.

2. Commitments

Operating Lease

The Company leases its office space under an operating lease that expired in January 2003. Rent expense under this operating lease amounted to approximately $157,000 during 2002 and was recognized on a straight-line basis over the term of the lease. The Company entered into another operating lease for a new facility in December 2002 that began in February 2003 and expires in May 2006.

Applied Semantics, Inc.

NOTES TO FINANCIAL STATEMENTS—(Continued)
December 31, 2002

Capitalized Leases

The Company leases certain equipment, which is accounted for as capital leases. The gross assets under capital lease at December 31, 2002, were $114,000, with accumulated depreciation of $21,000. The Company has recorded $12,000 of depreciation expense for leased assets during 2002, which is included in the accompanying statement of operations.

Future minimum lease payments as of December 31, 2002, under capital and noncancelable operating leases are as follows (in thousands):

	Capital Leases	Operating Lease
2003	$ 38	$ 256
2004	43	281
2005	26	286
2006	—	121
Total minimum payments required	107	$ 944
Less amounts representing interest	19	
Minimum future payments of principal	88	
Current portion	28	
Noncurrent portion	$ 60	

3. Property and Equipment

Property and equipment consist of the following (in thousands):

	December 31, 2002
Computers and equipment	$ 1,049
Computer software for internal use	567
Furniture and fixtures	24
Leasehold improvements	15
	1,655
Accumulated depreciation and amortization	(1,129)
Property and equipment, net	$ 526

4. Redeemable Convertible Preferred Stock

In August 2000, the Company issued 1,976,756 shares of Series B redeemable convertible preferred stock (the "Series B shares") for $2.76 per share and net proceeds of approximately $5.4 million. The declaration of dividends rests in the sole discretion of the Company's Board of Directors. The right to dividends is not cumulative. Each Series B share has a liquidation preference of $2.76 per share. Each Series B share may be converted at any time, at the holder's option, into a share of common stock at a conversion price of $2.76 per share. Such shares shall automatically convert into common stock immediately prior to the closing of an underwritten public offering, as defined. The holders of the Series B shares are entitled to vote on all matters and

F-49

Applied Semantics, Inc.

NOTES TO FINANCIAL STATEMENTS—(Continued)
December 31, 2002

are entitled to the number of votes equal to the number of full common shares into which such holders' series of preferred shares could be converted. The Series B shares are redeemable at the option of at least 20% of the holders if a qualified initial public offering, as defined, has not occurred five years subsequent to the Series B purchase date. Each Series B share is redeemable at a redemption price equal to the original Series B issue price plus any declared and unpaid dividends.

5. Net Capital Deficiency

Convertible Preferred Stock

In May 2000, the Company issued 500,000, 100,000, and 205,000 shares of Series A-1, A-2, and A-3 convertible preferred stock, respectively (collectively, the "Series A shares") in exchange for 1,610,000 shares of common stock representing a 1-for-2 ratio. The value of each Series A share is equal to the price originally paid for the share of common stock for which it was exchanged. The price per share was $1.00, $1.25, and $2.00 for a Series A-1, A-2, and A-3 share, respectively. The declaration of dividends rests in the sole discretion of the Company's Board of Directors, and the right to dividends is not cumulative. Each Series A share has a liquidation preference equal to the original issue price per share, as defined above, plus any declared and unpaid dividends. Each Series A share may be converted at any time, at the holder's option, into a share of common stock at a conversion price equal to the original issue price of the Series A share. Such shares shall automatically convert into common stock immediately prior to the closing of a firm commitment underwritten public offering, as defined. The holders of the Series A shares are entitled to vote on all matters and are entitled to the number of votes equal to the number of full common shares into which such holders' Series of preferred shares could be converted.

Founders Stock

Concurrent with the issuance of the Series B shares, the Company entered into Stock Restriction Agreements with the two founders of the Company. Pursuant to the terms of these agreements, all 10,200,000 common shares owned by the founders of the Company became restricted and subject to a right of repurchase by the Company at a per share amount equal to the original per share issuance price applicable to each share being repurchased. Such right of repurchase shall be exercisable only during the 60-day period following the date of the shareholder's termination. This right of repurchase shall lapse, with respect to the shares, over 48 equal monthly installments measured from January 1, 1999. The Company's management determined that at December 31, 2000, the Stock Restriction Agreements were compensatory. As of the date of execution of the Stock Restriction Agreements, 6,162,500 shares of common stock with a value of $2.3 million were subject to repurchase upon termination of the shareholders. Accordingly, the Company recorded deferred stock compensation in this amount, which was amortized to stock compensation expense, as the repurchase right lapses. Amortization for the year ended December 31, 2002, resulted in stock compensation charges of $956,000. As of December 31, 2002, no shares were subject to the restriction.

Additionally, on August 7, 2000, the Company and the purchasers of the Series B shares (the "Investors") entered into Right of First Refusal and Co-sale Agreements (the "Agreements") with the two founders of the Company. The Agreements state that should the founders propose to sell to a third party any shares held by them, the Company will have the first right to purchase such shares at the price and on the terms offered by the third party. If the Company does not exercise such right within the specified period of time, then the Investors will have the right to purchase all or a portion of such shares at the same price and terms offered by the third party. Should neither the Company nor the Investors purchase all the shares through their right of first refusal, then each Investor shall have the right to participate in the proposed sale (the "Co-Sale"). The Investor may sell up to

Applied Semantics, Inc.

NOTES TO FINANCIAL STATEMENTS—(Continued)
December 31, 2002

that number of common and/or preferred shares equal to the product of the number of shares under the Co-Sale agreement and the Investor's proportionate share of equity holdings. The rights under these Agreements expire on the earlier to occur of (i) the point in time at which the Investor no longer owns shares of the Company, (ii) the closing of a public offering, as defined, (iii) a sale of a majority of the Company shares, as defined, or (iv) 15 years.

1999 Stock Plan

Under the Company's 1999 Stock Option/Stock Issuance Plan (the "1999 Stock Plan"), incentive stock options and nonqualified options, as well as other stock-based awards, may be granted to employees, directors, and consultants. All awards have a maximum term of 10 years. Options are granted at exercise prices that approximated the fair value of the common stock and generally vest over four years or as specifically defined by the stock option agreement. All options granted through December 31, 2002, are immediately exercisable into restricted shares of common stock. Any shares issued upon the exercise of options are subject to a right of repurchase by the Company at the original exercise price, which right generally lapses over a four-year period. As of December 31, 2002, none of the options granted, subject to this repurchase right, had been exercised.

The following table summarizes the activity under the Company's 1999 Stock Plan (shares in thousands):

	Shares Available for Grant	Options Outstanding Number of Shares	Weighted-Average Exercise Price
Balance at December 31, 2001	3,180	2,820	$ 0.25
Options granted	(1,423)	1,423	$ 0.38
Options canceled	597	(597)	$ 0.35
Balance at December 31, 2002	2,354	3,646	$ 0.28

The following table summarizes additional information regarding outstanding and exercisable options as of December 31, 2002 (shares in thousands):

Exercise Price	Options Outstanding and Exercisable Number Outstanding	Weighted-Average Remaining Contractual Life (In years)
$0.15	1,706	7.44
$0.38	1,940	9.08
	3,646	8.83

Stock-Based Compensation

In 2002, the Company recorded deferred stock-based compensation cost totaling $460,000 in connection with stock option grants to employees. These amounts are being amortized over the vesting period of the related options using the straight-line vesting method. The amount represents the difference between the exercise price and the reassessed value for accounting purposes of the Company's common stock on the date the stock options were granted. Amortization of deferred stock-based compensation totaled $47,000 during 2002.

Applied Semantics, Inc.

NOTES TO FINANCIAL STATEMENTS—(Continued)
December 31, 2002

Options Granted to Nonemployees

The Company has granted options to nonemployees in exchange for services. These options have a vesting period of 36 months. The Company granted options under the 1999 Stock Plan to nonemployees to purchase 60,000 shares of common stock in 2001. No options were granted to nonemployees during 2002. The Company determined the value of the options granted to nonemployees using the Black-Scholes option pricing model using the following assumptions: 131% volatility, no dividends, risk-free interest rate of 3.83%, and an expected life of 10 years. For the year ended December 31, 2002, the Company recognized approximately $26,000 of stock-based compensation expense related to the fair value of options granted to nonemployees.

Warrants

In January 2001, the Company issued fully vested nonforfeitable warrants to purchase 36,142 shares of common stock at a purchase price of $0.38 per share in connection with recruitment fees. The Company determined the value of the warrants at the date of grant using the Black-Scholes option pricing model to be approximately $11,000 using the following assumptions: 119% volatility, 0% dividend yield, risk-free interest rate of 4.88%, and a contractual life of five years. The entire fair value of the warrants was expensed as stock-based compensation within general and administrative expenses during 2001, as it related to past services rendered. As of December 31, 2002, the warrants remain outstanding and unexercised.

In 2000, in conjunction with a convertible financing arrangement, the Company issued fully vested nonforfeitable warrants to purchase 12,655 shares of Series A-3 convertible preferred stock at a purchase price of $2.00 per share. These warrants, with a contractual life of three years, remain outstanding and unexercised at December 31, 2002. The Company determined the value of the warrants using the Black-Scholes option pricing model to be approximately $18,000 using the following assumptions: 116% volatility, no dividends, risk-free interest rate of 5.13%, and an expected life of three years.

Reserved Shares

Common stock reserved for future issuance was as follows at December 31, 2002 (in thousands):

Warrants	49
1999 Stock Plan	6,000
Conversion of preferred stock	2,781
Total common stock reserved for future issuance	8,830

6. 401(k) Plan

The Company has a 401(k) Savings Plan (the "401(k) Plan") that qualifies as a deferred salary arrangement under Section 401(k) of the Internal Revenue Code. Under the 401(k) Plan, participating employees may elect to contribute up to 15% of their eligible compensation, subject to certain limitations. The Company did not make any contributions for 2002.

Table of Contents

Applied Semantics, Inc.

NOTES TO FINANCIAL STATEMENTS—(Continued)
December 31, 2002

7. Income Taxes

The provision for income taxes consisted of the following (in thousands):

	Year ended December 31, 2002
Current:	
Federal	$ —
State	25
Total	25
Deferred:	
Federal	—
State	—
Total	—
Provision for income taxes	$ 25

The reconciliation of the federal statutory income tax rate to the Company's effective income tax rate is as follows (in thousands):

	Year ended December 31, 2002
Expected provision at federal statutory rate	$ 24
State taxes, net of federal benefit	25
Stock-based compensation expense	325
Valuation allowance	(351)
Other individually immaterial items	2
Provision for income taxes	$ 25

Deferred income taxes reflect the net tax effects of temporary differences between the carrying amounts of assets and liabilities for financial reporting purposes and the amounts used for income tax purposes. Significant components of the Company's deferred tax assets and liabilities are as follows (in thousands):

	December 31, 2002
Deferred tax assets:	
Net operating loss carryforwards	$ 1,277
Research and development credit carryforwards	83
Deferred compensation	37
State taxes	9
Accruals and reserves not currently deductible	30
Depreciation	14
Total deferred tax assets	1,450
Valuation allowance	(1,450)
Net deferred tax assets	$ —

Table of Contents

Applied Semantics, Inc.
NOTES TO FINANCIAL STATEMENTS—(Continued)
December 31, 2002

The net valuation allowance decreased by approximately $503,000 during the year ended December 31, 2002.

As of December 31, 2002, the Company had federal and state net operating loss carryforwards of approximately $3.0 million and $4.1 million, respectively. The Company also had federal research and development credit carryforwards of approximately $83,000. The net operating loss and credit carryforwards will begin to expire in 2020 if not utilized.

Utilization of the net operating loss carryforwards may be subject to substantial annual limitation due to the ownership change limitations provided by the Internal Revenue Code of 1986, as amended, and similar state provisions. The annual limitation may result in the expiration of net operating losses before utilization.

8. Subsequent Event

In April 2003, all of the outstanding shares of the Company were purchased by Google Inc. ("Google"). The Company was acquired for approximately 1.2 million shares of Google common stock and $41.5 million in cash.

Table of Contents

Applied Semantics Inc.
INDEX TO CONDENSED FINANCIAL STATEMENTS
Three Months ended March 31, 2003 (Unaudited)

Balance Sheet	F-56
Statements of Operations	F-57
Statements of Cash Flows	F-58
Notes to Condensed Financial Statements	F-59

Table of Contents

Applied Semantics, Inc.
BALANCE SHEET
(In thousands, except per share data)

	As of March 31, 2003
	(unaudited)
Assets	
Current assets:	
Cash and cash equivalents	$ 1,861
Accounts receivable, net of allowance of $11	2,933
Prepaid expenses and other current assets	72
Total current assets	4,866
Property and equipment, net	517
Other assets	23
Total assets	$ 5,406
Liabilities, redeemable convertible preferred stock, and net capital deficiency	
Current liabilities:	
Accounts payable	$ 804
Accrued revenue share	82
Accrued commissions	107
Other accrued expenses	206
Deferred revenue	178
Income taxes payable	157
Current portion of equipment leases	34
Total current liabilities	1,568
Noncurrent portion of equipment leases	92
Commitments	
Series B redeemable convertible preferred stock, par value $0.001 (liquidation preference of $5,453); 2,536 shares authorized; 1,976 issued and outstanding	5,394
Net capital deficiency:	
Undesignated preferred stock, par value $0.001; 6,504 authorized; none outstanding	
Series A-1 convertible preferred stock, par value $0.001; 500 shares authorized, issued, and outstanding (liquidation preference of $500)	500
Series A-2 convertible preferred stock, par value $0.001; 100 shares authorized, issued, and outstanding (liquidation preference of $125)	125
Series A-3 convertible preferred stock, par value $0.001; 360 shares authorized; 205 issued, and outstanding (liquidation preference of $410)	410
Common stock, par value $0.001; 40,000 shares authorized; 10,202 shares issued and outstanding	2,945
Deferred stock-based compensation	(384)
Accumulated deficit	(5,244)
Total net capital deficiency	(1,648)
Total liabilities, redeemable convertible preferred stock, and net capital deficiency	$ 5,406

See accompanying notes.

Applied Semantics, Inc.

STATEMENTS OF OPERATIONS
(In thousands)

	Three months ended March 31, 2002	Three months ended March 31, 2003
	(unaudited)	
Net revenues	$ 818	$ 2,228
Costs and expenses:		
Cost of revenues	130	180
Research and development expenses	423	419
Selling and marketing expense	300	426
General and administrative expenses(1)	454	533
Total costs and expenses	1,307	1,558
Income (loss) from operations	(489)	670
Interest income	2	3
Interest expense and other	—	(12)
Income (loss) before income taxes	(487)	661
Provision for income taxes	—	157
Net income (loss)	$ (487)	$ 504

(1) Includes stock-based compensation expense of $239 and $29, consisting of amortization of deferred stock-based compensation and the fair value of options and warrants issued to nonemployees for services rendered.

See accompanying notes.

F-57

Table of Contents

Applied Semantics, Inc.

STATEMENTS OF CASH FLOWS
(In thousands)

	Three months ended	
	March 31, 2002	March 31, 2003
	(unaudited)	
Operating Activities		
Net income (loss)	$ (487)	$ 504
Adjustments to reconcile net income (loss) to net cash provided by (used in) operating activities:		
Depreciation and amortization	120	129
Loss on disposal of property and equipment		12
Stock-based compensation	239	29
Changes in assets and liabilities:		
Accounts receivable	(292)	726
Prepaid expenses and other current assets	(5)	2
Accounts payable	(221)	768
Accrued revenue share	199	(2,196)
Other accrued expenses	11	(27)
Deferred revenue	159	(68)
Income taxes payable	—	132
Net cash provided by (used in) operating activities	(277)	11
Investing activities		
Purchases of property and equipment	(46)	(132)
Decrease in other assets	—	(17)
Net cash used in investing activities	(46)	(149)
Financing activities		
Payments of principal on equipment leases	(1)	(9)
Financing of equipment under capital lease	23	47
Proceeds from exercises of stock options	—	8
Net cash provided by financing activities	22	46
Net decrease in cash and cash equivalents	(301)	(92)
Cash and cash equivalents at beginning of period	832	1,953
Cash and cash equivalents at end of period	$ 531	$ 1,861

See accompanying notes.

F-58

Applied Semantics, Inc.

NOTES TO CONDENSED FINANCIAL STATEMENTS
(Unaudited)

NOTE 1. The Company and Basis of Presentation

Applied Semantics, Inc. (the "Company"), a California corporation, formerly known as Oingo, Inc., is a developer and provider of software technology solutions that enable businesses, their customers, and their employees to create value by better organizing, managing, and retrieving unstructured information in enterprise, Web-enabled, and e-commerce environments. The Company's solutions are based on its CIRCA Technology, which understands, organizes, and extracts knowledge from unstructured content in a way that mimics human thought and language, allowing for more effective information retrieval. Focusing on specific markets, the Company has introduced products through each of its business units: Naming Solutions (DomainAppraise, DomainPark, DomainSense, Error Page Assistant) and Enterprise Solutions (Auto-Categorizer, Metadata Creator, and Page Summarizer).

The preparation of financial statements in conformity with accounting principles generally accepted in the United States requires management to make estimates and assumptions that affect the amounts reported and disclosed in the financial statements and the accompanying notes. Actual results could differ materially from these estimates.

Certain information and footnote disclosures normally included in financial statements prepared in accordance with generally accepted accounting principles have been condensed or omitted. The results of operations for such periods are not necessarily indicative of the results expected for the full fiscal year or for any future period. These financial statements should be read in conjunction with our audited financial statements and notes for the year ended December 31, 2002.

NOTE 2. Commitments

Operating Leases

The Company leases its office lease under an operating lease that expired in January 2003. The Company entered into another operating lease for a new facility in December 2002 that began in February 2003 and expires in May 2006.

Capital Leases

The Company leases certain equipment, which is accounted for as capital leases. The company entered into a capital lease in the current period. The gross assets under lease at March 31, 2003, were $159,000, with accumulated depreciation of $29,000. The Company has recorded $9,000 of depreciation expense for leased assets during the first quarter 2003, which is included in the accompanying statement of operations.

NOTE 3. Subsequent Events

In April 2003, all of the outstanding shares of the Company were purchased by Google Inc. The Company was acquired for 1,191,497 shares of Google common stock and $41.5 million in cash.

In connection with the acquisition, the vesting of stock options for certain employees of the Company was accelerated by Google. The stock-based compensation charge related to the acceleration of vesting was included in the total purchase price of the Company by Google.

Applied Semantics, Inc.

UNAUDITED PRO FORMA COMBINED CONDENSED CONSOLIDATED
STATEMENT OF INCOME

The following unaudited pro forma combined condensed consolidated statement of income has been prepared to give effect to the acquisition of Applied Semantics, Inc. (ASI) by Google Inc. (Google) using the purchase method of accounting, and the assumptions and adjustments described in the accompanying notes to the unaudited pro forma combined condensed consolidated statement of income. This unaudited pro forma statement of income was prepared as if the acquisition had been completed at January 1, 2003 by combining the respective historical statements of income for both Google and ASI.

The unaudited pro forma combined condensed consolidated statement of income is presented for illustrative purposes only and is not necessarily indicative of the results of operations that would have actually been reported had the acquisition occurred on January 1, 2003, nor are they necessarily indicative of future results of operations. The pro forma combined condensed consolidated statement of income includes pro forma adjustments. The pro forma adjustments are based upon available information and certain assumptions that we believe are reasonable under the circumstances. The acquisition was accounted for under the purchase method of accounting. The allocation of the purchase price was based upon the estimated fair value of the acquired assets and liabilities in accordance with Statement of Financial Accounting Standard (SFAS) No. 141, *Business Combinations*.

Applied Semantics, Inc.

UNAUTED PRO FORMA COMBINED CONDENSED CONSOLIDATED STATEMENT OF INCOME

Year Ended December 31, 2003
(in thousands, except per share amounts)

	Google	ASI(1)	Pro forma Adjustments		Pro forma Combined
Net revenues	$1,465,934	$2,819	$ —		$1,468,753
Costs and expenses:					
Cost of revenues	625,854	227	1,722	(b)	627,803
Research and development	91,228	526			91,754
Sales and marketing	120,328	577	628	(b)	121,533
General and administrative	56,699	1,065			57,764
Stock-based compensation(2)	229,361	29	203	(b)	229,593
Total costs and expenses	1,123,470	2,424	2,553		1,128,447
Income from operations	342,464	395	(2,553)		340,306
Interest income, expense and other, net	4,190	(9)	(141)	(a)	4,040
Income before income taxes	346,654	386	(2,694)		344,346
Provision for income taxes	241,006	154	(1,886)	(c)	239,274
Net income	$ 105,648	$ 232	$ (808)		$ 105,072
Income per share—basic	$ 0.77				$ 0.76
Income per share—diluted	$ 0.41				$ 0.41
Shares used in per share calculation—basic	137,697				138,153
Shares used in per share calculation—diluted	256,638				257,225

(1) The ASI statement of income data is for the period from January 1, 2003 through April 23, 2003, the date of the acquisition.

(2) Stock-based compensation, consisting of amortization of deferred stock-based compensation and the fair value of options and warrants issued to non-employees for services rendered, is allocated as follows:

	Google	ASI	Pro forma Adjustments	Pro forma Combined
Cost of revenues	$ 8,557	$ —	$ 16	$ 8,573
Research and development	138,377	—	23	138,401
Sales and marketing	44,607	—	104	44,711
General and administrative	37,820	29	60	37,908
	$ 229,361	$ 29	$ 203	$ 229,593

Pro Forma Adjustments

a) To reflect decrease in interest income resulting from cash payment of $41.5 million for the acquisition.

b) To eliminate the amortization of ASI historical deferred compensation and reflect amortization of the amortizable intangible assets and deferred compensation resulting from the acquisition. The weighted average life of amortizable intangible assets approximates 3 years and the remaining vesting period of unvested employee stock options ranges from three to 47 months.

c) To adjust the provision for taxes to reflect the impact of ASI's net income and the pro forma adjustments. The pro forma adjustment for income taxes was determined based upon the effective tax rate.

Applied Semantics, Inc.

NOTES TO UNAUDITED PRO FORMA COMBINED CONDENSED CONSOLIDATED STATEMENT OF INCOME

1. Basis of Pro Forma Presentation

The unaudited pro forma combined condensed statement of income of Google and ASI for the year ended December 31, 2003 is presented as if the transaction had been consummated on January 1, 2003. The unaudited pro forma combined condensed statement of income for the twelve months ended December 31, 2003 combines the results of operations of Google and ASI for the fiscal year ended December 31, 2003.

The total purchase price was $102.4 million. The fair value of Google stock options to be issued was determined using the Black-Scholes option-pricing model. For the unvested options assumed, the intrinsic value was recorded as unearned stock-based compensation and will be amortized as compensation expense on an accelerated basis over the related vesting periods of one to forty-seven months contingent upon each stockholder's continued employment with the Company. The total purchase price of the ASI acquisition is as follows (in thousands):

Cash consideration (including $350K of merger related costs)	$ 41,451
Fair value of Google common stock issued	47,383
Fair value of options issued to purchase Google common stock	13,603
Aggregate purchase price	$102,437

The total purchase price is allocated to ASI's net tangible and intangible assets based upon their estimated fair value at the merger date. The purchase price allocation is as follows (in thousands):

Goodwill	$ 84,192
Identified intangible assets	20,700
Deferred stock-based compensation	1,933
Net tangible assets	3,612
Deferred tax liabilities	(8,000)
Aggregate purchase price	$102,437

$84.2 million has been allocated to Goodwill. Goodwill represents the excess of the purchase price over the fair value of the net tangible and intangible assets acquired. In accordance with Statement of Financial Accounting Standards No. 142, "Goodwill and Other Intangible Asset", goodwill will not be amortized and will be tested for impairment at least annually.

Identified intangible assets acquired were valued using assistance from an appraiser. Identified intangible assets are comprised of the following (in thousands):

	Fair Value	Estimated Useful Life
Developed Technology	$16,600	3 years
Customer contracts	$ 3,700	2 years
Trademark	$ 200	3 years
Non-compete agreement	$ 200	2 years

2. Pro Forma Combined Net Income Per Share

Shares used to calculate unaudited pro forma net income per basic share were adjusted to reflect 1,825,226 shares issued in exchange for the outstanding ASI shares to Google's weighted average shares outstanding. Shares used to calculate unaudited pro forma net income per diluted share were adjusted to reflect 1,825,226 shares and 493,959 options (using the treasury stock method) issued as part of the acquisition.

APPENDIX I GOOGLE INC. FORM S-1 REGISTRATION STATEMENT

Table of Contents

Appendix A

Thanks for your interest in Google

- You should view this presentation together with the more detailed information included elsewhere in the Prospectus.

- **An investment in Google involves significant risks.** We're not just saying that. There are many risk factors listed in the prospectus. You should review them carefully before going any further.

Google

Voice: Thanks for your interest in Google. You should view this presentation together with the more detailed information included elsewhere in the prospectus. An investment in Google involves significant risks. We're not just saying that. There are many risk factors listed in the prospectus. You should review them carefully before going any further.

A-1

Table of Contents

Note from our Lawyers

The following presentation contains certain forward-looking statements regarding the Company's long term strategy and growth prospects as well as the projected growth of the Internet advertising market, drivers of the Company's business and its competitive position which are subject to risks and uncertainties.

Google

Voice: Note from our lawyers. The following presentation contains certain forward-looking statements regarding the Company's long-term strategy and growth prospects as well as the projected growth of the Internet advertising market, drivers of the Company's business and its competitive position which are subject to risks and uncertainties.

A-2

Table of Contents

> **Note from our Lawyers, Continued**
>
> These forward-looking statements are subject to a number of risks, uncertainties and assumptions, including those described in the "Risk Factors" section of our Prospectus, including but not limited to the significant competition we face in web search and keyword-targeted Internet advertising markets and from traditional media companies, our expectation that our future revenue growth rate will decline and that there will be downward pressure on our operating margin, our ability to successfully innovate and provide new products and services to our users, advertisers and Google Network members.
>
> Google

Voice: These forward-looking statements are subject to a number of risks, uncertainties and assumptions, including those described in the "Risk Factors" section of our prospectus, including but not limited to the significant competition we face in web search and keyword-targeted Internet advertising markets and from traditional media companies, our expectation that our future revenue growth rate will decline and that there will be downward pressure on our operating margin, our ability to successfully innovate and provide new products and services to our users, advertisers and Google Network members.

A-3

Table of Contents

> **Note from our Lawyers, Continued**
>
> In light of these risks, uncertainties and assumptions, the forward-looking events and circumstances in the presentation may not occur and actual results could differ materially and adversely from those anticipated or implied in the forward-looking statements.
>
> Google

Voice: In light of these risks, uncertainties and assumptions, the forward-looking events and circumstances in the presentation may not occur and actual results could differ materially and adversely from those anticipated or implied in the forward-looking statements.

A-4

APPENDIX I GOOGLE INC. FORM S–1 REGISTRATION STATEMENT

Table of Contents

Google™

Meet the Management

Google

Meet the Management

A-5

Table of Contents

Eric Schmidt
Chief Executive Officer

Google

Eric: Well, hello and welcome. My name is Eric Schmidt and I am the CEO of Google. We're delighted to have you be part of this presentation. In a few minutes, you will be hearing from Larry Page and Sergey Brin, our founders, and George Reyes, our Chief Financial Officer, on important aspects of our business.

Eric Schmidt Chief Executive Officer

A-6

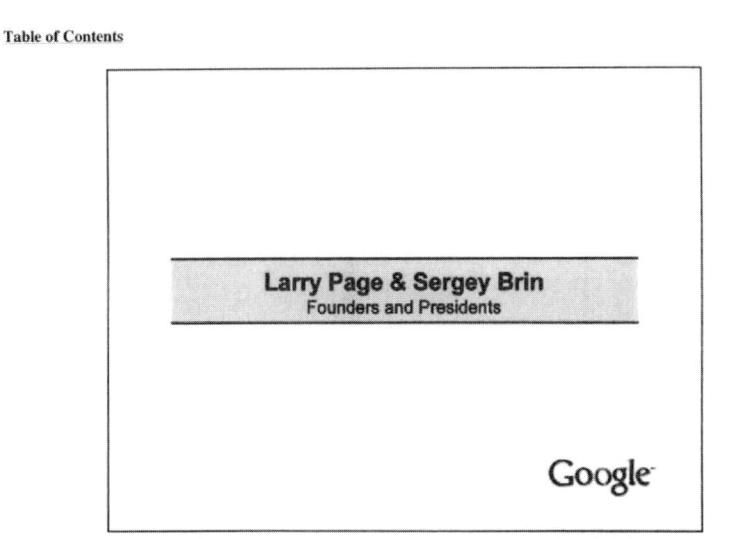

Table of Contents

> **Larry Page & Sergey Brin**
> Founders and Presidents
>
> Google

Sergey: Hello, I'm Sergey Brin. I'm one of the founders of Google and also currently the President of Technology.

Larry: I'm Larry Page, co-founder and President of Google, and I'm delighted to have this opportunity to communicate with our potential shareholders.

Larry Page & Sergey Brin Founders and Presidents

A-7

Table of Contents

> **Why Run an Auction for the Google IPO?**
>
> Google

Voice: Why run an auction for the Google IPO?

Larry: As we embarked on the process of going public we started to look at the ways in which people actually do the offering. And one thing we're interested in is making the process more democratic; making our shares available to more investors and to do that in sort of a rational way that would work. And this led us naturally to pursue an auction-based IPO which, although unusual in the United States, has been used in other countries more. And, it's something that we're hopeful that will work well and will serve both the Company and the investor, as well.

Why Run an Auction for the Google IPO?

A-8

Table of Contents

Why Have You Chosen a Dual-Class Structure?

Google

Voice: Why have you chosen a dual-class structure?

Sergey: While this kind of dual class structure is somewhat unusual in technology, it's not at all unusual in the media industry and in fact the Washington Post and The New York Times; their parent companies both have such dual class structures. Also, there are other prestigious companies in other spaces, such as Berkshire-Hathaway, that also have this structure. The reason that companies put in place these kinds of dual class structures is to preserve their core values, their editorial integrity, any kind of corporate culture they want to preserve for the long term and want to insulate against short term market forces which may sway them one way or the other. And in this way, we are trying to preserve what we think is important about Google. We never want, for example, there to be a short term revenue or profit opportunity that makes us do something that we feel compromises the integrity of our website or of our company. And by having this dual class structure, we feel that it's much less likely that something like that would happen.

Table of Contents

The Company's Mission

Google

Voice: What is Google's mission?

Table of Contents

Google's Mission

To organize the world's
information and make it universally
accessible and useful

Google

Larry: Google's mission is to organize the world's information and make it universally accessible and useful. When we started Google in 1998 out of Stanford University, we searched about 30 million web pages. And at the time that was pretty competitive. That was about as big as most search engines, not quite as big as the biggest, but we soon overcame those. Now we're searching many billions of web pages, so over a hundred times bigger, and Google works well. You can find a lot of things you're interested in using Google, but we hope to make it much, much better over time, and to really understand the query that you type, to really understand all the information that's available, and while there's a lot of information on the web, not all the information in the world is currently on the web, and so making more information available, understanding it better, understanding what you want better, are all important goals for us, and things that we think we can make a lot of progress on using technology and things that will really matter to people. You'll have an easier time finding the information you're interested in. There might be important medical or financial decisions or other things that you do.

Googles Mission To organize the worldsinformation and make it universallyaccessible and useful

Table of Contents

> **Google's Mission**
>
> What is the Company trying to accomplish?
>
> Google

Voice: We've heard from Larry now. How would you characterize Google's mission? What is the Company trying to accomplish?

Sergey: I think today the technology world, and Google as a part of it, stands on the place of great opportunity. I think the Internet is just the beginning of the kinds of ways that we can use technologies to affect peoples' everyday lives. And we want to encourage people at Google to really look at problems that really matter. Google, I think, really matters today because information really matters to people. Sometimes people have something related to their health or something related to their family, their career, their education. These are the kinds of information people search for on Google and it can affect them. We want to make sure that the problems we focus on and the products we develop or products that we try to develop will always have a large effect on a large number of people and will ultimately, leave a lasting legacy for the products we've developed.

Table of Contents

> Google's Mission
>
> What are some of the implications of that mission and those goals?
>
> How do they affect how you run the business?
>
> Google

Voice: What are some of the implications of that mission and those goals? How do they affect how you run the business?

Larry: With Google's long term focus, we do expect that we're going to take on a number of projects which, while we hope succeed, some of them will not, and they'll use up some short term capital. So as investors I think that you should request of us that we take that long term view, that we're willing to make investments and we might have a little bit more fluctuation in our results than other companies. But we actually believe that's the right way to optimize for the long term, and we'll have the fortitude to do that and we do request that of our investors as well.

Google's Mission What are some of the implications of that mission and those goals? How do they affect how you run the business?

Table of Contents

Google and the Community

Google

Voice: You've talked about loftier goals for the Company. Could you talk more specifically about how you aim to have an even broader impact?

Sergey: I believe that a successful corporation has a responsibility that's greater than simply growing itself as large as it can be. I believe large, successful corporations, have a number of resources and have an obligation to apply some of those resources to at least try to solve or ameliorate a number of the world's problems and ultimately to make the world a better place. The small way in which Google's doing this right now is through the Google Grants program, and this is a program we have that provides non-profits advertising credits in the Google ad system. We have close to 300 charities participating right now in areas ranging from the environment to poverty to education really across the board and affecting issues around the world. Now that's just really the tip of the iceberg of what I hope Google can accomplish. The next step will be the establishment of the Google Foundation. And we're working to put that together and to create a structure that we will initially endow with, in some way, with a value of roughly 1% of Google's equity, and we plan to continue to contribute to it with a small percentage of profits and also a way for our employees to spend time at the Google Foundation. I hope eventually that this can develop into a substantial organization that really produces a great outcome for the people of the world.

Table of Contents

> **The Beginning**
> Born at Stanford, raised in a garage
>
> STANFORD UNIVERSITY
> (c) Stanford University
> 1995: Google – A research project at Stanford University
>
> Google

Eric: Thank you Larry and Sergey. As many of you know, Google was founded at Stanford—literally in Larry's dorm room. Larry and Sergey went out and bought dozens of servers and terabytes of storage and used that to create a service that is now used by millions of people. The principles that they established at the very beginning drive the company today and still affect the way we make our decisions.

The BeginningBorn at Stanford, raised in a garage (c) Stanford University 1995: Google A research project at Stanford University

Table of Contents

Google products connect users, advertisers, and web sites

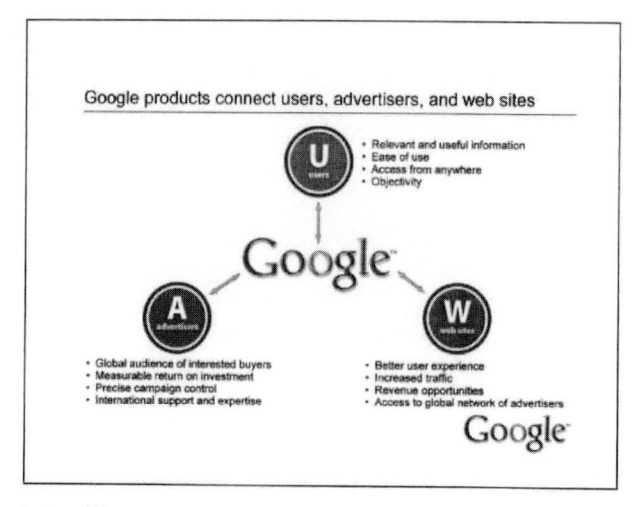

U — users
- Relevant and useful information
- Ease of use
- Access from anywhere
- Objectivity

A — advertisers
- Global audience of interested buyers
- Measurable return on investment
- Precise campaign control
- International support and expertise

W — web sites
- Better user experience
- Increased traffic
- Revenue opportunities
- Access to global network of advertisers

Google is organized around three important constituencies:

The first and by far the most important is our users. We spend hours and hours everyday trying to think of things that will make our products and services even more useful to our users. We focus on helping them more easily and efficiently solve problems, gather information and communicate more clearly.

We also serve advertisers. Through Google AdWords, advertisers are able to deliver relevant ads cost-effectively to Internet users.

The businesses these advertisers are building with Google, as a result of effective targeting, are changing the way advertising works and the way advertisers approach their markets.

For example, we don't help advertisers find 24 to 36 year old males. Instead, we help them find consumers interested in purchasing flat panel televisions.

These advertisers pay us only when a user clicks on one of their ads.

Now, the third very important group we serve includes the growing collection of independent third-party web sites or publishers.

We have not created the content on these sites. Rather, we simply provide a mechanism by which the publishers can offer their viewers access to our search technology or can display targeted advertisements from our global network of advertisers.

It is this unique mix of users, advertisers and web sites that drives our business.

Table of Contents

> **Value to Users**
> Fast, accurate and easy to use
>
> Google
>
> Web Images Groups News Froogle more >>
> [Google Search] [I'm Feeling Lucky]
> Advanced Search
> Preferences
> Language Tools
>
> Advertising Programs - Business Solutions - About Google
>
> Make Google Your Homepage!
>
> ©2004 Google - Searching 4,285,199,774 web pages
>
> Google

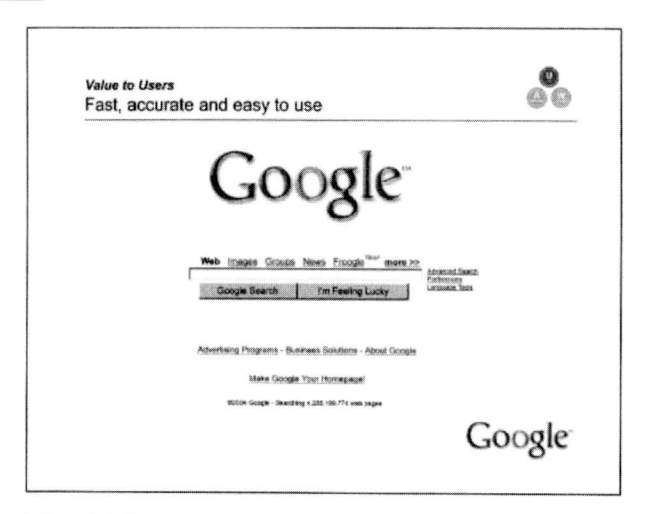

Google is organized around the simple screen that you see before you. This very simple user interface has made a big difference in the way people think about how to access information through computers.

We believe that the more powerful technology becomes, the easier it should be to use.

The service attempts to figure out exactly what you're looking for. If we don't get it right the first time, maybe we'll get it the second or third time. Our goal is to get it right every time.

Using our technology, as well as what we have learned and continue to learn about operating these very large data centers, we strive to make the search experience even better.

Value to UsersFast, accurate and easy to use

Table of Contents

Value to Users
Google connects users to many kinds of information

WebSearch	Google Image Search	Google News	Gmail
Froogle	Google Groups	Google Catalogs	Orkut
Google Local	Google Toolbar	Google Wireless	Blogger

Google

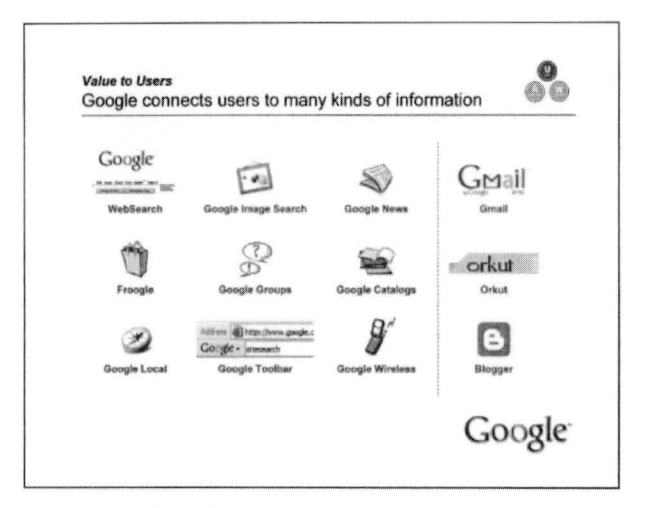

What Google does is more than just "search" in the sense of that simple interface.

As you can see, we do websearch but we also do image search. In fact, we have many new products and services in our portfolio, and we expect to continue to introduce more over time.

Each product or service reflects our effort to address a new opportunity with respect to the growth of the Internet and the availability of information around us.

One of the things that we believe at Google is that the Internet is in its infancy in terms of how information will be developed, analyzed and made useful.

In fact, the goal of the Company is to organize all of the world's information, whether it's images (of which we have 880 million searchable images today); or information on web sites, where we have the largest index; or, other content - like local information or e-mail messages, like Gmail.

We develop and improve new products with many rounds of testing. Some of them start off working better than others.

We strive to continuously improve them or replace them with something even better as we learn more, and the technology just gets better and better.

Table of Contents

Value to Users
Consistently #1 in search

World's largest online index of web sites – more than 4 billion web pages

Leading Internet Search Destinations

Total Audience Minutes per Month (MM)

Site	Minutes
Google	1,373
Yahoo! Search	721
AOL Search	685
MSN Search	438

Source: ComScore MediaMetrix, June 2004

Google

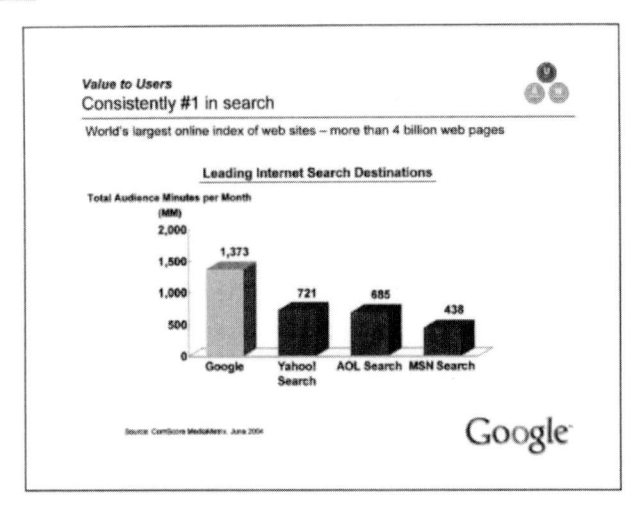

As you can see, the Company is the clear leader in search. The data you see is from Media Metrix by the way. We're very proud of these results. Still, we know that it's a very competitive market and that we have to work hard if we hope to maintain that lead, but that is our goal. We work very hard with new algorithms and new approaches to make our results better and better, and more relevant to the world.

A-19

Table of Contents

Value to Advertisers
The Internet is where the growth is

- Internet +101.9%
- Radio +16.2%
- TV +8.8%
- Newspapers (6.7)%
- Magazines (11.9)%

Notes:
1. Change in media consumption by U.S. consumers
2. Data for 2000-2007 as a % increase/(decrease) in absolute terms

Source: Veronis Suhler Stevenson Communications Industry Forecast (2003)

Google

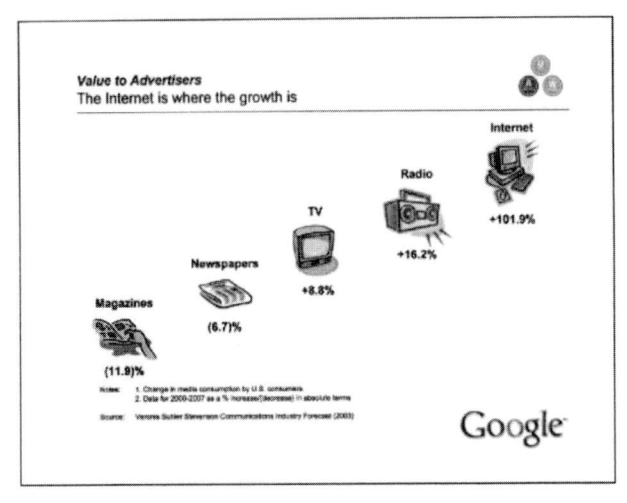

Now, why would advertisers be so interested in this area? Why would it be such a big deal?

If you take a look at this slide, you will see that the relative industry growth trends for the Internet versus other media.

As you can see, in the U.S. today, the Internet is the fastest growing medium for advertisers. This data shows a 102% projected growth rate between 2000 and 2007 in consumer usage of the Internet compared with single digit growth or declines in most media types. Not surprisingly, in addition to Google, there are a number of other companies that recognize that this is a big opportunity for advertisers.

Now let me explain to you a little bit about how our advertising actually works.

A-20

Table of Contents

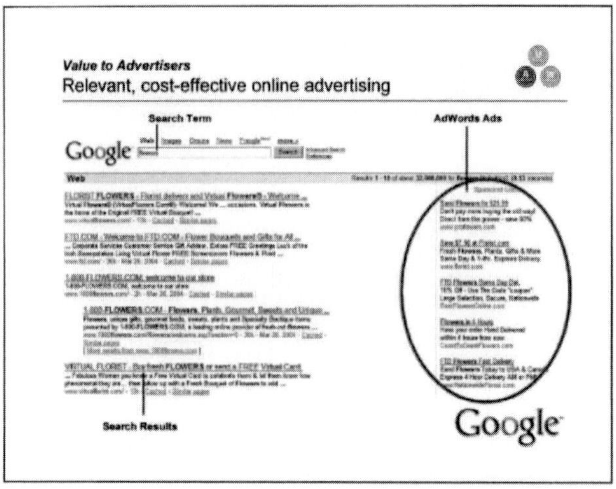

Here is the typical Google search results page. You can see that this relevant and cost-effective online advertising makes a difference. On the left, you see the results of a search. On the right, you can see the targeted and associated ads.

Now, unlike the earlier Internet advertising efforts, we didn't just show any ad along with the search. We used special technology invented by Google, to take a search term and figure out which ads were most likely to be relevant. Whereas people tend to ignore untargeted ads, we found that people actually like these ads because they provide additional, relevant information.

In addition to providing general information about a search topic, our ads also display information on how to learn more about or purchase the product. This extra information works well for both the user and the advertiser. That's really the secret of why the model has worked so well for us. We found a way to make advertising useful, not annoying.

Now, how do we choose which ads to run where? Well, we run auctions to gauge how interested each advertiser is in each search term. Advertisers bid for keywords and then we determine the order of the ads on the right based on the advertisers' willingness to pay and users' demonstrated interest in clicking on those ads.

Now, we're very careful at Google to maintain a separation between the left and the right, of course. On the left, nothing involving money or Google's policies or outside pressure influences those rankings. Rankings are done by the computers based on what the world thinks is most relevant. On the right – or on the advertising side – the answers are very much influenced by how much the advertisers are willing to pay.

That separation is not very different from what you'd see say in a newspaper where the writers write and submit their stories, but the advertisers can advertise right next to that content and the newspapers get paid for it. It's the same division, but now it's much more targeted on the Internet.

That's how our business works on Google and the other sites that we control.

However, we also have other businesses.

Value to AdvertisersRelevant, cost-effective online advertising Search Term AdWords Ads Search Results

Table of Contents

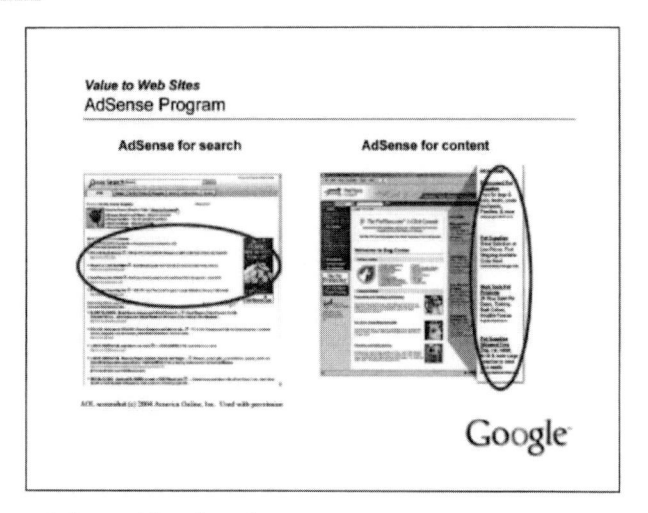

Value to Web Sites
AdSense Program

AdSense for search

AdSense for content

Google

We also offer a service known as AdSense for search.

AdSense makes targeted advertising available not just to Google, but also to other important companies like AOL and Ask Jeeves, and hundreds of other partners.

This Google network of AdSense partners is an important part of our business success as it helps us to help our advertisers reach an ever wider audience.

Yet another option we offer the members of the Google network is a service called AdSense for content, which you see pictured on the right.

With this product, we try to provide financial incentives to make it easier for people to publish content. It's not free to put up just a web site and keep it up to date.

By running AdSense for Content on their sites, these publishers can use ads from the Google network of advertisers to generate revenue and offset some of their operating costs that they have.

We partner with them to run targeted ads on their sites, and thanks to our 'revenue sharing' program, both of us generate revenue in a new way.

George will talk to you more about this, but we share the revenue from these ads with the publishers.

We hope this program will enable the publishing of additional web content that would not have otherwise been available on the Internet and we're very excited about the growth there.
Value to Advertisers Relevant, cost-effective online advertising Search Term AdWords Ads Search Results

A-22

Table of Contents

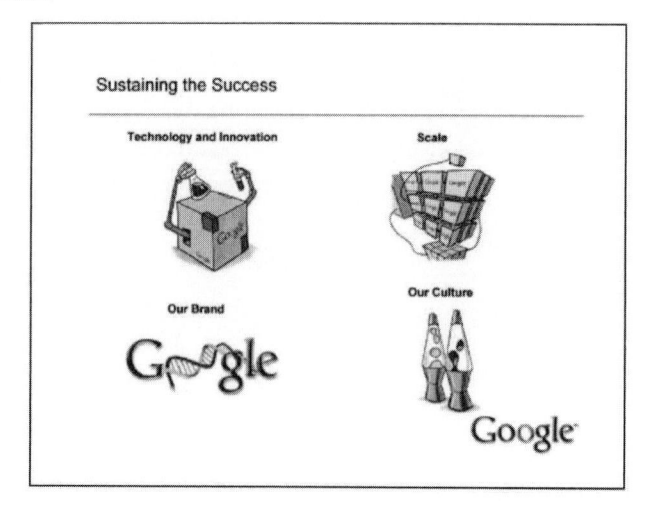

Sustaining the Success Technology and Innovation Scale Our Brand Our Culture

Table of Contents

So, how does Google do it and, more importantly for investors, how will Google sustain its edge?

We rely on four important elements of the business to keep us ahead.

For starters, this company is first and foremost a technology company. We're organized around the inventions and capabilities of these new platforms that are becoming available by virtue of inexpensive personal computers, new software technologies, new algorithms, new approaches to understanding information. Our technology is our first proprietary competitive advantage.

Second is how we have learned to use that technology. This is a very large operation. We have not only invested in the technology, but we've also learned how to make these technologies scale. As you have seen elsewhere in the prospectus, we spend a tremendous amount of money on hardware that goes into the data centers where we run our business. Coordinating the machines, in multiple locations, to run our many ad auctions for many advertisers while constantly answering search queries is very much a non-trivial exercise. In fact, we believe that the technology required is one of our most important proprietary advantages.

Third is our brand. We are so proud to have been named "Brand of the Year" two years running by Interbrand and we work very hard to make sure that the name Google is well-known and well thought of around the world.

Fourth, and truly important, is our culture. We want the very best people to want to work here. We offer them benefits from meals to on-site health care and laundry facilities to let them know how much we value their contributions and to keep them, frankly, from ever leaving the office. Our people are definitely one of our most important advantages and we rely on them to help us stay ahead of the pack.

Now as healthy as our business is today and as many advantages as we have, we believe it is important to you, the potential investor, to understand the significant risks we face as we work to grow our Company. I don't have time to go through all of them here, but I strongly, strongly recommend that you read the risk factors section in this prospectus to get a full understanding of the challenges that lie ahead.

I want to make sure that you fully understand the risks of your investment before you make a decision to bid on Google shares, so please, please review them carefully.

And with that, I would like to turn the presentation over to our, on our financial performance, by introducing you to our Chief Financial Officer, George Reyes.

Table of Contents

> **George Reyes**
> Chief Financial Officer
>
> Google

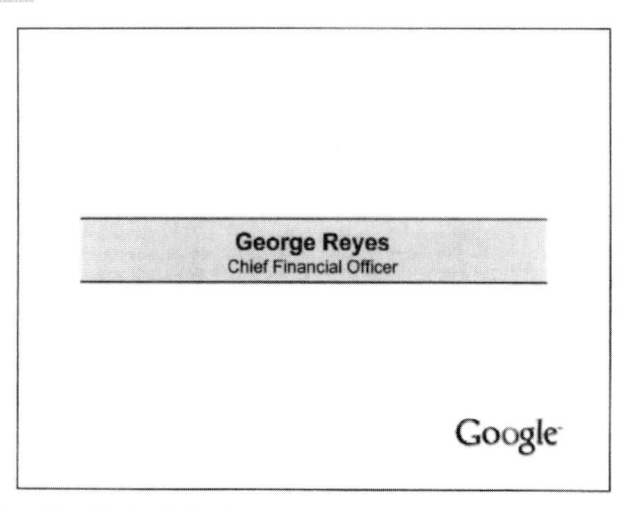

George: Thank you Eric and thanks to all of you for joining us today. I would like to take the next few minutes to talk to you about our business. Specifically, I want to address three topics with you: how Google makes money, how Google invests or spends the money it makes, and finally, I'd like to discuss our auction process with you. Hopefully, much of what you will hear today will be a refresher based upon what you have already read in the rest of our prospectus. If not, I encourage you to read this very important document. So, how does Google make money?

George Reyes Chief Financial Officer

A-25

Table of Contents

> **Value to Advertisers**
> Relevant, cost-effective online advertising
>
> [Google search results page showing Search Term, Search Results on the left, and AdWords Ads circled on the right]
>
> Google

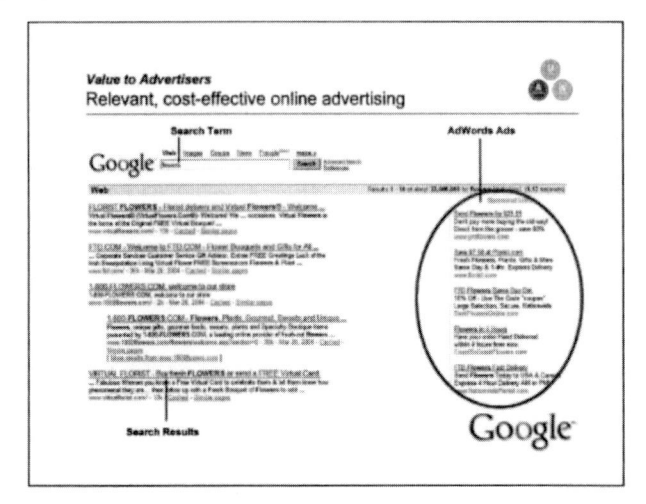

What we see on this slide is a Google.com search results page. As users seek answers, their search queries return not only relevant search results but highly relevant and targeted ads as well. The search results appear on the left-hand side of the page. The highly-targeted and relevant ads appear on the right-hand side of the page. We make money each time a user clicks on an ad. Through the first half of 2004, Google.com represented roughly 48% of our total revenues. Now let's look at how we make money for our network advertising members.

Value to AdvertisersRelevant, cost-effective online advertising Search Term AdWords Ads Search Results

A-26

Table of Contents

Value to Web Sites
AdSense Program

AdSense for search | AdSense for content

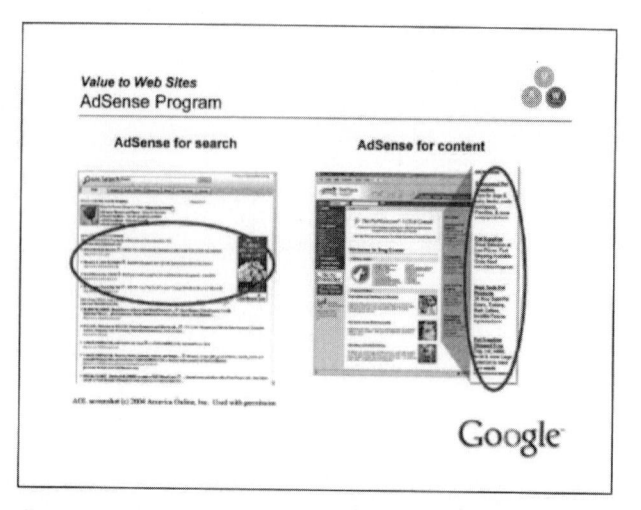

We make money for our network advertising members in two ways: first, through our AdSense for search program, second, through our AdSense for content program. Let's start first with AdSense for search. With our AdSense for search program, we are showing targeted and very relevant ads from our advertisers just below the search results of our network advertising member, in this case AOL. Each time a user clicks on an ad, we get paid and we share the majority of that revenue with our advertising network member. Let's now look at AdSense for content. As you can see in this example, a user is reading an article on a website, in this case, PetPlace.com. AdSense for content focuses on serving targeted and relevant ads based upon the content that the user is reading. Similar to AdSense for search, we get paid each time a user clicks on an ad, and we share the majority of that revenue with our advertising network member. Our AdSense program has become our largest source of revenue, generating about 50% of our revenues through the first half of 2004, up from 24% in 2002. Let's now look at how these advertising programs have driven our overall revenue growth.

Value to Web Sites AdSense Program AdSense for search AdSense for content

A-27

Table of Contents

Strong Revenue Growth

Revenues ($MM)
- 2001: $86
- 2002: $440
- 2003: $1,466
- 2004 1H: $1,352

(International / Domestic)

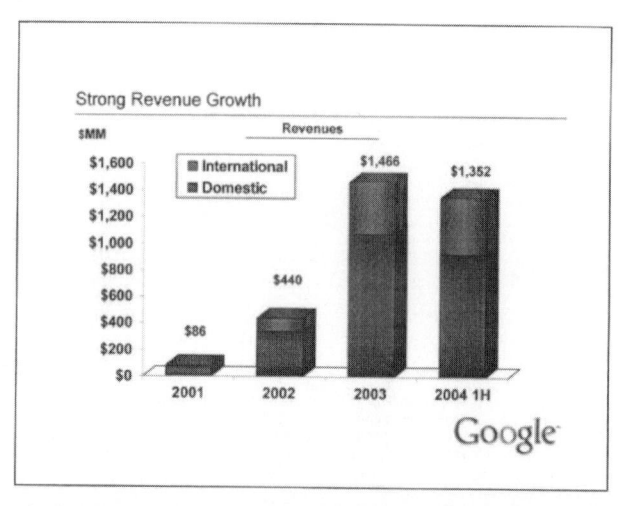

As you can see from this slide, Google has grown its revenue rapidly since 2001. The revenue growth has been primarily driven by Google.com and our AdSense business. Additionally, our international revenues have increased from 18% of revenue in 2001 to 31% of revenue through the first half of 2004. So, that is where the money comes from. Let's now talk about how we invest or spend it. I'd like to spend a few moments talking about Google's cost structure.

Strong Revenue Growth Revenues Domestic International 2001 $86, 2002 $440, 2003 $1,466, 2004 1H $1,352

A-28

Table of Contents

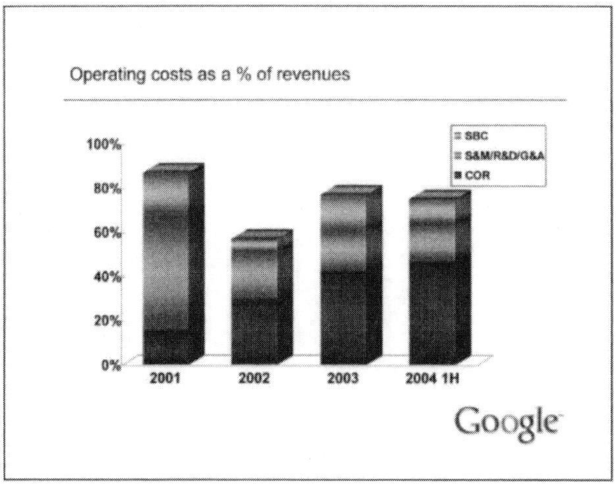
Operating costs as a % of revenues
100%
80%
60%
40%
20%
0%
SBC
S&M/R&D/G&A
COR
2001
2002
2003
2004 1H
Google

What we see on this slide is Google's cost structure: cost of revenues, operating expenses and stock-based compensation. Let's start with cost of revenue, in blue. The largest components of our cost of revenue are traffic acquisitions costs, followed by operating expenses, in yellow, which really comprise the sales and marketing, R&D and G&A functions of the company. And lastly, stock-based compensation expense shown in grey, which represents a non-cash charge that reflects the difference between the exercise prices of the options granted to employees and the reassessed values of the underlying shares on the dates they were granted. The reassessed values of the shares were determined based on a number of factors, including input from advisors, our historical and forecasted operating results and cash flows, and comparisons to publicly held companies in the internet sector. To give you some context on the size of this charge, stock-based compensation increased from $22 million in 2002 to $229 million in 2003 and to $151 million in the first half of 2004. In addition to all of the expenses shown on this chart, we also pay a lot of income taxes due to our high levels of profitability and the fact that stock-based compensation is not deductible for tax purposes. Now, let's look at the growth in our net income.

Operating costs as a % of revenues

Table of Contents

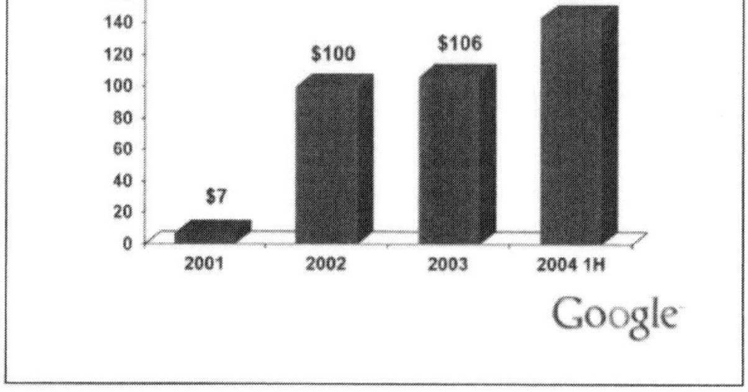
Strong Profitability
Attractive business model with significant financial scale
Net Income
$MM
160
140
120
100
80
60
40
20
0
$7
$100
$106
$143
2001
2002
2003
2004 1H
Google

As you can see from this chart, we have also been growing our net income each year. The apparent slowing in net income growth between 2002 and 2003 is caused by a $208 million increase in stock-based compensation, year over year, a non-cash charge. Similarly, the growth in net income for the first half of 2004 was reduced by $151 million for stock-based compensation charges. Before we wrap up, I would like to say a few words about our auction process.

Strong ProfitabilityAttractive business model with significant financial scale Net Income

Table of Contents

The auction process

- You will need an account with one of our underwriters in order to participate
- If you bid, you will be asked to specify both the number of shares and the price per share you are willing to pay
- You should read the sections in the prospectus titled "Auction Process" and "How to Participate in the Auction for our IPO" to understand how our auction will work.
- You should also understand that stocks can be volatile and Google's stock could go down after the IPO.

Google

First, you need an account with one of our underwriters. If you do bid, you will be asked to specify both the number of shares and the price per share you are willing to pay. You should read the sections in the prospectus linked to "Auction Process" and "How to Participate in our IPO" to understand how our auction will work. You should also understand that stocks can be volatile and Google's stock could go down after the IPO. I hope this discussion has helped you to better understand our financial results. Now, I'd like to turn it back to Eric.

A-31

Table of Contents

Google = mc²

Google Inc.

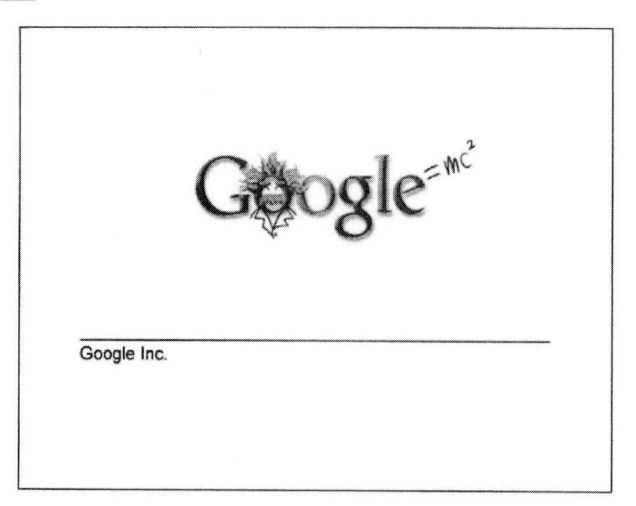

So, thank you very much George and to all of you who have spent some time getting to know our business better.

Just to summarize: our **fundamental goal** is to connect people to relevant information and conversely to connect that relevant information to the people who need it.

We believe that helping businesses grow through these connections, and making this all work seamlessly will make the world very much a better place.

And we love building the technology that capitalizes on the tremendous opportunity opened up to us by the Internet.

Thank you very, very much.

Google Inc.

A-32

Table of Contents

Appendix B

Please see *"Risk Factors—If our involvement in a September 2004 magazine article about Google were held to be in violation of the Securities Act of 1933, we could be required to repurchase securities sold in this offering. You should rely only on statements made in this prospectus in determining whether to purchase our shares"* for certain information in the following article that has been modified or updated.

PLAYBOY INTERVIEW: GOOGLE GUYS

A candid conversation with America's newest billionaires about their oddball company, how they tamed the web and why their motto is "Don't be evil"

Just five years ago a googol was an obscure, unimaginable concept: the number one followed by 100 zeros. Now respelled and capitalized, Google is an essential part of online life. From American cities to remote Chinese villages, more than 65 million people use the Internet search engine each day. It helps them find everything from the arcane to the essential, and Google has become a verb, as in, "I Googled your name on the Internet and, uh, no thanks, I'm not interested in going out Friday night."

In addition to being the gold standard of Internet search engines, Google is setting a new example for business. It's difficult to imagine Enron or WorldCom with a creed similar to Google's: "Don't be evil," a motto the company claims to take seriously.

This maxim was perhaps most apparent in May when the company announced it was going public. Google founders Sergey Brin and Larry Page explained their lofty ambitions. "Searching and organizing all the world's information is an unusually important task that should be carried out by a company that is trustworthy and interested in the public good," they wrote in an unprecedented letter to Wall Street. With the release of the letter, Newsweek reported, "The century's most anticipated IPO was on, and the document, revealing the search giant's financial details, business strategy and risk factors, instantly eclipsed Bob Woodward's Iraq book as the most talked about tome in the nation."

Page, 31, is the son of Carl Page, a pioneer in computer science and artificial intelligence at the University of Michigan. Larry was surrounded by computers when he was growing up and once built a programmable ink-jet printer out of Legos. Reticent but wide-eyed and reflective, he is Google's clean-cut geek in chief, the brilliant engineer and mathematician who oversees the writing of the complex algorithms and computer programs behind the search engine. His partner, Brin, 30, is a native of Moscow, where his father was a math professor. As Jews, the Brins where discriminated against and taunted when they walked down the street. "I was worried that my children would face the same discrimination if we stayed there," his father told Reuters. "Sometimes the love for one's country is not mutual." The family emigrated to the U.S. when Brin was six. A part-time trapeze artist. Brin is the company's earnest and impassioned visionary—a quieter, nerdier Steve Jobs. Early on, when Google CEO Eric Schmidt was asked how the company determines what exactly is and is not evil, he answered, "Evil is whatever Sergey says is evil."

Page and Brin met as graduate students at Stanford University. After years of analyzing the mathematics, the computer science and the psychological intricacies involved in searching for useful information on the ever-growing World Wide Web, they came up with the Google search engine in 1998. It was far superior to existing engines, and many companies, including Yahoo and MSN, licensed it. (Yahoo recently severed its ties with Google, introducing its own search engine. Bill Gates, who once admitted that "Google kicked our butts" on search-engine technology, has announced that Microsoft will launch its own search engine next year.) With its simple design and unobtrusive ads, Google has quickly become one of the most frequented websites on the Internet, and the company is one of the fastest growing in history. The financial press has estimated that after the initial public offering, Google will be valued at $30 billion, and Brin and Page, each of whom owns about 15 percent, will be worth more than $4 billion apiece.

B-1

Table of Contents

The two are unlikely billionaires. They seem uninterested in the accoutrements of wealth. Both drive Priuses, Toyota's hybrid gas-and-electric car. It is impossible to imagine them in Brioni suits. Brin often wears a T-shirt and shorts. Page usually dresses in nondescript short-sleeve collared shirts. Both rent modest apartments. Their only indulgences so far fall into the realm of technology, such as Brin's Segway Human Transporter, which he occasionally rides around the Googleplex, the company's Silicon Valley headquarters. (Page often scoots around on Rollerblades or rides a bike.) Page bought a digital communicator that employs voice-recognition technology to place phone calls. Both men are notorious workaholics, though The Wall Street Journal, which uncharacteristically did some sleuthing into their personal lives, reported that they have girlfriends. "Mr. Page has been dating an employee at Google, according to people close to the company," the Journal reported. "Mr. Brin has started going out with the sister of a Google employee."

Contributing Editor David Sheff met with the Google founders at the Googleplex. It is unlike most other offices, with free Odwalla juice, random toys, a pool table, a courtyard lined with scooters and bikes, and an on-site masseuse. In the company's airy cafeteria, the former chef to the Grateful Dead prepares lunch. Sheff arrived at Google just before the company entered the quiet period prior to its IPO, but he found Brin and Page less interested in the billions of dollars on the horizon than in the day-to-day challenge of running a hugely successful company that provides a valuable service, does good in the world and is fun to work for.

"When I arrived, Brin was indeed having fun, playing a sweaty game of volleyball in an open-air plaza," reports Sheff. "Dragged in shoeless from the court, he contemplated questions with great seriousness while occasionally stabbing at a salad. Throughout our conversation, he and Page, who wore shoes, rarely sat down. Instead they stood up, leaned on their chair backs, climbed on their chairs and wandered about the windowed conference room. It's apparently impossible to sit still when you're engaged in changing the world."

PLAYBOY: Google has emerged as one of the most watched companies in the world. Since deciding to go public, have you worried that Google could become less fun because of quarterly reports and the scrutiny of thousands of investors?

PAGE: I worry, but I've worried all along. I worried as we got bigger and there were new pressures on the company. It wasn't so long ago that we were all on one floor. Then we moved to a new, larger office building and were on two floors. We added salespeople. Each change was huge and happened over a very short period of time. I learned you have to pay a lot of attention to any company that's changing rapidly. When we had about 50 people, we initiated weekly TGIF meetings on Friday afternoons so everyone would know what had happened during the week. But those meetings have broken down because we now have too many people, about 1,000, including many who work in different time zones. We try to have a summation of the week's work via e-mail, but it's not the same. When you grow, you continually have to invent new processes. We've done a pretty good job keeping up, but it's an ongoing challenge.

PLAYBOY: It's one thing to have volleyball games, refrigerators full of free juice and massages when you're a start-up, but can you maintain such a laid-back culture as a public company?

PAGE: We think a lot about how to maintain our culture and the fun elements. I don't know if other companies care as much about those things as we do. We spent a lot of time getting our offices right. We think it's important to have a high density of people. People are packed together everywhere. We all share offices. We like this set of buildings because it's more like a densely packed university campus than a typical suburban office park.

PLAYBOY: We read that you originally wanted a building without telephones.

BRIN: That was Larry. He was making the argument that you call most people on their cell phones because you're not sure if they're at their desk. Why bother having land lines? We decided to have them, though, because the quality is better. It's nice to have them.

B-2

Table of Contents

PLAYBOY: Do you subscribe to any particular management theories, or do you make them up as you go?

PAGE: We try to use elements from different companies, but a lot is seat-of-your-pants stuff.

PLAYBOY: How will you avoid the mistakes of many other dot-coms? After their IPOs, employees became more focused on the stock price than on their jobs. Many of those companies are gone.

PAGE: Those companies are not good analogues for Google.

PLAYBOY: But like you, they were Internet-focused technology companies. What's the difference?

PAGE: A lot of those companies were around for less than a year or two before they went public. We've been around for five. We're at a pretty significant scale, too. We have more than 150,000 advertisers and a lot of salespeople. Millions of people use Google. It's a completely different thing.

PLAYBOY: And you're profitable.

PAGE: That's a difference, yes. The dot-com period was difficult for us. We were dismayed in that climate.

PLAYBOY: What dismayed you?

PAGE: We knew a lot of things people were doing weren't sustainable, and that made it hard for us to operate. We couldn't get good people for reasonable prices. We couldn't get office space. It was a hypercompetitive time. We had the opportunity to invest in 100 or more companies and didn't invest in any of them. I guess we lost a lot of money in the short term—but not in the long term.

PLAYBOY: Companies tried to buy you, too. Did you ever consider selling Google?

PAGE: No. We think we're an important company, and we're dedicated to doing this over the long term. We like being independent.

PLAYBOY: Is your company motto really "Don't be evil"?

BRIN: Yes, it's real.

PLAYBOY: Is it a written code?

BRIN: Yes. We have other rules, too.

PAGE: We allow dogs, for example.

BRIN: As for "Don't be evil," we have tried to define precisely what it means to be a force for good—always do the right, ethical thing. Ultimately, "Don't be evil" seems the easiest way to summarize it.

PAGE: Apparently people like it better than "Be good."

BRIN: It's not enough not to be evil. We also actively try to be good.

PLAYBOY: Who ultimately decides what is evil? Eric Schmidt, your CEO, once said, "Evil is whatever Sergey decides is evil."

PAGE: That was not one of his best quotes, though it's memorable.

PLAYBOY: How does it work?

BRIN: We deal with all varieties of information. Somebody's always upset no matter what we do. We have to make a decision; otherwise there's a never-ending debate. Some issues are crystal clear. When they're less

B-3

Table of Contents

clear and opinions differ, sometimes we have to break a tie. For example, we don't accept ads for hard liquor, but we accept ads for wine. It's just a personal preference. We don't allow gun ads, and the gun lobby got upset about that. We don't try to put our sense of ethics into the search results, but we do when it comes to advertising.

PLAYBOY: Who decides that wine is all right but hard liquor isn't?

BRIN: We collect input. I think we do a good job of deciding. As I said, we believe that "Don't be evil" is only half of it. There's a "Be good" rule also.

PLAYBOY: How are you good?

BRIN: We have Google grants that give advertising to nonprofit organizations. A couple hundred nonprofits—ranging from the environment to health to education to preventing various kinds of abuse by governments—receive free advertising on Google.

PAGE: We're also working to set up a Google foundation that will have even broader initiatives. The "Be good" concept also comes up when we design our products. We want them to have positive social effects. For example, we just released Gmail, a free e-mail service. We said, "We will not hold your e-mail hostage." We will make it possible for you to get your e-mail out of Gmail if you ever want to.

BRIN: You won't have to stay with us just to keep your address.

PAGE: Which is something we view as a social good.

BRIN: Another social good is simply providing a free and powerful communication service to everyone in the world. A schoolchild in Cambodia can have a Gmail account.

PLAYBOY: But Yahoo and MSN's Hotmail already offer free e-mail accounts.

BRIN: This one has one gigabyte of storage—200 times more.

PLAYBOY: But there's a catch. You have stated that you will scan e-mail in order to target advertisements based on its content. As a *San Jose Mercury News* columnist wrote, "If Google ogles your e-mail, could Ashcroft be far behind?"

BRIN: When people first read about this feature, it sounded alarming, but it isn't. The ads correlate to the message you're reading at the time. We're not keeping your mail and mining it or anything like that. And no information whatsoever goes out.

PLAYBOY: Regardless, it's analogous to someone looking over our shoulder as we write private messages.

PAGE: You should trust whoever is handling your e-mail.

BRIN: We need to be protective of the mail and of people's privacy. If you have people's e-mail, you have to treat that very seriously. We do. Everyone who handles e-mail has that responsibility.

PLAYBOY: The Electronic Privacy Information Center equates such monitoring with a telephone operator listening to your conversations and pitching ads while you talk.

BRIN: That's what Hotmail and Yahoo do, don't forget. They have big ads that interfere with your ability to use your mail. Our ads are more discreet and off to the side. Yes, the ads are related to what you are looking at, but that can make them more useful.

PAGE: During Gmail tests, people bought lots of things using the ads.

Table of Contents

BRIN: Today I got a message from a friend saying I should prepare a toast for another friend's birthday party. Off to the side were two websites I could go to that help prepare speeches. I like to make up my own speeches, but it's a useful link if I want to take advantage of it.

PLAYBOY: Even that sounds ominous. We may not want anyone—or any machine—knowing we're giving a speech at a friend's birthday party.

BRIN: Any web mail service will scan your e-mail. It scans it in order to show it to you; it scans it for spam. All I can say is that we are very up-front about it. That's an important principle of ours.

PLAYBOY: But do you agree that it raises a privacy issue? If you scan for keywords that will trigger ads, you could easily scan for political content.

BRIN: All we're doing is showing ads. It's automated. No one is looking, so I don't think it's a privacy issue. To me, if it's a choice between big, intrusive ads and our smaller ones, it's a pretty obvious choice. I've used Gmail for a while, and I like having the ads.

PLAYBOY: Do the ads pay for the extra storage space?

BRIN: Yes. Targeted advertising is an important component. We could have had glaring videos appear before you look at every message. That could generate revenue too. Our ads aren't distracting; they're helpful.

PAGE: I find it works well. And it's an example of the way we try to do good. It's a high-quality product. I like using it. Even if it seems a little spooky at first, it's useful, and it's a good way to support a valuable service.

PLAYBOY: Did the outcry about the privacy issue surprise you?

BRIN: Yes. The Gmail thing has been a bit of a lesson.

PAGE: We learned a few things. There was a lot of debate about whether we were going to delete people's mail if they wanted it to be deleted. Obviously, you want us to have backups of your mail to protect it, but that raises privacy issues. We created a policy statement about privacy, and the attorneys probably got a little ahead of themselves. The lawyers wrote something that was not very specific. It said something like, "If you request that we delete your e-mail, it may remain on a backup system for a while." It led people to say, "Google wants to keep my deleted mail." That's not our intent at all. Since then we have added some language explaining it. We intend to try to delete it.

PLAYBOY: That's not reassuring.

PAGE: But you wouldn't want us to lose your mail, either. There's a trade-off. So yes, we learned some things. We could have done a better job on the messaging. In its earliest testing stages Gmail was available only to a small number of people. People started talking about it before they could try it. I didn't expect them to be so interested. We released the privacy policy, and they were very interested in that. It was all they had access to, so it sparked a lot of controversy. The more people tried Gmail, however, the more they understood it.

BRIN: Journalists who tried it wrote positive reviews.

PLAYBOY: With the addition of e-mail, Froogle—your new shopping site- and Google news, plus your search engine, will Google become a portal similar to Yahoo, AOL or MSN? Many Internet companies were founded as portals. It was assumed that the more services you provided, the longer people would stay on your website and the more revenue you could generate from advertising and pay services.

PAGE: We built a business on the opposite message. We want you to come to Google and quickly find what you want. Then we're happy to send you to the other sites. In fact, that's the point. The portal strategy tries to own all of the information.

Table of Contents

PLAYBOY: Portals attempt to create what they call sticky content to keep a user as long as possible.

PAGE: That's the problem. Most portals show their own content above content elsewhere on the web. We feel that's a conflict of interest, analogous to taking money for search results. Their search engine doesn't necessarily provide the best results; it provides the portal's results. Google conscientiously tries to stay away from that. We want to get you out of Google and to the right place as fast as possible. It's a very different model.

PLAYBOY: Until you launched news, Gmail, Froogle and similar services.

PAGE: These are just other technologies to help you use the web. They're an alternative, hopefully a good one. But we continue to point users to the best websites and try to do whatever is in their best interest. With news, we're not buying information and then pointing users to information we own. We collect many news sources, list them and point the user to other websites. Gmail is just a good mail program with lots of storage.

BRIN: Ironically, toward the end of the 1990s most of the portals started as search engines. Yahoo was the exception, but Excite, Infoseek, HotBot and Lycos began as search engines. They diversified and didn't take searching as seriously as they should have. Searching was viewed as just another service, one of 100 different services. With 100 services, they assumed they would be 100 times as successful. But they learned that not all services are created equal. Finding information is much more important to most people than horoscopes, stock quotes or a whole range of other things—which all have merit, but searching is substantially more important. They lost sight of that. It's why we started Google in the first place. We decided that searching is an important problem that requires serious concentration. That continues to be our focus.

PLAYBOY: What does Google do that early search engines didn't?

BRIN: Before Google, I don't think people put much effort into the ordering of results. You might get a couple thousand results for a query. We saw that a thousand results weren't necessarily as useful as 10 good ones. We developed a system that determines the best and most useful websites. We also understood that the problem of finding useful information was expanding as the web expanded. In 1993 and 1994, when Mosaic, the predecessor of Netscape, was launched, a "What's New" page listed new websites for the month and then, when more began appearing, for the week. At the time, search engineers had to deal with a relative handful of sites, first thousands and then tens of thousands. By the time we deployed our initial commercial version of Google in late 1998, we had 25 million or 30 million pages in our index. Today we have billions—more than 4 billion, in fact. That volume requires a different approach to search technology.

PLAYBOY: How do you refine the results when there are so many websites?

BRIN: We had to solve several problems. One was relevance: How do we determine if a web page relates to what you ask? Next, although many results may be relevant, which are the most relevant and the most useful? That's something we continue to work hard on. Another important consideration is that the kinds of questions people ask have changed. They have become far more challenging and complex. People's expectations have grown. They ask for unusual things that have a variety of associated linguistic challenges. We have to deal with all of those situations.

PLAYBOY: Specifically, how do you deal with them?

BRIN: It's so complex—there's not one way but many ways. We worked hard to understand the link structure of the web. It's analogous to the way people provide references to one another. If I'm looking for a doctor in the area, I might go around and ask my friends to recommend good doctors. They in turn may point me to other people who know more than they do—"This guy knows the whole field of Bay Area doctors." I would then go to that person and ask him. The same thinking applies to websites. They refer to one an other with links, a system that simulates referrals. The web is far more expansive and broad, however, so there must be refinements to the system. We have to look at who is doing the referring. It presents a new challenge: How do you decide the importance of the links on a site? We do it with mathematical formulas that go deeper and weigh many factors.

Table of Contents

PAGE: That's a small part of how we actually link pages. It's very complex.

BRIN: We have to consider many other challenges. How do you deal with different words that refer to the same concept? How do you help people find websites in languages they understand? Can we translate pages for them? Google is all about getting the right information to people quickly, easily, cheaply—and for free. We serve the world—all countries, at least 100 different languages. It's a powerful service that most people probably couldn't have dreamed of 20 years ago. It's available to the rich, the poor, street children in Cambodia, stock traders on Wall Street—basically everybody. It's very democratic.

PLAYBOY: Tim Berners-Lee, who designed the World Wide Web, worried that commercial content would prevail on the Internet, pushing aside open and free conversation and information from individuals. Does Google have a bias toward commercial websites?

BRIN: One thing that's important to us is the distinction between advertising and pure search results. We make it clear when something is paid for. Our advertising is off to the side and in a couple of slots across the top. Ads are clearly marked. There's a clear, large wall between the objective search results and the ads, which have commercial influence. Other search engines don't necessarily distinguish. Beyond ads, with other search engines, payment affects the results. We think that's a slippery slope. At Google, the search results cannot be bought or paid for.

PLAYBOY: Will that distinction be protected after the IPO? What if your shareholders push you to accept payment for better placement in search results?

BRIN: It doesn't make sense. Why don't you, as a magazine, accept payment for your articles? Why are advertisements clearly separate?

PLAYBOY: Our editorial content retains its credibility only if it isn't influenced by advertisers. If that line were unclear, our readers would rebel.

PAGE: There you go. It's no different for Google. People use Google because they trust us.

PLAYBOY: With search engines, however, the line between editorial content and advertisements may become less obvious than in magazines. As you note, some search engines do not clearly identify results that are paid for. How can users know the difference?

PAGE: It's a problem for us because some people assume we blur the distinction as well. But people are smart. They can distinguish pure results. We will continue to make it clear.

BRIN: It's an important issue, something people should be concerned about. We're dedicated to separating advertising and search results, and we want people to understand the distinction. The more awareness among the entire world's people about these questions —their ability to understand results that are tainted versus those that are not- the better. It's not enough for us to improve the search engine so it provides better results from more web pages; we must also protect it from people who attempt to manipulate the results. People try to find ways around our system, and we continue to work on the problem.

PLAYBOY: And yet an entire industry of optimizers seeks to influence Google search results. They claim they can help companies place higher in your rankings, but sometimes they resort to treachery. How do you counteract them?

BRIN: You have to distinguish among optimizers. Some do perfectly legitimate things—they're just trying to create informative sites.

PAGE: They help people find what they're looking for.

BRIN: But some people do surreptitious things They try to influence the system.

Table of Contents

PLAYBOY: What are some examples of new techniques people use to influence your search results?

BRIN: People send us web pages to review that are different from the ones they'll send to users. It's known as cloaking. They'll put stuff on their web pages that the user can't see—black-on-black text, for example. We consider that manipulative and work to combat it.

PLAYBOY: Playing cat and mouse like this, how can you be sure to stop them?

PAGE: We have a lot of people devoted to stopping them. We do a good job.

BRIN: People try new things all the time. By now, the people who succeed have to be very sophisticated. All the obvious or trivial things one might think of have been done many times, and we've dealt with them.

PAGE: It's going to get harder and harder to do these things. However, the benefits are obviously large, so some people will try to manipulate the results. Ultimately, it's not worth it. If you're spending time, trouble and money promoting your results, why not just buy advertising? We sell it, and it's effective. Use that instead. Advertising is more predictable and probably more effective.

PLAYBOY: Yet it may not carry the weight of a search that appears to be unaffected by money.

PAGE: Yes. So people will try, and we will continue to stop them. Eventually people may realize that it's more efficient just to pay to promote their things, if that's what they want to do.

BRIN: That's absolutely true, because ads on Google work. We know that when people are looking for commercial things, they use the ads. They know they're ads and they know they're just commercial, yet they use them.

PLAYBOY: How do you fight Google bombing, a tactic some people use to manipulate search results by linking words? For instance, if they have their way, the query "world's dumbest man" might lead you to the White House web page.

BRIN: That's in a different category. We call it spam but not in the sense of e-mail. People try to make political statements using search results. They want to affect the results when you search for something obscure and specific, say "French military victories." They get tons of people to link the phrase to a website that pushes their political point of view. These queries are rare. The number of people interested in French military victories is tiny. There may be no other websites dedicated to that topic, so people create a page with the idea of controlling a message.

PAGE: People do it because it's like discovering fire: "We can affect the web!" Well, you are the web, so of course you can affect it.

BRIN: Typically Google bombs don't affect people looking for information.

PAGE: They're more like entertainment.

PLAYBOY: How can you balance the more modest sites of nonprofits or consumer groups with those of enormous companies and industries? If we research a controversial topic, how can Google be certain to point us to sites that reflect both sides of an issue?

BRIN: I agree that diversity of sources is a desirable goal, and in fact the results naturally tend to be diverse. We do some simple things to increase the diversity. If you check almost any topic, you will get diverging viewpoints. Everyone on any side of an issue will typically complain, though. Environmentalists will say, "Why aren't you showing our results first?" An industrial group will say, "Why aren't you showing *our* results first?" They all want to be number one. We think it's good for us to encourage diverse viewpoints, and the search engine presents them. It happens naturally as a response to queries.

B-8

Table of Contents

PLAYBOY: But don't companies with enormous budgets have the ability to pay for deep sites with lots of links and overwhelm the opposition?

PAGE: Actually, given the factors the search engines take into consideration, opposition groups do well in search results. For example, environmental groups tend to be very active on the Internet. That's how they organize. They have good websites with a lot of activity. All of that is factored into the search results. Thus their sites will be prominent in the listings.

BRIN: Yes. On such a search, you would likely get the best environmental sites as well as the best sites representing the industry, for two sides of the issue. I'm sure there are counterexamples, and I'm sure we could do a better job.

PAGE: In general we're trying to use the web's self-organizing properties to decide which things to present. We don't want to be in the position of having to decide these things. We take the responsibility seriously. People depend on us.

PLAYBOY: Yet you've been criticized for caving to pressure from organizations that objected to some of your search results. In one famous case, the Church of Scientology pressured you to stop pointing out a website critical of it.

PAGE: That was more of a legal issue.

BRIN: The Scientologists made a copyright claim against an anti-Scientology site. It had excerpts from some of their texts. The counter-Scientology site, Xenu.net, didn't file an appeal. It sort of folded. Consequently, we were forced to omit their results, but we explain what happened on the search. If things are missing from a search, we often link to websites that explain the controversies. So now, if you do a generic search on Scientology, you get a link to a site that discusses the legal aspects of why the anti-Scientology site isn't listed. In addition, this independent site links to the anti-Scientology site. As a result, if you search for Scientology, you will be armed with anti-Scientology materials as well as pro-Scientology material.

PAGE: A Stanford University organization has volunteer lawyers posting complaints about cases like this related to web searches. We're able to link to this site. It's a nice compromise. In general, though, few things get removed in this way. It's not a practical problem.

PLAYBOY: How did you respond when the Chinese government blocked Google because your search engine pointed to sites it forbade, including Falun Gong and pro-democracy websites?

BRIN: China actually shut us down a couple of times.

PLAYBOY: Did you negotiate with the Chinese government to unblock your site?

BRIN: No. There was enough popular demand in China for our services—information, commerce and so forth—that the government re-enabled us.

PLAYBOY: Have you ever agreed to conditions set by the Chinese government?

BRIN: No, and China never demanded such things. However, other search engines have established local presences there and, as a price of doing so, offer severely restricted information. We have no sales team in China. Regardless, many Chinese Internet users rely on Google. To be fair to China, it never made any explicit demands regarding censoring material. That's not to say I'm happy about the policies of other portals that have established a presence there.

PLAYBOY: Which sites cooperate with Chinese government censors?

Table of Contents

BRIN: I've heard various things, but I don't want to spread secondhand rumors. There is a Harvard site that lists what you can and can't get from different places around the world.

PAGE: Search for "censorship" and "Berkman" and you can get the website. [Editor's note: The website is at cyber.law.harvard.edu/home.] It has some cool programs that automatically track what is and isn't available on the web.

PLAYBOY What would you do if you had to choose between compromising search results and being unavailable to millions of Chinese?

BRIN: There are difficult questions, difficult challenges. Sometimes the "Don't be evil" policy leads to many discussions about what exactly is evil. One thing we know is that people can make better decisions with better information. Google is a useful tool in people's lives. There are extreme cases, we're told, when Google has saved people's lives.

PLAYBOY: How has Google saved lives?

BRIN: When people look up information in a life-threatening situation. Someone wrote that he was having chest pains and wasn't sure of the cause. He did a Google search, decided he was having a heart attack and called the hospital. He survived and wrote to us. To help in situations like that, Google has to be quick and correct. Other people have written us with similar stories. We get postcards and pictures of them with their family. Those are extremes, but there are countless other examples. People are helped with their careers. Students are helped when they study. It's a powerful tool.

PLAYBOY: When someone is having chest pains and searches the web for information about them, for example, it's essential that the information be correct. How does Google know about the veracity of a website's information?

BRIN: Similar to other media—books, magazines, whatever—you have to use judgment.

PLAYBOY: But isn't the Net, where anyone can put up a web page, more likely to have erroneous information?

BRIN: Yes. Joe Blow can write something in a few hours, post it and it's on the Net. It could be about neuroscience, and he may know nothing about neuroscience. More typical inaccuracies in other media are from out-of-date material. In both cases, you have to apply judgment. The Internet helps because you can quickly check a number of different sources. If I were seriously interested in something important to me, I wouldn't just click on the first search result, read it and take it as God's word.

PAGE: Which is a great thing about the Internet, because you can read information from many sources and decide. Libraries might have some of the information but probably not all—and not necessarily the most up-to-date.

PLAYBOY: Librarians must hate Google. Will you put them out of business?

BRIN: Actually, more and more librarians love Google. They use it. They do an excellent job helping people find answers on the Internet in addition to using their book collections. Finding information still requires skill. It's just that you can go much further now. Google is a tool for librarians just as it's a tool for anyone who wants to use it.

PLAYBOY: Much has been made of the fact that *Google* has now become a verb. When did you begin to fathom the scale of Google's success?

PAGE: I don't remember exactly. Pretty early on I saw a newspaper story about Googling dates. People were checking out who they were dating by Googling them. I think it's a tremendous responsibility. If you think

Table of Contents

everybody is relying on us for information, you understand the responsibility. That's mostly what I feel. You have to take that very seriously.

PLAYBOY: Are you still surprised by the ways people use Google?

PAGE: We hear surprising stories all the time. The amazing thing is that we're part of people's daily lives, like brushing their teeth. It's just something they do throughout the day while working, buying things, deciding what to do after work and much more. Google has been accepted as part of people's lives. It's quite remarkable. Most people spend most of their time getting information, so maybe it's not a complete surprise that Google is successful.

PLAYBOY: Though you have cataloged 4 billion websites, there are more than 10 billion, and the number grows each day. Is it possible for Google to catch up and keep up?

PAGE: We have to. The increasing volume of information is just more opportunity to build better answers to questions. The more information you have, the better.

PLAYBOY: Yet more isn't necessarily better.

BRIN: Exactly. This is why it's a complex problem we're solving. You want access to as much as possible so you can discern what is most relevant and correct. The solution isn't to limit the information you receive. Ultimately you want to have the entire world's knowledge connected directly to your mind.

PLAYBOY: Is that what we have to look forward to?

BRIN: Well, maybe. I hope so. At least a version of that. We probably won't be looking up everything on a computer.

PLAYBOY: How will we use Google in the future?

BRIN: Probably in many new ways. We're already experimenting with some. You can call a phone number and say what you want to search for, and it will be pulled up. At this stage it's obviously just a toy, but it helps us understand how to develop future products.

PLAYBOY: Is your goal to have the entire world's knowledge connected directly to our minds?

BRIN: To get closer to that—as close as possible.

PLAYBOY: At some point doesn't the volume become overwhelming?

BRIN: Your mind is tremendously efficient at weighing an enormous amount of information. We want to make smarter search engines that do a lot of the work for us. The smarter we can make the search engine, the better. Where will it lead? Who knows? But it's credible to imagine a leap as great as that from hunting through library stacks to a Google session, when we leap from today's search engines to having the entirety of the world's information as just one of our thoughts.

Table of Contents

Google

Table of Contents

PART II

INFORMATION NOT REQUIRED IN PROSPECTUS

Item 13. Other Expenses of Issuance and Distribution.

The following table sets forth all expenses to be paid by the registrant, other than estimated underwriting discounts and commissions, in connection with this offering. All amounts shown are estimates except for the registration fee.

	Amount to be Paid
SEC registration fee	$ 505,474.87
NASD listing fee	30,500.00
Printing and engraving	200,000.00
Legal fees and expenses	2,350,000.00
Accounting fees and expenses	1,500,000.00
The Nasdaq National Market fee	150,000.00
Blue sky fees and expenses (including legal fees)	7,500.00
Transfer agent and registrar fees	15,000.00
Miscellaneous	41,525.13
Total	$4,800,000.00

Item 14. Indemnification of Officers and Directors.

Section 145 of the Delaware General Corporation Law authorizes a court to award, or a corporation's board of directors to grant, indemnity to officers, directors and other corporate agents in terms sufficiently broad to permit such indemnification under certain circumstances and subject to certain limitations.

As permitted by Section 145 of the Delaware General Corporation Law, the registrant's amended and restated certificate of incorporation includes a provision that eliminates the personal liability of its directors for monetary damages for breach of their fiduciary duty as directors.

In addition, as permitted by Section 145 of the Delaware General Corporation Law, the bylaws of the registrant provide that:

- The registrant shall indemnify its directors and officers for serving the registrant in those capacities or for serving other business enterprises at the registrant's request, to the fullest extent permitted by Delaware law, if such person acted in good faith and in a manner such person reasonably believed to be in or not opposed to the best interests of the registrant, and, with respect to any criminal proceeding, had no reasonable cause to believe such person's conduct was unlawful.

- The registrant may, in its discretion, indemnify employees and agents in those circumstances where indemnification is not required by law.

- The registrant is required to advance expenses, as incurred, to its directors and officers in connection with defending a proceeding, except that such director or officer shall undertake to repay such advances if it is ultimately determined that such person is not entitled to indemnification.

- The registrant will not be obligated pursuant to the bylaws to indemnify a person with respect to proceedings initiated by that person, except with respect to proceedings authorized by the registrant's board of directors or brought to enforce a right to indemnification.

- The rights conferred in the bylaws are not exclusive, and the registrant is authorized to enter into indemnification agreements with its directors, officers, employees and agents and to obtain insurance to indemnify such persons.

Table of Contents

- The registrant may not retroactively amend the bylaw provisions to reduce its indemnification obligations to directors, officers, employees and agents.

The registrant's policy is to enter into separate indemnification agreements with each of its directors and executive officers that provide the maximum indemnity allowed to directors and executive officers by Section 145 of the Delaware General Corporation Law and which allow for certain additional procedural protections. The registrant also maintains directors and officers insurance to insure such persons against certain liabilities.

The Investor Rights Agreement between the registrant and certain investors provides for cross-indemnification in connection with registration of the registrant's common stock on behalf of such investors.

These indemnification provisions and the indemnification agreements entered into between the registrant and its officers and directors may be sufficiently broad to permit indemnification of the registrant's officers and directors for liabilities (including reimbursement of expenses incurred) arising under the Securities Act.

The underwriting agreement filed as Exhibit 1.1 to this registration statement provides for indemnification by the underwriters of the registrant and its officers and directors for certain liabilities arising under the Securities Act, or otherwise. Reference is made to the following documents filed as exhibits to this registration statement regarding relevant indemnification provisions described above and elsewhere herein.

Document	Exhibit Number
Form of Underwriting Agreement	1.01
Second Amended and Restated Certificate of Incorporation (currently in effect)	3.01
Third Amended and Restated Certificate of Incorporation (to be in effect after offering)	3.01.1
Bylaws (currently in effect)	3.02
Amended and Restated Bylaws (to be in effect after offering)	3.02.1
Form of Indemnification Agreement	10.01
Investor Rights Agreement	4.01

Item 15. Recent Sales of Unregistered Securities.

The following sets forth information regarding securities sold by the registrant since January 1, 2001.

1. In January 2001, the registrant sold 9,000 shares of Series C preferred stock for cash consideration of $21,083 to an accredited investor.

2. In January 2001, the registrant issued 30,000 shares of Class B common stock to a consultant that is an accredited investor in consideration for consulting services valued at $9,000.

3. Between February 2001 and July 2004, the registrant issued an aggregate of 3,300,742 shares of common stock with an aggregate value of $13,734,865 in connection with various mergers and acquisitions involving the registrant during this period. These issuances are described more fully below.

    - In February 2001, the registrant issued 80,000 shares of common stock with an aggregate value of $24,000 to a privately-held technology corporation as consideration for the acquisition of certain assets from such corporation.

    - In June 2001, the registrant issued 20,000 shares of common stock with an aggregate value of $6,000 to a privately-held technology corporation as consideration for the acquisition of certain assets from such corporation.

    - In February 2003, the registrant issued 300,000 shares of common stock with an aggregate value of $90,000 to a privately-held technology corporation as consideration for the acquisition of certain assets from such corporation.

II-2

Table of Contents

- In February 2003, the registrant issued 46,000 shares of common stock with an aggregate value of $13,800 to a privately-held technology corporation as consideration for a license of technology from such corporation.

- In April 2003, the registrant issued 2,382,881 shares of common stock, which includes 557,655 shares issuable upon exercise of options, with an aggregate value of $4,765,762 to the former shareholders of a privately-held technology corporation in connection with the registrant's acquisition of such corporation.

- In April 2003, the registrant issued 120,000 shares of common stock with an aggregate value of $240,000 to the former shareholders of a privately-held technology corporation in connection with the registrant's acquisition of such corporation.

- In September 2003, the registrant issued 254,994 shares of common stock with an aggregate value of $1,784,958 to the former shareholders of a privately-held technology corporation in connection with the registrant's acquisition of such corporation.

- In April 2004, the registrant issued 20,867 shares of common stock, which includes 2,141 shares issuable upon exercise of options, with an aggregate value of $730,345 to the former shareholders of a privately-held technology corporation in connection with the registrant's acquisition of such corporation.

- In July 2004, the registrant issued 76,000 shares of common stock, which includes 16,018 shares issuable upon exercise of options, with an estimated approximate aggregate value of $6,080,000 to the former shareholders of a privately-held technology corporation in connection with the registrant's acquisition of such corporation.

4. In July 2001, the registrant issued 426,892 shares of Series C preferred stock for an aggregate purchase price of $999,995 to an accredited investor.

5. Since January 2001, the registrant has issued to directors, officers, employees and consultants options to purchase 63,230,957 shares of common stock with an aggregate exercise price of $118,292,482, and has issued 42,013,513 shares of common stock for an aggregate purchase price of $27,123,241 upon exercise of such options.

6. Since January 2001, the registrant issued warrants to purchase shares of our capital stock to the following investors:

    - From June 2001 through June 2002, we issued to accredited investors warrants to purchase an aggregate of 179,956 shares of Series C preferred stock for an aggregate exercise price of $421,547.

    - In July 2001, we issued to an accredited investor a warrant to purchase 1,194,308 shares of Class B common stock for an aggregate exercise price of $358,292.

    - In May 2002, we issued to an accredited investor a warrant to purchase 7,437,452 shares of Series D preferred stock for an aggregate exercise price of $21,642,985.

7. Since January 2001, the registrant issued shares of our capital stock to the following investors:

    - In June 2003, we issued to an accredited investor 1,229,944 shares of Series C Preferred Stock for an aggregate purchase price of $2,881,144 upon the net-issue exercise by the investor of a warrant to purchase shares of Series C Preferred Stock.

    - In May 2004, we issued to an accredited investor upon exercise of a warrant 7,437,452 shares of Series D Preferred Stock for an aggregate purchase price of $21,642,985.

    - In May 2004, we issued to an accredited investor upon exercise of a warrant 100,000 shares of Class B common stock for an aggregate purchase price of $234,250.

    - In August 2004, we issued to an accredited investor 2,700,000 shares of Class A common stock for an estimated aggregate purchase price of $243,000,000 based on an assumed price of $90.00 in connection with a settlement arrangement.

Table of Contents

Except as noted below, the issuance of securities described above were deemed to be exempt from registration under the Securities Act in reliance on Section 4(2) of the Securities Act as transactions by an issuer not involving any public offering. The recipients of securities in each such transaction represented their intention to acquire the securities for investment only and not with a view to or for sale in connection with any distribution thereof and appropriate legends were affixed to the share certificates and other instruments issued in such transactions. The sale of these securities were made without general solicitation or advertising.

The option grants and stock issuances described in paragraph 5 above include the issuance of 37,079,623 options and 23,702,819 shares of our common stock that may not have been exempt from registration or qualification requirements under federal or state securities laws. Consequently, certain of the options we granted and the shares issued upon exercise of these options may have been issued in violation of federal or state securities laws, or both, and may be subject to rescission. In order to address this issue, we intend to make a rescission offer soon after the effective date of this offering to all holders of any outstanding options and shares subject to rescission, pursuant to which we will offer to repurchase these options and shares then outstanding from the holder. If our rescission offer is accepted by all offerees, we could be required to make an aggregate payment to the holders of these options and shares of up to approximately $25.9 million, which includes statutory interest. There are no assurances that we will not be subject to penalties or fines relating to these issuances. We believe our anticipated rescission offer could provide us with additional meritorious defenses against any future claims relating to these shares.

Item 16. Exhibits and Financial Statement Schedules.

(a) Exhibits. The following exhibits are included herein or incorporated herein by reference:

Exhibit Number	Exhibit Title
1.01	Form of Underwriting Agreement
2.01**	Merger Agreement and Plan of Reorganization by and among Google Technology Inc., Bermuda Acquisition Inc., Applied Semantics Inc. and other parties signatory hereto dated as of April 18, 2003
3.01**	Amended and Restated Certificate of Incorporation of Registrant as filed August 27, 2003
3.01.1***	Second Amended and Restated Certificate of Incorporation of Registrant as filed July 6, 2004
3.01.2**	Form of Third Amended and Restated Certificate of Incorporation of Registrant, to be filed upon the closing of the offering
3.02**	Bylaws of Registrant
3.02.1**	Form of Amended and Restated Bylaws of Registrant, to be effective upon the closing of the offering
4.01**	Investor Rights Agreement dated May 31, 2002
4.01.1	Amendment to Investor Rights Agreement dated August 17, 2004
4.02	Specimen Class A common stock certificate
4.03*	Specimen Class B common stock certificate
5.01	Opinion of Wilson Sonsini Goodrich & Rosati, Professional Corporation
10.01**	Form of Indemnification Agreement entered into between Registrant, its affiliates and its directors and officers
10.02**	1998 Stock Plan, as amended, and form of stock option agreement
10.03**	1999 Stock Option/Stock Issuance Plan, as amended, and form of stock option agreement
10.04**	2000 Stock Plan, as amended, and form of stock option agreement
10.05**	2003 Stock Plan, as amended, and form of stock option agreement

II-4

Table of Contents

Exhibit Number	Exhibit Title
10.06**	2003 Stock Plan (No. 2) and form of stock option agreement
10.07**	2003 Stock Plan (No. 3) and form of stock option agreement
10.08**	2004 Stock Plan
10.09**	Google Technology Sublease Agreement dated July 9, 2003 by and between Silicon Graphics, Inc. and Registrant
10.09.1**	Amendment No. 1 to Sublease dated November 18, 2003 by and between Silicon Graphics, Inc. and Registrant
10.09.2**	Amendment No. 2 to Sublease dated December 17, 2003 by and between Silicon Graphics, Inc. and Registrant
10.09.3**	Landlord-Subtenant Agreement dated July 9, 2003 by and among WXIII/Amphitheatre Realty, L.L.C., Silicon Graphics, Inc. and Registrant
10.09.4**	Second Amendment to Commercial Lease dated July 9, 2003 by and among WXIII/Amphitheatre Realty, L.L.C., Silicon Graphics, Inc. and Registrant
10.09.5**	Amendment to Commercial Lease dated April 19, 2001 by and among the Goldman Sachs Group, Inc., Silicon Graphics, Inc. and Silicon Graphics Real Estate, Inc.
10.09.6**	Lease between the Goldman Sachs Group, Inc. and Silicon Graphics, Inc. dated December 29, 2000
10.09.7**	Nondisturbance and Attornment Agreement between Registrant and WXIII/Amphitheatre Realty, L.L.C.
10.10†**	Amended and Restated License Agreement dated October 13, 2003 by and between The Board of Trustees of the Leland Stanford Junior University and Registrant
10.10.1	License Agreement dated July 2, 2001 by and between The Board of Trustees of the Leland Stanford Junior University and Registrant
10.11**	Employment Agreement dated March 14, 2001 by and between Eric Schmidt and Registrant
10.12**	2003 Equity Incentive Plan and form of stock option agreement
21.01**	List of subsidiaries of Registrant
23.01	Consent of Ernst & Young LLP, Independent Registered Public Accounting Firm
23.02	Consent of Ernst & Young LLP, Independent Registered Public Accounting Firm
23.03**	Consent of Wilson Sonsini Goodrich & Rosati, Professional Corporation (included in Exhibit 5.01)
24.01**	Power of Attorney

*   To be filed by amendment.
** Previously filed.
*** Incorporated herein by reference to the Registrant's current report on Form 8-K filed on July 9, 2004.
†   Confidential treatment has been requested for portions of this exhibit. These portions have been omitted from the Registration Statement and submitted separately to the Securities and Exchange Commission.

(b) Financial Statement Schedules.

The following schedule required to be filed by Item 16(b) is contained on page II-8 of this Report:

Schedule II—Valuation and Qualifying Accounts for each of the three years in the period ended December 31, 2003.

All other schedules have been omitted because they are either inapplicable or the required information has been given in the consolidated financial statements or the notes thereto.

Table of Contents

Item 17. Undertakings.

The undersigned registrant hereby undertakes to provide to the underwriters at the closing specified in the underwriting agreement certificates in such denominations and registered in such names as required by the underwriters to permit prompt delivery to each purchaser.

Insofar as indemnification by the registrant for liabilities arising under the Securities Act may be permitted to directors, officers and controlling persons of the registrant pursuant to the provisions described in Item 14 above or otherwise, the registrant has been advised that in the opinion of the Securities and Exchange Commission such indemnification is against public policy as expressed in the Securities Act, and is, therefore, unenforceable. In the event that a claim for indemnification against such liabilities (other than the payment by the registrant of expenses incurred or paid by a director, officer, or controlling person of the registrant in the successful defense of any action, suit or proceeding) is asserted by such director, officer or controlling person in connection with the securities being registered, the registrant will, unless in the opinion of its counsel the matter has been settled by controlling precedent, submit to a court of appropriate jurisdiction the question whether such indemnification by it is against public policy as expressed in the Securities Act and will be governed by the final adjudication of such issue.

The undersigned registrant hereby undertakes that:

For purposes of determining any liability under the Securities Act, the information omitted from the form of prospectus filed as part of this registration statement in reliance upon Rule 430A and contained in a form of prospectus filed by the registrant pursuant to Rule 424(b)(1) or (4) or 497(h) under the Securities Act shall be deemed to be part of this registration statement as of the time it was declared effective.

For the purpose of determining any liability under the Securities Act, each post-effective amendment that contains a form of prospectus shall be deemed to be a new registration statement relating to the securities offered therein, and the offering of such securities at the time shall be deemed to be the initial bona fide offering thereof.

APPENDIX I   GOOGLE INC. FORM S-1 REGISTRATION STATEMENT

Table of Contents

SIGNATURES

Pursuant to the requirements of the Securities Act of 1933, the registrant has duly caused this amendment to the registration statement on Form S-1 to be signed on its behalf by the undersigned, thereunto duly authorized, in the City of Mountain View, County of Santa Clara, State of California, on the 18th day of August, 2004.

GOOGLE INC.

By: /s/ ERIC E. SCHMIDT
          Eric E. Schmidt
          Chairman of the Executive Committee
          and Chief Executive Officer

Pursuant to the requirements of the Securities Act of 1933, this amendment to the registration statement on Form S-1 has been signed by the following persons in the capacities and on the dates indicated:

Signature	Title	Date
/s/ ERIC E. SCHMIDT Eric E. Schmidt	Chairman of the Executive Committee and Chief Executive Officer (*Principal Executive Officer*)	August 18, 2004
/s/ GEORGE REYES George Reyes	Chief Financial Officer (*Principal Financial and Accounting Officer*)	August 18, 2004
* Sergey Brin	President of Technology, Assistant Secretary and Director	August 18, 2004
* Larry Page	President of Products, Assistant Secretary and Director	August 18, 2004
* L. John Doerr	Director	August 18, 2004
* Michael Moritz	Director	August 18, 2004
* K. Ram Shriram	Director	August 18, 2004
* John L. Hennessy	Director	August 18, 2004
* Arthur D. Levinson	Director	August 18, 2004
* Paul S. Otellini	Director	August 18, 2004

*By: */s/ GEORGE REYES
             George Reyes
             Attorney-in-Fact

Table of Contents

Schedule II—Valuation and Qualifying Accounts

Allowance for doubtful accounts and sales credits	Balance at Beginning of Year	Charged to Expenses/ against Revenue	Write-Offs Net of Recoveries	Balance at End of Year
		(in thousands)		
Year ended December 31, 2001	$ 437	$ 2,065	$ (942)	$ 1,560
Year ended December 31, 2002	$ 1,560	$ 7,024	$ (6,287)	$ 2,297
Year ended December 31, 2003	$ 2,297	$ 6,106	$ (3,733)	$ 4,670

Note: Additions to the allowance for doubtful accounts are charged to expense. Additions to the allowance for sales credits are charged against revenues.

II-8

Table of Contents

EXHIBIT INDEX

Exhibit Number	Exhibit Title
1.01	Form of Underwriting Agreement
2.01**	Merger Agreement and Plan of Reorganization by and among Google Technology Inc., Bermuda Acquisition Inc., Applied Semantics Inc. and other parties signatory hereto dated as of April 18, 2003
3.01**	Amended and Restated Certificate of Incorporation of Registrant as filed August 27, 2003
3.01.1***	Second Amended and Restated Certificate of Incorporation of Registrant as filed July 6, 2004
3.01.2**	Form of Third Amended and Restated Certificate of Incorporation of Registrant, to be filed upon the closing of the offering
3.02**	Bylaws of Registrant
3.02.1**	Form of Amended and Restated Bylaws of Registrant, to be effective upon the closing of the offering
4.01**	Investor Rights Agreement dated May 31, 2002
4.01.1	Amendment to Investor Rights Agreement dated August 17, 2004
4.02	Specimen Class A common stock certificate
4.03*	Specimen Class B common stock certificate
5.01	Opinion of Wilson Sonsini Goodrich & Rosati, Professional Corporation
10.01**	Form of Indemnification Agreement entered into between Registrant, its affiliates and its directors and officers
10.02**	1998 Stock Plan, as amended, and form of stock option agreement
10.03**	1999 Stock Option/Stock Issuance Plan, as amended, and form of stock option agreement
10.04**	2000 Stock Plan, as amended, and form of stock option agreement
10.05**	2003 Stock Plan, as amended, and form of stock option agreement
10.06**	2003 Stock Plan (No. 2) and form of stock option agreement
10.07**	2003 Stock Plan (No. 3) and form of stock option agreement
10.08**	2004 Stock Plan
10.09**	Google Technology Sublease Agreement dated July 9, 2003 by and between Silicon Graphics, Inc. and Registrant
10.09.1**	Amendment No. 1 to Sublease dated November 18, 2003 by and between Silicon Graphics, Inc. and Registrant
10.09.2**	Amendment No. 2 to Sublease dated December 17, 2003 by and between Silicon Graphics, Inc. and Registrant
10.09.3**	Landlord-Subtenant Agreement dated July 9, 2003 by and among WXIII/Amphitheatre Realty, L.L.C., Silicon Graphics, Inc. and Registrant
10.09.4**	Second Amendment to Commercial Lease dated July 9, 2003 by and among WXIII/Amphitheatre Realty, L.L.C., Silicon Graphics, Inc. and Registrant
10.09.5**	Amendment to Commercial Lease dated April 19, 2001 by and among the Goldman Sachs Group, Inc., Silicon Graphics, Inc. and Silicon Graphics Real Estate, Inc.
10.09.6**	Lease between the Goldman Sachs Group, Inc. and Silicon Graphics, Inc. dated December 29, 2000
10.09.7**	Nondisturbance and Attornment Agreement between Registrant and WXIII/Amphitheatre Realty, L.L.C.
10.10†**	Amended and Restated License Agreement dated October 13, 2003 by and between The Board of Trustees of the Leland Stanford Junior University and Registrant
10.10.1	License Agreement dated July 2, 2001 by and between The Board of Trustees of the Leland Stanford Junior University and Registrant
10.11**	Employment Agreement dated March 14, 2001 by and between Eric Schmidt and Registrant
10.12**	2003 Equity Incentive Plan and form of stock option agreement

Table of Contents

Exhibit Number	Exhibit Title
21.01**	List of subsidiaries of Registrant
23.01	Consent of Ernst & Young LLP, Independent Registered Public Accounting Firm
23.02	Consent of Ernst & Young LLP, Independent Registered Public Accounting Firm
23.03**	Consent of Wilson Sonsini Goodrich & Rosati, Professional Corporation (included in Exhibit 5.01)
24.01**	Power of Attorney

* To be filed by amendment.
** Previously filed.
*** Incorporated herein by reference to the Registrant's current report on Form 8-K filed on July 9, 2004.
† Confidential treatment has been requested for portions of this exhibit. These portions have been omitted from the Registration Statement and submitted separately to the Securities and Exchange Commission.

APPENDIX II

PIXAR, Underwriting Agreement, November 28, 1995

6,000,000 Shares

PIXAR

Common Stock

UNDERWRITING AGREEMENT

November 28, 1995

ROBERTSON, STEPHENS & COMPANY, L.P.
HAMBRECHT & QUIST LLC
COWEN & COMPANY
 As Representatives of the several Underwriters
c/o Robertson, Stephens & Company, L.P.
555 California Street
Suite 2600
San Francisco, California 94104

Ladies/Gentlemen:

Pixar, a California corporation (the "Company"), addresses you as the Representatives of each of the persons, firms and corporations listed in Schedule A hereto (herein collectively called the "Underwriters") and hereby confirms its agreement with the several Underwriters as follows:

1. <u>Description of Shares</u>. The Company proposes to issue and sell 6,000,000 shares of its authorized and unissued Common Stock, no par value (the "Firm Shares"), to the several Underwriters. The Company also proposes to grant to the Underwriters an option to purchase up to 900,000 additional shares of the Company's Common Stock, no par value (the "Option Shares"), as provided in Section 7 hereof. As used in this Agreement, the term "Shares" shall include the Firm Shares and the Option Shares. All shares of Common Stock of the Company to be outstanding after giving effect to the sales contemplated hereby, including the Shares, are hereinafter referred to as "Common Stock."

2. <u>Representations, Warranties and Agreements of the Company</u>.

The Company represents and warrants to and agrees with each Underwriter that:

(a) A registration statement on Form S-1 (File No. 33-97918) with respect to the Shares, including a prospectus subject to completion, has been prepared by the Company in conformity with the requirements of the Securities Act of 1933, as amended (the "Act"), and the applicable rules and regulations (the "Rules and Regulations") of the Securities and Exchange Commission (the "Commission") under the Act and has been filed with the Commission; such amendments to such registration statement, such amended prospectuses subject to completion and such abbreviated registration statements pursuant to Rule 462(b) of the Rules and Regulations as may have been required prior to the date hereof have been similarly prepared and filed with the Commission; and the Company will file such additional amendments to such registration statement, such amended prospectuses subject to completion and such abbreviated registration statements as may hereafter be required. Copies of such registration statement and amendments, of each related prospectus subject to completion (the "Preliminary Prospectuses") and of any abbreviated registration statement pursuant to Rule 462(b) of the Rules and Regulations have been delivered to you.

If the registration statement relating to the Shares has been declared effective under the Act by the Commission, the Company will prepare and promptly file with the Commission the information omitted from the registration statement pursuant to Rule 430A(a) or, if Robertson, Stephens & Company, L.P., on behalf of the several Underwriters, shall agree to the utilization of Rule 434 of the Rules and Regulations, the information required to be included in any term sheet filed pursuant to Rule 434(b) or (c), as applicable, of the Rules and Regulations pursuant to subparagraph (1), (4) or (7) of Rule 424(b) of the Rules and Regulations or as part of a post-effective amendment to the registration statement (including a final form of prospectus). If the registration statement relating to the Shares has not been declared effective under the Act by the Commission, the Company will prepare and promptly file an amendment to the registration statement, including a final form of prospectus, or, if Robertson, Stephens & Company, L.P., on behalf of the several Underwriters, shall agree to the utilization of Rule 434 of the Rules and Regulations, the information required to be included in any term sheet filed pursuant to Rule 434(b) or (c), as applicable, of the Rules and Regulations. The term "Registration Statement" as used in this Agreement shall mean such registration statement, including financial statements, schedules and exhibits, in the form in which it became or becomes, as the case may be, effective (including, if the Company omitted information from the registration statement pursuant to Rule 430A(a) or files a term sheet pursuant to Rule 434 of the Rules and Regulations, the information deemed to be a part of the registration statement at the time it became effective pursuant to Rule 430A(b) or Rule 434(d) of the Rules and Regulations) and, in the event of any amendment thereto or the filing of any abbreviated registration statement pursuant to Rule 462(b) of the Rules and Regulations relating thereto after the effective date of such registration statement, shall also mean (from and after the effectiveness of such amendment or the filing of such abbreviated registration statement) such registration statement as so amended, together with any such abbreviated registration statement. The term "Prospectus" as used in this Agreement shall mean the prospectus relating to the Shares as included in such Registration Statement at the time it becomes effective (including, if the Company omitted information from the Registration Statement pursuant to Rule 430A(a) of the Rules and Regulations, the information deemed to be a part of the Registration Statement at the time it became effective pursuant to Rule 430A(b) of the Rules and Regulations); provided, however, that if in reliance on Rule 434 of the Rules and Regulations and with the consent of Robertson, Stephens & Company, L.P., on behalf of the several Underwriters, the Company shall have provided to the Underwriters a term sheet pursuant to Rule 434(b) or (c), as applicable, prior to the time that a confirmation is sent or given for purposes of Section 2(10)(a) of the Act, the term "Prospectus" shall mean the "prospectus subject to completion" (as defined in Rule 434(g) of the

Rules and Regulations) last provided to the Underwriters by the Company and circulated by the Underwriters to all prospective purchasers of the Shares (including the information deemed to be a part of the Registration Statement at the time it became effective pursuant to Rule 434(d) of the Rules and Regulations). Notwithstanding the foregoing, if any revised prospectus shall be provided to the Underwriters by the Company for use in connection with the offering of the Shares that differs from the prospectus referred to in the immediately preceding sentence (whether or not such revised prospectus is required to be filed with the Commission pursuant to Rule 424(b) of the Rules and Regulations), the term "Prospectus" shall refer to such revised prospectus from and after the time it is first provided to the Underwriters for such use. If in reliance on Rule 434 of the Rules and Regulations and with the consent of Robertson, Stephens & Company, L.P., on behalf of the several Underwriters, the Company shall have provided to the Underwriters a term sheet pursuant to Rule 434(b) or (c), as applicable, prior to the time that a confirmation is sent or given for purposes of Section 2(10)(a) of the Act, the Prospectus and the term sheet, together, will not be materially different from the prospectus in the Registration Statement.

(b) The Commission has not issued any order preventing or suspending the use of any Preliminary Prospectus or instituted proceedings for that purpose, and each such Preliminary Prospectus has conformed in all material respects to the requirements of the Act and the Rules and Regulations and, as of its date, has not included any untrue statement of a material fact or omitted to state a material fact necessary to make the statements therein, in the light of the circumstances under which they were made, not misleading; and at the time the Registration Statement became or becomes, as the case may be, effective and at all times subsequent thereto up to and on the Closing Date (hereinafter defined) and on any later date on which Option Shares are to be purchased, (i) the Registration Statement and the Prospectus, and any amendments or supplements thereto, contained and will contain all material information required to be included therein by the Act and the Rules and Regulations and will in all material respects conform to the requirements of the Act and the Rules and Regulations, (ii) the Registration Statement, and any amendments or supplements thereto, did not and will not include any untrue statement of a material fact or omit to state a material fact required to be stated therein or necessary to make the statements therein not misleading, and (iii) the Prospectus, and any amendments or supplements thereto, did not and will not include any untrue statement of a material fact or omit to state a material fact necessary to make the statements therein, in the light of the circumstances under which they were made, not misleading; provided, however, that none of the representations and warranties contained in this subparagraph (b) shall apply to information contained in or omitted from the Registration Statement or Prospectus, or any amendment or supplement thereto, in reliance upon, and in conformity with, written information relating to any Underwriter furnished to the Company by such Underwriter specifically for use in the preparation thereof.

(c) The Company has been duly incorporated and is validly existing as a corporation in good standing under the laws of California with full power and authority (corporate and other) to own, lease and operate its properties and conduct its business as described in the Prospectus; the Company is duly qualified to do business as a foreign corporation and is in good standing in each jurisdiction in which the ownership or leasing of its properties or the conduct of its business requires such qualification, except where the failure to be so qualified or be in good standing would not have a material adverse effect on the condition (financial or otherwise), earnings, operations or business of the Company; no proceeding has been instituted in any such jurisdiction, revoking, limiting or curtailing, or seeking to revoke, limit or curtail, such power and authority or qualification; the Company is in possession of and operating in compliance with all authorizations, licenses, certificates, consents, orders and permits from state, federal and other regulatory authorities which are material to the conduct of its business, all of which are valid and in full force and effect; the Company is not in violation of its respective charter or bylaws or in material default in the performance or observance of any material obligation, agreement, covenant or condition contained in any material bond, debenture, note or other evidence of indebtedness, or in any material lease, contract, indenture, mortgage, deed of trust, loan agreement, joint venture or other agreement or instrument to which the Company is a party or by which its properties may be bound; and the Company is not in material violation of any law, order, rule, regulation, writ, injunction, judgment or decree of any court, government or governmental agency or body, domestic or foreign, having jurisdiction over the Company or over its properties of which it has knowledge. The Company does not own or control, directly or indirectly, any corporation, association or other entity.

(d) The Company has full legal right, power and authority to enter into this Agreement and perform the transactions contemplated hereby. This Agreement has been duly authorized, executed and delivered by the Company and is a valid and binding agreement on the part of the Company, enforceable in accordance with its terms, except as rights to indemnification hereunder may be limited by applicable law and except as the enforcement hereof may be limited by applicable bankruptcy, insolvency, reorganization, moratorium or other similar laws relating to or affecting creditors' rights generally or by general equitable principles; the performance of this Agreement and the consummation of the transactions herein contemplated will not result in a material breach or violation of any of the terms and provisions of, or constitute a default under, (i) any material bond, debenture, note or other evidence of indebtedness, or under any material lease, contract, indenture, mortgage, deed of trust, loan agreement, joint venture or other agreement or instrument to which the Company is a party or by which its properties may be bound, (ii) the charter or bylaws of the Company, or (iii) any law, order, rule, regulation, writ, injunction, judgment or decree of any court, government or governmental agency or body, domestic or foreign, having jurisdiction over the Company or over its properties. No consent, approval, authorization or order of or qualification with any court, government or governmental agency or body, domestic or foreign, having jurisdiction over the Company or over its properties is required for the execution and delivery of this Agreement and the consummation by the Company of the transactions herein contemplated, except such as may be required under the Act or under state or other securities or Blue Sky laws, all of which requirements have been satisfied in all material respects.

(e) There is not any pending or, to the best of the Company's knowledge, threatened action, suit, claim or proceeding against the Company, or any of its officers or any of its properties, assets or rights before any court, government or governmental agency or body, domestic or foreign, having jurisdiction over the Company or over its officers or properties or otherwise which (i) might result in any material adverse change in the condition (financial or otherwise), earnings, operations or business of the Company or might materially and adversely affect its properties, assets or rights, (ii) might prevent consummation of the transactions contemplated hereby or (iii) is required to be disclosed in the Registration Statement or Prospectus and is not so disclosed; and there are no agreements, contracts, leases or documents of the Company of a character required to be described or referred to in the Registration Statement or Prospectus or to be filed as an exhibit to the Registration Statement by the Act or the Rules and Regulations which have not been accurately described in all material respects in the Registration Statement or Prospectus or filed as exhibits to the Registration Statement.

(f) All outstanding shares of capital stock of the Company have been duly authorized and validly issued and are fully paid and nonassessable, have been issued in compliance with all federal and state securities laws, were not issued in violation of or subject to any preemptive rights or other rights to subscribe for or purchase securities, and the authorized and outstanding capital stock of the Company is as set forth in the Prospectus under the caption "Capitalization" and conforms in all material respects to the statements relating thereto contained in the Registration Statement and the Prospectus (and such statements correctly state the substance of the instruments defining the capitalization of the Company in all material respects); the Firm Shares and the Option Shares have been duly authorized for issuance and sale to the Underwriters pursuant to this Agreement and, when issued and delivered by the Company against payment therefor in accordance with the terms of this Agreement, will be duly and validly issued and fully paid and nonassessable, and will be sold free and clear of any pledge, lien, security interest, encumbrance, claim or equitable interest; and no preemptive right, co-sale right, registration right, right of first refusal or other similar right of shareholders exists with respect to any of the Firm Shares or Option Shares or the issuance and sale thereof other than those that have been expressly waived prior to the date hereof and those that will automatically expire upon or will not apply to the consummation of the transactions contemplated on the Closing Date. No further approval or authorization of any shareholder, the Board of Directors of the Company or others is required for the issuance and sale or transfer of the Shares except as may be required under the Act or under state or other securities or Blue Sky laws. Except as disclosed in or contemplated by the Prospectus and the financial statements of the Company, and the related notes thereto, included in the Prospectus, the Company does not have outstanding any options to purchase, or any preemptive rights or other rights to subscribe for or to purchase, any securities or obligations convertible into, or any contracts or commitments to issue or sell, shares of its capital stock or any such options, rights, convertible securities or obligations. The description of the Company's stock option, stock bonus and other stock plans or arrangements, and the options or other rights granted and exercised thereunder, set forth in the Prospectus accurately and fairly presents in all material respects the information required to be shown with respect to such plans, arrangements, options and rights.

(g) KPMG Peat Marwick LLP, which has examined the financial statements of the Company, together with the related schedules and notes, as of December 31, 1993 and 1994 and as of September 30, 1995 and for each of the years in the three (3) years ended December 31, 1994 and for the nine month period ended September 30, 1995 filed with the Commission as a part of the Registration Statement, which are included in the Prospectus, are independent accountants within the meaning of the Act and the Rules and Regulations; the audited financial statements of the Company, together with the related schedules and notes, and the unaudited financial information, forming part of the Registration Statement and Prospectus, fairly present the financial position and the results of operations of the Company at the respective dates and for the respective periods to which they apply; and all audited financial statements of the Company, together with the related schedules and notes, and the unaudited financial information (other than the selected and summary financial and statistical data included in the Registration Statement), filed with the Commission as part of the Registration Statement, have been prepared in accordance with generally accepted accounting principles consistently applied throughout the periods involved except as may be otherwise stated therein. The selected and summary financial and statistical data included in the Registration Statement present fairly the information shown therein and have been compiled on a basis consistent with the audited financial statements presented therein. No other financial statements or schedules are required to be included in the Registration Statement.

(h) Subsequent to the respective dates as of which information is given in the Registration Statement and Prospectus, there has not been (i) any material adverse change, or any development involving a prospective material adverse change, in the condition (financial or otherwise), earnings, operations or business of the Company, (ii) any transaction that is material to the Company, except transactions entered into in the ordinary course of business, (iii) any obligation, direct or contingent, that is material to the Company, incurred by the Company, except obligations incurred in the ordinary course of business, (iv) any change in the capital stock or outstanding indebtedness of the Company that is material to the Company, (v) any dividend or distribution of any kind declared, paid or made on the capital stock of the Company, or (vi) any loss or damage (whether or not insured) to the property of the Company which has been sustained or will have been sustained which has a material adverse effect on the condition (financial or otherwise), earnings, operations or business of the Company.

(i) Except as set forth in the Registration Statement and Prospectus, (i) the Company has good and marketable title to all properties and assets described in the Registration Statement and Prospectus as owned by it, free and clear of any pledge, lien, security interest, encumbrance, claim or equitable interest, other than such as would not have a material adverse effect on the condition (financial or otherwise), earnings, operations or business of the Company, (ii) the agreements to which the Company is a party described in the Registration Statement and Prospectus are valid agreements, enforceable by the Company, except as the enforcement thereof may be limited by applicable bankruptcy, insolvency, reorganization, moratorium or other similar laws relating to or affecting creditors' rights generally or by general equitable principles and, to the best of the Company's knowledge, the other contracting party or parties thereto are not in material breach or material default under any of such agreements, and (iii) the Company has valid and enforceable leases for all properties described in the Registration Statement and Prospectus as leased by it, except as the enforcement thereof may be limited by applicable bankruptcy, insolvency, reorganization, moratorium or other similar laws relating to or affecting creditors' rights generally or by general equitable principles. Except as set forth in the Registration Statement and Prospectus, the Company owns or leases all such properties as are necessary to its operations as now conducted or as proposed to be conducted.

(j) The Company has timely filed all necessary federal, state and foreign income and franchise tax returns and has paid all taxes shown thereon as due, and there is no tax deficiency that has been or, to the best of the Company's knowledge, might be asserted against the Company that might have a material adverse effect on the condition (financial or otherwise), earnings, operations or business of the Company; and all tax liabilities are adequately provided for on the books of the Company.

(k) The Company maintains insurance with insurers of recognized financial responsibility of the types and in the amounts generally deemed adequate for its businesses and consistent with insurance coverage maintained by similar companies in similar businesses, including, but not limited to, insurance covering real and personal property owned or leased by the Company against theft, damage, destruction, acts of vandalism and all other risks customarily insured against, all of which insurance is in full force and effect; the Company has not been refused any insurance coverage sought or applied for; and the Company does not have any reason to believe that it will not be able to renew its existing insurance coverage as and when such coverage expires or to obtain similar coverage from similar insurers as may be necessary to continue its business at a cost that would not materially and adversely affect the condition (financial or otherwise), earnings, operations or business of the Company.

(l) To the best of the Company's knowledge, no labor disturbance by the employees of the Company exists or is imminent; and the Company is not aware of any existing or imminent labor disturbance by the employees of any of its principal suppliers or at The Walt Disney Company that might be expected to result in a material adverse change in the condition (financial or otherwise), earnings, operations or business of the Company. No collective bargaining agreement exists with any of the Company's employees and, to the best of the Company's knowledge, no such agreement is imminent.

(m) The Company owns or possesses adequate rights to use all patents, patent rights, inventions, trade secrets, know-how, trademarks, service marks, trade names and copyrights which are necessary to conduct its businesses in all material respects as described in the Registration Statement and Prospectus; the expiration of any patents, patent rights, trade secrets, trademarks, service marks, trade names or copyrights would not have a material adverse effect on the condition (financial or otherwise), earnings, operations or business of the Company; the Company has not received any notice of, and has no knowledge of, any infringement of or conflict with asserted rights of the Company by others with respect to any patent, patent rights, inventions, trade secrets, know-how, trademarks, service marks, trade names or copyrights (other than Silicon Graphics Inc., which the Company alleges is infringing its patents in rendering software); and the Company has not received any notice of, and has no knowledge of, any infringement of or conflict with asserted rights of others with respect to any patent, patent rights, inventions, trade secrets, know-how, trademarks, service marks, trade names or copyrights which, singly or in the aggregate, if the subject of an unfavorable decision, ruling or finding, would have a material adverse effect on the condition (financial or otherwise), earnings, operations or business of the Company.

(n) The Common Stock has been approved for quotation on The Nasdaq National Market, subject to official notice of issuance.

(o) The Company has been advised concerning the Investment Company Act of 1940, as amended (the "1940 Act"), and the rules and regulations thereunder, and has in the past conducted, and intends in the future to conduct, its affairs in such a manner as to ensure that it will not become an "investment company" or a company "controlled" by an "investment company" within the meaning of the 1940 Act and such rules and regulations.

(p) The Company has not distributed and will not distribute prior to the later of (i) the Closing Date, or any date on which Option Shares are to be purchased, as the case may be, and (ii) completion of the distribution of the Shares, any offering material in connection with the offering and sale of the Shares other than any Preliminary Prospectuses, the Prospectus, the Registration Statement and other materials, if any, permitted by the Act.

(q) The Company has not at any time during the last five (5) years (i) made any unlawful contribution to any candidate for foreign office or failed to disclose fully any contribution in violation of law, or (ii) made any payment to any federal or state governmental officer or official, or other person charged with similar public or quasi-public duties, other than payments required or permitted by the laws of the United States or any jurisdiction thereof.

(r) The Company has not taken and will, for a period of 30 days after the date hereof, not take, directly or indirectly, any action designed to or that might reasonably be expected to cause or result in stabilization or manipulation of the price of the Common Stock to facilitate the sale or resale of the Shares.

(s) Each officer and director of the Company has agreed in writing that such person will not, for a period of 180 days from the date that the Registration Statement is declared effective by the Commission (the "Lock-up Period"), offer to sell, contract to sell, or otherwise sell, dispose of, loan, pledge or grant any rights with respect to (collectively, a "Disposition") any shares of Common Stock, any options or warrants to purchase any shares of Common Stock or any securities convertible into or exchangeable for shares of Common Stock (collectively, "Securities") now owned or hereafter acquired directly by such person or with respect to which such person has or hereafter acquires the power of disposition, otherwise than (i) as a bona fide gift or gifts, provided the donee or donees thereof agree in writing to be bound by this restriction, (ii) as a distribution to limited partners or shareholders of such person, provided that the distributees thereof agree in writing to be bound by the terms of this restriction, or (iii) with the prior written consent of Robertson, Stephens & Company, L.P. The foregoing restriction has been expressly agreed to preclude the holder of the Securities from engaging in any hedging or other transaction which is designed to or reasonably expected to lead to or result in a Disposition of Securities during the Lock-up Period, even if such Securities would be disposed of by someone other than such holder. Such prohibited hedging or other transactions would include, without limitation, any short sale (whether or not against the box) or any purchase, sale or grant of any right (including, without limitation, any put or call option) with respect to any Securities or with respect to any security (other than a broad-based market basket or index) that includes, relates to or derives any significant part of its value from Securities. Furthermore, such person has also agreed and consented to the entry of stop transfer instructions with the Company's transfer agent against the transfer of the Securities held by such person except in compliance with this restriction. The Company has provided to counsel for the Underwriters a complete and accurate list of all securityholders of the Company and the number and type of securities held by each securityholder. The Company has provided to counsel for the Underwriters true, accurate and complete copies of all of the agreements pursuant to which its officers, directors and shareholders have agreed to such or similar restrictions (the "Lock-up Agreements") presently in effect or effected hereby. The Company hereby represents and warrants that it will not release any of its officers, directors or other shareholders from any Lock-up Agreements currently existing or hereafter effected without the prior written consent of Robertson, Stephens & Company, L.P. In addition, each other beneficial owner of Common Stock and each other optionee has agreed in writing that such person shall not sell or otherwise transfer any shares or other securities of the Company during a period of up to 180 days following the effective date of a Registration Statement of the Company filed under the Securities Act; provided, however, that such restriction shall only apply to the first Registration Statement of the Company to become effective under the Securities Act which includes securities to be sold on behalf of the Company to the public in an underwritten public offering under the Securities Act. Each such beneficial owner and optionee has further agreed that the Company may impose stop-transfer instructions with respect to securities subject to the foregoing restrictions until the end of such 180-day period.

(t) Except as set forth in the Registration Statement and Prospectus, (i) the Company is in compliance with all rules, laws and regulations relating to the use, treatment, storage and disposal of toxic substances and protection of health or the environment ("Environmental Laws") which are applicable to its business, (ii) the Company has received no notice from any governmental authority or third party of an asserted claim under Environmental Laws, which claim is required to be disclosed in the Registration Statement and the Prospectus, (iii) the Company will not be required to make future material capital expenditures to comply with Environmental Laws and (iv) no property which is owned, leased or occupied by the Company has been designated as a Superfund site pursuant to the Comprehensive Response, Compensation, and Liability Act of 1980, as amended (42 U.S.C. § 9601, et seq.), or otherwise designated as a contaminated site under applicable state or local law.

(u) The Company maintains a system of internal accounting controls sufficient to provide reasonable assurances that (i) transactions are executed in accordance with management's general or specific authorizations, (ii) transactions are recorded as necessary to permit preparation of financial statements in conformity with generally accepted accounting principles and to maintain accountability for assets, (iii) access to assets is permitted only in accordance with management's general or specific authorization, and (iv) the recorded accountability for assets is compared with existing assets at reasonable intervals and appropriate action is taken with respect to any differences.

(v) There are no outstanding loans, advances (except normal advances for business expenses in the ordinary course of business) or guarantees of indebtedness by the Company to or for the benefit of any of the officers or directors of the Company or any of the members of the families of any of them, except as disclosed in the Registration Statement and the Prospectus.

(w) The Company has complied with all provisions of Section 517.075, Florida Statutes relating to doing business with the Government of Cuba or with any person or affiliate located in Cuba.

3. **Purchase, Sale and Delivery of Shares**. On the basis of the representations, warranties and agreements herein contained, but subject to the terms and conditions herein set forth, the Company agrees to sell to the Underwriters, and each Underwriter agrees, severally and not jointly, to purchase from the Company, at a purchase price of $20.51 per share, the respective number of Firm Shares as hereinafter set forth. The obligation of each Underwriter to the Company shall be to purchase from the Company that number of Firm Shares which is set forth opposite the name of such Underwriter in Schedule A hereto (subject to adjustment as provided in Section 10).

Delivery of definitive certificates for the Firm Shares to be purchased by the Underwriters pursuant to this Section 3 shall be made against payment of the purchase price therefor by the several Underwriters by certified or official bank check or checks drawn in next-day funds, payable to the order of the Company (and the Company agrees not to deposit any such check in the bank on which it is drawn, and not to take any other action with the purpose or effect of receiving immediately available funds, until the business day following the date of its delivery to the Company, and, in the event of any breach of the foregoing, the Company shall reimburse the Underwriters for the interest lost and any other expenses borne by them by reason of such breach), at the offices of Wilson Sonsini Goodrich & Rosati, 650 Page Mill Road, Palo Alto, CA 94304 (or at such other place as may be agreed upon among the Representatives and the Company), at 7:00 A.M., San Francisco time (a) on the third (3rd) full business day following the first day that Shares are traded, (b) if this Agreement is executed and delivered after 1:30 P.M., San Francisco time, the fourth (4th) full business day following the day that this Agreement is executed and delivered or (c) at such other time and date not later than seven (7) full business days following the first day that Shares are traded as the Representatives and the Company may determine (or at such time and date to which payment and delivery shall have been postponed pursuant to Section 10 hereof), such time and date of payment and delivery being herein called the "Closing Date;" provided, however, that if the Company has not made available to the Representatives copies of the Prospectus within the time provided in Section 4(d) hereof, the Representatives may, in their sole discretion, postpone the Closing Date until no later than two (2) full business days following delivery of copies of the Prospectus to the Representatives. The certificates for the Firm Shares to be so delivered will be made available to you at such office or such other location including, without limitation, in New York City, as you may reasonably request for checking at least one (1) full business day prior to the Closing Date and will be in such names and denominations as you may request, such request to be made at least two (2) full business days prior to the Closing Date. If the Representatives so elect, delivery of the Firm Shares may be made by credit through full fast transfer to the accounts at The Depository Trust Company designated by the Representatives.

It is understood that you, individually, and not as the Representatives of the several Underwriters, may (but shall not be obligated to) make payment of the purchase price on behalf of any Underwriter or Underwriters whose check or checks shall not have been received by you prior to the Closing Date for the Firm Shares to be purchased by such Underwriter or Underwriters. Any such payment by you shall not relieve any such Underwriter or Underwriters of any of its or their obligations hereunder.

After the Registration Statement becomes effective, the several Underwriters intend to make an initial public offering (as such term is described in Section 11 hereof) of the Firm Shares at an initial public offering price of $22.00 per share. After the initial public offering, the several Underwriters may, in their discretion, vary the public offering price.

The information set forth in the last paragraph on the front cover page (insofar as such information relates to the Underwriters), under the last paragraph on page 2, concerning stabilization and over-allotment by the Underwriters, and under the first paragraph (including the table below such paragraph), second, sixth and seventh paragraphs under the caption "Underwriting" in any Preliminary Prospectus and in the final form of Prospectus filed pursuant to Rule 424(b) constitutes the only information furnished by the Underwriters to the Company for inclusion in any Preliminary Prospectus, the Prospectus or the Registration Statement, and you, on behalf of the respective Underwriters, represent and warrant to the Company that the statements made therein do not include any untrue statement of a material fact or omit to state a material fact required to be stated therein or necessary to make the statements therein, in the light of the circumstances under which they were made, not misleading.

4. <u>Further Agreements of the Company</u>. The Company agrees with the several Underwriters that:

(a) The Company will use its best efforts to cause the Registration Statement and any amendment thereof, if not effective at the time and date that this Agreement is executed and delivered by the parties hereto, to become effective as promptly as possible; the Company will use its best efforts to cause any abbreviated registration statement pursuant to Rule 462(b) of the Rules and Regulations as may be required subsequent to the date the Registration Statement is declared effective to become effective as promptly as possible; the Company will notify you, promptly after it shall receive notice thereof, of the time when the Registration Statement, any subsequent amendment to the Registration Statement or any abbreviated registration statement has become effective or any supplement to the Prospectus has been filed; if the Company omitted information from the Registration Statement at the time it was originally declared effective in reliance upon Rule 430A(a) of the Rules and Regulations, the Company will provide evidence satisfactory to you that the Prospectus contains such information and has been filed, within the time period prescribed, with the Commission pursuant to subparagraph (1) or (4) of Rule 424(b) of the Rules and Regulations or as part of a post-effective amendment to such Registration Statement as originally declared effective which is declared effective by the Commission; if the Company files a term sheet pursuant to Rule 434 of the Rules and Regulations, the Company will provide evidence satisfactory to you that the Prospectus and term sheet meeting the requirements of Rule 434(b) or (c), as applicable, of the Rules and Regulations, have been filed, within the time period prescribed, with the Commission pursuant to subparagraph (7) of Rule 424(b) of the Rules and Regulations; if for any reason the filing of the final form of Prospectus is required under Rule 424(b)(3) of the Rules and Regulations, it will provide evidence satisfactory to you that the Prospectus contains such information and has been filed with the Commission within the time period prescribed; it will notify you promptly of any request by the Commission for the amending or supplementing of the Registration Statement or the Prospectus or for additional information; as promptly as practicable upon your request, it will prepare and file with the Commission any amendments or supplements to the Registration Statement or Prospectus which, in the reasonable opinion of counsel for the several Underwriters ("Underwriters' Counsel"), may be necessary or advisable in connection with the distribution of the Shares by the Underwriters; it will promptly prepare and file with the Commission, and promptly notify you of the filing of, any amendments or supplements to the Registration Statement or Prospectus which may be necessary to correct any statements or omissions, if, at any time when a prospectus relating to the Shares is required to be delivered under the Act, any event shall have occurred as a result of which the Prospectus or any other prospectus relating to the Shares as then in effect would include any untrue statement of a material fact or omit to state a material fact necessary to make the statements therein, in the light of the circumstances under which they were made, not misleading; in case any Underwriter is required to deliver a prospectus nine (9) months or more after the effective date of the Registration Statement in connection with the sale of the Shares, it will prepare as promptly as practicable upon request, but at the expense of such Underwriter, such amendment or amendments to the Registration Statement and such prospectus or prospectuses as may be necessary to permit compliance with the requirements of Section 10(a)(3) of the Act; and it will file no amendment or supplement to the Registration Statement or Prospectus which shall not previously have been submitted to you a reasonable time prior to the proposed filing thereof or to which you shall reasonably object in writing, subject, however, to compliance with the Act and the Rules and Regulations and the provisions of this Agreement.

(b) The Company will advise you, promptly after it shall receive notice or obtain knowledge, of the issuance of any stop order by the Commission suspending the effectiveness of the Registration Statement or of the initiation or threat of any proceeding for that purpose; and it will promptly use its best efforts to prevent the issuance of any stop order or to obtain its withdrawal at the earliest possible moment if such stop order should be issued.

(c) The Company will endeavor to qualify the Shares for offering and sale under the securities laws of such jurisdictions as you may reasonably designate and to continue such qualifications in effect for so long as may be required for purposes of the distribution of the Shares, except that the Company shall not be required in connection therewith or as a condition thereof to qualify as a foreign corporation or to execute a general consent to service of process in any jurisdiction in which it is not otherwise required to be so qualified or to so execute a general consent to service of process. In each jurisdiction in which the Shares shall have been qualified as above provided, the Company will make and file such statements and reports in each year as are or may be reasonably required by the laws of such jurisdiction.

(d) The Company will furnish to you, as soon as available, and, in the case of the Prospectus and any term sheet or abbreviated term sheet under Rule 434, in no event later than the first (1st) full business day following the first day that Shares are traded, copies of the Registration Statement (four of which will be signed and which will include all exhibits), each Preliminary Prospectus, the Prospectus and any amendments or supplements to such documents, including any prospectus prepared to permit compliance with Section 10(a)(3) of the Act, all in such quantities as you may from time to time reasonably request. Notwithstanding the foregoing, if Robertson, Stephens & Company, L.P., on behalf of the several Underwriters, shall agree to the utilization of Rule 434 of the Rules and Regulations, the Company shall provide to you copies of a Preliminary Prospectus updated in all respects through the date specified by you in such quantities as you may from time to time reasonably request.

(e) The Company will make generally available to its securityholders as soon as practicable, but in any event not later than the forty-fifth (45th) day following the end of the fiscal quarter first occurring after the first anniversary of the effective date of the Registration Statement, an earnings statement (which will be in reasonable detail but need not be audited) complying with the provisions of Section 11(a) of the Act and covering a twelve (12) month period beginning after the effective date of the Registration Statement.

(f) During a period of three (3) years after the date hereof, the Company will furnish to its shareholders as soon as practicable after the end of each respective period, annual reports (including financial statements audited by independent certified public accountants) and unaudited quarterly reports of operations for each of the first three quarters of the fiscal year, and will furnish to you and the other several Underwriters hereunder, upon request (i) concurrently with furnishing such reports to its shareholders, statements of operations of the Company for each of the first three (3) quarters in the form furnished to the Company's shareholders, (ii) concurrently with furnishing to its shareholders, a balance sheet of the Company as of the end of such fiscal year, together with statements of operations, of shareholders' equity, and of cash flows of the Company for such fiscal year, accompanied by a copy of the certificate or report thereon of independent certified public accountants, (iii) as soon as they are available, copies of all reports (financial or other) mailed to shareholders, (iv) as soon as they are available, copies of all reports and financial statements furnished to or filed with the Commission, any securities exchange or the National Association of Securities Dealers, Inc. ("NASD"), (v) every material press release and every material news item or article in respect of the Company or its affairs which was generally released to shareholders or prepared by the Company or any of its subsidiaries, and (vi) any additional information of a public nature concerning the Company or its subsidiaries, or its business which you may reasonably request. During such three (3) year period, if the Company shall have active subsidiaries, the foregoing financial statements shall be on a consolidated basis to the extent that the accounts of the Company and its subsidiaries are consolidated, and shall be accompanied by similar financial statements for any significant subsidiary which is not so consolidated.

(g) The Company intends to apply the net proceeds from the sale of the Shares being sold by it in the manner set forth under the caption "Use of Proceeds" in the Prospectus.

(h) The Company will maintain a transfer agent and, if necessary under the jurisdiction of incorporation of the Company, a registrar (which may be the same entity as the transfer agent) for its Common Stock.

(i) The Company will file Form SR in conformity with the requirements of the Act and the Rules and Regulations.

(j) If the transactions contemplated hereby are not consummated by reason of any failure, refusal or inability on the part of the Company to perform any agreement on its part to be performed hereunder or to fulfill any condition of the Underwriters' obligations hereunder, or if the Company shall terminate this Agreement pursuant to Section 11(a) hereof, or if the Underwriters shall terminate this Agreement pursuant to Section 11(b)(i) (other than for noncompliance with paragraph (e) of Section 6 hereof), the Company will reimburse the several Underwriters for all out-of-pocket expenses (including fees and disbursements of Underwriters' Counsel) incurred by the Underwriters in investigating or preparing to market or marketing the Shares.

(k) If at any time during the twenty-five (25) day period after the Registration Statement becomes effective, any rumor, publication or event relating to or affecting the Company shall occur as a result of which in your reasonable opinion the market price of the Common Stock has been or is likely to be materially affected (regardless of whether such rumor, publication or event necessitates a supplement to or amendment of the Prospectus), the Company will, after written notice from you advising the Company to the effect set forth above, forthwith prepare, consult with you concerning the substance of and disseminate a press release or other public statement, reasonably satisfactory to you, responding to or commenting on such rumor, publication or event.

(l) During the Lock-up Period, the Company will not, without the prior written consent of Robertson Stephens & Company, L.P., effect the Disposition of, directly or indirectly, any Securities other than the sale of the Firm Shares and the Option Shares hereunder and the Company's issuance of options or Common Stock under the Company's presently authorized 1995 Stock Plan and 1995 Director Option Plan (collectively, the "Option Plan") or the issuance of Common Stock under stock options presently outstanding.

(m) For a period of 180 days from the date hereof, the Company will issue no options or warrants that may be exercised during such period unless any shares of the Company's capital stock issued upon the exercise of such options or warrants are subject to lock-up agreements identical to those to which the Company's other optionees are currently subject, unless such optionee is an officer or director, in which case such officer or director will be subject to lock-up agreements identical to those to which the Company's other officers and directors are currently subject.

(n) The Company will enforce all lock-up agreements that it has with existing shareholders and optionees.

5. Expenses.

(a) The Company agrees with each Underwriter that:

(i) The Company will pay and bear all costs and expenses in connection with the preparation, printing and filing of the Registration Statement (including financial statements, schedules and exhibits), Preliminary Prospectuses and the Prospectus and any amendments or supplements thereto; the printing of this Agreement, the Agreement Among Underwriters, the Selected Dealer Agreement, the Preliminary Blue Sky Survey and any Supplemental Blue Sky Survey, the Underwriters' Questionnaire and Power of Attorney and any instruments related to any of the foregoing; the issuance and delivery of the Shares hereunder to the several Underwriters, including transfer taxes, if any, the cost of all certificates representing the Shares and transfer agents' and registrars' fees; the fees and disbursements of counsel for the Company; all fees and other charges of the Company's independent certified public accountants; the cost of furnishing to the several Underwriters copies of the Registration Statement (including appropriate exhibits), Preliminary Prospectus and the Prospectus, and any amendments or supplements to any of the foregoing; NASD filing fees and the cost of qualifying the Shares under the laws of such jurisdictions as you may designate (including filing fees and fees and disbursements of Underwriters' Counsel in connection with such NASD filings and Blue Sky qualifications); and all other expenses directly incurred by the Company in connection with the performance of their obligations hereunder.

(ii) In addition to its other obligations under Section 8(a) hereof, the Company agrees that, as an interim measure during the pendency of any claim, action, investigation, inquiry or other proceeding described in Section 8(a) hereof, it will reimburse the Underwriters on a monthly basis for all reasonable legal or other expenses incurred in connection with investigating or defending any such claim, action, investigation, inquiry or other proceeding, notwithstanding the absence of a judicial determination as to the propriety and enforceability of the Company's obligation to reimburse the Underwriters for such expenses and the possibility that such payments might later be held to have been improper by a court of competent jurisdiction. To the extent that any such interim reimbursement payment is so held to have been improper, the Underwriters shall promptly return such payment to the Company together with interest, compounded daily, determined on the basis of the prime rate (or other commercial lending rate for borrowers of the highest credit standing) listed from time to time in The Wall Street Journal which represents the base rate on corporate loans posted by a substantial majority of the nation's thirty (30) largest banks (the "Prime Rate"). Any such interim reimbursement payments which are not made to the Underwriters within thirty (30) days of a request for reimbursement shall bear interest at the Prime Rate from the date of such request.

(b) In addition to their other obligations under Section 8(b) hereof, the Underwriters severally and not jointly agree that, as an interim measure during the pendency of any claim, action, investigation, inquiry or other proceeding described in Section 8(b) hereof, they will reimburse the Company on a monthly basis for all reasonable legal or other expenses incurred in connection with investigating or defending any such claim, action, investigation, inquiry or other proceeding, notwithstanding the absence of a judicial determination as to the propriety and enforceability of the Underwriters' obligation to reimburse the Company for such expenses and the possibility that such payments might later be held to have been improper by a court of competent jurisdiction. To the extent that any such interim reimbursement payment is so held to have been improper, the Company shall promptly return such payment to the Underwriters together with interest, compounded daily, determined on the basis of the Prime Rate. Any such interim reimbursement payments which are not made to the Company within thirty (30) days of a request for reimbursement shall bear interest at the Prime Rate from the date of such request.

(c) It is agreed that any controversy arising out of the operation of the interim reimbursement arrangements set forth in Sections 5(a)(ii) and 5(b) hereof, including the amounts of any requested reimbursement payments, the method of determining such amounts and the basis on which such amounts shall be apportioned among the reimbursing parties, shall be settled by arbitration conducted under the provisions of the Constitution and Rules of the Board of Governors of the New York Stock Exchange, Inc. or pursuant to the Code of Arbitration Procedure of the NASD. Any such arbitration must be commenced by service of a written demand for arbitration or a written notice of intention to arbitrate, therein electing the arbitration tribunal. In the event the party demanding arbitration does not make such designation of an arbitration tribunal in such demand or notice, then the party responding to said demand or notice is authorized to do so. Any such arbitration will be limited to the operation of the interim reimbursement provisions contained in Sections 5(a)(ii) and 5(b) hereof and will not resolve the ultimate propriety or enforceability of the obligation to indemnify for expenses which is created by the provisions of Sections 8(a) and 8(b) hereof or the obligation to contribute to expenses which is created by the provisions of Section 8(d) hereof.

6. <u>Conditions of Underwriters' Obligations</u>. The obligations of the several Underwriters to purchase and pay for the Shares as provided herein shall be subject to the accuracy, as of the date hereof and the Closing Date and any later date on which Option Shares are to be purchased,

as the case may be, of the representations and warranties of the Company herein, to the performance by the Company of its obligations hereunder and to the following additional conditions:

(a) The Registration Statement shall have become effective not later than 2:00 P.M., San Francisco time, on the date following the date of this Agreement, or such later date as shall be consented to in writing by you; and no stop order suspending the effectiveness thereof shall have been issued and no proceedings for that purpose shall have been initiated or, to the knowledge of the Company or any Underwriter, threatened by the Commission, and any request of the Commission for additional information (to be included in the Registration Statement or the Prospectus or otherwise) shall have been complied with to the reasonable satisfaction of Underwriters' Counsel.

(b) All corporate proceedings and other legal matters in connection with this Agreement, the form of Registration Statement and the Prospectus, and the registration, authorization, issue, sale and delivery of the Shares, shall have been reasonably satisfactory to Underwriters' Counsel, Fenwick & West, and such counsel shall have been furnished with such papers and information as they may reasonably have requested to enable them to pass upon the matters referred to in this Section.

(c) Subsequent to the execution and delivery of this Agreement and prior to the Closing Date, there shall not have been any change in the condition (financial or otherwise), earnings, operations, business or business prospects of the Company from that set forth in the Registration Statement or Prospectus, which, in your sole judgment, is material and adverse and that makes it, in your sole judgment, impracticable or inadvisable to proceed with the public offering of the Shares as contemplated by the Prospectus.

(d) You shall have received on the Closing Date and on any later date on which Option Shares are purchased, as the case may be, the following opinion of Company's Counsel, Wilson Sonsini Goodrich & Rosati, dated the Closing Date or such later date on which Option Shares are purchased addressed to the Underwriters and with reproduced copies or signed counterparts thereof for each of the Underwriters, to the effect that:

(i) The Company has been duly incorporated and is validly existing as a corporation in good standing under the laws of California;

(ii) The Company has the corporate power and authority to own, lease and operate its properties and to conduct its business as described in the Prospectus;

(iii) The Company is duly qualified to do business as a foreign corporation and is in good standing in each jurisdiction, if any, in which the ownership or leasing of its properties or the conduct of its business requires such qualification, except where the failure to be so qualified or be in good standing would not have a material adverse effect on the condition (financial or otherwise), earnings, operations or business of the Company. To such counsel's knowledge, the Company does not own or control, directly or indirectly, any corporation, association or other entity;

(iv) The authorized, issued and outstanding capital stock of the Company is as set forth in the Prospectus under the caption "Capitalization" as of the dates stated therein, the issued and outstanding shares of capital stock of the Company have been duly and validly issued and are fully paid and nonassessable, and, to such counsel's knowledge, will not have been issued in violation of or subject to any preemptive right, co-sale right, registration right, right of first refusal or other similar right;

(v) The Firm Shares or the Option Shares, as the case may be, to be issued by the Company pursuant to the terms of this Agreement have been duly authorized and, upon issuance and delivery against payment therefor in accordance with the terms hereof, will be duly and validly issued and fully paid and nonassessable, and, to such counsel's knowledge, will not have been issued in violation of or subject to any preemptive right, co-sale right, registration right, right of first refusal or other similar right of shareholders;

(vi) The Company has the corporate power and authority to enter into this Agreement and to issue, sell and deliver to the Underwriters the Shares to be issued and sold by it hereunder;

(vii) This Agreement has been duly authorized by all necessary corporate action on the part of the Company and has been duly executed and delivered by the Company and, assuming due authorization, execution and delivery by you, is a valid and binding agreement of the Company, enforceable in accordance with its terms, except insofar as indemnification provisions may be limited by applicable law and except as enforceability may be limited by bankruptcy, insolvency, reorganization, moratorium or similar laws relating to or affecting creditors' rights generally or by general equitable principles;

(viii) The Registration Statement has become effective under the Act and, to such counsel's knowledge, no stop order suspending the effectiveness of the Registration Statement has been issued and no proceedings for that purpose have been instituted or are pending or threatened under the Act;

(ix) The Registration Statement and the Prospectus, and each amendment or supplement thereto (other than the financial statements (including supporting schedules) and financial and statistical data derived therefrom as to which such counsel need express no opinion), as of the effective date of the Registration Statement, complied as to form in all material respects with the requirements of the Act and the applicable Rules and Regulations;

(x) The information in the Prospectus under the caption "Description of Capital Stock," to the extent that it constitutes matters of law or legal conclusions, has been reviewed by such counsel and is a fair summary of such matters and conclusions; and the forms of certificates evidencing the Common Stock and filed as exhibits to the Registration Statement comply with California law;

(xi) The description in the Registration Statement and the Prospectus of the charter and bylaws of the Company and of statutes are accurate and fairly present the information required to be presented by the Act and the applicable Rules and Regulations;

(xii) To such counsel's knowledge, there are no agreements, contracts, leases or documents to which the Company is a party of a character required to be described or referred to in the Registration Statement or Prospectus or to be filed as an exhibit to the Registration Statement which are not described or referred to therein or filed as required;

(xiii) The performance of this Agreement and the consummation of the transactions herein contemplated (other than performance of the Company's indemnification obligations hereunder, concerning which no opinion need be expressed) does not (a) result in any violation of the Company's charter or bylaws or (b) to such counsel's knowledge, result in a material breach or violation of any of the terms and provisions of, or constitute a default under, any material bond, debenture, note or other evidence of indebtedness, or under any material lease, contract, indenture, mortgage, deed of trust, loan agreement, joint venture or other agreement or instrument known to such counsel to which the Company is a party or by which its properties are bound, or any applicable federal or state statute, rule or regulation known to such counsel or, to such counsel's knowledge, any order, writ or decree of any court, government or governmental agency or body having jurisdiction over the Company or over any of its properties or operations;

(xiv) No consent, approval, authorization or order of or qualification with any court, government or governmental agency or body having jurisdiction over the Company, or over any of its properties or operations is necessary in connection with the consummation by the Company of the transactions herein contemplated, except such as have been obtained under the Act or such as may be required under state or other securities or Blue Sky laws in connection with the purchase and the distribution of the Shares by the Underwriters;

(xv) To such counsel's knowledge, there are no legal or governmental proceedings pending or threatened against the Company of a character required to be disclosed in the Registration Statement or the Prospectus by the Act or the Rules and Regulations, other than those described therein;

(xvi) To such counsel's knowledge, except as set forth in the Registration Statement and Prospectus, no holders of Common Stock or other securities of the Company have registration rights with respect to securities of the Company and, except as set forth in the Registration Statement and Prospectus, all holders of securities of the Company having rights known to such counsel to registration of such shares of Common Stock or other securities, because of the filing of the Registration Statement by the Company have, with respect to the offering contemplated thereby, waived such rights or such rights have expired by reason of lapse of time following notification of the Company's intent to file the Registration Statement or have included securities in the Registration Statement pursuant to the exercise of and in full satisfaction of such rights.

In addition, such counsel shall state that such counsel has participated in conferences with officials and other representatives of the Company, the Representatives, Underwriters' Counsel and the independent certified public accountants of the Company, at which such conferences the contents of the Registration Statement and Prospectus and related matters were discussed, and although they have not verified the accuracy or completeness of the statements contained in the Registration Statement or the Prospectus, nothing has come to the attention of such counsel which leads them to believe that, at the time the Registration Statement became effective and at all times subsequent thereto up to and on the Closing Date and on any later date on which Option Shares are to be purchased, the Registration Statement and any amendment or supplement thereto (other than the financial statements including supporting schedules and other financial and statistical information derived therefrom, as to which such counsel need express no comment) contained any untrue statement of a material fact or omitted to state a material fact required to be stated therein or necessary to make the statements therein not misleading, or at the Closing Date or any later date on which the Option Shares are to be purchased, as the case may be, the Prospectus and any amendment or supplement thereto (except as aforesaid) contained any untrue statement of a material fact or omitted to state a material fact necessary to make the statements therein, in the light of the circumstances under which they were made, not misleading.

Counsel rendering the foregoing opinion may rely as to questions of law not involving the laws of the United States or the State of California upon opinions of local counsel, and as to questions of fact upon representations or certificates of officers of the Company, and of government officials, in which case their opinion is to state that they are so relying and that they have no knowledge of any material misstatement or inaccuracy in any such opinion, representation or certificate. Copies of any opinion, representation or certificate so relied upon shall be delivered to you, as Representatives of the Underwriters, and to Underwriters' Counsel.

(e) You shall have received on the Closing Date and on any later date on which Option Shares are to be purchased, as the case may be, an opinion of Fenwick & West, in form and substance satisfactory to you, with respect to the sufficiency of all such corporate proceedings and other legal matters relating to this Agreement and the transactions contemplated hereby as you may reasonably require, and the Company shall have furnished to such counsel such documents as they may have requested for the purpose of enabling them to pass upon such matters.

(f) You shall have received on the Closing Date and on any later date on which Option Shares are to be purchased, as the case may be, a letter from KPMG Peat Marwick LLP addressed to the Company and the Underwriters, dated the Closing Date or such later date on which Option Shares are to be purchased, as the case may be, confirming that they are independent certified public accountants with respect to the Company within the meaning of the Act and the applicable published Rules and Regulations and based upon the procedures described in such letter delivered to you concurrently with the execution of this Agreement (herein called the "Original Letter"), but carried out to a date not more than five (5) business days prior to the

Closing Date or such later date on which Option Shares are to be purchased, as the case may be, (i) confirming, to the extent true, that the statements and conclusions set forth in the Original Letter are accurate as of the Closing Date or such later date on which Option Shares are to be purchased, as the case may be, and (ii) setting forth any revisions and additions to the statements and conclusions set forth in the Original Letter which are necessary to reflect any changes in the facts described in the Original Letter since the date of such letter, or to reflect the availability of more recent financial statements, data or information. The letter shall not disclose any change in the condition (financial or otherwise), earnings, operations or business of the Company from that set forth in the Registration Statement or Prospectus, which, in your sole judgment, is material and adverse and that makes it, in your sole judgment, impracticable or inadvisable to proceed with the public offering of the Shares as contemplated by the Prospectus. The Original Letter from KPMG Peat Marwick LLP shall be addressed to or for the use of the Underwriters in form and substance satisfactory to the Underwriters and shall (i) represent, to the extent true, that they are independent certified public accountants with respect to the Company within the meaning of the Act and the applicable published Rules and Regulations, (ii) set forth their opinion with respect to their examination of the balance sheets of the Company as of December 31, 1994 and September 30, 1995 and related statements of operations, shareholders' equity, and cash flows for the twelve (12) months ended December 31, 1994, and nine (9) months ended September 30, 1995, (iii) state that KPMG Peat Marwick LLP has performed the procedure set out in Statement on Auditing Standards No. 71 ("SAS 71") for a review of interim financial information on the financial statements for the nine month period ended September 30, 1994, and (iv) address other matters agreed upon by KPMG Peat Marwick LLP and you. In addition, you shall have received from KPMG Peat Marwick LLP a letter addressed to the Company and made available to you for the use of the Underwriters stating that their review of the Company's system of internal accounting controls, to the extent they deemed necessary in establishing the scope of their examination of the Company's financial statements as of December 31, 1994 and September 30, 1995, did not disclose any weaknesses in internal controls that they considered to be material weaknesses.

(g) You shall have received on the Closing Date and on any later date on which Option Shares are to be purchased, as the case may be, a certificate of the Company, dated the Closing Date or such later date on which Option Shares are to be purchased, as the case may be, signed by the Chief Executive Officer and Chief Financial Officer of the Company, to the effect that, and you shall be satisfied that:

(i) The representations and warranties of the Company in this Agreement are true and correct, as if made on and as of the Closing Date or any later date on which Option Shares are to be purchased, as the case may be, and the Company has complied with all the agreements and satisfied all the conditions on its part to be performed or satisfied at or prior to the Closing Date or any later date on which Option Shares are to be purchased, as the case may be;

(ii) No stop order suspending the effectiveness of the Registration Statement has been issued and, to the best knowledge of the Company, no proceedings for that purpose have been instituted or are pending or threatened under the Act;

(iii) When the Registration Statement became effective and at all times subsequent thereto up to the delivery of such certificate, the Registration Statement and the Prospectus, and any amendments or supplements thereto, contained all material information required to be included therein by the Act and the Rules and Regulations and in all material respects conformed to the requirements of the Act and the Rules and Regulations, the Registration Statement, and any amendment or supplement thereto, did not and does not include any untrue statement of a material fact or omit to state a material fact required to be stated therein or necessary to make the statements therein not misleading, the Prospectus, and any amendment or supplement thereto, did not and does not include any untrue statement of a material fact or omit to state a material fact necessary to make the statements therein, in the light of the circumstances under which they were made, not misleading, and, since the effective date of the Registration Statement, there has occurred no event required to be set forth in an amended or supplemented Prospectus which has not been so set forth; and

(iv) Subsequent to the respective dates as of which information is given in the Registration Statement and Prospectus, there has not been (a) any material adverse change in the condition (financial or otherwise), earnings, operations, business or business prospects of the Company, (b) any transaction that is material to the Company considered as one enterprise, except transactions entered into in the ordinary course of business, (c) any obligation, direct or contingent, that is material to the Company, incurred by the Company, except obligations incurred in the ordinary course of business, (d) any change in the capital stock or outstanding indebtedness of the Company that is material to the Company, (e) any dividend or distribution of any kind declared, paid or made on the capital stock of the Company, or (f) any loss or damage (whether or not insured) to the property of the Company which has been sustained or will have been sustained which has a material adverse effect on the condition (financial or otherwise), earnings, operations or business of the Company.

(h) The Company shall have obtained and delivered to you an agreement from each officer and director of the Company in writing prior to the date hereof that such person will not, during the Lock-up Period, effect the Disposition of any Securities now owned or hereafter acquired directly by such person or with respect to which such person has or hereafter acquires the power of disposition, otherwise than (i) as a bona fide gift or gifts, provided the donee or donees thereof agree in writing to be bound by this restriction, (ii) as a distribution to limited partners or shareholders of such person, provided that the distributees thereof agree in writing to be bound by the terms of this restriction, or (iii) with the prior written consent of Robertson, Stephens & Company, L.P. The foregoing restriction shall have been expressly agreed to preclude the holder of the Securities from engaging in any hedging or other transaction which is designed to or reasonably expected to lead to or result in a Disposition of Securities during the Lock-up Period, even if such Securities would be disposed of by someone other than the such holder. Such prohibited hedging or other transactions would include, without limitation, any short sale (whether or not against the box) or any purchase, sale or grant of any right (including, without limitation, any put or call option) with respect to any Securities or with respect to any security (other than a broad-based market basket or index) that includes, relates to or derives any significant part of its value from Securities. Furthermore, such person will have also agreed and consented to the entry of stop transfer instructions with the Company's transfer agent against the transfer of the Securities held by such person except in compliance with this restriction. In addition, the Company shall have obtained and delivered to you an agreement from each other beneficial owner of Common Stock and each other optionee in writing that such person shall not sell or otherwise transfer any shares or other securities of the Company during a period of up to 180 days following the effective date of a Registration Statement of the Company filed under the Securities Act; provided, however, that such restriction shall only apply to the first Registration Statement of the Company to become effective under the Securities Act which includes securities to be sold on behalf of the Company to the public in an underwritten public offering under the Securities Act. Each such beneficial owner and optionee will have further agreed that the Company may impose stop-transfer instructions with respect to securities subject to the foregoing restrictions until the end of such 180-day period.

(i) The Company shall have furnished to you such further certificates and documents as you shall reasonably request, including certificates of officers of the Company as to the accuracy of the representations and warranties of the Company herein, as to the performance by the Company of its obligations hereunder and as to the other conditions concurrent and precedent to the obligations of the Underwriters hereunder.

All such opinions, certificates, letters and documents will be in compliance with the provisions hereof only if they are reasonably satisfactory to Fenwick & West. The Company will furnish you with such number of conformed copies of such opinions, certificates, letters and documents as you shall reasonably request.

7. Option Shares.

(a) On the basis of the representations, warranties and agreements herein contained, but subject to the terms and conditions herein set forth, the Company hereby grants to the several Underwriters, for the purpose of covering over-allotments in connection with the distribution and sale of the Firm Shares only, a nontransferable option to purchase up to an aggregate of 900,000 Option Shares at the purchase price per share for the Firm Shares set forth in Section 3 hereof. Such option may be exercised by the Representatives on behalf of the several Underwriters on one (1) or more occasions in whole or in part during the period of thirty (30) days after the date on which the Firm Shares are initially offered to the public, by giving written notice to the Company. The number of Option Shares to be purchased by each Underwriter upon the exercise of such option shall be the same proportion of the total number of Option Shares to be purchased by the several Underwriters pursuant to the exercise of such option as the number of Firm Shares purchased by such Underwriter (set forth in Schedule A hereto) bears to the total number of Firm Shares purchased by the several Underwriters (set forth in Schedule A hereto), adjusted by the Representatives in such manner as to avoid fractional shares.

Delivery of definitive certificates for the Option Shares to be purchased by the several Underwriters pursuant to the exercise of the option granted by this Section 7 shall be made against payment of the purchase price therefor by the several Underwriters by certified or official bank check or checks drawn in next-day funds, payable to the order of the Company (and the Company agrees not to deposit any such check in the bank on which it is drawn, and not to take any other action with the purpose or effect of receiving immediately available funds, until the business day following the date of its delivery to the Company). In the event of any breach of the foregoing, the Company shall reimburse the Underwriters for the interest lost and any other expenses borne by them by reason of such breach. Such delivery and payment shall take place at the offices of Wilson Sonsini Goodrich & Rosati, 650 Page Mill Road, Palo Alto, CA 94304 or at such other place as may be agreed upon among the Representatives and the Company (i) on the Closing Date, if written notice of the exercise of such option is received by the Company at least two (2) full business days prior to the Closing Date, or (ii) on a date which shall not be later than the third (3rd) full business day following the date the Company receives written notice of the exercise of such option, if such notice is received by the Company less than two (2) full business days prior to the Closing Date.

The certificates for the Option Shares to be so delivered will be made available to you at such office or such other location including, without limitation, in New York City, as you may reasonably request for checking at least one (1) full business day prior to the date of payment and delivery and will be in such names and denominations as you may request, such request to be made at least two (2) full business days prior to such date of payment and delivery. If the Representatives so elect, delivery of the Option Shares may be made by credit through full fast transfer to the accounts at The Depository Trust Company designated by the Representatives.

It is understood that you, individually, and not as the Representatives of the several Underwriters, may (but shall not be obligated to) make payment of the purchase price on behalf of any Underwriter or Underwriters whose check or checks shall not have been received by you prior to the date of payment and delivery for the Option Shares to be purchased by such Underwriter or Underwriters. Any such payment by you shall not relieve any such Underwriter or Underwriters of any of its or their obligations hereunder.

(b) Upon exercise of any option provided for in Section 7(a) hereof, the obligations of the several Underwriters to purchase such Option Shares will be subject (as of the date hereof and as of the date of payment and delivery for such Option Shares) to the accuracy of and compliance with the representations, warranties and agreements of the Company herein, to the accuracy of the statements of the Company and officers of the Company made pursuant to the provisions hereof, to the performance by the Company of its obligations hereunder, and to the condition that all proceedings taken at or prior to the payment date in connection with the sale and transfer of such Option Shares shall be reasonably satisfactory in form and substance to you and to Fenwick & West, and you shall have been furnished with all such documents, certificates and opinions as you may reasonably request in order to evidence the accuracy and completeness of any of the representations, warranties or statements, the performance of any of the covenants or agreements of the Company or the compliance with any of the conditions herein contained.

8. Indemnification and Contribution.

(a) The Company agrees to indemnify and hold harmless each Underwriter against any losses, claims, damages or liabilities, joint or several, to which such Underwriter may become subject (including, without limitation, in its capacity as an Underwriter or as a "qualified independent underwriter" within the meaning of Schedule E of the Bylaws of the NASD), under the Act or otherwise, specifically including, but not limited to, losses, claims, damages or liabilities, insofar as such losses, claims, damages or liabilities (or actions in respect thereof) arise out of or are based upon (i) any breach of any representation, warranty, agreement or covenant of the Company herein contained, (ii) any untrue statement or alleged untrue statement of any material fact contained in the Registration Statement or any amendment or supplement thereto, or the omission or alleged omission to state therein a material fact required to be stated therein or necessary to make the statements therein not misleading, or (iii) any untrue statement or alleged untrue statement of any material fact contained in any Preliminary Prospectus or the Prospectus or any amendment or supplement thereto, or the omission or alleged omission to state therein a material fact necessary to make the statements therein, in the light of the circumstances under which they were made, not misleading, and agrees to reimburse each Underwriter for any legal or other expenses reasonably incurred by it in connection with investigating or defending any such loss, claim, damage, liability or action; provided, however, that the Company shall not be liable in any such case to the extent that any such loss, claim, damage, liability or action arises out of or is based upon an untrue statement or alleged untrue statement or omission or alleged omission made in the Registration Statement, such Preliminary Prospectus or the Prospectus, or any such amendment or supplement thereto, in reliance upon, and in conformity with, written information relating to any Underwriter furnished to the Company by such Underwriter, directly or through you, specifically for use in the preparation thereof and, provided further, that the indemnity agreement provided in this Section 8(a) with respect to any Preliminary Prospectus shall not inure to the benefit of any Underwriter from whom the person asserting any losses, claims, damages, liabilities or actions based upon any untrue statement or alleged untrue statement of material fact or omission or alleged omission to state therein a material fact purchased Shares, if a copy of the Prospectus in which such untrue statement or alleged untrue statement or omission or alleged omission was corrected had not been sent or given to such person within the time required by the Act and the Rules and Regulations, unless such failure is the result of noncompliance by the Company with Section 4(d) hereof.

The indemnity agreement in this Section 8(a) shall extend upon the same terms and conditions to, and shall inure to the benefit of, each person, if any, who controls any Underwriter within the meaning of the Act or the Exchange Act. This indemnity agreement shall be in addition to any liabilities which the Company may otherwise have.

APPENDIX III

Master Agreement Among Underwriters

MASTER AGREEMENT AMONG UNDERWRITERS

October 1, 1997

BANCAMERICA ROBERTSON STEPHENS
555 California Street
Suite 2600
San Francisco, CA 94104

Ladies/Gentlemen:

1. <u>General</u>. We understand that from time to time you may act as Representative or as one of the Representatives of the several underwriters of offerings of securities of various issuers. This Agreement shall apply to any such offering of securities (hereinafter, an "Offering") in which we elect to act as an underwriter after receipt of an invitation from your Syndicate Department which shall identify the issuer, contain information regarding certain terms of the securities to be offered and specify the amount of our proposed participation (subject to increase as provided in the applicable Underwriting Agreement, as hereinafter defined), and the names of the other Representatives, if any. At or prior to the time of an Offering, you will advise us, to the extent applicable, as to the expected offering date, the expected closing date, the initial public offering price, the expected number of securities to be offered, the interest or dividend rate (or the method by which such rate is to be determined), the conversion price, the underwriting discount, the management fee, the selling concession and the reallowance, except that if the public offering price of the securities is to be determined by a formula based upon the market price of certain securities (such procedure being hereinafter referred to as "Formula Pricing"), you shall so advise us and shall specify the maximum underwriting discount, management fee and selling concession. Such information may be conveyed by you in one or more communications in the form of letters, wires, telexes or other written communications or by telephone calls (provided any such telephone calls are promptly confirmed in writing) (such communications received by us with respect to an offering are collectively referred to as the "Invitation"). If the Underwriting Agreement provides for the granting of an option to purchase additional securities to cover over-allotments, you will notify us, in the Invitation, of such option.

This Agreement, as amended or supplemented by the Invitation, shall become effective with respect to our participation in an Offering if you have received our oral or written acceptance and you do not subsequently receive a written communication revoking our acceptance prior to the time and date specified in the Invitation (our unrevoked acceptance after expiration of such time and date being hereinafter referred to as our "Acceptance"). Our Acceptance will constitute (i) our representation that our commitment to purchase Securities (as hereinafter defined) pursuant to the Underwriting Agreement will not result in a violation of the financial responsibility requirements of Rule 15c3-1 under the Securities Exchange Act of 1934, as amended (the "Exchange Act"), or of the National Association of Securities Dealers, Inc. (the "NASD"), if we are a member, or of any securities exchange to which we belong, and (ii) our confirmation that, except as otherwise stated in such Acceptance, each statement included in the Master Underwriters' Questionnaire set forth as Exhibit A hereto (or otherwise furnished to us) is correct. We agree to notify you immediately before the termination of this Agreement with respect to any Offering of any development which makes untrue or incomplete any information that we have given or are deemed to have given in response to the Master Underwriters' Questionnaire. You reserve the right to reject any Acceptance in whole or in part.

The issuer of the securities in any offering of securities made pursuant to this Agreement is hereinafter referred to as the "Company." If the Underwriting Agreement does not provide for an over-allotment option, the securities the Underwriters (as hereinafter defined) are obligated to purchase pursuant to the Underwriting Agreement are hereinafter referred to as the "Securities"; if the Underwriting Agreement provides for an over-allotment option, the securities the Underwriters (as hereinafter defined) are initially obligated to purchase pursuant to the Underwriting Agreement are hereinafter called the "Firm Securities" and any additional securities which may be purchased upon exercise of the over-allotment option are hereinafter called the "Additional Securities," with the Firm Securities and all or any part of the Additional Securities being collectively referred to as the "Securities." Any underwriters of Securities under this Agreement, including the Representative (as hereinafter defined), are hereinafter collectively referred to as the "Underwriters." The term "underwriting obligation," as used in this Agreement with respect to any Underwriter, shall refer to the amount of Securities, including any Additional Securities (plus such additional Securities as may be required by the Underwriting Agreement in the event of a default by one or more of the Underwriters) which such Underwriter is obligated to purchase pursuant to the provisions of the Underwriting Agreement. All references herein to "you" or to the "Representative" or to the "Representatives" shall mean BancAmerica Robertson Stephens and the other firm or firms, if any, which are named as Representatives in the Invitation. The Securities to be offered may, but need not be, registered for a delayed or continuous offering pursuant to Rule 415 under the Securities Act of 1933, as amended (the "Securities Act").

The following provisions of this Agreement shall apply separately to each individual Offering. This Agreement may be supplemented or amended by you by written notice to us and, except for supplements or amendments set forth in an Invitation relating only to a particular Offering, any such supplement or amendment to this Agreement shall be effective without further action by us with respect to any Offering to which this Agreement applies after this Agreement has been so amended or supplemented.

2. <u>Underwriting Agreement; Authority of Representatives</u>. We authorize you to execute and deliver an underwriting or purchase agreement and any amendment or supplement thereto and any associated pricing agreement or other similar agreement (collectively, the "Underwriting Agreement") on our behalf with the Company and/or any selling securityholder(s) with respect to Securities in such form as you determine. We will be bound by all terms of the Underwriting Agreement as executed. We understand that changes may be made in the firms that are to be Underwriters and in the amount of Securities to be purchased by them, but the amount of Securities to be purchased by us in accordance with the terms of this Agreement and the Underwriting Agreement, including the amount of Additional Securities, if any, which we may become obligated to purchase by reason of the exercise of any over-allotment option provided in the Underwriting Agreement, shall not be changed without our consent. Without limiting the foregoing, we authorize you to (a) determine all matters relating to advertising and communications with dealers or others, (b) extend the time within which the Registration Statement (as hereinafter defined) may become effective, (c) postpone the closing date or dates for any Offering, and (d) exercise any right of cancellation or termination. We also authorize you to file with any governmental agency or regulatory body any reports required to be filed by the Representatives or the Underwriters in connection with the transactions contemplated by the Underwriting Agreement or this Agreement, and we shall furnish any information in our possession that is needed for such reports.

As Representatives of the Underwriters, you are authorized to take such action as you deem necessary or advisable to carry out this Agreement, the Underwriting Agreement, and the purchase, carrying, sale and distribution of the Securities, and to agree to any waiver or modification of any provision of the Underwriting Agreement. To the extent applicable, you are also authorized to determine (i) the amount of Additional Securities, if any, to be purchased by the Underwriters to any over-allotment option, and (ii) with respect to offerings using Formula Pricing, the initial public offering price and the price at which the Securities are to be purchased by the Underwriters in accordance with the Underwriting Agreement. Authority with respect to matters to be determined by you, or by you and the Company pursuant to the Underwriting Agreement, shall survive the termination of this Agreement. Your authority hereunder and under the Underwriting Agreement may be exercised by the Representatives jointly or by BancAmerica Robertson Stephens acting alone.

3. <u>Registration Statement and Prospectus</u>. You will furnish to us, to the extent made available to you by the Company, copies of the registration statement, the related prospectus and the amendment(s) thereto (excluding exhibits but including any documents incorporated by reference therein) filed with the Securities and Exchange Commission (the "Commission") in respect of the Securities, and our Acceptance of the Invitation with respect to an Offering will serve to confirm that we are willing to accept the responsibility of an Underwriter thereunder and to proceed as therein contemplated. Our Acceptance will further confirm that the statements made under the heading "Underwriting" in the proposed final form of prospectus, insofar as they relate to us, do not

contain any untrue statement of a material fact or omit to state any material fact required to be stated therein or necessary to make the statements therein not misleading. We understand that in connection with the Offering we are not authorized to give any information or make any representation that is not contained in the registration statement or any such preliminary prospectus, prospectus or prospectus supplement, as amended or supplemented. By our Acceptance we agree that, if requested by you as Representative, we will furnish a copy of any amended preliminary prospectus, prospectus, or prospectus supplement to each person to whom we shall have furnished a previous preliminary prospectus, prospectus or prospectus supplement. By our Acceptance we confirm that we have delivered and agree that we will deliver all preliminary and final prospectuses required for compliance with the provisions of Rule 15c2-8 (or any successor provision) under the Exchange Act. As hereinafter mentioned, the "Registration Statement" and the "Prospectus" refer to the Registration Statement and Prospectus included as a part thereof, in the form in which the Registration Statement becomes effective (including all information deemed to be a part thereof pursuant to Rule 430A promulgated under the Securities Act), and any Registration Statement filed pursuant to Rule 462(b) under the Securities Act and, the form in which the Prospectus is filed pursuant to Rule 424(b) under the Securities Act or, if no such filing is required, the form in which the Prospectus is in at the time the Registration Statement in which it is contained becomes effective, with respect to the Securities. Each preliminary prospectus with respect to the Securities is herein referred to as a "Preliminary Prospectus." You have our consent to the use of our name in the Prospectus and any Preliminary Prospectus as one of the Underwriters. You are authorized, with the approval of counsel for the Underwriters, to approve on our behalf any further amendments or supplements to the Registration Statement or the Prospectus which you deem necessary or appropriate.

4. _Compensation_. As our share of the compensation to be paid for your services in the Offering, we will pay you, and we authorize you to charge our account therefor, a management fee as specified in the Invitation. If there is more than one Representative, such compensation will be divided among the Representatives in such proportion as you may determine.

5. _Public Offering_. In connection with the public offering of the Securities, we authorize you, in your discretion:

(a) to determine the time of the initial public offering, the initial public offering price, the purchase price of the Securities to the Underwriters, and the concessions and discounts to Selected Dealers (as defined below), to change the public offering price and such concessions and discounts (and we agree to be bound by any such change), to furnish the Company with the information to be included in the Registration Statement and any amendment or supplement thereto with respect to the terms of the Offering, and to determine all matters relating to advertising and communications with Selected Dealers and others;

(b) to reserve for sale to dealers selected by you, among whom any of the Underwriters may in your determination be included ("Selected Dealers"), who shall be either (i) members of the NASD who agree in writing to comply with Rule 2740 of the NASD's Conduct Rules or (ii) foreign brokers or dealers not eligible for membership in the NASD who agree in writing not to make sales within the United States, its territories or possessions or to persons who are citizens or residents therein, to comply with the NASD's Interpretation with respect to Free-Riding and Withholding, and to comply with Rules 2420, 2730, 2740 (as such Rules apply to foreign non-members of the NASD) and Rule 2750 of the NASD's Conduct Rules, and to others, all or any part of the Securities to be purchased by us, such reservations for sales to Selected Dealers to be in such proportions as you may determine and such reservations for sales to others to be as nearly as practicable in proportion to the respective underwriting obligations of the Underwriters unless you agree to a smaller proportion at the request of any Underwriter, and from time to time to add to the reserved Securities any Securities retained by us remaining unsold and to release to us any of our Securities reserved but not sold;

(c) to sell reserved Securities as nearly as practicable in proportion to the respective reservations, (i) to Selected Dealers, under Selected Dealers Agreements in substantially the form attached hereto as Exhibit B or otherwise, at the public offering price less the applicable Selected Dealers' concession, and (ii) to others at the public offering price; and

(d) to buy Securities for our account from Selected Dealers at the initial public offering price less such amount not in excess of the applicable Selected Dealers' concession as you determine.

After, and only after, advice from you that the Securities are released for public offering, we will offer to the public in conformity with the terms of the Offering as set forth in the Prospectus or any amendment or supplement thereto such of the Securities to be purchased by us as you advise us are not reserved.

We will comply with any and all restrictions which may be set forth in the Invitation. The initial public advertisement with respect to the Securities shall appear on such date, and shall include the names of such of the Underwriters, as you may determine.

6. Additional Provisions Regarding Sales. Any Securities sold by us (otherwise than through you) which you purchase in the open market or otherwise prior to the termination of this Agreement as provided in Section 12(b), shall be repurchased by us on demand at the cost to you of such purchase plus commissions and taxes on redelivery. Securities delivered on such repurchase need not be the identical Securities so purchased. In lieu of such repurchase, you may, in your discretion, sell for our account the Securities so purchased and debit or credit our account for the loss or profit resulting from such sale, or charge our account with an amount not in excess of the Selected Dealers' concession with respect to such Securities.

Sales of Securities among the Underwriters may be made with your prior consent or as you deem advisable for state securities law purposes.

In connection with offers to sell and sales of the Securities, we will comply with all applicable laws and all applicable rules, regulations and interpretations of all governmental agencies and self-regulatory organizations.

7. Payment and Delivery. At or before the time and date as you may specify in the Invitation and at your offices unless you otherwise specify in the Invitation, we will deliver to you a certified or bank cashier's check in such funds as are specified in the Invitation, payable to the order of BancAmerica Robertson Stephens (unless otherwise specified in the Invitation) in an amount equal to, as you direct, either (i) the public offering price or prices plus accrued interest, amortization of original issue discount or dividends, if any, set forth in the Prospectus less the concession to Selected Dealers, in respect of the amount of Securities to be purchased by us in accordance with the terms of this Agreement and the Underwriting Agreement, or (ii) the amount set forth in the Invitation with respect to the Securities to be purchased by us. We authorize you to make payment for our account of the purchase price for the Securities to be purchased by us against delivery to you of such Securities (which, in the case of Securities which are debt obligations, may be in temporary form), and the difference between such purchase price of the Securities and the amount of our funds delivered to you therefor shall be applied against our account.

You may, in your discretion, make payment of such purchase price on our behalf as provided in Section 8 hereof, but any such payment shall not relieve us of any of our obligations under this Agreement or the Underwriting Agreement and we agree to pay you on demand the amount so advanced for our account. We authorize you, as our custodian, to take delivery of the Securities to be purchased by us and to hold the same for our account, in your name or otherwise subject to the provisions of this Agreement, and to deliver our reserved Securities against sales. Delivery to us of Securities retained by us for direct sale shall be made by you as soon as practicable after your receipt of the Securities. Upon termination of the provisions of this Agreement as provided in Section 12(b), you shall deliver to us any Securities reserved for our account for sale to Selected Dealers and others which remain unsold at that time, except that if, upon such termination, the aggregate of all reserved and unsold Securities of all Underwriters does not exceed 10% of the total amount of Securities underwritten, you are authorized in your discretion to sell such Securities for the accounts of the several Underwriters at such price or prices as you may determine. After you receive payment for reserved Securities sold for our account, you shall remit to us the purchase price paid by us for such Securities and debit or credit our account with the difference, if any, between the sale price and such purchase price.

If we are a member of The Depository Trust Company or any other depository or similar facility, you are authorized to make appropriate arrangements through its facilities for payment for and/or delivery of the Securities to be purchased by us, or, if we are not a member, settlement may be made through a correspondent that is a member pursuant to our timely instructions to you.

In the event that the Underwriting Agreement for an Offering provides for the payment of a commission or other compensation to the Underwriters, we authorize you to receive such commission or other compensation for our account.

8. <u>Authority to Borrow</u>. In connection with the purchase or carrying for our account of any of the Securities to be purchased by us under this Agreement or the Underwriting Agreement or any other securities purchased for our account pursuant to Section 9 hereof, we authorize you, in your discretion, in your individual capacity, to advance your own funds for our account, charging current interest rates (but not in excess of the amount permitted by law), and as Representatives to arrange and make loans on our behalf and for our account, and in connection therewith to execute and deliver any notes or other instruments and hold or pledge as security any of our Securities or other securities purchased for our account, as may be necessary or advisable in your discretion. Any lender may rely upon your instructions in all matters relating to any such loan.

Any Securities held by you for our account may be delivered to us for carrying purposes, and if so delivered, will be redelivered to you upon demand.

9. <u>Stabilization and Over-Allotment</u>. We authorize you, in your discretion, to make purchases and sales of the Securities, any other Securities of the Company of the same class and series, any securities of the Company into which the Securities are convertible or exchangeable and any other securities of the Company which you may designate, in the open market or otherwise, on a when-issued basis or otherwise, for long or short account, on such terms and for such prices as you may determine, and to over-allot in arranging sales. Such purchases and sales and over-allotments will be made for the account of the Underwriters as nearly as practicable in proportion to their respective underwriting obligations. It is understood that you may have made purchases of securities of the Company for stabilization purposes prior to the time when we become one of the Underwriters, and we agree that any securities so purchased shall be treated as having been purchased for the respective accounts of the Underwriters pursuant to the foregoing authorization. We authorize you, in your discretion, to cover any short position or liquidate any long position incurred pursuant to this Section 9 by purchasing or selling Securities on such terms and at such times and prices during the term of this Agreement or after its termination as you deem advisable. At no time will the amount of our net commitment either for long or short account under this Section 9 exceed 15% of our underwriting obligation. Solely for the purposes of the immediately preceding sentence, our "underwriting obligation" shall be deemed to exclude any Securities which we are obligated to purchase solely by virtue of the exercise of an over-allotment option. We will on demand take up and pay at cost Securities so purchased and deliver any Securities so sold or over-allotted for our account and deliver on demand any of the Securities sold or over-allotted for our account. In the event of default by one or more Underwriters in respect of their obligations under this paragraph, each non-defaulting Underwriter will assume its proportionate share of the obligation of such defaulting Underwriter without relieving the defaulting Underwriter of its liability hereunder. The provisions of this Section 9 do not constitute an assurance that the price of the Securities will be stabilized or that stabilization, if commenced, may not be discontinued at any time.

We authorize you, as our Representative, to file with the Commission or any other governmental or regulatory agency any notices and reports which may be required as a result of any transactions made by you for the accounts of the Underwriters pursuant to this Section 9.

If you engage in any stabilizing transactions on behalf of the Underwriters, you shall notify us of that fact. We agree that stabilizing by us may be effected only with your consent, and we will furnish you with such information and reports relating to such stabilization as are required by the rules and regulations of the Commission and other governmental or regulatory agencies.

We agree to advise you, upon your request, of the Securities retained by or released to us and remaining unsold, and will, upon your request, release to you for the account of one or more of the Underwriters such of the unsold Securities retained by us and at such price, not less than the applicable net price to Selected Dealers nor more than the public offering price, as you may determine.

10. Open Market Transactions. Until termination of this Agreement as provided in Section 12(b), unless this restriction is sooner terminated by you, we agree not to bid for, purchase, sell or attempt to induce others to purchase or sell, directly or indirectly, either before or after issuance of the Securities, any of the Securities or securities exchangeable for, or convertible into, or exercisable against the Securities, any security of the same class and series as the Securities and any right to purchase or sell the Securities or any such security, including trading in any put or call option on any such security other than (a) as provided for in this Agreement or in the Underwriting Agreement or (b) as a broker in executing unsolicited orders.

We represent that we have not participated in any transaction prohibited by the preceding paragraph and that we have at all times complied with and will at all times comply with the provisions of Rule 139 of the Securities Act and Regulation M of the Exchange Act, each as interpreted by the Commission.

11. Expenses and Settlement. You may charge our account with all transfer taxes on sales or purchases made of Securities purchased for our account and with our proportionate share (based upon our underwriting obligation or upon sales for our accounts, as you shall determine in your sole discretion) of all other expenses incurred by you and arising under this Agreement or the Underwriting Agreement or in connection with the purchase, carrying, sale or distribution of the Securities. With respect to each Offering to which this Agreement applies, the respective accounts of the Underwriters shall be settled as promptly as practicable after the termination of this Agreement as provided in Section 12(b), but you may reserve such amount as you deem advisable for additional expenses. Your determination of the amount and allocation of such expenses shall be final and conclusive. You may at any time make partial distribution of credit balances or call for payment of debit balances. Any of our funds in your hands may be held with your general funds without segregation and without accountability for interest. Notwithstanding any settlement, we will remain liable for taxes on transfers for our account and for our proportionate share (based upon our underwriting obligation) of all expenses and liabilities which may be incurred by or for the accounts of the Underwriters with respect to each Offering to which this Agreement applies. In the event of the default of one or more Underwriters in carrying out their obligations hereunder, the expenses chargeable to such Underwriter pursuant to this Agreement and not paid by it, as well as any additional losses or expenses arising from such default, may be proportionately charged (based upon underwriting obligations) against the other Underwriters not so defaulting without, however, relieving such defaulting Underwriter from its liability therefor.

12. Termination.

(a) This Agreement may be terminated by either party hereto upon five business days' written notice to the other party; provided, however, that with respect to any particular offering, if you receive any such notice from us after our Acceptance, this Agreement shall remain in full force and effect as to such Offering and all previous Offerings only in accordance with the provisions of paragraph (b) of this Section 12.

(b) With respect to each Offering to which this Agreement applies, all limitations in this Agreement on the price at which the Securities may be sold, the periods of time referred to in Sections 7 and 18, the authority granted by the first sentence of Section 9, and the restrictions contained in Sections 6 and 10, shall terminate at the close of business on the 30th day after the initial public offering of the Securities or at the close of business on the day of the closing of the purchase of the Securities, whichever is later, or in any event, at such earlier time as you determine in your discretion, by notice to us stating that the offering provisions are terminated. All other provisions of this Agreement shall survive the termination of such provisions and shall remain operative and in full force and effect with respect to such Offering.

13. Default by Underwriters. Default by one or more Underwriters in respect of their obligations hereunder or under the Underwriting Agreement shall not release us from any of our obligations or in any way affect the liability of any defaulting Underwriter to the other Underwriters for damages resulting from such default. If one or more Underwriters default under the Underwriting Agreement, you may (but shall not be obligated to)

arrange for the purchase by others, including you or other non-defaulting Underwriters, of the Securities not taken up by the defaulting Underwriter or Underwriters.

In the event that such arrangements are made, the respective underwriting obligations of the non-defaulting Underwriters and the amounts of the Securities to be purchased by others, if any, shall be taken as the basis for all rights and obligations hereunder; but this shall not in any way affect the liability of any defaulting Underwriter to the other Underwriters for damages resulting from its default nor shall any such default relieve any other Underwriter of any of its obligations hereunder or under the Underwriting Agreement except as herein or therein provided. In addition, in the event of default by one or more Underwriters in respect of their obligations under the Underwriting Agreement to purchase the Securities agreed to be purchased by them thereunder and, to the extent that arrangements shall not have been made by you for any person to assume the obligations of such defaulting Underwriter or Underwriters, we agree, if provided in the Underwriting Agreement, to assume our proportionate share, based upon our underwriting obligation, of the obligations of each such defaulting Underwriter (subject to the limitations contained in the Underwriting Agreement) without relieving such defaulting Underwriter of its liability therefor.

In the event of default by one or more Underwriters in respect of their obligations under this Agreement to take up and pay for any Securities purchased by you for their respective accounts pursuant to Section 9 hereof, or to deliver any such Securities sold or over-allotted by you for their respective accounts pursuant to any provision of this Agreement, and to the extent that arrangements shall not have been made by you for other persons to assume the obligations of such defaulting Underwriter or Underwriters, each non-defaulting Underwriter shall assume its proportionate share of the aforesaid obligations of each such defaulting Underwriter without relieving any such defaulting Underwriter of its liability therefor.

14. <u>Liability of Representatives; No Liability for Certain Matters</u>. Except as this Agreement specifically provides, you shall have full authority to take such action as you deem necessary or advisable in respect of all matters pertaining to the Underwriting Agreement and this Agreement in connection with the purchase, carrying, sale and distribution of the Securities. However, you shall be under no liability to us for any act or omission except for your lack of good faith in the performance of the obligations expressly assumed by you in this Agreement. No obligations on your part shall be implied or inferred herefrom. Without limiting the foregoing, you shall be under no liability for or in respect of the validity or value of, or title to, the Securities; the form of, or the statements contained in, or the validity of, the Registration Statement as initially filed, any Preliminary Prospectus, the Registration Statement or the Prospectus, or any amendment or supplement to any of them, or any other letters or instruments executed by or on behalf of the Company and/or any selling securityholder(s) or others; the form or validity of the Underwriting Agreement, the Selected Dealers Agreement or this Agreement; the delivery of the Securities; the performance by the Company and/or any selling securityholder(s) or others of any agreement on its or their part to be performed; the qualification of the Securities for sale under the laws of any jurisdiction; or any matter in connection with any of the foregoing. The rights and liabilities of the Underwriters are several and not joint and nothing shall constitute the Underwriters a partnership, association or separate entity.

If the Underwriters are deemed to constitute a partnership for federal income tax purposes, we elect to be excluded from the application of Subchapter K, Chapter 1, Subtitle A, of the Internal Revenue Code of 1986, as amended, and agree not to take any position inconsistent with such election, and you are authorized, in your discretion, to execute on behalf of the Underwriters such evidence of such election as may be required by the Internal Revenue Service.

Notwithstanding any settlement of accounts under this Agreement, we agree to pay our underwriting proportion of the amount of any tax, claim, demand or liability which may be asserted against and discharged by the Underwriters, or any of them, based on the claim that the Underwriters, or any of them, constitute a partnership, association, or separate entity, and also to pay our underwriting proportion of expenses approved by you incurred by the Underwriters, or any of them, in contesting any such taxes, claims, demands, or liabilities.

15. <u>Indemnification</u>. We will indemnify and hold harmless each other Underwriter (including you) and each person, if any, who controls such Underwriter within the meaning of Section 15 of the Securities Act, to

the extent and upon the terms upon which each Underwriter agrees to indemnify the Company and other specified persons as set forth in the Underwriting Agreement.

If at any time a claim or claims (whether alone or together with another claim or claims) shall be asserted against you, individually or as Representative of the Underwriters, or against any other Underwriter, or against any person who controls either you or such other Underwriter within the meaning of Section 15 of the Securities Act, which claim or claims arise out of or are based in whole or in part upon (i) any actual or alleged or misleading statement in or omission from any version of the Registration Statement or Prospectus, or any amendment or supplement to any of them, (ii) any actual or alleged action or omission to act by you or any such Underwriter or any other person in connection with the preparation for and management or other effectuation of any of the transactions contemplated by this Agreement, the Selected Dealers Agreement or the Underwriting Agreement or (iii) any other actual or alleged action or omission in connection with or related to the offer or sale of the Securities, we authorize you to make such investigation, to retain or arrange for or approve the retaining of such attorneys (including, in your discretion, separate attorneys for any single Underwriter or group of Underwriters) and to take such other action as you shall deem necessary or desirable under the circumstances, including settlement of any such claim or claims. We will pay you, on request, our proportionate share (based upon the underwriting obligation of all Underwriters participating in such indemnification) of all expenses by you to the date of each such request (including, without limitation, cost of investigation and the fees and disbursements of your attorneys and any other attorneys or experts retained by you or whose retaining you arrange for or approve) in investigating, defending against and negotiating with respect to such claim or claims, and our similar proportionate share of any liability incurred to the date of each such request by you, by any such other Underwriter or by any such controlling person in respect of such claim or claims, whether such liability shall be the result of a judgment or the result of any such settlement. In determining the amount of our obligation under this paragraph, appropriate adjustment may be made by you to reflect any amounts received by any one or more Underwriters in respect of such claim from the Company pursuant to the Underwriting Agreement or otherwise. If any Underwriter or Underwriters default in their obligation to make any payments under this second paragraph of Section 15, each non-defaulting Underwriter shall be obligated to pay its proportionate share of all defaulting payments, based upon such Underwriter's underwriting obligation as related to the underwriting obligations of all non-defaulting Underwriters. Nothing herein shall relieve a defaulting Underwriter from liability for its default. No person guilty of fraudulent misrepresentation (within the meaning of Section 11(f) of the Securities Act) shall be entitled to contribution from any person who was not guilty of such fraudulent misrepresentation.

In addition and without limiting the foregoing, we will indemnify and hold harmless you, each other Underwriter and each person, if any, who controls you and each Underwriter within the meaning of Section 15 of the Securities Act, against any claim or claims, liabilities and expenses (including, without limitation, costs of investigation, attorneys' fees and disbursements and amounts paid upon judgment or settlement) to which you, any such other Underwriters and any such controlling persons may become subject or incur, in whole or in part, as a result of our actual or alleged failure to timely perform our obligations under this Agreement, the Underwriting Agreement or under applicable law or the inaccuracy of any of our representations in this Agreement or the Master Underwriters' Questionnaire (attached hereto as Exhibit A), and we will, upon such request as may be made from time to time, pay to you, each such other Underwriter and each such controlling person (i) such expenses as have been incurred by you, such other Underwriters and such controlling persons to the date of each such request (including, without limitation, costs of investigation and attorneys' fees and disbursements) in whole or in part in investigating, defending against and negotiating with respect to such claim or claims, and (ii) any liabilities incurred by you, such other Underwriters or such controlling persons to the date of each such request, in whole or in part, as a result of such claim or claims, whether such liability shall be the result of a judgment or other determination or the result of any settlement made by you, such other Underwriter or such controlling person.

You shall give us reasonably prompt notice of the assertion of any such claim or claims referred to in this Section 15, as well as such reports from time to time as you deem reasonable as to the status thereof and as to the actions taken by you in respect thereof pursuant to the foregoing authorizations and indemnifications, although your failure to do so shall not affect our obligations hereunder. In addition, we will cooperate with you and attorneys retained by you (or which you arranged for or approved the retaining of) in investigating and defending against any such claim or claims referred to in this Section 15 and will make available all relevant records and documents and appropriate personnel. We understand that the discharge of any obligations that we may have under the provisions of the preceding two paragraphs of this Section 15 shall not relieve us of any obligation that we may have under the first paragraph of this Section 15. The foregoing indemnifications will be in addition to, and will not supersede, any other indemnification to which you, any such other Underwriter and any such controlling person shall be entitled from us by virtue of this Agreement, the Underwriting Agreement, by operation of law or otherwise.

Notwithstanding any other provision herein to the contrary, the provisions of Section 14 hereof and our agreements contained in this Section 15 shall remain in full force and effect regardless of any investigation made by or on behalf of you, any other Underwriter or any controlling person and shall survive the delivery of the Securities and the termination of this Agreement and the similar agreements entered into with the other Underwriters.

16. <u>Reports and Blue Sky Matters</u>. We authorize you to file with the Commission and any other governmental or regulatory agency any reports required to be filed by you in connection with any transactions effected by you for our account pursuant to this Agreement and the Underwriting Agreement, and we will furnish any information in our possession needed for such reports. As provided in Section 9 hereof, we agree to notify you in writing of the information specified in Rule 17a-2(d) of the Commission promulgated under the Exchange Act. You shall not have any responsibility with respect to the right of any Underwriter or other person to sell the Securities in any jurisdiction, notwithstanding any information you may furnish in that connection.

We are familiar with Rule 15c2-8 promulgated under the Exchange Act relating to the distribution of preliminary and final prospectuses for securities of an issuer (whether or not the issuer is subject to the requirements of Section 13 or 15(d) of the Exchange Act) and confirm that we will comply therewith in connection with any sale of Securities.

17. <u>NASD Membership</u>. We understand that you are a member in good standing of the NASD. We confirm that we are actually engaged in the investment banking or securities business and are either a member in good standing of the NASD or a foreign broker or dealer not eligible for membership in the NASD who has agreed not to make sales within the United States, its territories or possessions or to persons who are citizens thereof or residents therein, to comply with the requirements of the NASD's Interpretation with Respect to Free-Riding and Withholding in making sales of the Securities and not to use any means of interstate commerce to effect such sales unless we are registered under the Exchange Act. In connection with our sale of the Securities, and without limiting the foregoing, we specifically agree to comply with Rule 2740 of the Conduct Rules of the NASD or, if we are a foreign dealer not a member of the NASD, we agree to comply as though we were a member with Rules 2730, 2740 and 2750 of said Rules and with Rule 2740 of said Rules as that Rule applies to non-member brokers or dealers in a foreign country.

We authorize you to file on our behalf with the NASD such documents and information, if any, which are available or have been furnished to you for filing pursuant to applicable rules, statements and interpretations of the NASD.

18. <u>Representations and Agreements</u>.

(a) We understand that it is our responsibility to examine the Registration Statement, the Prospectus, any amendment or supplement thereto, or any preliminary prospectus and the material, if any, incorporated by reference therein, and we will familiarize ourselves with the terms of the Securities and the other terms of the Offering which are to be reflected in the Prospectus and the Invitation with respect thereto. You are authorized, with the approval of counsel for the Underwriters, to approve on our behalf any amendments or supplements to the Registration Statement or the Prospectus.

(b) We confirm that the information that we have given or are deemed to have been given in response to the Master Underwriters' Questionnaire attached as Exhibit A hereto (which information has been furnished to the Company for use in the Registration Statement or the Prospectus) is correct. We will notify you immediately if any development occurs before the termination of this Agreement under Section 12(b) as to the

Offering which makes untrue or incomplete any information that we have given or are deemed to have been given in response to the Master Underwriters' Questionnaire.

(c) Unless we have promptly notified you in writing otherwise, our name as it should appear in the Prospectus and our address are as set forth on the signature page hereof.

(d) We agree that if we are advised by you that the Company was not, immediately prior to the filing of the Registration Statement, subject to the requirements of Section 13(a) or 15(d) of the Exchange Act, we will not, without your consent, sell any of the Securities to an account over which we exercise discretionary authority.

(e) With respect to each offering of Securities, we will not advertise over our name until after the first public advertisement made by you and then only at our own expense and risk. We authorize you to exercise complete discretion with regard to the first public advertisement.

(f) In accordance with Securities Act Release No. 4968, we will deliver copies of each Preliminary Prospectus to all our salesmen before they offer Securities to their clients, and we will deliver a Preliminary Prospectus to all persons to whom we expect to mail confirmations of sales not less than 48 hours prior to the time we expect to mail such confirmations.

19. Capital Requirements. We confirm that our net capital and the ratio of our aggregate indebtedness to our net capital is such that we may, in accordance with and pursuant to Rule 15c3-1 promulgated by the Commission under the Exchange Act, and other applicable laws, rules and regulations relating to us, and agree to purchase the Securities that we are obligated to purchase hereunder and under the Underwriting Agreement.

20. Notices. All notices to us will be considered duly given if mailed or telegraphed to our address as set forth on the signature page hereof (as such address may be changed by written notice to you). All notices to you will be considered duly given if mailed or telegraphed to BancAmerica Robertson Stephens at the address set forth above, directed to the attention of the Syndicate Department, or to such other address as you may specify to us in writing from time to time.

21. General Provisions. Subject to the provisions of Section 1 hereof, this Agreement may be amended or modified by notification in writing by you to us. This Agreement will be governed by and construed in accordance with the laws of the State of California without regard to that State's conflict of law principles. The invalidity or unenforceability of any provision or portion of this Agreement shall not affect the validity or enforceability of the other provisions hereof. If any provision or portion of this Agreement shall be invalid or unenforceable for any reason, there shall be deemed to be made such minor changes (and only such minor changes) as are necessary to make it valid and enforceable.

Neither this Agreement nor any rights hereunder may be directly or indirectly assigned (whether by merger, reverse merger, sale of stock or assets, operation of law or, without limitation, otherwise) by us. This Agreement shall inure to the benefit of and be binding upon the permissible successors and assigns and the heirs, executors and administrators of the parties hereto. No such assignment will relieve us of our obligations hereunder.

In this Agreement, the masculine, feminine and neuter genders and the singular and the plural include one another. The section headings in this Agreement are for the convenience of the parties only and will not affect the construction or interpretation of this Agreement. This Agreement may be executed in several counterparts, each one of which shall be an original and all of which shall constitute one and the same document.

Very truly yours,

_____
Name of Firm

By:_____

Name:_____

Title:_____

Address:

_____

_____

_____

Confirmed as of the date
first above written:

BANCAMERICA ROBERTSON STEPHENS

By:_____
     Authorized Signatory

EXHIBIT A

MASTER UNDERWRITERS' QUESTIONNAIRE

In connection with each Offering to which the foregoing Master Agreement Among Underwriters dated March 14, 1997 between BancAmerica Robertson Stephens and the Underwriter executing the same relates, except as otherwise disclosed to the Representative(s) in a written Acceptance, such Underwriter advises the Representative(s) as follows and authorizes the Representative(s) to use the information furnished in response to this Master Underwriters' Questionnaire in the Registration Statement relating to the Securities:

(a) Neither such Underwriter nor any of its directors, officers or partners, individually or as a part of a "group" (as that term is used in Section 13(d)(3) of the Exchange Act), (i) has a "material" relationship (as defined in Rule 405 under the Securities Act) with the Company or any other seller of Securities in the Offering or (ii) is a director, officer or holder (of record or beneficially, determined in accordance with Rule 13d-3 under the Exchange Act) of 5% or more of any class of voting securities of the Company or any other seller of Securities in the Offering, or (iii) other than as may be stated in the Registration Statement, has any knowledge that more than 5% of any class of voting securities of the Company is held or is to be held subject to any voting trust or similar agreement;

(b) With reference to the Interpretation of the Board of Governors of the NASD with respect to the Review of Corporate Financing, neither such Underwriter nor any of its "related persons" (as defined by the NASD) (i) has purchased or otherwise acquired from the Company any warrants, options or other securities of the Company within 18 months prior to the date that the Registration Statement was initially filed or subsequent to that date, and there are no existing arrangements for any such purchase or (ii) has had any dealings with the Company (except those with respect to the Underwriting Agreement) or any "affiliate" of the Company (as defined in Rule 405 under the Securities Act) as to which documents or other information are required to be furnished to the NASD pursuant to such Interpretation;

(c) Neither such Underwriter or any of its "related persons" (as defined by the NASD) is an "affiliate" of the Company as that term is defined in Rule 2720(b) of the Conduct Rules of the NASD or has a "conflict of interest" with the Company under Rule 2720 of such Rules or under Rule 2710 of the NASD's Conduct Rules;

(d) Other than as may be stated in the Registration Statement, a copy of which has been examined by us, any Prospectus, the Master Agreement Among Underwriters, or the Underwriting Agreement, such Underwriter does not know of any arrangements made or to be made for limiting or restricting the sale of the Securities, for withholding commissions or otherwise to hold each Underwriter or dealer responsible for the distribution of their participation in the Securities, or for discounts or commissions, including any cash, securities, contract or other consideration to be received by any dealer in connection with the sale of the Securities, or of any intention to over-allot the Securities or to stabilize the price of any security to facilitate the offering of the Securities;

(e) If the Securities are to be issued pursuant to a trust indenture, such Underwriter is not, directly or indirectly, in control of, directly or indirectly, controlled by, or under direct or indirect common control with the Trustee, any other trustee under a trust indenture relating to securities of the Company and qualified under the Trust Indenture Act of 1939, as amended (an "Other Trustee") or any of their respective affiliates, and none of said companies or affiliates, or any of their respective directors or executive officers, is a director, officer, partner, employee, appointee or representative of such Underwriter;

(f) If the Securities are to be issued pursuant to a trust indenture, such Underwriter and its directors, executive officers and partners, taken as a group, did not, on the date of the Trustee's Statement of Eligibility and qualification on Form T-1, own beneficially more than 1% of the outstanding voting securities of the Trustee, the Trustee's parent, any Other Trustee or the parent of any Other Trustee;

(g) If the Registration Statement is on Form S-1, such Underwriter has not prepared or had prepared for it within the past 12 months any engineering, management or similar report or memorandum relating to the broad aspects of the business, operations or products of the Company except for reports solely comprising recommendations to buy, sell or hold the Company's securities, unless such recommendations have changed within the past six months;

(h) If the Registration Statement is on either Form S-2 or Form S-3, such Underwriter has not prepared any report or memorandum for external use by it or by the Company in connection with the Offering;

(i) If the Company does not have any securities registered under Section 12 of the Exchange Act and is not subject to Section 15(d) of the Exchange Act, such Underwriter does not intend to confirm sales of the Securities to any accounts over which it exercises discretionary authority; and

(j) Such Underwriter's proposed commitment to purchase Securities will not result in a violation by it of the financial responsibility requirements of Rule 15c3-1 under the Exchange Act and is not prohibited or restricted by any action of the Commission, the NASD or of any national securities exchange applicable to such Underwriter;

(k) Such Underwriter is familiar with the rules, regulations and releases of the Commission dealing with the dissemination of information prior to and during registration and has not distributed nor will it distribute any written information outside of its organization relating to the Company or its securities other than in accordance with such rules, regulations and releases; and

(l) If the Company is a "public utility" such Underwriter is not a "holding company" or a "subsidiary company" or an "affiliate" of a "holding company" or of a "public utility," each as defined in the Public Utility Holding Company Act of 1935, as amended.

All capitalized items in this Questionnaire not otherwise defined herein are used as defined in the foregoing Master Agreement Among Underwriters.

March 14, 1997

Very truly yours,

_____
(Name of Firm)

By:_____

Name:_____

Title:_____

Appendix IV

Master Selected Dealers Agreement

EXHIBIT B

MASTER SELECTED DEALERS AGREEMENT

March 14, 1997

BANCAMERICA ROBERTSON STEPHENS
555 California Street
Suite 2600
San Francisco, CA 94104

Ladies and Gentlemen:

1. <u>General</u>. We understand that BancAmerica Robertson Stephens is entering into this Agreement with us and other firms who may be offered the right to purchase as principal a portion of securities being distributed to the public. The terms and conditions of this Agreement shall be applicable to any public offering of securities ("Securities") pursuant to a registration statement filed under the Securities Act of 1933, as amended (the "Securities Act") wherein BancAmerica Robertson Stephens (acting for its own account or for the account of any underwriting or similar group or syndicate) is responsible, alone or with another manager, for managing or otherwise implementing the sale of the Securities to selected dealers ("Selected Dealers") and has expressly informed us that such terms and conditions shall be applicable. Any such offering of Securities to us as a Selected Dealer is hereinafter called an "Offering." In the case of any Offering in which you are acting for the account of any underwriting or similar group or syndicate ("Underwriters"), the terms and conditions of this Agreement shall be for the benefit of, and binding upon, such Underwriters, including, in the case of any Offering in which you are acting with others as representatives of Underwriters, such other representatives. As used herein, the term "Preliminary Prospectus" means any preliminary prospectus relating to an Offering or any preliminary prospectus supplement together with a prospectus relating to an Offering; the term "Prospectus" means the prospectus, together with the final prospectus supplement, if any, relating to an Offering, either filed pursuant to Rule 424(b) or Rule 424(c) under the Securities Act or, if no such filing is required, the form of final prospectus contained in the related registration statement at the time that it first becomes effective.

2. <u>Conditions of Offering; Acceptance and Purchase</u>. Any Offering will be subject to delivery of the Securities and their acceptance by you and any other Underwriters, may be subject to the approval of certain legal matters by counsel and the satisfaction of other conditions, and may be made on the basis of reservation of Securities or an allotment against subscription. You will advise us by telegram, telex, or other form of written communication ("Written Communication") of the particular method and supplementary terms and conditions (including, without limitation, the information as to prices and offering date referred to in Section 3(b)) of any Offering in which we are invited to participate. To the extent such supplementary terms and conditions are inconsistent with any provision herein, such terms and conditions shall supersede any such provision. Unless otherwise indicated in any such Written Communication, acceptances and other communications by us with respect to any Offering should be sent to BancAmerica Robertson Stephens, 555 California Street, Attention: Syndicate Department, Suite 2600, San Francisco, CA 94104. You reserve the right to reject any acceptance in whole or in part. Payment for Securities purchased by us is to be made at such office as you may designate, at the public offering price, or, if you shall so advise us, at such price less the concession to dealers or at the price set forth or indicated in a Written Communication, on such date as you may designate, on one day's prior notice to us, by certified or official bank check payable in next day funds to the order of BancAmerica Robertson Stephens against delivery of certificates evidencing such Securities. If payment is made for Securities purchased by us at the public offering price, the concession to which we shall be entitled will be paid to us upon termination of the provisions of Section 3(b) hereof with respect to such Securities.

Unless we promptly give you written instructions otherwise, transactions in the Securities may be settled through the facilities of The Depository Trust Company, payment for and delivery of Securities purchased by us will be made through such facilities if we are a member, or if we are not a member, settlement may be made through our ordinary correspondent who is a member.

3. Representations, Warranties, and Agreement.

(a) Prospectuses. You shall provide us with such number of copies of each Preliminary Prospectus, the Prospectus and any supplement thereto relating to each Offering as we may reasonably request for the purposes contemplated by the Securities Act and the Securities Exchange Act of 1934, as amended (the "Exchange Act") and the applicable rules and regulations of the Securities and Exchange Commission (the "Commission") thereunder. We represent that we are familiar with Rule 15c2-8 under the Exchange Act relating to the distribution of preliminary and final prospectuses and agree that we will comply therewith. We agree to keep an accurate record of our distribution (including dates, number of copies, and persons to whom sent) of copies of the Prospectus or any Preliminary Prospectus (or any amendment or supplement to any thereof), and promptly upon request by you, to bring all subsequent changes to the attention of anyone to whom such material shall have been furnished. We agree to deliver copies of each Preliminary Prospectus to our salesmen before they offer Securities to their clients, and we will deliver a Preliminary Prospectus to all persons to whom we expect to mail confirmations of sales not less than 48 hours prior to the time we expect to mail such confirmations. We agree that in purchasing Securities in an Offering we will rely upon no statement, written or oral, not in the Prospectus delivered to us by you. We will not be authorized by the issuer or other seller of Securities offered pursuant to a Prospectus or by any Underwriters to give any information or to make any representation not contained in the Prospectus in connection with the sale of such Securities. We agree that we will not confirm sales to any account over which we have discretionary authority, or make allocations of the type discussed in Release No. 4150 under the Securities Act.

(b) Offer and Sale to the Public. With respect to any Offering of Securities, you will inform us by a Written Communication of the public offering price, the selling concession, the reallowance (if any) to dealers, and the time when we may commence selling Securities to the public. After such public offering has commenced you may change the public offering price, the selling concession, and the reallowance to dealers. With respect to each Offering, until the provisions of this Section 3(b) shall be terminated pursuant to Section 4, we agree to offer Securities to the public only at the public offering price and in conformity with the terms of offering set forth in the Prospectus, except that if a reallowance is in effect, a reallowance from the public offering price not in excess of such reallowance may be allowed as consideration for services rendered in distribution to dealers who are actually engaged in the investment banking or securities business, who execute the written agreement prescribed by Rule 2740(c) of the Conduct Rules of the National Association of Securities Dealers, Inc. (the "NASD") and who are either members in good standing of the NASD or foreign brokers or dealers not eligible for membership in the NASD who represent to us that they will promptly reoffer such Securities at the public offering price and will abide by the conditions with respect to foreign brokers and dealers set forth in Section 3(e) hereof.

(c) Stabilization and Overallotment. You may, with respect to any Offering, be authorized to overallot in arranging sales to Selected Dealers, to purchase and sell Securities, any other securities of the issuer of the Securities of the same class and series and any other securities of such issuer that you may designate for long or short account, and to stabilize or maintain the market price of the Securities. We agree to advise you from time to time upon request, prior to the termination of the provisions of Section 3(b) with respect to any Offering, of the amount of Securities purchased by us hereunder remaining unsold and we will, upon your request, sell to you, for the account or the accounts of one or more Underwriters, such amount of such unsold Securities as you may designate, at the public offering price thereof less an amount to be determined by you not in excess of the concession to dealers. If, prior to the later of (i) the termination of the provisions of Section 3(b) with respect to any Offering, or (ii) the covering by you of any short position created by you in connection with such Offering for your account or the account of one or more Underwriters, you purchase or contract to purchase for your account or the account of one or more Underwriters, in the open market or otherwise, any Securities theretofore delivered to us, you reserve the right to withhold the above-mentioned concession to dealers on such Securities if sold to us at the public offering price, or if such concession has been allowed to us through purchase at a net price, we agree to repay

B-2

such concession upon your demand, plus in each case any taxes on redelivery, commissions, accrued interest, and dividends paid in connection with such purchase or contract to purchase.

(d) <u>Open Market Transactions</u>. We agree not to bid for, purchase, attempt to purchase, or sell, directly or indirectly, any Securities, any other securities of the issuer of Securities of the same class and series, or any other securities of such issuer as you may designate, except pursuant to Regulation M of the Exchange Act, as interpreted by the Commission or as otherwise provided in this Agreement. If the Securities are or include common stock or securities convertible into common stock we agree not to effect, or attempt to induce others to effect, directly or indirectly, any transactions, except to the extent permitted by Regulation M under the Exchange Act as interpreted by the Commission.

(e) <u>NASD</u>. We represent that we are actually engaged in the investment banking or securities business and we are either a member in good standing of the NASD, or if not such a member, a foreign dealer or broker not eligible for membership. If we are such a member, we agree that in making sales of the Securities we will comply with all applicable rules of the NASD, including, without limitation, the NASD's Interpretation with Respect to Free-Riding and Withholding and Rule 2740 of the Conduct Rules. If we are such a foreign dealer, we agree not to offer or sell any Securities in the United States of America, its territories or possession or to persons who are citizens thereof or residents therein, except through you, and in making sales of Securities outside the United States of America we agree to comply as though we were a member with such interpretation and with Rules 2730, 2740 and 2750 of the NASD's Conduct Rules and to comply with Rule 2420 of such Rules as it applies to a non-member broker or dealer in a foreign country.

(f) <u>Relationship among Underwriters and Selected Dealers</u>. You may buy Securities from or sell Securities to any Underwriter or Selected Dealer and, with your consent, the Underwriters (if any) and the Selected Dealers may purchase Securities from and sell Securities to each other at the public offering price less all or any part of the concession. We are not authorized to act as agent for you or any Underwriter or the issuer or other seller of any Securities in offering securities to the public or otherwise. Nothing contained herein or in any Written Communication from you shall constitute the Selected Dealers an association or partners with you or any Underwriter or with one another. If the Selected Dealers, among themselves or with the Underwriters, should be deemed to constitute a partnership for Federal income tax purposes, then we elect to be excluded from the application of Subchapter K, Chapter 1, Subtitle A, of the Internal Revenue Code of 1986, as amended, and agree not to take any position inconsistent with that election, and you are authorized, in your discretion, to execute and file on our behalf such evidence of that election as may be required by the Internal Revenue Service. Neither you nor any Underwriter shall be under any obligation to us except for obligations assumed hereby or in any Written Communication from you in connection with any Offering. In connection with any Offering, we agree to pay our proportionate share of any tax, claim, demand or liability asserted against us, alone or against one or more Selected Dealers participating in such Offering, or against you or the Underwriters, if any, based on any claim that such Selected Dealers or any of them constitute an association, unincorporated business, or other separate entity, including, in each case, our proportionate share of any expense incurred in defending against any such tax, claim, demand, or liability.

(g) <u>Blue Sky Laws</u>. Upon application to you, you will inform us as to any advice you have received from counsel concerning the jurisdictions in which you believe the Securities have been qualified for sale or are exempt under the respective securities or "blue sky" laws of such jurisdictions. We understand and agree that compliance with the securities or "blue sky" laws in each jurisdiction in which we shall offer or sell any of the Securities shall be our sole responsibility and that you assume no responsibility or obligations as to the eligibility of the Securities for sale or our right to sell the Securities in any jurisdiction.

(h) <u>Compliance with Law</u>. We agree that in selling Securities pursuant to any Offering (which agreement shall also be for the benefit of the issuer or other seller(s) of such Securities), we will comply with all applicable laws, rules and regulations, including the applicable provisions of the Securities Act and the Exchange Act, the applicable rules and regulations of the Commission thereunder and the applicable rules and regulations of the NASD and any securities exchange having jurisdiction over the Offering. You shall have full authority to take such action as you may deem advisable in respect of all matters pertaining to any Offering.

Neither you nor any Underwriter shall be under any liability to us, except for lack of good faith and for obligations expressly assumed by you in this Agreement; provided, however, that nothing in this sentence shall be deemed to relieve you from any liability imposed by the Securities Act.

      4.   Termination; Supplements and Amendments. This Agreement may be terminated by either party hereto upon five business days' written notice to the other party; provided that with respect to any Offering for which a Written Communication was sent and accepted prior to such notice, this Agreement as it applies to such Offering shall remain in full force and effect and shall terminate with respect to such Offering in accordance with the last sentence of this Section. This Agreement may be supplemented or amended by you by written notice thereof to us, and any such supplement or amendment to this Agreement shall be effective with respect to any Offering to which this Agreement applies after the date of such supplement or amendment. Each reference to "this Agreement" herein shall, as appropriate, be to this Agreement as so amended and supplemented. The terms and conditions set forth in Sections 3(b) and (d) hereof with regard to any Offering will terminate at the close of business on the thirtieth day after the date of the initial public offering of the Securities or at the close of business on the day of the closing of the purchase of the Securities by the Underwriters, whichever is later, or in any event, at such later date as you shall have advised us in writing.

      5.   Successor and Assigns. This Agreement shall be binding on, and inure to the benefit of, the parties hereto and other persons specified or indicated in Section 1 hereof, and the respective successors and assigns of each of them; provided, however, that we may not assign our rights or delegate any of our duties under this Agreement without your prior written consent.

      6.   Governing Law. This Agreement and the terms and conditions set forth herein with respect to any Offering together with such supplementary terms and conditions with respect to such Offering as may be contained in any Written Communication from you to us in connection therewith shall be governed by, and construed in accordance with, the laws of the State of California without regard to that State's conflicts of law principles.

By signing this Agreement we confirm that our subscription to, or our acceptance of any reservation of, any Securities pursuant to an Offering shall constitute (i) acceptance of and agreement to the terms and conditions of this Agreement (as supplemented and amended pursuant to Section 4) together with and subject to any supplementary terms and conditions contained in any Written Communication from you in connection with such Offering, all of which shall constitute a binding agreement between us and you, individually, or as representative of any Underwriters, (ii) confirmation that our representations and warranties set forth in Section 3 hereof are true and correct at that time (iii) confirmation that our agreements set forth in Sections 2 and 3 hereof have been and will be fully performed by us to the extent and at the times required thereby, and (iv) acknowledgment that we have requested and received from you sufficient copies of the Prospectus in order to comply with our undertaking in Section 3(a) hereof.

Very truly yours,

_____
(Name of Firm)

By:_____

Name:_____

Title:_____

Confirmed, as of the date first above written

BANCAMERICA ROBERTSON STEPHENS

By:_____
    Authorized Signatory